Fodor's 2014

BRAZIL

WELCOME TO BRAZIL

Whether you go during Carnival or not, Brazil is always a party. You can tan and mingle with the locals on the country's seemingly endless beaches, from Rio's glamorous Ipanema to the unspoiled treasures along the northeastern shores. In the vast interior, outdoor adventures thrill: take a spray-soaked boat ride into Iguaçu's raging waterfalls or spot exotic wildlife in the Pantanal. On rugged treks through the Amazon rain forest or on shopping expeditions in São Paulo's chic boutiques, you will plunge into a vibrant mix of colors, rhythms, and cultures.

TOP REASONS TO GO

★ **Cool Cities:** Brasília, Rio de Janeiro, São Paulo, Salvador, to name just a few.

★ **Beaches:** Glitzy or secluded, there's a strand here to suit every taste.

★ **Amazon Excursions:** Jungle lodges and river tours entice with adventures aplenty.

★ **Soccer:** Chanting with the fans at an iconic stadium is a truly memorable experience.

★ **Architecture:** From Salvador's baroque gems to Brasília's modernism, Brazil dazzles.

★ **Brazilian Beats:** Samba, bossa nova, and forró rhythms pulse through the country.

12
TOP EXPERIENCES

Brazil offers terrific experiences that should be on every traveler's list. Here are Fodor's top picks for a memorable trip.

1 Postcard-Perfect Beaches

Slip into your beachwear for a day of sunbathing and people-watching on Brazil's most beautiful beaches, including Copacabana (above), Ipanema, and Búzios. *(Ch. 2, 3, 5, 9, 10)*

2 Carnival

Brazilians can throw a party like no one else, and Carnival is the biggest party of the year—a raucous bacchanal of music, drink, and flesh. *(Ch. 2, 9)*

3 Brasília's Architecture

Built from scratch in less than five years in the late 1950s, Brasília, the country's planned capital, is an architecture buff's dream. *(Ch. 8)*

4 Brazilian Beats

Music is woven into the fabric of Brazilian life, and no trip here is complete without catching a live show, whether samba, bossa nova, axé, or forró. *(Ch. 1)*

5 Brazilian Wildlife

The biodiversity in Brazil is astonishing. With any luck, you'll spot capybaras and anteaters in the Pantanal, and toucans and pink dolphins in the Amazon. *(Ch. 8, 11)*

6 Food and Drink

From black bean stews to Amazonian fish dishes, Brazil's cuisines will delight your taste buds. Start your meal with a caipirinha, the national cocktail. *(Ch. 1)*

7 Iguaçu Falls

Iguaçu's raging, jungle-fringed waterfalls will leave you speechless, especially on a spray-soaked boat tour. *(Ch. 6)*

8 Christ the Redeemer

Don't leave Rio without making a trip to the statue of Christ the Redeemer, arms outstretched to embrace the city from its perch on Corcovado Mountain. *(Ch. 2)*

9 Ouro Preto

This former gold-rush town is nestled in the Minas Gerais mountains, with cobblestoned streets and red-roofed buildings that climb the hills. *(Ch. 7)*

10 Soccer Matches

Soccer is a national passion and an art form in Brazil. It's a blast to sit among thousands of cheering, chanting fans in one of the country's iconic stadiums. *(Ch. 1)*

11 São Paulo Nightlife

São Paulo's nightlife options are seemingly endless, and the numerous bars and nightclubs prove worthy venues for even the feistiest nighthawk. *(Ch. 4)*

12 Jungle Lodges

There's no better way to explore the Amazon rain forest than by staying right in the middle of it in an all-inclusive riverside lodge. *(Ch. 11)*

CONTENTS

MAPS

ABOUT
THIS GUIDE

Fodor's Recommendations

Everything in this guide is worth doing—
we don't cover what isn't—but exceptional sights, hotels, and restaurants are
recognized with additional accolades.
Fodor's Choice★ indicates our top recom-
mendations; and **Best Bets** calls attention
to notable hotels and restaurants in various categories. Care to nominate a new
place? Visit Fodors.com/contact-us.

Trip Costs

We list prices wherever possible to help
you budget well. Hotel and restaurant
price categories from **$** to **$$$$** are noted
alongside each recommendation. For
hotels, we include the lowest cost of a
standard double room in high season.
For restaurants, we cite the average price
of a main course at dinner or, if dinner
isn't served, at lunch. For attractions,
we always list adult admission fees; dis-
counts are usually available for children,
students, and senior citizens.

Hotels

Our local writers vet every hotel to recom-
mend the best overnights in each price cat-
egory, from budget to expensive. Unless
otherwise specified, you can expect pri-
vate bath, phone, and TV in your room.
For expanded hotel reviews, facilities, and
deals visit Fodors.com.

Restaurants

Unless we state otherwise, restaurants are
open for lunch and dinner daily. We men-
tion dress code only when there's a specific
requirement and reservations only when
they're essential or not accepted. To make
restaurant reservations, visit Fodors.com.

Credit Cards

The hotels and restaurants in this guide
typically accept credit cards. If not, we'll
say so.

Top Picks	Hotels &
★ **Fodor's** Choice	**Restaurants**
	⊡ Hotel
Listings	⤴ Number of
✉ Address	rooms
✉ Branch address	‖○‖ Meal plans
☎ Telephone	✕ Restaurant
🖷 Fax	◿ Reservations
⊕ Website	⚲ Dress code
✑ E-mail	▱ No credit cards
◈ Admission fee	$ Price
⊙ Open/closed	
times	**Other**
Ⓜ Subway	⇨ See also
⊹ Directions or	☞ Take note
Map coordinates	🏌 Golf facilities

EXPERIENCE
BRAZIL

BRAZIL TODAY

Brazil is immensely diverse—socially, culturally, racially, economically—and rife with profound contradictions that are not always evident at first. All this makes for a complex nation that eludes easy definitions—but is fascinating to discover.

Culture

Brazil's contrasts are everywhere. Take a look around when you land. Dense forests that are home to pint-sized monkeys and birds found nowhere else brush up against gleaming high-rises, which in turn border *favelas* (shantytowns). Juxtapositions of this sort can make any experience breathtaking and shocking at once.

A stroll through any Brazilian town will show you this is one of the most racially mixed populations anywhere. The country was shaped not only by the Portuguese, who brought their religion and language, but also by millions of enslaved Africans, the native indigenous, and waves of European, Arabic, and Japanese immigrants. Most Brazilians include elements from several of these backgrounds in their cultural and ethnic heritage.

Brazil never had the Jim Crow laws and institutionalized discrimination that marked the U.S., yet it is far from being a color-blind society. In spite of the recent economic boom, blacks and the indigenous still face stiff discrimination and underrepresentation in government. They also far outweigh whites at the broad base of Brazil's economic pyramid.

Brazilians are known for their warmth, their tiny bikinis, their frequent public displays of affection—it's not uncommon to see couples kissing at length on a park bench or a beach blanket—and their riotous displays of joie de vivre in annual Carnival celebrations. But the country is also home to the world's largest Catholic population, and conservative sexual mores shape the culture more than visitors might imagine.

Politics

Brazil's current president, Dilma Rouseff, is an example of how Brazil defies stereotypes. The fact that she is a woman—and twice divorced at that, currently living without a husband—was scarcely discussed during her 2010 campaign for president, even though this is a country were *machismo* (male chauvinism) still thrives.

Of far greater importance to voters was that she is a member of the Partido dos Trabalhadores (PT) or Workers Party, and had the support of the immensely popular outgoing president, Luiz Inácio Lula da Silva, who has towered over the political landscape for the last decade.

Lula's story is fascinating. Born into poverty in the country's northeast, he rose to prominence in São Paulo as a union leader while the country was still under the rule of a military dictatorship that had seized power in 1964. Buoyed by his charisma and his appeal to poor Brazilians, Lula was elected to the presidency in 2003, then again to a second four-year term.

Rousseff, the no-nonsense administrator who succeeded him, has maintained similarly high approval ratings by keeping in place transfer-of-wealth policies that have helped alleviate poverty, and by cultivating the image of a leader who brooks no corruption with public money of the sort that have long been a hallmark of Brazilian politics.

Economy

After punishing years of economic instability and hyperinflation in the 1980s and 90s, Brazil's GDP began to grow along with prices and demand for the commodities that make up the base of its economy, including soybeans, sugar, iron ore, and oil.

The last decade of social progress has created real improvement in the quality of life for Brazil's new middle class. About 35 million Brazilians have hoisted themselves out of poverty in that time. Over half of the country's 194 million people now officially belong to the middle class. However, many still hover perilously close to the bottom, and many more live in neighborhoods that still don't have such services as trash collection, sewage treatment, and safety. But the improvement is real and visible.

Religion

Brazil has the world's largest Catholic population, although Roman Catholicism has been losing worshippers to Evangelical churches. These churches are booming, especially in poorer communities where it is not uncommon to see several modest storefront churches on a single street.

In religion, like in so many other aspects of Brazil, the reality is more complex than it first appears. The country's rich ethnic and cultural heritage means that the dominant Christianity is often blended with other sects and religions, creating fascinating local variants that are unique to Brazil.

The most widespread examples of this blending happen within Afro-Brazilian religious practices. Forbidden from worshipping the deities they brought with them from Africa, enslaved men and women established connections between their *orixas*, or gods, and saints from the Catholic faith of their masters. This way, they could pay homage to their own gods while keeping up appearances by seeming to pray to Catholic saints.

While freedom of religion is enshrined in the Constitution, Brazil's many contradictions surface in attitudes toward Afro-Brazilian faiths such as Candomble, the more orthodox of the variations, and Umbanda, an even more syncretic religion incorporating elements of French-based spiritualism. Although some Afro-Brazilian practices are popular, including wearing white on New Year's Eve and leaving gifts of flowers and fruit on the beach to honor Iemanja, the orixa of oceans and seas, serious practitioners can be frequent targets of discrimination.

Sports

You don't even have to set foot in Brazil to know that soccer—or *futebol*—is king here. The country's mad about it, and there's good reason: Brazil has produced some of the world's best players, and it is the only nation to have won five World Cups. The displays of passion seen during major games make them worthy of a visit. Although there is criticism over the way soccer is run—and there have been wide-ranging protests about the costs of hosting the 2014 FIFA World Cup—love for the "jogo bonito," or beautiful game, is unabated.

Volleyball is also a favorite. Beaches are often settings for spectacular displays of beach volleyball, and of a Brazilian combination of the two: futevolei, where the players can use only their feet, chest, and head to touch the volleyball.

WHAT'S WHERE

The following numbers refer to chapters.

2 Rio de Janeiro.
This verdant city cascades down dramatic mountains and out to beaches that line the metropolitan area. The breathtaking landscapes are glorious in all seasons.

3 Side trips from Rio.
Inland from Rio de Janeiro are several historical towns in refreshing mountainous settings along with quieter beach destinations.

4 São Paulo. This huge metropolis is lined with skyscrapers and buzzes with fast-paced urban life. It also has some of the country's best restaurants, boutiques, theaters, and museums.

5 Side Trips from São Paulo. São Paulo's heartland includes mountainous regions with charming resort towns, and beautiful beaches that offer a range of water sports.

6 The South. The three southernmost states include charming European architecture, a subdued pace of life, and the mighty rushing waterfalls of Foz do Iguaçu.

ARIBO
●Cayenne
H
A   50°W

40°W

Macapá   *Equator*   0°

○Belem
        São Luís

                        Fortaleza

        Caxias
          Teresina   Natal
○Maraba   **10**

BRAZIL
                        Recife○

                Petrolina
                            ○Maceio
                                        10°S
SERRA GERAL DO GOIAS
○Alvorada   ○Barreiras   ○Feira de Santana

    BRASILIA   **9** ○Salvador
8   ○Vitoria da Conquista
★
○Goiania   ○Montes Claros

  ○Uberlandia
        BRAZILIAN HIGHLANDS
                ○Belo Horizonte   20°S
rande   **7**   ○Vila Velha
            2
○Campinas   ○Rio de Janeiro
○Sorocabo   **4**   **3**
onta Grossa **5**○Sao Paulo
    ○Curitiba

        ○Florianopolis

SERRA DO MAR
  ○Caxias do Sul
                            30°S
○Porto Alegre
  ○Pelotas
AY

ATLANTIC OCEAN

7 Minas Gerais. This inland
state is dotted with picturesque gold and mineral spa
towns all within a short drive
of one another.

8 Brasília and the West.
Built from scratch in five
years, Brasília has become
a global model of urbanism.
Farther west, the Pantanal
is an untamable mosaic of
swamp and forest teeming
with wildlife.

9 Salvador and the Bahia
Coast. The epicenter of Afro-
Brazilian culture, Salvador
teems with life, history, and
flavor. Along Bahia's southern
coast are some of Brazil's
most beautiful beaches.

10 The Northeast.
On Brazil's curvaceous
northeast coast are gorgeous
colonial cities and beaches
lapped by warm waters and
cooling breezes.

11 The Amazon. Flowing for
more than 4,000 miles, the
gargantuan Amazon River is
banked by a rain forest that
houses the greatest variety of
life on earth.

BRAZIL PLANNER

Visitor Information

While you can enjoy Brazil's large cities on your own, a guide can help facilitate multi-day trips among several cities. Official municipal tour offices offer basic information:

Rio de Janeiro Riotur ⊕ www.rio.rj.gov.br ☎ +55–21/2542–8080, +55–21/2542–8004

São Paulo Turismo ⊕ www.cidadedesaopaulo.com/sp ☎ +55–11/2226–0400

Salvador Saltur ⊕ www.saltur.salvador.ba.gov.br ☎ +55–71/3176–4200

Brasília SETUR ⊕ www.setur.df.gov.br ☎ +55–61/3214–2744

Tour Companies

South American Tours will plan week-plus trips that include Rio de Janeiro, Iguaçu Falls, and neighboring countries. ✉ Av. Princesa Isabel 323, 8th floor, Copacabana, Rio de Janeiro ☎ +55–21/3147–2599 ⊕ www.southamericantours.com.

Havas Creative Tours, based in Rio de Janeiro, will take you to some of Brazil's hard-to-reach corners. ✉ Avenida das Américas 3434, Bloco 5 grupo 520, Rio de Janeiro ☎ +55–21/2430–1101 ⊕ www.havasbrazil.com.br.

Getting Here and Around

Getting Here: International flights largely arrive in Rio de Janeiro's Galeão airport or São Paulo's Guarulhos. Some nationalities, Americans and Canadians included, require a visa issued from a consulate abroad to enter Brazil—the country operates on the principle of reciprocity, meaning that if a country requires a visa of Brazilian citizens, Brazil will require one of them. Visas are not granted on arrival. Tourist visas are generally valid for three months, and able to be extended for another three months by visiting the Federal Police and paying a small fee.

Getting Around: When planning trips in Brazil, keep in mind its vastness: The country occupies nearly half the South American landmass. Flights between large and medium-sized cities are frequent and reasonably priced. But be ready for some frustrations: You may need to buy your tickets through a tour agency or at the airline's booking office, since many airlines do not accept foreign credit cards or payments online without a CPF, a Brazilian ID number.

Bus trips are a good option for short trips, such as exploring Rio de Janeiro's coastal beaches or traveling from São Paulo to Rio. But comfortable travel to Iguaçu Falls or the Amazon region will likely require flying. Brazil does not have a developed intermunicipal train system, though a bullet train from São Paulo to Rio is predicted to be ready by 2020. Sparse infrastructure, especially as you leave Brazil's densely populated coast and head to the interior, makes travel times by land even longer.

TYPICAL TRAVEL TIMES FROM RIO DE JANEIRO

	Hours by Car	Hours by Plane
São Paulo	5 hrs.	50 min.
Brasília	13 hrs.	1 hr. 45 min.
Salvador	20 hrs.	2 hrs. 15 min.
Belo Horizonte	5½ hrs.	1 hr.
Recife	28 hrs.	2 hrs. 50 min.
Florianópolis	13 hrs.	1 hr. 40 min.
Foz do Iguaçu	17 hrs.	2 hrs.
Manaus	N/A	4 hrs.

Staying Safe in Brazil

Throngs of tourists have perfectly safe vacations in Brazil each year. Still, crime and violence are sad realities throughout the country. A few common sense tips can help you have a safe trip.

PETTY CRIME

Keep your belongings close to you and be aware of what you do and do not need as you go out each day. Stashing some cash and a camera in a small *pochette* (as Brazilians affectionately call fanny packs) will make for a worry-free, hands-off day. Carry only a copy of your passport as an ID with you—you won't need the actual document, except when making large purchases like airline tickets. In the case of a mugging, do not resist and give up all belongings immediately. Should you be the victim of a crime, many Brazilian cities have specialized tourist police stations, where police are bilingual and take extra care with your case.

WALKING

In Brazilian cities, stick to areas with high pedestrian traffic. When hiking or in the forest, bring minimal belongings and consult local guides about the safety of a path. In touristy areas, avoid walking in alleyways and closed-off areas that are empty. At night, only walk if you are in a well-lit area with heavy pedestrian traffic.

PUBLIC TRANSPORTATION

Taxis in major cities are regulated, safe, fairly priced, and obediently run on the meter. The subway is also a safe and fast way to get around many cities. Buses are a widely used form of transport both within and between cities, but are occasionally the target of robberies. Avoid the informal vans that locals commonly use. After dark, take only cabs.

MONEY AND CREDIT CARDS

Watch your bank account after using debit cards in ATM machines, since card cloning is common. Making payments with credit cards is generally fine, but keep an eye on your account.

Lodging: The Basics

1

Brazil's large cities have a variety of lodging options, ranging from luxurious to no-frills budget hotels and bed-and-breakfasts. Beachside hotels in Ipanema or Leblon offer world-class rooms and services, as do São Paulo lodgings in posh neighborhoods like Jardins. In Brasília, demand often exceeds supply, and centrally located hotels are pricey. Treat yourself to a night in the late Oscar Niemeyer's Brasília Palace to immerse yourself in the city's modernism.

You'll also have a chance to immerse yourself in your surroundings through alternative lodgings, such as floating dock inns in the Amazon and family-owned bed-and-breakfasts on the beach. Nothing caps off a Brazil trip like a night sleeping in a hammock on a boat cruise, where body-to-body passengers swing in unison through the breezy night.

WHEN TO GO

Prices in beach resorts are invariably higher during the Brazilian summer season (December–February) and in July, when schools take a monthlong break. Expect crowds and try to book in advance. If you're looking for a bargain, stick to May–June and August–October. Rio and beach resorts along the coast, especially in the northeast, sizzle with heat November–April, but in Rio the temperature can drop to uncomfortable levels for swimming June–August. If you want sun and hot weather and to enjoy beaches and cities in the south, come in the high season, as temperatures can be very low from May–December.

Seasons below the equator are the reverse of the north—summer in Brazil runs from December to March and winter from June to September. The rainy season in Brazil occurs at the end of the summer months. Showers can be torrential but usually last no more than an hour or two. The Amazon and the Pantanal have the most pronounced rainy seasons, running roughly from November to May and marked by heavy, twice-daily downpours.

Rio de Janeiro is on the tropic of Capricorn, and its climate is just that—tropical. Summers are hot and humid. Be extra careful with sun exposure and use a high SPF sunscreen. The same pattern holds true for the entire Brazilian coastline north of Rio, although temperatures are slightly higher year-round in Salvador and the northeastern coastal cities.

In the Amazon, where the equator crosses the country, temperatures in the high 80s to the 90s (30s C) are common all year. In the south, São Paulo, and parts of Minas Gerais, winter temperatures can fall to the low 40s (5°–8° C). In the southern states of Santa Catarina and Rio Grande do Sul, snowfalls occur in winter, although they're seldom more than dustings.

Festivals and Events

Festa Junina: Throughout June, Brazilians celebrate country culture, dressing their kids in blooming dresses and painting freckles on their cheeks. Enjoy rustic music while sipping *quentãos*, cocktails with wine, ginger, clove, and cinnamon.

Oktoberfest: Brazil's vast German community (remember Gisele Bündchen?) parties in the country's south, in the states of Santa Catarina and Rio Grande do Sul.

Reveillon: Brazilians take New Year's Eve seriously—it doesn't hurt that it takes place in the middle of the hot summer. Rio's Copacabana beach overflows with more than a million revelers each year for a fireworks and live music show. Traditionalists wear all white.

Forecasts Weather Channel Connection ⊕ *www.weather.com.*

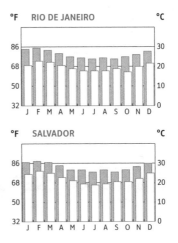

FLAVORS OF BRAZIL

Food, for Brazilians, has much to do with fellowship—portions are often heaping and, rather than coming individually on one plate, arrive in a series of platters meant to be shared among diners.

Meat and Carbs

Perhaps the most well-known Brazilian staple is meat, especially those that come from *churrascarias* (grills): sizzling cuts of beef, some lined generously with fat, served on skewers by men in aprons and boots called *gaúchos*. (The name refers to the southern state of Rio Grande do Sul, with which the style is associated, though churrascarias are found throughout Brazil.)

Churrascarias also serve up sausages (*linguiça*), chicken (*frango*), and various types of fish. Expect little in the way of spice—just salt and garlic. The natural flavors of the meat are meant to carry the meal. In a rodízio-style churrascaria, you get all the meat and side dishes you can eat at a fixed price. Rodízio means "going around," which explains the *gaúchos* who constantly circle the restaurant, only resting their skewers to slice another strip of meat onto your plate.

Feijoada, black beans stewed with fatty pork parts, is a popular party food synonymous with carefree weekend afternoons spent digesting the heavy dish. The dish is often topped with *farofa* (toasted manioc root) and served with *couve* (collard greens) and rice. Brazilians traditionally give guests an orange slice after the meal to help with the aching belly that ensues from its consumption.

Native Fruits and Vegetables

Beyond the meat-and-carbs crowd-pleasers, Brazil's tropical expanse allows for a diversity of fruits and vegetables. Visitors will find these on display in colorful *feiras* (fresh food fairs) throughout the country. Tropical citrus fruits include *maracujá* (passion fruit), *abacaxi* (pineapple), *mamão* (papaya), *tangerine* (tangerine), and *lima-da-pérsia* (something like a sweet, crisp version of an orange). All are frequently found as mixers in *caipirinhas*, Brazil's national drink made with *cachaça*, a sugarcane-based liquor.

Visitors should make a point to sample some of the unique flavors of the Amazon, such as *cupuaçú*, a fragrant yellow fruit, or *mangaba*, something of a cross between a honeydew and a durian. At *lanchonetes*, no-frills snack bars that consist of metal chairs lined along a bar, you'll often find velvety ice drinks made with açai, a purple Amazonian berry that is touted for its health benefits. These drinks are usually mixed with *guaraná*, an energy-packed red berry used as a sweetener.

Bahian Specialties

Bahian food from Brazil's northeast revolves around seafood and is normally spicy and hot. Specialties include *moqueca*, a seafood stew cooked quickly in a clay pot over a high flame, and *acarajé*, a patty deep-fried in *dendê* oil and filled with sun-dried shrimp and hot-pepper sauce. Brazilians from around the country lick their chops at the mention of *pirão de peixe*, a thick blended stew often made with fish heads and manioc flour.

Coffee Break

No trip here is complete without an afternoon snack of Brazilian coffee, often served without milk and heavy on sugar, and *pão frances*, freshly baked white bread, or *pão de queijo*, chewy cheese buns. By the end of your trip you'll understand why Brazilians use the same word to describe not only tasty food but any life experience that is enjoyable: *gostoso*.

BEACHGOING IN BRAZIL

Close your eyes, say the word "Brazil," and one of the first images to float up in your mind most likely will be of a tropical beach: white sands, azure water, and a fringe of palm trees. There's good reason for that. The country boasts 8,000 kilometers of coastline, and most of the population is concentrated along the coast, where the ocean's moderating influence tempers the tropical sun.

Beaches are often the center of social life, and there is one to suit every taste: kitsch paradises where you can sip juice cocktails under brightly colored umbrellas, chichi playgrounds for the rich, windswept gems, hard-to-reach fishing villages, and surfer havens with pounding waves.

In short, beaches are places to tan, strut, eat, drink, play sports, catch up with friends, and chat with strangers. Even if you're not interested in spending hours in the sun, beaches are worth a visit for people-watching and experiencing this quintessential aspect of Brazilian culture.

What to Expect

Brazilians are well known for being comfortable wearing very little. This goes for all ages and body types. Men often wear *sungas,* Speedo-style swimming trunks, though they avoid high-cut models that show too much leg. In recent years, the popular *sungao,* a wider model that is around 6 inches at the side, has taken over as the outfit of choice. Surfers wear board shorts, and these are acceptable on and off the beach (and a more discreet alternative for bathers unwilling to go the sunga route.)

Women generally wear two-piece bathing suits. Since details such as size, print, and design vary year to year, fashionistas will buy several bikinis to alternate during the summer. Window-shop a little if you want to get a sense of this year's models.

Although the infamous string bikini can still be found, it is no longer as common as it was during the 1990s.

Men and women will generally wear light, easy-to-remove clothes over their bathing suit so that they can undress easily at the beach and then compose themselves enough at the end of the day to make a stop at a beachside restaurant with friends. *Havaianas,* rubber flip-flops that come in a rainbow of colors, are ubiquitous at the beach.

Finally, *cangas* (beach towels) are a must. The large rectangles of cloth come in a variety of prints and can be used to sit on the sand and to drape over your lounge chair or around your shoulders after the sun sets.

Forget your canga at the hotel? Never fear, Brazil's inventive beach vendors will happily sell you one, along with everything from sunblock, light summer dresses, bikinis, and even grilled shrimp. Usually, you can rent lounge chairs and sun umbrellas from them as well.

Food vendors offer cheese grilled over live coals, popsicles in myriad fruit flavors, savory pastries like *esfihas* stuffed with spinach, meat, or cheese, frozen açaí slushies, and slices of fresh fruit. Drinks range from the conventional—water, beer, sodas—to the uniquely Brazilian, such as fresh green coconuts, sweet maté tea, and caipirinhas.

While beaches in Brazil are relatively free of hazards—no sharks or jellyfish to worry about—conditions vary throughout the country. Always heed local warnings about riptides. When in Rio, check the newspaper in the section next to the weather to see if the beach you're planning to go to is clean. Heavy rain showers often wash sewage and trash into the ocean, rendering otherwise beautiful beaches unfit for bathing for at least 24 hours.

Where to Go

Around Rio de Janeiro. Rio's culture revolves around the beach. For a lively, urban experience (in the summer, think beach-goers packed canga-to-canga, with scores of vendors touting their wares), go to Copacabana, Ipanema, or Leblon. Praia Vermelha, at the foot of the Sugar Loaf Mountain, is a tiny, gorgeous beach that is well protected by massive boulders, ideal if you prefer calmer water. The western suburbs of Barra da Tijuca and Recreio offer quieter experiences on sparkling white sands. But the surf here is bigger, so beware of the waves and the undertow even if you're a strong swimmer.

Three hours to the west of Rio is Buzios, a jutting peninsula with 17 beaches. Once the site of fishing villages, it is now expensive and extensively developed, with a pulsing nightlife, high-end restaurants, and a cobblestoned shopping district that overflows with well-to-do Brazilians on vacation.

Around São Paulo. Worth a visit along the Litoral Paulista, or São Paulo coast, is the breathtaking, well-preserved Ilhabela. Its name means beautiful island, and it certainly lives up to the reputation. Its looming peaks are blanketed in dense tropical foliage that harbors parakeets, toucans, and capuchin monkeys.

Southern Brazil. The south boasts a sunny, temperate climate, making its beaches a massive draw during the summer months. Many of the best are around Ilha de Santa Catarina, an island that is home to the state's capital, Florianopolis. The island's north coast is family friendly, with calm waters and many easily accessed hotels and restaurants. For challenging surf and great white dunes, head east to Praia da Joaquina.

Northern Brazil. A quick flight from Natal or Recife, the archipelago of Fernando de Noronha is a marine national park with limited visitation and a required environmental preservation tax. It presents visitors with a dreamscape of untouched beaches, great hikes, surfing, snorkeling, and wildlife-sighting, with the gold star going to the spinner dolphins that pirouette alongside boats.

The Amazon. A surprisingly great beach can be found far from the Atlantic. If you're visiting the Amazon region and want a place to unwind, Alter do Chao is your best bet. Here the Tapajos River forms a white sand bank island, the Ilha do Amor. Locals call it the Amazon's answer to the Caribbean, and during the dry season (June–December) when the water is low and clear, it is easy to see why.

CARNIVAL IN BRAZIL

Brazilians can throw a party like no one else, and Carnival is the biggest party of the year. From dancing in the streets of the nation's smallest towns to the full-throttle revelry of Rio de Janeiro, this raucous bacchanal of music, drink, and flesh takes over the country. This is a time of transgression, when excesses are encouraged and lines are crossed: men dress as women, the poor dress as kings, strangers kiss in the streets, and rules are bent, if only for a few days.

Like Mardi Gras, Carnival has its origins in pagan festivals of spring. These were co-opted by the advent of Christianity into a period of lenience, when one could rack up as many sins as possible before the 40 days of abstinence and withdrawal that comes with Lent.

Carnival is supposed to last five days, from the Friday until the Tuesday before Ash Wednesday. But the reality is that pre-Carnival parties begin to stoke the wild atmosphere for a few weeks before the official opening ceremony. This is when the Mayor gives the keys of the city to the rotund King Momo, a jester-like figure who presides over the chaos and debauchery. The fun often continues for days after Ash Wednesday.

It can be an unforgettable experience if you're ready to plunge headlong into the joyful mayhem: Be prepared for days and nights fueled by light Brazilian beer and potent caipirinhas, and streets jammed with revelers following sound floats playing old-fashioned samba songs morning to night.

The crowds are surprisingly peaceful, but keep your wits about you. This is generally the hottest time of the year, so drink plenty of water and bring sunblock. The streets can get very crowded, making it easy to lose members of your party. Avoid traveling great distances through the city because traffic can turn nightmarish.

Since pickpockets work the masses, carry only cash you plan to spend that day and leave home any nice watches, jewelry, or sunglasses. Groping can be a real hassle for women, especially in Salvador. Travel in groups and avoid wearing a skirt—hands might get up there.

Plan your Carnival visit well in advance; be sure to make your hotel reservations early, and prepare to pay steeper prices. Lastly, do your research. The party takes on various regional flavors. Finding the best fit is important to enjoying the experience.

Rio de Janeiro

The best-known celebration is in Rio de Janeiro, which hosts the lavish culmination of the festival: the Carnival parades, in which *escolas de samba* (samba groups) compete for the top prize with elaborate, mechanized floats, sequin-and-spangled dancers, and huge percussion sections.

During the season, Rio's neighborhoods are also taken over by *blocos*—brass bands or sound trucks that parade through the streets, dragging behind them throngs of faithful revelers in a variety of costumes. There are nearly 500 of these spread around town. For many Rio residents, they are the heart of Carnival.

Most attract a mixed crowd, but some target a particular audience or have special characteristics: the traditional Banda de Ipanema draws a plethora of drag queens; among the Carmelitas, in the Santa Teresa neighborhood, you'll see many partygoers dressed as nuns. There are blocos for children, for journalists, for Michael Jackson lovers—you name it. Street blocos are impossible to miss. In fact, if you are not interested in full-immersion Carnival,

avoid Rio during this time period, because the party is unavoidable.

Carnival balls are good option for those who prefer an enclosed, less chaotic setting. These are massive parties of mostly costumed revelers with live music, and can range from more staid, black-tie affairs like the famous (and pricey) Copacabana Palace ball, to gay balls, balls for children, and smaller ones in samba joints like Rio Scenarium.

Planning: To learn more about Carnival, from the schedules of the parading escolas de samba to where to find the street bloco of your dreams, visit the Riotur website (⊕ *www.rioguiaoficial.com.br*), or pick up their free Carnaval de Rua (street Carnival) guide. *Veja* magazine, sold at all newsstands, also has a Rio insert, *Veja Rio*, with a lot of good information about events during Carnival.

For tickets to see the Carnival parade, go to official league site: ⊕ *liesa.globo.com*. They go on sale as early as December. Alternately, you can check in with travel agencies. They snap up most of the tickets, and resell them at a higher cost in the months preceding Carnival.

Salvador

What makes Salvador's Carnival distinctive is the strong Afro-Brazilian presence in its music and traditions. While Rio's samba also derives from African rhythms, in Salvador this influence feels more immediate.

The centerpieces of Carnival in the Bahian capital are the *trios elétricos,* which are decorated sound trucks that parade through town at the head of a densely packed throng of dancers; and the *afoxes,* which are Afro-Brazilian groups that perform the rhythms and dances of *candomble,* the main Afro-Brazilian religion.

Getting close to the trio elétrico requires buying an *abada*, an outfit that allows the person wearing it to access a roped-off area. Those dancing around outside the cordoned area are called *pipoca*, or popcorn. It's cheaper and easier to "go popcorn," but the crowds can be suffocating. If you want to avoid the crush entirely, buy a ticket to the walled-off bleachers.

Planning: You can find more information at the official tourist office's website (⊕ *www.bahiatursa.ba.gov. br*). Tickets for camarotes and abadas are for sale year-round at ⊕ *home. centraldocarnaval.com.br*.

Elsewhere in Brazil

A multitude of smaller towns offer picturesque and lively Carnival bashes without the crowds. In Recife in Brazil's Northeast, people attend *baile* (dance) and *bloco* (percussion group) practice for months prior to the main Carnival festivities. The beat of choice is *frevo* (a fast-pace rhythm accompanied by a dance performed with umbrellas). Galo da Madrugada, the largest of Recife's 500 blocos, opens Carnival and has included up to 1,500,000 costumed revelers. The blocos are joined by *escolas de samba* (samba schools or groups), *caboclinhos* (wearing traditional Indian garb and bright feathers), and *maracatus* (African percussionists).

In addition, historic gold mining era towns, like Paraty in Rio state and Ouro Preto in Minas Gerais, have plenty of dancing in their cobblestoned streets. Laidback beach resorts like Arraial d'Ajuda in Bahia or Jericoacoara in Ceará offer a mellower atmosphere with more than enough fun to go around.

BRAZIL AND THE ENVIRONMENT

Since Brazil's colonization some five centuries ago, inhabitants have largely congregated along the country's coastline. The majority of Brazil's largest cities—Rio de Janeiro, São Paulo, Curitiba, Porto Alegre, Salvador, Recife—are along or very near the coast. Brazilian leaders grew so worried that its population did not "take advantage of its space" that former President Juscelino Kubitschek constructed and inaugurated in 1960 the planned capital city of Brasília in the country's center as a means to draw population inward.

Pushing Into the Interior

Take advantage of the interior they did, often to a fault. Brazilian agriculturalists, extraction industries, and infrastructure planners have long seemed to suffer from the mentality that land is extensive and cheap, and that pushing into new areas is easier than proper stewardship of the ones they already have. Deforestations has left the Atlantic Forest (*Mata Atlântica*) along Brazil's coast a tiny fraction of its original size, while the *cerrado* savanna in the country's center has lost an estimated half of its original territory. The Amazon rain forest loses thousands of square miles each year, in part because growing global demand for soy and cotton in Brazil's interior then pushes cattle farming into the Amazon.

In addition to deforestation, bitter land disputes between commercial farmers and indigenous populations have a long and deadly history in Brazil. Killings of rural activists and indigenous leaders are common and justice can be scarce. In one of the most famous and chilling cases, the American nun and environmental activist Dorothy Stang was assassinated on her way to a meeting in the Amazon state of Pará. Another front for conflict has been the Brazilian government's push to build dozens of hydroelectric dams across the Amazon, which it says is necessary to satisfy urban Brazilians' growing demand for electricity.

Move Toward Sustainability

Despite the conflicts, the good news is that the tide is turning. Deforestation peaked in 2004, at more than 10,000 square miles per year, and has since dramatically declined to less than a third of that total.

A new seriousness about environmental causes was reflected by the political ascendency of Marina Silva. Born to an impoverished family in the Amazonian state of Acre, and illiterate until her teenage years, Silva later moved to the state's capital city and became an environmental activist alongside Chico Mendes, a famous rubber tapper and trade union leader who was assassinated in 1988. A former senator from the state of Acre and the environmental minister under former President Luiz Inácio Lula da Silva, she left his cabinet in protest over lack of commitment to environmental issues, and had a surprisingly strong performance as a third-party candidate in Brazil's 2010 elections. With rumors of another presidential run, she remains a force to be reckoned with, especially as a greater number of Brazilians embrace what was once seen as a fringe cause.

Sustainability has become a mainstream value over the past two decades, especially since Brazil hosted the 1992 United Nations Earth Summit in Rio de Janeiro, then resurrected it 20 years later at the Rio+20 United Nations Conference on Sustainable Development. A more telling gauge of popular public opinion were

the protests that erupted across Brazil in 2012 to fight against proposed changes in the national forestry code, which would have retroactively "amnestied" years of deforestation.

Such protests highlight how Brazil's civil society has learned to use the tools of accountability and manifestations. Social media has fueled the environmental movement by bringing urbanite organizers in Brazil's coastal cities in line with activists across Brazil's interior.

The Rise of Ecotourism

As a visitor, you will be able to appreciate the fruits of Brazil's sustainability efforts. Take note when you explore a park to see if it is a protected forest. Look at the map of Rio de Janeiro to understand just how large the Tijuca and Pedra Branca national parks are—all the more impressive in a city pressed for space, with real estate prices spiraling and green space coveted.

Many experts claim that Brazil still has few options for true ecotourism that involves education, study, and appreciation of local cultures and the environment. While ecotourism became a priority following the 1992 Earth Summit, the practice has taken some time to get off the ground in Brazil.

During the 1990s, economic turmoil and inconsistent government actions hampered the national industry. In addition, the high price of access to Brazil's Amazon region made it an expensive market in comparison with other destinations. A plane ticket from Rio or São Paulo to Manaus is often as expensive as one to Europe or Miami, and overland access to the Amazon is shaky, at best, with the Transamazônica highway,

meant to cross the country's north and northeast, still largely unpaved.

What Brazil has built up in the meantime is nature-based tourism, which includes responsible and respectful tourism that often lacks an educational component. The Instituto EcoBrasil is a superb resource for planning an eco-friendly trip to Brazil. On their informative, bilingual website (⊕ *www.ecobrasil.org.br*), you can browse a database of "Responsible Companies" and tour operators for the area that you hope to visit.

Overall, there are numerous options available for tourists who want to explore the country's vast natural wonders in an environmentally responsible manner. All visitors should simply keep in mind a phrase that rain forest activist Dorothy Stang often wore emblazoned on her shirt: "The death of the forest is the end of our lives." Brazil's forests are a verdant treasure to be enjoyed, open to those willing to tread lightly.

WILDLIFE IN BRAZIL

Brazil's biodiversity is a wonder to behold. The country itself occupies nearly half the South American continent, and Brazil's Amazon rain forest alone is larger than India. Its distinct ecosystems—the Pantanal wetlands in the center-west, the Pampas temperate grasslands in the south, the Mata Atlântica tropical decid-uous forest along the Atlantic coast, the *cerrado* savanna in the heart of the coun-try, the *caatinga* tropical scrublands in the northeast, and the Amazon rain forest in the north—contain more than 100,000 animal species and roughly 45,000 plant species. According to the Brazilian gov-ernment, some 700 new animals are dis-covered in the country each year. A new plant species is unearthed every two days.

Anaconda: The only contact that tourists most likely will have with this nocturnal snake is through the local's hyperbolic stories about its mammoth size. Tall tales of giant anacondas abound, and for good reason. The green anaconda is the world's heaviest snake, and also one of the longest, sometimes growing up to 16 feet. Anacondas lurk in the waters of the Amazon rain forest, although they rarely make their large presence known.

Capybara: The world's largest rodent, this scurrying beaver-like creature with a nar-row head and rotund behind is prevalent in the Pantanal and Rio de Janeiro's parks.

Giant Anteater: This bushy-tailed creature with outsized claws and an undersized snout and head was once found in all Bra-zilian states; it has since become extinct in populous states like Rio de Janeiro and Espirito Santo, but is well represented in the Pantanal and Amazon area. The giant anteater digs up ants and termites with its claws and then laps them up with its long, sticky tongue.

Jaguar: This elegant big cat is one of the most alluring and elusive animals in Brazil. The largest feline species in the

Americas, the jaguar is recognizable by its golden fur and scattered black spots. Often solitary, they prowl about Brazil's Amazon region in search of prey, and are particularly adept at remaining in the jungle's shadows.

Pink dolphin: Tourists will likely spot these playful creatures during cruises along the Amazon River. The pink river dolphin, or boto, is an exclusively freshwater mammal with sharp rows of teeth on each side of its jaw. These animals catch fish by using echolocation, or sonar, and are particularly adept at prying fish out of the Amazon River's murky vegetation. In local lore, pink river dolphins can take human form as handsome men and seduce beautiful women.

Piranhas: These sharp-toothed freshwater fish are the stuff of legend. Visitors undoubtedly have heard unfounded tales of how piranhas can devour cows in seconds. Most jungle excursions include stops along the Amazon River to fish for piranhas, most likely to eat that night for dinner.

Tapir: This hefty mammal looks like a pig or a small rhino with a characteristically curved snout. Surprisingly exceptional swimmers, tapirs in Brazil largely live close to the river in the Amazon rain forest.

Three-banded armadillo: The official mascot of the 2014 World Cup, the three-banded armadillo resides in the savanna and tropical scrublands. It's most renowned for its ability to roll up into a perfectly spherical, scaly ball.

Toco Toucan: Unmistakable for its large, orange beak, this black-and-white bird can be seen in Brazil's cerrado and Pantanal, and even in Brasília, an unexpected site among its traffic jams and concrete. Perhaps the country's most emblematic animal, the toco toucan uses its distinctive bill to snatch fruit from trees.

IF YOU LIKE

Beaches

Along its 4,654-mile coastline, Brazil has thousands of breathtaking beaches, so you're bound to find a little slice of paradise wherever you are. In the northeast you find sweeping, isolated expanses of dunes; warm aquamarine waters; and constant breezes. Rio's famous beaches are vibrant, social, and beautiful. The south has glorious sands and cooler climes. A short list doesn't do them justice, but these are some of our favorite beach destinations:

Rio de Janeiro. Barra da Tijuca, Prainha, and Grumari are the most naturally beautiful beaches in the city of Rio. Copacabana and Ipanema are the best beach "scenes." Itacoatiara in Rio's sister city Niterói is a hidden paradise locals sneak off to on the weekends to avoid crowds. Farther out of the city, Búzios has some of the country's most gorgeous beaches.

Ceará. Canoa Quebrada, near Fortaleza, and Jericoacoara are our two favorite northeastern beaches for sheer beauty and relaxation.

Paraná. Ilha do Mel is known as the Paradise of the South Atlantic, and is one of the best ecotourism destinations in Brazil.

Santa Catarina. It's difficult to choose one beach to recommend on Ilha de Santa Catarina and Florianópolis. Garopaba, Praia dos Ingleses, and Praia Mole are the most famous, and Jurerê Internacional is the favorite among the well-to-do.

São Paulo. Ilhabela is a paradise of more than 25 beaches.

Bahia. Praia do Forte has plenty of leisure activities, and is the number-one place to see sea turtles in Brazil.

Nature

This is one of the best places on earth for nature-lovers. There are so many places to see that you will need to carefully plan your itinerary. The Amazon and the Pantanal, Brazil's two ecological wonderlands, are givens, but some lesser-known gems are waiting to be discovered by tourists, like Curitiba, known as the "ecological city" because of its many parks and green areas. Our favorite nature destinations follow.

Pantanal Wetlands. This vast floodplain is the best place to see wildlife outside sub-Saharan Africa. Its savannas, forests, and swamps are home to more than 600 bird species as well as anacondas, jaguars, monkeys, and other creatures.

The Amazon Rain Forest. A visit to the world-famous Amazon is one of those "life-list" experiences. Its scope and natural wealth are truly awe-inspiring.

Parque Nacional da Chapada Diamantina, west of Salvador. One of Brazil's most spectacular parks, Chapada Diamantina was a former diamond mining center where intrepid tourists now camp amongst its plateaus and hidden pools.

Parque Nacional do Iguaçu. This preserve has one of the world's most fantastic waterfalls, in addition to winding hiking trails to take you to the fall's lookout points.

Projeto Tamar, Praia do Forte. Each year, September through March, more than 400,000 baby turtles are hatched along this beach northeast of Salvador.

Nightlife

Brazilians are famous for their Carnival, but any time of year is occasion for revelry here. Even small towns have multitudes of festivals that may start out with a Catholic mass and end with dancing in the streets. Nearly every town has live-music venues playing samba, axé, forró, and MPB (Brazilian pop music) year-round. Brazilians—men and women alike—seem to have been born shaking their hips. If you can't dance the wild-yet-elegant samba, don't worry, a lot of Brazilians can't either—they just know how to fake it.

Rio de Janeiro. Music and dance clubs stay open all night long here, especially in Lapa. Brazilians arrive for their nights out late—expect the houses to fill around midnight. This is one of the top places in Brazil to hear great samba and Brazilian jazz, called bossa nova. Carnival is the biggest party of the year, but New Year's Eve in Rio is also a fabulous celebration on the Copacabana beach.

Salvador. The center of axé (Brazilian pop) music and Afro-Brazilian culture, Salvador has an easygoing party scene, but its Carnival is considered one of Brazil's best parties, where you can dance in the streets for eight days straight.

Belo Horizonte. With more bars per capita than any other Brazilian city, it's obvious that BH knows how to party. Expect to find fine sipping cachaça. The music scene is quite lively here.

São Paulo. If you crave elite clubs and rubbing elbows with Brazilian cosmopolitan millionaires and sipping martinis at rooftop skyscraper bars, head to São Paulo. It's Brazil's poshest place to party.

Food and Drink

You will have your pick of diverse dishes to try in Brazil. Each region has its own specialties: exotic fish dishes and fruit juices in the Amazon; African spiced casseroles in Bahia; and the seasoned bean paste tutu in Minas Gerais.

Feijoada. The national dish is a thick stew with a base of black beans, combined with sausage, bacon, pork loin, and other meats. Traditional versions may include pig's feet, ears, and other "choice" meats. Feijoada is usually accompanied by *farofa* (toasted manioc flour), rice, and garlicky collard greens.

Churrasco. Served at churrascarias, churrasco is meat, poultry, or fish roasted on spits over an open fire. In a rodízio-style churrascaria, you get all the meat and side dishes you can eat at a fixed price.

Caipirinha. The national drink is caipirinha—crushed lime, ice, sugar—and cachaça, a liquor distilled from sugarcane.

Açaí. This purple energy-packed berry from the Amazon makes a velvety, icy drink that wins addicts much as coffee does. Amazonians take it bitter, often accompanying savory dishes, whereas urbanite Brazilians in Rio and São Paulo sweeten it and drink it with granola or peanut dust, called *paçoca*.

Guaraná. Be sure to try this carbonated soft drink made with the Amazonian fruit of the same name. It has a unique but subtle flavor.

Cafezinhos. These thimble-size cups of coffee with tons of sugar keep Brazilians going between meals. They are also offered after rodízios to sooth an achingly full stomach.

GREAT ITINERARIES

BEACH, BRASÍLIA, AND IGUAÇU

Day 1: Arrival

Land in Rio de Janeiro and enjoy the view on the way in from the airport to the Zona Sul, where you will likely pass several favelas (squatter settlements) rich with history, the Guanabara Bay and Rio's packed commercial port, the city's colonial-era downtown, and finally arrive at the beachside, where the open Atlantic greets you. Cool down with an icy açaí berry drink at sunset.

Logistics: Wear your breeziest clothes on the flight so that you can keep cool when you arrive in sunny Rio de Janeiro, where summer temperatures are the norm most of the year.

Day 2: Christ Statue, Sugarloaf, Ipanema Beach

Take the train up Corcovado to the Christ Statue, where the 360 views of the city never fail to impress. Once you descend, a short trip through the charming neighborhood of Botafogo will take you to Urca. There, ride a cable car to the top of the iconic Sugar Loaf mount, where you can enjoy a different perspective on the city. End your day at the Praia do Arpoador, right between Copacabana and Ipanema. Locals applaud there as the sun sets.

Logistics: Check the weather to make sure the Christ Statue will not be above the clouds. Wear comfortable shoes for hiking, especially on rocky Arpoador. You can also hike the hill that leads up to the second tram station of the Sugar Loaf mount.

Day 3: Rio's Hidden Corners

Since Rio bursts with beauty, travelers often overlook many of the city's indoor treasures. Try the Roberto Burle Marx Farm, a plantation-turned-museum dedicated to Brazil's most famous landscape designer. You should also make time for the Museu de Arte Contemporânea, designed by the one and only Oscar Niemeyer, in Rio's sister city, Niterói, across the Guanabara Bay. Top the night off with live music in Rio's grunge-chic party district, Lapa.

Logistics: Enjoy the view as you cross the bay to Niterói, either by the Rio-Niterói bridge or the ferry from Praça 15.

Day 4: Beach bum

Rio's long coastline offers a beach for every taste. Want crowds and people-watching? Try Copacabana, with lunch in the Confeitaria Colombo along the Forte de Copacabana. A surfer's beach? The Prainha past Barra da Tijuca is for you. A beach for families? You can't go wrong at the low-key Praia do Leblon.

Logistics: Beyond Copacabana and Ipanema, you will need a car or long bus rides to get to the beaches farther southwest along the coast.

Days 5–6: Onward to Brasília

Make your way to the airport in Rio for a short flight to Brasília. Enjoy the view of Brasília at night—the Esplanada dos Ministérios is generally empty and feels elegant and massive lit in the dark. Remember that Brasília was the city of the future—half a century ago. Enjoy Oscar Niemeyer's modernism and the clean lines of the government buildings of the Esplanada dos Ministérios. If you don't stay in Niemeyer's Brasília Palace, at least have dinner in the elegant Oscar restaurant to enjoy the grounds. Feel free to enter the boisterous Congress—just show an ID to get in.

Logistics: Take note of whether your flight leaves in Rio from Santos Dumont, the domestic airport, or Galeão, which is

both international and domestic. The former is usually preferable and closer to Zona Sul hotels. Brasília has a speedy metro, but a taxi is a better option if you have difficulty orienting yourself on Brasília's highly organized map, which involves cardinal directions, "sectors," and numbered streets.

Day 7: Brasília to Foz do Iguaçu
Fly into Foz do Iguaçu, Brazil's side of the famous South American falls. Remember that the city is but a launching pad to the falls.

Logistics: Talk with local tour operators to decide whether to take a bus into the falls or a private taxi, which means you'll pay your own entrance fee separately. If you arrive early enough in the city, head straight to the falls—the Brazilian side has fewer trails and can be enjoyed in a few hours.

Day 8: The Falls from Argentina
The general wisdom is the following: Brazil's side of Iguaçu offers the best views, while Argentina's side offers the fun winding hikes that often directly overlook the falls. A boat trip into the falls is a thrilling way to enjoy its majesty.

Logistics: Crossing the border is a cinch, but make sure your Brazilian visa is in order so that you can return to Brazil afterward. Bring a towel if you plan on doing a boat ride.

Day 9: Into the Big City
Fly from Iguaçu to São Paulo to enjoy a day in the country's frenetic commercial capital. Wander anywhere in the city and you're likely to find a museum, top-notch restaurant, or a world-class boutique. Don't miss the outstanding collection at the Museu de Arte de São Paulo.

Day 10: Market Day

Stroll along Avenida Paulista, the packed heart of commercial São Paulo. The Jardins neighborhood will take you to more mouthwatering restaurants than you can handle. Check out the bustling Mercado Municipal for a light lunch and, if time permits, take a taxi to the massive CEAGESP wholesale market. The warehouses of fresh foods and endless stream of buyers will make you appreciate what breadbasket Brazil has to offer.

Logistics: The metro in São Paulo is extensive, so make sure you grab a map before riding. Remember that distances in São Paulo can be quite far. Give yourself plenty of time between outings.

Day 11: Return to Rio

Try to fly in through the Santos Dumont airport so that you can hop out for an extra afternoon in Rio. Sunsets are glorious year-round.

Logistics: Give yourself cushion time, especially during holidays. Long lines for emigration can hold you back.

ADVENTURE RIO, SALVADOR, AND THE AMAZON

Day 1: Arrive in Rio de Janeiro

Spend your first afternoon visiting either Corcovado and the Christ Statue or Sugar Loaf. Relax at night with caipirinhas from a beachside kiosk.

Logistics: To keep days in Rio stress-free, consult a map to see the distances between your outings. Remember that rush hour is not just in São Paulo—try to make sure you are set to wait out the worst afternoon traffic.

Day 2: Hiking

Explore Rio de Janeiro's Tijuca forest, a sprawling national park in the middle of the municipality. Hike up the Pedra Bonita for great views. If you're feeling especially adventurous, you can then hang-glide down to the São Conrado beach.

Logistics: Start early to avoid the hottest part of the day. Wear sunscreen since the sun burns strong in Rio.

Day 3: Beach Day

Take a break after a strenuous day by lounging on either Copacabana or Ipanema Beach. Take several leisurely strolls to fully appreciate Rio's beach culture. The city's lagoon, called the Lagoa, offers a series of chic bars and restaurants behind Ipanema beach.

Logistics: Be careful with Rio's strong undertow and waves. Bring only the bare minimum of belongings to the beach, and make sure someone from your group keeps an eye on them.

Day 4: Rio to Salvador

Say good-bye to Rio with breakfast at the Confeitaria Colombo, one of the city's oldest restaurants and known for its sweets, before flying to Salvador, the bayside capital of Bahia State. If you start in Pelourinho, you won't have to look hard to find live music in the evening.

Logistics: Keep in mind the difference it makes to fly from Rio de Janeiro's Santos Dumont, the centrally located domestic airport, or Galeão, the international airport about 45 minutes from it. Traffic leading toward Galeão during rush hour is often at a standstill.

Days 5–6: Historical Salvador

Stroll along Pelourinho, the center of historical Salvador, and the surrounding churches, art galleries, and museums.

Start in the Largo do Pelourinho, where you can visit the impressive Museu da Cidade. Head up Rua Maciel de Baixo and stroll the cobblestone streets of the colonial district, flanked by houses in pastel shades. Continue through Praça da Sé to the Municipal Square towering above the Lower City, which offers spectacular views. Have a snack of acarajé, the traditional fried snack with shrimp and spicy peppers.

Logistics: Wear comfortable shoes—you may need to hike up one of Salvador's steep streets.

Day 6: Afro-Brazilian Culture

Bahia is a seedbed of Brazilian culture. To learn more, visit the comprehensive Museu Afro-Brasileiro (Afro-Brazilian Museum) next to the Catedral Basilica. Many of the country's top musicians have come from here. Make a point to find live music and *capoeira*, a highly rhythmic form of martial arts. The Balé Folclórico de Bahia, for example, stages exhilarating dance shows that showcase the region's Afro-Brazilian culture.

Logistics: Salvador's life often happens on the streets. Carry only what you need so that you can have your hands free.

Day 7: Salvador to Manaus

Manaus, the gateway to the Amazon region, is not just a hop from Brazil's coastal cities. Remember that distances in Brazil's Amazon region are far, and flight service is sparse. You'll need to reserve at least half a day for this leg of the trip, since there are no direct flights from Salvador. When you arrive late in the day, check out a few Manaus sites, such as the iconic Opera House whose dome is tiled in the colors of Brazil's flag.

Logistics: Make an effort in advance to find a close connecting flight, often via Brasília, that will minimize your trip time. Flight service from Northeastern cities remains minimal to none.

Days 8–9: Cruise on the Amazon

Here, your options are limited only by your time. With five or more days, you can plan an excursion to a lonely river reserve, such as the breathtaking Mamirauá, with floating guest homes on the river and with pink dolphins jumping outside your window. A shorter trip could involve seeing the two-colored "Meeting of the Waters," where the dark waters of the Rio Negro meets the sandy-colored Rio Solimões to form the mighty Rio Amazonas. If you don't have the time for a long trip on the river, try a short day trip, such as the Praia do Tupé, a half-hour riverboat ride along the Rio Negro from the center of Manaus. Gird yourself and hire a guide for a day of tree climbing up a 130-foot Amapazeiro.

Logistics: A normal "barco" (boat) will take you at the leisurely speed of a regular riverboat, often several days to get to popular Amazonian destinations, whereas the speedboat "lancha," sometimes called an "ajato," will fraction the time of your rides, albeit without the ability to lounge around on the deck. Generously apply bug spray, as mosquitoes are a real threat. It is also highly recommended that you get a yellow fever vaccine before going to the Amazon.

Day 10: Shopping and Departure

Look for some of the only-in-the-Amazon products, such as the healing copaiba oil or the "milk" of the Amapazeiro tree, used for medicinal purposes. A bar of the energetic guaraná, which locals grind into a fine powder using the hard, dried tongue of the pirarucu fish, will keep you awake during your next adventure.

SOUNDS OF BRAZIL

Music is woven into the fabric of Brazilian life and is the art form that most completely translates this diverse nation's creativity and richness. Travelers will be exposed to it throughout their visit, whether it is an upbeat *forro* playing on the radio of your taxi or a traditional samba coming from a local bar where musicians have gathered for an afternoon jam session. You'll learn much about the country and the region you're in from music, since local rhythms usually say much about the place's unique ethnic makeup and history.

Samba

Samba, the music most associated with Brazil, was born in the mostly black neighborhoods near Rio de Janeiro's docks among stevedores and other laborers in the early 20th century. There are many varieties of it, generally all fast-paced and driven by percussion instruments including the deep bass *bumbo* and the smaller *atabaque*, tambourines, and complemented by stringed instruments like the *cavaquinho*, which looks like a tiny guitar.

There are great venues to see traditional samba in Rio's bohemian Lapa neighborhood, among them Semente and Carioca da Gema. Trapiche Gamboa, in the port-side neighborhood of Saude, has great bands in a beautifully restored old warehouse.

One of the real delights of Rio is to see samba played outdoors in samba circles much as it was over a century ago. These circles often spring up without notice, but there are parts of town where musicians traditionally gather. These include Ouvidor Street in downtown, which generally has music on Wednesdays and Saturdays, and Pedra do Sal, an outdoor space in Saude that hosts hugely popular samba circles on Monday and Friday evenings.

Bossa Nova

Bossa Nova, which means "new trend," is a fresh, jazzy take on percussion-heavy samba. Where samba is cathartic and communal and built on drums and powerful voices, bossa nova is intimate and contemplative, with the melody up front and percussion in the background, often played with brushes for a softer texture.

Bossa Nova was born in the bars of Rio's posh south side neighborhoods like Ipanema in the 1950s. It became famous worldwide with the song "The Girl from Ipanema." A good place to hear Bossa Nova is Rio's Vinicius Piano Bar, across the street from the Ipanema bar where the song's authors watched their muse saunter by.

Forro

Brazil's northeast has the country's richest musical tradition. From these arid backlands sprung *coco, xaxado, baiao, xote, axe,* and *frevo*, among many others. The best known across Brazil is the *forro*, a fast, syncopated rhythm driven by the accordion and the *zabumba*, a rustic drum. It was brought to wealthier São Paulo and Rio de Janeiro by Northeastern migrants who left their impoverished hometowns in search of work.

Derided for years as the "music of maids and doormen," forro has gained a mainstream following. Good places to check it out are São Paulo's Canto da Ema or Feira Moderna, a charming little bar with Northeastern fare and music. In Rio de Janeiro, the Feira de Sao Cristovao—a huge indoor fair with about 700 stands selling Northeastern food, arts, and crafts—is the place to go.

RIO DE JANEIRO

Updated by
Lucy Bryson

Welcome to the Cidade Maravilhosa, or the Marvelous City, as Rio is known in Brazil. Synonymous with the girl from Ipanema, the dramatic views from Christ the Redeemer atop Corcovado Mountain, and famous Carnival celebrations, Rio is a city of stunning architecture, abundant museums, and marvelous food. Rio is also home to 23 beaches, an almost continuous 73-km (45-mile) ribbon of sand.

As you leave the airport and head to Ipanema or Copacabana, you'll drive for about 40 minutes on a highway from where you'll begin to get a sense of the dramatic contrast between beautiful landscape and devastating poverty. In this teeming metropolis of 12 million people (6.2 million of whom live in Rio proper), the very rich and the very poor live in uneasy proximity. But by the time you reach Copacabana's breezy, sunny Avenida Atlântica—flanked on one side by white beach and azure sea and on the other by condominiums and hotels—your heart will leap with expectation as you begin to recognize the postcard-famous sights. Now you're truly in Rio, where *cariocas* (Rio residents) and tourists live life to its fullest.

Enthusiasm is contagious in Rio. Prepare to have your senses engaged and your inhibitions untied. Rio seduces with a host of images: the joyous bustle of vendors at Sunday's Feira Hippie (Hippie Fair); the tipsy babble at sidewalk cafés as patrons sip their last glass of icy beer under the stars; the blanket of lights beneath the Pão de Açúcar (Sugar Loaf) morro; the bikers, joggers, strollers, and power walkers who parade along the beach each morning. Borrow the carioca spirit for your stay; you may find yourself reluctant to give it back.

ORIENTATION AND PLANNING

GETTING ORIENTED

Cariocas divide their city into four main sections: the suburban Zona Norte (North Zone), the chic Zona Sul (South Zone), the sprawling Zona Oeste (West Zone), and the urban Centro.

Most tourist activity takes place in the Zona Sul, amid its mix of residential areas, office buildings, shops, restaurants, bars, hotels, and beaches. This is the city's most affluent section, with fancy condos housing Rio's middle and upper class, and dozens of theaters and music halls.

Centro and neighboring Lapa and Santa Teresa are filled with the remnants of the old Portuguese colony, including some impressive neoclassical structures housing churches, museums, and art galleries. The vast Zona Norte is primarily residential and lower class, but the international airport and the soccer stadium are here. Zona Oeste is the "up and coming" part of Rio, occupied by the newly rich, and replete with malls, superstores, and untouched beaches.

TOP REASONS TO GO

■ **Stunning Beaches:** Unpack your Speedo or thong bikini and join the masses at Rio's miles of gorgeous beaches.

■ **Carnival:** Head to the streets or the Sambódromo, and revel in the celebration of Rio's biggest party.

■ **Brazilian Beats:** Tap your feet to the uniquely Brazilian styles of music such as samba, bossa nova, funk, and pagode that echo from the myriad clubs and live-music venues.

■ **Scrumptious Meals:** Tickle your taste buds with delicious dining experiences—there's a lot to like for meat lovers and vegetarians at Rio's diverse restaurants.

■ **Breathtaking landscapes:** Bask in the beauty of the endlessly breathtaking landscapes that unfold between mountain and ocean.

CENTRO

Architectural gems left behind from the days of Portuguese colonialism share space with modern high-rises in Rio's financial district. Ornately decorated churches, museums, and palaces are just some of the highlights. The neighborhood is a virtual ghost town from Saturday afternoon until Monday morning, when the workweek begins. Have a look in one of Centro's many used bookstores for good buys on Brazilian literature and English-language titles.

CATETE AND GLÓRIA

Historic Catete and Glória, two largely residential neighborhoods close to Centro, are well worth an afternoon's sightseeing. The national government formerly operated out of Catete, which still has its beautiful palaces and old residences, and Glória is famous for its beautiful hilltop church.

SANTA TERESA AND LAPA

One of Rio's first residential neighborhoods, Santa Teresa is worth a visit to explore its narrow, cobblestone streets. Many of the beautiful colonial mansions lining them have been converted into stylish guesthouses and boutique hotels. This charming neighborhood also contains excellent restaurants, craft stores, and art galleries. Adjacent to Centro, the Lapa neighborhood has some of the best music halls and dance clubs in the city. If you've come to Rio to explore its nightlife, you'll become intimately familiar with Lapa.

FLAMENGO AND BOTAFOGO

The middle class neighborhoods of Flamengo and Botafogo, both good places to find value lodgings, are famed for their rival soccer teams, two of Brazil's biggest teams. Sports rivalry aside, the Parque de Flamengo, designed by the world-famous landscape architect Roberto Burle Marx, is an oasis of calm and a popular spot for walkers and joggers, while Botafogo is home to some of Rio's best independent bars and restaurants. The beaches in both neighborhoods aren't the greatest, but a five-minute hop on the metro will bring you to Copacabana and Ipanema.

URCA

East of Botafogo is tiny, mainly residential Urca, where you can ascend the huge morro Sugar Loaf by cable car. Few visitors linger in this peaceful neighborhood, but it's worth exploring. Praia Vermelha, a small, sheltered beach beneath Sugar Loaf, is a wonderful spot for sunbathing, and on the easy walking trail nearby there's a good chance you'll see marmoset monkeys at play.

COPACABANA

Copacabana Beach is the main attraction in the city's most tourist-packed neighborhood. It's the perfect place to sunbathe, stroll, people-watch, buy souvenirs at the open-air night market, sip a caipirinha at a beach kiosk, or gaze in awe at the giant apartment buildings and hotels (including the Copacabana Palace) that line the Avenida Atlântica.

> ### WHAT'S A CARIOCA?
>
> The term *carioca* was an indigenous word meaning "white man's house" and was used in the city's early history to describe the Portuguese colonizers. Today the word is used more broadly, to identify residents of the city of Rio. But the word defines much more than birthplace, race, or residence: it represents an ethos of pride, a sensuality, and a passion for life. Poor or rich, cariocas share a common identity and a distinct local accent, considered by many foreigners and Brazilians alike to be the most beautiful within the Portuguese language.

IPANEMA AND LEBLON

Famously the place where "The Girl from Ipanema" caught the eye of bossa nova songwriters Tom Jobim and Vinicius de Moraes in the 1960s, this affluent neighborhood is a collection of tree-lined streets harboring smart condos, fabulous restaurants, and trendy boutiques. The gorgeous beach, framed by the towering Dois Irmaos (Two Brothers) mountains, is the sunbathing spot of choice for Rio's young and beautiful. Extending west from Ipanema, affluent, intimate Leblon borrows some of its neighbor's trendy charms, but is slightly funkier. Leblon's beach, an extension of Ipanema, is popular with families, but the water is often too dirty for swimming.

SÃO CONRADO AND BARRA DA TIJUCA

West of Leblon, the well-heeled neighborhoods of São Conrado and Barra da Tijuca have long stretches of unspoiled beach. São Conrado contains some striking mansions, while towering condos and vast shopping malls have earned Barra da Tijuca the nickname Estados Unidos da Barra (United States of Barra). It's best to take a cab straight to the beaches, which are quieter than Copacabana and Ipanema and are especially recommended for families with children.

THE LUSH INLAND

The middle-class residential neighborhoods of Jardim Botânico, Gávea, Lagoa, and Cosme Velho are worth visiting for their stunning scenery and opportunities for peaceful strolls and nature-spotting rambles. The highlights here include the botanical garden in Jardim Botânico, the cable-car ride to the Christ statue in Cosme Velho, Gávea's planetarium, Tijuca's samba school, and massive city lake in Lagoa, good for a brisk stroll, run, or bike ride.

PLANNING

WHEN TO GO

Rio is a year-round destination, but Carnival, which usually takes place in February, is the best time to soak up the city's energy. Arrive a few days before the celebrations begin, or stay a few days after they end to enjoy the museums and other sights that close for the four days of revelry. Prices rise substantially during Carnival season, and accommodations need to be booked several months in advance.

Temperatures in Rio tend to be the highest from January to March, when they often soar above 100 degrees. The city generally sees the most rain during December, when it might pour for days at a time. To tour the city at a quieter time with gentler temperatures and at lower prices, come in the off-season, from May to October (Brazil's winter). The temperature in the winter tends to be in the upper 70s during the day and rarely falls below 50 degrees at night.

SAFETY AND PRECAUTIONS

IN THE CITY

As with any city its size, crime occurs in Rio, but taking a few basic precautions should keep you from becoming a victim of it. Most violent crime is related to drug trafficking, so tourists are more likely to run afoul of petty thieves than anyone more sinister. Crimes involving visitors generally occur in crowded public areas: beaches, busy sidewalks, intersections, and city buses. Pickpockets, usually children, work in groups. One will distract you while another grabs a wallet, bag, or camera. Be particularly wary of children who thrust themselves in front of you and ask for money or offer to shine your shoes. Another member of the gang may strike from behind, grabbing your valuables and disappearing into the crowd. Another tactic is for criminals to approach your car at intersections. Always keep doors locked and windows partially closed. Leave valuables in your hotel safe, don't wear expensive jewelry or watches, and keep cameras hidden except when snapping shots.

ON THE BEACH

Don't shun the beaches because of reports of crime, but *do* take precautions. Leave jewelry, passports, and large sums of cash at your hotel; don't wander alone and at night; and be alert if groups of seemingly friendly youths attempt to engage you in conversation. They may be trying to distract you while one of their cohorts snatches your belongings. A big danger is actually the sun. From 10 am to 3 pm the rays are merciless, making heavy-duty sunscreen, hats, cover-ups, and plenty of liquids essential; you can also rent a beach umbrella from vendors on the beach or your hotel. Vendors stroll the beaches with beverages, food, and trinkets. These guys are no-nonsense salespeople, and quickly move on if you shake your head no, but if you express interest in their wares they will press you to buy. Most beachgoers take advantage of their services. Beach vendors generally charge about R$4 for an ice-cold beer, R$3 for water, and up to R$5 for a coconut water. Lifeguard stations, with bathrooms and showers, are found every kilometer.

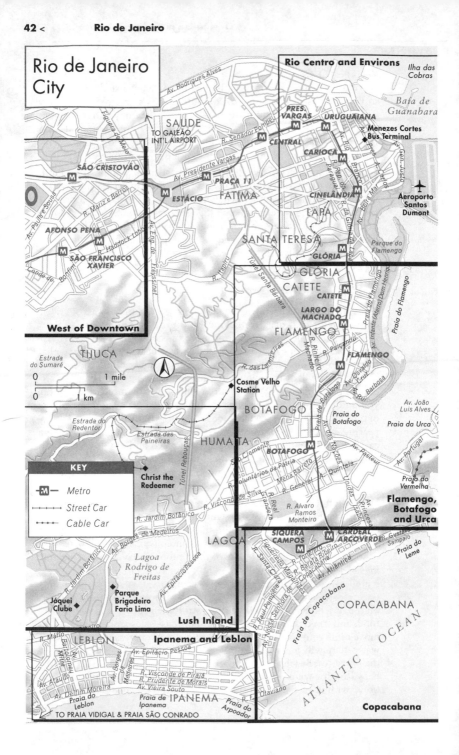

Rio de Janeiro City

Rio Centro and Environs

Ilha das Cobras

Baía de Guanabara

SAUDE
TO GALEÃO INT'L AIRPORT

PRES. VARGAS

URUGUAIANA

Menezes Cortes Bus Terminal

CENTRAL

CARIOCA

SÃO CRISTOVÃO

PRAÇA 11

CINELÂNDIA

ESTÁCIO

FATIMA

Aeroporto Santos Dumont

AFONSO PENA

LAPA

SÃO FRANCISCO XAVIER

SANTA TERESA

Parque do Flamengo

GLÓRIA

Praia do Flamengo

GLÓRIA

West of Downtown

CATETE

CATETE

LARGO DO MACHADO

FLAMENGO

FLAMENGO

Estrada do Sumaré

TIJUCA

0 ——— 1 mile
0 ——— 1 km

Cosme Velho Station

BOTAFOGO

Praia do Botafogo

Praia da Urca

Estrada do Redentor

Estrada das Paineiras

HUMAITÁ

Av. João Luis Alves

KEY

Christ the Redeemer

BOTAFOGO

Praia do Vermelha

🅼— *Metro*

Flamengo, Botafogo and Urca

┼┼┼┼ *Street Car*

•••• *Cable Car*

LAGOA

SIQUERA CAMPOS

CARDEAL ARCOVERDE

Praia do Leme

Lagoa Rodrigo de Freitas

Jóquei Clube

Parque Brigadeiro Faria Lima

COPACABANA

Lush Inland

Praia de Copacabana

LEBLON

Ipanema and Leblon

ATLANTIC OCEAN

IPANEMA

Praia do Leblon

Praia de Ipanema

Praia do Arpoador

TO PRAIA VIDIGAL & PRAIA SÃO CONRADO

Copacabana

2

GETTING HERE AND AROUND

Rio's shuttle system currently extends from the Zona Norte to Ipanema, with shuttles to areas west of the final stop. By 2014 work to extend the metro as far as Barra da Tijuca may have been completed. Within Ipanema and Copacabana, it's easy to get around on foot, but some attractions are far apart, so a taxi might be in order. After dark you should always take a taxi if you're venturing into unexplored territory. It's easy to hail taxis on every main street. Public buses are cheap and cover every inch of the city, but can be difficult to figure out if you don't speak Portuguese. Vans are a form of informal public transportation that are more frequent and quicker than buses, but for basic safety reasons, it is not recommended that tourists use them.

AIR TRAVEL

Nearly three-dozen airlines regularly serve Rio, but most flights from North America stop first in São Paulo. Several international carriers offer Rio–São Paulo flights.

AIRPORTS All international flights and most domestic flights arrive and depart from the Aeroporto Internacional Antônio Carlos Jobim, also known as Galeão (GIG). The airport is about 45 minutes northwest of the beach area and most of Rio's hotels. Aeroporto Santos Dumont (SDU), 20 minutes from the beaches and within walking distance of Centro, is served by the Rio–São Paulo air shuttle and a few air-taxi firms.

Airport Information Aeroporto Internacional Antônio Carlos Jobim (*Galeão, GIG*) ✉ *Av. 20 de Janeiro s/n, Ilha do Governador* ☎ *021/3398–2288* ⊕ *www.aeroportogaleao.net.* **Aeroporto Santos Dumont** (*SDU*) ✉ *Praça Senador Salgado Filho s/n, Centro* ☎ *021/3814–7262* ⊕ *www.aeroportosantosdumont.net.*

AIRPORT TRANSFERS: BUSES AND TAXIS Most visitors arrive at Rio International Airport, about a 40-minute car ride from the tourist destinations. The speediest way to reach Centro and the Zona Sul is to take a taxi. Prices are steep, however. Expect to pay up to R$90 to reach Copacabana, and slightly more to Ipanema and Leblon. There are taxi booths in front of the airport, and passengers pay a set fare in advance, though drivers may charge extra if you have lots of luggage. Also trustworthy are the white radio taxis parked in the same areas; these metered vehicles cost an average of 20% less than the airport taxis. Three taxi firms are Transcoopass, Cootramo, and Coopertramo (⇨ *See Taxi Travel, below, for contact information*).

Comfortable, air-conditioned buses run by Real (marked Real Premium) park curbside outside the arrivals lounge; there is plenty of luggage storage space, and staff will safely stow your luggage beneath the bus. The buses (R$12) make the hour-long trip from Galeão to the Zona Sul, following the beachfront drives and stopping at major hotels along the way. If your hotel is inland, the driver will let you off at the nearest corner. Buses operate from 5:30 am to 11:45 pm (⇨ *See Bus Travel, below, for contact information*).

BUS TRAVEL

Regular service is available to and from Rio. Long-distance and international buses leave from the Rodoviária Novo Rio. Any local bus marked "rodoviária" will take you to the station. You can buy tickets at the depot or, for some destinations, from travel agents. To buy online you will need a CPF (Brazilian Social Security) number. A staff member at your hotel may be able to help you with online purchases.

Bus Stations Menezes Cortes Terminal ⊠ *Rua São José 35, Centro* ☎ *021/2544–6667* ⊕ *www.tgmc.com.br.* **Rodoviária Novo Rio** ⊠ *Av. Francisco Bicalho 1, Santo Cristo* ☎ *021/3213–1800* ⊕ *www.transportal.com.br/rodoviaria-novorio.*

Rio's urban buses are cheap, frequent, and generally safe to use, but do not show cameras or wallets, and do not wear expensive-looking clothes or jewelry. Wear backpacks on your front, and avoid getting on or off the bus in deserted areas. Local buses have a fixed price (R$2.80), and can take you anywhere you want to go. Route maps aren't available, but local tourist offices (⇨ *See Visitor Information, below*) have route lists for the most popular sights. Enter buses at the front, pay the attendant, and pass through a turnstile. Have your fare in hand when you board to avoid flashing bills or your wallet. When you want to get off, pull the overhead cord and the driver will pause at the next designated stop. Exit from the rear of the bus.

The comfortable, privately run, and air-conditioned **Real VIP** buses serve the beaches, downtown, and Rio's two airports. These vehicles, which look like highway buses, stop at regular bus stops but also may be flagged down wherever you see them. Expect to pay around three times the price of the regular bus. Minivans, known as "combis," run back and forth along beachfront avenues. Fares start at about R$2.50.

Bus Contact Real ☎ *021/3035–6700, 021/3086–1700* ⊕ *www.realautoonibus.com.br.*

CAR TRAVEL

The carioca style of driving is passionate to the point of abandon: traffic jams are common, the streets aren't well marked, and red lights are often more decorative than functional. Although there are parking areas along the beachfront boulevards, finding a spot can still be a problem. If you do choose to drive, exercise extreme caution, wear seat belts at all times, and keep the doors locked.

Car rentals can be arranged through hotels or agencies and at this writing cost between R$140 and R$250 a day for standard models. Major agencies include Avis, Hertz, and Unidas. Localiza is a local agency. Hertz and Unidas have desks at the international and domestic airports. (⇨ *See Car Travel in the Travel Smart chapter for car-agency contact information.)*

Turismo Clássico Travel, one of Brazil's most reliable travel and transport agencies, can arrange for a driver to get you around the city, with or without an English-speaking guide (US$50 per hour). Clássico's owners, Liliana and Vera, speak English, and each has more than 20 years of experience in organizing transportation. They also lead sightseeing tours.

SUBWAY TRAVEL

Metrô Rio, the subway system, is clean, relatively safe, and efficient— a delight to use—but it's not comprehensive. The metro is a great option to get from Centro to Ipanema, for instance, but not to Leblon, because the southernmost metro stop, Ipanema/General Osório, is on the opposite side of Ipanema. The metro shuttle can get you to and from Ipanema/General Osório to Gávea, Lagoa, and farther west to Barra da Tijuca. (At this writing, work was underway to extend the metro as far as Barra da Tijuca in time for the 2014 FIFA World Cup.) Reaching sights distant from metro stations can be a challenge, especially in summer, when beach traffic increases. Tourism offices and some metro stations have maps.

Trains operate daily between 5 am and midnight except on Sundays and holidays, when they run between 7 am and 11 pm. A single metro ticket costs R$3.20.

Subway Information Metrô Rio ⊠ *Av. Presidente Vargas 2000, Centro* ☎ *021/3211–6300 information line* ⊕ *www.metrorio.com.br.*

TAXI TRAVEL

Taxis are plentiful in Rio, and in most parts of the city you can easily flag one down on the street. Yellow taxis have meters that start at a set price and have two rates. The "1" rate applies to fares before 8 pm, and the "2" rate applies to fares after 8 pm, on Sunday, on holidays, throughout December, in the neighborhoods of São Conrado and Barra da Tijuca, and when climbing steep hills, such as those in Santa Teresa. Drivers are required to post a chart noting the current fares on the inside of the left rear window. CentralTaxi has a fare calculator on its website that will give you a general idea of what the fare from one destination to another might be.

Radio taxis and several companies that routinely serve hotels (and whose drivers often speak English) are also options. They charge 30% more than other taxis but are reliable and usually air-conditioned. Other cabs working with the hotels also charge more, normally a fixed fee that you should agree on before you leave. Reliable radio-cab companies include Coopacarioca and Coopatur.

Most carioca cabbies are pleasant, but there are exceptions. If flagging down a taxi on the street, check to see that an official phone number is displayed on the side and that the driver's official identity card is displayed. Remain alert and trust your instincts. Unless you've negotiated a flat fee with the driver, be sure the meter is turned on.

■ **TIP→** Few cab drivers speak English, so it's a good idea to have your destination written down to show the driver, in case there's a communication gap.

Taxi Companies CentralTaxi ☎ *021/2195–1000* ⊕ *www.centraltaxi.com.br.* **Coopacarioca** ☎ *021/2518–3857, 021/2158–1818* ⊕ *www.coopacarioca.com.br.* **Coopatur** ☎ *021/3885–1000.*

TRAIN TRAVEL

Few visitors to Rio travel by rail. The urban network serves the North Zone of the city, which is less visited by tourists, and trains tend to be hot, overcrowded and uncomfortable. Long distance trips are generally made by bus or plane. Should you have reason to take a local train, these leave from the central station, Estação Dom Pedro II Central do Brasil.

Train Information Estação Dom Pedro II Central do Brasil
✉ *Praça Cristiano Otoni, Av. Presidente Vargas s/n, Centro* ☎ *0800/726–9494*
⊕ *www.supervia.com.br.*

CONTACTS AND RESOURCES

EMERGENCIES AND MEDICAL ASSISTANCE
The Tourism Police station is open 24 hours.

Contacts Tourism Police ✉ *Av. Afrânio de Melo Franco 159, Leblon*
☎ *021/2332–2924.*

TOURS
CITY TOURS
Be a Local conducts walking tours of Rocinha that make various stops inside the community. On Sunday nights, the fun favela funk-party tour (R$65) includes transport, entrance, and admission to a VIP area. The company accepts donations of clothing, food, and medicine on behalf of favela residents. Brazil Expedition runs trips to soccer games, samba-school rehearsals, and has a speedy city tour (R$95), a great option for time-pressed travelers, that takes in the Christ Statue as well as Santa Teresa, Lapa, and Tijuca National Park.

Favela Tour, led by Marcelo Armstrong, conducts tours twice daily through Rocinha and Vila Canoas. Marcelo pioneered favela tourism in Rio, has an impeccable reputation and offers tours in English, Spanish, French and Portuguese. Tours (R$70) are informative, not voyeuristic, and there are opportunities to buy locally produced arts and crafts as you tour the communities. Hotel pickup and drop-off are included in the price.

Private Tours' jeeps can whisk you around old Rio, the favelas, Corcovado, Floresta da Tijuca, and the hard-to-reach beaches of Prainha and Grumari. Guides are available who speak English, French, German, and Hungarian. Rio Hiking not only takes groups on jungle hikes, but also on nightlife tours to clubs and bars beyond the regular tourist circuit.

Tour Contacts Be a Local ☎ *021/7816–9581* ⊕ *www.bealocal.com.* **Brazil Expedition** ☎ *021/9998–2907, 021/9376–2839* ⊕ *www.brazilexpedition.com.* **Favela Tour** ☎ *021/3322–2727, 021/9989–0074* ⊕ *www.favelatour.com.br.* **Private Tours** ☎ *021/2232–9710* ⊕ *www.privatetours.com.br.* **Rio Hiking** ✉ *Rua Coelho Neto 70, Sala 401, Laranjeiras* ☎ *021/2552–9204* ⊕ *www.riohiking.com.br.*

2

HELICOPTER TOURS

Helisight conducts helicopter tours that pass over the Christ the Redeemer statue, the beaches of the Zona Sul, and other iconic sights. Prices start at R$210 for a seven-minute flight from Sugar Loaf's landing pad.

Information Helisight ⊠ *Conde de Bernadotte 26, Leblon* ☎ *021/2511– 2141, 021/2542–7935, 021/2259–6995* ⊕ *www.helisight.com.br.*

VISITOR INFORMATION

The Rio de Janeiro city tourism department, Riotur, has an information booth in Copacabana that is open daily from 8 to 5. There are also city tourism desks at the airports and the Novo Rio bus terminal. The Rio de Janeiro state tourism board, Turisrio, is open weekdays from 9 to 6. You can also try contacting Brazil's national tourism board, Embatur, via its Visit Brasil website.

Information Riotur ⊠ *Rua da Assembléia 10, near Praça 15 de Novembro, Centro* ☎ *021/2542–8080* ⊕ *www.rio.rj.gov.br/riotur.* **Riotur information booth** ⊠ *Kiosk 15, Av. Atlantica, in front of Rua Hilário Gouveia, Copacabana* ☎ *No phone.* **Turisrio** ⊠ *Rua da Ajuda 5, Centro* ☎ *021/2215–0011* ⊕ *www.turisrio.rj.gov.br.*

THE COPS

Once known as the murder capital of the world, Rio is now much less dangerous than it was a decade ago. Simple changes such as installing lights on the beaches have improved safety. An increased police presence has also helped. In Rio there are three types of police: the gray-uniformed Military Police, the beige-uniformed Municipal Guard, and the black-uniformed special forces called the BOPE (pronounced "boppy"). For a glimpse at Rio's SWAT team, the BOPE, check out the film *Tropa de Elite (Elite Squad)* (2007) and its Oscar-nominated sequel, *Tropa de Elite 2* (2010).

RESTAURANTS

With nearly a thousand restaurants, Rio's dining choices are broad, from low-key Middle Eastern cafés to elegant contemporary eateries with award-winning kitchens and first-class service. The succulent offerings in the *churrascarias* (restaurants specializing in grilled meats) can be mesmerizing for meat lovers—especially the places that serve *rodízio* style (grilled meat on skewers is continuously brought to your table— until you can eat no more). Hotel restaurants often serve the national dish, *feijoada* (a hearty stew of black beans and pork), on Saturdays— sometimes on Fridays, too. Wash it down with a *chopp* (the local draft beer; pronounced "shop") or a caipirinha (Brazilian rum, lime, and sugar). *Prices in the reviews are the average cost of a main course at dinner or, if dinner is not served, at lunch.*

HOTELS

Lodgings in Rio de Janeiro are among the most expensive in the world, though the price-to-quality ratio often disappoints. That said, there are some wonderful accommodation options in all price ranges if you know where to look. Copacabana and Ipanema are awash with lodgings and are the best bet for sun seekers, but expect to get more bang for your buck the further you travel from the famous beaches. Leafy Santa Teresa contains many charming guesthouses and chic boutique hotels, while Centro, Flamengo and Botafogo have solid options for business travelers. ⚠ Note that "motels" are not aimed at tourists. They attract couples looking for privacy and usually rent by the hour.

Expect to pay a premium for a room with a view. Most hotels include breakfast in the rate, and Brazilian breakfasts are usually a lavish affair involving everything from fresh fruit and juices to cakes, cold meats, and cheeses. If you're traveling during peak periods—from December to March—make reservations as far ahead of your visit as possible. *Prices in the reviews are the lowest cost of a standard double room in high season. For expanded reviews, facilities, and current deals, visit Fodors.com.*

EXPLORING

When in Rio, don't be afraid to follow the tourist trail—the major attractions really are "must-sees." Contrary to tourist-board images, the sun doesn't always shine on the city, so when it does, make the most of it. If the skies are clear, waste no time in heading for Cosme Velho to visit the Christ the Redeemer statue atop Corcovado mountain, or to Urca to make the cable car ascent to the peak of Sugar Loaf. Time-pressed travelers will find that whistle-stop city tours are a good way to see many attractions in one day, while those lucky enough to spend a week or more here can afford to take a more leisurely approach. Cloudy days are a good time to visit the attractions of leafy Lagoa and Jardim Botânico and the breezily bohemian hilltop neighborhood of Santa Teresa. The historic buildings, museums, and cultural centers of Centro, Catete, Glória, and Lapa are ideal rainy-day options.

CENTRO

Rio's settlement dates back to 1555. You can experience much of the city's rich history by visiting churches, government buildings, and villas in and around Centro. The metro is a good way to get downtown, but wear comfortable shoes and be ready to walk multiple blocks as you explore this historic city center. If you're not up for a long walk, consider taking an organized bus tour.

What locals generally refer to as Centro is actually several sprawling districts containing the city's oldest neighborhoods, churches, and most enchanting cafés. Rio's beaches, broad boulevards, and modern architecture may be impressive; but its colonial structures, old narrow streets, and alleyways in leafy inland neighborhoods are no less so. The metro stations that serve Centro are Cinelândia, Carioca, Uruguaiana, Presidente Vargas, Central, and Praça Onze.

TOP ATTRACTIONS

Biblioteca Nacional. Corinthian columns adorn the neoclassical National Library (built between 1905 and 1908), the first such establishment in Latin America. Its original archives were brought to Brazil by King João VI in 1808. The library contains roughly 13 million books, including two 15th-century printed Bibles, manuscript New Testaments from the

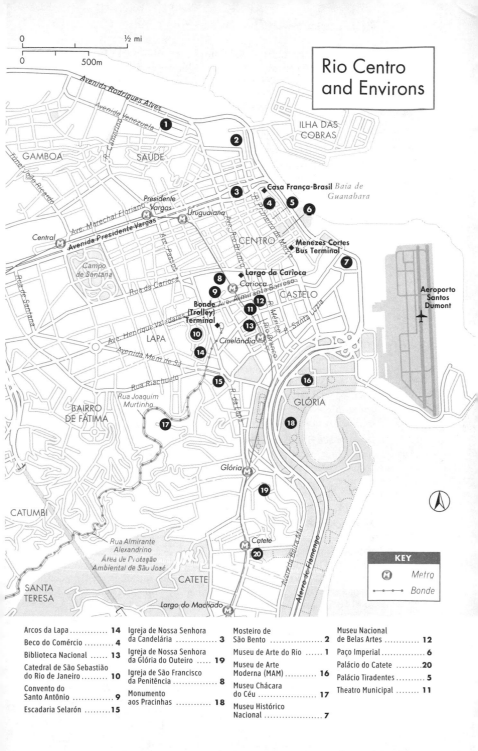

Rio Centro and Environs

0 ½ mi
0 500m

Avenida Rodrigues Alves

Avenida Venezuela

Túnel João Ricardo

GAMBOA

SAÚDE

ILHA DAS COBRAS

① Museu de Arte do Rio

② Mosteiro de São Bento

Presidente Vargas

Uruguaiana

③ Igreja de Nossa Senhora da Candelária

Casa França-Brasil *Baía de Guanabara*

④ ⑤ ⑥

Central

Ave. Marechal Floriano

Avenida Presidente Vargas

Rua de Santana

Campo de Sántana

Rua da Carioca

CENTRO

Menezes Cortes Bus Terminal

⑦

Aeroporto Santos Dumont

Largo da Carioca

⑧ ⑨

Carioca

Almirante Barroso

CASTELO

Bonde (Trolley) Terminal

⑫ ⑪

Ave. Henrique Valadares

LAPA

⑩ ⑬

Cinelândia

México

R. Santa Luzia

Rua Branco

Avenida Mem de Sá

⑭

Rua Riachuelo

⑮

⑯

BAIRRO DE FÁTIMA

Rua Joaquim Murtinho

⑰

GLÓRIA

⑱

Glória Ⓜ

⑲

CATUMBÍ

Rua Almirante Alexandrino

Área de Proteção Ambiental de São José

Catete

⑳

Aterro de Flamengo

Avenida Beira Mar

SANTA TERESA

CATETE

Largo do Machado Ⓜ

KEY

Ⓜ Metro
•→•→• Bonde

11th and 12th centuries, and volumes that belonged to Empress Teresa Christina. Also here are first-edition Mozart scores, as well as scores by Carlos Gomes, who adapted the José de Alencar novel about Brazil's Indians, *O Guarani,* into an opera of the same name. Tours are available in English. ⊠ *Av. Rio Branco 219, Centro* ☎ *021/3095–3879* ⊕ *www. bn.br* ✉ *Tours R$2* ⊘ *By guided tour only, weekdays 10–5, weekends 12:30–4 on the hour* Ⓜ *Cinelândia.*

Catedral de São Sebastião do Rio de Janeiro (*Catedral Metropolitana*). The exterior of this circa-1960 metropolitan cathedral, which looks like a concrete beehive, divides opinion. The daring modern design stands in sharp contrast to the baroque style of other churches in Rio, but don't judge until you've stepped inside. When light floods through the colorful stained-glass windows it transforms the interior—which is 80 meters (263 feet) high and 96 meters (315 feet) in diameter—into a warm, serious place of worship that accommodates up to 20,000 people. An 8½-ton granite rock lends considerable weight to the concept of an altar. ⊠ *Av. República do Chile 245, Centro* ☎ *021/2240–2669* ⊕ *www. catedral.com.br* ✉ *Free* ⊘ *Daily 7–6* Ⓜ *Carioca or Cinelândia.*

Convento do Santo Antônio. The Convent of St. Anthony was completed in 1780, but some parts date from 1615, making it one of Rio's oldest structures. Its baroque interior contains priceless colonial art, including wood carvings and wall paintings. The sacristy is covered with traditional Portuguese *azulejos* (ceramic tiles). The church has no bell tower: its bells hang from a double arch on the monastery ceiling. An exterior mausoleum contains the tombs of the offspring of Dom Pedro I and Dom Pedro II. ⊠ *Largo da Carioca 5, Centro* ☎ *021/2262–0129* ⊕ *www. conventosantoantonio.org.br* ✉ *Free* ⊘ *By appointment only, call ahead or email conventorj@franciscanos.org.br to set up a visit* Ⓜ *Carioca.*

Igreja de São Francisco da Penitência. The church was completed in 1737, nearly four decades after construction began. Today it's famed for its wooden sculptures and its rich gold-leaf interior. The nave contains a painting of St. Francis, the patron of the church—reportedly the first painting in Brazil done in perspective. ⊠ *Largo da Carioca 5, Centro* ☎ *021/2262–0197* ✉ *R$2* ⊘ *Tues.–Fri. 9–noon and 1–4* Ⓜ *Carioca.*

Mosteiro de São Bento. Just a glimpse of the Monastery of St. Benedict's main altar can fill you with awe. Layer upon layer of curvaceous woodcarvings coated in gold lend the space an opulent air, while spiral columns whirl upward to capitals topped by the chubbiest of cherubs and angels that appear lost in divine thought. Although the Benedictine monks arrived in 1586, work didn't begin on this church and monastery until 1617. It was completed in 1641, but artisans that included Mestre Valentim (who designed the silver chandeliers) continued to add details almost to the 19th century. ■TIP→ Sunday mass at 10 am is accompanied by Gregorian chants. ⊠ *Rua Dom Gerardo 68, Centro* ☎ *021/2206–8100* ⊕ *www.osb.org.br* ✉ *Free* ⊘ *Daily 7–6.*

Museu de Arte do Rio. Rio's once rundown port zone is now the focus of a major investment and regeneration program, and the 2013 opening of the Museu de Arte do Rio (MAR) has provided a compelling reason for visitors to head to this part of town. The attention-grabbing museum structures—a colonial palace and a modernist former bus station, united visually by a wavelike postmodern form that floats on stilts above them—represent an impressive feat of architectural reimagination. The eight gallery spaces inside the buildings contain permanent collections of surrealist, modernist, and *naïf* artworks, along with painted depictions of Rio. The temporary exhibitions here are generally quite good. ✉ *Praça Mauá 5, Centro* ☎ *021/2203–1235* ⊕ *www.museudeartedorio. org.br* ✍ *R$8, free on Tues.* ☉ *Tues.–Sun. 10–5* Ⓜ *Uruguiana.*

Museu de Arte Moderna (MAM). A great place to take the pulse of the vibrant Brazilian fine-arts scene, the Museum of Modern Art occupies a striking concrete-and-glass modernist building. Augmenting the permanent collection of about 6,400 works by Brazilian and international artists is the slightly larger Gilberto Chateaubriand Collection of modern and contemporary Brazilian art. MAM has earned respect over the years for its bold, often thought-provoking exhibitions. The venue also hosts events such as music performances and DJ sessions. Its theater screens Brazilian and international independent and art-house films. ✉ *Av. Infante Dom Henrique 85, Centro* ☎ *021/3883–5600* ⊕ *www.mamrio.org.br* ✍ *R$8* ☉ *Tues.–Fri. noon–6, weekends and holidays noon–7* Ⓜ *Cinelândia.*

Museu Histórico Nacional. The building that houses the National History Museum dates from 1762, though some sections—such as the battlements—were erected as early as 1603. It seems appropriate that this colonial structure should exhibit relics that document Brazil's history. Among its treasures are rare papers, Latin American coins, carriages, cannons, and religious art. ✉ *Praça Marechal Âncora, Centro* ☎ *021/2550–9224, 021/2220–2328* ⊕ *www.museuhistoriconacional. com.br* ✍ *Tues.–Sat. R$6, Sun. free* ☉ *Tues.–Fri. 10–5:30, weekends and holidays 2–6* Ⓜ *Carioca or Cinelândia.*

Museu Nacional de Belas Artes. Works by Brazil's leading 19th- and 20th-century artists fill the space at the National Museum of Fine Arts. The most notable canvases are those by the country's best-known modernist, Cândido Portinari, but be on the lookout for such gems as Leandro Joaquim's heartwarming 18th-century painting of Rio (a window to a time when fishermen still cast nets in the waters below the landmark Igreja de Nossa Senhora da Glória do Outeiro). After wandering the picture galleries, tour the extensive collections of folk and African art. ✉ *Av. Rio Branco 199, Centro* ☎ *021/2262–6067* ⊕ *www.mnba.gov.br* ✍ *R$8, free Sun.* ☉ *Tues.–Fri. 10–6, weekends noon–5* Ⓜ *Carioca or Cinelândia.*

Theatro Municipal. If you visit one place in Centro, make it the Municipal Theater, modeled after the Paris Opera House and opened in 1909. Now restored to its sparkling best, the theater boasts Carrara marble, stunning mosaics, glittering chandeliers, bronze and onyx statues, gilded mirrors, German stained-glass windows, and brazilwood inlay floors. Murals by Brazilian artists Eliseu Visconti and Rodolfo Amoedo further enhance the opulent feel. The main entrance and first two galleries are particularly ornate. As you climb to the upper floors, the decor becomes simpler, a reflection of a time when different classes entered through different doors and sat in separate sections, but also due in part to the exhaustion of funds toward the end of the project. The theater seats 2,357—with outstanding sight lines—for its dance performances and classical music concerts. English-speaking guides are available. ⊠ *Rua Marechal Floriano s/n, Centro* ☎ *021/2332–9228* ⊕ *www. theatromunicipal.rj.gov.br* 🎫 *Tours R$10* ⊙ *Guided tours Tues.–Fri. on the hour 11–4, Sat. at 11, 1, and 9 pm* Ⓜ *Cinelândia or Carioca.*

WORTH NOTING

Beco do Comércio. A network of narrow streets and alleys centers on this pedestrian thoroughfare, also called the Travessa do Comércio, whose name translates to Alley of Commerce. The area is flanked by restored 18th-century homes, now converted to offices, shops, and galleries. The best-known sight here is the Arco de Teles, a picturesque archway named in honor of the wealthy Teles de Menezes family, who built many of the street's most handsome buildings. ■ TIP→ **Beco do Comércio is a good place to stop for lunch**—the street is lined with everything from simple pay-by-weight buffet spots and casual bars to more upmarket restaurants and cafés. ⊠ *Praça 15 de Novembro, Centro* Ⓜ *Uruguaiana/Carioca.*

Igreja de Nossa Senhora da Candelária. The classic symmetry of Candelária's white dome and bell towers casts an unexpected air of tranquility over the chaos of downtown traffic. The church was built on the site of a chapel founded in 1610 by Antônio de Palma after he survived a shipwreck; paintings in the present dome tell his tale. Construction on the present church began in 1775, and although the emperor formally dedicated it in 1811, work on the dome wasn't completed until 1877. The sculpted bronze doors were exhibited at the 1889 World's Fair in Paris. ⊠ *Praça Pio X, Centro* ☎ *021/2233–2324* 🎫 *Free* ⊙ *Weekdays 7:30–4* Ⓜ *Uruguaiana.*

Paço Imperial. This two-story building with thick stone walls and an ornate entrance was built in 1743, and for the next 60 years was the headquarters for Brazil's captains (viceroys), appointed by the Portuguese court in Lisbon. When King João VI arrived, he made it his royal palace. After Brazil's declaration of independence, emperors Dom Pedro I and II called the palace home, and when the monarchy was overthrown, the building became Rio's central post office. Restoration work in the 1980s transformed the palace into a cultural center and concert hall. The building houses a restaurant, a bistro, and a bit of shopping. The square on which the palace sits, Praça 15 de Novembro, known in colonial days as Largo do Paço, has witnessed some of Brazil's most significant historic moments: here two emperors were crowned, slavery was abolished, and Emperor Pedro II was deposed. The square's modern name is a reference to the date of the declaration of the Republic of Brazil: November 15, 1889. ⊠ *Praça 15 de Novembro 48, Centro* ☎ *021/2533–4359* ⊕ *www. pacoimperial.com.br* 🎫 *Free* ⊙ *Weekdays 1–5.*

Palácio Tiradentes. The Tiradentes Palace contains a permanent exhibit describing its history as the seat of the Brazilian parliament before Brasília was built in the late 1950s. Getúlio Vargas, Brazil's president for almost 20 years and by far the biggest force in 20th-century Brazilian politics, used the palace in the 1940s as a nucleus for disseminating propaganda. Tours are given in Portuguese, English, and Spanish. ⊠ *Rua Primeiro de Março s/n, Centro* ☎ *021/2588–1000* 🎫 *Free* ⊙ *Mon.–Sat. 10–7, Sun. noon–5.*

CATETE AND GLÓRIA

Though a little run-down, historic, residential Catete and Glória are well worth an afternoon's sightseeing. The Palácio do Catete, the presidential palace until the government moved to Brasília, itself warrants at least two hours. In addition to its hilltop church, Glória has a lovely marina that's perfect for a picnic or stroll, especially on a Sunday, when the main road is closed to traffic.

TOP ATTRACTIONS

Igreja de Nossa Senhora da Glória do Outeiro. The aptly named Church of Our Lady of the Glory of the Knoll (Church of Glory for short) is visible from many spots in the city, making it a landmark that's truly cherished by the cariocas. Its location was a strategic point in the city's early days. Estácio da Sá took this hill from the French in the 1560s and then went on to expand the first settlement and to found a city for the Portuguese. The baroque church, which wasn't built until 1739, is notable for its octagonal floor plan, large dome, ornamental stonework, and vivid tile work. The small museum here contains baroque art. Tours are given by appointment only. ⊠ *Praça Nossa Senhora da Glória 135, Glória* ☎ *021/2225–2869* ⊕ *www.outeirodagloria.org.br* 🖃 *Church free, museum R\$2* ⊙ *Tues.–Fri. 9–noon and 1–5, weekends 9–noon* Ⓜ *Glória.*

Fodor's Choice **Palácio do Catete.** Once the villa of a German baron, the elegant, 19th-
★ century granite-and-marble palace became the presidential residence after the 1889 coup overthrew the monarchy and established the Republic of Brazil. Eighteen presidents lived here. Gaze at the palace's gleaming parquet floors and intricate bas-relief ceilings as you wander through its **Museu da República** (Museum of the Republic). The permanent exhibits include a shroud-draped view of the bedroom where President Getúlio Vargas committed suicide in 1954 after the military threatened to overthrow his government. Presidential memorabilia, furniture, and paintings that date from the proclamation of the republic to the end of Brazil's military regime in 1985 are also displayed. A small contemporary art gallery, a movie theater, a restaurant, and a theater operate within the museum. ⊠ *Rua do Catete 153, Catete* ☎ *021/3235–3693* ⊕ *www.museus.gov.br/os-museus* 🖃 *Tues. and Thurs.–Sat. R\$6, Wed. and Sun. free* ⊙ *Tues., Thurs., and Fri. noon–5, Wed. 2–5, weekends 2–6* Ⓜ *Catete.*

WORTH NOTING

Monumento aos Pracinhas. The Monument to the Brazilian Dead of World War II—the nation sided with the Allies during the conflict—is actually a combination museum and monument. The museum houses military uniforms, medals, stamps, and documents belonging to soldiers, and two soaring columns flank the tomb of an unknown soldier. ■ **TIP➔ The best time to visit is on a Sunday, when the road in front of the monument is closed to traffic, and joggers, dog-walkers, and strolling families fill the area.** ⊠ *Parque Brigadeiro Eduardo Gomes, Glória* ☎ *021/2240–1283* 🖃 *Free* ⊙ *Tues.–Sun. 10–4* Ⓜ *Glória.*

SANTA TERESA AND LAPA

With its cobblestone streets and bohemian atmosphere, Santa Teresa is a delightfully eccentric neighborhood. Gabled Victorian mansions sit beside alpine-style chalets as well as more prosaic dwellings—many hanging at unbelievable angles from the flower-encrusted hills. Cafés, galleries, and antiques shops have nudged their way into nooks and crannies between the colorful homes, many of which house artists and their studios. Downhill from Santa Teresa, Lapa has some of the oldest buildings in the city, and is home to the imposing Arcos da Lapa (Lapa Aqueduct) and the colorful Escadaria Selarón, also called the Lapa Steps, as well as the city's oldest street, the café-paved Rua do Lavradio. By night, Lapa is transformed into the party heart of Rio, with countless bars and clubs and a notoriously wild weekend street party.

TOP ATTRACTIONS

Arcos da Lapa. Formerly the Aqueduto da Carioca (Carioca Aqueduct), this structure with 42 massive stone arches was built between 1744 and 1750 to carry water from the Carioca River in the hillside neighborhood of Santa Teresa to Centro. In 1896 the city transportation company converted the aqueduct, by then abandoned, into a viaduct, laying trolley tracks along it. For decades, Santa Teresa's rattling yellow streetcars (the "bonde" or "bondinho") passed over the aqueduct as they carried passengers from Centro up to the hillside neighborhood of Santa Teresa. After an accident in 2011, however, when the tram's brakes failed and six passengers were killed, the bonde was shut down pending major upgrades. New trams are expected to be in service by 2014, though this target may not be met. ⊠ *Estação Carioca, Rua Professor Lélio Gama, Lapa* Ⓜ *Carioca or Cinelândia.*

Escadaria Selarón. After traveling the world and living in more than 50 countries, Chilean painter Selarón began working in 1990 on the iconic tile staircase that is now one of the highlights of Lapa. With tiles from around the world, Selarón's staircase is the product of years of dedication, artistic vision, and donations of tiles from places far and near. Sadly, in early 2013 Selarón was found murdered at his nearby home. ■TIP→ **The colorful stairs provide a great photo opportunity—Snoop Dogg and Pharell Williams shot the video for their song "Beautiful" here.** ⊠ *Escadaria Selarón 24, Lapa.*

Museu Chácara do Céu. The collection of mostly modern works at the Museum of the Small Farm of the Sky was left—along with the hilltop house that contains it—by one of Rio's greatest arts patrons, Raymundo de Castro Maya. Included are originals by 20th-century masters Picasso, Braque, Degas, Matisse, Modigliani, and Monet. The Brazilian holdings include priceless 17th- and 18th-century maps and works by leading modernists. ■TIP→ **The views of the aqueduct, Centro, and the bay are splendid from the museum's grounds.** ⊠ *Rua Murtinho Nobre 93, Santa Teresa* ☎ *021/3970–1126* ⊕ *www.museuscastromaya.com.br/chacara.htm* ⊡ *R$5, free on Wed.* ☉ *Wed.–Mon. noon–5.*

WORTH NOTING

Largo do Guimarães (*Guimarães Square*). Much of the activity in close-knit Santa Teresa takes place around its village-like squares, among them Largo do Guimarães, a social hub that frequently hosts street parties. The informal restaurant Bar do Arnaudo (⇨ *Where to Eat)* is a popular hangout for the neighborhood's artistic types, and Cafecito (⇨ *Where to Eat)* is nearby. If you follow the tram track 1.2 km (¾ mile) northwest from here you'll come to **Largo das Neves** (Neves Square), with its picturesque whitewashed church. Families and other locals gather in this square until late at night. ⊠ *Rua Paschoal Carlos Magno, Ladeira do Castro, and Rua Almirante Alexandrino, Santa Teresa.*

FLAMENGO AND BOTAFOGO

These largely residential neighborhoods connect the southern beach districts and Centro via a series of highways that intersect here. It's easy to reach these neighborhoods by metro. Apartment buildings dominate, but Rio Sul—one of the city's most popular shopping centers—is here, as are some of the city's best museums and public spaces.

The eponymous beach at Flamengo no longer draws swimmers (its gentle waters look appealing but are polluted; the people you see are sunning, not swimming). A marina sits on a bay at one end of the beach, which is connected via a busy boulevard to the smaller beach (also polluted), at Botafogo. The city's yacht club is here, and when Rio was Brazil's capital, it was also the site of the city's glittering embassy row. The embassies relocated to Brasília long ago, but the mansions that housed them remain. Among Botafogo's more interesting mansion- and tree-lined streets are Mariana, Sorocaba, Matriz, and Visconde e Silva.

TOP ATTRACTIONS

Museu Carmen Miranda. This tribute to the Brazilian bombshell Carmen Miranda is in a circular building that resembles a concrete spaceship (its door even opens upward rather than out). On display are some of the elaborate costumes and incredibly high platform shoes worn by the actress, who was viewed as a national icon by some and as a traitor to true Brazilian culture by others. Hollywood photos of Miranda, who was only 46 when she died of a heart attack in 1955, show her in her trademark turban and jewelry Also here are her records and movie posters and such memorabilia as the silver hand mirror she was clutching when she died. Guided tours are given by appointment, but the guides do not speak English. ⊠ *Parque do Flamengo, Av. Rui Barbosa s/n, across from Av. Rui Barbosa 560, Flamengo* ☎ *021/2334–4293* ✉ *Free* ☉ *Weekdays 10–5, Sat. and holidays 1–5* Ⓜ *Flamengo.*

Museu das Telecomunicações. Inside the Oi Futuro (Hi, Future), the high-tech Telecommunications Museum delivers a unique multimedia adventure—lots of monitors, blinking lights, and media artifacts—to each visitor. After you've been oriented in the use of the MP3 headsets, a light- and mirror-filled airlock-like room awaits. The sights in this tiny exhibit space will likely mesmerize you, and if you don't

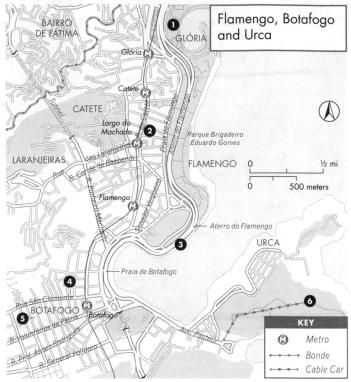

Flamengo, Botafogo and Urca

speak Portuguese, the English guide will explain what you can't figure out from the visual cues. The other floors of the Oi Futuro building house cultural spaces devoted to theater performances, film screenings, and art exhibits. There's also a café whose rooftop terrace is a pleasant place to enjoy an iced cappuccino on a balmy day. ⊠ *Rua Dois de Dezembro 63, Flamengo* ☎ *021/3131–3060* ⊕ *www.oifuturo. org.br/cultura/oi-futuro-flamengo* ⊠ *Free* ⊙ *Weekdays 11–5* Ⓜ *Largo do Machado or Catete.*

Museu do Índio. The Indian Museum pays homage to Brazil's many indigenous tribes. Entrance to the first floor is free; the admission fee is to visit the second, which contains the main exhibition. ■**TIP→ Stop at the gift shop to browse native handicrafts and purchase your tickets before heading up the stairs to the main exhibition.** ⊠ *Rua das Palmeiras 55, Botafogo* ☎ *021/3214–8700* ⊕ *www.museudoindio.org.br* ⊠ *R$3 Tue.–Sat., free Sun.* ⊙ *Tues.–Fri. 9–5:30, weekends 1–5* Ⓜ *Botafogo.*

WORTH NOTING

Casa Rui Barbosa. Slightly inland from Parque de Flamengo is a museum in the former home of the 19th-century Brazilian statesman, writer, and scholar Rui Barbosa, a liberal from Bahia State who drafted one of Brazil's early constitutions. The pink mansion, which dates from 1849, is itself worth a visit. Stepping inside instantly transports you to the period when writers and other intellectuals inhabited this street's grand houses. Among the memorabilia and artifacts on display are Barbosa's 1913 car and legal, political, and journalistic works. The bucolic gardens are a pleasant place to take respite from the rush and crush of the city. ⊠ *Rua São Clemente 134, Botafogo* ☎ *021/3289–4600* ⊕ *www.casaruibarbosa.gov.br* ⌧ *R$2, free on Sun.* ☉ *Tues.–Fri. 10–6, weekends and holidays 2–6* Ⓜ *Botafogo.*

Parque do Flamengo. The landscape architect Roberto Burle Marx designed this waterfront park that flanks the Baía de Guanabara from the Glória neighborhood to Flamengo. Frequently referred to as "Aterro do Flamengo," it gets its nickname from its location atop an *atêrro* (landfill). The park contains playgrounds and public tennis and basketball courts, and paths used for jogging, walking, and hiking wind through it. ■**TIP→** On weekends the freeway beside the park is closed to traffic and the entire area becomes one enormous public space. For safety reasons, avoid wandering the park after dark. ⊠ *Inland of beach from Glória to Botafogo* ⌧ *Free* Ⓜ *Glória or Flamengo.*

URCA

Tiny, sheltered Urca is home to one of Rio's most famous attractions, the Pão de Açúcar morro. As tranquil and bucolic as the rest of Rio is fast-paced and frenetic, Urca is a wonderful place for an afternoon's wandering. Fishing boats bob on a bay set against a spectacular view of Christ the Redeemer on his mountaintop perch, and the neighborhood contains some wonderful colonial architecture. The Pão de Açúcar separates Urca's tree-lined streets from Praia Vermelha, its small, coarse-sand beach. This beach is, in turn, blocked by the Urubu and Leme mountains from the 1-km (½-mile) Leme Beach at the start of the Zona Sul.

TOP ATTRACTION

Fodor's Choice ★ **Pão de Açúcar** (*Sugar Loaf*). The indigenous Tupi people originally called the soaring 396-meter (1,300-foot) granite block at the mouth of Baía de Guanabara *pau-nh-acugua* (high, pointed peak). To the Portuguese the phrase seemed similar to *pão de açúcar*, itself fitting because the rock's shape reminded them of the conical loaves in which refined sugar was sold. Italian-made bubble cars holding 75 passengers each move up the mountain in two stages. The first stop is at Morro da Urca, a smaller, 212-meter (705-foot) mountain; the second is at the summit of Pão de Açúcar itself. The trip to each level takes three minutes. In high season long lines form for the cable car; the rest of the year the wait is seldom more than 30 minutes. ■**TIP→** Consider visiting Pão de Açúcar before climbing the considerably higher Corcovado, as the view here may seem anticlimactic if experienced second. ⊠ *Av. Pasteur 520, near Praia Vermelha, Urca* ☎ *021/2546–8400* ⊕ *www.bondinho.com. br* ⌧ *R$53 adults, R$26 children under 13, free for children under 6* ☉ *Daily 8 am–7:50 pm.*

CLOSE UP

Gay Rio

Gay Rio rocks almost every night with a whole menu of entertainment options. During the day, dedicated areas of the beach in Copacabana (Posto 6) and Ipanema (in front of Rua Farme de Amoedo, near Posto 8) are gay and lesbian havens. After dark, the nightlife is welcoming and inclusive. Kick off the evening at **Galeria Café**, in Ipanema, or **Rainbow Kiosk**, right on the sands in front of the Copacabana Palace. As the night nudges 1 am, head toward **Le Boy**, the more intimate **La Girl**, or deservedly popular **The Week**. **La Cueva** is one of Copacabana's longest-running gay venues, and most of the livelier underground clubs (**Casa Rosa, Fosfobox**, and **Bunker**) run GLS (Gay/Lesbian/Sympathizer) nights during the week. The downtown party district of Lapa has long been lacking in GLS action, but **Sinônimo** has perked up the scene with a three-story club incorporating live music, DJs, and a cocktail lounge. The sporadic circuit party B.I.T.C.H (Barbies in Total Control ⊕ *www.bitch.com.br*) has been one of the biggest events on the gay calendar since the 1980s.

COPACABANA

Copacabana is Rio's most famous tourist neighborhood thanks to its fabulous beach and grande-dame hotels such as the Copacabana Palace. The main thoroughfare is Avenida Nossa Senhora de Copacabana, two blocks inland from the beach. The commercial street is filled with shops, restaurants, and sidewalks crowded with colorful characters. Despite having some of the best hotels in Rio, Copacabana's heyday is over, and the neighborhood is grittier than Ipanema or Leblon. It's no secret to thieves that tourists congregate here, so keep your eyes peeled for shady types when walking around after dark. ⇨ *For a description of Copacabana Beach, see Beaches, below.*

TOP ATTRACTION

Forte de Copacabana and Museu Histórico do Exército. Copacabana Fort was built in 1914 as part of Rio's first line of defense, and many original features, such as the thick brick fortification and old Krupp cannons, are still visible. In the '60s and '70s, during Brazil's military dictatorship, political prisoners were kept here. The fort is impressive in itself, and the entrance archway perfectly frames a postcard view of Sugar Loaf. The on-site military-history museum is worth a stop, as is the café (excellent coffee, pastries, and desserts), which has sweeping beach vistas. ⊠ *Praça Coronel Eugênio Franco 1, Copacabana* ☎ *021/2287–3781* ⊕ *www.fortedecopacabana.com* ☒ *R$6* ⊙ *Tues.–Sun. 10–6.*

IPANEMA AND LEBLON

Ipanema, Leblon, and the blocks surrounding Lagoa Rodrigo de Freitas are part of Rio's money belt. For an up-close look at the posh apartment buildings, stroll down beachfront Avenida Vieira Souto and its extension, Avenida Delfim Moreira, or drive around the lagoon on Avenida Epitácio Pessoa. The tree-lined streets between Ipanema Beach and the lagoon are as peaceful as they are attractive. The boutiques along Rua Garcia D'Ávila make window-shopping a sophisticated endeavor. Other chic areas near the beach include Praça Nossa Senhora da Paz, which is lined with wonderful restaurants and bars; Rua Vinicius de Moraes; and Rua Farme de Amoedo. Gourmands should make a beeline for Leblon's Rua Dias Ferreira, where top-notch restaurants thrill diners daily. The lively bar scene here encompasses everything from exclusive lounges and wine bars to relaxed post-beach watering holes. ⇨ *For descriptions of Ipanema Beach and Leblon Beach, see Beaches, below.*

TOP ATTRACTION

Museu H.Stern. Hans Stern started his gem empire in 1945 with an initial investment of about $200. Today his company's interests include mining and production operations, as well as stores in Europe, the Americas, and the Middle East. The world headquarters of H.Stern contains a small museum that exhibits rare gems. On the self-guided workshop tour you'll learn about the entire process of cutting, polishing, and setting stones. Afterward, you get a personal consultation with a salesperson, although you should not feel obliged to buy. The museum can arrange free transport to and from your hotel. ⊠ *Rua Garcia D'Avila 113, Ipanema* ☎ *021/2106–0000* ⊕ *www.hsterninrio. com* ⊠ *Free* ☺ *Tours by appointment only; booking form on website.*

SÃO CONRADO AND BARRA DA TIJUCA

West of the Zona Sul lie the largely residential (and considerably affluent) neighborhoods of São Conrado and Barra da Tijuca. If you're accustomed to the shop-lined and restaurant-filled streets of Copacabana and Ipanema, you're in for a shock if you head to these neighborhoods, dominated mainly by towering, modern apartment buildings. São Conrado's main attractions are the beach, which serves as a landing point for hang gliders and paragliders, and the chic Fashion Mall. Barra da Tijuca, often likened to Miami because of its wide avenues, towering condos, and sprawling malls, offers ample high-end dining opportunities as well as a white sand beach that stretches for a staggering 9 miles.

TOP ATTRACTIONS

Fodor's Choice **Sítio Roberto Burle Marx** (*Roberto Burle Marx Farm*). It's a cab ride out ★ of town, but nature lovers and architecture buffs will find it worth the effort to visit this plantation-turned-museum honoring Roberto Burle Marx, Brazil's legendary landscape architect. Marx, the mind behind Rio's swirling mosaic beachfront walkways and the Aterro do Flamengo, was said to have "painted with plants," and he was the first designer to use Brazilian flora in his projects. More than 3,500 species—including some discovered by and named for Marx, as well as many on the endangered list—flourish at this 100-acre estate. Marx grouped his plants not only according to their soil and light needs but also according to their shape and texture. He also liked to mix the modern with the traditional—a recurring theme throughout the property. The results are both whimsical and elegant. In 1985 he bequeathed the farm to the Brazilian government, though he remained here until his death in 1994. His house is now a cultural center full of his belongings, including collections of folk art, and the beautiful gardens are a tribute to his talents. The grounds also contain his ultramodern studio (he was a painter, too) and a small, restored colonial chapel dedicated to St. Anthony. ⊠ *Estrada Roberto Burle Marx 2019, Pedra da Guaratiba* ☎ *021/2410–1412* ⊕ *sitioburlemarx.blogspot.com.br* ⊡ *R$10* ⊘ *Tues.– Sun. by appointment only; tours at 9:30 am and 1:30 pm.*

Museu Casa do Pontal. If you're heading toward Prainha or beyond to Grumari, consider taking a detour to Brazil's largest folk-art museum. One room houses a wonderful mechanical sculpture that represents all of the *escolas de samba* (samba schools) that march in the Carnival parades. Another mechanical "scene" depicts a circus in action. This private collection is owned by a French expatriate, Jacques Van de Beuque, who has been collecting Brazilian treasures—including religious pieces—since he arrived in the country in 1946. ⊠ *Estrada do Pontal 3295, Grumari* ☎ *021/2490–3278* ⊕ *www.museucasadopontal. com.br* ⊡ *R$10* ⊘ *Tues.–Sun. 9:30–5.*

WORTH NOTING

São Conrado. The juxtaposition of the "haves" and "have nots" couldn't be more stark, or more startling, than it is in São Conrado, where mansions and expensive condos sit right next to sprawling favelas. As you approach the neighborhood heading west from Ipanema, Avenida Niemeyer, blocked by the imposing Dois Irmãos Mountain, snakes along rugged cliffs that offer spectacular sea views on the left. The road returns to sea level again in São Conrado, a natural amphitheater surrounded by forested mountains and the ocean. Development of this upper-class residential area began in the late 1960s with an eye on Rio's high society. A short stretch along the beach includes the condominiums of a former president, the ex-wife of another former president, an ex-governor of Rio de Janeiro State, and a one-time Central Bank president. The towering Pedra da Gávea, a huge flattop granite boulder, marks the western edge of São Conrado. North of the boulder lies Pedra Bonita, the mountain from which gliders depart. ⊠ *Just west of Leblon.*

THE LUSH INLAND

In the western portion of the city north of Leblon, trees and hills dominate the landscape in the neighborhoods of Jardim Botânico, Lagoa, Cosme Velho, and Tijuca. In addition to their parks and gardens, these primarily residential neighborhoods have marvelous museums, seductive architecture, and tantalizing restaurants. The architecture is a blend of modern condominiums and colonial houses. These neighborhoods tend to be quieter during the day because they're not on the beachfront, but they do have some of the hippest nightclubs in Rio. You can't say you've seen Rio until you've taken in the view from Corcovado and then strolled through its forested areas or beside its inland Lagoa (Lagoon) Rodrigo de Freitas—hanging out just like a true carioca.

Public transportation doesn't conveniently reach the sights here; take a taxi or a tour.

CLOSE UP

Favelas

A BIT OF HISTORY

Named after the flowers that grow on the hills of Rio, the first favela began as a squatter town for homeless soldiers at the end of the 19th century. Later, freed slaves illegally made their homes on these undeveloped government lands. The favelas flourished and expanded in the 1940s as the population in Brazil shifted from a rural-based to an urban-based one. In the 1970s, during the military dictatorship, the government moved favela dwellers into public housing projects.

RIO'S LARGEST FAVELA

Rocinha is Rio's largest and most developed favela. Between 150,000 and 300,000 people reside in this well-developed community (there are three banks, a nightclub, and many shops and small markets). Brace yourself for a variety of smells, both good and bad: you'll find savory-smelling, grilled churrasquinho (meat skewers) sold in the street, and any number of delicious aromas drifting out of nearby restaurants. On the flip side, residents dump their trash on the side of the road (in designated areas) and in some places, raw sewage flows in open canals.

EXPLORING

The main thoroughfare, the Estrada da Gávea, begins in São Conrado and ends on the other side of Rocinha, in Gávea. Anyone can take a stroll up this street, and visitors are likely to hear English being spoken. If you're feeling intrepid and want to explore Rocinha on foot without a guide, be aware of the following: In 2012 police wrested control of Rocinha from the drug faction Amigos dos Amigos (ADA) as part of an ongoing citywide pacification project. Though UPPs (Police Pacification Units) have largely kept the peace since then, shoot-outs between police and faction members are not unheard of. Crime against tourists in the favela is rare, but unguided visitors stand a real chance of getting lost in the maze of streets. By far the safest way to visit Rocinha or other favelas is to take an organized tour. ⇨ *For information about favela tours, see Tours, in Rio de Janeiro Planning, above.*

TOP ATTRACTIONS

Fodor's Choice
★
Corcovado. Rio's iconic *Cristo Redentor* (Christ the Redeemer) statue stands arms outstretched atop 690-meter-high (2,300-foot-high) Corcovado Mountain. There's an eternal argument about which city view is better, the one from Pão de Açúcar (Sugar Loaf) or the one from here. In our opinion, it's best to visit Sugar Loaf *before* you visit Corcovado, or you may experience Sugar Loaf only as an anticlimax. Corcovado has two advantages: it's nearly twice as high, and it offers an excellent view of Pão de Açúcar itself. The sheer 300-meter (1,000-foot) granite face of Corcovado (the name means "hunchback" and refers to the mountain's shape) has always been a difficult undertaking for climbers.

It wasn't until 1921, the centennial of Brazil's independence from Portugal, that someone had the idea of placing a statue atop Corcovado. A team of French artisans headed by sculptor Paul Landowski was assigned the task of erecting a statue of Christ with his arms apart as if embracing the city. (Nowadays, mischievous cariocas say Christ is getting ready to clap for his favorite escola de samba.) It took 10 years, but on October 12, 1931, Christ the Redeemer was inaugurated by then-president Getúlio Vargas, Brazil's FDR. The sleek, modern figure rises more than 30 meters (100 feet) from a 6-meter (20-foot) pedestal and weighs 700 tons. In the evening a powerful lighting system transforms it into an even more dramatic icon.

There are three ways to reach the top: by cogwheel train, by minibus, or on foot (not recommended without a guide for safety reasons). The train, built in 1885, provides delightful views of Ipanema and Leblon from an absurd angle of ascent, as well as a close look at thick vegetation and butterflies. (You may wonder what those oblong medicine balls hanging from the trees are, the ones that look like spiked watermelons tied to ropes—they're *jaca,* or jackfruit.) Trains leave the Cosme Velho station (⊠ *Rua Cosme Velho 513, Cosme Velho* ☎ *021/2558–1329* ⊕ *www.corcovado.com.br*) for the steep, 5-km (3-mile), 17-minute ascent. Late-afternoon trains are the most popular; on weekends be prepared for a long wait. After disembarking you can climb up 220 steep, zigzagging steps to the summit, or take an escalator or a panoramic elevator. If you choose the stairs, you pass little cafés and shops selling film and souvenirs along the way. Save your money for Copacabana's night market; you'll pay at least double atop Corcovado. Once at the top, all of Rio stretches out before you. ■ TIP→ Visit Corcovado on a clear day; clouds often obscure the Christ statue and the view of the city. Go as early in the morning as possible, before people start pouring out of tour buses, and before the haze sets in. ⊠ *Estrada da Redentor, Cosme Velho* ⊕ *www.corcovado.com.br* ⊡ *R$48 by train, R$40 by minibus, R$30 on foot with guide* ۞ *Daily 8–7; trains run every 30 minutes.*

FAMILY   **Fundação Planetário.** Rio's planetarium is a great escape if your vacation gets rained on, or if you simply have a passion for astronomy. The adjoining interactive Museu do Universo (Museum of the Universe) illustrates the history of space exploration and travel in a futuristic exhibition area. The planetarium has two projection domes: a 23-meter-diameter Carl Zeiss Universarium VIII as well as a 12.5-meter-diameter Galileu Galilei Spacemaster. The larger dome, projecting around 9,000 stars, is among the most modern in Latin America. The planetarium frequently updates its programming, which consists of a mixture of fictitious adventures in space (recommended for kids) and nonfiction shows about the constellations and our solar system. If your aim is stargazing without the voice-over and music, the Praça dos Telescópios is open for sky observation from Tuesday to Friday, between 7:30 pm and 9:30 pm. ⊠ *Rua Vice-Governador Ruben Bernardo 100, Gávea* ☎ *021/2274–0046* ⊕ *www.planetariodorio.com.br* ⊡ *Museum R$4; museum and planetarium session R$16; weekends half price* ۞ *Tues.– Fri. 9–5, weekends and holidays 2:30–6.*

FAMILY   **Jardim Botânico.** The 340-acre Botanical Garden contains more than
Fodor's Choice   5,000 species of tropical and subtropical plants and trees, including
★   900 varieties of palms (some more than a century old) and more than 140 species of birds. The shady garden, created in 1808 by the Portuguese king João VI during his exile in Brazil, offers respite from Rio's

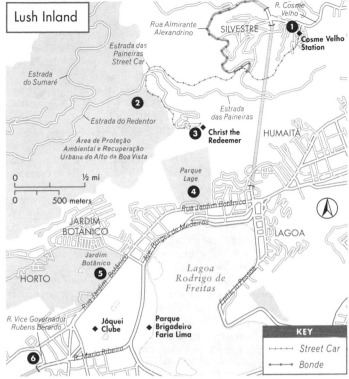

2

sticky heat. In 1842 the garden gained its most impressive adornment, the Avenue of the Royal Palms, a 720-meter (800-yard) double row of 134 soaring royal palms. Elsewhere, the Casa dos Pilões, an old gunpowder factory, has been restored and displays objects pertaining to the nobility and their slaves. Also on the grounds are a museum dedicated to environmental concerns, a library, two small cafés, and a gift shop. ⊠ *Rua Jardim Botânico 1008, Jardim Botânico* ☎ *021/3874–1808, 021/3874–1214* ⌨ *R$6* ☉ *Daily 8–5. Guided tours in English, Spanish, and Portuguese by appointment weekdays 9–3:30.*

Parque Lage. This lush green space down the road from Jardim Botânico was acquired by Antônio Martins Lage Jr., whose grandson, Henrique Lage, fell head-over-heels in love with the Italian singer Gabriela Bezanzoni. The magnificent palace he had constructed for her was completed in 1922; the impressive mansion and grounds were turned into a public park in 1960. A visual-arts school and a café occupy the mansion. On the grounds are small aquariums and a few caves that have stalactites and stalagmites. ■TIP→ If you want to tackle Corcovado on foot to make your pilgrimage to see Christ the Redeemer, start in Parque Lage; trails are clearly marked, though you shouldn't go alone. ⊠ *Rua Jardim Botânico 414, Jardim Botânico* ☎ *021/3257–1800* ⊕ *www.eavparquelage.rj.gov. br* ⌨ *Free* ☉ *Daily 8–5.*

WORTH NOTING

Floresta da Tijuca (*Tijuca Forest*). Surrounding Corcovado is the dense, tropical Tijuca Forest, also known as the Parque Nacional da Tijuca. Once part of a Brazilian nobleman's estate, it's studded with exotic trees and thick jungle vines and has several waterfalls, including the delightful Cascatinha de Taunay (Taunay Waterfall). About 180 meters (200 yards) beyond the waterfall is the small pink-and-purple Capela Mayrink (Mayrink Chapel), with painted panels by the 20th-century Brazilian artist Cândido Portinari.

The views are breathtaking from several points along this national park's 96 km (60 miles) of narrow winding roads. Some of the most spectacular are from Dona Marta, on the way up Corcovado; the Emperor's Table, supposedly where Brazil's last emperor, Pedro II, took his court for picnics; and, farther down the road, the Chinese View, the area where Portuguese king João VI allegedly settled the first Chinese immigrants to Brazil, who came in the early 19th century to develop tea plantations. A great way to see the forest is by jeep; you can arrange tours through several agencies, among them Brasil Active Ecoturismo & Aventura (☎ *021/2425–8441* ⊕ *www.brasilactive.com. br*), known for its fun programs and well-trained guides (request an English-speaking one when booking). Jeep Tour (☎ *021/2108–5800* ⊕ *www.jeeptour.com.br*) is another option. ⊠ *Estrada da Cascatinha, 850, Alta da Boa Vista* ☎ *021/2492–2252* ⊕ *www.parquedatijuca.com. br* 🖰 *Free* ⊙ *Daily 8–5.*

Museu Internacional De Arte Naïf do Brasil (*International Museum of Naïve Art from Brazil*). More than 6,000 art naïf works by Brazil's best self-taught painters, along with some by their counterparts from around the world, grace the walls of a colonial mansion that was once the studio of painter Eliseu Visconti. The museum, near the station for the train to Corcovado, grew out of a collection started decades ago by a jewelry designer. The works on display date from the 15th century to the present. ■TIP→ Don't miss the colorful, colossal 7×4-meter (22×13-foot) canvas that depicts the city of Rio; it reportedly took five years to complete. ⊠ *Rua Cosme Velho 561, Cosme Velho* ☎ *021/2205–8612, 021/2205– 8547* 🖰 *R$16* ⊙ *Tues.–Fri. 10–6, weekends and holidays noon–6.*

WEST OF DOWNTOWN

Neighborhoods west of downtown are mainly residential. Some are middle-class and some are poor. Unless you're a local, it's hard to know which areas are safe and which are not, so you should avoid wandering around. One exception is pleasant Quinta da Boa Vista, which is fine to wander. You can easily get here by metro, but avoid coming after dark.

TOP ATTRACTIONS

FAMILY **Museu Nacional.** A little off Rio's main tourist track, the National Museum is well worth the metro ride to view its exhibits of botanical, anthropological, and animal specimens. With a permanent collection of 20 million objects (give or take a few), the supply is nearly endless. Temporary exhibitions focus on subjects such as meteorites, tribal art, and animal evolution. The opulent museum building—a former imperial palace—itself merits a visit, and the vast grounds are home to Rio's city zoo. ☒ *Quinta da Boa Vista, São Cristóvão* ☎ *021/2.562–6900* ⊕ *www.museunacional.ufrj.br* ☒ *R$3* ☉ *Tue.–Fri. 10–4* Ⓜ *Estação São Cristóvão.*

Quinta da Boa Vista (*Farm of the Good View*). Complete with lakes and marble statuary, this vast public park on a former royal estate's landscaped grounds is a popular spot for family picnics. You can rent boats to pedal on the water, and bicycles to pedal on land. The former imperial palace now houses the Museu Nacional (⇨ *above*). The city zoo (⇨ *below*) sits adjacent to the park, which often hosts live-music events. ☒ *Av. Paulo e Silva and Av. Bartolomeu de Gusmão, São Cristóvão* ☒ *Free* ☉ *Daily 10–6* Ⓜ *São Cristóvão.*

WORTH NOTING

Jardim Zoológico. For children and others with an interest in seeing birds and beasts up close, Rio's city zoo makes for a diverting day out. Colorful native birds and a variety of South American monkeys are among the attractions; the "nursery" for baby animals and the reptile house are always popular with younger visitors. The zoo has received criticism for the somewhat small enclosures the larger animals—including lions and bears—endure, but conditions overall have improved in recent years. ☒ *Quinta da Boa Vista, São Cristóvão* ☎ *021/3878–4200* ⊕ *www.rio. rj.gov.br/web/riozoo* ☒ *R$6* ☉ *Wed.–Sun. 9–4:30* Ⓜ *São Cristovão.*

BEACHES

Rio's circuit of *praias* (beaches) begins in the north with Flamengo, on Guanabara Bay, but the best strands are farther south. Beaches are the city's pulse points: exercise centers, gathering places, lovers' lanes. Although cariocas wander into the water to cool off, most spend their time sunning and socializing, not swimming. Copacabana and Ipanema are the most active areas. As you head west from Barra da Tijuca the beaches become increasingly isolated and have little tourist infrastructure. Ruggedly beautiful, they are popular with surfers.

For beaches not accessible by metro, consider taking a taxi. City buses and chartered minivans drop you off along the shore, but they can be confusing if you don't speak Portuguese. Most beaches have parking lots—look for attendants in green-and-yellow vests. Turismo Clássico (⇨ *See Car Travel in the Rio de Janeiro Planner, above*) can arrange for drivers and guides.

THE ZONA SUL

Praia do Flamengo. This small curved beach is much busier from 5 to 7 in the morning than on a sunny afternoon. That's because Flamengo Beach is a great place to go for a walk, jog, run, or stroll, but not such a great place for a dip in the (usually brown) water. ■**TIP→ Vying with the beach for the attention of locals is Porção Rio's, a not-to-be-missed churrascaria. Amenities:** food and drink. **Best for:** walking. ☒ *Rua Praia do Flamengo, Flamengo* Ⓜ *Flamengo.*

Praia do Botafogo. Though very much a strand, the Zona Sul's most polluted beach doesn't attract swimmers and sunbathers. Locals joke that the fish here come ready-coated in oil for frying, but don't let that stop you from jogging along the sidewalk if you're staying nearby. ■TIP→ **Early risers are often rewarded with a stunning sunrise from this shore. Amenities:** none. **Best for:** sunrise. ⊠ *Between Praça Praia Nova and Praça Marinha do Brasil, Botafogo* Ⓜ *Botafogo.*

Praia Vermelha. Right at the foot of Sugar Loaf, this sheltered, rough-sand beach (the name means "red beach," a reference to the distinctive coarse sand here) is one of the safest places in the city for sunbathing thanks to its location next to a military base. Frequented more by local families than by tourists, and with only a few vendors, Vermelha is a tranquil spot to catch some rays. ■TIP→ **The water here is calm, but it's often too dirty for swimming. Amenities:** food and drink. **Best for:** sunset. ⊠ *Praça General Tibúrcio, Urca.*

Praia do Leme. Leme Beach is a natural extension of Copacabana Beach to the northeast, toward Pão de Açúcar. A rock formation juts into the water here, forming a quiet cove that's less crowded than the rest of the beach. Along a sidewalk, at the side of the mountain overlooking Leme, anglers stand elbow to elbow with their lines dangling into the sea. ■TIP→ **Many locals swim here, but be wary of the strong undertow, and never head into the water when the red flag is displayed on the beach. Amenities:** food and drink; toilets; showers; lifeguards. **Best for:** walking; sunset. ⊠ *From Av. Princesa Isabel to Morro do Leme, Leme* ⊕ *Cardeal Arcoverde.*

Fodor's Choice **Praia de Copacabana.** Maddening traffic, noise, packed apartment
★ blocks, and a world-famous beach—this is Copacabana, or, Manhattan with bikinis. Walk along the neighborhood's classic crescent to dive headfirst into Rio's beach culture, a cradle-to-grave lifestyle that begins with toddlers accompanying their parents to the water and ends with silver-haired seniors walking hand in hand along the sidewalk. Copacabana hums with activity: you're likely to see athletic men playing volleyball using only their feet and heads, not their hands—a sport Brazilians have dubbed *futevôlei.* As you can tell by all the goal nets, soccer is also popular, and Copacabana has been a frequent host to the annual world beach soccer championships. You can swim here, although pollution levels and a strong undertow can sometimes be discouraging. Pollution levels change daily and are well publicized; someone at your hotel should be able to get you the information.

NEW YEAR'S EVE IN RIO

Rio's New Year's celebration, or *Réveillon* as it's known in Brazil, is a whirling dervish of a party in which an estimated 3 million people truck over to Copacabana for drinks, dancing, and a spectacular fireworks show in Guanabara Bay. A word of warning: stay away from the stage. The area immediately surrounding the temporary stage on the beach becomes packed with people, and you run the risk of getting pickpocketed. Plan your hotel stay months in advance, and be prepared to pay more. Prices at least double, and rooms fill quickly.

2

Copacabana's privileged live on beachfront Avenida Atlântica, famed for its wide mosaic sidewalks designed by Roberto Burle Marx, and for its grand hotels—including the Copacabana Palace Hotel—and cafés with sidewalk seating. On Sunday two of the avenue's lanes are closed to traffic and are taken over by joggers, rollerbladers, cyclists, and pedestrians. **Amenities:** food and drink; lifeguards; showers; toilets. **Best for:** sunset; walking. ⊠ *Av. Princesa Isabel to Rua Francisco Otaviano, Copacabana* Ⓜ *Cardeal Arcoverde, Siqueira Campos, and Cantagalo.*

NEED A BREAK?

Manoel & Juaquim. For a cooling drink after a walk along the beach, drop by this air-conditioned *boteco* (casual bar-restaurant) whose windows face the sand. Part of a chain whose branches you'll find elsewhere in Copacabana and in Ipanema, this is a fine place to settle in with a cold draft beer, order a few *empadas* (little pies filled with shrimp, chicken, or cheese), and watch carioca life unfold. ⊠ *Av. Atlântica 1936, Copacabana* ☎ *021/2236–6768* ⊕ *manoelejuaquim.com.br/copacabanaposto3* Ⓜ *Siqueira Campos.*

Praia do Diabo. A barely noticeable stretch of sand tucked away between Arpoador and a natural rock wall that extends to Copacabana's fort, Praia do Diabo is popular with local *surfistas* (surfers) but the dangerous waves, which can smash an unskilled surfer into the nearby rocks, leave no mystery as to why this beach is called the Devil's Beach in Portuguese. Take advantage of the exercise bars, but stay out of the water unless you are a very experienced surfer. Toilets and showers can be found at nearby Arpoador and Copacabana. **Amenities:** none. **Best for:** surfing. ⊠ *Between Arpoador rock and Copacabana Fort, Copacabana* Ⓜ *Ipanema/General Osório.*

Praia do Arpoador. At the point where Ipanema Beach meets Copacabana, Praia do Arpoador has great waves for surfing. They're so great that nonsurfers tend to avoid the water for fear of getting hit by boards. A giant rock jutting out into the waves provides panoramic views over the beaches and out to sea. Not surprisingly, the rock is a favorite haunt of romantic couples looking to catch the sunset. ■**TIP→** With more elbow room and fewer vendors than Ipanema, this beach is a prime spot for a relaxed sunbathing session. **Amenities:** food and drink; toilets; showers; lifeguards. **Best for:** sunset; surfing. ⊠ *Rua Francisco Otaviano, Arpoador* Ⓜ *Ipanema/General Osório or Cantagalo.*

Fodor's Choice
★

Praia de Ipanema. As you stroll this world-famous beach you'll encounter a cross section of the city's residents, each favoring a particular stretch. Families predominate in the area near Posto (Post) 10, for instance, and the gay community clusters near Posto 8. Throughout the day you'll see groups playing beach volleyball and soccer, and if you're lucky you might even come across the Brazilian Olympic volleyball team practicing here. ■**TIP→** At kiosks all along the boardwalk, you can sample all sorts of food and drink, from the typical coconut water to fried shrimp and turnovers. **Amenities:** food and drink; lifeguards; showers; toilets. **Best for:** walking; sunset. ⊠ *Avenida Viera Souto to Praça do Arpoador, Ipanema* Ⓜ *Ipanema/General Osório.*

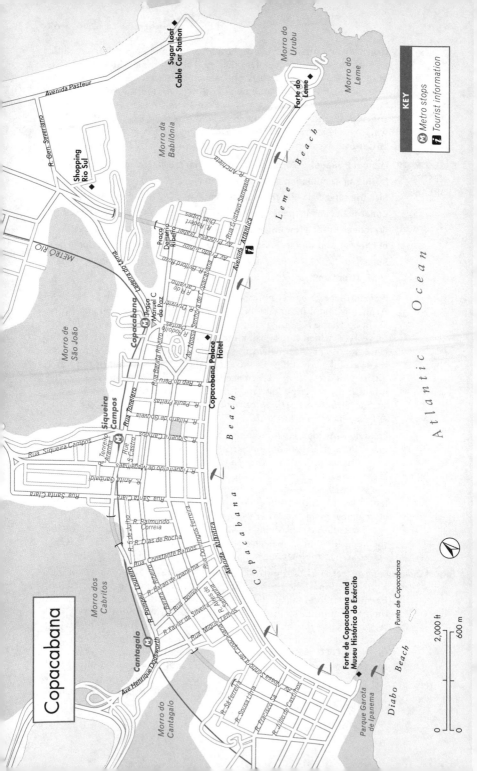

What's Your Beach Style?

To cariocas, where you hang out on the beach says a lot about you. Each of Rio's beaches has its own style, and the longer stretches of sand are themselves informally divided according to social groupings and lifestyles. There are sections of beach for singles, families, sporty types, and those looking for a quiet time. Cariocas who choose to bronze their bodies at Ipanema are generally considered to be more chic than those who catch their rays at Copacabana, with Ipanema's Posto Nove (lifeguard post 9) the hangout of choice for a young, fashionable crowd. Nearby, a vast rainbow flag in front of Rua Farme do Amoeda marks Ipanema Beach's gay and lesbian section. Families and beachgoers who prefer working on their tans to making new friends, on the other hand, largely populate Leblon Beach.

Wherever you choose to make your beach base, note that bringing along a beach towel constitutes a social faux pas. Women should equip themselves with a colorful sarong, and men are expected to remain either standing or engaged in sporting activity.

Praia do Leblon. At the far end of Ipanema lies Praia do Leblon, a stretch of beach usually occupied by families and generally less lively as far as beach sports are concerned. The water tends to be rough and a strong undertow makes swimming unwise, but this is a nice place for a paddle and a splash. Vendors pass by selling everything from ice-cold beer and coconut water to bikinis and sarongs, so come with a few reais to spend. As you stroll along the beautifully tiled sidewalk, take note of the sprawling Vidigal favela, which perches on the hillside overlooking the area. ■TIP→ Continue up the road a bit to one of Leblon's mirantes, boardwalklike areas that offer a great view of the entire beach from Leblon to Arpoador. **Amenities:** food and drink; lifeguards; toilets; showers. **Best for:** walking; sunset. ⊠ *Av. Epitácio Pessoa to Praça Escritor Antônio Callado, Leblon.*

Praia do Vidigal. Calm, clean Vidigal Beach is next to the Sheraton hotel. The small stretch of sand was the playground of residents of the nearby Vidigal favela until the hotel was built in the 1970s. These days it's practically a private beach for hotel guests. **Amenities:** food and drink. **Best for:** swimming. ⊠ *Av. Niemeyer at Sheraton, Vidigal.*

Praia de São Conrado. Arguably Rio's safest beach, Praia de São Conrado sits empty during the week but is often packed on weekends and holidays. The strand of soft sand attracts both wealthy locals and residents of the nearby Rocinha favela, and it provides a soft landing for hang gliders swooping over the city. Surfers love the crashing waves, but swimmers should be cautious because of the undertow. ■TIP→ It's worth remaining until sunset; the pumpkin sun often performs a dazzling show over Pedra da Gávea (Gávea Rock). **Amenities:** food and drink; water sports; lifeguards. **Best for:** sunset; surfing. ⊠ *Av. Niemeyer, São Conrado.*

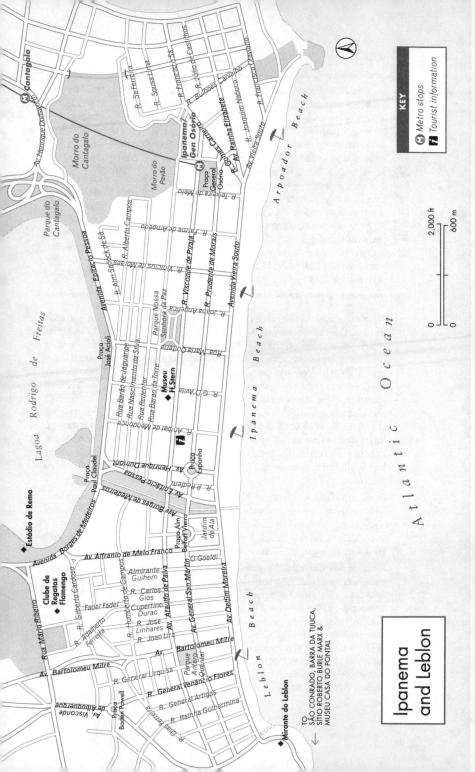

BEYOND THE ZONA SUL

Praia da Barra. Some cariocas consider the beach at Barra da Tijuca to be Rio's best, and the 18-km-long (11-mile-long) sweep of sand and jostling waves certainly is dramatic. Pollution isn't generally a problem, and in many spots neither are crowds. Barra's water is cooler and its breezes more refreshing than those at other beaches. The strong waves in some sections attract surfers, windsurfers, and jet skiers, so you should swim with caution. The beach is set slightly below a sidewalk, where cafés and restaurants beckon. Condos have also sprung up here, and the city's largest shopping centers and supermarkets have made inland Barra their home. **Amenities:** food and drink; toilets; showers. **Best for:** walking; surfing. ⊠ *Av. Sernambetiba to Av. Lúcio Costa, Barra da Tijuca.*

FAMILY **Recreio dos Bandeirantes.** At the far end of Barra's beachfront avenue— the name of the street was changed a few years back to Avenida Lúcio Costa, but locals still call it Sernambetiba—is this 1-km (½-mile) stretch of sand anchored by a huge rock that creates a small, protected cove. Recreio's quiet seclusion makes it popular with families. Although busy on weekends, the beach here is wonderfully quiet during the workweek. ■ **TIP→** The calm, pollution-free water, with no waves or currents, is good for bathing, but don't try to swim around the rock—it's bigger than it looks. **Amenities:** food and drink. **Best for:** swimming; walking. ⊠ *Av. Lúcio Costa, Recreio dos Bandeirantes.*

Prainha. The length of two football fields, Prainha is a vest-pocket beach favored by surfers, who take charge of it on weekends. The swimming is good, but watch out for surfboards. On weekdays, especially in the off-season, the beach is almost empty; on weekends, particularly in peak season, the road to and from Prainha and nearby Grumari is so crowded it almost becomes a parking lot. **Amenities:** toilets; showers. **Best for:** swimming; surfing; sunset. ⊠ *35 km (22 miles) west of Ipanema on coast road; accessible only by car from Av. Lúcio Costa (Av. Sernambetiba), Grumari.*

Praia de Grumari. A bit beyond Prainha, off Estrada de Guaratiba, is Grumari, a beach that seems a preview of paradise. What it lacks in amenities—it has only a couple of groupings of thatch-roof huts selling drinks and snacks—it makes up for in natural beauty: the glorious red sands of its quiet cove are backed by low, lush hills. Weekends are extremely crowded. ■ **TIP→** Take a lunch break at Restaurante Point de Grumari (⇨ *Where to Eat, below*), which serves excellent fish dishes. If you've ventured this far, you might as well take a slight detour to the Museu Casa do Pontal, Brazil's largest folk-art museum, and, for an in-depth look at one of the world's greatest landscape artists, the Sítio Roberto Burle Marx. **Amenities:** food and drink. **Best for:** surfing; sunset. ⊠ *Av. Estado de Guanabara, Grumari.*

West of Recreio. If you continue walking west from Recreio, you'll notice that this part of Rio is largely untouched; in fact, you'll see just three things: the mountains on your right, the road ahead, and the beach to your left. Numerous trails maintained by city workers lead to the hidden beaches west of Recreio. You'll see Rio's nude beach, Praia do Abricó, among the many short stretches of sand. Many of these beaches can be reached only on foot or by car, and are practically deserted during the week. Grumari (⇨ *above*) is a favorite with surfers, but there is always lots of room on the sands during the workweek.

WHERE TO EAT

Rio de Janeiro is world famous for its *churrascarias* (grilled-meat restaurants) but there's more to its dining scene than sizzling cuts of meat: the city embraces all types of cuisine, from traditional set meals of meat, rice, and black beans to upscale French cuisine. Unlike the states of Bahia and Minas Gerais, Rio doesn't have an identifiable cuisine, though its coastal location ensures that fish and seafood dishes are a staple of many menus here. Vegetarian cuisine has become more visible over the past half-decade. Non-carnivores can feast on a vast range of vividly colored fruits and vegetables at a number of health-food spots. Don't leave Rio without enjoying a relaxed meal and drinks at a traditional *boteco* (casual bar-restaurant), or taking your pick from the heaping buffets at a *comida-a-kilo* (pay-by-weight) restaurant.

CENTRO

$$$$ SEAFOOD
🍴 **Albamar Restaurante.** Open since 1933, the Albamar is not hard to spot: this outstanding seafood house is inside a distinctive green octagonal building with 360-degree views of Guanabara Bay. Chef Luiz Incao arrived here from Copacabana Palace in 2009 with a major reputation—he's cooked for Princess Diana, Bill Clinton, and Mick Jagger, among others—and he works wonders with dishes such as sautéed lobster with asparagus and saffron risotto. Most main dishes are large enough for two people to share. ■ **TIP→ If you're just looking to nibble, order a cocktail and some classic codfish balls, sit back, and take in the spectacular view across the bay.** [$] *Average main: R$90* ✉ *Praça Marechal Âncora 186, Centro* ☎ *021/2240–8478* 🌐 *www.albamar.com.br* 🕑 *No dinner* [M] *Carioca* ✥ *F1.*

$$ BRAZILIAN
🍴 **Amarelinho.** The best spot for city-center people-watching, this vast pavement *boteco* (bar) sits directly in front of the Biblioteco Nacional, and to the side of the Theatro Nacional. An institution that's been around since 1921, the bar attracts hordes of lunchtime and afterwork diners, competing for the tables and chairs that sit directly on the flagstones of the busy Praça do Floriano. Waitstaffers in bright yellow waistcoats and bow ties flit among the tables delivering simple Brazilian dishes such as the mixed grill served with rice and fries. Pizzas are also popular here, as is the ice-cold draft beer, and the fresh fruit salad is a nice option on a hot day. Given the prime location, prices are surprisingly reasonable. ■ **TIP→ Don't confuse Amerelinho with the adjoining bar, Vermelhino. Both have yellow roof canopies and yellow plastic chairs, but Amerelinho serves superior food.** [$] *Average main: R$30* ✉ *Praça Floriano 55 B, Cinelândia, Centro* ☎ *021/2240–8434* 🌐 *www.amarelinhodacinelandia.com.br* 🕑 *Closed Sun.* [M] *Cinelândia* ✥ *F2.*

$$ GERMAN
🍴 **Bar Luiz.** It's been well over a century since Bar Luiz first opened its doors—it's been at this location since 1927—and you could be excused for thinking that little has changed since, including the affable waiters. Claiming the best *chopp* (draft beer) in the city would arouse controversy from a lesser venue, but few in Rio would bother to argue. Tasty sausages and other German favorites are the culinary specialty; locals pop in for simple meals such as white bratwurst with potato salad

dressed in a singular homemade mayonnaise. The chopp comes in light and dark varieties, both served *estupidamente gelado* (stupidly cold). The wooden tables, tiled floor, and wall-mounted photographs of old Rio combine to create a pleasingly nostalgic ambience. [$] *Average main: R$40* ✉ *Rua da Carioca 39, Centro* ☎ *021/2262–6900* 🌐 *www.barluiz.com.br* ⏲ *Closed Sun.* [M] *Carioca* ✥ *F1.*

2

$$ INTERNATIONAL 🍴 **Bistrô do Paço.** Inside the cool, whitewashed Emporio do Paço Cultural Center, this is a good option for a light lunch. The vegetarian-friendly menu includes a lunchtime salad buffet that incorporates healthy options such as the carrot salad with oranges, potatoes, and apples. The à la carte menu, which changes daily, might include such pan-European selections as goulash with polenta and beef stroganoff with spaetzle. Close to the Palacio Tirandentes and inside the Cultural Center itself, the bistro is well placed for Centro sightseers. [$] *Average main: R$35* ✉ *Praça Quinze de Novembro 48, Centro* ☎ *021/2262–3613* 🌐 *www.bistro.com.br* ⏲ *No dinner (closes at 7 or 7:30 pm)* [M] *Uruguaiana* ✥ *F1.*

$$ CAFÉ Fodor's Choice ★ 🍴 **Confeitaria Colombo.** At the turn of the 20th century, the belle epoque structure that houses Colombo Confectionery was Rio's preeminent café, the site of elaborate balls, afternoon teas for upper-class *senhoras,* and a center of political intrigue and gossip. Enormous jacaranda-framed mirrors from Belgium, stained glass from France, and tiles from Portugal are among the art-nouveau decor's highlights. Diners come to nibble on above-average *salgados* (savory snacks) and melt-in-the-mouth sweet treats. The waffles here are a local legend. Savory pastries are stuffed with shrimp and chicken, and vegetarian nosh includes spinach and ricotta quiche and heart-of-palm pie. You can wash it all down with a creamy coffee, a European lager, or a fruity cocktail (served virgin or laced with alcohol). ■ **TIP→ If you want to experience the opulent side of city life, do so the way Rio's high society did a century ago: with *chá da tarde*, or afternoon tea. R$75 buys a lavish spread for two.** [$] *Average main: R$45* ✉ *Rua Gonçalves Dias 32, Centro* ☎ *021/2505–1500* 🌐 *www.confeitariacolombo.com.br* ⏲ *Closed Sun. Closes at 8 pm on weekdays, 5 pm on Sat.* [M] *Carioca* ✥ *F1.*

$$$$ SEAFOOD 🍴 **Rio Minho.** Enjoy a slice of history along with your afternoon snack. This downtown restaurant said to be the oldest in the city has been serving up seafood to hungry cariocas since 1884. The simple blue-and-white facade of its pretty colonial building harks back to that time, as do the uniforms of the attentive waiters who show you to your seats. For a real taste of culinary history, order the Sopa Leáo Veloso—this fortifying Brazilian soup was created in honor of the Brazilian ambassador. It's an adaptation of the French seafood broth bouillabaisse marselhesa, and combines every type of seafood imaginable, along with onion, garlic, and herbs. It's now a staple on menus across Rio de Janeiro State, but Minho still serves up the best version. [$] *Average main: R$80* ✉ *Rua do Ouvidor 10, Centro* ☎ *021/2509–2338* ⏲ *Closed weekends. No dinner* [M] *Uruguaiana* ✥ *F1.*

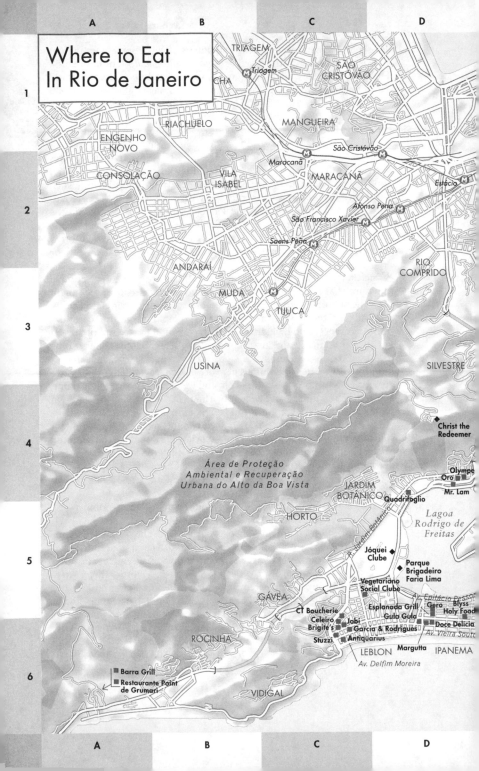

Where to Eat In Rio de Janeiro

TRIAGEM
Triagem
SÃO CRISTÓVÃO
CHA
RIACHUELO
MANGUEIRA
ENGENHO NOVO
São Cristóvão
CONSOLAÇÃO
VILA ISABEL
Maracanã
MARACANÃ
Estácia
Afonso Pena
São Francisco Xavier
Saens Peña
ANDARAÍ
RIO COMPRIDO
MUDA
TIJUCA
USINA
SILVESTRE
Christ the Redeemer
Área de Proteção Ambiental e Recuperação Urbana do Alto da Boa Vista
JARDIM BOTÂNICO
Olympe
Oro
Mr. Lam
Quadrifoglio
HORTO
Lagoa Rodrigo de Freitas
Jóquei Clube
Parque Brigadeiro Faria Lima
Vegetariano Social Clube
GÁVEA
Av. Epitácio Pessoa
Esplanada Grill
Gero
Blyss
Gula Gula
Holy Food
CT Boucherie
Jobi
Doce Delicia
Celeiro
Garcia & Rodrigues
Brigite's
Antiquarius
Av. Vieira Souto
ROCINHA
Stuzzi
Margutta
IPANEMA
LEBLON
Av. Delfim Moreira
Barra Grill
Restaurante Point de Grumari
VIDIGAL

COPACABANA AND LEME

$$ BRAZILIAN 🍴 **Boteco Belmonte.** A block back from the beach, the Copacabana branch of this Rio chain is a great place for a relaxed meal and a drink after a hard day's sunbathing. On the menu are dependably good versions of traditional Brazilian dishes such as dried beef served with rice and spring greens, as well as pizzas and an extensive line of finger foods. For a light lunch we recommend three or four *empadas* with different fillings—they're delicious little pies with a light, buttery pastry. Wash it all down with a *Chopp Black* (dark draft beer). **■ TIP→ The line to get a table snakes out into the street on weekend evenings, but you'll have plenty of elbow room on weekday afternoons.** [$] *Average main: R$45* ✉ *Rua Domingos Ferreira 242, Copacabana* ☎ *021/2255–9696* 🌐 *www.botecobelmonte.com.br* [M] *Cantagalo* ✣ *E5.*

$$$$ ITALIAN 🍴 **Cipriani.** This restaurant is housed in the plush environs of Copacabana Palace, overlooking the hotel's enormous pool. Start with a Cipriani—champagne with fresh peach juice (really a Bellini)—and then take your pick from an extensive Northern Italian menu that includes appetizers such as shiitake carpaccio with goat-cheese gratin and excellent mains such as potato-encrusted snapper fillet with broad-bean cream. The dishes with freshly made pasta are prepared with great care, and meat and fish entrées, such as wild boar, are appropriate to their lavish surroundings. Service, as one would expect, is excellent. The degustation menu costs R$208, or R$352 with wine. [$] *Average main: R$85* ✉ *Copacabana Palace Hotel, Av. Atlântica 1702, Copacabana* ☎ *021/2545–8747* 🌐 *www.copacabanapalace.com.br* ✍ *Reservations essential* [M] *Cardeal Arcoverde* ✣ *F5.*

$$$$ ITALIAN 🍴 **D'Amici.** A world away from the touristy restaurants that line Copacabana's beachfront, this small Italian restaurant is easily overlooked but well worth seeking out. The menu celebrates Italy's diverse regional cuisines. The fish-stuffed ravioli with saffron sauce stands out among many wonderful pastas, and the meat cuts are uniformly top-quality. The knowledgeable staff can advise you about the proper wines to pair with your food—you might find yourself gladly accepting it, as the list is extensive. **■ TIP→ The baskets of bread placed on the table aren't free. Ask the waiter to remove them if you don't want to pay for them.** [$] *Average main: R$75* ✉ *Rua Antônio Vieira 18, Leme* ☎ *021/2541–4477* 🌐 *www.damiciristorante.com.br* ✍ *Reservations essential* [M] *Cardeal Arcoverde* ✣ *F4.*

$$$$ FRENCH 🍴 **Le Pré-Catalan.** In an elegant space overlooking Copacabana Beach, this carioca version of the same-named Parisian restaurant serves some of Rio's best haute cuisine. Chef Roland Villard, who's won numerous awards acknowledging his culinary skills, offers two prix-fixe menus. For the first he creates dazzling dishes using ingredients from the Amazon region; for the second he puts a chic French spin on traditional Brazilian cuisine. Each meal consists of a staggering nine courses and costs R$290. You can also order à la carte and feast on sophisticated plates such as rigatoni stuffed with quail, foie gras, and wild mushrooms, or duck breast with manioc balls and duck-thigh confit. [$] *Average main: R$90* ✉ *Sofitel Rio Palace, Av. Atlântica 4240, Copacabana* ☎ *021/2525–1160* 🌐 *www.leprecatelan.com.*

br ⚐ *Reservations essential* ◷ *No lunch* Ⓜ *Cantagalo* ✛ *E6.*

$$$$ ✕ **Marius Carnes.** This well-regarded
BRAZILIAN churrascaria overlooks Leme beach and serves more than a dozen types of sizzling meats—all from organic farms—rodízio style. Your choices also include an extremely tempting seafood buffet and a salad bar. The borderline-kitsch decor incorporates items recovered from 19th-century *fazendas* (coffee farms), but don't let that distract you from the task of eating as much as you possibly can. ■ **TIP→ For those who prefer the flavors of the sea to the flavors of the farm, Marius Crustacoes sits right next door and offers the same rodizio-style service, but this time with seafood, and at a slightly higher price tag (R$170).** Ⓢ *Average main: R$115* ⊠ *Av. Atlântica 290A, Leme* ☎ *021/2104–9000* ⊕ *www.marius.com.br* ✛ *F4.*

$$$$ ✕ **Restaurante Shirley.** Homemade Spanish seafood casseroles and splen-
SEAFOOD did soups are the main draws at this small restaurant on a shady street. A line snakes around the block at peak hours, but it's worth the wait to find a table: the food is terrific. Seafood paella is among the most popular of the generously portioned traditional dishes. The waiters, clad in white suits, add to the old-time atmosphere. ■ **TIP→ The restaurant doesn't accept credit cards, so be sure to have cash.** Ⓢ *Average main: R$80* ⊠ *Rua Gustavo Sampaio 610, loja A, Leme* ☎ *021/2275–1398* ⚐ *Reservations not accepted* ▭ *No credit cards* Ⓜ *Cardeal Arcoverde* ✛ *F4.*

$$$$ ✕ **Siri Mole & Cia.** This restaurant takes its name from a soft-shell crab
BRAZILIAN native to Brazil, and the signature dish here is moqueca—a Bahian stew that combines dendê oil and coconut milk with seafood. Beware, though: This dish from the northeastern state of Bahia is delicious, but it's very high in saturated fat and can have disastrous effects on the digestion to those not used to it. For your stew, you can choose from squid, lobster, fish, or, of course, siri mole crab. Another delicious dish is *acaraje,* for which bean-flour patties are deep fried, split in two, and filled with shrimp, an okra paste, chili, and tomato. Vegetarians can opt for a shrimp-free version. ■ **TIP→ This is one of Rio's best places for seafood served Bahian style.** Ⓢ *Average main: R$75* ⊠ *Rua Francisco Otaviano 50, Copacabana* ☎ *021/2267–0894* ⊕ *www.sirimole.com.br* ◷ *No lunch Mon.* Ⓜ *Ipanema/General Osório.* ✛ *E6*

FLAMENGO AND BOTAFOGO

$$$ ✕ **Miam Miam.** Blink and you could miss this hip Botafogo eatery
ECLECTIC housed in a tiny white colonial building and furnished entirely with pieces from the 1950s to the 1970s. The French–Brazilian owners have created a relaxed, casual dining space where they prepare hearty portions of tasty comfort food. The fettuccine with mushrooms, roasted garlic, and lime is a treat for vegetarians, and the fish and meat dishes

---

DINING TIPS

Some restaurants in Rio serve a *couvert* (a little something to nibble), usually bread, olives, or another type of munchie. The couvert is not free. If you don't want to pay for it, just hand it to your waiter. Also, restaurants will include a 10% service charge, only half of which is distributed among the restaurant staff. Feel free to leave some bills on the table for your server.

2

are unfailingly good. Leave room for dessert: the hot chocolate mousse with mango ice cream is an indulgent treat. The relaxed vibe and kitsch decor ensures Miam Miam's popularity with Rio's bohemian crowd, and the award-winning cocktail list includes the *basel julep,* a vivacious concoction of rum, tangerine juice, and basil. Ⓢ *Average main: R$55* ✉ *Rua General Góes Monteiro 34, Botafogo* ☎ *021/2244–0125* ⊕ *www.miammiam.com.br* ⌕ *Reservations essential* ⊘ *Closed Mon. No lunch* Ⓜ *Botafogo* ✛ *F4.*

$$$
BRAZILIAN
FAMILY
Fodor's Choice
★

✕ **Porcão Rio's.** At lively Porcão, the ultimate in Brazilian churrascaria experiences, bow-tied waiters wielding giant skewers slip nimbly between linen-draped tables, slicing off portions of sizzling barbecued beef, pork, and chicken until you can eat no more. The buffet is huge, with salads, sushi, and pasta and rice dishes, and enough meat-free sides to keep the staunchest of vegetarians happy. Porcão is a chain, with three restaurants in Rio—including one in Ipanema *(⇨ below)*—but the nearly floor-to-ceiling windows with a view over Guanabara Bay to the Sugar Loaf make the Flamengo branch, known as Porcão Rio's, the top choice. Ⓢ *Average main: R$106* ✉ *Av. Infante Dom Henrique, Parque do Flamengo, Flamengo* ☎ *021/3461–9020* ⊕ *www.porcao. com.br* Ⓜ *Flamengo* ✛ *F3.*

$$$
AFRICAN

✕ **Yorubá.** Named after the West African tribe of the same name, Yorubá specializes in Afro-Brazilian cuisine that goes beyond the traditional Bahian dishes. Spice lovers are in for a treat, as many of the small restaurant's dishes have a strong chili kick. Chef and owner Neide Santos stays true to the West African practice of spicing up dishes such as moqueca, a seafood stew that at here is prepared with rice, *farofa* (manioc flour), and *vatapa,* a rich sauce made with coconut milk, palm oil, and shrimp. Brightly colored tribal art pays homage to Africa's cultural contributions to Brazil with the same verve that the food celebrates the culinary ones. Ⓢ *Average main: R$58* ✉ *Rua Arnaldo Quintela 94, Botafogo* ☎ *021/2541–9387* ⊘ *Closed Mon. and Tues., no lunch Wed.–Fri., no dinner Sat.* Ⓜ *Botafogo* ✛ *F4.*

IPANEMA AND LEBLON

$$$$
PORTUGUESE
Fodor's Choice
★

✕ **Antiquarius.** This pricey but much-loved establishment is famous for its flawless rendering of Portuguese classics, including many cod dishes. The couvert includes tasty cod-and-potato balls, seafood rissoles, and imported cheeses. Seafood dishes are by far the best options. The chef prepares the shrimp cocktail simply but elegantly, and the vast seafood risotto is a knockout. The wine list is impressive, if predictably expensive, and the knowledgeable sommelier is always on hand to give tips on food and wine pairings. Ⓢ *Average main: R$190* ✉ *Rua Aristides Espínola 19, Leblon* ☎ *021/2294–1049* ⌕ *Reservations essential* ✛ *C6.*

$$$
SEAFOOD

✕ **Azul Marinho.** You'll catch superb sunsets from the beachside tables at this quiet little spot in Arpoador that serves high-quality seafood and pasta dishes for lunch and dinner and assembles a lavish breakfast buffet each morning. Across from the beach on the Arpoador Inn's ground floor, the restaurant has a giant window with panoramic views. *Moqueca* is the house specialty, made with shrimp, cod, lobster, crab, or octopus—or a mix of them all. The service at Azul Marinho is excellent and the seafood is ultrafresh, but an even better reason to come here is to sit at one of the outdoor tables next to the sand and enjoy early-evening appetizers, drinks, and a marvelous sunset. $ *Average main: R$58* ⊠ *Av. Francisco Bhering s/n, Arpoador* ☎ *021/3813–4228* ⊕ *www.cozinhatipica.com.br* Ⓜ *Ipanema/General Osório* ✛ *E6.*

$ ✕ **Blyss Holy Foods.** Hidden away in a small arcade off Ipanema's main
VEGETARIAN   square, Blyss Holy Foods provides culinary delights for vegetarians, vegans, and anyone who fancies a break from the meat-centric Brazilian diet. The restaurant's organic lunch buffet is laden with fresh vegetable soups, colorful salads, fish-free sushi, savory pies and tarts, and a host of other dishes that are as tasty as they are nourishing. For a guilt-free feast after marveling at the parade of perfect beach bodies on Ipanema Beach, look no further. The friendly owners run yoga groups in the neighborhood and welcome out-of-towners to join the classes. $ *Average main: R$16* ⊠ *Rua Visconde de Pirajá 180, Loja H, Ipanema* ☎ *021/9218–5511* ⊙ *Closed Sun. No lunch* Ⓜ *Ipanema/General Osório* ✛ *D6.*

$$$$ ✕ **Brigite's.** Leblon's Rua Dias Ferreira is becoming a go-to street for
ECLECTIC   foodies, and the upmarket bar-restaurant Brigite's is a major reason
Fodor's Choice why. As one might expect in body-conscious Leblon, there's an emphasis
★   on fresh, organic ingredients, and vegetarians fare well here with dishes such as goat cheese–stuffed risotto and hot tomato sauce. Meat, fish, and seafood lovers will find a lot to like, too. The octopus is a popular dish, as is the fresh pasta with a lamb ragout. The wine choices are extensive, and delicious, if pricey, cocktails can be enjoyed at the long balcony bar. Floor-to-ceiling plate-glass windows allow sunlight to flood Brigite's by day, and dim lighting creates a more atmospheric mood for after-dark drinking and dining. $ *Average main: R$70* ⊠ *Rua Dias Ferreira 247 A, Leblon* ☎ *021/2274–5590* ✛ *C6.*

$$$ ✕ **Capricciosa.** Rio fairly bursts with pizza places, but this upmarket
ITALIAN   chain's Ipanema branch emerges at the top of the list. Wood-fired, thin-crust pizzas are made with imported Italian flour, and the toppings—from wild mushrooms and handmade buffalo mozzarella to wafer-thin Parma ham and fresh tuna—are of the highest quality. Capricciosa has branches in Jardim Botânico, Barra da Tijuca, Copacabana, and the beach resort of Búzios, but the Ipanema venue stands out for its location and tall glass windows that are perfect for people-watching. $ *Average main: R$50* ⊠ *Rua Vinicius de Moraes 134, Ipanema* ☎ *021/2523–3394* ⊕ *www. capricciosa.com.br* ⊙ *No lunch* Ⓜ *Ipanema/General Osório* ✛ *E6.*

$$$$ ✕ **Casa da Feijoada.** Restaurants traditionally serve feijoada, Brazil's
BRAZILIAN   savory national dish, on Saturday, but here the huge pots of the stew simmer every day. You can choose which of the nine types of meat you want in your stew, but if it's your first time, waiters will bring you a "safe" version with sausage, beef, and pork—sans feet and ears. The feijoada comes with the traditional side dishes of rice, collard greens, *farofa* (toasted and seasoned manioc flour), *aipim* (cassava), *toresminho* (pork rinds), and orange slices. The set meal price includes an appetizer portion of black-bean soup and sausage, a choice of dessert, and a lime or passion-fruit *batida* (creamy cachaça cocktail). The menu also features options such as baked chicken, shrimp in coconut milk,

grilled trout, and filet mignon. Desserts include *quindim* (a yolk-and-sugar pudding with coconut crust) and Romeo and Juliet (guava compote with fresh cheese). The caipirinhas are made not only with lime but also with tangerine, passion fruit, pineapple, strawberry, or kiwi. Be careful—they're strong. [$] *Average main: R$75* ✉ *Rua Prudente de Morais 10, Ipanema* ☏ *021/2247–2776* Ⓜ *Ipanema/ General Osório* ✛ *E6.*

$$ ✕ **Celeiro.** One of an increasing
VEGETARIAN number of organic eateries in Rio, Celeiro is a combination café and health-food store that's popular with models and other body-conscious locals. The restaurant operates on a pay-by-weight system, and the buffet features a staggering 50 types of salad, as well as oven-baked pies, wholemeal pastries, fish and chicken dishes, and low-calorie desserts. The homemade breads are delicious. [$] *Average main: R$35* ✉ *Rua Dias Ferreira 199, Leblon* ☏ *021/2274–7843* ⊕ *www. celeiroculinaria.com.br* ☾ *Closed Sun. No dinner* ✛ *C6.*

> ## PIZZA RIO STYLE
>
> Cariocas love pizza, and they've added some touches of their own to the established formula. As well as sharing the pan-Brazilian penchant for pizza bases covered in chocolate, Rio residents are also known to indulge in unusual topping combinations such as cheese with pepperoni, banana, and cinnamon. In one last break with tradition, many cariocas eschew the idea of tomato sauce *beneath* the cheese, in favor of squirting ketchup on the surface.

$$ ✕ **Colher de Pau.** Upscale Ipanema is short on affordable lunch options,
BRAZILIAN but this notable exception serves generous portions at accessible prices. The chilled-out little spot is just two blocks from Ipanema Beach, and it's a good stop before, during, or after a day in the sun. Open for breakfast, lunch, and dinner, it serves *prato feitos* (daily set meals), tasty sandwiches, and salads, plus healthful grilled fish or steak. Indulge your sweet tooth after your meal with the *brigadeiro*, a Brazilian treat made of condensed milk, butter, and chocolate. Colher de Pau's version is among the city's best. [$] *Average main: R$30* ✉ *Rua Farme de Amoedo 39, Ipanema* ☏ *021/2523–3018* Ⓜ *Ipanema/General Osório* ✛ *E6.*

$$$$ ✕ **CT Boucherie.** The city's most celebrated chef—Claude Troisgros—has
FRENCH changed the face of the all-you-can-eat churrascaria with this chic bistro whose kitchen is led by his talented son Thomas. Unlike at traditional rodizios, where waiters deliver cut after cut of meat, here they dash from table to table with steaming plates of roasted palm hearts, stuffed tomatoes, creamy mashed potatoes, and other meat-free sides. These delicious dishes accompany meaty mains, among them the substantial prime rib and the more accessibly priced house burger, that diners choose from the menu. ■ **TIP→ As tempting as they are, consider skipping the entrées to save room for the never-ending flow of vegetable plates.** [$] *Average main: R$85* ✉ *Rua Dias Ferreira 636, Leblon* ☏ *021/2529–2329* ⊕ *www.ctboucherie.com.br* ✛ *C6.*

$$ ✕ **Doce Delícia.** Diners at the Sweet Delight build a meal by selecting
ECLECTIC from more than three-dozen combinations of vegetables, side dishes, hot mains, and fruits. Choices include quiche, salmon, grilled tenderloin, chicken, and cold pasta, which can be dressed with anything from

yogurt-based sauces to fanciful creations that combine mustard, lemon, and herbs. The many vegetarian plates lure in the health-conscious set, as do desserts such as the 240-calorie chocolate cheesecake and banana strudel and apple tartlets, both of which tally a mere 180 calories. There are plenty of high-cal desserts to entice traditionally sweet-toothed types as well. ■TIP→ **Doce Delícia hosts seasonal food festivals—a strawberry one in June and a shrimp one in August—that local foodies have enthusiastically embraced.** Ⓢ *Average main: R$35* ⊠ *Rua Aníbal de Mendonça 55, Ipanema* ☎ *021/2540–0000* ⊕ *www.docedelicia.com.br* Ⓜ *Ipanema/ General Osório* ✢ *D6.*

$$$$ ✕ **Esplanada Grill.** This churrascaria is famed for the quality of its meats,
BRAZILIAN among them T-bone steak and *picanha*, a tasty Brazilian cut of beef marbled with a little fat. All the grilled dishes come with fried palm hearts, seasoned rice, and a choice of fried, baked, or sautéed potatoes. Ⓢ *Average main: R$80* ⊠ *Rua Barão da Torre 600, Ipanema* ☎ *021/2512– 2970* ⊕ *www.esplanadagrill.com.br* Ⓜ *Ipanema/General Osório* ✢ *D6.*

$$ ✕ **Garcia & Rodrigues.** Cariocas rave about the breakfast, served until
CAFÉ midday, at this cozy combination café, delicatessen, and liquor shop. R$38 helps you kick-start your day with a feast of sweet and savory breads, freshly squeezed orange juice, croissants, cold meats, cheeses, cereals, and strong Brazilian coffee. From lunchtime until 6 pm the fare includes sandwiches (the pastrami with Gruyère is superb) and omelets. There's no formal dinner, but after 6 pm the café serves delicious thin-crust Provençal-style pizzas in addition to cakes, tarts, and sweet and savory pastries. Ⓢ *Average main: R$35* ⊠ *Rua Dias Ferreira 50, Leblon* ☎ *021/3521–2938* ⊕ *www.garciaerodrigues.com.br* ✢ *C6.*

$$$$ ✕ **Gero.** This chic, beautifully appointed restaurant serves wonderful
ITALIAN pastas and risottos along with excellent fish and meat dishes. Vegetarian options are plentiful, and the tiramisu is a perfect blend of creamy, espresso-laced mascarpone. The restaurant is owned by the Italian Fasano chain, and the high-ceiling, wooden-floor building exhibits the clean, contemporary design that is the Fasano hallmark. ■TIP→ **A second Rio branch operates in Barra da Tijuca, but the Ipanema location is a better option for Zona Sul–based visitors.** Ⓢ *Average main: R$90* ⊠ *Rua Anibal de Mendonca 157, Ipanema* ☎ *021/2239–8158* ⊕ *www.fasano. com.br* ⌕ *Reservations essential* ✢ *D6.*

$$ ✕ **Gula Gula.** The salads at the upscale café chain Gula Gula are anything
CAFÉ but boring. Beyond classics such as Caesar and chicken pesto, fresh local fruits and veggies are mixed into curried quinoa with tomatoes and marinated eggplant and bean sprouts, and the organic palm-heart salad comes with tomatoes, watercress, and raisins. Grilled fish or steak, baked potatoes, and soups are good nonsalad options, and there are some very fine desserts. ■TIP→ **Gula Gula operates a dozen restaurants in Rio, plus one in Niterói, but its location a few blocks from the beach makes the Ipanema branch an excellent choice.** Ⓢ *Average main: R$35* ⊠ *Rua Henrique Dumont 57, Ipanema* ☎ *021/2259–3084* ⊕ *www.gulagula. com.br* Ⓜ *Ipanema/General Osório* ✢ *D6.*

$$ ✕ **Jobi.** The post-beach hangout of choice for neighborhood locals, Jobi
BRAZILIAN serves good coffee, super-chilled draft beer, and lip-smackingly delicious seafood. The bar's *bolinhos de bacalhau* (cod and potato balls) may well

be the best in town. Because the restaurant is so small and unassuming, it's only after you step inside and see the many awards hanging on the walls that you realize just how special Jobi is. This Leblon institution is open from 9 am to 4 am, so you should be able to squeeze it into your schedule. ■ **TIP→ A cocktail favorite here is the caipitequila,** a variation on the classic caipirinha that's made with tequila instead of sugarcane rum. [$] *Average main: R$30* ✉ *Rua Ataulfo de Paiva 1166, Leblon* ☎ *021/2274–0547* ✣ *C6.*

$$$ ITALIAN 🍴 **Margutta.** A block from Ipanema Beach, Margutta has a reputation for outstanding Mediterranean-style seafood, such as mussels cooked in red wine and lobster baked with butter and saffron rice. Vegetarian options include homemade rigatoni with dried wild mushrooms and olive oil flavored with white truffles. [$] *Average main: R$55* ✉ *Av. Henrique Dumont 62, Ipanema* ☎ *021/2259–3718* 🌐 *www.margutta.com.br/ipanema* ⏲ *No lunch weekdays* [M] *Ipanema/General Osório* ✣ *D6.*

$ BRAZILIAN 🍴 **New Natural.** One of many restaurants in Rio where you pay per kilo, this one stands out for its use of natural and organic products and its delicious fruit juices. The food is mainly vegetarian, with many soy-based dishes, but there are fish and chicken options. ■ **TIP→ On hot days seek out the somewhat hidden upstairs dining room, which is air-conditioned.** Attached to the restaurant is Emporia Natural—a health-food shop that sells oven-baked pastries to go. The palm heart with soft and creamy *catupiry* cheese is a winning combination. [$] *Average main: R$28* ✉ *Rua Barão da Torre 169, Ipanema* ☎ *021/2247–1335* [M] *Ipanema/General Osório* ✣ *E6.*

$$$$ BRAZILIAN 🍴 **Porcão Rio's.** A convenient location makes this branch of Rio's famous churrascaria the most popular one with travelers, though the Flamengo branch *(⇨ above)* has a fabulous view. You'll get the same excellent service and quality of food here, but in a smaller space with no view. [$] *Average main: R$95* ✉ *Rua Barão da Torre 218, Ipanema* ☎ *021/3202–9158* 🌐 *www.porcao.com.br* [M] *Ipanema/General Osório* ✣ *E5.*

$$$$ SEAFOOD Fodor's Choice ★ 🍴 **Satyricon.** Some of the best seafood in town is served at this eclectic Italian restaurant that has impressed the likes of Madonna and Sting. A tank of snapping lobsters at the entrance gives diners an indication of the freshness of the fare served here. The carpaccio entrée is a specialty—it and the daily specials, such as red snapper baked in red wine and herbs, are rendered beautifully. Grilled swordfish and sea bass are other popular orders, and the homemade Italian-style ice cream is a sweet way indeed to round off a meal. [$] *Average main: R$90* ✉ *Rua Barão da Torre 192, Ipanema* ☎ *021/2521–0627* 🌐 *www.satyricon.com.br* [M] *Ipanema/General Osório* ✣ *E6.*

$$$ ITALIAN 🍴 **Stuzzi.** Bringing the concept of Italian *stuzzichini* (tapas-style small plates of food for sharing), Stuzzi has evolved into a star of Leblon's Rua Dias Ferreira foodie strip. Chef Paula Prandini trained in Italy and France, arriving here fresh from a stint at the double-Michelin-starred Il Griso in Italy. Start with the mixed antipastos, which include a basket of baked breads and authentic Grana Padano cheese, Parma ham, marinated eggplant, and other light bites. Among the other don't-miss dishes are the fried balls of rice filled with meat ragout and the polenta *grissini* (breadsticks) with tomato chutney and Gorgonzola sauce. For

something more substantial, head here on a Sunday for the Buffet da Mamma, a serve-yourself comfort-food feast. ■ **TIP→ Arrive here early to get a table on the leafy patio, and relax with a tangy apple martini as you peruse the menu.** [$] *Average main: R$55* ✉ *Rua Dias Ferreira 48, Leblon* ☎ *021/2274–4017* 🌐 *www.stuzzibar.com.br* ⏲ *No lunch Mon.–Sat.* ✥ *C6.*

$ VEGETARIAN ✕ **Vegetariano Social Clube.** Vegan restaurants are a growing trend in body-conscious Rio, but few are as established and well loved as the Vegetarian Social Club. The serve-yourself lunch buffet (R$28) includes tasty and wholesome soups, whole-grain rice, colorful salads, and many soy-based dishes. Dining in the evening is à la carte, with options such as quinoa with seasonal vegetables and tofu cream. The tempeh burgers with soya mayonnaise are a post-beach treat. Detoxifying juices and smoothies are on the drinks menu, along with organic wines and cachaças for those less in need of a cleansing. ■ **TIP→ The Sunday feijoada, made with smoked tofu instead of pork, attracts vegetarians from across the city.** [$] *Average main: R$28* ✉ *Rua Conde de Bernadotte 26, Loja L, Leblon* ☎ *021/2294–5200* 🌐 *www.vegetarianosocialclube.com.br* ✥ *C5.*

FOOD ON THE GO

There's a street snack for every taste in Rio—from low-cal treats such as corn on the cob and chilled pineapple slices to less virtuous, but absolutely delicious, barbecued sticks of grilled cheese served with or without herbs. Tasty bags of roasted and salted peanuts and cashews are found everywhere, as are giant hot dogs, served on a stick and covered in manioc flour. Barbecued chicken heart (*coraçao*) is not for the fainthearted, and the grilled shrimp at the beach is best avoided unless you want a side order of food poisoning.

THE LUSH INLAND

$$$$ CHINESE ✕ **Mr Lam.** In a city where Chinese food has long been associated with low-budget dining, this restaurant tossed out the rule book, attracting a discerning clientele with top-quality Peking-style cuisine. The head chef here is the famous Mr. Lam, formerly of Mr Chow, first at the London branch and then in New York City. The downstairs dining room of his Rio venue is spacious and well illuminated by enormous windows, but for the ultimate experience book a table on the top floor. At night the roof retracts to allow dining beneath the stars, and you can request a spot directly beneath the gaze of Christ the Redeemer. The satay chicken and Peking duck are two of the signature dishes. ■ **TIP→ You can dine à la carte, but most patrons choose from one of the set menus (from R$95 to R$145 per person).** [$] *Average main: R$85* ✉ *Av. Maria Angélica 21, Lagoa* ☎ *021/2286–6661* 🌐 *www.mrlam.com.br* ✍ *Reservations essential* ⏲ *No lunch Mon.–Sat.* ✥ *D4.*

$$$$ FRENCH Fodor's Choice ★ ✕ **Olympe.** Claude Troisgros, of the celebrated Michelin-starred Troisgros family of France, runs this top-notch venue whose line chefs apply nouvelle-cooking techniques to meals with all-Brazilian ingredients. From the crab or lobster flan to chicken, fish, and stuffed qualu, the dishes here are exceptionally light. If you find yourself unable to make

a selection, consider the degustation menu (R$260). ■TIP→ Olympe's signature dessert, a passion-fruit crepe, deserves the raves it receives. $ *Average main: R$130* ✉ *Rua Custódio Serrão 62, Jardim Botânico* ☎ *021/2539–4542* ⊕ *www.claudetroisgros.com.br* ☛ *Reservations essential* ✛ *D4.*

$$$$
CONTEMPORARY
Fodor's Choice
★

✕ **Oro.** Food as theater is the theme of the restaurant of celebrity chef Felipe Bronze, who has created an avant-garde dining experience like no other in the city. A pink-hued glass wall allows diners to watch his culinary team prepare ultra-contemporary dishes, many using traditional Brazilian ingredients. Starters include savory profiteroles stuffed with handmade Brazilian cheeses; a hummus-style dip for which edamame beans replace the chickpeas (brilliant); and smoked salmon wrapped in a crispy cone fashioned from manioc flour. The "mains" are really a series of small, elaborately prepared dishes, including a tiny burger made of duck confit and foie-gras powder and served with guava "ketchup." Clever tricks such as using liquid nitrogen to "freeze" chocolate mousse add to the stylish-yet-playful atmosphere, as do the waitstaff's uniforms, designed by Lenny Niemeyer, famous for his high-fashion bikinis. $ *Average main: R$100* ✉ *Rua Frei Leandro 20, Jardim Botânico* ☎ *021/2266–7591* ⊕ *www.ororestaurante. com* ☛ *Reservations essential* ☾ *Closed Sun. No lunch* ✛ *D4.*

$$$$
ITALIAN
Fodor's Choice
★

✕ **Quadrifoglio.** Many locals consider cozy Quadrifoglio to be Rio's best Italian restaurant. The restaurant has been around since 1991, and the service and the food are impeccable, the former perhaps because much of the original waitstaff still works here. The standout dishes include foie gras ravioli and some fabulous salads, but the ravioli stuffed with palm heart and served with a sauce of shrimp and fine herbs is also a treat. Ice cream with baked figs is among the justly famous desserts. $ *Average main: R$75* ✉ *Rua J.J. Seabra 19, Jardim Botânico* ☎ *021/2294–1433* ⊕ *www.quadrifogliorestaurante.com.br* ☾ *No dinner Sun. No lunch Sat.* ✛ *D4.*

SANTA TERESA

$$$$
ECLECTIC

✕ **Aprazível.** A tropical garden filled with exotic plants, monkeys, and birds is the spectacular setting for this family restaurant serving pan-Brazilian dishes. The owner and chef, Ana Castilha, hails from Minas Gerais but received her formal training at New York City's French Culinary Institute. As a delightful consequence, there's a French twist to the traditional Brazilian dishes she's adapted, among them a salad made with mixed lettuce, mango, whole green peppercorns, Minas cheese, and sun-dried tomatoes. All the wines at Aprazível are made in Brazil; their high quality may surprise those who have dismissed the country's wines. The outdoor tables enjoy excellent views of downtown and Guanabara Bay during the day, and by night hanging lanterns illuminate the garden. ■TIP→ Call ahead to make your booking, as opening hours can be erratic. $ *Average main: R$65* ✉ *Rua Aprazível 62, Santa Teresa* ☎ *021/2508–9174* ⊕ *www.aprazivel.com. br* ☛ *Reservations essential* ☾ *Closed Mon.* ✛ *E2.*

$$ BRAZILIAN Fodor's Choice ★ 🍴 **Bar do Arnaudo.** A neighborhood favorite for more than three decades, this informal tavern serves excellent Northeastern cuisine in more than ample portions. Sun-dried beef is a popular choice among carnivores, and vegetarians will love the set meal of *queijo coalho* (grilled white cheese, similar to halloumi) with brown beans, rice, and seasoned farofa. Reservations aren't necessary, but the restaurant is always packed on weekend evenings. It's quieter at lunchtime, when you may be able to occupy one of the two tables that have views down to Guanabara Bay. Though the friendly staffers are speedy, the service never feels rushed. ■ **TIP→ Wine isn't sold here, but your waiter will happily uncork any bottle you bring.** [$] *Average main: R$35* ✉ *Rua Almirante Alexandrino 316-B, Santa Teresa* ☎ *021/2252–7246* 🕓 *Closed Mon.* ✥ *E2.*

2

$$ CAFÉ 🍴 **Cafecito.** Coffee culture is only just taking off in Rio, and Cafecito is among the few places so far to capture the essence of "café society." A leafy terrace overlooking Santa Teresa's main eating, drinking, and shopping strip provides a relaxed setting for brunches, lunches, and early-evening nibbles and cocktails. The knickknack-strewn café serves what's arguably the city's best cappuccino—with a dusting of cinnamon and a morsel of gooey chocolate brownie—but the food menu also has plenty to recommend it. The standouts include the toasted ciabatta sandwiches (the ham and Minas cheese is a simple but tasty option) and some pleasingly rustic baked mushrooms with melted Gorgonzola. ■ **TIP→ Cafecito is a great place to start your evening before making the descent to the boisterous bars of nearby Lapa.** [$] *Average main: R$30* ✉ *Rua Pashcoal Carlos Magno 121, Santa Teresa* ☎ *021/2221–9439* 🌐 *www.cafecito.com.br* 🕓 *Closed Wed. Closes at 8 pm Mon., Tues., and Thurs.* ✥ *E2.*

SÃO CONRADO, BARRA DA TIJUCA, AND BEYOND

$$$$ BRAZILIAN 🍴 **Barra Grill.** A nice place to stop after a long day at Praia Barra, this informal and popular steak house serves some of the best meat in town, and the buffet of salads and sides is always impressive in range and quality. Prices for the rodízio-style feasts are slightly higher on weekends than during the week. ■ **TIP→ Reservations are essential on weekends.** [$] *Average main: R$65* ✉ *Av. Ministro Ivan Lins 314, Barra da Tijuca* ☎ *021/2493–6060* 🌐 *www.barragrill.com.br* ✥ *A6.*

$$$ SEAFOOD 🍴 **Restaurante Point de Grumari.** From Grumari Beach, Estrada de Guaratiba climbs up through dense forest, emerging atop a hill above the vast Guaratiba flatlands. Here you'll come upon this restaurant famed for its moqueca, the traditional seafood stew. With its shady setting, glorious vistas, and live music (samba, bossa nova, jazz), this a fine spot for an early lunch after a morning on the beach and before an afternoon visit to the Sítio Roberto Burle Marx or the Museu Casa do Pontal. Or come here in the early evening to catch the spectacular sunset. [$] *Average main: R$58* ✉ *Estrada do Grumari 710, Grumari* ☎ *021/2410–1434* 🌐 *www.pointdegrumari.com.br* 🕓 *No dinner* ✥ *A6.*

URCA

$$ ✕ **Bar e Restaurante Urca.** Dine indoors in this relaxed spot, or make like
BRAZILIAN the locals and enjoy your meal alfresco, propped against the harbor wall
across the street: the wall doubles as a makeshift table, and waiters run to
and fro delivering orders. You can enjoy a cold beer and some finger food
while you contemplate the menu—cold dishes, such as the tomato and
palm-heart salad are good, as are the Portuguese-influenced hot dishes,
among them fried fish fillet with rice and creamed spinach. ■ **TIP→ Bar e
Restaurante Urca breaks with tradition and serves feijoada on Friday instead
of Saturday, and at a good price for what you get: R$64 for two.** $ *Aver-
age main: R$38* ⊠ *Rua Cândido Gaffrée 205, Urca* ☎ *021/2295-8744*
⊕ *www.barurca.com.br* ☉ *No dinner Sun. (closes at 7:30)* ✛ *G3.*

WHERE TO STAY

Rio's accommodations are among the most expensive in the world, with
beachfront lodgings in particular charging a premium for their envi-
able locations. Expect hotel rates to be the most expensive during high
season (from December through February), especially during Carnival
and New Year's, and for special events such as the 2014 FIFA World
Cup and 2016 Rio Olympics. For stays during these times it would be
wise to book ahead as far as possible. The low season (from March to
November) sees prices fall across the city.

As for the types of lodgings available, there are some excellent luxury
options on the beachfront—most notably the Copacabana Palace and
Ipanema's Fasano Rio—as well as standard chain hotels. Ipanema and
neighboring Leblon are more expensive than Copacabana, but they are
also safer and more pleasant to walk around at night. Rio's expand-
ing boutique-hotel scene centers largely around the Santa Teresa and
Gávea neighborhoods, while Botafogo and Flamengo offer some decent
mid-range options.

CENTRO

$$$ ⊞ **Windsor Guanabara.** The Windsor Guanabara is one of the few solid
HOTEL hotel choices right in Centro. **Pros:** great views from pool; close to down-
town attractions and nightlife; good value. **Cons:** far from beaches;
Centro is nearly deserted on Sundays. $ *Rooms from: R$386* ⊠ *Av. Presidente Vargas 392, Centro* ☎ *021/2195-5000* ⊕ *www.windsorhoteis.com.
br* ➳ *510 rooms, 3 suites* ⦿ *Breakfast* Ⓜ *Uruguaiana* ✛ *G1.*

COPACABANA AND LEME

These neighborhoods can be dangerous at night, so it's wise to get
around by taxi after dark.

$$$$ ⊞ **Copacabana Palace.** Built in 1923 for the visiting king of Belgium and
HOTEL inspired by Nice's Negresco and Cannes's Carlton, the Copacabana
Fodor's Choice was the first luxury hotel in South America, and it's still one of the top
★ hotels on the continent. **Pros:** historic landmark; front-facing rooms
have spectacular views; great on-site restaurant. **Cons:** area is a little

seedy at night; need to take taxis to best bars and restaurants; "city view" rooms have poor views of backstreets. $ *Rooms from: R$1490* ✉ *Av. Atlântica 1702, Copacabana* ☎ *021/2548–7070, 0800/21–1533, 800/237–1236 in U.S.* ⊕ *www.copacabanapalace.com.br* ⤳ *129 rooms, 116 suites* ¶◎ *Breakfast* Ⓜ *Cardeal Arcoverde* ⊕ *F4.*

$$$ ⛌ **Copacabana Rio Hotel.** Brightly decorated in blues, yellows, and
HOTEL reds, the rooms here are nicer than ones at more expensive places in Copa. **Pros:** good price; comfortable rooms; handy to Copacabana and Ipanema beaches; fine breakfasts. **Cons:** busy and noisy street; minimum seven-day stay in high season. $ *Rooms from: R$470* ✉ *Av. Nossa Senhora de Copacabana 1256, Posto 6, Copacabana* ☎ *021/3043–1111* ⊕ *www.copacabanariohotel.com.br* ⤳ *90 rooms, 8 suites* ¶◎ *Breakfast* Ⓜ *Ipanema/General Osório* ⊕ *E6.*

$$$ ⛌ **Excelsior.** This hotel, part of the Windsor chain, may have been
HOTEL built in the 1950s, but its look is sleek and contemporary—from the sparkling marble lobby to the guest-room closets paneled in gleaming Brazilian redwood. **Pros:** top-notch service; rooftop pool; elaborate buffets. **Cons:** slightly impersonal chain feel; busy street can be dangerous at night. $ *Rooms from: R$402* ✉ *Av. Atlântica 1800, Copacabana* ☎ *021/2195–5800, 0800/704–2827* ⊕ *www.windsorhoteis.com. br* ⤳ *233 rooms, 12 suites* ¶◎ *Breakfast* Ⓜ *Cardeal Arcoverde* ⊕ *F4.*

$$$$ ⛌ **Golden Tulip Regente Hotel.** The excellent location in front of Copa-
HOTEL cabana Beach is this hotel's main draw. **Pros:** good location; good breakfast; small but well-equipped gym; pool. **Cons:** some rooms have poor view; Copacabana isn't the safest area. $ *Rooms from: R$600* ✉ *Av. Atlântica 3716, Copacabana* ☎ *021/2525–2070, 0800/16–5322* ⊕ *www.goldentulip.com.br* ⤳ *228 rooms, 2 suites* ¶◎ *Breakfast* Ⓜ *Cantagalo* ⊕ *E6.*

$$$$ ⛌ **JW Marriott Rio de Janeiro.** You could be walking into a Marriott
HOTEL anywhere in the world, which is a comfort for some and a curse for others: expect spotlessly clean rooms and public areas, an efficient English-speaking staff, and modern (and expensive) services and facilities. **Pros:** close to beach; efficient service; bountiful breakfasts; modern facilities. **Cons:** lacks character; expensive; street noise heard in some rooms. $ *Rooms from: R$1000* ✉ *Av. Atlântica 2600, Copacabana* ☎ *021/2545–6500* ⊕ *www.marriott.com* ⤳ *229 rooms, 16 suites* ¶◎ *Breakfast* Ⓜ *Siqueira Campos* ⊕ *E5.*

$$$ ⛌ **Leme Othon Palace.** Adequate rather than luxurious, this hotel has
HOTEL large rooms and a quiet beachfront location. **Pros:** quiet location; safer than many parts of Copacabana; metro access; reasonable rates for the area; helpful, English-speaking staff. **Cons:** far from Ipanema and Leblon nightlife; uninspired interiors. $ *Rooms from: R$403* ✉ *Av. Atlântica 656, Leme* ☎ *021/2106–1500* ⤳ *163 rooms, 28 suites* ¶◎ *Breakfast* Ⓜ *Cardeal Arco Verde* ⊕ *G4.*

$$ ⛌ **Mercure Rio de Janeiro Arpoador Hotel.** This apartment-hotel is just steps
RENTAL from Copacabana Beach and a few-minutes' walk from Ipanema. **Pros:** great location; good price for this. **Cons:** small rooms; some units have limited views; some traffic noise. $ *Rooms from: R$370* ✉ *Rua Francisco Otaviano 61, Copacabana* ☎ *021/3222–9603* ⊕ *www.mercure. com* ⤳ *52 apartments* ¶◎ *No meals* Ⓜ *Ipanema/General Osório* ⊕ *E6.*

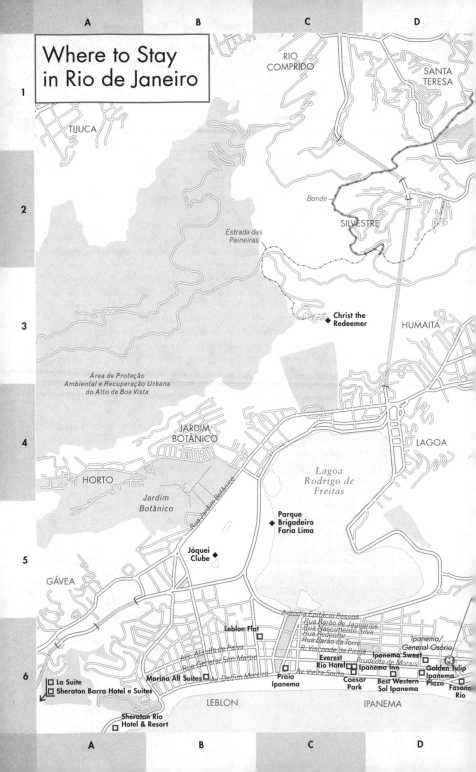

Where to Stay in Rio de Janeiro

A   **B**   **C**   **D**

RIO COMPRIDO

SANTA TERESA

TIJUCA

Bonde

SILVESTRE

Estrada das Paineiras

♦ Christ the Redeemer

HUMAITÁ

Área de Proteção Ambiental e Recuperação Urbana do Alto da Boa Vista

JARDIM BOTÂNICO

LAGOA

HORTO

Jardim Botânico

Lagoa Rodrigo de Freitas

Rua Jardim Botânico

♦ Parque Brigadeiro Faria Lima

Jóquei Clube ♦

GÁVEA

Avenida Epitácio Pessoa
Rua Barão de Jaguaripe
Rua Nascimento Silva
Rua Redentor
Rua Barão da Torre
R. Visconde de Piratá

Leblon Flat

Ipanema/
General Osório

Everest Rio Hotel
 Av. Atáulfo de Paiva
Rua General San Martin

Ipanema Sweet
Ipanema Inn
Av. Vieira Souto

Golden Tulip Ipanema Plaza

Marina All Suites

Av. Delfim Moreira

Praia Ipanema

Caesar Park

Best Western Sol Ipanema

Fasano Rio

La Suite
Sheraton Barra Hotel e Suites

LEBLON

IPANEMA

Sheraton Rio Hotel & Resort

A   **B**   **C**   **D**

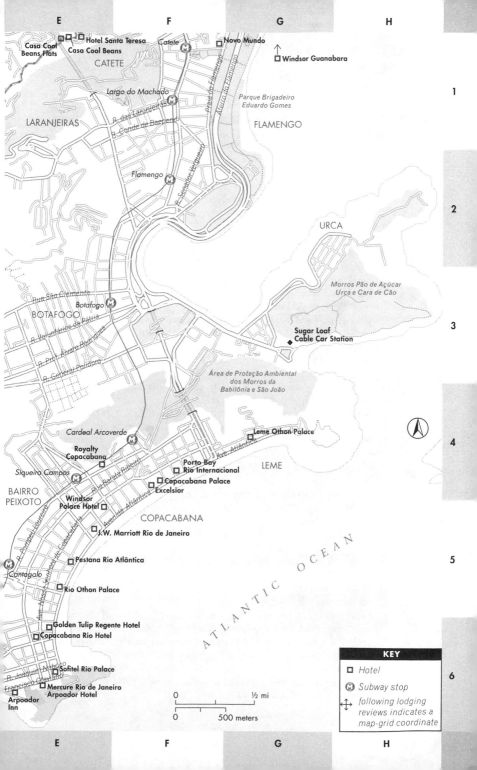

$$$$ **HOTEL** ⛶ **Pestana Rio Atlântica.** This well-located hotel offers friendly service, a great breakfast and a good location opposite Copacabana Beach, but the real stars of the show are the rooftop pool and bar. **Pros:** good value for the area; rooftop pool and bar; good beachfront location. **Cons:** some rooms need revamping; can feel a little crowded. Ⓢ *Rooms from: R$705* ⊠ *Av. Atlântica 2964, Copacabana* ☎ *21/2548–6332* ⊕ *www.pestana.com* ⇨ *109 rooms, 105 suites* ⫯◯⫯ *No meals* Ⓜ *Cantagalo* ⊹ *E5.*

$$$$ **HOTEL** ⛶ **Porto Bay Rio Internacional.** All rooms at this Copacabana landmark hotel have balconies with sea views, a rarity on Avenida Atlântica. **Pros:** good design and tasteful decor; excellent service; good views; beachfront location. **Cons:** some rooms quite small; Copacabana not as safe as Ipanema after dark. Ⓢ *Rooms from: R$792* ⊠ *Av. Atlântica 1500, Copacabana* ☎ *021/2546–8000* ⊕ *www.portobay.com* ⇨ *117 rooms, 11 suites* ⫯◯⫯ *Breakfast* Ⓜ *Cardeal Arcoverde* ⊹ *F4.*

$$$$ **HOTEL** ⛶ **Rio Othon Palace.** The flagship of the Brazilian Othon chain, this 30-story hotel is not new, and its ambience is functional rather than luxurious. **Pros:** good beach views from front-facing rooms and pool; handy to the beach. **Cons:** some rooms dated; some fixtures and fittings past their prime. Ⓢ *Rooms from: R$580* ⊠ *Av. Atlântica 3264, Copacabana* ☎ *021/2522–1522* ⊕ *www.othon.com.br/en/hoteis/rio-othon-palace#o-hotel* ⇨ *556 rooms, 30 suites* ⫯◯⫯ *Breakfast* Ⓜ *Cantagalo* ⊹ *E5.*

$$ **HOTEL** ⛶ **Royalty Copacabana.** Three blocks from the beach and handy to the metro, this hotel is in a relatively quiet, semi-residential area. **Pros:** great view from the pool; fairly quiet location; good price for Copacabana. **Cons:** basic amenities; not on the beach; looks dated. Ⓢ *Rooms from: R$350* ⊠ *Rua Tonelero 154, Copacabana* ☎ *021/2548–5699* ⊕ *www.royaltyhotel.com.br/royalty-copacabana* ⇨ *123 rooms, 13 suites* ⫯◯⫯ *Breakfast* Ⓜ *Siqueira Campos* ⊹ *E4.*

$$$$ **HOTEL** ⛶ **Sofitel Rio Palace.** Anchoring one end of Copacabana Beach, and close to Ipanema, this huge hotel has an "H" shape that provides breathtaking views of the sea, the mountains, or both, from all the rooms' balconies. **Pros:** handy to Ipanema and Arpoador beaches and nightlife; fantastic views. **Cons:** very large; somewhat impersonal; small bathrooms in some rooms. Ⓢ *Rooms from: R$750* ⊠ *Av. Atlântica 4240, Copacabana* ☎ *021/2525–1232* ⊕ *www.sofitel.com/gb/hotel-1988-sofitel-rio-de-janeiro-copacabana/index.shtml* ⇨ *388 rooms, 53 suites* ⫯◯⫯ *No meals* Ⓜ *Canto Galo* ⊹ *E6.*

ALTERNATIVE HOUSING

Rio has accommodations to suit virtually every taste and wallet. There are plenty of self-catering options for those who value their own space over hotel luxury. Agencies specialize in everything from luxury Ipanema penthouses to pokey Copacabana digs. One good one, Alex Rio Flats (⊕ *www.alexrioflats.com*), has 10 air-conditioned studios and apartments, many with beachfront locations and full sea views, that cost R$200 and up per night. Alex, the English-speaking owner, provides friendly, personalized service and can help book trips and tours.

$$$ 📺 **Windsor Palace Hotel.** Close to Copacabana's main shopping area,
HOTEL   the Windsor Palace is a solid mid-range option with decent services
and standard, cookie-cutter hotel rooms. **Pros:** rooftop views; good
amenities; two blocks from metro. **Cons:** bland rooms; so-so location.
💲 *Rooms from: R$385* ✉ *Rua Domingos Ferreira 6, Copacabana*
☎ *021/2195–6600* ⊕ *www.windsorhoteis.com* ➴ *73 rooms, 1 suite*
🍴 *Breakfast* Ⓜ *Siqueira Campos* ✛ *F5.*

FLAMENGO

$$$$ 📺 **Novo Mundo.** A short walk from the Catete metro station and five min-
HOTEL   utes by car from Santos Dumont Airport, this traditional hotel occupies
an attractive art deco building overlooking Guanabara Bay. **Pros:** good
for business travelers; some rooms have good views. **Cons:** metro ride
away from the best beaches; some rooms past their prime. 💲 *Rooms
from: R$630* ✉ *Praia do Flamengo 20, Flamengo* ☎ *021/2105–7000,
0800/25–3355* ⊕ *www.hotelnovomundo-rio.com.br* ➴ *209 rooms, 22
suites* 🍴 *Breakfast* Ⓜ *Catete* ✛ *F1.*

IPANEMA AND LEBLON

$$$ 📺 **Arpoador Inn.** This pocket-size hotel occupies the stretch of sand known
HOTEL   as Arpoador. **Pros:** great sunsets; right-on-the-beach location; good res-
taurant; reasonable prices. **Cons:** front rooms can be noisy; hotel often
busy with groups of surfers. 💲 *Rooms from: R$410* ✉ *Rua Francisco
Otaviano 177, Ipanema* ☎ *021/2523–0060* ⊕ *www.arpoadorinn.com.
br* ➴ *50 rooms* 🍴 *Breakfast* Ⓜ *Ipanema/General Osório* ✛ *E6.*

$$$ 📺 **Best Western Sol Ipanema.** Another of Rio's tall, slender hotels, this one
HOTEL   has a great location at the eastern end of Ipanema Beach between Rua
Vinicius de Moraes and Farme de Amoedo. **Pros:** great beach location;
near several happening bars; friendly staff; modern. **Cons:** standard
facilities; tiny pool. 💲 *Rooms from: R$570* ✉ *Av. Vieira Souto 320,
Ipanema* ☎ *021/2525–2020* ⊕ *www.solipanema.com.br* ➴ *90 rooms*
🍴 *Breakfast* Ⓜ *Ipanema/General Osório* ✛ *D6.*

$$$$ 📺 **Caesar Park.** In the heart of Ipanema, close to high-class shops and
HOTEL   gourmet restaurants, this beachfront hotel has established itself among
business travelers, celebrities, and heads of state, who appreciate its impec-
cable service. **Pros:** great location; good business facilities; good views.
Cons: no balconies; small pool; uninspired decor. 💲 *Rooms from: R$840*
✉ *Av. Vieira Souto 460, Ipanema* ☎ *021/2525–2525, 0800/21–0789,
877/223–7272 in U.S.* ⊕ *www.sofitel.com* ➴ *221 rooms, 24 suites* ✛ *C6.*

$$ 📺 **Casa Cool Beans Flats.** In 2013 the team that developed the much-
RENTAL   raved-about Santa Teresa guesthouse Casa Cool Beans (⇨ *below*) opened
a second lodging a block from the beach in Ipanema. **Pros:** affordable;
close to beach, bars, restaurants, shopping, and the metro; complimentary beach towels; gay friendly. **Cons:** no breakfast; two-night minimum
(three for major holidays and events); no guests under age 18. 💲 *Rooms
from: R$350* ✉ *Rua Vinicius de Moraes 72, Ipanema* ☎ *021/2262–0552,
202/470–3548 in the U.S.* ⊕ *flats.casacoolbeans.com* ➴ *4 rooms, 4
suites* 🍴 *No meals* Ⓜ *Ipanema/General Osório* ✛ *E1.*

$$$ **Everest Rio Hotel.** With standard accommodations and in-room ame-
HOTEL nities but a great rooftop view—a postcard shot of Corcovado and
the lagoon—this recently refurbished hotel is in the heart of Ipanema's
shopping and dining district, a block from the beach. **Pros:** rooftop
views; rooftop pool; good business amenities; fine location. **Cons:**
noisy air-conditioning; other buildings hamper some views. $ *Rooms
from: R$480* ⊠ *Rua Prudente de Morais 1117, Ipanema* ☎ *021/2525–
2200, 0800/709–2220* ⊕ *www.everest.com.br* ↝ *148 rooms, 8 suites*
|○| *Breakfast* Ⓜ *Ipanema/General Osório* ✢ *C6.*

$$$$ **Fasano Rio.** The Italian-owned Fasano Group is renowned for its
HOTEL stylish, elegant hotels and restaurants, and Fasano Rio has the added
glamour of having been crafted by the French designer Philippe Starck.
Pros: chic decor; wonderful views from pool; glamorous clientele. **Cons:**
standard rooms lack views; expensive. $ *Rooms from: R$1500* ⊠ *Av.
Viera Souto 80, Ipanema* ☎ *021/3202–4000* ⊕ *www.fasano.com.br* ↝ *82
rooms, 10 suites* |○| *Breakfast* Ⓜ *Ipanema/General Osório* ✢ *E6.*

$$$$ **Golden Tulip Ipanema Plaza.** The location close to Ipanema Beach
HOTEL is the main reason to stay at this hotel, which provides guests with
beach chairs and umbrella service free of charge. **Pros:** excellent loca-
tion; fabulous views from pool; good breakfast; bars and restaurants
nearby. **Cons:** rooms are basic for the price; decor and fixtures are
dated. $ *Rooms from: R$710* ⊠ *Rua Farme de Amoedo 34, Ipanema*
☎ *021/3687–2000* ⊕ *www.ipanemaplazahotel.com* ↝ *118 rooms, 13
suites* |○| *Breakfast* Ⓜ *Ipanema/General Osório* ✢ *D6.*

$$$ **Ipanema Inn.** If you want to stay in Ipanema and avoid the high prices
HOTEL of beachfront accommodations, this no-frills hotel with great service
is a wise choice. **Pros:** great location; good value. **Cons:** basic rooms;
no views. $ *Rooms from: R$415* ⊠ *Rua Maria Quitéria 27, Ipanema*
☎ *021/2523–6092, 021/2529–1000* ⊕ *www.ipanemainn.com.br* ↝ *56
rooms* |○| *Breakfast* Ⓜ *Ipanema/General Osório* ✢ *C6.*

$$$ **Ipanema Sweet.** In this smart residential building in the heart of
RENTAL Ipanema, owners rent out their units by the night, week, or month. **Pros:**
unbeatable location; stylish public areas; more space than standard
hotel rooms; kitchens; grocery store nearby. **Cons:** not all apartments
have safe boxes; small pool; maid service costs extra. $ *Rooms from:
R$400* ⊠ *Rua Visconde de Pirajá 161, Ipanema* ☎ *021/8201–1458,
021/8277–4815 Sonia Maria Cordeiro* ⊕ *www.ipanemasweet.com.br*
🚫 *No credit cards* |○| *No meals* Ⓜ *Ipanema/General Osório* ✢ *D6.*

$$$$ **Leblon Flat.** Simply decorated, small furnished apartments with one or
RENTAL two bedrooms and balconies are offered at this hotel-like complex that has
a pool. **Pros:** good rate for Leblon area; kitchens; near shopping, restau-
rants, and nightlife. **Cons:** unattractive building. $ *Rooms from: R$550*
⊠ *Rua Professor Antônio Maria Teixeira 33, Leblon* ☎ *021/2127–7700
for information, 021/3722–5053 for reservations* ⊕ *www2.protel.com.br/
protel/hoteis/leblon_flat* ↝ *120 apartments* |○| *Breakfast* ✢ *C6.*

$$$$ **Marina All Suites.** In front of Leblon Beach and surrounded by
HOTEL designer stores and upmarket restaurants, this hotel is a favorite with
chic vacationers (Gisele Bundchen and Calvin Klein are regulars). **Pros:**
good location; spacious, well-equipped suites; excellent service; pool
with sea views. **Cons:** expensive; Leblon Beach is not quite as pretty

as Ipanema. $ *Rooms from: R$730* ⊠ *Avenida Delfim Moreira 696, Leblon* ☎ *021/2172–1001* ⊕ *www.hoteismarina.com.br* ☞ *37 suites* ❍❘ *No meals* ✛ *B6.*

$$$$ 🛏 **Praia Ipanema.** This hotel between Ipanema and Leblon may not be
HOTEL   deluxe, but it's across from the beach, and you can see the sea from all the rooms. **Pros:** great views; beachfront location; close to Ipanema and Leblon shopping and nightlife. **Cons:** some furnishings a little shabby. $ *Rooms from: R$710* ⊠ *Av. Vieira Souto 706, Ipanema* ☎ *021/2141–4949* ⊕ *www.praiaipanema.com* ☞ *103 rooms* ❍❘ *Breakfast* ✛ *C6.*

$$$$ 🛏 **Sheraton Rio Hotel & Resort.** Between the upmarket neighborhoods of
RESORT   São Conrado and Leblon, this is the only hotel in Rio with a "private"
FAMILY   beach. **Pros:** great for families; wonderful beach; good amenities. **Cons:** isolated; close to Vidigal favela; some furnishings past their prime. $ *Rooms from: R$686* ⊠ *Av. Niemeyer 121, Leblon* ☎ *021/2274–1122, 800/325–3589 in U.S.* ⊕ *www.sheraton-rio.com* ☞ *500 rooms, 59 suites* ❍❘ *Breakfast* ✛ *A6.*

SANTA TERESA

$$ 🛏 **Casa Cool Beans.** American expats Lance and David opened Casa Cool
B&B/INN   Beans in 2010, determined to raise the bar for accommodations in Rio,
Fodor's Choice   and their guests' raves about the attentive service, chilled-out atmosphere,
★   and gorgeous decor testify to the high level of success. **Pros:** excellent service; characterful building; peaceful neighborhood; breakfast alfresco. **Cons:** difficult for taxis to find; far from the beach; two-night minimum stay. $ *Rooms from: R$340* ⊠ *Rua Laurinda Santos Lobo 136, Santa Teresa* ☎ *021/2262–0552, 202/470–3548 for calls from the U.S.* ⊕ *www. casacoolbeans.com* ☞ *10 rooms* ❍❘ *Breakfast* ✛ *E1.*

$$$$ 🛏 **Hotel Santa Teresa.** This five-star hotel in the historic hilltop neighbor-
HOTEL   hood of Santa Teresa is the ideal spot for travelers keen to discover Rio's
Fodor's Choice   artistic side. **Pros:** stylish setting; excellent restaurant; 24-hour room ser-
★   vice; close to Santa Teresa's drinking and dining scene. **Cons:** it's a cab ride to the beach; hotel bar sometimes closed for private events. $ *Rooms from: R$870* ⊠ *Rua Almirante Alexandrino 660, Santa Teresa* ☎ *021/3380–0204* ⊕ *www.santa-teresa-hotel.com* ☞ *44 rooms* ❍❘ *Breakfast* ✛ *E1.*

SÃO CONRADO, BARRA DA TIJUCA, AND BEYOND

$$$$ 🛏 **La Suite.** If you're looking for an extra-special place to spend a roman-
HOTEL   tic night in Rio, this luxurious cliffside hideaway is the one to book.
Fodor's Choice   **Pros:** impossibly scenic location; exclusive feel; romantic ambience.
★   **Cons:** it's a cab ride to bars and restaurants. $ *Rooms from: R$860* ⊠ *R. Jackson de Figueiredo, 501, Joatinga* ☎ *021/2484–1962* ☞ *7 rooms* ❍❘ *Breakfast* ✛ *A6.*

$$$$ 🛏 **Sheraton Barra Hotel e Suites.** Each room in this mammoth, gleaming-
HOTEL   white hotel has a balcony overlooking Barra Beach. **Pros:** good facili-
ties; Barra Beach is quieter than Zona Sul. **Cons:** traffic is bad; poor transportation options; neighborhood is more like Miami than Rio. $ *Rooms from: R$645* ⊠ *Av. Lúcio Costa 3150, Barra da Tijuca* ☎ *021/3139–8000* ⊕ *www.sheraton.com/barra* ☞ *264 rooms, 28 suites* ❍❘ *Breakfast* ✛ *A6.*

NIGHTLIFE AND THE ARTS

Rio supports a rich variety of cultural activity and cutting-edge nightlife. The classic rhythms of samba can be heard in many clubs and bars, and on street corners, but it's possible to find something to suit every kind of musical taste almost every night of the week. Major theater, opera, ballet, and classical-music performances are plentiful, and smaller, more intimate events happen in most neighborhoods. Arts enthusiasts should pick up the bilingual *Guia do Rio* published by Riotur, the city's tourist board. The Portuguese-language newspapers *Jornal do Brasil* and *O Globo* publish schedules of events in the entertainment supplements of their Friday editions, which can be found online at ⊕ *www.jb.com.br* and ⊕ *www.oglobo.com.br*. For an up-to-date look at happenings in party-focused Lapa, check out ⊕ *www.lanalapa.com.br*. Finally, *Veja Rio* is the city's most comprehensive entertainment guide, published every Saturday and available at all newsstands.

NIGHTLIFE

It's sometimes said that cariocas would rather expend their energy on the beach and that nighttime is strictly for recharging their batteries and de-sanding their swimsuits, but witnessing the masses swarming into Lapa at 10 pm on a Friday night make this a tricky argument to endorse. New nightclubs and bars continue to sprout up with remarkable regularity, and there are cutting-edge underground rhythms and musical styles competing with samba, chorro, and MPB for the locals' hearts.

A much-loved local pastime is drinking a well-chilled *chopp* (draft beer) and enjoying the lively atmosphere of a genuine Rio *botequim* (bar). Every neighborhood has its share of upmarket options (branches of Belmonte, Devassa, and Conversa Fiada are dotted around town), but no less enjoyable are the huge number of hole-in-the-wall spots offering ice-cold bottles of *cerveja* (beer) and the chance to chat with down-to-earth regulars.

Live music is Rio's raison d'être, with street corners regularly playing host to impromptu renditions. During Carnival the entire city can feel like one giant playground. The electronic-music scene is also very much alive, and the underground popularity of Funk (the city's own X-rated genre, not to be confused with the James Brown version) is slowly seeping into the mainstream, down from the huge *bailes* or open-air parties held weekly in the city's favelas. In addition to samba and Brazilian pop (MPB), hip-hop, electronica, and rock can be heard in clubs around the city.

COPACABANA

BARS

Bip Bip. Here the *roda de samba*—where musicians sit and play instruments around a central table (in fact the *only* table in this tiny bar)—is legendary, as is the help-yourself beer policy. The gnarled old owner makes drink notations and keeps the crowd in check. The standards of the music here are as high as the bar is simple: big name Brazilian musicians have known to drop in for a jam session, and on weekend evenings the revelry often spills out onto the street. ⊠ *Rua Almirante Gonçalves 50, Copacabana* ☎ *021/2267–9696.*

Cervantes. This no-frills Copacabana institution marries great beer with great sandwiches made with fresh beef, pork, and cheese crammed into French bread (with the obligatory pineapple slice). It's closed on Mondays, but merely to give the staff a chance to recover: the rest of the week everyone's up until all hours catering to the lively late night–early morning crowd. ⊠ *Rua Barata Ribeiro 7, Loja B, Copacabana* ☎ *021/2275–6147* ⊕ *www.restaurantecervantes.com.br* ⊘ *Closed Mon.*

NIGHTCLUBS AND LIVE MUSIC

Fosfobox. For the more serious dance-music enthusiast, Fosfobox, in the heart of Copacabana, plays the best underground tunes, as well as rock and pop. It's in an industrial-feeling basement. ⊠ *Rua Siqueira Campos 143, Loja 22 A, Copacabana* ☎ *021/2548–7498* ⊕ *www.fosfobox.com. br* ⊘ *Closed Mon. and Tues.*

La Girl. A well-known women-only lesbian club, La Girl attracts the famous and fabulous females of Rio. ⊠ *Rua Raul Pompéia 102, Posto 6, Copacabana* ☎ *021/2247–8342* ⊕ *www.lagirl.com.br.*

Le Boy. Right next door to La Girl, this is, unsurprisingly, a gay-male mecca. DJs play pop and house music nightly, and outrageous stage shows often take place. ⊠ *Rua Paul Pompéia 102, Posto 6, Copacabana* ☎ *021/2513–4993* ⊕ *www.leboy.com.br.*

FLAMENGO AND BOTAFOGO

BARS

Belmonte. If you find yourself in need of refreshment after a stroll through the beautiful Parque Do Flamengo, then your best stop is Belmonte. The original outlet of a now successful chain, it keeps the carioca spirit alive and well with its carefree air, great food, and icy chopp. ⊠ *Praia Do Flamengo 300, Flamengo* ☎ *021/2552–3349* ⊕ *www.botecobelmonte.com.br.*

The Cobal. More than just a single venue, this collection of bars, restaurants, and shops in the style of an open-air market is always lively and has great views of Cristo Redentor. ⊠ *Cobal do Humaitá, Rua Voluntarios Da Patria 446, Loja 3/4 A, Humaitá* ☎ *021/2266–5599* ⊕ *www. espiritodochopp.com.br.*

Maldita. The name of this interesting bar translates, somewhat curiously, as "the Cursed," but don't let that put you off: the cocktails are excellent, and great electronic music can be heard here. ⊠ *Rua Voluntarios Da Patria 10, Loja 2, Botafogo* ☎ *021/2527–2456.*

NIGHTCLUBS AND LIVE MUSIC

Casa Da Matriz. With its multi-room layout, old-school arcade games, and small junk shop, this shabby-chic venue has the look and feel of a house party. The club's youngish crowd appreciates the adventurous musical policy: don't be surprised if the DJ follows a 1960s Beatles track with down-and-dirty favela funk. ⊠ *Rua Henrique de Novaes 107, Botafogo* ☎ *021/2226–9691.*

Cinemathèque. Take in Brazilian music old and new at the live shows upstairs (from 10:30 pm on), or simply relax in the open-air garden downstairs. ⊠ *Rua Voluntários da Pátria 53, Botafogo* ☎ *021/2286–5731.*

IPANEMA AND LEBLON
BARS

Ipanema is better equipped with clothes shops and restaurants than bars, but there are some great ones here. Rua Vinicius De Moraes has some upmarket options. Studio RJ, in the Arpoador neighborhood, between Ipanema and Copacabana, is an action-packed dance club, and the gay community congregates at smart bars along Rua Farme do Amoeda. Things are tamer in Leblon, but its cool places to congregate include Academia da Cachaça, specialists in the potent liquor, and down-to-earth Jobi.

PLAYING IT SAFE

Safety after dark is a paramount concern in Rio. Be aware of your surroundings at all times. Always take a taxi after dark, and be sure it has the company name and phone number painted on the outside before you get in. Pickpockets love Copacabana and Lapa, so keep valuables either at the hotel or well hidden.

Fodor's Choice ★ **Academia da Cachaça.** Not merely *the* place in Rio to try caipirinhas (made here with a variety of tropical fruits), Academia da Cachaça is a veritable temple to cachaça. The small bar sells close to 100 brands of cachaça by the glass or bottle, as well as mixing the famous sugarcane rum into dangerously drinkable concoctions such as the *cocada geladinha*—frozen coconut, coconut water, brown sugar, and cachaça. The Northeastern bar snacks here include sun-dried beef, baked palm hearts, and delicious black-bean soup. ✉ *Rua Conde de Bernadotte 26, Leblon, Leblon* ☎ *21/2239–1542* ⊕ *www.academiadacachaca.com.br.*

Bar D'Hotel. It's hard to escape the fact that this is just a good, if hip, hotel bar with a nice view of the sea. Expect to find actors, models, sports stars, and socialites rubbing shoulders over drinks, cocktails, and food at steep prices they can afford. ✉ *Marina All Suites, Av. Delfim Moreira 696, Leblon* ☎ *021/2172–1100* ⊕ *www.marinaallsuites.com.br.*

Bar Garota de Ipanema. This is the original Garota (there are branches all over the city), where Tom Jobim and Vinicius de Moraes penned the timeless song "The Girl from Ipanema." The place serves well-priced food and drink that no doubt originally appealed to the two songsmiths. Occasional live-music events take place in the upstairs lounge. ✉ *Rua Vinicius de Moraes 39, Ipanema* ☎ *021/2523–3787* Ⓜ *Ipanema/General Osório.*

Bracarense. A trip to Bracarense after a hard day on the beach is what Rio is all about. Crowds spill onto the streets while parked cars double as chairs and the sandy masses gather at sunset for ice-cold chopp and some of Leblon's best pork sandwiches, fish balls, and empadas. ✉ *Rua José Linhares 85, Leblon* ☎ *021/2294–3549* ⊕ *www.bracarense.com.br.*

Devassa. Another cross-city bar chain, Devassa is notable for its ownbrand beers, including delicious Pale Ales and *Chopp Escuro* (dark beer). The bar also has a great menu of meat-related staples. This branch has a plum location a block from Ipanema Beach. ✉ *Rua Prudente de Moraes 416, Ipanema* ☎ *021/2522–0627* ⊕ *www.devassa.com.br* Ⓜ *Ipanema/General Osório.*

Jobi Bar. Authentically carioca and a fine place to experience Rio spirit, the bar at down-to-earth Jobi (⇨ *Where to Eat, above*) stays open on weekends until the last customer leaves. ⊠ *Av. Ataulfo de Paiva 1166, Loja B, Leblon* ☎ *021/2274–0547.*

NIGHTCLUBS AND LIVE MUSIC

Melt. It's no longer the upper-class hangout it once was, but Melt is arguably all the more appealing for it. The club used to attract models, soap stars, and others looking to see and be seen, but these days attracts a more relaxed crowd of backpackers, well-to-do locals, and young bohemians. The live music ranges from MPB to rock, and the Tuesday night samba-thons are quite fun. ⊠ *Rua Rita Ludolf 47, Leblon* ☎ *021/2249–9309* ⊕ *www.meltbar.com.br.*

> **BAR TALK**
>
> A few useful Portuguese words under your belt will make the bar experience even more enjoyable and help to make you feel like a local. *Chopp* is the ubiquitous draft beer served in small glasses, while *cerveja* is the universal word for bottled beer. A simple *mais uma* will get you "one more," and a *saideira* will get you "one for the road." Finally, ask for *a conta* or "the bill" when you want to settle your tab.

Plataforma. Although Plataforma is very tourist-oriented, if you're in Rio outside of Carnival season, then seeing the shows here will give you a taste of the festival's costumes, music, and energy. Capoeira martial-arts displays complete an enjoyable if expensive look at some great Brazilian traditions. Reservations can be made on the venue's website (also for the restaurant). The smaller, adjoining Bar do Tom is a good place to hear bossa nova and jazz. ⊠ *Rua Adalberto Ferreira 32, Leblon* ☎ *021/2274–4022* ⊕ *www.plataforma.com.*

Studio RJ. Live bands, diverse DJ sets, and dancing to stunning sea views are the draw at this welcome addition to the Zona Sul nightlife scene. The ample space is ideally suited to dancing, and the bar that anchors one end serves excellent cocktails. In a nod to the area's hip musical past—this space operated for decades as the bar–restaurant Barril 1800—Studio RJ has revived the Jazzmania nights that had locals donning their dancing shoes during the 1980s and 1990s. ⊠ *Avenida Vieira Souto 110, Arpoador* ☎ *021/2523–1204* ⊕ *www.studiorj.org* Ⓜ *Cantagalo.*

THE LUSH INLAND

BARS

Caroline Cafe. One of several laid-back bars in the Jardim Botânico area, Caroline Cafe attracts a hip, friendly crowd for straightforward drinking and some unusual snacks. There's an open balcony upstairs. ⊠ *Rua J. J. Seabra 10, Jardim Botânico* ☎ *021/2540–0705* ⊕ *www.carolinecafe.com.br.*

Lagoa. Rio's beautiful city lake is flanked with bars and informal kiosks. Along with the usual beers and cocktails, the food—Italian, Arabian, burgers, and other nontraditional Brazilian—may not be spectacular, but the view of surrounding water and mountains, with Cristo Redentor lighted up in the distance, most certainly is. The kiosks close down around 1 am. ⊠ *Parque Brigadeiro Faria Lima, turnoff near BR gas station, Av. Epitácio Pessoa 1674, Lagoa* ☎ *021/2523–1135.*

NIGHTCLUBS AND LIVE MUSIC

00 (Zero Zero). Alongside the Gávea Planetarium, 00 is at once a buzzing nightclub, chic sushi restaurant, and open-air bar. Music at this special place ranges from modern Brazilian samba and house to drum and bass. ⊠ *Av. Padre Leonel Franca 240, Gávea* ☎ *021/2540–8041* ⊕ *www.00site.com.br.*

Casa Rosa. A former brothel in a bright-pink mansion in the Laranjeiras hillside is now a hot spot for live music and dancing. The Sunday-afternoon *feijoada* and samba on the terrace is a must for anyone seeking out a true carioca experience. ⊠ *Rua Alice 550, Laranjeiras* ☎ *021/2557–2562* ⊕ *www.casarosa.com.br.*

SANTA TERESA AND LAPA

BARS

> **THE REAL GIRL FROM IPANEMA**
>
> Have you ever wondered if there really *was* a girl from Ipanema? The song was inspired by schoolgirl Heloisa Pinheiro, who caught the fancy of songwriter Antônio Carlos (aka Tom) Jobim and his pal, lyricist Vinicius de Moraes, as she walked past the two bohemians sitting in their favorite bar. They then penned one of last century's classics. That was in 1962, and today the bar has been renamed **Bar Garota de Ipanema.** Its owners have further capitalized on their venue's renown, with "Garota de . . ." bars across the city, with the appropriate neighborhood names appended.

Bar do Gomez. Officially Armazem São Thiago, this neighborhood institution is universally referred to by its nickname, Bar do Gomez, in honor of the owner, whose family has run the business for close to 100 years. Pictures documenting the bar's history adorn the high wooden walls, and surveying the scene in the present, you get the pleasant impression that little has changed over the years. The draft beer flows like water, locals swap stories at the long wooden bar, and new friendships are forged at the outdoor drinking posts. Favorites among the bar snacks include the giant olives, a pastrami sandwich, and the shrimp plate. ■TIP➔ **Early on a Friday night, this is a good place to strike up a conversation with locals before heading down the hill to Lapa.** ⊠ *Rua Aurea 26, Santa Teresa* ☎ *021/2232–0822* ⊕ *www.armazemsaothiago.com.br.*

Bar do Mineiro. By far the liveliest of Santa Teresa's many drinking dens and the hub of much social activity, this enduringly popular *boteco* anchors one end of the neighborhood's main drinking and dining strip. The whitewashed walls are hung with posters and artworks honoring the *Tropicalia* arts movement of the 1970s, and Bar do Mineiro continues to attract the kinds of artists and intellectuals that lived in Santa Teresa at that time. Some excellent snacks are served here—the *pasteis de feijao* (fried pastries filled with black beans) being a firm favorite with locals—as well as hearty plates of meat-based *comida mineira* (cuisine from Minas Gerais State). ■TIP➔ **A street-party atmosphere prevails on Sunday afternoons, when the bar is standing-room only and revelers spill out onto the road outside.** ⊠ *Rua Paschoal Carlos Magno 99, Santa Teresa* ☎ *021/2221–9227.*

Mangue Seco Cachaçaria. Specializing in some of Brazil's finest institutions—strong and unusual cachaças (Brazilian rum), mouthwatering *moquecas* (stews), and, of course, live samba—Mangue Seco's location on the popular Rua do Lavradio makes it a perfect place to start a night out. Arrive at sundown, grab one of the sidewalk tables, and watch Lapa life unfold as you sip a caipirinha and browse the menu. ⊠ *Rua do Lavradio 23, Centro* ☏ *021/3852–1947* ⊕ *www.mangueseccocachacaria.com.br.*

NIGHTCLUBS AND LIVE MUSIC

Carioca da Gema. A favorite among local *sambistas*, Carioca da Gema is one of Lapa's liveliest spots, with talented musicians performing six nights a week. By 11 pm, finding a place to stand can be difficult, but regulars still find a way to samba. Call ahead and book a table if you are more keen to be a spectator. There's a good pizzeria downstairs. ⊠ *Rua Mem de Sá 79, Lapa* ☏ *021/2221–0043* ⊕ *www.barcariocadagema.com.br* ☉ *Closed Sun.*

Fodor's Choice **Circo Voador.** A great venue in an excellent location right by the Lapa
★ arches, Circo Voador hosts club nights during the week, but it's the varied live shows that really stand out, with a big stage set under a huge open-sided circular tent and room for up to 1,500 people to dance the night away. ⊠ *Rua dos Arcos s/n, Lapa* ☏ *021/2533-0354* ⊕ *www.circovoador.com.br.*

Estrela da Lapa. One of the area's more upmarket nightspots, this club presents a mixture of cutting-edge music, classic samba, and MPB. ⊠ *Rua Mem de Sá 69, Lapa* ☏ *021/2507–6686* ☉ *Closed Sun. and Mon.*

Lapa Street Party. Lapa's transformation from no-go area to must-go party district has been dramatic, and the ongoing gentrification of this formerly neglected part of downtown has extended to the weekend street parties held in the area surrounding the Arcos da Lapa (Lapa Aqueduct). On Friday and Saturday, smart-looking canvas kiosks sprout up, offering everything from super-strong fruit cocktails to alcohol-absorbing pizzas and burgers, and thousands of revelers come to rub shoulders. The lively scene often involves impromptu music performances, and the party doesn't wind down until the sun rises. Both men and women should be prepared for an onslaught of attention from locals. If this attention is unwanted, be polite but clear and walk away—small talk may be perceived as flirting. ■TIP➡ An increased police presence has made Lapa safer than it was, but pickpocketing remains a problem, so don't bring valuables here. ⊠ *Rua dos Arcos, Lapa* Ⓜ *Carioca.*

Leviano. Lapa's nightlife scene encompasses virtually every type of music imaginable, and sleek Leviano has established itself as a prime venue for the sonically curious. On the packed upstairs dance floor, locals and tourists strut their stuff to everything from MPB (Brazilian pop music) to bass-heavy favela funk. *Sambistas* flock to Wednesday's roda de samba, and live jazz on Tuesdays has also proven popular. With its wooden floors, steel beams, and exposed brick walls, the downstairs lounge is typical of the chic bars replacing the hole-in-the-wall joints Lapa was famous for. ■TIP➡ Leviano's sidewalk patio is ideal for early-evening drinks and munchies. ⊠ *Av. Mem de Sá 49, Lapa* ☏ *021/2507–5779* ⊕ *www.levianobar.com.br* Ⓜ *Carioca or Cinelandia.*

Fodor's Choice
★

Rio Scenarium. Despite the hordes of samba-seeking tourists, Rio Scenarium somehow manages to retain its authenticity and magic. This is partly due to the incredible setting—a former junk shop still crammed to the rafters with old instruments, bikes, furniture, and puppets—but also to the great bands and persevering locals who love to show off their moves and entice novices onto the dance floor. ■ TIP→ On weekends arrive before 9 pm to avoid the lines, or call ahead and book a table. ⊠ *Rua do Lavrádio 20, Lapa* ☎ *021/3147–9005* ⊕ *www.rioscenarium.com.br.*

THE ARTS

Theater, classical music (*música erudita*), and opera may be largely the preserve of the affluent upper classes in Rio, but tickets remain reasonably priced by international standards and can be purchased easily from box offices. Although understanding Portuguese may prove difficult for some visitors, musicals provide a good opportunity to catch the glitzier side of Rio, and the international language of song and dance is considerably more comprehensible. Since many of the venues are in downtown or more out-of-the-way areas, use taxis to get to and from them, as the surrounding streets can feel dangerously deserted by night.

Cinema also remains big business in Rio, and the film industry benefited from one of the country's most talked-about films of all time when *Tropa De Elite* (named after the "Elite Troop" police force that patrols the favelas) hit movie theaters in 2007 and the favorable attention continued after the 2010 follow up was nominated for an Oscar as Best Foreign Film. The annual Rio International Film Festival (⊕ *www.festivaldorio.com.br*) carries a huge buzz every September, when the city's numerous small, private cinemas are awash with avant-garde short films and homegrown acting and directing talent. Multiplexes showing mainstream films can be found in most big malls across the city, and new releases are usually in English with Portuguese subtitles.

Visual-art venues and museums are also very well endowed, with privately funded cultural centers hosting a rich variety of exhibitions, specific details of which are again best sought out in the Friday editions of the Rio press.

CLASSICAL MUSIC

Centro Cultural Municipal Parque Das Ruinas. With a glorious view of Guanabara Bay and downtown, the Parque Das Ruinas houses the remains of a mansion building that was Rio's bohemian epicenter in the first half of the 20th century. Today, occasional music and art events take place during the summer. Check the press for details before heading here. ⊠ *Rua Murtinho Nobre 169, Santa Teresa* ☎ *021/2252–1039.*

Escola de Música da UFRJ. The music school auditorium, inspired by the Salle Gaveau in Paris, has 1,100 seats, and you can listen to chamber music, symphony orchestras, and opera, all free of charge. ⊠ *Rua do Passeio 98, Lapa* ☎ *021/2222–1029* ⊕ *www.musica.ufrj.br* Ⓜ *Cinelândia.*

Carnival in Rio

The four-day Carnival weekend, marked on every Brazilian's calendar, is by far the biggest event of the year, with planning and preparation starting months ahead. What began as a pre-Lent celebration has morphed into a massive affair of street parties, masquerades, and samba parades. Elaborate costumes, enormous floats, and intensive planning all unfurl magically behind the scenes as Brazilians from all walks of life save their money for the all-important *desfile* (parade) down the Sambódromo. Even though Carnival has set dates based on the lunar calendar that determine when Lent occurs, the *folia* (Carnival festivities) start at least a week before and end at least a week after the samba schools parade. Five-star hotels such as the Sheraton and Copacabana Palace have balls that are open to the public, as long as you can afford tickets (which run upward of R$3,000). A cheaper option is partying at the Carnival blocos (street parties), along the streets of Centro and Santa Teresa and the beaches of the Zona Sul. If you really want to get close to the action, then you'll need to buy tickets (well in advance) for a seat at the Sambódromo. Most samba schools begin their rehearsals around October; if you're in Rio from October to January, visit one of the samba schools *(see The Arts)* on a rehearsal day. Whether your scene is hanging out at the bars, partying in the street, parading along the beach, masked balls for the elite, or fun in a stadium, Rio's Carnival is an experience of a lifetime.

Instituto Moreira Salles. Surrounded by beautiful gardens, the institute creates the perfect atmosphere for classical music. Listen to musicians performing pieces from Bach, Chopin, Debussy, and other classical composers. ⊠ *Rua Marquês de São Vicente 476, Gávea* ☎ *021/3284–7400* ⊕ *www.ims.com.br.*

Sala Cecília Meireles. A popular concert venue for classical music in the city, the Sala hosts regular performances in a midsize hall. ⊠ *Largo da Lapa 47, Lapa* ☎ *021/2332–9223* ⊕ *www.salaceciliameireles.com.br* Ⓜ *Cinelândia.*

CONCERT HALLS

Canecão. The traditional venue for big names on the national, and sometimes the international, music scene seats up to 5,000 people, but if you can, reserve a table up front. Upcoming events are advertised on a huge billboard outside the main entrance. ⊠ *Av. Vencoslau Brás 215, Botafogo* ☎ *021/2105–2000.*

Citibank Hall. This huge venue has played host to Caetano Veloso, Luciano Pavarotti, Adele, and Lady Gaga, among many other stars and superstars. ⊠ *Via Parque Shopping, Av. Ayrton Senna 3000, Barra da Tijuca* ☎ *011/4003–5588* ⊕ *www.citibankhall.com.br.*

SAMBA-SCHOOL SHOWS

Weekly public rehearsals (*ensaio*) attract crowds of samba enthusiasts and visitors alike to the *escolas de samba* (samba schools) from August through to Carnival (February or March). As the schools frantically ready themselves for the high point of the year, the atmosphere in these packed warehouses is often electric, and with Mangueira and Beija Flor, always sweaty. This may prove one of your liveliest and most chaotic nights on the town. Ticket prices range from R$15 to R$35. The tour company Brazil Expedition *(⇨ See Tours, in the Rio de Janeiro Planner, above)* offers trips to samba school rehearsals, including transport and entrance, for R$65.

Acadêmicos do Salgueiro. The samba school Salguiero holds its pre-Carnival rehearsals only on Saturdays, at 10 pm. ⊠ *Rua Silva Teles 104, Andaraí* ☎ *021/2238–0389* ⊕ *www.salgueiro.com.br.*

Beija-Flor. The several-times winner of Rio's annual Samba School competition, Beija-Flor holds public rehearsals on Thursdays at 9 pm in the months leading up to Carnival. ⊠ *Pracinha Wallace Paes Leme 1025, Nilópolis* ☎ *021/2791–2866* ⊕ *www.beija-flor.com.br.*

Estação Primeira de Mangueira. One of the most popular schools and always a challenger for the Carnival title, Estação Primeira holds its rehearsals on Saturdays at 10 pm. ⊠ *Rua Visconde de Niterói 1072, Mangueira* ☎ *021/2567–4637* ⊕ *www.mangueira.com.br.*

FILM

Estação Ipanema. The charming two-screen Estação Ipanema cinema is part of a lively area of small restaurants and bookstores, perfect for hanging out before or after the films (the theater itself has a coffee shop). Other locations of the Estação chain of small art-house cinemas can be found on the Ipanema beachfront (Estação Laura Alvim), in Flamengo (Estação Paissandu), and in Botafogo (Estação Botafogo). ⊠ *Av. Visconde de Pirajá 605, Ipanema* ☎ *021/2279–4603* ⊕ *www. grupoestacao.com.br.*

Odeon BR. The last remaining movie palace in historic Cinelândia—once the focal point of moviegoing activity in Rio—is one of the most well preserved and important in the country. The luxurious theater has hosted premieres, exhibits, and events since opening in 1926. ⊠ *Praça Floriano 7, Cinelândia* ☎ *021/2240–1093.*

UCI New York City Center. This 18-screen, American-style multiplex comes complete with a fake Statue of Liberty outside. ⊠ *Av. das Américas 5000, Loja 301, Barra da Tijuca* ☎ *021/2461–1818* ⊕ *www. ucicinemas.com.br.*

OPERA

Fodor'sChoice **Theatro Municipal.** Built in 1909, the stunning Municipal Theater at
★   Cinelândia is the city's main performing-arts venue, hosting dance, opera, symphony concerts, and theater events for most of the year. The season officially runs from March to December, so don't be surprised to find the theater closed in January and February. The theater also has its own ballet company. ⊠ *Praça Floriano, Rua Manuel Carvalho s/n, Centro* ☎ *021/2332–9134, 021/2332–9191* ⊕ *www.theatromunicipal. rj.gov.br* Ⓜ *Cinelândia.*

THEATER

Fodor'sChoice ★ **Centro Cultural Banco do Brasil.** Formerly the headquarters of the Banco do Brasil, in the late 1980s this opulent six-story domed building with marble floors was transformed into a space for plays, art exhibitions, and music recitals. Today the CCBB is one of the city's most important cultural centers, with a bookstore, three theaters, a video hall, four individual video booths, a movie theater, two auditoriums, a restaurant, a coffee shop, and a tearoom. It's open daily except Monday between 10 am and 9 pm. ⊠ *Rua 1° de Março 66, Centro* ☎ *21/3808–2020* ⊕ *www. bb.com.br/cultura* Ⓜ *Uruguaiana.*

Teatro das Artes. The main theater in an unlikely shopping-mall setting is one of four in a complex that hosts popular productions. With one room for children-oriented shows and two smaller, more specialized theaters, you're apt to find something of interest here. ⊠ *Shopping Center da Gávea, Rua Marques de São Vicente 52, Loja 264, Gávea* ☎ *021/2540–6004* ⊕ *www.teatrodasartes.com.br.*

Teatro João Caetano. The city's oldest theater dates to 1813, and with the 1,200 seats and many inexpensive productions staged here, the place here is worth a look, especially since the once-seedy area around it has been smartened up. ⊠ *Praça Tiradentes, Centro* ☎ *021/2332–9166* ⊕ *www.cultura.rj.gov.br/espaco/teatro-joao-caetano* Ⓜ *Presidente Vargas.*

Teatro Villa-Lobos. This 463-seat theater close to Copacabana Beach presents excellent drama productions and occasional dance performances. ⊠ *Av. Princesa Isabel 440, Copacabana* ☎ *021/2334–7153, 021/2541–6799* ⊕ *www.cultura.rj.gov.br/espaco/teatro-villa-lobos.*

SPORTS AND THE OUTDOORS

Simply put, Rio de Janeiro is sports mad. Though much of the frenzy centers on soccer, other sports—among them volleyball, basketball, beach soccer, beach volleyball, and futevolei (a soccer-volleyball hybrid)—are taken extremely seriously. It is with a sense of fevered anticipation, then, that Rio awaits the 2014 FIFA World Cup soccer championship games and the 2016 Olympics. Their impact on the city cannot be understated. In addition to the vast sums spent to renovate the legendary Maracanã soccer stadium and create new sports facilities and an Olympic village in the city's West Zone, significant investments are being made to upgrade the public-transportation system, and extra efforts to reduce crime are underway as well.

ON THE SIDELINES

HORSE RACING

Jóquei Clube. This beautiful old racetrack conjures up a bygone era of grandeur with its impeccably preserved betting hall, 1920s grandstand, and distant beach views framed by Cristo Redentor and the Dois Irmaos mountain. When the big event of the year, the Grande Premio, comes around in August, expect the crowds to swell and everyone to be dressed to the nines. Entry is free year-round, but you need to dress smart–casual, with no shorts or flip-flops allowed in the main stand. ✉ *Praça Santos Dumont 31, Gávea* ☎ *021/2512–9988* ⊕ *www.jcb.com.br.*

SOCCER

Estádio Maracanã. The vast stadium is nothing short of legendary, and watching a soccer game here is a must if the season (from mid-January to November) is in swing. As entertaining as some of the games are the obsessive supporters, devoted to their team colors but not afraid to trash their own players, the opposition, other fans, and of course the referee, are also fun to watch. The huge flags and fireworks are always spectacular. Tickets are available in advance and often on game day from the stadium ticket office. The *branco* or white section of the *archibancado,* or upper tier, is the safest option for the neutral fan. Expect to pay around R$35 for a ticket there, and arrive in good time to grab the best seats and soak up the atmosphere. Major refurbishments were made to prepare the 78,838-seat stadium for the FIFA 2014 World Cup. ✉ *Rua Prof. Eurico Rabelo s/n, Maracanã* ☎ *021/8871–3950.*

PARTICIPATORY SPORTS

Rio is an incredibly active city, with people of all ages cycling, jogging, or walking along the beachfront paths, swimming across Ipanema to Leblon, and using municipal tennis courts and football pitches into the early hours of the morning. Given the natural amenities the city is blessed with, an energetic visitor won't be at a loss for activities.

BOATING AND SAILING

Dive Point. Schooner tours around the main beaches of Rio and as far afield as Búzios and Angra are offered here, as well as deep-sea and wreck diving. ■TIP→ **Be sure to ask if prices include all the necessary equipment and training (if required).** ✉ *Av. Ataulfo da Paiva 1174, SS 04, Leblon* ☎ *021/2239–5105* ⊕ *www.divepoint.com.br.*

Saveiro's Tour. Catch one of the daily cruises around Guanabara Bay— views of Sugar Loaf, Botafogo Bay, and the Rio-Niterói Bridge are the highlights. Saveiro's also hires out speedboats and sailboats by the day. ✉ *Marina da Glória, Av. Infante Dom Henrique S/N, Lojas 13 e 14, Glória* ☎ *021/2225–6064* ⊕ *www.saveiros.com.br.*

GOLF

Gávea Golf Club. Nonmembers can play this upmarket golfing club's impeccably groomed course on weekdays. The greens fee is steep, but you can get a discount if you're staying at the Copacabana Palace, Inter-Continental, or Sheraton hotel. ✉ *Estrada da Gávea 800, São Conrado* ☎ *021/3322–4141* ⊕ *www.gaveagolf.com.br* ⅃ *Course: 18 holes. 5990 yds. Par 69. Greens fee: R$350/R$450* ☞ *Facilities: Driving range, putting green, pitching area, golf carts, pull carts, caddies, rental clubs, pro-shop, restaurant, bar.*

Golden Green Golf Club. It may only have six holes, but given the exclusivity and prices of the alternatives, this could be your best option for getting in a little play in Rio. Nonmembers are welcome every day. ✉ *Avenida Prefeito Dulcídio Cardoso 2901, Barra da Tijuca*

☏ 021/2434–0696 🎿 *Course: 6 holes. 2637 yds. Par 18. Greens fee: R$80/R$100* ☞ *Facilities: Driving range, putting green, pitching area, rental clubs, restaurant.*

HANG GLIDING

Just Fly. This outfit will collect you from your hotel, take you through the basics, and then run you off Pedra Bonita mountain into the sky high above Tijuca Forest. The excellent instructors can also film or photograph the experience for an extra charge. ⊠ *Rua Barão da Torre 175, Ipanema* ☏ *21/2268–0565, 021/9985–7540* ⊕ *www.justfly.com.br.*

> ### CYCLE RIO
>
> With its many bike paths, Rio is a great place to explore by bicycle, and Bike Rio, a citywide bicycle-sharing system, has made it easier than ever to do so. Locals and visitors can pick up one of hundreds of bicycles at rental stations along the beachfront and at other bike-friendly locations, returning the bikes to similar stations at journey's end. Daily passes cost R$5 and can be purchased online at ⊕ *www.mobilicidade.com.br.*

São Conrado Eco-Aventura. This reliable and experienced team can provide you with a bird's-eye view of Rio either by hang glider or paraglider. ⊠ *São Conrado* ☏ *021/2522–5586* ⊕ *www.saoconradoecoaventuras.com.br.*

HIKING AND CLIMBING

Given the changeable weather and the harsh terrain, guides are recommended for all major walks and climbs in Rio. Of particular note within the city itself are the hikes up Corcovado from Parque Lage and the trip through Tijuca Forest to Pico da Tijuca.

Brasil Active. These ecotourism specialists provide a wealth of options—including horse treks and yoga trails, along with climbing, mountain biking, and other standbys—for every age range. ⊠ *Rua Francisca Sales 645, Jacarepaguá* ☏ *021/2424–5455* ⊕ *www.brasilactive.com.br.*

Centro Excursionista Brasileiro. You can research and register for all upcoming tours on Centro Excursionista's website. The outfit, which leads treks throughout Rio State and as far away as Minas Gerais, provides guides, maps, and all the gear you'll need. ⊠ *Av. Almirante Barroso 2, Centro* ☏ *021/2252–9844* ⊕ *www.ceb.org.br.*

Rio Adventures. You need to book your adventures well in advance with this outfit that arranges caving, fishing, rafting, and hiking and mountain climbing trips. ⊠ *Praça Radial Sul 25, Botafogo* ☏ *021/2705–5747, 021/9768–5221* ⊕ *rioadventures.com.*

KARTING

Kartodromo Premium. This is the biggest recreational karting track in Rio (1.6 km/1 mile). Group parties are accepted. If you're solo, you can enter in a cup against other members of the public. ⊠ *Av Ayrton Senna 3010, Barra da Tijuca* ☏ *021/2431–9373, 021/9995–3535* ⊕ *www.kartodromopremium.com.br* 🎟 *R$45 weekdays, R$49 weekends and holidays* ⊙ *Daily 5 pm–midnight.*

SURFING

Surfing remains hugely popular in Rio, but kite surfing is growing rapidly, too, with several schools opening on Barra beachfront and out of town toward Cabo Frio.

Escola de Surf do Arpoador. The most consistent break in the city has its own surf school based on the beach; call up or stop by to book an early-morning appointment. ✉ *Avenida Francisco Bhering s/n, In front of Posto 7, Arpoador* ☎ *021/9180–2287* ⊕ *www.surfrio.com.br.*

Kitepoint Rio. One of several companies based in huts along Avenida do Pepê near Posto 7, Kitepoint provides all the equipment and training you'll need to master the sport of kite surfing. Wind conditions have to be just right, though, so patience is a virtue when seeking lessons. ✉ *Ave do Pepê, Kiosk 7, Next to Bombeiro, Barra* ☎ *021/8859–2112* ⊕ *www.kitepointrio.com.br.*

> ### RIO SURF BUS
>
> The Oi Surf Bus travels seven days a week from Botafogo to Prainha, which is considered to be the best surfing beach close to the city. The two-hour trip takes in the best surf breaks west of Rio, including all 12 km (7½ miles) of Barra, Recreio, and Macumba. There's no snobbery if you don't have a board and are just going along for the ride. Catch the bus from anywhere along the Copacabana, Ipanema, or Leblon beachfront for an easy route to some stunning out-of-town beaches. Check outward and return times at ⊕ *www.surfbus. com.br,* because you do not want to be left stranded.

TENNIS

Parque do Flamengo. Municipal tennis courts rare in Rio, so the two near Flamengo Beach, both in good condition, are popular. The courts can't be booked, but a half-hour wait is likely to be rewarded. ✉ *South of Parque Brigadeiro Eduardo Gomes, off Av. Infante D. Henrique, Flamengo* ☎ *021/2265–4990.*

SHOPPING

Rio shopping is most famous for its incomparable beachwear and gemstone jewelry, both of which are exported globally. Brazil is one of the world's largest suppliers of colored gemstones, with deposits of aquamarines, amethysts, diamonds, emeralds, rubellites, topazes, and tourmalines. If you're planning to go to Minas Gerais, do your jewelry shopping there; otherwise stick with shops that have certificates of authenticity and quality. Other good local buys include shoes, Havaianas flip-flops, arts and crafts, coffee, local music, and summer clothing in natural fibers. With lots of low-quality merchandise around, the trick to successful shopping in Rio is knowing where to find high-quality items at reasonable prices.

Ipanema is Rio's most fashionable shopping district. Its many exclusive boutiques are in arcades, with the majority along Rua Visconde de Pirajá. Leblon's shops, scattered among cafés, restaurants, and newspaper kiosks, are found mainly along Rua Ataulfo da Paiva. Copacabana has souvenir shops, bookstores, and branches of some of Rio's better shops along Avenida Nossa Senhora de Copacabana and connecting streets. For cheap fashion finds and Carnival costumes, head to the maze of shopping streets behind the Uruguaiana metro station.

CENTRO

DEPARTMENT STORE

Lojas Americanas. Rio's largest chain department store sells casual clothing, toys, records, candy, cosmetics, and sporting goods. ⊠ *Rua do Passeio 42–56, Centro* ☎ *021/2524–0284* ⊕ *www.americanas.com.br* Ⓜ *Cinelândia* ⊠ *Rua Visconde de Pirajá 526, Ipanema* ☎ *021/2274–0590* ⊕ *www.americanas.com.br* Ⓜ *Praça General Osório.*

MARKETS

Feira de Antiquários da Praça 15 de Novembro. This open-air antiques fair held on Saturdays attracts more locals than tourists—it's a good place to pick up vintage clothing, sunglasses, rare vinyl, and antique furniture and jewelry. Arrive early to get the best buys, and be prepared to haggle. ■**TIP**➜ **Serious collectors arrive as early as 6 am, often with an eye to grabbing a bargain and reselling it a few hours later at a higher price. Sellers begin to close up shop by early afternoon.** ⊠ *Praça Qunize de Novembro, Centro.*

Fodor's Choice ★ **Feira do Rio Antigo** (*Rio Antiques Fair*). Vendors at this outdoor fair sell antiques, rare books, records, and all types of objets d'art on the first Saturday afternoon of the month. New and vintage fashion is also a strong suit. Live samba music and capoeira performances create a festival-like atmosphere, and the pavement bars and restaurants buzz with locals and visitors. ⊠ *Rua do Lavradio, Centro* ☎ *021/2224–6693* ⊕ *www.polonovorioantigo.com.br.*

Feira Nordestina (*Northeastern Fair*). The crowded, lively Feira de São Cristóvão, better known as the Feira Nordestina, is a social hub for Brazilians from the country's northeast who live in Rio. They gather to hear their own distinctive music, eat regional foods, and buy arts, crafts, home furnishings, and clothing. With two stages for live music, the fair takes on a nightclub vibe after dark, and there are some seriously impressive displays of *forro* dancing. ■**TIP**➜ **This fair is at its busiest and most exciting on the weekends. It's best to take a taxi here.** ⊠ *Campo de São Cristóvão, Pavilhão de São Cristóvão, 7 km (4½ miles northwest of Centro), São Cristóvão* ☎ *021/2580–0501, 021/2580–5335* ⊕ *www.feiradesaocristovao.org.br* ☉ *Tues.–Thurs. 10–6, and Fri. 10 am–Sun. 8 pm (continuously).*

BOOKS

Livraria Leonardo da Vinci. One of Rio's best sources for foreign-language titles, this bookstore has a wide selection of titles in English, Spanish, and French. ⊠ *Av. Rio Branco 185, Subsolo, Centro* ☎ *021/2533–2237* ⊕ *www.leonardodavinci.com.br* Ⓜ *Carioca.*

CAHAÇA

Lidador. Deli goods and more than 30 types of cachaça are sold at Lidador. ⊠ *Rua da Assembléia 65, Centro* ☎ *021/2533–4988* ⊕ *www.lidador.com.br/loja* Ⓜ *Carioca* ⊠ *Rua Barata Ribeiro 505, Copacabana*

☎ *021/2549–0091* Ⓜ *Siqueira Campos* ✉ *Rua Vinicius de Morais 120, Ipanema* ☎ *021/2227–0593* Ⓜ *Ipanema/General Osório.*

MUSIC

Musical Carioca. A paradise for music lovers, Musical Carioca shares a street with many other music stores. Brazilian percussion instruments are also sold here. ✉ *Rua da Carioca 89, Centro* ☎ *021/2524–6029, 021/3814–3400* ⊕ *www. musicalcarioca.com.br.*

> ### BARGAINING IN RIO
>
> Bargaining in shops is unusual, but you can try your luck and ask if there's a discount for paying in cash, especially if it's a high-priced item. When granted, you can expect a 5% to 10% discount. Market or street-vendor shopping is a different story—bargain to your wallet's content.

COPACABANA AND LEME

CENTERS AND MALLS

Shopping Center Cassino Atlântico. Antiques shops, jewelry stores, art galleries, and souvenir outlets predominate at this mall adjoining the Rio Palace hotel. ✉ *Av. Nossa Senhora de Copacabana 1417, Copacabana* ☎ *021/2523–8709.*

MARKETS

Avenida Atlântica. In the evening and on weekends along the median of Avenida Atlântica, artisans spread out their wares. You can find paintings, carvings, handicrafts, handmade clothing, and hammocks. ✉ *Copacabana.*

Feirarte. This street fair similar to the Sunday Feira Hippie in Ipanema takes place on weekends from 8 to 6. Handmade clothes, jewelry, and artsy knickknacks can be found here. ✉ *Praça do Lido, Copacabana* Ⓜ *Cardeal Arcoverde.*

BEAUTY

Spa do Pé. If touring and shopping have left you in need of revival, stop by Spa do Pé for a massage, manicure, or a foot treatment. ✉ *Av. Nossa Senhora de Copacabana 680, Loja L, Copacabana* ☎ *021/2547–0459* ⊕ *www.spadope.com.br* Ⓜ *Siqueira Campos.*

COFFEE

Pão de Açúcar. The supermarket Pão de Açúcar is a good bet for coffee that's cheaper than you'd pay at a coffee shop. ✉ *Av. Nossa Senhora Copacabana 749, SB, Copacabana* ☎ *021/2547–0372* ⊕ *www.paodeacucar.com.br* Ⓜ *Siqueira Campos.*

SURF AND RADICAL SPORTS GEAR

Centauro. The massive Centauro store caters to the needs of all sorts of sporting enthusiasts. ✉ *Shopping Leblon, Av. Afrânio de Melo Franco 290, Loja 106 and 107 A, Leblon* ☎ *021/2512–1246* ⊕ *www.centauro.com.br.*

Galeria River. Stores at this arcade sell all the clothing and equipment you'll need for a surfing or sporting vacation. ✉ *Rua Francisco Otaviano 67, Copacabana* ☎ *21/2267–1709* ⊕ *www.galeriariver.com.br* Ⓜ *Ipanema/General Osório.*

FLAMENGO AND BOTAFOGO

CENTERS AND MALLS

Rio Sul. The popular Rio Sul retail complex has 400 stores, plus a cineplex and a giant food court. The complex offers free bus service to and from many hotels. ⊠ *Av. Lauro Müller 116, Botafogo* ☎ *021/2122–8070* ⊕ *www.riosul.com.br.*

SHOES, BAGS, AND ACCESSORIES

Mr. Cat. The stylish Mr. Cat carries handbags and leather shoes for men and women and has stores all over the city. ⊠ *Botafogo Praia Shopping, Praia de Botafogo 400, Lojas 124 and 125, Botafogo* ☎ *021/2552–5333* ⊕ *www.mrcat.com.br* Ⓜ *Botafogo* ⊠ *Rua Visconde de Pirajá 414, Loja D, Ipanema* ☎ *021/2227–6521* Ⓜ *Ipanema/General Osório.*

Victor Hugo. A Uruguayan who began making handbags when he came to Brazil in the 1970s, Victor Hugo has become famous nationally for leather handbags that are similar in quality to those of more expensive brands such as Louis Vuitton, Gucci, and Prada. ⊠ *Rio Sul, Av. Lauro Müller 116, Loja B19, Botafogo* ☎ *021/2542–2999* ⊕ *www. victorhugo.com.br.*

IPANEMA AND LEBLON

CENTERS AND MALLS

Shopping Leblon. Chanel, H.Stern, Juicy Couture, and 200 or so other stores do business at this mall that's easily accessible on foot for those in Ipanema and Leblon. It has a good food court and a modern four-screen cineplex. ⊠ *Av. Afrânio de Melo Franco 290, Leblon* ☎ *021/2430–5122* ⊕ *www.shoppingleblon.com.br.*

MARKETS

Feira Hippie (*Hippie Fair*). The colorful handicrafts street fair takes place on Sundays between 9 am and 7 pm. Shop for high-quality jewelry, hand-painted dresses, paintings, wood carvings, leather bags and sandals, rag dolls, knickknacks, furniture, and samba percussion instruments, among many other items. ■**TIP→** **It's fun to browse here even if you're not looking to buy anything.** ⊠ *Praça General Osório, Ipanema* ⊕ *www.feirahippieipanema.com* Ⓜ *Ipanema/General Osório.*

ART

Gam, Arte e Molduras. A good place to find high-quality modern and contemporary paintings and sculptures, this gallery, which ships items abroad for customers, also sells photographs that can be made to size. ⊠ *Rua Garcia D'Ávila 145, Loja C, Ipanema* ☎ *021/2247–8060* ⊕ *www.gamarteemolduras.com.br* Ⓜ *Ipanema/General Osório.*

BEACHWEAR

Bumbum Ipanema. Alcindo Silva Filho, better known as Cidinho, opened Bumbum in 1979 after deciding to create the smallest (and by some accounts, the sexiest) bikinis in town. Bumbum remains a solid beachwear brand. ⊠ *Rua Visconde de Pirajá 351, Loja B, Ipanema* ☎ *021/3259–8630* ⊕ *www.bumbum.com.br* Ⓜ *Ipanema/General Osório* ⊠ *Shopping Rio Sul, Rua Lauro Müller 116, Loja*

401, Botafogo ☎ *021/2542–9614* ✉ *Barra Shopping, Av. das Américas 4666, Loja 134B, Barra da Tijuca* ☎ *021/2431–8323.*

Espaço Brazilian Soul. For funky T-shirts and high-quality swimsuits, go to Brazilian Soul. The two-floor department store sells pricey but hip clothes and accessories from Brazilian designers and carries international brands such as Osklen. ✉ *Rua Prudente de Moraes 1102, Ipanema* ☎ *021/2522–3641* Ⓜ *Ipanema/General Osório.*

Garota de Ipanema Shop. Come here for T-shirts, tanks, colorful beach bags, and everything else you'll need to look fabulous at the beach. ✉ *Rua Vinicius de Moraes 53, Loja A, Ipanema* ☎ *021/2521–3168* ⊕ *www.garotadeipanemabrasil.com.br* Ⓜ *Ipanema/General Osório.*

Lenny. Upmarket swimwear store Lenny sells sophisticated pieces in comfortable sizes, and lots of fashionable beach accessories. Prices are high, but the bikinis are particularly creative. ✉ *Forum Ipanema, Rua Visconde de Pirajá 351, Loja 114/115, Ipanema* ☎ *021/2523–3796* ⊕ *www.lenny.com.br* Ⓜ *Ipanema/General Osório.*

Lenny Off. If you are looking for an affordably priced designer bikini and don't mind last season's models, check out Lenny Off, selling slashed-rate pieces from the celebrated bikini brand Lenny. ✉ *Rua Carlos Góis 234, Loja H, Leblon* ☎ *021/2511–2739* ⊕ *www.lenny.com.br*

BEAUTY
Farma Life. The drugstore Farma Life has a wide selection of beauty products. ✉ *Av. Ataulfo de Paiva 285, Loja B/C, Leblon* ☎ *021/2239–1178* ⊕ *www.farmalife.com.br* ✉ *Rua Visconde de Pirajá 559, Loja A, Ipanema* ☎ *021/2274–2017* Ⓜ *Ipanema/General Osório.*

O Boticario. This shop carries soaps, lotions, perfumes, shampoos, and cosmetics made from local plants and seeds. There are branches across the city, but the Ipanema branch is handy for post-beach shopping. ✉ *Rua Visconde de Pirajá 371, Ipanema* ☎ *021/2287–2944* ⊕ *www. oboticario.com.br* Ⓜ *Ipanema/General Osório.*

Shampoo. This shop sells local and imported beauty products. ✉ *Rua Visconde de Pirajá 581, Loja A, Ipanema* ☎ *021/2529–2518.*

BOOKS
Argumento. Its large selection of books in English has made this bookstore popular with expats and vacationers. There's also a CD section. The very fine Café Severino, in the back, has coffee, pastries, salads, crepes, and sandwiches. ✉ *Rua Dias Ferreira 417, Leblon* ☎ *021/2239–5294.*

CACHAÇA
Academia da Cachaça. You can buy close to 100 brands of cachaça here. The bar (⇨ *Nightlife*) serves amazing caipirinhas and other cachaça-based drinks. ✉ *Rua Conde Bernadote 26, Loja G, Leblon* ☎ *021/ 2239–1542.*

Garapa Doida. At Garapa Doida you can learn how to prepare a good caipirinha, and how to purchase everything you need to make it, including glasses, straws, barrels to conserve the alcohol, and cachaça from all over the country. ✉ *Rua Carlos Góis 234, Loja F, Leblon* ☎ *021/2274–8186.*

Garrafeira. The charming liquor store Garrafeira sells a wide range of cachaça, including excellent versions from Minas Gerais State. ⊠ *Rua Dias Ferreira 259, Loja A, Leblon* ☎ *021/2512–3336* ⊕ *www.agarrafeira.com.br.*

CLOTHING

Alessa. For fashion-forward designs, visit Alessa. Pay special attention to Alessa's fabulously fun underwear, which makes for great presents. ⊠ *Rua Nascimento Silva 399, Ipanema* ☎ *021/2287–9939* ⊕ *www.alessa.com.br.*

Animale. A favorite among local fashionistas, Animale carries casualwear and formalwear that's both sophisticated and sexy. If you want to make an impression in Rio's social scene, head here for slinky dresses, chic cover-ups, and show-stopping shoes and accessories. ⊠ *Rua Joana Angelica 116, Ipanema* ☎ *021/2227–3336* ⊕ *www.animale.com.br* Ⓜ *Ipanema/General Osório.*

Farm. Fun colors and bold patterns make Farm popular with cariocas. It's a great place to find feminine dresses and cute tops. ⊠ *Rua Visconde de Pirajá 365, Loja C-D, 202–204, Ipanema* ☎ *021/3813–3817* ⊕ *www.farmrio.com.br* Ⓜ *Ipanema/General Osório* ⊠ *Rio Design Leblon, Av. Ataulfo de Paiva 270, Loja 313 e 314, Leblon* ☎ *021/2540–0082.*

Osklen. Osklen is a synonym for sporty casual clothing with a fashionable flair. The clothes—from trousers to coats to tennis shoes—are designed for outdoor use. ⊠ *Rua Maria Quitéria 85, Ipanema* ☎ *021/2227–2911* ⊕ *www.osklen.com.br* Ⓜ *Ipanema/General Osório* ⊠ *São Conrado Fashion Mall, Estrada da Gávea 899, Loja 17 second floor, São Conrado* ☎ *021/3322–0317* ⊠ *Barra Shopping, Av. das Américas 4666, Loja 207 F, Barra da Tijuca* ☎ *21/2431–9553* ⊕ *www.osklen.com.*

Richards. One of the most traditional clothing stores in Brazil, Richards was originally just for men but now also carries women's clothing. It's the place to go to for good-quality linen clothing. ⊠ *Rua Maria Quitéria 95, Ipanema* ☎ *021/2522–1245* ⊕ *www.richards.com.br* Ⓜ *Ipanema/General Osório.*

COFFEE

Armazém do Café. The Armazém do Café chain has several branches in Rio, including ones in Ipanema and Leblon where you can enjoy a cappuccino or espresso and a pastry at the café before browsing the coffees and coffee-making devices for sale. ⊠ *Rua Visconde de Pirajá 595, Loja 101/102, Ipanema* ☎ *021/3874–2920* ⊕ *www.armazemdocafe.com.br* Ⓜ *Ipanema/General Osório* ⊠ *Rua Rita Ludolf 87, Loja B, Leblon* ☎ *021/3874–2609.*

THE BRAZILIAN BIKINI

Urban myth has it that Brazilian model Rose de Primo fashioned the Brazilian string bikini when she hurriedly sewed a bikini for a photo shoot with too little material. Whatever its history, the Tanga (string bikini) provides less than half the coverage of conventional bikinis, and makes the itsy bitsy teeny-weeny yellow polka-dot bikini look rather conservative. If you're looking to buy a Brazilian bikini, but are looking for a little more coverage, ask for a "sunkini." Happily for those reluctant to bare almost all, recent years have seen chic cariocas increasingly embrace one-piece swimwear.

Zona Sul. Branches of this upscale supermarket can be found throughout Rio's South Zone, and they're good places to pick up deli goods, coffee, chocolate, and fresh fruit and vegetables. ■TIP→ The promotional prices displayed usually apply only to those holding Zona Sul loyalty cards. ⊠ *Prudente de Morais 49, Ipanema* ☎ *021/2267–0361* Ⓜ *Ipanema/General Osório.*

JEWELRY

Amsterdam Sauer. One of Rio's top names in jewelry, this is the perfect place to pick up an elegant gift. The on-site gemstone museum is open weekdays between 10 and 6 and Saturday between 9 and 2 for free guided tours that can be booked online. ⊠ *Rua Visconde de Pirajá 484, Ipanema* ☎ *021/3539–0165, 021/2512–9878 for the museum* ⊕ *www.amsterdamsauer.com* Ⓜ *Ipanema/General Osório.*

Chloé Laclau. The beautiful jewelry pieces here make great gifts; the necklaces are a particularly good value. ⊠ *Rua Garcia d'Ávila 149, Ipanema* ☎ *021/2521–9545* ⊕ *Ipanema/General Osório.*

Francesca Romana Diana. The store's namesake designer, who has five shops in Rio, creates great gold and silver jewelry and works with semiprecious stones. Check out the great bangles featuring the famous Copacabana or Ipanema sidewalk pattern. ⊠ *Rua Visconde de Pirajá 547, Ipanema* ☎ *021/2274–8511* ⊕ *www.francescaromanadiana.com.*

H.Stern. The award-winning designers at H.Stern create distinctive contemporary pieces—the inventory runs to about 300,000 items. The shops downstairs sell more affordable pieces and folkloric items. Around the corner at the company's world headquarters *(⇨ Exploring Rio de Janeiro)*, you can see exhibits of rare stones and watch craftspeople transform rough stones into sparkling jewels. ⊠ *Rua Visconde de Pirajá 490, Ipanema* ☎ *0800/227–442* ⊕ *www.hstern.com.br.*

Sobral. Visit Sobral for chunky, colorful resin jewelry, accessories, and decorative items. Reclaimed materials are used to make the store's funky goods, and its owners invest in social projects such as jewelry-making classes for young people in disadvantaged communities. ⊠ *Forum Ipanema, Rua Visconde de Pirajá 351, Loja 105, Ipanema* ☎ *021/2267–0009* ⊕ *www.rsobral.com.br* Ⓜ *Ipanema/General Osório.*

MUSIC

Fodor'sChoice **Toca do Vinicius.** Tiny Toca do Vinicius bills itself as a "cultural space
★ and bossa nova salon," and indeed the shop feels like more than just a place of business. Bossa nova aficionados from around the world gather here, and if you're one of them, there's a good chance you'll leave with the email address of at least one new pal. You'll also find sheet music, T-shirts, CDs, and books on music, including a few in English. One Sunday a month the shop hosts an intimate bossa nova concert. ⊠ *Rua Vinicius de Moraes 129, Loja C, Ipanema* ☎ *021/2247–5227* ⊕ *www.tocadovinicius.com.br* Ⓜ *Ipanema/General Osório.*

THE 7 WONDERS OF RIO SHOPPING

Arts and crafts. The hills of Santa Teresa brim with arts and crafts stores selling paintings, colorful wooden animals, and other works by local artists. (R$10 and up)

Brazilian soccer shirt. You just can't leave Brazil without one of the country's most emblematic gifts. (R$35 and up)

Cachaça. While showing your friends your vacation pictures, you can impress them with a caipirinha made with genuine cachaça. (R$10 and up)

Chic swimwear. You can show off your Rio tan back home in a daringly revealing bikini—Lenny and Bumbum have some of the best designs—or a more modest, but still sexy, one-piece suit. (R$90 and up)

Gilson Martins bag. Whatever style or size you buy from the hip designer's stores will make a cool souvenir or gift. (R$30 and up)

Havaianas. The brand's stores in Ipanema and Centro sell its flip-flops at such low prices, how can you not take home a bagful? (R$17 and up)

Mini-Cristo. Sobral makes a colorful miniversion of one of the seven wonders of the modern world. (R$50)

SHOES, BAGS, AND ACCESSORIES

Constança Basto. Costly women's shoes made of crocodile and snake leather in original styles are the specialty of Constança Basto. ✉ *Shopping Leblon, Av. Ataulfo de Paiva 290, Loja 311j, Leblon* ☎ *021/2511–8801* ⊕ *www.constancabasto.com.*

Fodor's Choice ★ **Gilson Martins.** The shops of one of Brazil's most gifted and acclaimed designers sell his colorful Rio-inspired bags and accessories at affordable prices. ✉ *Rua Visconde de Pirajá 462, Ipanema* ☎ *021/2227–6178* ⊕ *www.gilsonmartins.com.br* ✉ *Rua Figueredo de Magalhães 304, Loja A, Copacabana* ☎ *021/3816–0552* ⊕ *Siqueira Campos* ✉ *Av. Atlântica 1998, Copacabana* ☎ *021/2235–5701* ⊕ *Siqueira Campos.*

Havaianas Store. The Ipanema Havaianas store carries the fun and funky flip-flops in all colors, styles, and sizes, for men, women, and kids. The range is staggering, from classic Brazil-flag designs to limited-edition gem-encrusted versions. The prices start at R$15 and creep over R$100. Alongside the legendary flops, the store also sells canvas deck shoes and sturdier sandals, as well as opinion-dividing "flip flop socks." Other locations around town include one in Centro. ✉ *Rua Farme de Amoedo 76A, Ipanema* ☎ *021/2267–7395* ⊕ *br.havaianas. com* Ⓜ *Ipanema/General Osório* ✉ *Rua da Alfandega, Loja 176, Centro* ☎ *021/2222–4634* Ⓜ *Uruguaiana.*

Via Mia. You'll find a large selection of reasonably priced shoes, bags, and accessories at Via Mia. ✉ *Rua Anibal de Mendonça 55, Loja F, Ipanema* ☎ *021/2274–9996* ⊕ *www.viamia.com.br* ✉ *Rio Design Leblon, Av. Ataulfo de Paiva 270, 3rd fl., Leblon* ☎ *021/2529–6941.*

THE LUSH INLAND

CENTERS AND MALLS

Shopping da Gávea. The brand-name stores and smaller boutiques at the fashionable Shopping da Gávea mall sell designer fashions, accessories, and swimwear, and there are several good cafés and coffee shops. ⊠ *Rua Marquês de São Vicente 52, Gávea* ☎ *021/2294–1096* ⊕ *www. shoppingdagavea.com.br.*

MARKETS

Babilônia Feira Hype (*Babylon Hype Fair*). This fair that takes place every other weekend from 2 pm to 10 pm combines fashion, design, art, and gastronomy. It's good not only for shopping, but also for watching the parade of beautiful people. ∎ **TIP→ The fair occasionally skips a weekend or two, so check before heading here.** ⊠ *Clube Monte Líbano, Avenida Borges de Medeiros s/n, Leblon* ☎ *021/2267–0066* ⊕ *www. babiloniafeirahype.com.br* 🖃 *R$10.*

ART

Contorno. The gallery Contorno exhibits and sells an eclectic selection of Brazilian art. ⊠ *Gávea Trade Center, Rua Marquês de São Vicente 124, Loja 102, Gávea* ☎ *021/2274–3832* ⊕ *www.contornoartes.com.br.*

HANDICRAFTS

Fodor's Choice
★ **O Sol.** Exhibiting Brazilian craftsmanship at its finest, O Sol is a nonprofit, nongovernmental shop promoting and selling the handiwork of artisans from all regions of Brazil. It's one of Rio's best handicraft stores, and well worth a visit. ⊠ *Rua Corcovado 213, Jardim Botânico* ☎ *021/2294–6198* ⊕ *www.artesanato-sol.com.br.*

Pé de Boi. A popular arts and crafts store that carries woodwork pieces, ceramics, weaving, and sculptures created by artists from around Brazil, Pé de Boi specializes in objects from the states of Pernambuco and Minas Gerais. ⊠ *Rua Ipiranga 55, Laranjeiras* ☎ *021/2285–4395* ⊕ *www.pedeboi.com.br.*

SANTA TERESA

CLOTHING

Eu Amo Vintage. Bohemian Santa Teresa is a hotbed of vintage fashions, and the style-savvy team behind I Love Vintage has put together the biggest and best collection of all. If you find yourself envying the effortless, thrift-store chic of the neighborhood's gals and guys about town, the staff here can help you join their ranks. The store sits right behind the hot Bar do Gomez, so you can slip into your new threads and instantly fit in with the bar's hipster throngs. ⊠ *Rua Monte Alegre 374, Loja R, Santa Teresa* ☎ *021/2221–2855* ⊕ *blogeuamovintage.blogspot.co.uk.*

HANDICRAFTS

La Vereda. Head to this Santa Teresa arts and crafts store for colorful ceramics, ornate mirrors, and original works by local artists. For the quality and inventiveness of the objects it sells, La Vereda warrants a lengthy browsing session. ⊠ *Rua Almirante Alexandrino 428, Santa Teresa* ☎ *021/2507–0317* ⊕ *www.lavereda.com.br.*

SÃO CONRADO AND BARRA DA TIJUCA

CENTERS AND MALLS

Barra Shopping. By far Rio's largest mall, this is the place to come for a serious shopping spree. There are some 600 stores here, ranging from high-street names such as C&A to small and seriously chic boutique fashion, jewelry, and lingerie stores. A branch of the legendary bikini store Bumbum Ipanema is here, and there's a wealth of good dining options. ⊠ *Av. das Américas 4666, Barra da Tijuca* ☏ *021/4003–4131* ⊕ *www.barrashopping.com.br.*

São Conrado Fashion Mall. The shops at Rio's least crowded and most sophisticated mall sell domestic and international fashions to a clientele that knows how to splurge. The high-end labels represented here include Jean-Paul Gaultier, Calvin Klein, Prada Sport, Diesel, and Emporio Armani. Some very decent restaurants do business here, and there's a four-screen movie theater. ⊠ *Estrada da Gávea 899, São Conrado* ☏ *021/2111–4444* ⊕ *www.fashionmall.com.br.*

SIDE TRIPS FROM RIO

Updated by
Lucy Bryson

While there's no shortage of things to do in Rio de Janeiro itself, visitors should make time to experience the many attractions in the surrounding area. The state of Rio de Janeiro is relatively small, but offers a broad range of distinctly Brazilian attractions. There are no better places to unwind after the frenetic pace of Rio than Búzios or Paraty. And nature lovers will greatly enjoy the idyllic Ilha Grande.

The verdant Costa Verde (Green Coast) south of the city provides virtually unlimited opportunities for beach hopping, hiking on nature trails, and just resting and relaxing. The vast nature-reserve island of Ilha Grande and the perfectly preserved colonial town of Paraty are just two of the gems to be found along this scenic stretch of coastline. Heading north of the city along the Blue Coast, meanwhile, will lead you to the hip resort town of Búzios, famed for its sunny weather, beautiful beaches, and lively drinking and dining scene. On a peninsula that enjoys more sunny days than anywhere else in Rio de Janeiro State, Búzios is very much a playground for Rio de Janeiro's *gente bonita* (beautiful people), who come here to relax on the 23 beaches by day and socialize in the buzzing bars and clubs by night.

En route to Búzios are the quieter beach resorts of Cabo Frio and Arraial do Cabo. These unpretentious fishing towns are top spots for surfing and diving in the crystal clear waters. Heading inland from Rio, the stifling temperatures drop a little as steep mountain roads deliver you to the Imperial City of Petrópolis. It is important to check weather forecasts before traveling into the mountains, as recent years have seen heavy rainfall cause major landslides in the mountainous regions. Petrópolis merits an overnight stay but can also be enjoyed as a day trip, and there are numerous adventure sports companies operating walking, climbing, and camping trips in the mountains.

ORIENTATION AND PLANNING

GETTING ORIENTED

THE BLUE COAST

The Blue Coast starts just across Guanabara Bay in Niterói, whose ancient forts stand in stark contrast to its ultramodern Museu de Arte Contemporânea. Farther east is Cabo Frio, one of the country's oldest settlements. Nearby Búzios, with its 23 beaches, temperate climate, and vibrant nightlife, is a popular weekend holiday destination for wealthy cariocas as well as foreign visitors to Rio.

TOP REASONS TO GO

■ **Glamorous Búzios:** Hang out with the young and beautiful on the beach at Búzios in the morning, then enjoy the sunset on Orla Bardot.

■ **Water Sports:** Sail a schooner to a deserted island for some scuba diving, then watch the dolphins play in your wake on the way home.

■ **Mountain Excursions:** Get lost in time at the Imperial Museum in mountainous Petrópolis.

■ **Glorious Ilha Grande:** Take an early-morning hike through the Atlantic rain forests of Ilha Grande.

■ **Fresh Beach Food:** Wash down some fresh shrimp with caipirinhas at the kiosks on the beach in Cabo Frio.

3

NORTH OF RIO DE JANEIRO

Northeast of Rio de Janeiro lies Petrópolis, whose opulent imperial palace was once the emperor's summer home. A twisting road through the mountains takes you to Teresópolis, named for Empress Teresa Christina. Nestled between these two towns is Parque Nacional da Serra dos Órgãos, famous for its unique rock formations.

THE GREEN COAST

West of Rio de Janeiro, Angra dos Reis is the jumping-off point for 365 islands that pepper a picturesque bay. The largest, Ilha Grande, is a short ferry ride from Angra dos Reis and is still somewhat unspoiled. Paraty, a UNESCO World Heritage Site, is a well-preserved imperial town. Its 18th-century Portuguese architecture and proximity to secluded beaches make it the region's highlight.

PLANNING

WHEN TO GO

The towns along the Blue and Green coasts are packed solid between Christmas and Carnival, so reservations should be made well in advance. The populations of Paraty and Búzios can more than double as young people arrive from nearby Rio de Janeiro and São Paulo on the weekend. Paraty books up well ahead of its annual literary festival (July) and cachaça festival (August).

The weather along the coast is fairly predictable: summers are hot. During low season, from March to June and September to November, the weather is mild and the beaches are practically deserted. To top it off, prices can be half of what they are in high season. In the interior, Petrópolis and Teresópolis provide a refreshing change from the oppressive heat of the coast.

GETTING HERE AND AROUND

While most resort towns boast an airport of some kind, the state of Rio is small enough that few people fly to destinations within the state. The roads along the Blue and Green coasts and to the resort towns in the mountains tend to be well maintained, so most Brazilians travel by car or bus.

Driving within the city of Rio can be a daunting experience, but outside the city it's fairly easy to get around. The roads, especially to the major tourist destinations, are well signposted. To get to Ilha Grande you'll need to leave your car in Angra dos Reis and catch a 90-minute passenger ferry or 50-minute catamaran to the island. Buses are cheap, comfortable, and efficient, but the terminal in Rio can be intimidating. It's best to travel light so you can get to your bus on time.

⚠ Avoid leaving the city on a Friday afternoon, when residents flee the city en mass and the traffic is horrific.

BUS TRAVEL

As a rule, private buses in Rio such as 1001 and Costa Verde tend to be clean, punctual, air-conditioned, and comfortable. Buses leave from the Rodoviária Novo Rio, and most destinations are within three hours of the city. Expect to catch a taxi from the bus station to your hotel.

Local bus service within towns, or districts, tends to be regular and cheap, but buses rarely have air-conditioning and are not well maintained. There are few routes, and the bus driver will either nod or shake his head if you tell him where you want to go. You can buy your ticket on the bus, but don't use large notes. Bus terminals and stands are easy to spot. Beware of pickpockets if the stand or bus is particularly crowded.

Bus Contacts 1001 ☎ 022/2623–2050 ⊕ www.autoviacao1001.com.br. **Costa Verde** ☎ 021/3622–3123 ⊕ www.costaverdetransportes.com.br.

CAR TRAVEL

The roads in Rio de Janeiro State are generally in good condition and well marked, especially in the areas frequented by holidaymakers. If you plan to travel around and spend a few nights in different towns, it makes sense to rent a car in Rio, although it can be a bit tricky finding your way out of the city. Remember that if you travel to Ilha Grande, you will have to leave your car in the parking lot near the ferry terminal in Angra or Mangaratiba, so be sure to remove all valuables from sight.

■ TIP➜ Car-rental prices in resort towns can be exorbitant, so if you plan to rent a car, do it in Rio.

TOURS

A fun way for time-pressed travelers to see as much of Rio's coastline as possible is to cruise it with Cruz the Coast Brazil. This hassle-free hop-on, hop-off service makes a four-day loop from Rio to Paraty and Ilha Grande, or from Rio to Cabo Frio and Búzios, with all travel and accommodations prearranged and excursions such as boating trips and surfing lessons included. Cruz the Coast also arranges adventure tours, as do the friendly, professional guides of Rio Xtreme. This outfit's tours range from the relatively mild (hiking Ilha Grande, for instance) to the adventurous and wild (rappelling in dense rain forests).

Tour Operators Cruz the Coast Brazil ☎ *021/3251–5833* ⊕ *www. cruzthecoastbrazil.com.* **Rio Xtreme** ☎ *021/8105–7335* ⊕ *www.rioxtreme.com.*

RESTAURANTS

The food here is nothing if not eclectic. Coastal towns serve a large selection of fresh seafood, and most have a local specialty that's worth trying. Beachfront restaurants, especially the ubiquitous *baracas* (kiosks), can be a pleasant surprise. Paraty and Búzios have excellent restaurants serving international cuisine. During high season they fill up beginning at 10 pm and may not close until after sunrise. Restaurants in Petrópolis and Teresópolis serve European cuisine and *comida mineira,* the hearty fare from Minas Gerais. Dinner starts at seven, and restaurants generally close around midnight. *Prices in the reviews are the average cost of a main course at dinner or, if dinner is not served, at lunch.*

■ TIP➔ **To be on the safe side, don't buy seafood from venders strolling along the beach. Be especially careful about the oysters in Búzios and Cabo Frio, which may not be as fresh as the vendor claims.**

HOTELS

There are hotels for all budgets and all tastes, from pousadas lining the beaches along the Blue and Green coasts that offer simple rooms—with barely more than a bed and a ceiling fan—to boutique hotels with luxurious amenities and on-site spas. Paraty and Petrópolis have gorgeous 18th-century inns, some of which can be a bit drafty. *Prices in the reviews are the lowest cost of a standard double room in high season. For expanded reviews, facilities, and current deals, visit Fodors.com.*

■ TIP➔ **Staffers at the region's smaller hotels speak very little English, so bring along a phrase book. It also helps to arrange as much as your trip as possible while you're still in Rio de Janeiro.**

THE BLUE COAST

Also known as the Cost Região dos Lagos (Lake District), this stretch of coastline is where you'll find the resort towns of Cabo Frio, Arraial do Cabo, and Búzios. The most popular of the three is Búzios, reminiscent of the French Riviera gone tropical. On its 8-km (5-mile) peninsula are 23 beaches. Cabo Frio is a family resort famous for its bikini shops and blue water. Arraial do Cabo, jutting into the Atlantic Ocean, still retains the rustic charms of a fishing village. The wind blows year-round, and sports such as windsurfing, kite surfing, and sailing are popular.

■ TIP➔ **Currency exchange rates outside the city of Rio can be exorbitant. Use credit cards and cash machines where you can because the rates, even with the charges, will be better than those at hotels and exchange bureaus.**

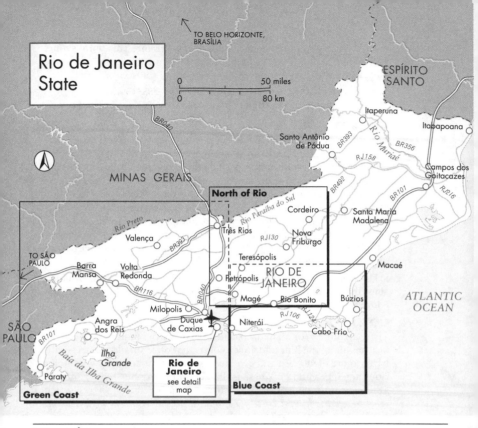

NITERÓI

14 km (9 miles) east of Rio.

Cariocas joke that the best thing about Niterói is the view—on a clear day you can see Rio de Janeiro with the Corcovado and Sugarloaf across the bay. But Niterói has the last laugh, as the city is ranked as having the highest quality of life in the state.

Catch a ferry from Rio's Praça 15 de Novembro and cross the bay in 20 minutes. From the Praça Araribóia or at the Terminal Hidroviário de Charitas, walk along the esplanade to the Forte de Gragoatá and then walk to Museu de Arte Contemporânea, whose Oscar Niemeyer–designed building and views of Rio are more impressive than the art. Icaraí beach is a smaller, less touristy version of Copacabana. If you have time, enjoy a beer on the beach and watch the sunset over Rio and the Corcovado. Don't plan to spend more than one afternoon in Niterói. Instead head up the Blue Coast to Búzios or Cabo Frio. The tourist office is located next to the ferry terminal.

GETTING HERE AND AROUND

The best way to get to Niterói is by passenger ferry from the Praça 15 de Novembro in Rio de Janeiro. The trip takes about 20 minutes with Barcas S/A boats (R$4.80). Don't travel here by car unless you have

A Bit of History

The history of Rio de Janeiro State is as colorful as it is bloody. The first Portuguese trading post was established in 1502 in Cabo Frio to facilitate the export of *Pau-Brasil* (Brazil Wood). This led to confrontations with Tamoios Indians and their French allies.

The discovery of gold in the state of Minas Gerais in 1696 and the construction of the "Caminho de Ouro" (Path of Gold) from the mines to Paraty brought prosperity. In its wake came pirates and corsairs who used the islands and bays of Angra dos Reis as cover while they plundered the ships bound for Rio de Janeiro.

The mines gave out in the late 1700s, but the relatively new crop called coffee, introduced to the state around 1770, brought another boom. In the mid-19th century the state produced more than 70% of Brazil's coffee. Sadly, vast tracts of Atlantic rain forest were destroyed to make room for the crop across the interior of the state.

In 1808, threatened by Napoléon, King Dom João VI of Portugal moved his court to Rio. He returned to Portugal in 1821 and left his son, Dom Pedro I, behind as prince regent. The following year Dom Pedro I was called back to Portugal, but he refused to leave. Instead, he declared Brazil an independent state and himself its emperor. In 1847, his son, Dom Pedro II, inaugurated Petrópolis as the summer capital of Brazil.

3

somebody driving for you. The roads in Niterói are even more confusing than in Rio. Auto Viação Mauá's Bus 100 (R$4.35) departs for Niterói from Praca IV de Novembro (in front of the ferry terminal). The trip takes 15 minutes, not counting traffic delays.

ESSENTIALS

Boat Contact Barcas S/A ⊠ *Praça Aráriboia 6–8, Centro* ☎ *021/2620–6756* ⊕ *www.barcas-sa.com.br.*

Bus Contact Auto Viação Mauá ☎ *021/2127–4000* ⊕ *www.vmaua.com.br.*

Taxi Contact Rádio Táxi Niterói ☎ *021/2610–0609* ⊕ *www.radiotaxiniteroi.com.*

Visitor Information Niterói Tourism Office ⊠ *Estrada Leopoldo Fróes 773, São Francisco* ☎ *021/2710–2727* ⊕ *www.neltur.com.br* ☉ *Daily 9–5.*

EXPLORING

Fortaleza de Santa Cruz. Built in 1555, the impressive Fortaleza de Santa Cruz was the first fort on Guanabara Bay. The cannons are distributed over two levels, but more impressive are the 17th-century sun clock and Santa Barbara Chapel. It takes 15 minutes by taxi to reach the fort from downtown Niterói. The ride costs about R$30. ■**TIP→ On hot days, it's best to visit the fort during the morning, when it's cooler.** ⊠ *Estrada General Eurico Gaspar Dutra s/n, Jurujuba* ☎ *021/2710–2354* ☎ *R$4* ☉ *Tues.–Sun. 9–5.*

Museu de Arte Contemporânea. Oscar Niemeyer designed the Museum of Contemporary Art to looks something like a spaceship. The museum's art collection is underwhelming; to see the exterior is the reason to visit. The museum is five minutes from Praça Araribóia in downtown Niterói. ⊠ *Mirante de Boa Viagem s/n* ☎ *021/2620–2400* ⊕ *www.macniteroi. com.br* ⊠ *R$6, free Wed.* ☉ *Tues.–Sun. 10–6.*

CABO FRIO

155 km (101 miles) east of Rio.

One of the oldest settlements in Brazil, Cabo Frio was established in the early 1500s as a port from which wood was shipped to Portugal. Today it's best known for its lovely seaside setting and fresh seafood. Cabo Frio is a popular weekend getaway for residents of Rio de Janeiro and a favorite destination for water-sports enthusiasts. Don't miss the chance to go diving in Arraial do Cabo, which has some of the clearest water in Brazil.

Although they tend to be cheaper, Cabo Frio hotels are not as nice as those in nearby Búzios. If you are looking for chic lodgings, you're better off staying in Búzios and taking a day trip to Cabo Frio.

GETTING HERE AND AROUND

From Rio de Janeiro, drive across the Rio–Niterói Bridge (officially the President Costa e Silva Bridge) and bear left, following the BR 101. At Rio Bonito take the exit to the Region dos Lagos and follow the signs to Cabo Frio. The trip takes approximately two hours. Cabo Frio-bound 1001 buses leave the Rodoviária every half hour. The trip takes two hours and 40 minutes and costs R$53. Shuttle transfers from Rio hotels can be arranged for around R$80—speak to hotel staff.

ESSENTIALS

Bus Contact Terminal Rodoviário Cabo Frio ⊠ *Av. Julia Kubitschek s/n, Parque Riviera* ⊕ *www.cabofrio.rj.gov.br/rodoviaria.aspx.*

Taxi Contact Associação dos Taxistas de Cabo Frio ⊠ *Av. Júlia Kubitschek 35, Parque Riviera* ☎ *022/2645–5463* ⊕ *www.cabofriotaxi.com.br.*

Visitor Information Cabo Frio Tourism Office ⊠ *Avenida do Contorno s/n* ☎ *022/2647–1689* ⊕ *cabofrioturismo.com.br* ☉ *Daily 8–7.*

EXPLORING

Arraial do Cabo. Quiet Arraial do Cabo, a beautiful fishing village with pristine beaches, clear warm waters, and the Gruta Azul—a 15-meter-tall cave over the blue sea—lies just 10 km (6 miles) south of Cabo Frio. The sunsets over the small beach Prainha Pontal do Atalaia are often quite stunning. ⊠ *Arraial do Cabo.*

BEACHES

Praia do Forte. Its calm, clear waters and long stretch of sand make Praia do Forte very popular. On summer weekends it's jammed with colorful beach umbrellas, swimmers, sun lovers, and food kiosks that extend their services to tables on the sand. Be prepared to deal with all kinds of vendors, some of them obnoxiously insistent, some of them selling unique souvenirs. After dark during the summer, there's live music (and dancing) on the beach. **Amenities:** food and drink. **Best for:** swimming; partiers. ⊠ *Praia do Forte.*

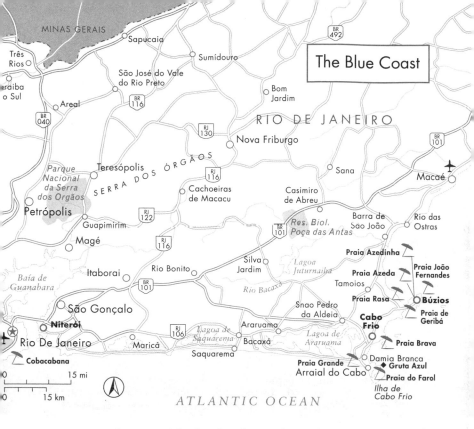

The Blue Coast

Praia do Foguete. This beach is famous for its almost transparent soft white sand and the equally clear waters that shelter sea creatures such as turtles, dolphins, and even penguins. The 6-km (4-mile) strand is almost deserted in low season, and while even in summer the water is chilly, the constant strong breeze here creates waves that are perfect for surfing and bodyboarding. ■TIP→ **During summer, a few vendors operate kiosks with food and drink, but if you visit between March and November you should bring your own refreshments. Amenities:** food and drink (in summer). **Best for:** solitude, surfing. ⊠ *Ogiva*.

WHERE TO STAY

$ ⊡ **Hotel Joalpa.** Three blocks from Praia do Forte, but in front of not-
HOTEL   as-crowded Praia das Dunas, the Joalpa has rooms that can accommodate five people. **Pros:** close to the beach; Wi-Fi connection. **Cons:** uninspired decor; street noise. *$ Rooms from: R$150*⊠ *Rua dos Cravos 2* ☎ *022/2645–4848* ⊕ *www.joalpa.com.br* ➥ *68 rooms* ⊧⊙⊧ *Breakfast.*

$ ⊡ **Malibu Palace Hotel.** Cabo Frio's most convenient option sits across
HOTEL   the avenue from Praia do Forte and mere blocks from the shops and restaurants of the town center. **Pros:** rooms have great views; hotel provides umbrellas on the beach; delicious breakfast. **Cons:** can be noisy at night; beach is across the street; property showing signs of wear

and tear. [$] *Rooms from: R$245* ✉ *Av. do Contorno 900, Praia do Forte* ☎ *022/2647–8000* 🌐 *www.malibupalace.com.br* 🛏 *102 rooms, 6 suites* 🍴 *Breakfast.*

SPORTS AND THE OUTDOORS

TOUR OPERATOR

Tridente Dive Center. This full-service dive center offers sports-adventure trips, including diving, climbing, and rappelling. Ask for Frederico, who speaks fluent English. ✉ *Praça da Bandeira 362, Passagem* ☎ *022/2645–1705* 🌐 *www.tridente.tur.br* 🕓 *Daily 9–6.*

> **BATHING BEAUTIES**
>
> No visit to Cabo Frio is complete without a walk past the bikini shops along Rua das Biquínis. Local lore has it that everything began with a woman selling her homemade bathing suits on the street here. Today more than 70 stores—the largest collection of bikini stores in Latin America, according to the Guinness World Records—sell all manner of beach fashions. In summer, many shops stay open past midnight.

BÚZIOS

24 km (15 miles) northeast of Cabo Frio; 176 km (126 miles) northeast of Rio.

Fodor's Choice ★

Little more than two hours from Rio de Janeiro, Búzios is a string of beautiful beaches on an 8-km-long (5-mile-long) peninsula. It was the quintessential sleepy fishing village until the 1960s, when the French actress Brigitte Bardot holidayed here to escape the paparazzi and the place almost instantly transformed into a vacation sensation. Búzios has something for everyone. Some hotels cater specifically to families and provide plenty of activities and around-the-clock child care. Many have spa facilities, and some specialize in weeklong retreats. For outdoor enthusiasts, Búzios offers surfing, windsurfing, kite surfing, diving, hiking, and mountain biking, as well as leisurely rounds of golf.

GETTING HERE AND AROUND

From Rio de Janeiro, drive across the Rio–Niterói Bridge and bear left, following the BR 101. At Rio Bonito take the exit to the Region dos Lagos. At São Pedro de Aldeia, turn left at the sign for Búzios. The trip takes about two hours.

Búzios-bound 1001 buses leave from Rio every half hour. The trip takes 2 hours and 50 minutes and costs R$46. Transfers from Rio hotels can be arranged for around R$80—speak to hotel staff.

ESSENTIALS

Airport Information Aeroporto Umberto Modiano ✉ *Av. José Bento Ribeiro Dantas s/n, Rasa* ☎ *022/2629–1225.*

Taxi Information Búzios Radio Taxi ☎ *22/2623–2509.*

Visitor Information Búzios Tourism Office ✉ *Pórtico da Cidade s/n, Centro* ☎ *022/2633–6200* 🌐 *www.buziosonline.com.br* 🕓 *Daily 8–noon.*

SAFETY AND PRECAUTIONS

A few simple rules: don't eat fresh oysters sold anywhere but in a restaurant, and make sure the drinks you buy from street vendors are made with filtered ice. (The easiest way to check is to look for a circular hole through the middle.) Crime here is rare, but don't walk along dark and deserted streets after dark, and don't leave your belongings unattended on the beach.

BEACHES

Búzios boasts 23 beautiful beaches, which can be reached by schooner boat trips or speedier taxi boats. There is a taxi boat "terminal" on Orla Bardot, with skippers ready to whisk passengers off to any of the beaches on the island. Prices

POUSADA DEFINED
Wherever you travel in Rio de Janeiro State, you're likely to stay in a *pousada*. The name translates as "rest stop," and a pousada may be anything from a simple guesthouse to a luxury boutique lodging with pool and spa. The one thing they have in common is that they are independently run and managed. Generally smaller than hotels, pousadas tend to offer more personalized service. For detailed listings of pousadas throughout Brazil, visit the website of Hidden Pousadas Brazil ⊕ *www.hiddenpousadasbrazil.com*.

are per person and start at R$10 to get to the closest beaches, rising to around R$40 for farther-flung sands. There's a minimum two-person fare but solo travelers can wait for others to come along and bump up the numbers. Schooners depart from the end of a small pier, and take groups on beach-hopping trips that might last from a couple of hours to a full day. Prices start at around R$30 per person for a two-hour trip, rising to around R$80 for a full-day trip with stops for swimming and snorkeling.

Praia Azeda. Two beaches, Praia Azeda and its smaller neighbor, Praia Azedinha, have clear, calm waters and are accessible via a trail from Praia dos Ossos, or by taxi boat (R$10). The view as you descend to the beach on foot is breathtaking. Vendors at kiosks on the beach sell coconut water and frozen caipirinhas, and you can rent beach chairs and umbrellas. This is one of the few beaches here where women can sunbathe topless. ■ TIP➔ During summer, arrive early to secure a good spot—the beach starts to get crowded by 11 am. Amenities: food and drink; toilets. Best for: swimming. ⊠ *João Fernandes*.

FAMILY **Praia da Ferradura.** On a cove that protects it from the winds that often blow elsewhere on the peninsula, Praia da Ferradura has calm waters that make it a perfect choice for families with children. The beach adjoins one of the Búzios area's most exclusive sections—some mansions back right onto it—but the kiosks and beach bars have a relaxed ambience. Chairs and umbrellas can be rented here. ■ TIP➔ Arrive early on summer weekends, when the beach is very popular. Amenities: food and drink; toilets; water sports. Best for: swimming. ⊠ *Ferradura*.

Praia de Geribá. This long half-moon of white sand is fashionable with a young crowd, and its breaks and swells make it popular with surfers and windsurfers. The walk from one end to the other takes 30 minutes, so there's plenty of elbow room here even in high season. The relaxed bars and beach kiosks make it easy to while away whole days here. With many good pousadas nearby, this a good base for beach lovers. **Amenities:** food and drink; water sports. **Best for:** walking; surfing. ⊠ *Geribá.*

Praia João Fernandes. Praia João Fernandes and the smaller adjoining beach, Praia João Fernandinho, are a short taxi-boat ride (R$10) from the center of town; both are beloved for their crystal waters and soft sands. The sounds of live samba music at nearby restaurants and bars can be heard on the beach, and you can bring cocktails out to your chosen spot on the sand if you're not ready to abandon your sun lounger. ■ TIP→ **This beach can get a little busy, but the sunset here is spectacular.** **Amenities:** food and drink; toilets; water sports. **Best for:** sunset; swimming. ⊠ *João Fernandes.*

WHERE TO EAT

$$
BRAZILIAN

✕ **Buzin.** Behind fashionable Rua das Pedras is a buffet restaurant featuring many varieties of seafood, steaks, salads, and pizzas. The reasonable prices, ample choices, and casual atmosphere make it a great post-beach stop. Try the shrimp fried in oil and garlic or the *picanha* beef, a very tender cut found in every churrascaria. The house opens at noon and closes when the last person leaves in the evening. $ *Average main: R$32*⊠ *Rua Manoel Turíbio de Farias 273, Centro* ☎ *022/2633–7051* ⚘ *Reservations essential.*

$$$
PIZZA

✕ **Capricciosa.** The Búzios branch of this pizzeria serves the same high-quality pies as the main location in Rio. The Margarita Gourmet is a must, with a thin crust topped with tomatoes and buffalo mozzarella. $ *Average main: R$50*⊠ *Orla Brigitte Bardot 500, Centro* ☎ *022/2623–2691* ⊕ *www.capricciosa.com.br* ☾ *No lunch.*

$
FRENCH

✕ **Chez Michou.** This Belgian-owned *crêperie* is the best place for a quick, light, inexpensive bite, and with about 50 savory and sweet fillings you're sure to find one to match your precise desire. At night the streetside tables buzz with locals and visitors congregating to drink and people-watch. $ *Average main: R$20*⊠ *Rua das Pedras 90, Centro* ☎ *022/2623–2169* ⊕ *www.chezmichou.com.br* ▭ *No credit cards.*

$$$
EUROPEAN

✕ **Cigalon.** Widely considered the best restaurant in Búzios, Cigalon is an elegant establishment with a veranda overlooking the beach. Though the waiters are bow-tied and the tables covered with crisp linens and lighted by flickering candles, the place still has a casual feel. The food is French-inspired, and includes lamb steak, braised duck breast, and prawns in a lemongrass sauce with almonds. Set menus start at R$55 including a starter, a main, and a dessert, and are a terrific value. $ *Average main: R$55*⊠ *Rua das Pedras 199, Centro* ☎ *022/2623–6284* ⊕ *www.cigalon.com.br.*

$$$$
SEAFOOD

✕ **Rocka.** Overlooking beautiful Praia Brava, relaxed but sophisticated Rocka is one of Búzios's gastronomic highlights. Superbly fresh seafood is combined with seasonal fruits, vegetables, and herbs to wonderful effect. Order a frozen cocktail, or splurge on a bottle of Veuve Clicquot, and soak up the ambience as you wait for your food. The lobster dishes are terrific, while the chocolate fondant with hazelnut makes for an appropriately decadent closer. If you're here for lunch (all that's served during low season), you can enjoy your meal from the comfort of a sun bed—literally, a bed, not a plastic lounger—on a grassy slope with perfect beach views. [$] *Average main: R$70* ✉ *Praia Brava 13, Brava* ☎ *022/2623–6159* ✍ *Reservations essential* ⏲ *No dinner Mar.–Nov.*

$$$$ SEAFOOD 🍴 **Satyricon.** The Italian fish restaurant famous in Rio has opened up shop here as well. The dishes are expensive, but always excellent. Go all out and try the grilled mixed seafood plate with cream-of-lemon risotto. On weekends, reservations are normally required for parties of four or more. [$] *Average main: R$100* ✉ *Av. José Bento Ribeiro Dantas (Orla Bardot) 500, Centro* ☎ *022/2623–2691* 🌐 *www.satyricon.com.br* ⏲ *No lunch.*

BRIGITTE & BÚZIOS

A walk along the Orla Bardot will bring you to the bronze statue of a seated woman looking out over the cobalt-blue waters. This is the statue of the actress Brigitte Bardot, who put Búzios on the map when she came here on holiday. Bardot, world famous at the time for her role in director Roger Vadim's provocative *And God Created Woman* and other films, declared the city the one place where she was able to relax. She stayed in Búzios until photographer Denis Albanèse's candid shots allowed the international press to discover her and, in turn, Búzios.

WHERE TO STAY

Be sure to book well in advance if you plan to visit Búzios on a weekend between Christmas and Carnival. You'll find good accommodation options in the center of town—handy for nightlife, shopping, and organized tours—but there's no real beach there. For beachfront lodgings, you'll have to head a little out of town.

$$ B&B/INN 🏨 **Abracadabra.** Rooms at this gorgeous, centrally located boutique hotel are simply but stylishly appointed and have soft white linens and fresh flowers, but the crowning glory is an infinity pool that has stunning views over the bay and out to sea. **Pros:** stunning views; wonderful breakfasts; excellent service. **Cons:** the best beaches are a taxi boat ride away. [$] *Rooms from: R$340* ✉ *Alto do Humaitá 13* ☎ *022/2623–1217* 🌐 *www.abracadabrapousada.com.br* 🛏 *16 rooms* 🍽 *Breakfast.*

$$$ B&B/INN 🏨 **Aquabarra Boutique Hotel and Spa.** A zenlike calm pervades the rooms and living spaces at this casual-chic spot just a few-minutes' walk from Geriba beach. **Pros:** gorgeous space; excellent spas; most rooms have lovely views; close to beach. **Cons:** need to cab or bus to get to Centro. [$] *Rooms from: R$380* ✉ *Rua de Corina 16, Centro* ☎ *022/2623–6186* 🌐 *www.aquabarra.com* 🛏 *15 rooms* 🍽 *Breakfast.*

$$$$ B&B/INN Fodor's Choice ★ 🏨 **Casas Brancas.** Each of the 32 rooms at this timelessly chic hotel is unique, and many have deep baths, beach views, and private balconies. **Pros:** unique accommodations; friendly service; multilingual staff; pool with stunning views; beautiful setting; excellent spa and restaurants; relaxed ambience. **Cons:** no children under the age of five permitted. [$] *Rooms from: R$620* ✉ *Alto do Humaitá 10, Centro* ☎ *022/2623–1458* 🌐 *www.casasbrancas.com.br* 🛏 *32 rooms, 3 suites* 🍽 *Breakfast.*

$$$$ HOTEL 🏨 **Galápagos Inn.** Overlooking the charming Orla Bardot—the continuation of Rua das Pedras, where people congregate at night—this hotel also has a view of the sea and, best of all, a view of the sunset. **Pros:** all rooms have ocean views; close to center. **Cons:** beach is crowded during

high season; lots of steps to climb. $ *Rooms from: R$580*⊠ *Praia João Fernandes s/n, João Fernandes* ☎ *022/2623-2245* ⊕ *www.galapagos. com.br* 💬 *39 rooms, 5 suites* ❖❘ *Breakfast.*

$$$
HOTEL

▥ **Hotel le Relais de la Borie.** Imagine a country house with a tropical bent and stairs right down to the beach and you've got La Borie. **Pros:** on the beach; great restaurant; friendly staff. **Cons:** it's a bus or cab ride from the center. $ *Rooms from: R$495*⊠ *Rua dos Gravatás 1374, Geribá* ☎ *022/2620-8504* ⊕ *www.laborie.com.br* 💬 *38 rooms, 1 suite* ❖❘ *Breakfast.*

$
B&B/INN
FAMILY

▥ **Maresia de Búzios.** Small but stylish, this guesthouse close to Geribá beach provides clean, budget-friendly accommodations. **Pros:** friendly staff; contemporary decor; fine buffet breakfast; pleasant communal spaces; children welcome. **Cons:** small rooms; no TVs in rooms; need to take a taxi to get to town. $ *Rooms from: R$150*⊠ *Rua das Pitangueiras 12, Bosque de Geribá, Geribá* ☎ *022/8822-2384* 💬 *6 rooms* ❖❘ *Breakfast.*

$$$
HOTEL

▥ **Rio Búzios Beach Hotel.** This hotel has a great location a few steps from João Fernandes Beach. **Pros:** on João Fernandes Beach; intimate setting; fantastic breakfast. **Cons:** 20-minute walk to the center; uninspired decor. $ *Rooms from: R$400*⊠ *Praia de João Fernandes s/n, João Fernandes* ☎ *022/2633-6400* ⊕ *www.riobuzios.com.br* 💬 *63 rooms* ❖❘ *Breakfast.*

NIGHTLIFE
BARS

Anexo. A low-key alternative to the city's more frenetic clubs, Anexo has a veranda where you can kick back and enjoy one of the many specialty cocktails. ⊠ *Av. José Bento Ribeiro Dantas 392, Centro* ☎ *022/2623-6837* ⊕ *www.anexobarbuzios.com.br.*

Cervejaria Devassa. The Buzios branch of this Rio-based chain specializes in microbrews, with names such as *loira* (blonde), *ruiva* (redhead), and *negra* (black). There's a good menu of bar snacks, and the pitchers of cocktails make this a good place for groups of friends to start a night out. ⊠ *Av. José Bento Ribeiro Dantas 550, Manguinhos* ☎ *022/2623-4992* ⊕ *www.devassa.com.br.*

Terraço no Morro. Head here in the early evening for relaxed drinks and *petiscos* (light snacks) on the wooden patio and enjoy a perfect view as the pumpkin sun dips over the harbor. A place where you won't feel out of place in beachwear and Havaianas, this casual bar holds regular *"Churrasquinho e Futebol"* (barbecue and soccer) evenings, during which patrons dine on grilled meats—steaks, chicken, burgers, hot dogs, and kebabs—and down ice-cold beer and caipirinhas while watching the sports action on big-screen TVs. ⊠ *Av. José Bento Ribeiro Dantas 575, Centro* ☎ *022/2623-0859.*

DANCE CLUBS

Pacha. If you want to sip potent cocktails with beautiful people in scanty clothing, this slick beachfront nightclub is the place to do it. The party set dances here until dawn to contemporary tunes spun by visiting DJs from Europe and the United States, as well as some of the biggest names on the Brazilian dance-music circuit. With room for 1,000 party people, the vast, colorfully lit space can feel a little empty in the low season, but it's packed to the rafters during the summer high season. ⊠ *Rua das Pedras 151, Centro* ☎ *022/2633–0592* ⊕ *www.pachabuzios.com* ☉ *Thurs.–Sat. 10 pm–7 am* ☉ *Closed Sun.–Wed.*

Privilège. With space for more than 1,000 people, Privilège is the city's top nightclub. Resident DJs play techno on Thursdays and Sundays, while top DJs from around the world fly in to spin tunes on Fridays and Saturdays. This is a late-night hangout for the rich and famous, who head to the exclusive VIP area. ⊠ *Av. José Bento Ribeiro Dantas 550, Orla Bardot, Manguinhos* ☎ *022/2620–8585* ⊕ *www.privilegenet.com.br* ☉ *Closed Mon.–Wed. except for Carnival and other major holidays.*

SPORTS AND THE OUTDOORS
BOATING

FAMILY **Babylon Park.** The Babylon Park schooner whisks passengers to 12 of the peninsula's best beaches, as well as three nearby islands. The two-and-a-half-hour trips include stops for swimming and snorkeling (masks provided). A great option for families, the vessel is equipped with a splash pool and a water slide that flows right into the ocean. Boats depart three times daily from the main pier in Búzios. ⊠ *Pier do Centro, Centro* ☎ *022/2623–2350* ⊠ *R$120* ☉ *Daily departures 11:45, 2:45, 5:45.*

DIVING

The clear waters of Búzios teem with colorful marine life, making the peninsula a thrilling place to dive.

Casamar Dive Center. This very professional dive center operates classes—from beginners' "baptism" courses and guided dives through to advanced scuba diving courses. Courses run from 30-minute theory classes to five-day intensive training. Prices start at R$150. The center rents and sells all necessary equipment, and conducts day and night trips out to sea. There's a guesthouse next door, with basic but comfortable lodgings. ⊠ *Rua das Pedras 242, Centro* ☎ *022/2623–2441* ⊕ *www.casamar.com.br.*

Elite Dive Center. This PADI-accredited dive school offers diving classes from beginner to Dive Master level, rents out equipment, and runs daytime and nocturnal diving excursions to numerous places around the island. ⊠ *Travessa Bouganville, loja 1, Vila do Abraão, Ilha Grande* ☎ *024/9999–9789* ⊕ *www.elitedivecenter.com.br.*

GOLF

Búzios Golf Club and Resort. Designed by the acclaimed American golf-course architect Pete Dye, this well-maintained 18-hole course is challenging thanks to the winds that blow here, but the scenic backdrop of hills, natural pools, and tropical vegetation makes a round here worth the effort. The course is about 10 km (6 miles) from the town center, but it's easily accessed by car or taxi. ⊠ *Av. José Bento Ribeiro Dantas 9* ☎ *022/2629–1240* ⊕ *www.buziosgolf.com.br* ⸎ *Course: 18 holes. 6652 yards. Par 72. Greens fee R$165* ⚐ *Facilities: Driving range, putting green, pitching area, golf carts, caddies, rental clubs, pro shop, bar.*

KITE SURFING

Buzios Kitesurf School. The certified instructors here are an upbeat team dedicated to helping you get the most out of your lessons. ⊠ *José Bento Ribeiro Dantas 9, Praia Raza* ☎ *022/9956–0668* ⊕ *www.kitenews.com.br.*

SURFING

Surf schools set up tents along Geribá Beach, and also rent out boards. Expect to pay around R$60 an hour for a private lesson, including board rental, and R$20 to rent a board for an hour.

Shark's Surf School. Next to the Fishbone restaurant and nightspot, this outfit rents equipment and offers personalized classes for children and adults of all experience levels. The energetic, enthusiastic instructor, Marcio, has years of experience, and the school has International Surfing Association accreditation. ⊠ *Praia de Geribá* ☎ *022/2623–1134* ⊕ *www.sharksurfschool.com.br.*

TOURS

FAMILY **Tour Shop.** The largest tour operator in Búzios conducts white-water rafting and boat trips, 4X4 adventures in the dunes, and a popular trolley tour that takes in 12 of the peninsula's best beaches. There are other activities, too, many of them geared to children. ⊠ *Orla Bardot 550, Centro* ☎ *022/2623–4733, 022/2623–0292* ⊕ *www.buziostrolley.com.br.*

NORTH OF RIO

Petrópolis is a charming historical village that was once the summer home of the imperial family. If you enjoy hiking, visit the Parque National da Serra dos Órgãos between Teresópolis and Petrópolis. Temperatures in the mountains are low by Brazilian standards—an average of 55°F (13°C) in winter—providing a welcome change from the stifling heat of the city.

PETRÓPOLIS

68 km (42 miles) northeast of Rio.

The highway northeast of Rio de Janeiro rumbles past forests and waterfalls en route to a mountain town so refreshing and picturesque that Dom Pedro II, Brazil's second emperor, moved there with his summer court. From 1889 to 1899 it was the country's year-round seat of government. Horse-drawn carriages clip-clop between the sights, passing flowering gardens, shady parks, and imposing pink mansions. Be sure to visit the Crystal Palace and the Gothic cathedral, São Pedro de Alcântara. The city is also home to the Encantada—literally "Enchanted"— the peculiar house created by Santos Dumont, an inventor and early aviator. Fashion-conscious bargain hunters from across Rio de Janeiro State generally make a beeline for Rua Teresa, a hilly street just outside the historic center that's lined with discount clothing stores.

GETTING HERE AND AROUND

From Rio by car head north along BR 040 to Petrópolis. The picturesque drive (once you leave the city) takes about an hour if traffic isn't heavy. Única buses leave every 40 minutes—less often on weekends—from

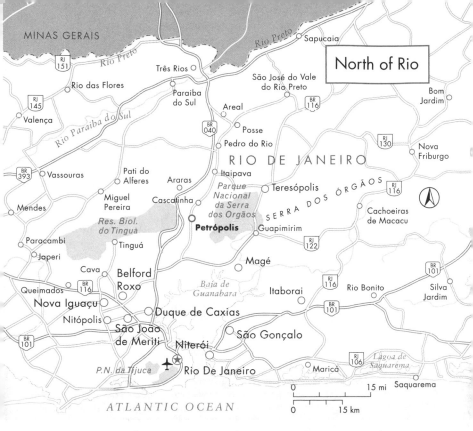

Rio's Rodoviária Novo Rio. The 90-minute journey costs R$17. Upon arrival at Rodoviária Petrópolis, the bus station, you'll be several miles from downtown, so you'll need to take a taxi (R$15–30, depending on traffic), especially if you're laden with luggage.

The easiest and safest way to get to Petrópolis from Rio, though, is to arrange a shuttle at your hotel. The tour company Rio Turismo Radical conducts guided day tours from Rio of Petrópolis and other off-the-beaten-track destinations and provides English-speaking guides. The cost is about R$100, including transportation and admission to the main sights.

ESSENTIALS

Bus Contacts Rodoviária Petrópolis ✉ *Rua Doutor Porciúncula 75* ☎ *024/2237-0101.* **Única** ☎ *021/2263-8792* ⊕ *www.unica-facil.com.br.*

Taxi Contact Ponto de Taxi Elite ☎ *0800/282-1412, 024/2242-4090.*

Visitor and Tour Information Petrópolis Tourism Office ✉ *Centro de Cultura Raul de Leoni, Praça Visconde de Mauá 305, Centro* ☎ *024/2233-1200* ⊕ *www.petropolis.rj.gov.br* ☾ *Mon.–Sat. 9–6, Sun. 9–5.* **Rio Turismo Radical** ☎ *021/2548-2592, 021/9224-6963* ⊕ *www.rioturismoradical.com.br/ petropolis.htm.*

EXPLORING

TOP ATTRACTIONS

Catedral São Pedro de Alcântara. The imposing Cathedral of Saint Peter of Alcantara, a fine example of Gothic architecture, sits at the base of a jungle-clad hill. Inside the building, whose construction began in 1884, lie the tombs of Dom Pedro II; his wife, Dona Teresa Cristina; and their daughter, Princesa Isabel. Elegant sculptures and ornate stained-glass windows add to the visual appeal indoors, and if you take the trip up the tower (don't pass this up) you'll be rewarded with panoramic city views. ■ **TIP→ Drift further back in time by arriving via a horse-drawn carriage, easily hailed in the historic center of town.** ✉ *Rua São Pedro de Alcântara 60, Centro* ☎ *024/2242–4300* 🎟 *Cathedral free, tower R$8* ⏲ *Cathedral daily 8–6, tower Tues.–Sat. 10–5.*

Museu Imperial. The Imperial Museum is the magnificent 44-room palace that was the summer home of Dom Pedro II, emperor of Brazil, and his family in the 19th century. The colossal structure is filled with polished wooden floors, artworks, and grand chandeliers. You can also see the diamond-encrusted gold crown and scepter of Brazil's last emperor, as well as other royal jewels. ✉ *Rua da Imperatriz 220, Centro, Centro* ☎ *024/2245–5550* 🌐 *www.museuimperial.gov.br* 🎟 *R$8* ⏲ *Tues.–Sun. 11–6.*

Palácio de Cristal. The Crystal Palace, a stained-glass and iron building made in France and assembled in Brazil, was a wedding present to Princess Isabel from her consort, the French Count d'Eu. Their marriage was arranged by their parents—Isabel, then 18, learned of Dom Pedro II's choice only a few weeks before her wedding. The count wrote to his sister that his bride to be was "ugly," but after a few weeks of marriage decided he rather liked her. During the imperial years the palace was used as a ballroom: the princess held a celebration dance here after she abolished slavery in Brazil in 1888. ✉ *Praça da Confluência, Rua Alfredo Pachá s/n, Centro* ☎ *024/2247–3721* 🎟 *R$5* ⏲ *Tues.–Sun. 9–6.*

WORTH NOTING

Casa de Santos Dumont. The Santos Dumont House was built in 1918 by one of the world's first aviators. Santos Dumont's inventions fill the house, including a heated shower he developed before most homes even had running water. The home doesn't have a kitchen because Dumont ordered his food from a nearby hotel—the first documented restaurant delivery service in Brazil. ✉ *Rua do Encantado 22, Centro* ☎ *024/2247–3158* 🎟 *R$5* ⏲ *Tues.–Sun. 9:30–5.*

WHERE TO EAT AND STAY

$$ SEAFOOD

🍴 **Trutas do Rocio.** Trout, trout, and more trout is served at this restaurant next to a river teeming with—you guessed it—trout. The fish is prepared as appetizers in pâté or in a cassava-dough pastry. Entrées include grilled trout and trout cooked in almond sauce, mustard sauce, or orange sauce. The rustic restaurant (its name is Portuguese for trout, by the way) seats only 22, so reservations are a must. ■ **TIP→ On weekdays, Trutas is open only to parties of six or more that have booked in advance.** [$] *Average main: R$33* ✉ *Estrada da Vargem Grande 6333,*

Rocio ☎ *024/2291–5623* 🌐 *www.trutas.com.br* ✍ *Reservations essential* ⏲ *No dinner.*

$$$$ B&B/INN 🏨 **Locanda Della Mimosa.** This cozy pousada sits in a valley with trails winding through colorful bougainvillea trees. **Pros:** spacious rooms; great restaurant; massages and afternoon tea service are included in the rates. **Cons:** need to book well in advance; some suites have traffic noise; minimum two-night stay. [$] *Rooms from: R$840* ✉ *BR 040, Km 71.5, Alameda das Mimosas 30, Vale Florido* ☎ *024/2233–5405* 🌐 *www.locanda.com.br* 🛏 *6 suites* ⏲ *Hotel closed Mon.–Thurs.* 🍴 *Breakfast.*

$$$ B&B/INN 🏨 **Pousada de Alcobaça.** Just north of Petrópolis, this is considered by many the region's loveliest inn. **Pros:** tasty food; great views. **Cons:** need to book far in advance; inn is a 15-minute drive from the city. [$] *Rooms from: R$380* ✉ *Agostinho Goulão 298, Correias* ☎ *024/2221–1240* 🌐 *www.pousadadaalcobaca.com.br* 🛏 *11 rooms* 🍴 *Breakfast.*

$$ B&B/INN 🏨 **Pousada Monte Imperial.** A 10-minute walk from downtown, this Bavarian-style inn has a lobby with a fireplace and a comfortable restaurant and bar area. **Pros:** close to downtown; friendly, attentive staff; great sunset views. **Cons:** spartan rooms; chilly in winter; uphill walk from the city. [$] *Rooms from: R$300* ✉ *Rua José de Alencar 27, Centro* ☎ *024/2237–1664* 🌐 *www.pousadamonteimperial.com.br* 🛏 *15 rooms* 🍴 *Breakfast.*

$$$ HOTEL FAMILY Fodor's Choice ★ 🏨 **Solar do Imperio.** Occupying a tastefully restored 1875 neoclassical building and smaller outlying houses amid Petrópolis's historic center, this elegant hotel provides stylish, comfortable accommodations. **Pros:** excellent location; good in-house restaurant; great service; modern spa facilities. **Cons:** breakfast not as lavish as others in this price range. [$] *Rooms from: R$420* ✉ *Av. Koeler 376, Centro* ☎ *024/2242–0034* 🌐 *www.solardoimperio.com.br* 🛏 *24 rooms* 🍴 *Breakfast.*

WALKING IN THE CLOUDS

The Parque Nacional da Serra dos Órgãos, created in 1939 to protect the region's natural wonders, covers more than 39 square miles of mountainous terrain between Petrópolis and Teresópolis. Overseen by the Brazilian Institute for Environmental Protection, it's one of the best-managed national parks in the country. The Petrópolis to Teresópolis trail—a tough three-day hike with spectacular views—is a must for hardcore hikers. Inexperienced hikers should go with a guide, but everyone should check weather forecasts in advance as heavy rainfall in the region has caused mudslides in recent years.

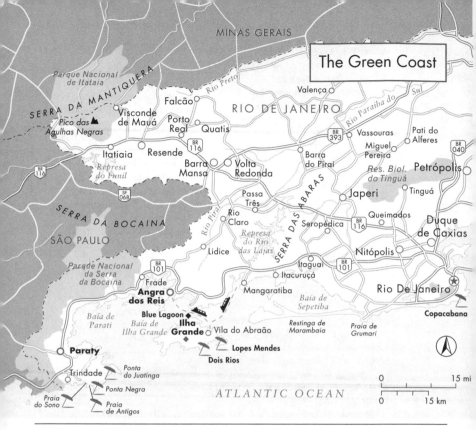

THE GREEN COAST

Italy has the charming Costa Azzura, but Brazil has the Costa Verde. The emerald waters in the bay at Angra dos Reis have fabulous diving spots, with abundant marine life and near year-round visibility. If you're not a diver, though, don't fret. There are plenty of boat tours to places like Ilha Grande. With its unspoiled beaches and rough-hewn nature trails, the bay's biggest island attracts sun seekers and adventure tourists alike.

During Carnival, pristine nature takes a back seat when the normally quiet Paraty celebrates its roots with Bloco da Lama, a parade for which participants get down and dirty—literally—and smear mud from local Praia do Jabaquara on one another. The ritual reenacts one the region's prehistoric tribes practiced to drive away evil spirits.

ANGRA DOS REIS

168 km (91 miles) west of Rio.

Angra dos Reis (Bay of Kings) has it all: colonial architecture, beautiful beaches, and clear green waters. Schooners, yachts, sailboats, and fishing skiffs drift among the bay's 365 islands, one for every day of the year. Indeed, Angra dos Reis' popularity lies in its strategic location near the islands. Some are deserted stretches of sand, others patches of Atlantic rain forest surrounded by emerald waters perfect for swimming or snorkeling.

GETTING HERE AND AROUND

Angra dos Reis-bound Costa Verde buses leave Rio every hour. The 2½-hour trip costs R$42. Ferries leave the terminal at Angra dos Reis for Ilha Grande every day at 3:30 pm. The 90-minute trip costs R$4.

From Rio by car, get onto the Rio-Santos highway (BR 101) and follow it south for 190 km until you get to Angra dos Reis. Expect the trip to take between two and three hours, depending on traffic.

ESSENTIALS

Bus Contact Rodoviária Angra dos Reis ⊠ *Av. Almirante Jair Toscano de Brito 110, Balneário* ☎ *024/3365–2041* ⊕ *www.socicam.com.br/terminais/terminais_rodoviarios.php?ID=15.*

Taxi Contact Ponto de Táxi ⊠ *Rua do Comércio 201, Centro* ☎ *024/3365–2792.*

Visitor Information Angra dos Reis Tourism Office ⊠ *Av. Ayrton Senna da Silva 580, Praia do Anil* ☎ *024/3367–7826* ⊕ *www.turisangra.com.br* ⊙ *Daily 8–8.*

EXPLORING

Associação dos Barqueiros. This group runs boat tours to the islands around Angra dos Reis. One great tour is to Ilha da Gipóia and its beautiful beaches, such as the famous Jurubaíba, which is perfect for snorkeling or diving. ■**TIP**➔ **Some boats have a reputation for playing loud music. Check before you book if you prefer a tranquil environment.** ⊠ *Rua Júlio Maria, 92, Centro* ☎ *024/3365–3165* ⊕ *www.turisangra. com.br/associacao-dos-barqueiros-de-angra-dos-reis/44-705.*

Mar de Angra. This reliable outfit sails its schooners, catamarans, and other boats on day trips to the islands around Angra dos Reis. ⊠ *Av. Júlio Maria 16* ☎ *024/3365–1097* ⊕ *www.mardeangra.com.br.*

WHERE TO STAY

$$$$ ⊡ **Hotel do Bosque.** Inside Parque Perequê, this hotel has boat service
HOTEL to its private beach across the river. **Pros:** plenty of activities; private beach; spacious rooms. **Cons:** out-of-the-way location. $ *Rooms from: R$2150* ⊠ *BR 101, Km 533, Praia de Mambucaba, Mambucaba* ☎ *024/3362–3130* ⊕ *www.hoteldobosque.com.br* ↪ *98 rooms, 4 suites* ⊙ *Some meals.*

$ ⊡ **Pousada dos Corsarios.** Its location right on the beach at scenic Praia do
HOTEL Bonfim makes this simple hotel a great option for its price range. **Pros:** beachfront location; abundant breakfast; friendly service. **Cons:** few frills; a half-hour walk or 10-minute taxi ride to town center. $ *Rooms from: R$170* ⊠ *Praia do Bonfim, 5, Bonfim* ☎ *024/3365–4445* ⊕ *www. corsarios.com.br* ↪ *10 rooms* ⊙ *Breakfast.*

ILHA GRANDE

21 km (13 miles) south of Angra dos Reis or Mangaratiba via 90-minute ferry ride.

Ilha Grande, 90 minutes via ferry from Angra dos Reis, is one of the most popular island destinations in Brazil. It boasts 86 idyllic beaches, some of which are sandy ribbons with backdrops of tropical foliage, while others are densely wooded coves with waterfalls tumbling down from the forest.

Ilha Grande once provided refuge for pirates and corsairs, and was the first point of entry for many slaves brought here from Africa. Later it became a leper colony, but for some its use as a political prison during the military dictatorship from 1964 to 1984 was its most insidious incarnation.

Ferries, catamarans, and schooners arrive at Vila do Abraão. As there are no cars, it's wise to take only what you can carry. Men waiting at the pier make a living helping tourists carry luggage for about R$10 per bag. Take cash out in Angra. There aren't any ATMs on the island, and credit cards aren't always accepted.

GETTING HERE AND AROUND

The long-distance bus station at Angra is several kilometers from the town center and ferry terminal—a hot 20-minute walk or a R$20 cab ride away. Ferries to Ilha Grande are run by Barcas S/A. The ferry for Vila do Abraão on Ilha Grande leaves Angra dos Reis daily at 3:30 pm and returns on weekdays at 10 am and on weekends at 11 am; the price is R$4 during the week and R$10 on weekends. Speedier but more expensive (R$25) catamarans make the trip every day at 9 am, 12:30 pm and 5 pm, arriving at the island in less than 50 minutes. Tickets can be bought at a kiosk in front of the pier. Throughout the day, schooners make the trip, charging R$20 per person. Note that the boats often wait until they are close to full before setting off.

ESSENTIALS

Visitor Information **Tourist Information Center** ⊠ *Rua da Praia s/n, Abraão* ☎ *024/3365–5186* ⊕ *www.ilhagrandeon.com.br.*

SAFETY AND PRECAUTIONS

Avoid taking unlicensed boats. Verify the condition of any boat you plan to board, and check that it has a life preserver for every person aboard.

EXPLORING

Visitors to Ilha Grande can follow well-marked nature trails that lead to isolated beaches and waterfalls and past the ruins of the former prison. Walks may last from 20 minutes to six hours, and there are maps at strategic points. Bring along water and insect repellent, and wear lightweight walking shoes. For a less taxing experience, take a schooner or taxi boat out to the unspoiled beaches. Schooners make regular trips out to the most popular beaches and lagoons, with stops for swimming and snorkeling, while the taxi boats whisk passengers to any point on the island.

Blue Lagoon. This natural pool that forms at low tide is home to thousands of small fish that will literally eat out of your hands. Blue Lagoon is popular with day-trippers from the mainland. ■ **TIP→ If you come here, be sure to bring a mask and snorkel.** ✉ *Lagoa Azul* 🌐 *www.ilhagrandeon.com.br/lagoaazul.htm.*

ILHA GRANDE'S SWEET SPOT

They appear late in the afternoon to tempt you with their sweet aromas and delicate flavors. We're talking about Vila do Abraão's sweet carts, of course. They first appeared in 1998, when a resident of the island started producing baked good at his home. His success inspired other dessert makers to sell their sweets on the streets of Abraão. The carts stay out late at night, tempting even the most resolute of travelers.

BEACHES

Dois Rios. With its pristine white sands and turquoise waters, this beautiful, unspoiled beach sits in stark contrast to the dark prison ruins that sit behind it. Visitors have the beach practically to themselves, as few people make the arduous 5-km (3-mile) trek through hot jungle to get here. Those who do are rewarded with one of the island's most gorgeous beaches, and the sense of achievement that comes with really getting off the beaten track. ■ **TIP→ The prison ruins are worth exploring, but be sure to head back several hours before sundown.** **Amenities:** none. **Best for:** solitude. ✉ *Dois Rios.*

Fodor's Choice ★ **Lopes Mendes.** Locals and visitors alike regard Lopes Mendes, a 3-km (2-mile) stretch of dazzling-white sand lapped by emerald waters, as the most beautiful beach on Ilha Grande. It's often cited as one of the most beautiful in all Brazil. Strict environmental protection orders have kept the jungle-fringed beach from being spoiled by development: expect makeshift beach kiosks, not upscale bars. Organize a boat trip from Vila do Abraão if you don't feel up to the two-hour hike through the forest, or hike here and take the boat back—the rough jungle trail and sticky heat can tax even the most hearty of ramblers. ■ **TIP→ While here, use plenty of sunblock, as the rays rebounding off the white sand are particularly strong.** **Amenities:** food and drink. **Best for:** swimming; walking. ✉ *Lopez Mendes* 🌐 *www.ilhagrandeon.com.br.*

WHERE TO EAT

$$ SEAFOOD 🍴 **Lua e Mar.** Expect fresh, well-prepared seafood at this longtime favorite. It's a casual establishment, so you can stroll in from the beach still wearing your Havaianas. Try Dona Cidinha's specialty, fish with half-ripe bananas, or the famous *moqueca* (seafood stew), which many islanders claim is the best in Rio de Janeiro state. [$] *Average main: R$35* ✉ *Rua da Praia, Vila do Abraão, Abraão* ☎ *024/3361–5113* 🌐 *www.ilhagrande.org/luaemar* ⏲ *Closed Wed.*

$$ SEAFOOD 🍴 **O Pescador.** Inside the pousada of the same name, this restaurant serves local seafood prepared using Italian cooking techniques. The specialty is grilled fish (the types vary according to the season) bought from local fishermen. After dark, you can dine alfresco on the beach by candlelight. [$] *Average main: R$40* ✉ *Rua da Praia 647, Abraão* ☎ *024/3361–5114.*

$$ PIZZA 🍴 **Pizza na Praça.** On the flagstones of Ilha Grande's main square itself, this simple restaurant serves up more than four-dozen types of pies, from simple margheritas to exotic seafood combinations. There are low-cal versions made with fresh vegetables and soft ricotta cheese on a whole-grain base, but also indulgent options such as the sweet pizzas with chocolate, *doce de leite* (thick sweet milk), or both. The pizza menu is available from 6 pm until the early hours, while at lunchtime the restaurant serves vast, tasty salads and good-value set meals. **■TIP→ This is a great spot for evening meals on Friday and Saturday nights, when live bands play in the square.** [$] *Average main: R$40* ✉ *Praça São Sebastião, Abraão* ☎ *024/3361–9566.*

WHERE TO STAY

$ HOTEL 🏨 **Farol dos Borbas.** The main advantage of Farol dos Borbas is its location near the disembarcation pier for the ferry from Angra dos Reis. **Pros:** walking distance from the pier; close to everything; attentive staff; private schooner. **Cons:** can be noisy at night. [$] *Rooms from: R$180* ✉ *Rua da Praia 881, Abraão* ☎ *024/3361–5832* 🌐 *www.ilhagrandetur.com.br* 🛏 *14 rooms* 🍽 *Breakfast.*

$$ B&B/INN FAMILY 🏨 **Pousada do Canto.** In a colonial-style house, this pousada with a tropical atmosphere faces lovely Praia do Canto. **Pros:** on the beach; short walk to the village; pretty pool. **Cons:** rooms can get chilly in winter; small bathrooms. [$] *Rooms from: R$280* ✉ *Rua da Praia 121, Vila do Abraão* ☎ *021/3717–3262* 🌐 *www.canto-ilhagrande.com* 🛏 *11 rooms* 🍽 *Breakfast.*

$$ B&B/INN 🏨 **Pousada Naturalia.** A beachfront location, excellent service, and sumptuous breakfasts all contribute to the appeal of Pousada Naturalia. **Pros:** excellent service; sumptuous breakfasts; sea views; lush tropical gardens. **Cons:** 10-minute walk to the ferry terminal means that you may need to pay a carrier at the harbor R$20 to transport your luggage. [$] *Rooms from: R$260* ✉ *Rua da Praia 149, Abraão* ☎ *024/3361–9583* 🌐 *www.pousadanaturalia.net* 🛏 *14 rooms* 🍽 *No meals.*

PARATY

99 km (60 miles) southwest of Angra dos Reis; 261 km (140 miles) southwest of Rio.

Fodor's Choice ★ This stunning colonial city—also spelled Parati—is one of South America's gems. Giant iron chains hang from posts at the beginning of the mazelike grid of cobblestone streets, closing them to all but pedestrians, horses, and bicycles. Until the 18th century this was an important transit point for gold plucked from the Minas Gerais—a safe harbor protected by a fort. (The cobblestones are the rock ballast brought from Lisbon, then unloaded to make room in the ships for their gold cargoes.) In 1720, however, the colonial powers cut a new trail from the gold mines straight to Rio de Janeiro, bypassing the town and leaving it isolated. It remained that way until contemporary times, when artists, writers, and others "discovered" the community and UNESCO placed it on its list of World Heritage Sites.

Paraty isn't a city peppered with lavish mansions and opulent palaces; rather, it has a simple beauty. By the time the sun breaks over glorious Paraty Bay each morning—illuminating the whitewashed, colorfully trimmed buildings—the fishermen have begun spreading out their catch at the outdoor market. The best way to explore is simply to begin walking winding streets banked with centuries-old buildings that hide quaint inns, tiny restaurants, shops, and art galleries. Paraty holds Brazil's largest literary festival, FLIP (Festival Literaria de Paraty) each July, followed in quick succession by the more raucous Festival da Pinga (Cachaça Festival), at

> **A POTENT BREW**
>
> One telling has it that cachaça was invented around 1540 by slaves working on the sugarcane plantations. A liquid called *cagaço* was removed from the sugarcane to make it easier to transport. The slaves noticed that after a few days this liquid would ferment into a potent brew.

which cachaça producers from around the country unveil their latest brews. Book well in advance if you plan to visit during the festivals.

GETTING HERE AND AROUND

From Rio de Janeiro, it's a four-hour drive along the BR 101 to Paraty. Costa Verde buses leave Rio daily every two hours. The journey costs R$62.

ESSENTIALS

Bus Contact Rodoviária Paraty ⊠ *Rua Jango Pádua, Centro* ☎ *024/3371–1238.*

Taxi Contact Tuim Taxi Service ⊠ *Centro* ☎ *024/9918–7834* ⊕ *www.eco-paraty.com/taxi.*

Visitor and Tour Information Paraty Tourism Office ⊠ *Rua Dr. Samuel Costa 29, Centro* ☎ *024/3371–1897* ⊕ *www.paraty.com.br* ☉ *Daily 9–9.* **Paraty Tours.** This outfit conducts six-hour jeep tours that head into Serra da Bocaina National Park, crossing rivers and visiting fantastic waterfalls. ⊠ *Av. Roberto Silveira 11, Centro* ☎ *024/3371–2651* ⊕ *www.paratytours.com.br.*

EXPLORING

TOP ATTRACTIONS

Forte Defensor Perpétuo. Paraty's only fort was built in the early 1700s, and rebuilt in 1822, as a defense against pirates. It's now home to a folk-arts center. ⊠ *Morro da Vila Velha* ☎ *024/3371–1038 No phone* ⊕ *www.paraty.com.br/forte_paraty.asp* ☜ *R$3* ☉ *Wed.–Sun. 9–5.*

Igreja de Nossa Senhora dos Remédios. The neoclassical Church of Our Lady of Sorrows was built in 1787. The small art gallery within, Pinacoteca Antônio Marino Gouveia, has paintings by modern artists such as Djanira, Di Cavalcanti, and Anita Malfatti. ⊠ *Rua da Matriz, Centro Histórico* ☎ *024/3371–1897* ⊕ *www.museus.gov.br/os-museus* ☜ *R$4* ☉ *Tues.–Sun. 9–noon and 2–5.*

Igreja de Santa Rita. The oldest church in Paraty, the simple Church of Santa Rita was built in 1722 by and for freed slaves. Today it houses a small religious art museum (Museu de Arte Sacra). It's a typical Jesuit church with a tower and three front windows. Religious art objects inside the church are constantly being restored. ⊠ *Largo de Santa Rita, Rua Santa Rita s/n, Centro Histórico* ☎ *024/3371–1206* ⊕ *www.museus.gov.br/os-museus* ☜ *R$4* ☉ *Wed.–Sun. 9–noon and 2–5.*

FAMILY **Trinidade.** About 30 km (20 miles) from Paraty, Trinidade was once a hippie hangout. Today Trinidade's several gorgeous beaches attract everybody from backpackers to cariocas on vacation, and the natural pools are perfect for children. Regular buses run from the bus station in Paraty. If you're looking to stay overnight, you'll find simple lodgings and campsites near the beaches. ✉ *Trindade.*

WORTH NOTING

Casa da Cultura. The museum in the Casa da Cultura is a good place to get acquainted with Paraty's history and culture. The gift shop downstairs, one of the best in town, sells crafts made by local artisans. ✉ *Rua Dona Geralda 177, at Rua Dr. Samuel Costa, Centro Histórico* ☎ *024/3371–2325* 🌐 *www.casadaculturaparaty.org.br* 🎟 *Museum R$8* 🕒 *Wed.–Mon. 10–6:30.*

Igreja de Nossa Senhora do Rosário. Paraty's slaves built the Church of Our Lady of the Rosary for themselves around 1725 because they were not welcome in the town's other churches. ✉ *Rua do Comércio s/n, Centro Histórico* ☎ *024/3371–8328* 🌐 *www.museus.gov.br/os-museus* 🎟 *R$4* 🕒 *Tues.–Sun. 9–5.*

BEACHES

Praia de Antigos. An environmental protection order keeps beautiful Antigos Beach wonderfully unspoiled—you can swim amid rugged nature here. The thick jungle reaches right down to the sands, and the beach is famous for the large rocks that jut into the transparent water, separating Antigos from the adjoining smaller beach, Antiginhos, whose calmer waters are better for swimming. The beach can be reached via a 20-minute walking trail from equally scenic Sono Beach, which in turn can be reached by boat from Paraty. **Amenities:** none. **Best for:** solitude; snorkeling; sunbathing. ✉ *Take trail from Sono Beach, Trindade.*

Praia do Sono. Secluded Sono Beach is one of the Paraty area's most beautiful strands, with thick jungle framing the crescent of light, soft sand bordering crystal clear waters teeming with colorful fish. Campers base themselves here during the summer, when there's a relaxed, bohemian air. In the off-season, the beach is virtually deserted—sunbathers bask in what feels like a private tropical paradise. Although Sono is a bit off the beaten track, the gorgeous setting makes it worth the effort to reach it. ■ **TIP→ The best way to access the beach is by boat from Paraty (about R$35); otherwise you must take a one-hour bus ride and then hike for about 40 minutes.** **Amenities:** food and drink (in high season). **Best for:** solitude, swimming, walking. ✉ *Trindade.*

WHERE TO EAT

$$$ BRAZILIAN 🍴 **Banana da Terra.** This is one of the best places in Paraty for colossal shrimp, a dish that's hard to find from February to May, during the shrimp spawning season. The restaurant is in a colonial house that's decorated with cachaça labels (the caipirinhas here are quite good) and 19th-century pictures of the city. The name of the place comes from another of its specialties: *banana da terra* (plantain), which is incorporated into many dishes, among them grilled fish with garlic butter, herbs, plantains, and rice. [$] *Average main: R$55* ✉ *Rua Doutor Samuel Costa 198, Centro* ☎ *024/3371–1725* 🕒 *No lunch.*

$$$
ITALIAN
Fodor's Choice
★
✕ Punto Divino. A covered outdoor space means that diners at Punto Divino can enjoy meals alfresco even when the famously torrential Paraty rains start to pour. Evening live-music performances lend a touch of festivity to the proceedings, and the crisp, generously topped pizzas here are the best in town. The salads are fresh and tasty, and dishes such as the risotto with squid, squid ink, and chili peppers will tempt adventurous eaters. The restaurant's convenient location, at the heart of the historic center opposite the main square, only adds to its popularity. $ *Average main: R$50* ⊠ *Rua Marechal Deodoro, 129, Centro* ⊘ *No lunch.*

$$
SEAFOOD
✕ Refúgio. Near the water in a quiet part of town, this seafood restaurant that serves excellent codfish cakes is a great place for a romantic dinner. On chilly days, heat lamps warm the café tables out front. $ *Average main: R$40* ⊠ *Praça do Porto 1, Centro* ☎ *024/3371–2447* ⊕ *www.restauranterefugio.com.*

$$$
BRAZILIAN
✕ Restaurante do Hiltinho. The specialty at one of the Paraty's most elegant restaurants is *camarão casadinho*, fried colossal shrimp stuffed with hot *farofa* (cassava flour). Even if you're familiar with jumbo shrimp, you might be astonished at the size of these beauties. Seafood outnumbers other dishes two to one, but the filet mignon is very good. Glass doors that open onto the street are both welcoming and lend a meal here a touch of grandeur, as does the gracious, professional service. $ *Average main: R$60* ⊠ *Praça da Matriz, Rua Marechal Deodoro 233, Centro* ☎ *024/3371–1432* ⊕ *www.hiltinho.com.br.*

WHERE TO STAY

$
B&B/INN
Fodor's Choice
★
Pousada do Príncipe. The great-grandson of Emperor Pedro II owns this aptly named inn at the edge of the colonial city. **Pros:** historic building; good location a short walk from the bus station; nice pool and courtyard; welcoming, attentive staff. **Cons:** noisy air-conditioning; some rooms need repainting. $ *Rooms from: R$226* ⊠ *Av. Roberto Silveira 289, Centro* ☎ *024/3371–2266* ⊕ *www.pousadadoprincipe.com.br* ⬡ *34 rooms, 3 suites* ⦿ *No meals.*

$$$$
B&B/INN
Pousada do Sandi. This welcoming, centrally located pousada offers terrific service and a great location close to the main square in Paraty's historic center. **Pros:** close to all the main sights; large rooms; welcoming lobby and pool area; noteworthy restaurant; great breakfasts. **Cons:** street noise; hard to maneuver for people with some disabilities. $ *Rooms from: R$633* ⊠ *Largo do Rosário 1, Centro* ☎ *24/3371 2100* ⊕ *www.pousadadosandi.com.br* ⬡ *25 rooms, 1 suite* ⦿ *Breakfast.*

$$$$
HOTEL
Pousada Literária. A totally renovated colonial mansion is the setting for this timelessly chic luxury guesthouse that celebrates the literary spirit of Paraty. **Pros:** elegant decor; great pool and location. **Cons:** books up well ahead of July literary festival; streets nearby can flood during rainy season. $ *Rooms from: R$860* ⊠ *Rua Ten Francisco Antônio 36, Centro* ☎ *024/3371–1568* ⊕ *www.pousadaliteraria.com.br/pousada-literaria* ⬡ *33 rooms* ⦿ *Breakfast.*

$$$
B&B/INN
Pousada Pardieiro. The houses that make up this property are decorated in 19th-century colonial style. **Pros:** close to the historic center; great pool and garden. **Cons:** no TVs in rooms; cold floors in winter.

§ *Rooms from: R$390*⊠ *Rua Tenente Francisco Antônio 74, Centro Histórico* ☎ *024/3371–1370* ⊕ *www.pousadapardieiro.com.br* ⤸ *27 rooms, 2 suites* ❚◎❚ *Breakfast.*

SHOPPING

Paraty is known countrywide for its fine cachaça, including brands like Coqueiro, Corisco, Vamos Nessa, Itatinga, Murycana, Paratiana, and Maré Alta.

Empório da Cachaça. This shop that stocks more than 300 brands—both local and national—of sugarcane liquor stays open well into the evening. ⊠ *Rua Doutor Samuel Costa 22, Centro Histórico* ☎ *024/3371–6329.*

Porto da Pinga. If you're looking for cachaça, Porto da Pinga is a worthy stop. It stocks many brands of the liquor, along with fiery bottled chilis, *doce de leite* (thick, sweet milk), and other local specialties. ⊠ *Rua da Matriz 12, Centro Histórico* ☎ *024/3371–1563.*

SÃO PAULO

Updated by
Joshua Eric
Miller

São Paulo is a megalopolis of nearly 20 million people, with endless stands of skyscrapers defining the horizon from every angle. The largest city in South America, São Paulo even makes New York City, with its population of about 8 million, seem small in comparison. And this nearly 500-year-old capital of São Paulo State gets bigger every year: it now sprawls across some 8,000 square km (3,089 square miles), of which 1,530 square km (591 square miles) make up the city proper.

São Paulo is Brazil's main financial hub and its most cosmopolitan city, with top-rate nightlife and restaurants and impressive cultural and arts scenes. Most of the wealthiest people in Brazil live here—and the rest of them drop by at least once a year to shop for clothes, shoes, accessories, luxury items, and anything else money can buy. *Paulistanos* (São Paulo inhabitants) work hard and spend a lot, and there's no escaping the many shopping and eating temptations.

Despite—or because of—these qualities, many tourists, Brazilian and foreigners alike, avoid visiting the city. Too noisy, too polluted, too crowded, they say, and they have a point. São Paulo is hardly a beautiful city with nothing as scenic as Rio's hills and beaches. But for travelers who love big cities and prefer nights on the town to days on the sand, São Paulo is the right place to go. It's fast-paced and there's a lot to do. So even as the sea of high-rise buildings obstructs your view of the horizon, you'll see there's much to explore here.

ORIENTATION AND PLANNING

GETTING ORIENTED

Situated 70 km (43 miles) inland from the Atlantic Ocean with an average elevation of around 800 meters (2,625 feet), São Paulo has a flat and featureless metropolitan area, apart from a few elevated areas, including those around Avenida Paulista and Centro. A major thoroughfare called the "Marginal"—two one-way expressways on either side of a smelly, Pinheiros river—divides the city from both north to south and east to west, with most business and tourist activity occurring in the southeastern, western, and central neighborhoods. No matter where you are, though, it's difficult to gain a visual perspective of your relative location, thanks to the legions of buildings in every direction. A good map or app is a necessity.

TOP REASONS TO GO

■ **Shop Till You Drop:** Shop along with Brazil's rich and famous in the Jardins or Itaim areas, or at one of the city's many fashion malls.

■ **Food, Glorious Food:** Adventurous eating is a sport in São Paulo. The 12,500 restaurants here serve more than four-dozen cuisines.

■ **Live Music:** Enjoy the music that flows through the streets and can be heard around every corner—dance, sing, or just take in the ambience.

■ **Hopping Nightlife:** Bars of all shapes, styles, and sizes beckon the thirsty traveler—quench your thirst with a cold beer or strong caipirinha.

■ **The Beautiful Game:** Futebol, or soccer, is truly "the beautiful game" in Brazil, and in São Paulo futebol is played everywhere.

4

CENTRO

This downtown area has the city's most interesting historic architecture and some of its most famous sights; however, many parts are also quite daunting and dirty, so be prepared. Area highlights include Praça da Sé, considered the vortex for the São Paulo municipal district, and attractions around the revitalized Vale do Anhangabaú. Some of São Paulo's prime guilty pleasures can be snacked on at Mercado Municipal. Parque da Luz is just to the north and next to a number of important buildings, including the Estação da Luz, the former headquarters of São Paulo Railway that now houses the Museum of the Portuguese Language.

LIBERDADE

Southeast of Centro, Liberdade (meaning "freedom" or "liberty" in Portuguese) is the center of São Paulo's Japanese, Korean, and Chinese communities, and features a range of Asian-style streetscapes and shopfronts. It's a popular area with travelers, thanks to the many culturally motivated markets and restaurants.

BARRA FUNDA

Once a desert of abandoned warehouses, this region has experienced a renaissance in recent years. The construction of various high-rise apartment buildings and trendy nightlife venues has returned life to a neighborhood boasting many of São Paulo's samba schools, architecture by Oscar Niemeyer, and the Palestra Itália, home to the Palmeiras soccer club.

AVENIDA PAULISTA

The imposing Avenida Paulista is home to some of the city's best hotels, biggest financial companies, and most important businesses. Many of São Paulo's cultural institutions center around this impressive, eight-lane-wide thoroughfare. Just 2.8-km (1.7-miles) long, the avenue begins west of Centro and spans several of the city's chicest neighborhoods as it shoots southeast toward the Atlantic.

BIXIGA

Officially called Bela Vista, this is São Paulo's Little Italy. Here are plenty of restaurants, theaters, and nightlife hot spots. Southwest of Centro and right next to Avenida Paulista, Bixiga is an old, working-class neighborhood—the kind of place where everybody knows everybody else's business.

JARDINS

On the southern side of Avenida Paulista sits Jardins, a trendy neighborhood that's ideal for shopping and eating out. The gently sloping, tree-filled area is one of the nicer parts of São Paulo for walking around; it's also one of the city's safest neighborhoods.

ITAIM BIBI

Moving farther south, Itaim (locals always drop the Bibi part) is similar to Jardins because it's also filled with fashionable bars, restaurants, and shops. Another of the city's most impressive roads transects the suburb, Avenida Brigadeiro Faria Lima, which, along with its many cross-streets, has a ton of expensive and exclusive nightlife options. At its western border, Itaim stretches down to the Marginal.

PINHEIROS

Just north of Itaim and west of Jardins sits Pinheiros (pine trees), another nightlife hot spot chock-full of bars, clubs, and late-night restaurants. The area, with some of the city's most expensive low-rise housing, is also traversed by the popular Avenida Brigadeiro Faria Lima and has the Marginal as its western boundary.

VILA MADALENA

One of the hillier parts of São Paulo with impressive views across the city from the uppermost buildings, Vila Madalena is a relatively small enclave just to the north of Pinheiros. It's yet another nightlife mecca with bohemian-style haunts that stay open until dawn. Bars are stacked one on top of the other, making it a great place for a pub crawl, particularly because it's also one of the city's safest after-dark spots. Scores of boutiques, bookstores, cafés, galleries, and street-art displays also contribute to the neighborhood's pull on the free-spirited.

PLANNING

WHEN TO GO

Cultural events—film and music festivals, and fashion and art exhibits—usually take place between April and December. In South American summer (from January through March) the weather is rainy, and floods can disrupt traffic. Be sure to make reservations for beach resorts as far in advance as possible, particularly for weekend stays. In winter (June and July), follow the same rule for visits to Campos do Jordão. Summers are hot—35°C (95°F). In winter temperatures rarely dip below 10°C (50°F). ■ TIP➜ **The air pollution might irritate your eyes, especially in July and August (dirty air is held in the city by thermal inversions), so pack eyedrops.**

SAFETY

Stay alert and guard your belongings at all times. Avoid wearing expensive sneakers or watches and flashy jewelry, and be careful with cameras, smart phones, and tablets—all of which attract attention. Muggers love to target the airports, tourist-frequented neighborhoods, and ATMs, so be vigilant while in these spaces.

If driving, stay alert during traffic jams and at stop signs, especially at night, and don't deviate from the main streets and beltways. Watch out for motorcycle drivers—many are express couriers, but some are robbers. You should always be wary when there are two people on one bike. It's best to keep your windows up and doors locked.

GETTING HERE AND AROUND

Navigating São Paulo is not easy, and staying either in the central areas or at least near an inner-city subway station is advisable, especially if you don't plan on renting a car or taking cabs. The subway is quick, easy, inexpensive, and covers much of the city, with stops near the most interesting sites for travelers. Buses can be hard to navigate if you don't speak Portuguese. Driving in São Paulo, particularly in peak hours, can be slow and difficult. For longer stays, obtain a provisional drivers license and a good map or GPS—with a little care and a lot of confidence, you can get by. Parking can be perplexing, so it's probably best to use a parking lot (*estacionamento*), which are numerous and relatively cheap. Cabs rates are reasonable and they're abundant in the popular neighborhoods.

AIR TRAVEL

Nearly all international flights stop in São Paulo, so it's easy to get from São Paulo to everywhere else in Brazil. There are flights every half hour covering the short (around one hour) trip between São Paulo and Rio (starting from around R$65 one-way). There are also multiple departures per day to other major cities such as Brasília and Belo Horizonte. *For airline information, see Air Travel in Travel Smart Brazil.*

AIRPORTS São Paulo's international airport, Aeroporto Internacional de São Paulo/ Guarulhos (GRU) or "Cumbica," is in the suburb of Guarulhos, 30 km (19 miles) and a 45-minute drive (longer during rush hour or on rainy days) northeast of Centro. Much closer to the Zona Sul region is Aeroporto Congonhas (CGH), 14 km (9 miles) south of Centro (a 15- to 45-minute drive, depending on traffic), which serves regional airlines, including the Rio–São Paulo shuttle.

Airports Aeroporto Internacional de Congonhas (CGH) ⬣ *Avenida Washington Luís s/n, Campo Belo* ☎ *011/5090–9000* ⊕ *www.infraero.gov.br.* **Aeroporto Internacional de São Paulo/Guarulhos** (GRU) ✉ *Rod. Hélio Smidt s/n, Guarulhos* ☎ *011/2445–2945* ⊕ *www.infraero.gov.br.*

AIRPORT TRANSFERS: BUSES AND TAXIS State government–operated EMTU buses (blue vehicles, with air-conditioning) shuttle between Guarulhos and Congonhas airports every 30 to 40 minutes from 5:30 am to midnight and every 60 to 90 minutes from midnight to 5:30 am (R$35). Look for the EMTU stand near the private bus and cab stalls outside the arrivals terminal. You may also be able to arrange a free transfer with your airline as part of your ticket.

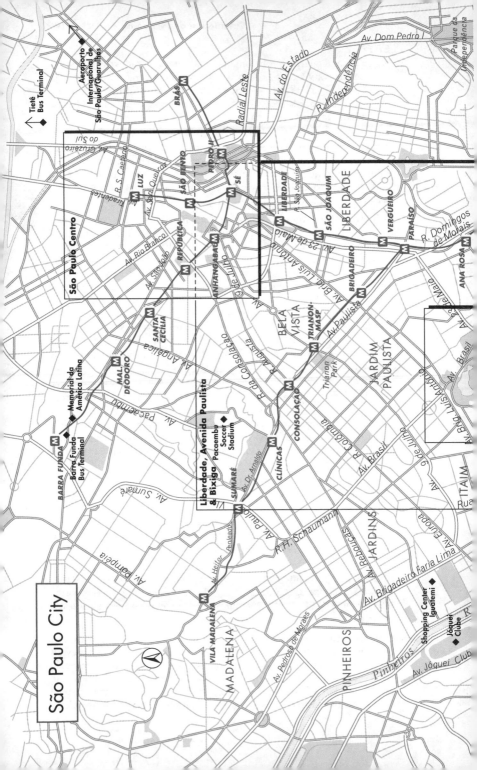

São Paulo City

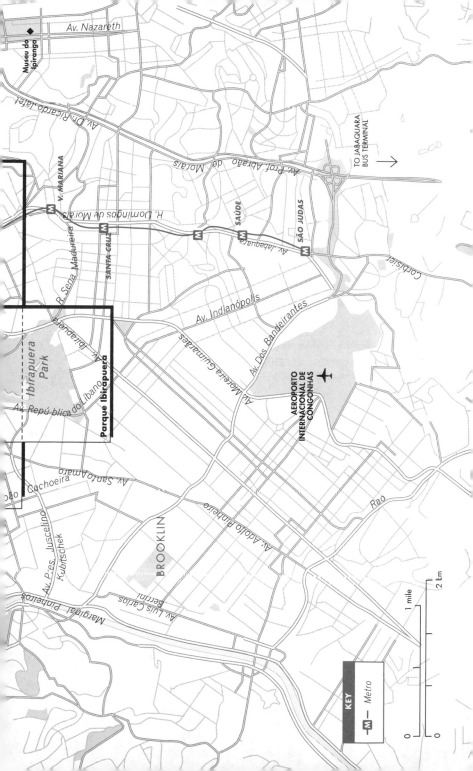

The blue, air-conditioned EMTU buses travel between Guarulhos and the Tietê bus terminal (which is also on the main subway line) from 5 am to midnight, every 30 to 60 minutes; the downtown Praça da República (5:40 am to midnight, every 60 to 90 minutes); and the Hotel Maksoud Plaza (5:50 am to 11:10 pm, every 60 to 70 minutes), stopping at most major hotels around Avenida Paulista. Lines also connect Guarulhos to the Barra Funda terminal and the Shopping Eldorado. The cost is R$35. The

> **A VIEW OF THE PAST**
>
> Although modern-day São Paulo is a tough place to navigate thanks to the jungle of tall buildings, this wasn't always the case. During the city's first few hundred years, before skyscrapers appeared, there were impressive views from Avenida Paulista, which runs along a natural ridge line, the highest part of the hilly Vila Madelena area.

blue-and-white, air-conditioned Guarucoop radio taxis are by far the most common taxis at the international airport and can take you from Guarulhos to Centro for around R$120. It can cost up to R$155 to the southern parts of the Zona Sul region. Congonhas is much closer to downtown and the Zona Sul, so it usually costs no more than R$50. The price is set before the trip based on your drop-off address or suburb and can take from 45 minutes to two hours in peak traffic. The line for the cabs forms just outside the arrivals terminal and moves quickly.

Transfer Contacts EMTU ☎ 0800/770–2287 ⊕ www.airportbusservice.com.br. **Guarucoop** ☎ 011/2440–7070 ⊕ www.guarucoop.com.br.

BUS TRAVEL
The three key bus terminals in the city of São Paulo are connected to metro (subway) stations and serve more than 1,100 destinations combined. The huge main station—serving all major Brazilian cities (with trips to Rio every 10 minutes during the day and every half hour at night, until 2 am) as well as Argentina, Uruguay, Chile, and Paraguay—is the Terminal Tietê in the north, on the Marginal Tietê Beltway. Terminal Jabaquara, near Congonhas Airport, serves coastal towns. Terminal Barra Funda, in the west, near the Memorial da América Latina, has buses to and from western Brazil. Socicam, a private company, runs all the bus terminals in the city of São Paulo.

Bus Contacts EMTU ☎ 0800/7702287 ⊕ www.airportbusservice.com.br. **Socicam** ☎ 011/3866–1100 ⊕ www.socicam.com.br. **Terminal Barra Funda** ✉ Rua Auro Soares de Moura Andrade, 664, Barra Funda ☎ 011/3866–1100 ⊕ www.socicam.com.br Ⓜ Barra Funda. **Terminal Jabaquara** ✉ Rua dos Jequitibás, s/n, Jabaquara ☎ 011/3866–1100 ⊕ www.socicam.com.br Ⓜ Jabaquara. **Terminal Tietê** ✉ Av. Cruzeiro do Sul, 1800, Santana ☎ 011/3866–1100 ⊕ www.socicam.com.br Ⓜ Tietê.

TRAVEL WITHIN SÃO PAULO Municipal bus service is frequent and covers the entire city, but regular buses are overcrowded at rush hour and when it rains. If you don't speak Portuguese, it can be hard to figure out the system and the stops. The stops are clearly marked, but routes are spelled out only on the buses themselves. Buses don't stop at every bus stop, so if you're waiting, you'll have to flag one down.

Bus fare is R$3. You enter at the front of the bus, pay the *cobrador* (fare collector) in the middle, and exit from the rear of the bus. To pay, you can use either money or the electronic card *bilhete único*. The card allows you to take four buses in three hours for the price of one fare. Cards can be bought and reloaded at special booths at major bus terminals or at lottery shops.

For bus numbers and names, routes, and schedules, go to the (Portuguese-language) website of Transporte Público de São Paulo (SPTrans), the city's public transport agency, or use its OlhoVivo application. The *Guia São Paulo Ruas,* published by Quatro Rodas and sold at newsstands and bookstores for about R$15, is another option.

Contact Transporte Público de São Paulo ☏ *156* ⊕ *www.sptrans.com.br.*

4

CAR TRAVEL

The principal highways leading into São Paulo are: the Dutra, from the northeast (and Rio); Anhangüera and Bandeirantes, from the north; Washington Luis, from the northwest; Raposo Tavares, from the west; Régis Bittencourt, from the south; and Anchieta-Imigrantes, from Santos in the southeast. Driving in the city isn't recommended, however, because of the heavy traffic (nothing moves at rush hour, especially when it rains), daredevil drivers, and inadequate parking. You'll also need to obtain a temporary driver's license from *Detran,* the State Transit Department, which can be a time-consuming endeavor.

MAJOR HIGHWAYS AND ROADS The high-speed beltways along the Rio Pinheiros and Rio Tietê rivers—called Marginal Tietê and Marginal Pinheiros—sandwich the main part of São Paulo. Avenida 23 de Maio runs south from Centro and beneath the Parque do Ibirapuera via the Ayrton Senna Tunnel. Avenida Paulista splits Bela Vista and Jardins with Higienópolis and Vila Mariana as bookends.

You can cut through Itaim en route to Brooklin and Santo Amaro by taking avenidas Brasil and Faria Lima southwest to Avenida Santo Amaro. Avenida João Dias and Viaduto José Bonifácio C. Nogueira cut across the Pinheiros River to Morumbi. The Elevado Costa e Silva, also called Minhocão, is an elevated road that connects Centro with Avenida Francisco Matarazzo in the west.

PARKING In most commercial neighborhoods you must buy hourly tickets (called Cartão Zona Azul) to park on the street during business hours. Buy them at newsstands, not from people on the street, who may overcharge or sell counterfeited copies. Booklets of 10 tickets cost R$28. Fill out each ticket—you'll need one for every hour you plan to park—with the car's license plate and the time you initially parked. Leave the tickets in the car's window so they're visible to officials from outside. After business hours or at any time near major sights, people may offer to watch your car. If you don't pay these "caretakers," there's a chance they'll damage your car (R$2 is enough to keep your car's paint job intact). But to truly ensure your car's safety, park in a guarded lot, where rates are R$5–R$7 for the first hour and R$1–R$2 each hour thereafter.

Invest in the *Guia São Paulo Ruas,* published by Quatro Rodas, which shows every street in the city. It's sold at newsstands and bookstores for about R$30.

SUBWAY TRAVEL

Five color-coded lines comprise the São Paulo Metrô, known simply as the Metrô by locals, which interconnects with six train lines administered by the Companhia Paulista de Trens Metropolitanos (CPTM) to blanket most of São Paulo in rail. The most glaring gaps exist around the Ibirapuera, Moema, and Morumbi neighborhoods, as well as near the airports. You can print maps of the entire network from the Metrô's English-language website, where you'll also find ticket prices and schedules. The first four lines are the most useful to tourists. Most notably they cover the center, Avenida Paulista, and Vila Madalena.

Kiosks at all Metrô and train stations sell tickets; vendors prefer small bills for payment. You insert the ticket into the turnstile at the platform entrance, and it's returned to you only if there's unused fare on it. Seniors (65 or older) ride without charge by showing photo IDs at the turnstiles. Transfers within the metro system are free. You can buy a bilhete único (combination ticket, good on buses and the metro) on buses or at metro stations for R$4.65.

Subway Information Metrô ☎ 0800/770–7722 ⊕ www.metro.sp.gov.br.

TAXI TRAVEL

Taxis in São Paulo are white. Owner-driven taxis are generally well maintained and reliable, as are radio taxis. Fares start at R$4.10 and run R$2.50 for each kilometer (½ mile) or R$0.55 for every minute sitting in traffic. After 8 pm and on weekends, fares rise by 30%. You'll pay a tax if the cab leaves the city, as is the case with trips to Cumbica Airport. Good radio-taxi companies, among them Coopertaxi, Ligue-Taxi, and Radio Taxi Vermelho e Branco, usually accept credit cards, but you must call ahead and request the service.

Taxi Contacts Coopertaxi ☎ 011/2095–6000, 011/3511–1919 ⊕ www.coopertax.com.br. **Ligue-Taxi** ☎ 011/2101–3030, 011/3873–3030 ⊕ www.ligue-taxi.com.br. **Radio Taxi Vermelho e Branco** ☎ 011/3146–4000 ⊕ www.radiotaxivermelhoebranco.com.br.

TRAIN TRAVEL

Coming to São Paulo via train is not really practical. The train only connects São Paulo with some nearby small towns in the interior of the state. Most travel to and from the interior of the state is done by bus or automobile.

Train Contacts Estação Barra Funda ✉ Av. Auro Soares de Moura Andrade 664, Barra Funda ☎ 011/770–7722 ⊕ www.metro.sp.gov.br Ⓜ Barra Funda. **Estação Brás** ✉ Rua Domingos Paiva, s/n, Brás ☎ 0800/770–7722 Ⓜ Brás. **Estação da Luz** ✉ Praça da Luz 1, Luz ☎ 0800/055–0121 ⊕ www.cptm.sp.gov. br Ⓜ Luz. **Estação Júlio Prestes** ✉ Praça Júlio Prestes 148, Campos Elíseos ☎ 0800/055–0121 ⊕ www.cptm.sp.gov.br.

CONTACTS AND RESOURCES

TOUR OPTIONS

You can hire a bilingual guide through a travel agency or a hotel concierge (about R$15 an hour with a four-hour minimum), or you can design your own itineraries. The São Paulo tourist board's Cidade São Paulo website offers various themed walking itineraries and English-language audio guides, and it outlines tours facilitated by subway through the TurisMetrô program. SPTuris conducts three half-day bus tours on Sundays, one covering the parks, one centered on the museums, and one focused on the historical downtown area. The prices beat those of most hotels. Officially, the board's guides don't speak English, but it's sometimes possible to arrange for an English speaker, so ask.

For general sightseeing tours, try Check Point, whose daily tours cost R$560 for four people. Easygoing has fly-and-dine tours that include a helicopter trip and dinner. You can book one in English if you reserve by phone. Gol Tour Viagens e Turismo arranges custom tours, as well as car tours for small groups. A half-day city tour costs about R$130 a person (group rate); a night tour—including a samba show, dinner, and drinks—costs around R$300; and day trips to the beach or the colonial city of Embu cost R$200–R$300. Sampa Bikers conducts city tours and excursions outside town. A day tour starts at R$30. Terra Nobre conducts four-hour car tours (R$528), including driver and English-speaking guide, for one or two people.

Information Check Point ⊠ *Rua Jacques Du Cerceau 84* ☎ *011/2791–1316 business hours, 011/99187–1393 after hours* ⊕ *www.checkpointtours.com.br.* **Easygoing** ⊠ *Rua Cristiano Viana 1182, Pinheiros* ☎ *011/3801–9540* ⊕ *www.easygoing.com.br.* **Gol Tour Viagens e Turismo** ⊠ *Av. São Luís, 187 Térreo, Lj. 08, Centro* ☎ *011/3256–2388* ⊕ *www.goltour.com.br* Ⓜ *República.* **Sampa Bikers** ⊠ *Rua Baluarte 672, Vila Olímpia* ☎ *011/5517–7733* ⊕ *www.sampabikers.com.br.* **Terra Nobre** ⊠ *Rua Tagipuru, 235, conj. 44, Perdizes* ☎ *011/3662–1505* ⊕ *www.terranobre.com.br.*

VISITOR INFORMATION

The most helpful contact is the São Paulo Convention and Visitors Bureau, open weekdays from 9 to 6. Branches of the city-operated Anhembi Turismo e Eventos da Cidade de São Paulo are open daily from 9 to 6. The Secretaria de Esportes e Turismo do Estado de São Paulo, open on weekdays from 9 to 6, is less helpful, but has maps and information about the city and state of São Paulo. SEST also has a booth at the arrivals terminal in Guarulhos airport; it's open daily from 9 am to 10 pm.

Visitor Information Anhembi Turismo e Eventos da Cidade de São Paulo ⊠ *Anhembi Convention Center, Av. Olavo Fontoura 1209, Santana* ☎ *011/2226– 0400* ⊕ *www.cidadedesaopaulo.com/sp/en/tourist-information-offices* ⊠ *Praça da República, Rua 7 de Abril, Centro* Ⓜ *República* ⊠ *Av. Paulista 1853, Cerqueira César* Ⓜ *Trianon-Masp* ⊠ *Av. Brigadeiro Faria Lima, in front of Shopping Center Iguatemi, Jardim Paulista* ⊠ *Bus station, Av. Cruzeiro do Sul, 1800, Tietê* Ⓜ *Tietê* ⊠ *Guarulhos Airport Terminals 1 and 2, Aeroporto de Guarulhos.* **São Paulo Convention and Visitors Bureau** ⊠ *Alameda Ribeirão Preto 130,* *conj. 121, Jardins* ☎ *011/3736–0600* ⊕ *www.visitesaopaulo.com.* **Secretaria de Esportes e Turismo do Estado de São Paulo** ✉ *Praça Antônio Prado 9, Centro* ☎ *011/3241–5822* ⊕ *www.selt.sp.gov.br.*

EXPLORING

CENTRO

The downtown district is one of the few places in São Paulo where a significant amount of pre-20th-century history remains visible. You can explore the areas where the city began and view examples of architecture, some of it beautifully restored, from the 19th century. Petty criminals operate in this area, so keep your wits about you while you tour. The best way to get here is by metro.

TOP ATTRACTIONS

Catedral da Sé. The imposing, 14-tower neo-Gothic Catedral da Sé occupies the official center of São Paulo—the 0 Km point, as it's called here. Tours of the church wind through the crypt that contains the remains of Tibiriçá, a native Brazilian who helped the Portuguese back in 1554. ✉ *Praça da Sé s/n, Centro* ☎ *011/3106–2709, 011/3107–6832 for tour information* ⊕ *www.catedraldase.org.br/site* ☎ *Tour R$5* ⊙ *Church weekdays 8–7, Sat. 8–5, Sun. 8–1 and 2–6; tours Tues.–Fri. 10–11:30 and 1–5:30, Sat. 10–11:30 and 1–4:30, Sun. 10–12:30 and 2–4:30* ⊙ *No tours Mon. or last Sun. of the month* Ⓜ *Sé.*

Edifício Itália. To catch the astounding view from atop the Itália Building, you must patronize the Terraço Itália restaurant, starting on the 41st floor. The main dining room gives off a formal feel featuring central columns, candlelit tables, and a terrace. A live band and dance floor, meanwhile, jazz up the panoramic parlor upstairs. The restaurant is expensive, making afternoon tea or a drink at the piano bar, with its upholstered seating and wood lining, the affordable strategy. ✉ *Av. Ipiranga 344, Centro* ☎ *011/2189–2929 restaurant* ⊕ *www.terracoitalia.com.br* ☎ *Piano bar R$30 entrance fee* ⊙ *Piano bar weekdays 3 until closing, weekends noon until closing; restaurant opens daily at 7* Ⓜ *República.*

Edifício Martinelli. Amid São Paulo's modern 1950s-era skyscrapers, the Gothic Martinelli Building is a welcome anomaly. Built in 1929 by Italian immigrant–turned–count Giuseppe Martinelli, it was the city's first skyscraper. The whimsical penthouse is worth checking out, and the rooftop has a great view. ■ **TIP➔ Building tours are by appointment only. Call to make a reservation, or fill out the online form.** ✉ *Av. São João 35, Centro* ☎ *011/3104–2477* ⊕ *www.prediomartinelli.com.br/visitas.php* ☎ *Free* ⊙ *Tour by appointment only, Mon., Tues., and Fri. 9:30–11:30 and 2:30–4:30, Sat. 9–1* Ⓜ *São Bento.*

Fodor's Choice ★ **Mercado Municipal.** The city's first grocery market, this huge 1928 neo-baroque-style building is the quintessential hot spot for gourmets and food lovers. The building, nicknamed Mercadão (Big Market) by locals, houses about 300 stands that sell just about everything edible, including meat, vegetables, cheese, spices, and fish from all over Brazil. It

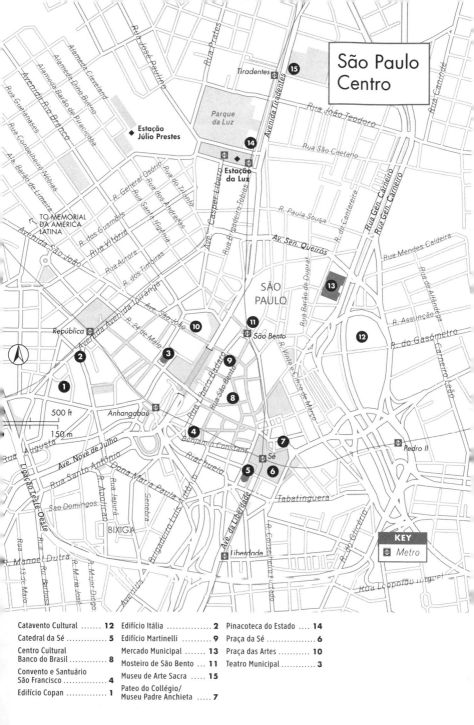

São Paulo Centro

Rua Prates

Tiradentes **15**

Rua João Teodoro

Parque
da Luz

Estação
Júlio Prestes

Rua São Caetano

14

Estação
da Luz

R. Paula Sousa

TO MEMORIAL
DA AMÉRICA
LATINA

Av. Sen. Queiros

Rua Mendes Caldeira

SÃO
PAULO

13

R. Assunção

R. do Gasómetro

República

10

11

São Bento

12

2

1

3

9

8

500 ft

150 m

Anhangabaú

4

7

Benjamin Constant

Pedro II

Sé

5 **6**

Praça da Sé

Tabatinguera

BIXIGA

KEY

Metro

Liberdade

Rua Leopoldo

also has restaurants and traditional snack places. ■TIP➜ The Hocca Bar is justly famous for its pastel de bacalhau (salt-cod pastry) and heaping mortadella sandwich. ⊠ *Rua da Cantareira 306, Sé, Centro* ☏ *011/3313–3365, 011/3313-7456* ⊕ *www.mercadomunicipal. com.br* 🖾 *Free* ⊗ *Mon.–Sat. 6–6, Sun. 6–4* ⊗ *Market is closed a few days a year for national holidays; check the website for the dates* Ⓜ *São Bento.*

Mosteiro de São Bento. The German architect Richard Berndl designed this Norman–Byzantine church that was completed in 1922. Ecclesiastical imagery abounds, and soaring archways extend skyward. The church's enormous organ has some 6,000 pipes, and its Russian image of the Kasperovo Virgin is covered with 6,000 pearls from the Black Sea. On the last Sunday of each month, paulistanos contest for space at the church's popular brunch. To join the party, call ☏ *011/2440–7837.* ■TIP➜ The don't-miss religious event at Mosterio de São Bento is Sunday mass at 10 am, when the sound of monks' Gregorian chants echoes through the chamber. ⊠ *Largo de São Bento, Centro* ☏ *011/3328–8799* ⊕ *www. mosteiro.org.br* 🖾 *Free* ⊗ *Weekdays 6–6, weekends 6–noon and 4–6* ⊗ *Closed Thurs. 8–11:30* Ⓜ *São Bento.*

Museu de Arte Sacra. If you can't get to Bahia or Minas Gerais during your stay in Brazil, you can get a taste of the fabulous baroque and rococo art found there at the Museum of Sacred Art. On display are 4,000 wooden and terra-cotta masks, jewelry, and liturgical objects from all over the country (but primarily Minas Gerais and Bahia), dating from the 17th century to the present. The on-site convent was founded in 1774. ⊠ *Av. Tiradentes 676, Centro* ☏ *011/5627–5393* ⊕ *www.museuartesacra.org.br* 🖾 *R$6, Sat. free* ⊗ *Tues.–Sun. 10–6* Ⓜ *Tiradentes or Luz.*

Pinacoteca do Estado. The highlights of the State Art Gallery's permanent collection include paintings by the renowned Brazilian artists Tarsila do Amaral and Cândido Portinari. Amaral, who died in São Paulo in 1973, applied avant-garde techniques, some of which she acquired while hanging out with the Cubists in 1920s Paris, with Brazilian themes and content. Portinari, born in São Paulo State and known for his neorealistic style, also dealt with social and historical themes. The museum occupies a 1905 structure that was renovated in the late 1990s. The exterior recalls a 1950s brick firehouse, while the view through the central courtyard's interior windows evokes the cliffs of Cuenca, Spain. ⊠ *Praça da Luz 2, Centro* ☏ *011/3324–1000* ⊕ *www.pinacoteca.org.br* 🖾 *R$6, Thurs. 6–10 and Sat. free* ⊗ *Tues.–Sun. 10–6, Thurs. until 10* Ⓜ *Luz.*

Praça da Sé. Two major metro lines cross under the busy Praça da Sé, the large plaza that marks the city's geographical center and holds its main cathedral (⇨ *Catedral da Sé, above*). Migrants from Brazil's poor northeast often gather here to enjoy their music and to purchase and

A Bit of History

São Paulo wasn't big and important right from the start. Jesuit priests founded it in 1554 and began converting native Indians to Catholicism. The town was built strategically on a plateau, protected from attack and served by many rivers. It remained unimportant to the Portuguese crown until the 1600s, when it became the departure point for the *bandeira* (literally, "flag") expeditions, whose members set out to look for gemstones and gold, to enslave Indians, and, later, to capture escaped African slaves. In the process, these adventurers established roads into vast portions of previously unexplored territory. São Paulo also saw Emperor Dom Pedro I declare independence from Portugal in 1822, by the Rio Ipiranga (Ipiranga River), near the city.

It was only in the late 19th century that São Paulo became a driving force in the country. As the state established itself as one of Brazil's main coffee producers, the city attracted laborers and investors from many countries. Italians, Portuguese, Spanish, Germans, and Japanese put their talents and energies to work. By 1895, 70,000 of the 130,000 residents were immigrants. Their efforts transformed the place from a sleepy mission post into a dynamic financial and cultural hub, with people of all colors and religions living and working together peacefully.

Avenida Paulista was once the site of many a coffee baron's mansion. Money flowed from these private domains into civic and cultural institutions. The arts began to flourish, and by the 1920s São Paulo was promoting such great artists as Mário and Oswald de Andrade, who introduced modern elements into Brazilian art.

In the 1950s the auto industry began to develop and contributed greatly to São Paulo's contemporary wealth—and problems. Over the next 30 years, people from throughout Brazil, especially the northeast, came seeking jobs, which transformed the city's landscape by increasing slums and poverty. Between the 1950s and today, the city's main revenue has moved from industry to banking and commerce.

Today, like many major European or American hubs, São Paulo struggles to meet its citizens' transportation and housing needs, and goods and services are expensive. Like most of its counterparts elsewhere in the world, it hasn't yet found an answer to these problems.

sell regional items such as medicinal herbs, while street children hang out and try to avoid the periodic police sweeps to remove them. ⊠ *Praça da Sé s/n, Centro* Ⓜ *Sé.*

WORTH NOTING

Caixa Cultural. In an art deco building abutting Praça da Sé, this lively cultural center celebrates Brazilian art, culture, and history. Recent temporary exhibitions have included the fantastic landscapes of João Suzuki and the edgy critiques of cartoonist Glauco Villas Boas. ■TIP→ **Vantage points on the upper floors afford superb views of surrounding sights.** ⊠ *Praça da Sé 111, Centro* ☎ *011/3321–4400* ⊕ *www.caixacultural. com.br* ☞ *Free* ☉ *Tues.–Sun. 9–9* Ⓜ *Sé.*

Casa da Imagem. This museum dedicated to São Paulo-themed photography opened in 2012 on the site of Casa No. 1, named for its original address in 1689. The 84,000-image collection, which traces the city's expansion and increasing complexity, includes flashbacks to the days when nearby park Vale do Anhangabaú hosted ceremonies for the rich and regal. Neighboring attractions such as the city museum and Páteo do Colégio speak to São

> **GAROA**
>
> One of São Paulo's most famous nicknames is *terra da garoa,* which basically means land of drizzling rain. Although some periods of the year are worse than others, no matter when you visit you'll more than likely get at least a little taste of garoa. An umbrella can be your best friend.

Paulo's earliest foundations, but the Casa da Imagem captures the its contemporary composition. ⊠ *Rua Roberto Simonsen 136-B, Centro* ☏ *011/3106–5122* ⊕ *www.museudacidade.sp.gov.br/casadaimagem. php* ⌦ *Free* ☉ *Tues.–Sun. 9–5* Ⓜ *Sé.*

FAMILY **Catavento Cultural.** Traveling families will find education and entertainment for their children at this interactive science museum in the former City Hall building. For architecture fans, the early-20th-century structure, with its interior courtyard, alone justifies a visit. Stepping into human-size soap bubbles or touching actual meteorites, meanwhile, are the big attractions for kids. The museum's exhibits are organized along four thematic lines: the universe, life, ingenuity, and society. ⊠ *Parque Dom Pedro II, Palácio das Indústrias s/n, Brás* ☏ *011/3315–0051* ⊕ *www.cataventocultural.org.br* ⌦ *R$6* ☉ *Tues.–Sun. 9–5* Ⓜ *Pedro II.*

Centro Cultural Banco do Brasil. The greenhouse-size skylight of this cultural center's 1901 neoclassical home makes the modern and contemporary art exhibits here seem almost to sprout organically. Past ones include "The Magic World of Escher." Plays and small film festivals, the latter celebrating filmmakers from Quentin Tarantino to Louis Malle, further broaden the venue's appeal. The center's facilities include a theater, an auditorium, a movie theater, a video room, and three floors of exhibition rooms. ⊠ *Rua Álvares Penteado 112, Centro* ☏ *011/3113–3651, 011/3113–3652* ⌦ *Free* ☉ *Tues.–Sun. 9–9* Ⓜ *Sé.*

Convento e Santuário São Francisco. One of the city's best-preserved Portuguese colonial buildings, this baroque structure—two churches, one run by Catholic clergy, and the other by lay brothers—was built between 1647 and 1790. The image inside of Saint Francis was rescued from a fire in 1870. ⊠ *Largo São Francisco 133, Centro* ☏ *011/3291–2400* ⊕ *www.franciscanos.org.br* ⌦ *Free* ☉ *Mon.–Sat. 7:30–5:50* Ⓜ *Sé or Anhangabaú.*

Edifício Copan. The architect of this serpentine apartment and office block, Oscar Niemeyer, went on to design much of Brasília, the nation's capital. The building has the clean, white, undulating curves characteristic of Niemeyer's work. The Copan was constructed in 1950, and its 1,160 apartments house about 5,000 people. At night the area is overrun by prostitutes and transvestites. ⊠ *Av. Ipiranga 200,*

Centro ☎ *011/3257–6169* ⊕ *www. copansp.com.br* Ⓜ *República.*

Pateo do Collegio / Museu Padre Anchieta. São Paulo was founded by the Jesuits José de Anchieta and Manoel da Nóbrega in the College Courtyard in 1554. The church was constructed in 1896 in the same style as the chapel built by the Jesuits. In the small museum you can see some paintings from the colonization period and an exhibition of early sacred art and relics. ✉ *Praça Pateo do Collegio 2, Centro* ☎ *011/3105–6899* ⊕ *www.pateocollegio.com. br* 🍽 *Museum R$5* ◷ *Museum Tues.–Sun. 9–4:30; church Mon.–Sat. 8:15–7, Sun. mass at 10* Ⓜ *Sé.*

> **CENTRO'S EVOLUTION**
>
> São Paulo's first inhabitants, Jesuit missionaries and treasure-hunting pioneers, lived in the largely pedestrians-only hilltop and valley areas, particularly Vale do Anhangabaú. Later these areas became Centro (downtown district), a financial and cultural center that's still home to the stock exchange and many banks. It's now the focus of revitalization efforts.

4

Praça das Artes. The center opened in 2012, adding another cultural attraction and architectural highlight to the Vale do Anhangabaú. The venue unites artistic bodies such as the municipal ballet company, choir, and orchestra, which were previously spread across the city. ✉ *Av. São João 281, Centro* ☎ *011/3337–9900* 🍽 *Free* Ⓜ *Anhangabaú.*

Teatro Municipal. Inspired by the Paris Opéra, the Municipal Theater was built between 1903 and 1911 with art nouveau elements. *Hamlet* was the first play presented, and the house went on to host such luminaries as Isadora Duncan in 1916 and Anna Pavlova in 1919. Plays and operas are still staged here; local newspapers, as well as the theater's website, have schedules and information on how to get tickets. The auditorium, resplendent with gold leaf, moss-green velvet, marble, and mirrors, has 1,500 seats and is usually open only to those attending cultural events, although prearranged visits are also available. A museum dedicated to the theater's history is located next door at Praça das Artes. ✉ *Praça Ramos de Azevedo, Centro* ☎ *011/3397–0300* ⊕ *www.teatromunicipal. sp.gov.br* 🍽 *Tickets from R$10* ◷ *Tours by appointment Tues. and Thurs. at 1 pm* Ⓜ *Anhangabaú.*

▪ NEED A BREAK?

Café Girondino. On weekdays, finance types and tourists crowd Café Girondino from happy hour until closing time. The friendly spot serves good draft beer and sandwiches. Pictures on the wall depict Centro in its early days. ✉ *Rua Boa Vista 365, Centro* ☎ *011/3229-4574* ⊕ *www. cafegirondino.com.br* ◷ *Mon.-Thurs. 7:30 am-10:30 pm, Fri. 7:30 am-11 pm, Sun. and holidays 8 am-7 pm* Ⓜ *São Bento.*

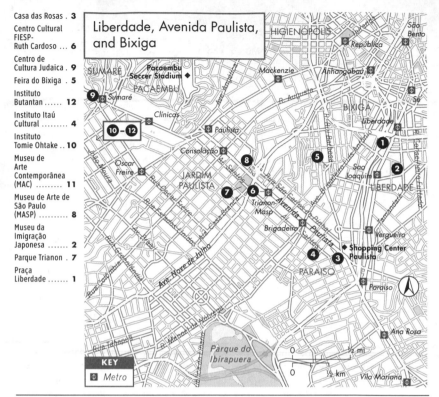

LIBERDADE

The red-porticoed entryway to Liberdade (which means "Freedom") is south of Praça da Sé, behind the cathedral. The neighborhood is home to many first-, second-, and third-generation Nippo-Brazilians, as well as to more recent Chinese and Korean immigrants. Clustered around Avenida Liberdade are shops with everything from imported bubble gum to miniature robots and Kabuki face paint.

The best time to visit Liberdade is on Sunday during the street fair at Praça Liberdade, where Asian food, crafts, and souvenirs are sold. The fair will very likely be crowded, so keep your wits about you and do not wander around at night.

TOP ATTRACTIONS

Museu da Imigração Japonesa. The three-floor Museum of Japanese Immigration has exhibits about Nippo-Brazilian culture and farm life, and about Japanese contributions to Brazilian horticulture. There are also World War II memorials. Relics and life-size re-creations of scenes from the Japanese diaspora line the walls, and paintings hang from the ceiling like wind chimes. ■**TIP**➔ **Most of the museum's labels are in Portuguese, so it's wise for English speakers to call ahead and arrange for an English-language tour.** ✉ *Rua São Joaquim 381, Liberdade*

☎ *011/3209–5465* ⊕ *www.museubunkyo.org.br* ✉ *R$6* ⊗ *Tues.–Sun. 1:30–5:30* Ⓜ *São Joaquim.*

WORTH NOTING

Praça Liberdade. To experience the eclectic cultural mix that keeps São Paulo pulsing, visit Praça Liberdade on a weekend, when the square hosts a sprawling Asian food and crafts fair. You might see Afro-Brazilians dressed in colorful kimonos hawking grilled shrimp on a stick, or perhaps a religious celebration such as April's Hanamatsuri, commemorating the birth of the Buddha. Many Japanese shops and restaurants worth a stop can be found near the square. ⊠ *Av. da Liberdade and Rua dos Estudantes, Liberdade* ⊗ *Fair weekends 10–7* Ⓜ *Liberdade.*

AVENIDA PAULISTA AND BIXIGA

Money once poured into and out of the coffee barons' mansions that lined Avenida Paulista, making it, in a sense, the financial hub. And so it is today, though the money is now centered in the major banks. Like the barons before them, many of these financial institutions generously support the arts. Numerous places have changing exhibitions—often free—in the Paulista neighborhood. Nearby Bixiga, São Paulo's Little Italy, is full of restaurants.

TOP ATTRACTIONS

Casa das Rosas. Peek into the Paulista's past at one of the avenue's few remaining early-20th-century buildings, the House of the Roses. A 1935 French-style mansion with gardens inspired by those at Versailles, it seems out of place next to the surrounding skyscrapers. The famous paulistano architect Ramos de Azevedo designed the home for one of his daughters, and the same family occupied it until 1986, when it was made an official municipal landmark. The site, now a cultural center, hosts classes and literary events. Coffee drinks and pastries are served at the restaurant on the terrace. ⊠ *Av. Paulista 37, Paraíso* ☎ *011/3285–6986, 011/3288–9447* ⊕ *www.casadasrosas-sp.org.br* ✉ *Free* ⊗ *Tues.–Sat. 10–10, Sun. 10–6; restaurant noon–5* Ⓜ *Brigadeiro.*

Centro Cultural FIESP–Ruth Cardoso. Adorned with LED lights, the cultural center's pyramid-shaped facade serves as an open-air digital-art gallery. Past exhibits at this facility of São Paulo State's Federation of Industry have broadcast towering games of Pacman and Space Invaders to pedestrians and nearby residents. The center has a theater, a library of art and photography, galleries that host temporary exhibitions, and areas for lectures, films, and other events. ⊠ *Av. Paulista 1313, Jardim Paulista* ☎ *011/3146–7405* ⊕ *www.sesisp.org.br/centrocultural* ✉ *Free* ⊗ *Mon. 11–8, Tues.–Sat. 10–8, Sun. 10–7* Ⓜ *Trianon-MASP.*

NEED A BREAK?

Ponto Chic. Stop here for a delicious *bauru*—a sandwich with roast beef, tomato, cucumber, and a mix of melted cheeses. This branch of the Paissandu restaurant that invented the bauru is a block east of the Instituto Itaú Cultural, across Avenida Paulista. ⊠ *Praça Osvaldo Cruz 26, Paraíso* ☎ *011/3289–1480* ⊕ *www.pontochic.com.br* ⊗ *Daily 11 am–2 am.*

Museu de Arte Contemporânea. The Museum of Contemprary Art expanded its Ibirapuera presence in 2012 by renovating and moving into the six-floor former Department of Transportation building. Now shorn of its bureaucratic coldness, the space ranks among the Parque Ibirapuera's architectural highlights. The museum already has moved much of its 10,000-piece collection, including works by Picasso, Modigliani, and Chagall, from its facility at the University of São Paulo. ■ TIP→ **One of the museum's most captivating visuals is the panoramic view of the park and its environs from the rooftop terrace.** ⊠ *Av. Pedro Álvares Cabral 1301, Parque Ibirapuera* ☎ *011/5573–9932 direct line, 011/3091–3039* ⊕ *www.macvirtual.usp.br* ⊑ *Free* ⊘ *Tues.–Sun. 10–6.*

Fodor's Choice
★

Museu de Arte de São Paulo (MASP). A striking low-rise building elevated on two massive concrete pillars holds one of the city's premier fine-arts collections. The highlights include works by Van Gogh, Renoir, Delacroix, Cézanne, Monet, Rembrandt, Picasso, and Degas. The baroque sculptor Aleijadinho, the expressionist painter Lasar Segall, and the expressionist/surrealist painter Cândido Portinari are three of the many Brazilian artists represented. The huge open area beneath the museum is often used for cultural events and is the site of a charming Sunday antiques fair. ⊠ *Av. Paulista 1578, Bela Vista* ☎ *011/3251–5644* ⊕ *www.masp.art.br* ⊑ *R$15* ⊘ *Tues.–Sun. 10–6; Thurs. 10–8* Ⓜ *Trianon-MASP.*

Parque Trianon. Created in 1892 as a showcase for local vegetation, the park was renovated in 1968 by Roberto Burle Marx, the Brazilian landscaper famed for Rio's mosaic-tile beachfront sidewalks. You can escape the noise of the street and admire the flora and the 300-year-old trees while seated on one of the benches sculpted to look like chairs. ⊠ *Rua Peixoto Gomide 949, Jardim Paulista* ☎ *011/3289–2160, 011/3253–4973* ⊑ *Free* ⊘ *Daily 6–6* Ⓜ *Trianon-MASP.*

WORTH NOTING

Centro da Cultura Judaica. A short cab or metro trip northwest of Avenida Paulista, this Torah-shape concrete building is one of the newest architectural hot spots in town. Inaugurated in 2003 to display Jewish history and culture in Brazil, it houses a theater and an art gallery and promotes exhibits, lectures, and book fairs. The center debuted a new café, inspired by New York delis and serving local Jewish cuisine, in 2013. ⊠ *Rua Oscar Freire 2500, Pinheiros* ☎ *011/3065–4333* ⊕ *www.culturajudaica.org.br* ⊑ *Free* ⊘ *Tues.–Sun. noon–7* Ⓜ *Sumaré.*

Feira do Bixiga. Strolling through this flea market is a favorite Sunday activity for paulistanos. Crafts, antiques, and furniture are among the wares. Walk up the São José staircase to see **Rua dos Ingleses**, a typical and well-preserved fin-de-siecle Bixiga street. ⊠ *Praça Dom Orione s/n, Bixiga* ⊑ *Free* ⊘ *Sun. 8–5.*

Instituto Itaú Cultural. Maintained by Itaú, one of Brazil's largest private banks, this cultural institute has art shows as well as lectures, workshops, and films. It also maintains an archive with the photographic history of São Paulo and a library that specializes in works on Brazilian art and culture. ⊠ *Av. Paulista 149, Paraíso* ☎ *011/2168–1777* ⊕ *www.itaucultural.org.br* ⊑ *Free* ⊘ *Tues.–Fri. 9–8, weekends 11–8* Ⓜ *Brigadeiro.*

TAKE A WALK

The imposing and almost dead-straight Avenida Paulista is a great place to explore on foot. Running from Paraiso (paradise) to Consolação (consolation), two bookending metro stations, the avenue also serves as paulistanos' tongue-in-cheek comparison to marriage, but many couples of all ages will be found strolling here hand-in-hand. The Museu de Arte de São Paulo (MASP) has one of Brazil's best collections of fine art. Right across the street is Parque Trianon, where locals hang out and eat lunch. Leaving the park, veer right and head for the Centro Cultural FIESP. Here you may be able to catch one of its art shows or performances. A few blocks away is the Instituto Itaú Cultural, a great place to see contemporary Brazilian art. Finally, rest your weary feet in Casa das Rosas, a beautiful Versailles-inspired garden.

PARQUE IBIRAPUERA

Ibirapuera is São Paulo's Central Park, though it's slightly less than half the size and is often more crowded on sunny weekends than its New York City counterpart. In the 1950s the land, which originally contained the municipal nurseries, was chosen as the site of a public park to commemorate the city's 400th anniversary. Architect Oscar Niemeyer and landscape architect Roberto Burle Marx joined the team of professionals assigned to the project. The park was inaugurated in 1954, and some pavilions used for the opening festivities still sit amid its 160 hectares (395 acres). It has jogging and biking paths, a lake, and rolling lawns. You can rent bicycles near some of the park entrances for about R$5 an hour.

TOP ATTRACTIONS

Museu de Arte Moderna (*MAM*). More than 4,500 paintings, installations, sculptures, and other works from modern and contemporary artists such as Alfredo Volpi and Ligia Clark are part of the Modern Art Museum's permanent collection. Temporary exhibits often feature works by new local artists. The giant wall of glass, designed by Brazilian architect Lina Bo Bardi, serves as a window beckoning you to glimpse inside; an exterior mural painted in 2010 by Os Gêmeos, São Paulo twin brothers famous for their graffiti art, shows a little of MAM's inner appeal to the outside world. ✉ *Av. Pedro Álvares Cabral s/n, Gate 3, Parque Ibirapuera* ☎ *011/5085–1300* ⊕ *www.mam.org.br* 🎫 *R$6, free Sun.* ☉ *Tues.–Sun. 10–6.*

NEED A BREAK?

Prêt no MAM. The café inside the Museum of Modern Art serves dishes from many lands, Brazil, France, and Italy among them. Except for hot-dog stands, this is one of the few places in Parque Ibirapuera to buy food. ✉ *Parque Ibirapuera* ☎ *011/5085–1306* ⊕ *www.mam.org.br.*

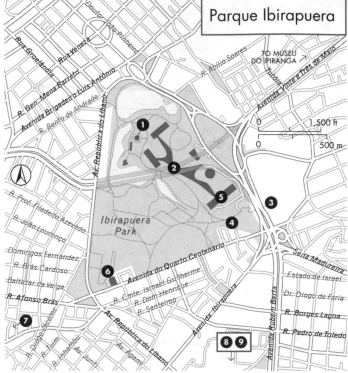

Oca. A spacecraft-like building that's pure Oscar Niemeyer, the Oca often hosts popular temporary art exhibitions. The building usually isn't open to the public when a show isn't on. ⊠ *Gate 3, Parque Ibirapuera* ☎ *011/3105–6118, 011/5082–1777* ⊕ *www.parqueibirapuera. org* ☞ *Price varies depending on show.*

Pavilhão da Bienal. In even-numbered years this pavilion hosts the *Bienal* (Biennial), an exhibition that presents the works of artists from more than 60 countries. The first such event was held in 1951 in Parque Trianon and drew artists from 21 countries. After Ibirapuera Park's inauguration in 1954, the Bienal was moved to this Oscar Niemeyer–designed building that's noteworthy for its large open spaces and floors connected by circular slopes. ⊠ *Parque Ibirapuera, Gate 3, Pavilhão Ciccillo Matarazzo, Ibirapuera* ☎ *011/5576–7600, 011/5576–7641* ⊕ *www.bienal.org.br.*

WORTH NOTING

FAMILY **Planetário.** Brazil's first planetarium when it opened in 1957, the Planetário has 280 seats under a 48-foot-high dome and features a state-of-the-art fiber-optic projection system. Shows last about 50 minutes. ⊠ *Gate 2, Av. Pedro Álvares Cabral, Parque Ibirapuera* ☎ *011/5575–5206* ☞ *Free* ☉ *Weekends at 3 and 5.*

ELSEWHERE IN SÃO PAULO

Several far-flung sights are worth a taxi ride to see. West of Centro is the Universidade de São Paulo (USP), which has two very interesting museums: a branch of the Museu de Arte Contemporânea and the Instituto Butantã, with its collection of creatures that slither and crawl. Close by, Parque Villa-Lobos is a smaller but still significant alternative to Ibirapuera for sporty locals. Head southwest of Centro to the Fundação Maria Luisa e Oscar Americano, a museum with a forest and garden in the residential neighborhood of Morumbi. In the Parque do Estado, southeast of Centro, are the Jardim Botânico and the Parque Zoológico de São Paulo.

TOP ATTRACTIONS

Fundação Maria Luisa e Oscar Americano. A beautiful, quiet private wooded estate is the setting for the Maria Luisa and Oscar Americano Foundation. Paintings, furniture, sacred art, silver, porcelain, engravings, tapestries, sculptures, and personal possessions of the Brazilian royal family are among the 1,500 objects from the Portuguese colonial and imperial periods on display here, and there are some modern pieces as well. Having afternoon high tea here is an event, albeit an expensive one, and Sunday concerts take place in the auditorium. ⊠ *Av. Morumbi 4077, Morumbi* ☎ *011/3742–0077* ⊕ *www.fundacaooscaramericano. org.br* ⊠ *R$10* ☼ *Tues.–Sun. 10–5:30.*

Memorial da América Latina. This massive cement hand, its fingers spread wide, reaching toward the São Paulo sky, is one of the city's signature images. Part of a 20-acre park filled with Oscar Niemeyer-designed structures, the Memorial da América Latina was inaugurated in 1989 in homage to regional unity and its greatest champions, among them Simón Bolívar and José Martí. Aside from the monument, the grounds' highlights include works by Cândido Portinari, and an auditorium dedicated to musical and theatrical performances. ⊠ *Av. Auro Soares de Moura Andrade, 664, Barra Funda* ☎ *011/3823–4600* ⊕ *www. memorial.org.br* ⊠ *Free* ☼ *Tues.–Sun. 9–6* Ⓜ *Barra Funda.*

Museu do Ipiranga. The oldest museum in town, Museu Paulista da Universidade de São Paulo, or Museu do Ipiranga, occupies an 1890 building constructed to honor Brazil's independence from Portugal, declared in the Ipiranga area in 1822 by then-emperor Dom Pedro I. The huge Pedro Américo oil painting depicting this very moment hangs in the main room of this French-inspired eclectic palace, whose famous gardens were patterned after those of Versailles. Dom Pedro's tomb lies under one of the museum's monuments. ⊠ *Parque da Independência, Ipiranga* ☎ *011/2065–8000* ⊕ *www.mp.usp.br* ⊠ *R$6* ☼ *Tues.–Sun. 9–5.*

FAMILY Parque Zoológico de São Paulo. The 200-acre São Paulo Zoo has more than 3,200 animals, and many of its 410 species—such as the *mico-leão-dourado* (golden lion tamarin monkey)—are endangered. ■ **TIP→ If you visit the zoo, don't miss the monkey houses, built on small islands in the park's lake, and the Casa do Sangue Frio (Cold-Blooded House), with reptilian and amphibious creatures.** ⊠ *Av. Miguel Stéfano 4241, Água Funda, Parque do Estado* ☎ *011/5073–0811* ⊕ *www.zoologico.com. br* ⊠ *R$18* ☼ *Tues.–Sun. 9–5* Ⓜ *Jabaquara.*

WORTH NOTING

Auditório do Ibirapuera. The final building in Oscar Niemeyer's design for the park, the Auditório opened in 2005. It has since become one of São Paulo's trademark images, with what looks like a giant red lightning bolt striking a massive white daredevil ramp. Seating up to 800, the concert hall regularly welcomes leading Brazilian and international musical acts. Its back wall can be retracted to reveal the stage to thousands more on the lawn outside. ⊠ *Gate 3, Av. Pedro Álvares Cabral, Parque Ibirapuera* ☎ *011/3629–1075* ⊕ *www.auditorioibirapuera.com.br* ⊠ *R$20.*

> ### LAP OF LUXURY
>
> Surrounding Parque Ibirapuera are some of the city's most expensive mansions and apartment buildings. Walk around the outskirts of the park and get an eyeful of the rich and famous of São Paulo. Better still, venture into one of the luxurious suburbs and join them for coffee or beer at a trendy *padaria* (part bakery, part bar).

FAMILY **Instituto Butantan.** In 1888 a Brazilian scientist, with the aid of the state government, turned a farmhouse into a center for the production of snake serum. Today the Instituto Butantan has more than 70,000 snakes, spiders, scorpions, and lizards in its five museums. It still extracts venom and processes it into serum that's made available to victims of poisonous bites throughout Latin America. ⊠ *Av. Vital Brasil 1500, Butantã* ☎ *011/3726–7222* ⊕ *www.butantan.gov.br* ⊠ *R$6* ☉ *Tues.–Sun. 9–4:30* Ⓜ *Butantã.*

Instituto Tomie Ohtake. The futuristic green, pink, and purple exterior of this contemporary art museum designed by Ruy Ohtake makes it one of the city's most recognizable buildings. The institute, named for Ohtake's mother, a renowned painter who emigrated from Japan to Brazil, mounts interesting photography and design-related exhibitions. The café serves a deservedly popular Sunday brunch. ⊠ *Av. Brigadeiro Faria Lima 201, Pinheiros* ☎ *011/2245–1900* ⊕ *www.institutotomieohtake. org.br* ⊠ *Free* ☉ *Tues.–Sun. 11–8* Ⓜ *Faria Lima.*

FAMILY **Jardim Botânico.** A great spot for a midday picnic, the Botanical Gardens contain about 3,000 plants belonging to more than 340 native species. Orchids, aquatic plants, and Atlantic rain-forest species thrive in the gardens' greenhouses. ■**TIP→ The hundred-plus bird species that have been observed at Jardim Botânico make it a favorite stopover of São Paulo birders.** ⊠ *Av. Miguel Stéfano 3031, Água Funda, Parque do Estado* ☎ *011/5073–6300* ⊕ *www.ibot.sp.gov.br* ⊠ *R$5* ☉ *Tues.–Sun. 9–5.*

WHERE TO EAT

São Paulo's dynamic social scene centers on dining out, and among the 12,500-plus restaurants, most of the world's cuisines are covered. The most popular options include Portuguese, Japanese, Italian, French, and Lebanese; contemporary fusions are popular and plentiful. The city also offers a massive selection of pizza and hamburger joints with some world-class offerings. Most places don't require jacket and tie, but paulistanos tend to dress to European standards, so if you're going to pricey establishments, looking elegant is key.

On the domestic front the Brazilian *churrascarias* are a carnivore's dream, with their all-you-can-eat skewers of barbecued meats and impressive salad buffets. For in-between times, just about every bar will offer a selection of grilled meats, sandwiches, and deep-fried favorites for casual grazing. On Wednesday and Saturday, head to a Brazilian restaurant for *feijoada*—the national dish of black beans and pork. Ask about the other traditional and regional Brazilian dishes as well. *Prices in the reviews are the average cost of a main course at dinner or, if dinner is not served, at lunch.*

STARCHITECT

World-famous paulistano landscape architect Roberto Burle Marx (1909–94) is responsible for the design of many of São Paulo's top sites, including a host of contemplative gardens and parks. Also an artist, ecologist, and naturalist, Burle Marx has been honored by the naming of a beautiful park in the Morumbi region southwest of the city: Parque Burle Marx features a number of weaving tracks among thick Atlantic Forest as well some fine examples of his design work.

4

BIXIGA

$$$$
ITALIAN
✗ **Cantina Roperto.** Wine casks and bottles adorn the walls at this typical Bixiga cantina, located on a street so charmingly human-scaled you'll hardly believe you're still in São Paulo. You won't be alone if you order the ever-popular fusilli—either *ao sugo* (with tomato sauce) or *ao frutos do mar* (with seafood)—or the traditional baby goat's leg with potatoes and tomatoes. Ⓢ *Average main: R$85 ☒ Rua 13 de Maio 634, Bixiga ☎ 011/3288-2573 ⊕ www.cantinaroperto.com.br* Ⓜ *Brigadeiro ✦ E3.*

$$
ITALIAN
✗ **Lazzerella.** Generous portions at reasonable prices and live music—that's the Lazzerella way. The cantina, a classic Italian joint founded in 1970, is hardly extravagant, but the rich flavors of a meal here and the Neapolitan stylings of the crooners circling among the red-and-white checkered tabletops linger in memory. The signature house lasagna dish, made old-style with ground beef and mozzarella in a Bolognese sauce, is meal enough for two. All the pastas here are worth a try. Ⓢ *Average main: R$40 ☒ Rua Treze de Maio 589, Bixiga ☎ 011/3289-3000 ⊕ www.lazzarella.com.br ✦ E3.*

$$$$
PIZZA
✗ **Speranza.** One of the most traditional pizzerias in São Paulo, this restaurant is famous for its margherita pie. In 2010, Speranza became the first pizzeria in Latin America to win recognition from the Italian pizza quality control board Associazione Verace Pizza Napoletana. The crunchy *pão de linguiça* (sausage bread) appetizers have a fine reputation as well. Pastas and chicken and beef dishes are also served. Ⓢ *Average main: R$70 ☒ Rua 13 de Maio 1004, Bela Vista ☎ 011/3288-8502 ⊕ www.pizzaria.com.br ✍ Reservations not accepted ✦ E3.*

$$$$
BRAZILIAN
✗ **Templo da Carne Marcos Bassi.** The brainchild of Marcos Bassi, a former butcher turned restaurateur and radio host, Templo da Carne (Temple of Meat) makes no bones about its specialty. *Contrafilé* (sirloin) and famed Brazilian *picanha* (rump cap) are among the highlights. Unlike at all-you-can-eat churrascarias, dining here is an à la carte experience. The

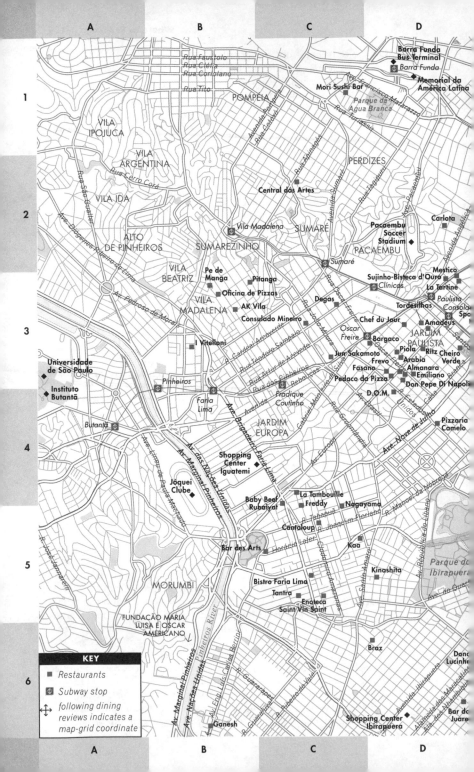

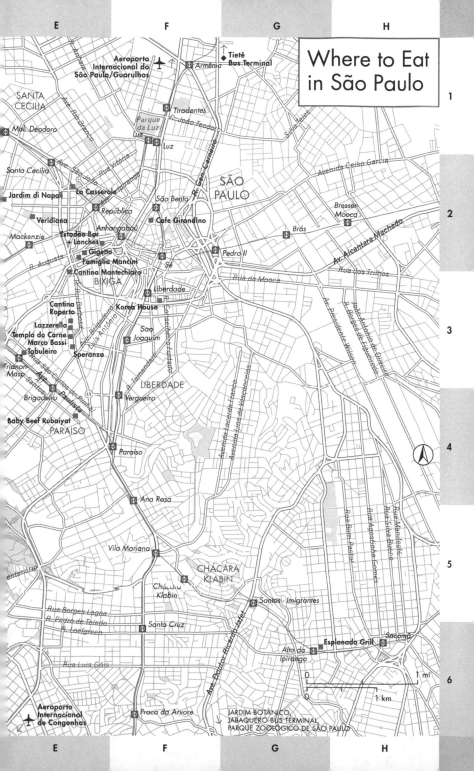

Where to Eat in São Paulo

E **F** **G** **H**

1

↑ Tietê
Bus Terminal

Aeroporto
Internacional do
São Paulo/Guarulhos

Armênia

SANTA
CECÍLIA

Mal. Deodoro

Tiradentes
João Teodoro

Parque
da Luz

Luz

Luz

Avenida Celso Garcia

Santa Cecília

Rua Vitória

2

SÃO
PAULO

Jardim di Napoli   La Casserole

São Bento

Bresser
Mooca

República

Café Girondino

Veridiana

Anhangabaú

Brás

Mackenzie

Estadão Bar
+ Lanches

Gigetto

Pedro II

Av. Alcântara Machada

Famiglia Mancini

Sé

Rua dos Trilhos

Cantina Montechiaro

BIXIGA

Rua da Mooca

Liberdade

3

Cantina
Roperto

Korea House

Lazzerella

São
Joaquim

Templo do Carne
Marco Bassi
Tabuleiro

Speranza

Trianon
Masp

LIBERDADE

Brigadeiro

Vergueiro

Baby Beef Rubaiyat

4

PARAÍSO

Paraíso

Ana Rosa

Vila Mariana

5

CHÁCARA
KLABIN

Chácara
Klabin

Santos - Imigrantes

Rua Borges Lagoa
R. Pedro de Toledo

Santa Cruz

R. Loefgreen

Esplanada Grill

Sacomã

Alto do
Ipiranga

Rua Luís Góis

0   1 mi

6

0   10 km

Aeroporto
Internacional
de Congonhas

Praça da Árvore

JARDIM BOTÂNICO,
JABAQUERO BUS TERMINAL,
PARQUE ZOOLÓGICO DE SÃO PAULO

E **F** **G** **H**

decor departs from the nostalgic interiors found in Bixiga's surrounding Italian cantinas without entirely abandoning the neighborhood's traditional coziness. ■ **TIP→ The wait for a table regularly exceeds an hour, so try to arrive before your hunger peaks.** [$] *Average main: R$150* ✉ *Rua. Treze de Maio 668, Bixiga* ☎ *011/3288–7045* 🌐 *www.marcosbassi.com.br* ✍ *Reservations essential* ⏲ *No dinner Sun.* ✣ *E3.*

CENTRO

$$ CAFÉ

🍴 **Café Girondino.** Photos of old São Paulo, a winding wooden bannister, and antique light fixtures transport Café Girondino's patrons back to the trolley-car era. On the ground floor is a coffee shop known for its espresso drinks and the wildly flavorful Miguel Couto (ice cream, espresso, bourbon, whipped cream, and cinnamon). Typical café fare and mouth-watering desserts are also served—the *arroz doce* (rice pudding) is among the city's best. A saloon occupies the second floor, and a full restaurant is on the third. [$] *Average main: R$30* ✉ *Rua Boa Vista 365, Centro* ☎ *011/3229–1287, 011/3229–4574* 🌐 *www.cafegirondino.com.br* ⏲ *Closes Sat. evening at 8, Sun. at 7* [M] *São Bento* ✣ *F2.*

$ DELI

🍴 **Estadão Bar & Lanches.** Quests for quick, cheap, and good food should start near São Paulo's origins at this greasy spoon that's open 24 hours a day. Estadão's recipe for staying in business for more than four decades is its succulent *pernil* (roast pork) sandwich, a staple of the local street-food scene. Depending on the hour, the clientele ranges from partygoers and bohemians to politicians and bus drivers. [$] *Average main: R$20* ✉ *Av. Nove de Julho 193, Centro* ☎ *011/3257–7121* 🌐 *www.estadaolanches.com.br* ✍ *Reservations not accepted* [M] *Anhangabau* ✣ *E2.*

$$$$ ITALIAN Fodor's Choice ★

🍴 **Famiglia Mancini.** This busy little cantina is well loved for both its cuisine and location. It's on an unforgettable restaurant-lined strip of Rua Avandhandava, where you may find yourself admiring the cobblestones on the street as you wait for a table. An incredible buffet with cheeses, olives, sausages, and much more makes finding a tasty appetizer a cinch. The menu has many terrific pasta options, such as the cannelloni with palm hearts and a four-cheese sauce. All dishes serve two people. [$] *Average main: R$80* ✉ *Rua Avanhandava 81, Bela Vista* ☎ *011/3256–4320* 🌐 *www.famigliamancini.com.br* ✍ *Reservations not accepted* [M] *Anhangabaú* ✣ *E2.*

$$$$ ITALIAN

🍴 **Gigetto.** When the menu of this São Paulo classic was slimmed down a few years back, dedicated locals successfully lobbied to have its more than 150 delicious options restored. Try the cappelletti *à romanesca* (pasta with chopped ham, peas, mushrooms, and white cream sauce) or osso buco with polenta. Main courses serve two people. [$] *Average main: R$70* ✉ *Rua Avanhandava 63, Centro* ☎ *011/3256–9804* 🌐 *www.gigetto.com.br* [M] *Anhangabaú* ✣ *E2.*

$$$$ FRENCH

🍴 **La Casserole.** Facing a little Centro flower market, this romantic Parisian-style bistro has been around for five decades and has witnessed more than its share of wedding proposals. Surrounded by wood-paneled walls decorated with art that nods at famous French artists, you can dine on such delights as *gigot d'agneau aux soissons* (roast leg of lamb in its own juices, served with white beans) and cherry strudel. [$] *Average main: R$90* ✉ *Largo do Arouche 346, Centro* ☎ *011/3331–6283* 🌐 *www.lacasserole.com.br* ⏲ *Closed Mon. No lunch Sat. No dinner Sun.* [M] *República* ✣ *E2.*

CERQUEIRA CÉSAR

$$
PIZZA

✗**Pedaço da Pizza.** At one of São Paulo's few pizzerias where you can order by the slice, the options for toppings range from pepperoni and other traditional favorites to shimeji mushrooms, kale, and other innovative ingredients. ■**TIP→ Open until 4 am on Friday and Saturday night, this is a good place to stop after clubbing.** $ *Average main: R$30* ⊠ *Rua Augusta 1463, Cerqueira César* ☎ *011/3061–0004* ⊕ *www. opedacodapizza.com.br* ⊙ *No lunch Sun.* Ⓜ *Consolação* ✥ *D3.*

$$$$
BRAZILIAN

✗**Tordesilhas.** Typically Brazilian from its decor to its daily specials, rustic-elegant Tordesilhas prides itself on spotlighting recipes from across the republic. *Feijoada* (black bean and pork stew) takes center stage on Wednesday and Saturday, while a Brazilian tasting menu is served from Tuesday through Saturday. Among the daily staples you'll find *tacacá* (shrimp soup), from Brazil's northern region, and *moqueca* (fish and shrimp stew), from Espírito Santo State. $ *Average main: R$75* ⊠ *Rua Bela Cintra 465, Cerqueira César* ☎ *011/3107–7444* ⊕ *www.tordesilhas.com* ⊙ *Closed Mon.* Ⓜ *Paulista* ✥ *D3.*

4

CONSOLAÇÃO

$$
FRENCH

✗**La Tartine.** An ideal place for an intimate dinner, this small bistro has a good wine selection and an upstairs bar furnished with mismatched sofas and armchairs. The menu changes daily; a favorite is the classic coq au vin, but you can also fill up on entrées such as beef tenderloin or soups and quiches. The frogs' legs come off like a Tangier-style chicken wing. If Moroccan couscous is being served, don't pass it up. ■**TIP→ The trendy set loves La Tartine; on weekends you might have to wait a bit to get a table.** $ *Average main: R$40* ⊠ *Rua Fernando de Albuquerque 267, Consolação* ☎ *011/3259–2090* ⊙ *Closed Sun. No lunch* Ⓜ *Consolação* ✥ *D3.*

$$$$
ECLECTIC

✗**Mestiço.** Even the fabulous people have to hang at the bar before being shown to a table in this large, sleek dining room, but especially for vegetarians, dishes such as the tofu and vegetable curry make the wait worthwhile. The restaurant makes a point of using free-range chicken and other ecologically responsible ingredients. The decidedly eclectic menu includes Italian, Brazilian, Bahian, and even Thai cuisine. $ *Average main: R$70* ⊠ *Rua Fernando de Albuquerque 277, Consolação* ☎ *011/3256–3165* ⊕ *www.mestico.com.br* ⌲ *Reservations essential* Ⓜ *Consolação* ✥ *D3.*

$$
BRAZILIAN

✗**Sujinho–Bisteca d'Ouro.** Occupying corners on both sides of the street, the modest Sujinho honors its roots as an informal bar by serving churrasco without any frills: this is the perfect place for diners craving a gorgeous piece of meat to down with a cold bottle of beer. The portions are so Jurassic in size that one dish can usually feed two. ■**TIP→ Sujinho stays open until 5 am, making it a leading stop on the post-bar circuit.** $ *Average main: R$35* ⊠ *Rua da Consolação 2078, Cerqueira César* ☎ *011/3231–1299* ⊕ *www.sujinho.com.br* ⊟ *No credit cards* Ⓜ *Consolação or Paulista* ✥ *D3.*

HIGIENÓPOLIS

$$$$ CONTEMPORARY 🍴 **Carlota.** TV host, author, and chef Carla Pernambuco introduces Brazilian elements to a multicultural array of recipes at her popular restaurant. The four-cheese polenta and the red-rice risotto with lobster are among the many well-calibrated dishes served here. All-white brick walls outside and inside lend Carlota a soothing, stylish feel. The clientele, befitting the neighborhood's demographics, tends to be older than elsewhere in town. ■ **TIP→ Save room for the signature dessert, a guava jam soufflé with melted-cheese sauce.** [$] *Average main: R$110* ✉ *Rua Sergipe 753, Higienópolis* ☎ *011/3661–8670* 🌐 *carlota.com.br* ⏲ *No dinner Sun. Dinner only Mon.* ✣ *D2.*

$$$$ ITALIAN 🍴 **Jardim di Napoli.** The classic neon sign that adorns this restaurant's exterior cues diners about what to expect inside: traditional Italian cuisine. No surprises here, but dishes such as the unchanging and unmatchable *polpettone alla parmigiana,* a huge meatball with mozzarella and tomato sauce, inspire devotion among the local clientele. Many other meat dishes can be found on the menu, along with pastas and pizzas. [$] *Average main: R$80* ✉ *Rua Doutor Martinico Prado 463, Higienópolis* ☎ *011/3666–3022* 🌐 *www.jardimdenapoli.com.br* ✣ *E2.*

$$$$ PIZZA Fodor's Choice ★ 🍴 **Veridiana.** Owner Roberto Loscalzo transformed a 1903 mansion into a remarkable dining space; expansive yet intimate, grandiose yet welcoming. At one end of the room chefs pull Napoli-style pizzas from the three mouths of a two-story brick oven that looms over diners like a cathedral organ. Different place-names lead to different taste combinations: Napoli in Beruit blends goat cheese and *za'atar*, a spice mixture that includes herbs and sesame seeds, while Napoli in Brasili contains sun-dried meat and Catupiry, the creamy Brazilian cheese invented in Minas Gerais a century ago. If you don't feel like globe-trotting, go for the Do Nonno, topped with juicy grilled tomatoes. A sister branch of Veridiana operates in the Jardins neighborhood. ■ **TIP→ The Higienópolis location is not well marked. The restaurant is directly across from the Iate Clube (Yacht Club) de Santos.** [$] *Average main: R$60* ✉ *Rua Dona Veridiana 661, Higienópolis* ☎ *011/3120–5050* 🌐 *www.veridiana.com.br* ⏲ *Closed Sun. No lunch* [M] *Santa Cecilia* [$] *Average main: R$60* ✉ *Rua José Maria Lisboa 493, Jardim Paulista* ☎ *011/3559–9151* ⏲ *No lunch* ✣ *E2.*

ITAIM BIBI

$$$$ BRAZILIAN 🍴 **Baby Beef Rubaiyat.** The family that owns and runs this restaurant serves meat from their ranch in Mato Grosso do Sul State. Charcoal-grilled fare—baby boar (on request at least two hours in advance), steak, chicken, salmon, and more—is served at the buffet, and a salad bar has all sorts of options. Wednesday and Saturday are feijoada nights, and on Friday the emphasis is on seafood. [$] *Average main: R$130* ✉ *Alameda Santos 86, Vila Mariana* ☎ *011/3170–5100* 🌐 *www.rubaiyat.com.br* ⏲ *No dinner Sun.* [M] *Paraíso* ✣ *E4* [$] *Average main: R$130* ✉ *Av. Brigadeiro Faria Lima 2954, Itaim Bibi* ☎ *011/3165–8888* 🌐 *www.rubaiyat.com.br* ⏲ *No dinner Sun.* [M] *Faria Lima* ✣ *C4.*

$$$$
ECLECTIC

$\times$ **Bar des Arts.** A great place for lunch or drinks and a favorite with business people, Bar des Arts is in a charming arcade with plenty of outdoor seating. Try the artichoke-filled ravioli in sage-and-tomato butter, or choose from the ample sushi menu. $ *Average main: R$110* ⊠ *Rua Pedro Humberto 9, at Rua Horacio Lafer, Itaim Bibi* ☏ *011/3074–6363* ⊕ *www.bardesarts.com.br* ⊗ *No dinner Sun.* ✛ *C5.*

> **MEAL TIME**
>
> Eating out in São Paulo can be an all-night affair, so most restaurants open late and close even later. The majority will officially throw their doors open around 8 pm but will only get busy after 9 pm, regardless of what day it is. Try a bar that has a good happy hour if you want to eat earlier.

4

$$
BRAZILIAN

$\times$ **Bar do Juarez.** With the look of an old-style saloon, Bar do Juarez has won awards for its draft beers and buffet of *petiscos* (small tapas-like dishes), but *picanha* (rump cap of beef) is this gastropub's calling card. Served raw on a mini-grill, the platter is perfect for small groups and gives individuals direct control over how their meat is done. Bow-tied waiters with A-plus attentiveness add to Juarez's appeal. The Itaim location is the best of four in the city, with the Moema, Pinheiros, and Brooklin houses coming close. $ *Average main: R$45* ⊠ *Av. Pres. Juscelino Kubitschek 1164, Itaim Bibi* ☏ *011/3078–3458* ⊕ *www.bardojuarez.com.br* ⊗ *No lunch weekdays* ✛ *D6.*

$$$$
EUROPEAN

$\times$ **Cantaloup.** That paulistanos take food seriously has not been lost on the folks at Cantaloup. The converted warehouse has two dining areas: oversize photos decorate the walls of the slightly formal room, while a fountain and plants make the second area feel more casual. Try the veal cutlet with blinis of yuca or the stuffed shrimp with clams. Save room for macerated strawberries in port wine sauce or a particularly velvety crème brûlée with ice cream. $ *Average main: R$110* ⊠ *Rua Manoel Guedes 474, Itaim Bibi* ☏ *011/3078–9884, 011/3078–3445* ⊕ *www.cantaloup.com.br* ⊗ *No dinner Sun.* ✛ *C5.*

$$$$
FRENCH

$\times$ **Freddy.** A pioneer in bringing French cuisine to São Paulo, Freddy opened originally in 1935. Despite moving from its original location, Freddy has managed to retain the feel of an upscale Parisian bistro, thanks to a number of small touches as well as some larger ones, like the grand chandeliers hanging from its ceiling. Try the duck with Madeira sauce and apple puree, coq au vin, or the hearty cassoulet with white beans, lamb, duck, and garlic sausage. $ *Average main: R$90* ⊠ *Rua Pedroso Alvarenga 1170, Itaim Bibi* ☏ *011/3167–0977* ⊕ *www.restaurantefreddy.com.br* ⊗ *No dinner Sun. No lunch Sat.* ✛ *C5.*

$$$$
ECLECTIC

$\times$ **La Tambouille.** This Italo-French restaurant with a partially enclosed garden isn't just a place for businesspeople and impresarios to see and be seen; it also has some of the best food in town. Among chef Giancarlo Bolla's recommended dishes are the linguine with fresh mussels and prawn sauce and the filet mignon *rosini* (served with foie gras and saffron risotto). $ *Average main: R$120* ⊠ *Av. Nove de Julho 5925, Itaim Bibi* ☏ *011/3079–6277, 011/3079–6276* ⊕ *www.tambouille.com.br* ✛ *C4.*

$$$$ JAPANESE **✕Nagayama.** Low-key, trustworthy, and well loved, Nagayama consistently serves excellent sushi and sashimi. The chefs like to experiment: the California *uramaki* Philadelphia has rice, cream cheese, grilled salmon, roe, cucumber, and spring onions rolled together. [$] *Average main: R$110 ✉ Rua Bandeira Paulista 369, Itaim Bibi ☎ 011/3079–7553 🌐 www.nagayama.com.br 🕒 Closed Sun.* [$] *Average main: R$110 ✉ Rua da Consolação 3397, Jardins ☎ 011/3064–0110 🌐 www.nagayama.com.br 🕒 Dinner only. Closed Sun. ✥ C5.*

A TASTE OF LEBANON

While in São Paulo, be sure to try a *beirute,* a Lebanese sandwich served hot on toasted Syrian bread and filled with roast beef, cheese, lettuce, and tomato. Another quick bite from Lebanon that has established itself in the city is *esfiha,* an open-faced pastry topped with cheese or spiced meat. Fast-food restaurants serving these snacks are scattered around the city.

JARDINS

$$ LEBANESE **✕Almanara.** Part of a chain of Lebanese semi-fast-food outlets, Almanara is perfect for a quick lunch of hummus, tabbouleh, grilled chicken, and rice. A full-blown restaurant also on the premises offers up Lebanese specialties *rodízio* style, meaning you're served continuously until you can ingest no more. [$] *Average main: R$40 ✉ Rua Oscar Freire 523, Jardins ☎ 011/3085–6916 🌐 www.almanara.com.br ✥ D3.*

$$$$ SEAFOOD **✕Amadeus.** Because São Paulo isn't on the ocean, most restaurants here don't base their reputations on seafood, but Amadeus is an exception. Appetizers such as fresh oysters and salmon and endive with mustard, and entrées like shrimp in cognac sauce make it a challenge to find better fruits of the sea elsewhere in town. The restaurant is popular with the business-lunch crowd. [$] *Average main: R$100 ✉ Rua Haddock Lobo 807, Jardins ☎ 011/3061–2859 🌐 restauranteamadeus.com.br 🕒 No dinner weekends* [M] *Consolação ✥ D3.*

$$$$ LEBANESE **✕Arábia.** For almost 20 years Arábia has served traditional Lebanese cuisine at this beautiful high-ceilinged restaurant. Simple dishes such as hummus and stuffed grape leaves are executed with aplomb. The lamb melts in your mouth. Meat-stuffed artichokes are great for sharing, and the reasonably priced "executive" lunch menu includes one appetizer, one cold dish, one meat dish, a drink, dessert, and coffee. **■ TIP→ Don't miss the crepelike ataife, filled with pistachio nuts or cream, for dessert.** [$] *Average main: R$80 ✉ Rua Haddock Lobo 1397, Jardins ☎ 011/3061–2203 🌐 www.arabia.com.br ✥ D3.*

$$$ ECLECTIC **✕Chef du Jour.** Despite the name, there's indeed a permanent chef installed here: Renato Frias, who hails from the state of Pernambuco, though his cuisine straddles France and Italy. Take your pick from a vast buffet with more than 30 different salads, along with sushi, risottos and pastas, and fish and meat dishes. Colorful tiles decorate the spacious dining room. [$] *Average main: R$50 ✉ Rua da Consolação 3101, Jardins ☎ 011/3845–6843 🕒 No dinner. Closed Sun. ✥ D3.*

$$ VEGETARIAN 🍴 **Cheiro Verde.** A São Paulo pioneer in meat-free dining, Cheiro Verde has attracted a devoted following over the past three decades for its simple but tasty vegetarian fare. (One couple fancied the restaurant so much they ended up buying it.) Whole-wheat mushroom pasta and delicious empanadas are among the many good bets here. [$] *Average main: R$35* ✉ *Rua Peixoto Gomide 1078, Jardim Paulista* ☎ *011/3289–6853* 🌐 *www.cheiroverderestaurante.com.br* 🕑 *No dinner* [M] *Trianon-MASP* ✥ *D3.*

$$$$ CONTEMPORARY 🍴 **D.O.M.** Regularly named among the best restaurants in South America and the world, D.O.M. is synonymous with exclusivity in São Paulo's gastronomic circles—its popularity is limited only by a self-imposed cap on the number of customers served. Prices that would make Shylock blush help bolster D.O.M.'s regal reputation. Celebrity chef Alex Atala stresses fare with a Brazilian flair, such as *filhote* (Amazonian catfish) with tapioca in *tucupi* sauce and sweet potato in a maté Béarnaise. ■ **TIP→ Try the tapas-esque tasting menu for the full experience. And make your reservations at least a week in advance.** [$] *Average main: R$250* ✉ *Rua Barão de Capanema 549, Jardins* ☎ *011/3088–0761* 🌐 *www.domrestaurante.com.br* ✍ *Reservations essential* 🕑 *Closed Sun. No dinner Sat.* ✥ *D4.*

$$$ BRAZILIAN 🍴 **Dona Lucinha.** Mineiro dishes are the specialties at this modest eatery with plain wooden tables. The classic cuisine is served as a buffet only: more than 50 stone pots hold dishes like *feijão tropeiro* (beans with manioc flour) and *frango com quiabo* (chicken with okra). Save room for a dessert of ambrosia. The menu is in English, French, and Spanish. [$] *Average main: R$58* ✉ *Av. Chibarás 399, Moema* ☎ *011/5051–2050* 🌐 *www.donalucinha.com.br* 🕑 *Closed Mon. No dinner Sun.* ✥ *D6.*

$$$$ ITALIAN 🍴 **Don Pepe Di Napoli.** Good and simple Italian food is what you'll find at this traditional spot. Choose from a great variety of pastas, salads, and meat dishes. A good option is *talharina a Don Pepe,* pasta with meat, broccoli, and garlic. [$] *Average main: R$80* ✉ *Rua Padre Joao Manoel 1104, Jardins* ☎ *011/3081–4080* 🌐 *www.donpepedinapoli.com.br* ✥ *D3.*

$$$$ ITALIAN 🍴 **Fasano.** A family-owned northern Italian classic subtly ensconced within the elegantly modern lobby of the hotel of the same name, this restaurant is as famous for its superior cuisine as for its exorbitant prices. Luca Gozzani added more seafood dishes to the menu after replacing longtime chef Salvatore Loi in 2012. The luxe decor oozes class—marble, mahogany, and mirrors, all crowned by a breathtaking skylight—and suggests that proof of one's captainship of industry or other such mastery of the universe must be shown at the door for entrance. [$] *Average main: R$180* ✉ *Rua Vittorio Fasano 88, Jardins* ☎ *011/3062–4000* 🌐 *www.fasano.com.br* ✍ *Reservations essential* 🕑 *Closed Sun. No lunch* ✥ *D3.*

$$ BRAZILIAN 🍴 **Frevo.** Paulistanos of all types and ages flock to this luncheonette on the stylish Rua Oscar Freire for its *beirute* sandwiches, filled with ham and cheese, tuna, or chicken, and for its draft beer and fruit juices in flavors such as *acerola* (Antilles cherry), passion fruit, and papaya. [$] *Average main: R$35* ✉ *Rua Oscar Freire 603, Jardins* ☎ *011/3082–3434, 011/4003–2665 delivery* 🌐 *www.frevinho.com.br* ✥ *D3.*

$$$
PIZZA
✗Piola. Part of a chain started in Italy, this restaurant serves pizzas loaded with toppings like Gorgonzola, Brie, ham, salami, mushrooms, and anchovies. It also has good pasta dishes, like the penne with smoked salmon in a creamy tomato sauce. The young, hip crowd matches the trendy contemporary decor, and there's also a place for kids to play while the grown-ups finish their meals. $ *Average main: R$65* ✉ *Alameda Lorena 1765, Jardins* ☎ *011/3064–6570, 011/3061–2221 delivery* ⊕ *www.piola.com.br* ☾ *No lunch* ✛ *D3.*

$$$
PIZZA
✗Pizzaria Camelo. Though it's neither fancy nor beautiful, Pizzaria Camelo has kept paulistanos enthralled for ages with its many thin-crust pies. The *chopp* (draft beer) is great, too. Avoid Sunday night unless you're willing to wait an hour for a table. $ *Average main: R$60* ✉ *Rua Pamplona 1873, Jardins* ☎ *011/3887–8764* ⊕ *www.pizzariacamelo.com.br* ☾ *No lunch* ✛ *D4.*

$$$
ECLECTIC
✗Ritz. An animated, gay-friendly crowd chatters at this restaurant with Italian, Brazilian, French, and mixed cuisine, as contemporary pop music plays in the background. Although Ritz serves some of the best hamburgers in the city, another popular dish is *bife à milanesa* (breaded beef cutlet) with creamed spinach and french fries. $ *Average main: R$58* ✉ *Alameda Franca 1088, Jardins* ☎ *011/3088–6808 delivery, 011/3062–5830* ⊕ *www.restauranteritz.com.br* Ⓜ *Consolação* ✛ *D3.*

> **PURPLE POWER**
>
> Açaí, an antioxidant-rich super fruit, has recently made its way to juice bars around the world. Don't miss your chance to get it close to the source, where it's cheaper and purer than the versions you'll find back home. Always frozen, scoops of it are blended together with syrup of the energy-filled guaraná berry. The most popular way to get it is *na tigela*, in a glass bowl with bananas and granola, though juice stands dedicated to the fruit should serve up a pure milkshake-thick *suco* (juice) as well.

LIBERDADE

$$
KOREAN
✗Korea House. Camper cooking meets Korean at this Liberdade mainstay. For the *bul go gui* (Korean barbecue), diners blend raw meat, spices, sauces, and veggies and cook them over small, do-it-yourself gas stoves. One order feeds two. You can prepare other Korean dishes, and there are Chinese options, including several involving tofu. Everything is reasonably priced. The design is unimpressive but the atmosphere is lively, with hipsters and gringos sprinkled among neighborhood residents. $ *Average main: R$30* ✉ *Rua Galvão Bueno 43, 1° andar, Liberdade* ☎ *011/3208–3052* Ⓜ *Liberdade* ✛ *F3.*

MOEMA

$$$
PIZZA
Fodor$Choice
★
✗Bráz. This restaurant's name comes from one of the most traditional Italian neighborhoods in São Paulo, and no one argues that Bráz doesn't have the right. The pies are of a medium thickness with high, bubbly crusts. And each of the nearly 20 varieties is delicious, from the traditional margherita to the house specialty, pizza *Bráz*, with tomato sauce, zucchini, and mozzarella and Parmesan cheeses.

The *chopp* (draft beer) is also very good. Reservations aren't accepted on weekends. [$] *Average main: R$60* ✉ *Rua Graúna 125, Moema* ☎ *011/5561–1736* 🌐 *www.brazpizzaria.com.br* ⏲ *No lunch* ✥ *D6.*

$$$$ JAPANESE Fodor's Choice ★ 🍴 **Kinoshita.** Contemporary Japanese plates with international influences are the draw at Kinoshita, where foie gras might accompany a Kobe beef hamburger or truffles might enliven salmon roe and shellfish. The freshness of the ingredients available on any given day determines the fare of chef Tsuyoshi Murakami, one of São Paulo's culinary superstars. Geishas serve guests in the Krug Room (available only for groups of 6 to 12), where slippers replace shoes and diners sit on floor mats. ■ **TIP→ For a real, if pricey, treat opt for one of the omakase (tasting) menus—seven or nine courses, plus dessert—and let chef Muramami decide what you eat.** [$] *Average main: R$200* ✉ *Rua Jacques Félix 405, Moema* ☎ *011/3849–6940, 011/5318–9014* 🌐 *restaurantekinoshita.com.br* ✍ *Reservations essential* ⏲ *Closed Sun.* ✥ *D5.*

> **WOK THIS WAY**
>
> In a street-food scene dominated by hamburgers and hot dogs, Yakisoba stands out—keep an eye peeled for the spectacle of stir-fried noodles tossed over an open flame in the middle of the crowded sidewalk. Another delicious option is homemade espetinhos or *churrascos,* wooden kebabs of beef, chicken, or pork whose juices send towers of fragrant smoke into the air. A calmer alternative is the corn cart. Rather than on the cob, try *pamonha,* steam-cooked sweetened cornmeal wrapped in a husk, or *curau,* sweet creamed corn.

4

MORUMBI

$$$$ BRAZILIAN 🍴 **Esplanada Grill.** The beautiful people hang out in the bar of this highly regarded churrascaria. The thinly sliced *picanha* (similar to rump steak) is excellent; it goes well with a house salad (hearts of palm and shredded, fried potatoes), onion rings, and creamed spinach. The version of the traditional *pão de queijo* (cheese bread) served here is widely viewed as among the city's best. [$] *Average main: R$90* ✉ *Morumbi Shopping Center, Av. Roque Petroni Jr. 1089, Morumbi* ☎ *011/5181–8156* ✥ *G6.*

$$$$ INDIAN 🍴 **Ganesh.** A good choice for vegetarians—but with plenty of dishes to satisfy meat lovers—this unassuming restaurant in a shopping center has a traditional menu that includes curries and tandoori dishes from many regions of India. Indian artwork and tapestries fill the interior. [$] *Average main: R$100* ✉ *Morumbi Shopping Center, Av. Roque Petroni Jr. 1089, Morumbi* ☎ *011/5181–4748* 🌐 *www.ganesh.com.br* ✥ *B6.*

PINHEIROS

$$$ BRAZILIAN 🍴 **Consulado Mineiro.** During and after the Saturday crafts and antiques fair in Praça Benedito Calixto, it may take an hour to get a table at this homey restaurant. Among the traditional *mineiro* (from Minas Gerais State) dishes are the *mandioca com carne de sol* (cassava with salted meat) appetizer and the *tutu* (pork loin with beans, pasta, cabbage, and rice) entrée. The cachaça menu is extensive, with rare,

premium, and homemade brands of the sugarcane-based spirits, and several types of *batidas* (fruit-and-alcohol mixtures) and caipirinhas are served. Ⓢ *Average main: R$50* ✉ *Rua Praça Benedito Calixto 74, Pinheiros* ☎ *011/3064–3882* ⊕ *www.consuladomineiro.com. br* ⊘ *Closed Mon.* ✉ *Rua Cônego Eugenio Leite 504, Pinheiros* ☎ *011/3898–3241, 011/3476–9556* ⊕ *www.consuladomineiro.com. br* ⊘ *No dinner Sun.* ✛ *C3.*

$$ ✕ **Degas.** Humble-looking Degas owes its more than 50 years in existence to word of mouth among the residents of São Paulo's western
ITALIAN
FAMILY
neighborhoods. Its famed filet mignon Parmigiana has gained near-legendary status, attracting foodies from across the city. The dish, along with almost anything else on the menu, easily feeds two, if not a family of four. Even the salads seem to be small vegetable gardens on a platter. Lunchtime usually brings a business crowd. Dinner, when the restaurant fires up its pizza ovens, is more of a family affair. Ⓢ *Average main: R$40* ✉ *Rua Teodoro Sampaio 568, Pinheiros* ☎ *011/3062–1276, 011/3085–3545* ⊕ *www.degasrestaurante.com.br* Ⓜ *Clinicas* ✛ *C3.*

$$$ ✕ **I Vitelloni.** At perhaps the most creative pizza restaurant in town,
PIZZA
owner Hamilton Mello Júnior combines disparate ingredients for his specialty pies, while serving up tasty classics as well. In the Pinheiros neighborhood, lively at night, the restaurant sits on a quiet residential street, away from the sidewalk bars an avenue away, so it's prized by locals and well worth searching out. We recommend the authentic rucola pie. There's a stand-up bar outside that's a nice place to finish your drinks before you head off. Ⓢ *Average main: R$50* ✉ *Rua Conde Sílvio Álvares Penteado 31, Pinheiros* ☎ *011/3819–0735* ⊕ *www.ivitelloni. com.br* ⊘ *No lunch. Closed Mon.* ✛ *B3.*

$$$$ ✕ **Jun Sakamoto.** Arguably the best Japanese restaurant in a town
JAPANESE
famous for them, Jun Sakamoto stands out for serving fish of the highest quality and for employing the most skillful of sushi chefs to slice them. This is haute gastronomy at its haughtiest. You're best served if you let the waiters wearing futuristic earpieces guide you through the menu based on what's freshest the day you visit. Ⓢ *Average main: R$150* ✉ *Rua Lisboa 55, Pinheiros* ☎ *011/3088–6019* ⊘ *No lunch. Closed Sun.* ✛ *C3.*

POMPÉIA

$$ ✕ **Central das Artes.** Come for the view, stay for the crepes. Or vice
ECLECTIC
versa. A back wall made of windows faces out to a verdant valley and, beyond that, Avenida Paulista. The panorama makes Central das Artes a popular place to grab drinks as well. Crepes are named for famous artists. The Cocteau, with salmon, shiitake, and cream, is as smooth on the taste buds as its namesake was with the written word. Ⓢ *Average main: R$30* ✉ *Rua Apinajés 1081, Pompéia* ☎ *011/3865–0116* ⊕ *www. centraldasartes.com.br* ⊘ *No lunch Sun.* ✛ *C2.*

$$$ ✕ **Mori Sushi Bar.** Sit at the counter for a bottomless supply of fresh
SUSHI
cuts. The service recalls your college dive-bar days, as sushi is served directly off the bar (no plates) in front of you. The sushi guys get creative with fish, fruit, and spices, but they also respond to individual

preferences, so don't be shy about stating yours. ■ **TIP→ Ask to start with a plate of thinly sliced salmon sashimi in soy sauce, lemon juice, olive oil, and hot sauce.** [$] *Average main: R$60* ✉ *Melo Palheta 284, Pompéia* ☎ *011/3872–0976, 011/3676–1917* 🌐 *www.morisushi1.com.br* ⏲ *Closed Sun.* ✥ *C1.*

VILA MADALENA

$$$$ CONTEMPORARY

🍴 **AK Vila.** Putting a premium on freshness, chef Andrea Kaufmann shifts her menu weekly to keep pace with seasonal ingredients. Her restaurant's multicultural, contemporary cuisine ranges from salads and sandwiches to ceviche and octopus couscous. The chef made her name cooking Jewish favorites, and she often makes room on her menu for bagels or salads with smoked salmon. A touch of the burlesque softens AK Vila's industrial-sleek design. ■ **TIP→ On nice nights, sit outside and soak in the Vila Madalena scene.** [$] *Average main: R$75* ✉ *Rua Fradique Coutinho 1240, Vila Madalena* ☎ *011/3231–4496, 011/3231–4497* 🌐 *www.akvila.com.br* ⏲ *No dinner Sun.* ✥ *B3.*

$$ PIZZA

🍴 **Oficina de Pizzas.** Both branches of this restaurant look like something designed by the Spanish architect Gaudí had he spent his later years in the tropics, but the pizzas couldn't be more Italian and straightforward. Try a pie with mozzarella and toasted garlic. [$] *Average main: R$40* ✉ *Rua Purpurina 517, Vila Madalena* ☎ *011/3816–3749* 🌐 *www.oficinadepizzas.com.br* ⏲ *No lunch weekends* [$] *Average main: R$40* ✉ *Rua Inácio Pereira da Rocha 15, Vila Madalena* ☎ *011/3813–8389* 🌐 *www.oficinadepizzas.com.br* ⏲ *No lunch weekends* ✥ *B3.*

$$ BRAZILIAN

🍴 **Pé de Manga.** The restaurant's name and charm come from a massive mango tree. Tables surrounding the trunk spread across a shaded patio, which is usually packed with professionals in their 30s and 40s. A two-story covered seating area lends the whole affair a Robinson Crusoe touch. High-end, Brazilian-style pub grub pad stomachs for Pé de Manga's beers and exotic cocktails. The *feijoada* (black bean and pork stew) buffet is a top option on Saturdays. [$] *Average main: R$40* ✉ *Rua Arapiraca 152, Vila Madalena* ☎ *011/3032–6068* 🌐 *www.pedemanga.com.br* ✥ *B3.*

VILA OLÍMPIA

$$ ECLECTIC

🍴 **Bistro Faria Lima.** Known for simple, straightforward bistro fare with a Brazilian twist like *bacalhau com natas* (salted cod with cream) this place guarantees a solid sit-down meal, even if you happen to be in a hurry. If you're not, stay for the coconut cake with strawberry sauce. [$] *Average main: R$45* ✉ *Avenida Brigadeiro Faria Lima 4150, Vila Olímpia* ☎ *011/3045–4040* 🌐 *www.bistrofarialima.com.br* ✥ *C5.*

$$$$ WINE BAR

🍴 **Enoteca Saint Vin Saint.** A snug bistro on as secluded a street as you're apt to find in São Paulo's hip southern neighborhoods, Enoteca triples as a wineshop, restaurant, and live-music venue. Marble-top tables fill two rooms brimming with bottle racks, bookshelves, and bullfighting posters. Friends and thirtysomething couples toast each other with an international array of wines, many from France, Spain, Italy, and Chile.

4

The kitchen's specialty is a risotto with wine-braised beef whose taste more than compensates for its plain appearance. **■TIP➔ There's an $R15 cover for live tango, jazz, and flamenco music from Wednesday through Saturday night, but it's well worth it.** [$] *Average main: R$110* ✉ *Rua Professor Atílio Innocenti 811, Vila Olímpia* ☎ *011/3846–0384* 🌐 *www.saintvinsaint.com.br* 🕒 *Closed Sun. No lunch* ✥ *C5.*

JAPANESE FRUIT

Along with the famous Japanese cuisine, which can be found just about everywhere in São Paulo, Brazil's Japanese immigrants are credited with introducing persimmons, azaleas, tangerines, and kiwis to Brazil.

$$$$ CONTEMPORARY Fodor's Choice ★ 🍴 **Kaá.** Contemporary cuisine, attentive service, and a luxurious, secret-garden charm help Kaá maintain its status as one of São Paulo's leading fine-dining establishments. The gorgeously designed restaurant, complete with fountains, a sunken bar, and a rain forest–like wall, attracts a mostly mature and well-to-do clientele. The crayfish au gratin in endive cream is a top choice among the appetizers; appealing entrées include rack of lamb ribs and beer-cooked duck. Though the wine list is extensive, many diners opt for the signature orchid martini. [$] *Average main: R$150* ✉ *Avenida Presidente Juscelino Kubitschek 279, Vila Olímpia* ☎ *011/3045–0043* 🌐 *kaarestaurante.com.br* ✥ *C5.*

$$ BRAZILIAN 🍴 **Tabuleiro do Marconi.** Owner Marconi Silva started his little slice of Bahia by selling *acarajé* (deep-fried bean balls usually stuffed with paste made from shrimp and other ingredients) on the sidewalk in front of where his restaurant now stands. Since moving indoors, he's expanded his menu to include favorites such as *escondadinho* (a lasagna-like dish with cheese, meat, and manioc) and shrimp risotto in a coconut shell. Kitsch is this tiny eatery's other calling card: keepsakes and curios line the walls. [$] *Average main: R$45* ✉ *Rue Ribeirao Claro, 319, Vila Olímpia* ☎ *011/3846–9593* 🌐 *www.tabuleirodomarconi.com.br* ✥ *E3.*

WHERE TO STAY

São Paulo puts an emphasis on business, and for the most part so do its hotels. Most of them are near Avenida Paulista, along Marginal Pinheiros, or in the charming Jardins neighborhood, where international businesses are located. But catering to business doesn't mean they've forgotten about pleasure. On the contrary, if you're willing to pay for it, the city can match London or New York for unfettered elegance.

Because of the business influence, rates often drop on weekends. Breakfast is a sumptuous affair and is oftentimes included in the room rate. International conventions and the annual Brazilian Grand Prix in November can book hotels completely, so it's wise to make reservations in advance. *Prices in the reviews are the lowest cost of a standard double room in high season. For expanded reviews, facilities, and current deals, visit Fodors.com.*

BELA VISTA

$ ▦ **Ibis São Paulo Paulista.** This large hotel is one of the best bargains on
HOTEL Avenida Paulista. **Pros:** a nonaffiliated airport shuttle bus has a stop
next door; close to major thoroughfares. **Cons:** heavy traffic all day
long. $ *Rooms from: R$200* ⊠ *Av Paulista 2355, Bela Vista* ☎ *011/
3523–3000* ⊕ *www.accorhotels.com.br* ⇌ *236 rooms* ❖❖| *No meals*
Ⓜ *Consolação or Paulista* ✛ *D3.*

$ ▦ **Pousada dos Franceses.** On rainy days young people lounge on the
B&B/INN couches in this classic backpacker's hostel that's complete with do-it-
yourself laundry facilities and a cook-for-yourself kitchen. **Pros:** Tips
of the Week board indicates cultural happenings; close to Bixiga restaurants; owners speak perfect English. **Cons:** long, dark walk from
Paulista means taking a taxi; spartan rooms. $ *Rooms from: R$125*
⊠ *Rua Dos Franceses 100, Bela Vista* ☎ *011/3288–1592* ⊕ *www.
pousadadosfranceses.com.br* ⇌ *15 rooms* ❖❖| *Breakfast* ✛ *E3.*

$ ▦ **San Gabriel.** Expect no frills at this budget hotel in a lively neighbor-
HOTEL hood close to Avenida Paulista. **Pros:** close to malls, bars, and restaurants; in-house convenience store. **Cons:** surrounding area isn't well
lighted; room rate doesn't include breakfast; no Internet. $ *Rooms
from: R$153* ⊠ *Rua Frei Caneca 1006, Bela Vista* ☎ *011/3253–2279*
⊕ *www.sangabriel.com.br* ⇌ *75 rooms, 25 suites* ❖❖| *No meals* Ⓜ *Pau-
lista* ✛ *E3.*

BROOKLIN

$$$$ ▦ **Hilton São Paulo Morumbi.** The brightest star in Brooklin and the hot
HOTEL spot of the São Paulo business world, this venue is one of three skyscrapers that form an office park loaded with Fortune 500 companies. **Pros:**
attached by tunnel to a shopping mall; art exhibits at Canvas bar; spa
uses treatments from the Amazon. **Cons:** far from anything cultural or
historical; charge for Internet access. $ *Rooms from: R$640* ⊠ *Av.das
Nações Unidas 12901, Torre Leste, Brooklin* ☎ *011/2845–0000* ⊕ *www.
hiltonmorumbi.com.br* ⇌ *503 rooms, 13 suites* ❖❖| *Breakfast* ✛ *B6.*

CENTRO

$ ▦ **Bourbon.** Rich woodwork runs at waist level throughout the halls of
HOTEL this small, classy hotel near Praça da República. **Pros:** great location
for exploring Centro; next door to metro. **Cons:** small workstations;
Praça da República can be dodgy at night. $ *Rooms from: R$235* ⊠ *Av
Vieira de Carvalho 99, Centro* ☎ *011/3337–2000* 🖷 *011/3331-8187*
☎ *011/3337–1414* ⊕ *www.bourbon.com.br* ⇌ *127 rooms* ❖❖| *Breakfast*
Ⓜ *República* ✛ *D2.*

$$ ▦ **Novotel Jaraguá.** Built in 1951 to be the headquarters of one of the
HOTEL main newspapers in the city, the building that now houses this hotel
is a landmark in downtown São Paulo. **Pros:** pleasant rooms at good
prices; close to many restaurants and sights; 10-minute taxi ride to
Paulista. **Cons:** no pool; weak water pressure; area can be spooky
at night. $ *Rooms from: R$320* ⊠ *Rua Martins Fontes 71, Centro*
☎ *011/2802–7000* ⊕ *www.novotel.com.br* ⇌ *315 rooms, 99 suites*
❖❖| *No meals* Ⓜ *Consolação* ✛ *B2.*

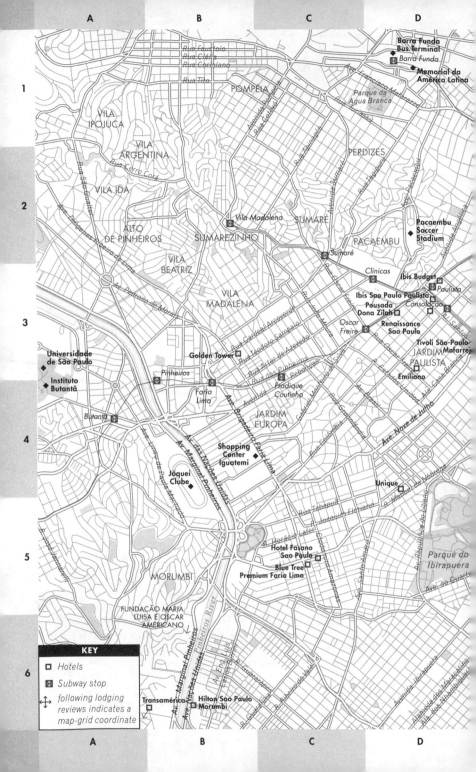

Where to Stay in São Paulo

E   F   G   H

1
2
3
4
5
6

Aeroporto Internacional de São Paulo/Guarulhos

↑ Tietê Bus Terminal

◆ Armênia

Tiradentes

Parque da Luz

Luz

Luz

R. João Teodoro

R. Gen. Carneiro

Suss. Julves

SANTA CECÍLIA

Mal. Deodoro

Santa Cecília

HIGIENÓPOLIS

Bourbon

Ville Hotel

Tryp Higienópolis

Mackenzie

R. Augusta

República

Anhangabaú

Novotel Jaraguá

São Bento

SÃO PAULO

Avenida Celso Garcia

Bresser Mooca

Brás

Av. Alcântara Machado

Sé

Pedro II

Rua dos Trilhos

BIXIGA

San Gabriel

Pousada dos Franceses

Rua São Carlos do Pinhal

Trianon-Masp

Maksoud Plaza

L'Hotel

Brigadeiro

InterContinental São Paulo

PARAÍSO

Liberdade

Liberdade

São Joaquim

LIBERDADE

Vergueiro

Rua da Mooca

R. Presidente da Quinto

R. Descendente Wisena

R. Barão de Itapetininga

Ave. Paulista

Paraíso

Ana Rosa

Hotel Pullman São Paulo Ibirapuera

Vila Mariana

Mercure Grand Hotel Parque do Ibirapuera

Chácara Klabin

CHÁCARA KLABIN

Santa Imigrantes

Rua Bom Pastor

Rua Agostinho Gomes

Rua Silva Bueno

Rua Manifesto

Centenário

Rua Borges Lagoa

R. Pedro de Toledo

R. Loefgren

Santa Cruz

Ave. Doutor Ricardo Jafet

Alto do Ipiranga

Sacomã

Rua Luís Góis

Aeroporto Internacional de Congonhas

Praça da Árvore

JARDIM BOTÂNICO, JABAQUERO BUS TERMINAL PARQUE ZOOLÓGICO DE SÃO PAULO

0   1 mi
0   1 km

E   F   G   H

CERQUEIRA CÉSAR

$$$$ HOTEL Fodor's Choice ★ 🏨 **Tivoli São Paulo - Mofarrej.** The five-star Tivoli Mofarrej reopened a few years ago after renovations that raised the standard of lavishness for São Paulo hotels. **Pros:** chance of meeting a prince or princess (literally); Thai spa's Rainmist Steam Bath; steps from Avenida Paulista. **Cons:** Wi-Fi access not included in price; the price itself. [$] *Rooms from: R$850* ✉ *Alameda Santos 1437, Cerqueira César* ☎ *011/3146–5900* 🌐 *www.tivolihotels.com* 🛏 *220, all suites* 🍴 *No meals* [M] *Tirianon-MASP* ✥ *D2.*

CONSOLAÇÃO

$ HOTEL 🏨 **Ibis Budget.** With hotels at both ends of Paulista and other properties in Jardins, Morumbi, and the city center, the Ibis Budget (formerly the Formule 1) is a great choice if you value location and price over luxury. **Pros:** close to metro and convenience stores; perfect for travelers who plan to be out and about. **Cons:** unspectacular breakfast; often fully booked; no pool. [$] *Rooms from: R$175* ✉ *Rua da Consolação, 2303, Consolação* ☎ *011/3123–7755* 🌐 *ibisbudgethotel.ibis.com* 🛏 *399 rooms* 🍴 *No meals* [M] *Consolação* [$] *Rooms from: R$175* ✉ *Rua Vergueiro, 1571, Paraíso* ☎ *011/5085–5699* 🛏 *300 rooms* 🍴 *No meals* [M] *Paraiso* ✥ *D3.*

HIGIENÓPOLIS

$$$$ HOTEL 🏨 **Tryp Higienópolis.** Tucked imperceptibly among stately apartment buildings in one of the city's oldest and most attractive residential neighborhoods, this hotel built in 2000 has bright and spacious rooms with contemporary light-wood furnishings. **Pros:** cool half-indoor, half-outdoor pool; breakfast menu in Braille; 10-minute taxi ride from Centro. **Cons:** small bathrooms; boring furniture. [$] *Rooms from: R$510* ✉ *Rua Maranhão 371, Higienópolis* ☎ *011/3665–8200, 0800/892–1356* 🌐 *www.melia.com* 🛏 *252 rooms* 🍴 *Breakfast* ✥ *E2.*

$$ HOTEL 🏨 **Ville Hotel.** In the lively Higienópolis neighborhood of apartment buildings, bars, and bookstores abutting Mackenzie University, this hotel has a small lobby with a black-and-pink-granite floor, recessed lighting, and leather sofas. **Pros:** walking distance to shopping mall; supermarket next door is open until midnight; university campus is pretty. **Cons:** only one person at desk on weekends; heavy evening-rush-hour traffic. [$] *Rooms from: R$310* ✉ *Rua Dona Veridiana 643, Higienópolis* ☎ *011/3257–5288* 🌐 *www.hotelville.com.br* 🛏 *54 rooms* 🍴 *Breakfast* [M] *Santa Cecilia* ✥ *E2.*

ITAIM BIBI

$ HOTEL 🏨 **Blue Tree Premium Faria Lima.** Techno beats enliven the lobby of this chic business hotel halfway between Paulista and Brooklin. **Pros:** courteous staff; on major thoroughfare close to many multinationals; close to restaurants. **Cons:** taxi needed to visit sights; heavy rush hour. [$] *Rooms from: R$200* ✉ *Avenida Brigadeiro Faria Lima 3989, Itaim Bibi* ☎ *011/3896–7544* 🌐 *www.bluetree.com.br* 🛏 *338 rooms* 🍴 *Breakfast* ✥ *C5.*

JARDINS

$$$$ HOTEL 🏨 **Emiliano.** Pure luxury, the Emiliano would fit in with any modern hotel in Europe's best cities. **Pros:** on São Paulo's version of 5th Avenue; pillow menus; complimentary wine bottles. **Cons:** stratospheric prices. [$] *Rooms from: R$1300* ✉ *Rua Oscar Freire 384, Jardins* ☎ *011/3069–4369* 🌐 *www.emiliano.com.br* 🛏 *57 rooms, 19 suites* 🍴 *No meals* ⊕ *D3.*

$$$$ HOTEL Fodor's Choice ★ 🏨 **Hotel Fasano São Paulo.** With a decor that hints at 1940s modern but is undeniably 21st-century chic, the Hotel Fasano caters to those for whom money is a mere detail. **Pros:** attentive, knowledgeable staff; top-floor pool with stunning view. **Cons:** paying for it all. [$] *Rooms from: R$1600* ✉ *Rua Vittorio Fasano 88, Jardins* ☎ *011/3896–4000* 🌐 *www.fasano.com.br* 🛏 *64 rooms, 10 suites* 🍴 *No meals* ⊕ *C5.*

MOTELS & POUSADAS

If you check into a reasonably priced motel with the hope of humble-but-cheap lodging alternative, you may be surprised to find a heart-shape bed and strategically placed mirrors. Yes, motels in Brazil are specifically set aside for romantic rendezvous. The market is large because most unmarried people live with their parents until well into their twenties or thirties, not to mention the soap-opera lives that many Brazilians lead. If you're looking for a bed that doesn't vibrate, the name of what you seek is *pousada.*

$$$$ HOTEL 🏨 **InterContinental São Paulo.** One of the city's most attractive top-tier establishments, the InterContinental consistently receives rave reviews because of the attention paid to every detail, including the pillows (guests choose among six different types). **Pros:** Japanese breakfast; Playstation in rooms; gym with personal trainers. **Cons:** suites aren't much bigger than regular rooms. [$] *Rooms from: R$945* ✉ *Al. Santos 1123, Jardins* ☎ *011/3179–2600, 0800/770–0858* 🌐 *www.intercontinental.com* 🛏 *195 rooms, 38 suites* 🍴 *No meals* [M] *Trianon-MASP* ⊕ *E3.*

$$$$ HOTEL 🏨 **L'Hotel.** Compared to the top-of-the line chain hotels on Paulista, L'Hotel stands out as truly special experience. **Pros:** small number of rooms makes for personalized service; L'Occitane bath products. **Cons:** expensive. [$] *Rooms from: R$1000* ✉ *Alameda Campinas 266, Jardins* ☎ *011/2183–0500* 🌐 *www.lhotel.com.br* 🛏 *83 rooms, 8 suites* 🍴 *No meals* [M] *Trianon-MASP* ⊕ *E3.*

$$$$ HOTEL 🏨 **Maksoud Plaza.** Once the top choice for luxury accommodations in São Paulo, Maksoud must now share the bill with a bevy of high-end hotels. **Pros:** four different full-service restaurants and five bars; huge atrium. **Cons:** dingy exterior; rush-hour traffic. [$] *Rooms from: R$650* ✉ *Alameda Campinas 1250, Jardins* ☎ *011/3145–8000, 1888/551–1333 U.S. toll free* 🌐 *www.maksoud.com.br* 🛏 *416 rooms* 🍴 *No meals* [M] *Trianon-MASP* ⊕ *E3.*

$ B&B/INN 🏨 **Pousada Dona Zilah.** Marvelously located in the retail-heavy part of the Jardins district, and easily navigable both to and from, this homey pousada, while not exactly cheap, might be a more affordable alternative if you're seeking to momentarily escape the skyscraper experience. **Pros:** close to Oscar Freire shopping; excellent breakfast.

Cons: can be noisy. [$] *Rooms from: R$235* ✉ *Alameda Franca 1621, Jardins* ☎ *011/3062–1444* 🌐 *www.zilah.com* 🛏 *14 rooms* 🍴 *Breakfast* [M] *Consolação* ✣ *D3.*

$$$$ HOTEL 🏨 **Renaissance São Paulo.** In case the rooftop helipad doesn't say it all, the striking lines of the red-and-black granite lobby announce one serious business hotel. **Pros:** you never have to leave hotel; professional staff. **Cons:** Internet and breakfast aren't free; uninspired decor. [$] *Rooms from: R$600* ✉ *Alameda Santos 2233, Jardins* ☎ *011/3069–2233, 888/236–2427 in U.S.* 🌐 *www.renaissancehotels.com* 🛏 *388 rooms, 56 suites, 45 clubrooms* 🍴 *No meals* [M] *Consolação* ✣ *D3.*

$$$$ HOTEL Fodor's Choice ★ 🏨 **Unique.** It's hard not see a familiar shape (some say watermelon, some say boat, but neither hits the mark) in the wild but harmonious design of this boutique hotel. **Pros:** steps from Ibirapuera Park and a taxi ride to many top restaurants. **Cons:** nonstop techno music in public spaces. [$] *Rooms from: R$1200* ✉ *Avenida Brigadeiro Luís Antônio 4700, Jardins* ☎ *011/3055–4700* 🌐 *www.unique.com.br* 🛏 *85 rooms* 🍴 *No meals* ✣ *D4.*

PINHEIROS

$$ HOTEL 🏨 **Golden Tower.** Proximity to important hubs and to Vila Madalena makes this a good choice. **Pros:** close to Marginal Pinheiros; quiet neighborhood. **Cons:** far from Centro. [$] *Rooms from: R$300* ✉ *Rua Deputado Lacerda Franco 148, Pinheiros* ☎ *011/3094–2200* 🌐 *www.goldentowerhotel.com.br* 🛏 *96 rooms, 8 suites* 🍴 *Breakfast* [M] *Faria Lima* ✣ *B3.*

SANTO AMARO

$$$$ HOTEL 🏨 **Transamérica.** Directly across the Pinheiros River from the Centro Empresarial office complex, the home of many U.S. companies, this hotel is a convenient choice for those working in the area. **Pros:** great location for business travelers; free Wi-Fi; tennis courts; 3-hole chip-and-putt golf course. **Cons:** Pinheiros River smells terrible; traffic paralyzes the area at rush hour. [$] *Rooms from: R$900* ✉ *Av. das Nações Unidas 18591, Santo Amaro* ☎ *011/5693–4050, 0800/012–6060* 🌐 *www.transamerica.com.br* 🛏 *396 rooms, 11 suites* 🍴 *Breakfast* ✣ *A6.*

VILA MARIANA

$$$ HOTEL 🏨 **Hotel Pullman São Paulo Ibirapuera.** Renovated in 2013 and looking fresh, the Pullman brings contemporary design and reasonable prices to the Ibirapuera area. **Pros:** near Ibirapuera Park, Avenida Paulista, and museums; affordable. **Cons:** considerable ride from main business and nightlife districts; small pool. [$] *Rooms from: R$400* ✉ *Rua Joinville 515, Vila Mariana* ☎ *011/5088–4000* 🌐 *www.pullmanhotels.com* 🛏 *350 rooms* 🍴 *No meals* ✣ *E5.*

$$ HOTEL [H] **Mercure Grand Hotel Parque do Ibirapuera.** Near the Congonhas Airport and Ibirapuera Park, this modern, luxury hotel is noted for its French style, and its restaurant serves French cuisine. **Pros:** many amenities; convenient helipad for millionaires. **Cons:** afternoon traffic; far from business centers. [$] *Rooms from: R$350* ✉ *Rua Sena Madureira 1355, Bloco 1, Vila Mariana* ☎ *011/3201–0800* 📠 *011/5575–4544* 🌐 *www.accorhotels.com.br* 🛏 *212 rooms* 🍴 *No meals* ⊕ *E5.*

NIGHTLIFE AND THE ARTS

NIGHTLIFE

4

São Paulo's nightlife options are seemingly endless, so knowing where to go is key. The chic and wealthy head for establishments, most of which serve food, in the Vila Olímpia, Jardins, and Itaim neighborhoods. The Pinheiros and Vila Madalena neighborhoods have a large concentration of youthful clubs and bars, and many trendy clubs have opened in Barra Funda. Jardins and Centro have many gay and lesbian spots, with the area around Rua Augusta catering to hipsters.

Some São Paulo music clubs host rock, jazz, and blues artists, but when it comes to Brazilian music, the options abound. On weekends you'll find MPB, samba, and *pagode* (similar to samba but with pop-music elements) in clubs throughout the city—many operating from early afternoon to early evening and accompanied by *feijoada* or other meals. At *forró* clubs, couples dance close to the fast beat and romantic lyrics of music that originated in the Northeast.

Most clubs open at 9 pm, but people tend to arrive late (around midnight), and dance until 5 or 6 am. Still, you should arrive early to be at the front of the lines. Don't worry if the dance floor appears empty at 11 pm; things will start to sizzle an hour or so later.

Clubbing can get expensive. Most clubs charge at least R$20 at the door (sometimes women are allowed in for free), and the most popular and upscale places as much as R$300 just for entry. At the hottest clubs, expect to wait in line for a bit, especially if you head out late.

São Paulo has a large and lively gay scene with a smorgasbord of bars, cafés, and mega nightclubs spread throughout the city. There's a good cluster of watering holes along Avenida Vieira de Carvalho and Rua Martinho Prada in República, and Ruas Frei Caneca, Augusta, and Bela Cintra in Consolação (10 minutes from the Consolação and Paulista metros on Avenida Paulista) is a regular rendezvous point and hangout.

A word about happy hour. Unlike in some countries, where the term refers to those few early-evening hours when drinks are cheaper, happy hour (pronounced and written in English) in Brazil simply means the time just after the work day ends, around 6 pm, when you might head to a bar for a drink with friends or colleagues. Despite the lack of discounted cocktails, paulistanos love to use the term, and many bars are judged purely on their suitability as a happy-hour venue.

BARRA FUNDA, ÁGUA BRANCA, AND LAPA

DANCE CLUBS

D.Edge. Electronic music is the main attraction at this popular club with a Death Star–meets–Studio 54 appeal. As many as nine DJs, often including internationally renowned turntabilists, spin music on Thursday, Friday, and Saturday nights; on Sunday the party starts at 6 am and runs into the afternoon, and Monday is rock night. The terrace here has views of a park of Oscar Niemeyer designs. Cover charges dip as low as R$20 but sometimes exceed R$100. Putting your name on the guest list through email reduces the cost. ⊠ *Av. Auro Soares de Moura Andrade 141, Barra Funda* ☎ *011/3665–9500, 011/3667–8799* ⊕ *www.d-edge. com.br* ☉ *Closed Tues. and Wed.* Ⓜ *Barra Funda.*

Villa Country. This is *the* place to dance to American country music and *sertanejo,* Brazilian country music. The huge club has a restaurant, bars, shops, game rooms, and a big dance floor. The decor is strictly Old West. ⊠ *Av. Francisco Matarazzo 774, Água Branca* ☎ *011/3868–5858* ⊕ *www.villacountry.com.br* ☒ *Cover varies* ☉ *Closed Mon.–Wed.* Ⓜ *Barra Funda.*

GAY AND LESBIAN BARS AND CLUBS

Blue Space. In a huge colonial blue house in an old industrial neighborhood, Blue Space is one of the largest gay nightclubs in São Paulo. Every Saturday and Sunday, two dance floors and four bars, along with lounge and private rooms, fill with a large crowd, mostly 40 and over, interested in the house DJs and go-go-boy and drag shows. ⊠ *Rua Brigadeiro Galvão 723, Barra Funda* ☎ *011/3666–1616, 011/3665–7157* ⊕ *www.bluespace.com.br* ☒ *R$32* ☉ *Closed weekdays* Ⓜ *Marechal Deodoro.*

The Week. Occupying a nearly 6,000-square-meter (64,500-square-foot) space, this club popular with gay men has two dance floors, three lounge rooms, a deck with a swimming pool, six bars, and a massage bed. Several DJs playing house, electro, and techno animate an often shirtless-crowd on Friday and Saturday nights. ⊠ *Rua Guaicurus 324, Lapa* ☎ *011/3868–9944* ⊕ *www.theweek.com.br* ☉ *Open Fri. and Sat. every week; other days vary.*

BELA VISTA

MUSIC CLUBS

Café Piu Piu. The café is best-known for its live-rock nights—Thursday, Friday, and Saturday. On other nights, it hosts groups that play rock jazz, blues bossa nova, and sometimes tango. Potato latkes are among the menu highlights. ⊠ *Rua 13 de Maio 134, Bela Vista* ☎ *011/3258–8066* ⊕ *www.cafepiupiu.com.br* ☉ *Closed Mon.*

CENTRO

BARS

Bar Brahma. First opened in 1948, Bar Brahma used to be the meeting place of artists, intellectuals, and politicians. The decor is a time warp to the mid-20th century, with furniture, lamps, and a piano true to the period. ■TIP→ **This is one of the best places in São Paulo for live music, with traditional samba and Brazilian pop groups scheduled every week.** Caetano Veloso immortalized the intersection of Ipiranga and São João avenues, where the bar is located, in his 1978 song "Sampa." ☒ *Av. São João 677, Centro* ☎ *011/3367–3600 reservations, 011/3367–3601* ⊕ *www.barbrahmasp.com* ⊙ *Closed Sun.* Ⓜ *República.*

DANCE CLUBS

Alberta #3. A linchpin of the nightlife revival pulling hipsters back to the Centro, this club across from the Novotel Jaraguá caters to crowds from happy hour to the bewitching hours. Head upstairs to the lounge for cocktails and imported beers or downstairs to shake it out on the dance floor to indie and classic rock. ☒ *Avenida São Luís 272, Centro* ☎ *011/3151–5299* ⊕ *www.alberta3.com.br* ⊙ *Closed Sun. and Mon.* Ⓜ *República.*

CONSOLAÇÃO

BARS

Drosophyla. Your creepy aunt's house filled with bizarre keepsakes meets quaint garden bar at Drosophyla. Young professionals and midlife free spirits assemble here for exotic caipirinhas, shots of vodka with cranberry syrup, and other zesty cocktails. If here for a meal, try the *huahine*, a French-Polynesian dish with marinated raw tuna, carrot, peppers, cherry tomatoes, and coconut milk. ☒ *Rua Pedro Taques 80, Consolação* ☎ *011/3120–5535* ⊕ *www.drosophyla.com.br* ⊙ *Closed Sun.* Ⓜ *Consolação or Paulista.*

GAY AND LESBIAN BARS AND CLUBS

A Lôca. A mixed gay, lesbian, and straight crowd often dances until dawn at A Lôca to everything from pop and rock to disco and techno. ☒ *Rua Frei Caneca 916, Consolação* ☎ *011/3159–8889* ⊕ *www.aloca.com.br* 💰 *R$25* ⊙ *Closed Mon.* Ⓜ *Consolação.*

FREGUESIA DO Ó

BARS

Frangó. A stop at off-the-beaten-path Frangó, northwest of Centro, makes you feel as if you've been transported to a small town. The bar has more than 300 varieties of beer, including the Brazilian craft beer Colorado. The Indica brew, an IPA made with sugarcane, nicely complements the bar's unforgettable *coxinhas de frango com queijo* (fried balls of chicken with cheese). ☒ *Largo da Matriz de Nossa Senhora do Ó 168, Freguesia do Ó* ☎ *011/3932–4818* ⊕ *www.frangobar.com.br* ⊙ *Closed Mon.*

ITAIM

BARS

BottaGallo. Italian-style tapas or *bottas*, many of them pasta based, accompany a selection of 130 wines at this gastropub. Try the risotto with burrata cheese or white wine–marinated ribs and Rosso di Montepulciano, the house wine imported from Tuscany. ☒ *Rua Jesuíno Arruda 520, Itaim* ☎ *011/3078–2858* ⊕ *www.bottagallo.com.br.*

GETTING AROUND AFTER DARK

For safety reasons, we strongly suggest taking cabs at night—it's convenient and relatively cheap. Ask your concierge about transportation if finding a cab proves difficult.

4

Na Mata Café. Close to the northern border of Itaim, Na Mata ranks among the city's best live-music venues. It's a great place to catch some upmarket Brazilian entertainment. ⊠ *Rua da Mata 70, Itaim* ☎ *011/3079–0300* ⊕ *www.namata. com.br* ☽ *Closed Mon. night.*

GAY AND LESBIAN BARS AND CLUBS

Vermont Itaim. A major lesbian hangout in Itaim, this venue offers dining, live music, and dancing. Ten acts divvy up the show

> ## GAY PRIDE PARADE
>
> São Paulo hosts one of the world's biggest and most famous gay parades each year on the Sunday of the Corpus Christi holiday, which generally falls at the end of May or in early June. The Gay Pride Parade, which was first held in 1997, runs along Avenida Paulista and attracts more than 2 million people.

times from Wednesday to Saturday; on Sunday a nine-piece all-girl samba band takes the stage. When the bands stop playing, DJs spin music late into the night. ⊠ *Rua Pedroso Alvarenga 1192, Itaim Bibi* ☎ *011/3071–1320, 011/3707–7721* ⊕ *www.vermontitaim.com.br* ☽ *Closed Mon. and Tues.*

MUSIC CLUBS

Kia Ora Pub. Rock and pop cover bands perform at this Down Under–themed pub. Seven international draft beers and happy hour specials make Kia Ora popular after businesses close. There's a second location in Barra Funda. ⊠ *R. Dr. Eduardo de Souza Aranha 377, Itaim* ☎ *011/3846–8300* ⊕ *www.kiaora.com.br* ▭ *Cover charge R$30–R$70* ☽ *Closed Sun. and Mon.*

JARDIM PAULISTA

BARS

Balcão. Balcão means "balcony" in Portuguese, and this artsy place has a sprawling one. If you'd like a little food to accompany your drinks and conversation, try one of the famous sandwiches on ciabatta bread. ⊠ *Rua Doutor Melo Alves 150, Jardim Paulista* ☎ *011/3063–6091* Ⓜ *Consolação.*

DANCE CLUBS

8 Bar. The DJs at this intimate space play electronic, disco, and hip-hop, often interacting with the crowd on the dance floor and accepting requests. The bar closes occasionally for private events, so call ahead to be sure it's open. ⊠ *Rua José Maria Lisboa 82, Jardim Paulista* ☎ *011/3889–9927, 011/97085–5718* ⊕ *www.8bar.com.br* ▭ *R$10* ☽ *Closed Sun. and Mon.*

JARDINS

BARS

O'Malley's. A self-proclaimed "gringo" hangout, this is a good place to catch international sporting events, perhaps that major one back home it's killing you to miss. O'Malley's has three bars, a game room, and more than a dozen TVs spread across two floors. Seven beers are on tap, along with more than four dozen by the bottle. Bands play nightly, so there's always a cover after happy hour ends. ⊠ *Alameda Itú 1529, Jardins* ☎ *011/3086–0780* ⊕ *www.omalleysbar.net* Ⓜ *Consolação.*

MOEMA
MUSIC CLUBS
Bourbon Street. With a name right out of New Orleans, it's no wonder that Bourbon Street is where the best jazz and blues bands, Brazilian and international, play. Performances start at 9:30 pm. On Sundays, you can merengue and mambo at the Caribbean dance party. ⊠ *Rua dos Chanés 127, Moema* ☎ *011/5095–6100* ⊕ *www.bourbonstreet.com.br* ☾ *Closed Mon.*

PARAÍSO
BARS
Barnaldo Lucrécia. Live *música popular brasileira* (MPB, popular Brazilian music) draws an intense but jovial crowd to this bohemian spot. ⊠ *Rua Abílio Soares 207, Paraíso* ☎ *011/3885–3425* ⊕ *www. barnaldolucrecia.com.br* Ⓜ *Paraíso.*

Fodor's Choice
★

Veloso. Tables here are as disputed as a parking spot in front of a downtown apartment. An intimate corner bar on a quiet cobblestone plaza, Veloso dispenses some of São Paulo's best caipirinhas, including exotic versions such as tangerine with red pepper, and *coxinhas* (fried balls of chicken with cheese). ⊠ *Rua Conceição Veloso 56, Paraíso* ☎ *011/5572–0254* ⊕ *www.velosobar.com.br* ☾ *Closed Mon.* Ⓜ *Ana Rosa.*

PINHEIROS
DANCE CLUBS
Bar Secreto. Madonna and band members from U2 are former patrons of this once esoteric and invitation-only dance club. Though entrance is no longer just for Bruce Wayne, to mingle with the moneyed partygoers you still have to be on the list—through the website or by email invitation—and pay a cover charge that might wade into the triple digits. Bar Secreto opens at 11 pm from Wednesday to Saturday, and at 7 on Sunday. Or does it? ⊠ *Rua Álvaro Anes 97, Pinheiros* ⊕ *barsecreto. com.br* Ⓜ *Faria Lima.*

Casa 92. Giving new meaning to the concept house party, Casa 92 was fashioned out of a converted domicile. The living room has been fitted with disco lighting. The patio and terrace each have bars. An upstairs dance floor resides where a bedroom otherwise would. The music is eclectic with an emphasis on (what else?) house. ⊠ *Rua Cristovão Gonçalves 92, Pinheiros* ☎ *011/3032–0371* ⊕ *www.casa92.com.br* ☾ *Doors open at 10:30 pm* ☾ *Closed Sun.–Wed.* Ⓜ *Faria Lima.*

Estúdio Emme. With a layout that evokes the Babylon Club from the movie *Scarface*, Estúdio Emme is a party and performance venue attached to the same-named clothing store and hair salon. The club opens from Wednesday through Saturday with a hodgepodge of themed parties rotating on weekly and monthly schedules. ⊠ *Av. Pedroso de Morais 1036, Pinheiros* ☎ *011/3031–3290* ☾ *Closed Sun.–Tues.* Ⓜ *Faria Lima.*

GAY AND LESBIAN BARS AND CLUBS
Bubu Lounge Disco. Disco balls dangle over the dance floor at gay Bubu, where shirtless is the new fully clothed. Drag performers strut their stuff at Sunday matinees, and the last Thursday of the month is girls-only night. ⊠ *Rua Dos Pinheiros 791, Pinheiros* ☎ *011/3081–9546, 011/3081–9659* ⊕ *www.bubulounge.com.br* ☾ *Closed Mon., Tues., Thurs.* Ⓜ *Faria Lima.*

MUSIC CLUBS

Canto da Ema. At what's widely considered the best place in town to dance forró you'll find people of different ages and styles coming together on the dance floor. *Xiboquinha* is the official forró drink, made with cachaça (a Brazilian sugarcane-based alcohol), lemon, honey, cinnamon, and ginger. The doors open at 10:30 pm from Wednesday through Saturday; the hours on Sunday are from 7 pm to midnight. ⊠ *Av. Brigadeiro Faria Lima 364, Pinheiros* ☎ *011/3813–4708* ⊕ *www. cantodaema.com.br* ⊠ *R$16–R$28* ⊘ *Closed Mon. and Tues.*

Carioca Club. A *carioca* is a person from Rio de Janeiro, and Carioca Club has the decor of old-style Rio clubs. Its large dance floor attracts an eclectic mix of up to 1,200 college students, couples, and professional dancers who move to samba, *gafieira*, and *pagode* from Thursday through Saturday starting at varying times. ⊠ *Rua Cardeal Arcoverde 2899, Pinheiros* ☎ *011/3813–8598, 011/3813–4524* ⊕ *www.cariocaclub. com.br* ⊠ *Cover charge R$30 and up* ⊘ *Closed Sun.–Wed.* Ⓜ *Faria Lima.*

Teta Jazz Bar. Uptempo jazz shows keep the mood perky at snug Teta, just outside the entrance to the Cemitério São Paulo. Bossa nova, soul, and blues also enter the rotation. The 15 tables make for a tight fit between the art-adorned red walls. ⊠ *Rua Cardeal Arcoverde 1265, Pinheiros* ☎ *011/3031–1641.*

VILA MADALENA

BARS

Astor. The 1960s and 1970s bohemian-chic decor here sends you back in time. The quality draft beer and tasty snacks and meals mean that Astor is always hopping—the menu is full of specialties from classic bars in Brazil. Don't miss the *picadinho:* beef stew with rice and black beans, poached eggs, banana, farofa, and beef *pastel* (a type of dumpling). To finish up, head downstairs, where SubAstor, a speakeasy-style sister bar, serves the kind of cocktails that inspire you to attempt knockoffs at your next house party. ⊠ *Rua Delfina 163, Vila Madalena* ☎ *011/3815–1364* ⊕ *www.barastor.com.br.*

Filial. When it comes to ending the night, Filial is considered the best bar in town. Many musicians stop by for an after-hours taste of its draft beer, along with the flavorful snacks (such as *bolinho de arroz,* or rice fritters) and meals (try *galinha afogada,* a stew with incredibly moist chicken and rice). ⊠ *Rua Fidalga 254, Vila Madalena* ☎ *011/3813–9226* ⊕ *www.barfilial.com.br.*

Gràcia. A flirtatious clientele frequents this hot spot. Named for a Barcelona neighborhood, Gràcia is clothed in Catalan imagery and serves tapas and Sangria from the region. Sidewalk seating is available when the weather cooperates. ⊠ *Rua Coropes 87, Vila Madalena* ☎ *011/3034–1481* ⊕ *graciabar.com.br* ⊘ *Closed Mon.* Ⓜ *Faria Lima.*

Posto 6. One of four comparable and fashionable bars at the corner of Mourato Coelho and Aspicuelta streets, Posto 6 pays homage to Rio de Janeiro and its Botafogo soccer club. The bar gets gold stars for its *chopp* (draft beer) and *escondidinho de camarão* (a lasagna-type dish with shrimp). ⊠ *Rua Aspicuelta 646, Vila Madalena* ☎ *011/3812–4342* ⊕ *www.posto6.com* ⊘ *Closed Mon.*

DANCE CLUBS

UP Club. DJs spin hip-hop and rap, and dancers pack the floor on Friday nights at the UP Club. If things get too steamy, you can take a breather in the backyard garden. ⊠ *Rua Harmonia 21, Vila Madalena* ☎ *011/2309–7159* ⊕ *www.upclubsp.com.br* ☉ *Fri. only.*

MUSIC CLUBS

Grazie a Dio. The fashionable patrons at this club may vary in age, but they all appreciate good music. The best time to go is at happy hour for daily live performances. Samba, soul, and jazz figure prominently, with Brazilian pop represented as well. The natural decorations, including trees and constellations, complement the Mediterranean food served in the back. ⊠ *Rua Girassol 67, Vila Madalena* ☎ *011/3031–6568* ⊕ *www.grazieadio.com.br.*

Fodor'sChoice **Madeleine.** The riffs heard at Madeleine place it in an exclusive stratum
★ of São Paulo music clubs, but it's the mix of music, food, drinks, and atmosphere that lends the bar its comprehensive appeal. Jazz ensembles play in the exposed-brick lounge, which has clear sightlines from the mezzanine. Better for chatting are the candlelit tables in the well-stocked wine cellar, and the seats on the veranda, with its panoramic views of Vila Madalena. Wherever you sit, the gourmet pizzas go great with the craft beers poured here. ⊠ *Rua Aspicuelta 201, Vila Madalena* ☎ *011/2936–0616* ⊕ *www.madeleine.com.br* ☉ *Closed Sun.*

VILA OLÍMPIA

BARS

Bar Do Arnesto. More than 500 types of the rumlike liquor cachaça—the main ingredient in caipirinhas, Brazil's national cocktail—line a huge wall at this traditional Brazilian *botequim*. These casual bars generally specialize in cold bottled beer, snack foods, and caipirinhas. ⊠ *Rua Ministro Jesuíno Cardoso, 207, Vila Olímpia* ☎ *011/3848–9432, 011/3848-6041 after 6 pm* ⊕ *www.bardoarnesto.com.br.*

DANCE CLUBS

Disco. Big names in electronic music command the turntables at Disco, where you might end up sharing the dance floor with members of the national glitterati—or just some very São Paulo playboys. ⊠ *Rua Professor Atílio Innocenti 160, Brooklin* ☎ *011/3078–0404* ⊕ *www.clubdisco.com.br* ☉ *Closed Mon.–Wed.*

Rey Castro. Salsa, merengue, zouk, and Latin pop predominate at Rey Castro, and during the breaks between live performances you can take dance classes. The Caribbean-influenced drinks and snacks include mojitos and ham croquettes. ⊠ *Rua Ministro Jesuíno Cardoso 181, Vila Olímpia* ☎ *011/3842–5279* ⊕ *www.reycastro.com.br* ☉ *Closed Sun.–Tues.*

MUSIC CLUBS

All of Jazz. People come here to listen quietly to good jazz and bossa nova in an intimate environment. Local musicians jam from 10 pm on except on Sunday. ■TIP➔ The club gets crowded on weekends, when it's best to reserve a table. ⊠ *Rua João Cachoeira 1366, Vila Olímpia* ☎ *011/3849–1345* ⊕ *www.allofjazz.com.br.*

THE ARTS

The world's top orchestras, opera and dance companies, and other troupes always include São Paulo in their South American tours. Many free concerts—with performances by either Brazilian or international artists—are presented on Sunday in Parque Ibirapuera. City-sponsored events are frequently held in Centro's Vale do Anhangabaú area or in Avenida Paulista.

The Centro Cultural São Paulo near Paraíso metro and ample network of Serviço Social do Comércio (SESC) cultural centers feature inexpensive dance, theater, and musical performances daily. Listings of events appear in the "Veja São Paulo" insert of the newsweekly *Veja*. The arts sections of the dailies *Folha de São Paulo* and *O Estado de São Paulo* also have listings and reviews. Both papers publish a weekly guide on Friday. The Portuguese-language website Catraca Livre is the authority on free entertainment options.

Tickets for many events are available at booths throughout the city, at theater box offices, or through the Ingresso Rápido, Ingresso, and Tickets for Fun websites. Many of these venues and sites offer ticket delivery to your hotel for a surcharge.

Ticket Information Ingresso Rápido ☎ *011/4003–1212* ⊕ *www.ingressorapido.com.br*. **Ingresso.com** ☎ *011/4003–2330* ⊕ *www.ingresso.com.br*. **Show Tickets.** This outfit sells tickets to the main concerts and performances in town. ✉ *Iguatemi São Paulo, Av. Brigadeiro Faria Lima 1191, 3rd fl., Jardim Paulistano* ☎ *011/3031–2098* ⊕ *www.showtickets. com.br* ⊗ *Mon.–Sat. 10–9, Sun. 2–7.* **Tickets for Fun** ☎ *011/4003–5588* ⊕ *premier.ticketsforfun.com.br*.

CLASSICAL MUSIC AND OPERA

Fodor's Choice ★ **Sala São Paulo.** Despite being housed in a magnificent old train station, Sala São Paulo is one of the most modern concert halls for classical music in Latin America. It's home to the **São Paulo Symphony** (OSESP). ✉ *Praça Júlio Prestes 16, Centro* ☎ *011/3367–9500* ⊕ *www. salasaopaulo.art.br* Ⓜ *Luz*.

Teatro São Pedro. Built in the neoclassical style in 1917, São Paulo's second-oldest theater is one of its best venues for chamber concerts and operas. Free morning events take place on Sundays and Wednesdays. ✉ *Rua Albuquerque Lins 207, Barra Funda* ☎ *011/3667–0499 ticket booth* ⊕ *www.teatrosaopedro.sp.gov.br* ⊗ *Closed Mon. and Tues.* Ⓜ *Marechal Deodoro*.

DANCE

Balé da Cidade. The City Ballet, São Paulo's official dance company, has performed for many years at the Theatro Municipal, but by 2014 it hopes to be dancing at a space on Rua Conselheiro Crispiniano in Praça das Artes. ✉ *Rua João Passaláqua 66, Bela Vista* ☎ *011/3241–3883, 011/3241–1740* Ⓜ *Anhangabaú*.

Ballet Stagium. The ballet performs contemporary works incorporating Brazilian pop and bossa nova music. Founded in 1971 during Brazil's period of dictatorship, the company made its name performing dances with political and social-justice themes. ⊠ *Rua Augusta 2985, 2nd fl., Cerqueira César* ☎ *011/3085–0151* ⊕ *www.stagium.com.br.*

São Paulo Companhia de Dança. The fine state dance company performs throughout the country and tours internationally. ⊠ *Rua Três Rios 363, Bom Retiro* ☎ *011/3224–1380* ⊕ *spcd.com.br* Ⓜ *Tiradentes.*

CONCERT HALLS

Credicard Hall. One of the biggest theaters in São Paulo, Credicard Hall can accommodate up to 7,000 people. The venue frequently hosts concerts by famous Brazilian and international artists. Tickets can be bought by phone or on the Internet using the services of Tickets for Fun. ⊠ *Av. das Nações Unidas 17995, Santo Amaro* ☎ *011/4003–5588* ⊕ *www.credicardhall.com.br.*

SESC Pompéia. Part of a chain of cultural centers throughout the city, SESC Pompéia incorporates a former factory into its design. There are multiple performance spaces, but the *choperia* (beer hall) and theater host the most prominent Brazilian and international musical acts—from jazz and soul to rock and hip-hop. ⊠ *Rua Clélia 93, Vila Olímpia* ☎ *011/3871–7700* ⊕ *www.sescsp.org.br.*

Teatro Alfa. International musicals and ballet, as well as occasional musical performances are held at Teatro Alfa, which seats more than a thousand people. The sound and lighting technology are top of the line. Tickets can be bought by phone and through Ingresso Rápido, then picked up a half hour before the performance. ⊠ *Rua Bento Branco de Andrade Filho 722, Santo Amaro* ☎ *011/5693–4000, 0300/789–3377* ⊕ *www.teatroalfa.com.br.*

Theatro Municipal. Most serious music, ballet, and opera is performed at Theatro Municipal, a classic theater built in 1911 with an intimate gilt and moss-green-velvet interior. Call the theater to arrange a free guided tour. ⊠ *Praça Ramos de Azevedo, Centro* ☎ *011/3397–0300, 011/3397–0327* ⊕ *www.prefeitura.sp.gov.br/cidade/secretarias/cultura/theatromunicipal* Ⓜ *Anhangabaú.*

Via Funchal. Capable of seating more than 3,000 people, Via Funchal is the site of many large international music, theater, and dance shows. ⊠ *Rua Funchal 65, Vila Olímpia* ☎ *011/3846–2300* ⊕ *www. viafunchal.com.br.*

SAMBA SHOWS

Escolas de samba or samba schools are the heart and soul of many communities. Most people only associate them with the dancing groups that perform during Carnival, but they keep busy all year round. In addition to samba lessons, they organize a range of community services, especially education and health outreach programs. Check them out anytime, but from November to February they're gearing up for Carnival, and often open their rehearsals to the public.

Mocidade Alegre. Up to 3,000 people at a time attend rehearsals at Mocidade Alegre just before Carnival. ⊠ *Av. Casa Verde 3498, Limão* ☎ *011/3857–7525* ⊕ *www.mocidadealegre.com.br.*

Rosas de Ouro. One of the most popular rehearsals takes place at Rosas de Ouro. ⊠ *Rua Coronel Euclides Machado 1066, Freguesia do Ó* ☏ *011/3931-4555* ⊕ *www.sociedaderosasdeouro.com.br.*

FILM

Centro Cultural São Paulo. The cultural center intends to become a key venue for alternative film screenings, particularly of Brazilian titles, but also presents plays, concerts, and art exhibits. Major renovations finished in 2013 added new projection and sound equipment and saw improvements in the lighting and acoustics. Admission is free or low-price for some events. ⊠ *Rua Vergueiro 1000, Paraíso* ☏ *011/3397–4002* ⊕ *www.centrocultural.sp.gov.br* Ⓜ *Vergueiro.*

Cidade Jardim Cinemark. The prices are elite but so are the amenities, such as gourmet food service. Cidade Jardim Cinemark set the bar much higher for blockbuster-screening, luxury theaters in São Paulo. ⊠ *Av. Magalhães de Castro 12000, Morumbi* ☏ *011/3552–1800* ⊕ *www. shoppingcidadejardim.com/cinema.*

CineSESC. Titles already out of other theaters and independent openings show for discounted prices at CineSESC. The screen is visible from the snack bar. ⊠ *Rua Augusta 2075, Cerqueira César* ☏ *011/3087–0500* ⊕ *www.sescsp.org.br/cinesesc* Ⓜ *Consolação.*

Espaço Itaú de Cinema. Brazilian, European, and other nonblockbuster films are shown at the Espaço Itaú. ⊠ *Rua Augusta 1475, Consolação* ☏ *011/3288–6780* ⊕ *www.itaucinemas.com.br* Ⓜ *Consolação.*

Reserva Cultural. The complex contains four movie theaters, a small café, a bar, and a deck-style restaurant from which you can see—and be seen by—pedestrians on Paulista Avenue. ⊠ *Av. Paulista 900, Jardim Paulista* ☏ *011/3287–3529* ⊕ *www.reservacultural.com.br* Ⓜ *Trianon-MASP or Brigadeiro.*

SPORTS AND THE OUTDOORS

Maybe it's the environment or maybe the culture, but participating in organized sports isn't usually a huge part of a paulistano's regime. An exception is soccer or "futebol," which you will see being played in most parks, either on full fields, half-size arenas, or even sandy courts, every weekend and on weeknights. Basketball and volleyball also have loyal, if smaller, followings at parks and SESC centers around the city.

ON THE SIDELINES

AUTO RACING

Brazilian Grand Prix. Racing fans from all over the world come to São Paulo in November for the Brazilian Grand Prix, a Formula 1 race that attracts massive national attention, especially when a Brazilian driver is in the mix. The race is held at Autódromo da Interlagos, which at other times hosts auto races on weekends. ⊠ *Autódromo da Interlagos, Av. Senador Teotônio Vilela 261* ☏ *021/2221–4895 tickets* ⊕ *www.gpbrasil.com.*

HORSE RACING

São Paulo Jockey Club. Thoroughbreds run at the São Paulo Jockey Club, which hosts races on weekends and Mondays. Card-carrying club members get the best seats, but you can also head to the elegant restaurant, which has a view of the track. ⊠ *Avenida Lineu de Paula Machado 1263, Cidade Jardim* ☎ *011/2161–8300* ⊕ *www.jockeysp. com.br* ⊙ *Weekends 2–8 pm, Mon. 6–11 pm.*

SOCCER

São Paulo State has several well-funded teams with some of the country's best players. The four main teams—Corinthians, São Paulo, Palmeiras, and Santos—attract fans from other states. Corinthians and Palmeiras will open new stadiums during the 2014 World Cup. São Paulo's Morumbi and the municipally run Pacaembu, meanwhile, will continue to host matchups featuring Brazilian clubs. Covered seats offer the best protection, not only from the elements but also from rowdy spectators. Buy tickets at the stadiums or online at ⊕ *www. ingressofacil.com.br.* Futebol Tour (⊕ *www.futeboltour.com.br*) also sells packages that include transportation to and from the stadiums, admission, and information folders. Regular games usually don't sell out, but finals and classicos between the big four—for which you can buy tickets up to five days in advance—generally do. For a history lesson on the "beautiful game," check out the interactive Soccer Museum at the Pacaembu stadium.

Arena Corinthians. The new R$850-million home of Corinthians soccer club is scheduled to host the opening of the 2014 World Cup. The seating capacity of 48,000 will expand temporarily to 68,000 for the Cup games. ⊠ *Av. Miguel Inácio Curi 111, Vila Carmosina* ☎ *011/2095–3000, 011/2095–3175* ⊕ *www.corinthians.com.br/arena* Ⓜ *Corinthians-Itaquera.*

Canindé. The home team, Portuguesa, is the main attraction here, though the *bolinhos de bacalhau* (salt-cod fritters), popular among the Portuguese immigrants, run a close second. ⊠ *Rua Comendador Nestor Pereira 33, Canindé* ☎ *011/2125–9400.*

Estádio da Javari. The 4,000-seat Estádio da Javari, also known as Estádio Conde Rodolfo Crespi, is where Juventus plays. It's an ideal place to soak up some Italian atmosphere—Moóca is an Italian neighborhood—and eat a cannoli while cheering for the home team. ⊠ *Rua Javari 117, Moóca* ☎ *011/2693-4688, 011/2292–4833* ⊕ *www. juventus.com.br* Ⓜ *Moóca.*

Morumbi. The home stadium of São Paulo Futebol Clube seats 67,000 people. When soccer isn't being played here, other events take place, including concerts by stars such as Lady Gaga. ⊠ *Praça Roberto Gomes Pedroza 1, Morumbi* ☎ *011/3742–3377, 011/3749–8000* ⊕ *www. saopaulofc.net.*

Nova Arena. This new arena, scheduled to open in 2014, is configured to seat about 45,000 people for soccer. The home team, Palmeiras, started playing at Estádio Palestra Itália, the stadium previously on this site, in 1920. ⊠ *Rua Turiassu 1840, Barra Funda* ☎ *011/3874-6500* ⊕ *www. novaarena.com.br* Ⓜ *Barra Funda.*

Pacaembu. The first games of the 1950 World Cup were played at this stadium. The plaza it inhabits is named for the Englishman who introduced Brazil to soccer. One interesting fact you'll learn at the Museu de Futebol (soccer museum), which is housed here, is that the soccer legend Pelé scored 115 goals in 119 career games at Pacaembu. ⊠ *Praça Charles Miller s/n, Pacaembú* ☎ *011/3664–4650, 011/3663–6888* Ⓜ *Clínicas.*

VOLLEYBALL

Brazilians love volleyball, both the traditional kind and the beach version. The country has a top-class national competition and hosts regular international matches.

Volleyball Federação Paulista. The Volleyball Federação Paulista has information about local volleyball courts. ☎ *011/3053–9560* ⊕ *www. fpv.com.br.*

PARTICIPATORY SPORTS

Check the air quality before you practice outdoor sports. During the dry season the air can be bad. Don't take your cues from the paulistanos—their lungs are made of steel.

BICYCLING AND JOGGING

Parque Ibirapuera. Going for a ride or a run in one of São Paulo's parks is a good choice if you want a little exercise. For cyclists there are usually plenty of rental options (from R$5 per hour) available and special lanes just for riders. Parque Ibirapuera gets busy on the weekends, but it's still worth coming here. ⊠ *Av. Pedro Álvares Cabral s/n, Parque Ibirapuera* ☎ *011/5574–5045* ⊕ *www.parqueibirapuera.org.*

Parque Villa-Lobos. Parque Villa-Lobos has fewer trees and less of a history than Parque Ibirapuera, but is big and has plenty of winding pathways wide enough to accommodate cyclists and runners. There are bike-rental stands inside the park, as well as a few soccer pitches and a big, concrete square with basketball half-courts. There are some food-and-drink options, too. ⊠ *Av. Professor Fonseca Rodrigues, 2001, Alto de Pinheiros* ☎ *011/3021–6285* ⊕ *www.ambiente.sp.gov. br/parquevillalobos* ⓥ *6–6.*

GOLF

Golf Center Interlagos. If you want to keep your swing from getting rusty while you're in São Paulo, head to the Golf Center, which has 48 covered tees on its 350-yard driving range. The price for 50 balls is R$10. There is also a putting green. ■TIP➔ **The center can arrange to transport you to and from your hotel.** ⊠ *Av. Robert Kennedy 2450, Interlagos* ☎ *011/5686–9722* ⊕ *www.golfcenterinterlagos.com.br.*

SHOPPING

Fashionistas from all over the continent flock to São Paulo for the clothes, shoes, and accessories. In fact, shopping is a tourist attraction in its own right. You can get a sampling of what's on offer six days a week: stores are usually open on weekdays from 9 to 6:30 and Saturdays from 9 to 1; many are closed on Sundays. Mall hours are generally weekdays and Saturdays from 10 am to 10 pm; some malls only open on Sundays around 2 pm.

Almost every neighborhood has a weekly outdoor food market, complete with loudmouthed hawkers, exotic scents, and mountains of colorful produce. Nine hundred of them happen every week in São Paulo, so you'll be able to hit at least one; ask around to find out when and where the closest one happens.

Antiques and secondhand furniture are the big draws at the Sunday flea market at the Praça Dom Orione in **Bela Vista**. You'll also find clothing, CDs, and other (mostly) reasonably priced items here. In **Centro**, Rua do Arouche is noted for leather goods. Rua Barão de Paranapiacaba is lined with jewelry shops and is nicknamed the "street of gold." The area around Rua João Cachoeira in **Itaim** has evolved from a neighborhood of small clothing factories into a wholesale- and retail-clothing sales district. Several shops on Rua Tabapuã sell small antiques. Also, Rua Dr. Mário Ferraz is stuffed with elegant clothing, gift, and home-decoration stores.

In **Jardins,** centering on Rua Oscar Freire, double-parked Mercedes-Benzes and BMWs point the way to the city's fanciest stores, which sell leather items, jewelry, gifts, antiques, and art. Shops that specialize in high-price European antiques are on or around Rua da Consolação. Lower-price antiques stores and thrift shops line Rua Cardeal Arcoverde in **Pinheiros**. Flea markets with secondhand furniture, clothes, and CDs take place on Saturday at the popular Praça Benedito Calixto in Pinheiros, where you can also eat at food stands and listen to music all day long. Arcades along Praça Benedito Calixto and many streets in neighboring **Vila Madalena,** like Ruas Aspicuelta and Harmonia, house boutique clothing stores.

BOM RETIRO

BEACHWEAR

Beira Mar Beachwear. This Brazillian brand, founded in 1948, is known for innovative and high-quality products. Beira Mar has its own factory and produces many types of bikinis and swimming suits. ⊠ *Rua Silva Pinto 254, 3rd fl., Bom Retiro* ☎ *011/3222–7999* ⊕ *www.maiosbeiramar.com.br* Ⓜ *Tiradentes.*

BROOKLIN

CENTERS AND MALLS

D&D Decoração & Design Center. The center shares a building with the World Trade Center and the Sheraton hotel. It's loaded with fancy home-decorating stores, full-scale restaurants, and fast-food spots. ⊠ *Av. das Nações Unidas 12555, Brooklin* ☎ *011/3043–9000* ⊕ *www. dedshopping.com.br.*

CENTRO

BEAUTY

O Boticário. The Brazilian brand O Boticário was founded by dermatologists and pharmacists from Curitiba in the 1970s. The company creates products for men, women, and children, and through its foundation funds ecological projects throughout Brazil. The shops can be found in most neighborhoods and malls in the city. ⊠ *R. Brig. Luis Antonio 282, Centro* ☎ *011/3115–0712* ⊕ *www.oboticario.com.br.*

LEATHER GOODS AND LUGGAGE

Inovathi. A shop you'll find in many malls all over town, Inovathi has leather accessories at good prices. ⊠ *Avenida Ipiranga 336, Centro* ☎ *011/2179–2050* ⊕ *www.inovathi.com.br* Ⓜ *República.*

MARKETS

Praça da República arts and crafts fair. Vendors sell jewelry, embroidery, leather goods, toys, clothing, paintings, and musical instruments at the Sunday-morning arts-and-crafts fair in Praça da República. ■TIP→ If you look carefully, you can find reasonably priced, out-of-the-ordinary souvenirs. ⊠ *Praça da República, Centro* Ⓜ *República.*

MUSIC

Baratos Afins. Heaven for music collectors, Baratos Afins opened in 1978 and is also a record label. The company was the brainchild of Arnaldo Baptista, guitar player in the influential 1960s Brazilian rock band Os Mutantes. The store sells all kinds of music, but it specializes in Brazilian popular music. If you're looking for rare records, ask for the owner, Luiz Calanca. ⊠ *Av. São João 439, 2nd fl., Centro* ☎ *011/3223–3629* ⊕ *www.baratosafins.com.br* Ⓜ *República.*

Ventania. Browse through more than 100,000 records at this huge store that specializes in Brazilian popular music. You can find old 78s, contemporary CDs, and everything in between. ⊠ *Rua 24 de Maio 188, 1st fl., Centro* ☎ *011/3331–0332* ⊕ *www.ventania.com.br* Ⓜ *República.*

CERQUEIRA CÉSAR

ANTIQUES

Patrimônio. Head to Patrimônio for Brazilian antiques at reasonable prices. The shop also sells Indian artifacts, as well as modern furnishings crafted from iron. ⊠ *Alameda Ministro Rocha Azevedo 1077, 1st fl., Cerqueira César* ☎ *011/99225–7570* ⊕ *www.patrimonioantiguidades. com* ☉ *Fri. and by appointment other days.*

CONSOLAÇÃO

JEWELRY

Antonio Bernardo. Carioca Antonio Bernardo is one of the most famous jewelry designers in Brazil. He creates custom pieces with gold, silver, and other precious metals and stones. ⊠ *Rua Bela Cintra 2063, Consolação* ☏ *011/3083–5622* ⊕ *www.antoniobernardo.com.br* ☻ *Closed Sun.*

HIGIENÓPOLIS

BEACHWEAR

Cia. Marítima. The Brazilian beachwear brand known for its bikinis and swimsuits has a presence in this and many other high-class malls. ⊠ *Shopping Pátio Higienópolis, Av. Higienópolis, Higienópolis* ☏ *011/3661–7602* ⊕ *www.ciamaritima.com.br.*

CENTERS AND MALLS

Shopping Pátio Higienópolis. One of the most upscale shopping malls in São Paulo, Shopping Pátio Higienópolis is a mixture of old and new architecture styles. It has plenty of shops and restaurants, as well as six movie theaters. ⊠ *Av. Higienópolis 618, Higienópolis* ☏ *011/3823–2300* ⊕ *www.patiohigienopolis.com.br.*

ITAIM BIBI

ANTIQUES

Pedro Corrêa do Lago. The shop's namesake owner, a consultant for Sotheby's auction house, sells and auctions rare and used books, as well as antique maps, prints, and drawings of Brazil. ⊠ *Rua Afonso Braz 473, conj. 31& 32, Itaim* ☏ *011/3063–5455* ⊕ *www.sothebys.com.*

CENTERS AND MALLS

JK Iguatemi. Natural light illuminates the atrium and walkways of this luxury mall for the elite, where international brands from AW Store to Zara mix it up with national brands like Animale and Carlos Miele. There are plenty of fancy dining spots. ■ **TIP→ For an added fee, the mall will supply you with a personal shopper.** ⊠ *Av. Presidente Juscelino Kubitschek 2041, Itaim Bibi* ☏ *011/3152–6800* ⊕ *www.jkiguatemi.com.br.*

JARDIM PAULISTA

HANDICRAFTS

Amoa Konoya Arte Indígena. Inspired by contact with indigenous peoples, Walter Gomes opened this store to promote awareness about and economic opportunities for Brazil's native communities. Artisans of 230 indigenous tribes create the crafts and artworks, from musical instruments to earthenware, sold here. ⊠ *Rua João Moura 1002, Jardim Paulista* ☏ *011/3061–0639* ⊕ *www.amoakonoya.com.br.*

JARDIM PAULISTANO

ANTIQUES

Juliana Benfatti. The antiques shop run by Juliana Benfatti and her two sons has inventory that dates back to the 18th century. The buyers have a discerning eye for what was unique and special in many lands over many generations. ✉ *Rua Sampaio Vidal 786, Jardim Paulistano* ☎ *011/3083–7858* ⊕ *www.julianabenfatti.com.br* Ⓜ *Faria Lima.*

BOOKS

Laselva. This bookstore usually receives magazines from abroad earlier than other ones. ✉ *Iguatemi São Paulo, Av. Brigadeiro Faria Lima 2232, Jardim Paulistano* ☎ *011/9460–3802.*

CENTERS AND MALLS

Iguatemi São Paulo. This may be the city's oldest mall, but it has the latest in fashion and fast food. Movie theaters often show films in English with Portuguese subtitles. The Gero Caffé, built in the middle of the main hall, has a fine menu. ■ TIP→ If you're in São Paulo at Christmastime, the North Pole–theme displays here are well worth a detour. ✉ *Av. Brigadeiro Faria Lima 2232, Jardim Paulistano* ☎ *011/3816–6116* ⊕ *www. iguatemisaopaulo.com.br.*

JEWELRY

Tiffany & Co. The world-famous store sells exclusive pieces for the very wealthy. Go for the diamonds—you know you want to. ✉ *Iguatemi São Paulo, Av. Brigadeiro Faria Lima 2232, Jardim Paulista* ☎ *011/3815–7000* ⊕ *www.tiffany.com.*

JARDINS

On Sunday there are antiques fairs near the Museu de Arte de São Paulo (MASP).

ANTIQUES

Legado. At this antiques showroom that holds monthly auctions you'll find plenty of heirlooms looking for new homes—Baccarat bowls and vases, art-nouveau and art-deco sideboards, and a slew of silver trays and tea sets among them—along with such oddities as the helmet of the late race-car legend Ayrton Senna. ✉ *Alameda Lorena 882, Jardins* ☎ *011/3063–3400* ⊕ *www.legadoantiguidades.com.br.*

Renée Behar Antiques. This shop has that prim and proper look one expects from a reputable, longtime dealer known for classic 18th- and 19th-century silver, ceramics, and other antiques. The craftsmanship in the items for sale here is consistently top-drawer. ✉ *Rua Peixoto Gomide 2088, Jardins* ☎ *011/3085–3622* ⊕ *www.reneebehar.com.br.*

ART GALLERIES

Arte Aplicada. A respected Jardins gallery, Arte Aplicada is known for its high-quality Brazilian paintings, sculptures, and prints. ✉ *Rua Haddock Lobo 1406, Jardins* ☎ *011/3062–5128, 011/3064–4725* ⊕ *www. arteaplicada.com.br.*

Bel Galeria. Paintings and sculptures from Brazilian and international artists go up for auction at Bel Galeria. ⊠ *Rua Paraguaçú 334, Perdizes* ☎ *011/3663–3100* ⊕ *www.belgaleriadearte.com.br.*

Galeria Renot. At this gallery you'll find oil paintings by such Brazilian artists as Vicente Rego Monteiro, Di Cavalcanti, Cícero Dias, and Anita Malfatti. ⊠ *Alameda Ministro Rocha Azevedo 1327, Jardins* ☎ *011/3083–5933* ⊕ *www.renot.com.br.*

Mônica Filgueiras & Eduardo Machado Galeria. Many a trend has been set at this gallery, which sells all types of art but mostly paintings and sculpture. ⊠ *Rua Bela Cintra 1533, Jardins* ☎ *011/3082–5292.*

BEAUTY

Granado. As with the other locations of this Brazilian beauty-supplies chain that dates back to 1870, the Jardins shop maintains the old-time appearance of an apothecary. ⊠ *Rua Haddock Lobo 1353, Jardins* ☎ *011/3061–0891* ⊕ *www.granado.com.br.*

BEACHWEAR

Track & Field. This brand's shops, which you'll find in nearly every mall in São Paulo, are good places to buy beachwear and sports clothing. The store sells bikinis and swimsuits from Cia. Marítima, a famous Brazilian beachwear brand. ⊠ *Rua Oscar Freire 959, Jardins* ☎ *011/3062–4457* ⊕ *www.tf.com.br.*

BOOKS

Livraria Cultura. São Paulo's best selection of travel literature can be found here, along with many maps. ⊠ *Av. Paulista 2073, Jardins* ☎ *011/3170–4033* ⊕ *www.livrariacultura.com.br* Ⓜ *Consolação.*

CLOTHING

Alexandre Herchcovitch. The Brazilian designer Alexandre Herchcovitch sells prêt-à-porter and tailor-made clothes at his store. ⊠ *Rua Melo Alves 561, Jardins* ☎ *011/3063–2888* ⊕ *www.herchcovitch.com.br.*

BO.BÔ. Brazilian models and soap-opera stars wear this brand, which blends bohemian and bourgeois (coincidentally, the type of bank account needed to shop here). ⊠ *Rua Oscar Freire 1039, Jardins* ☎ *011/3062–8145* ⊕ *www.bobo.com.br.*

Fórum. Evening attire for young men and women is the specialty of Fórum, which also sells sportswear and shoes. ⊠ *Rua Oscar Freire 916, Jardins* ☎ *011/3085–6269* ⊕ *www.forum.com.br.*

Le Lis Blanc. This chain is Brazil's exclusive purveyor of the French brand Vertigo. Look for party dresses in velvet and sheer fabrics. ⊠ *Rua Oscar Freire 1119, Jardins* ☎ *011/3809–8950* ⊕ *www.lelis.com.br.*

Lita Mortari. The designer Lita Mortari sells her feminine festive wear in four stores in São Paulo, including two in Jardins. ⊠ *Rua Bela Cintra 2195, Jardins* ☎ *011/3064–3021* ⊕ *litamortari.com.br.*

Maria Bonita. If you have money burning a hole in your pocket, shop at Maria Bonita, which has elegant and fun women's clothes. At Maria Bonita Extra, right next door, the prices are a little lower. ⊠ *Rua Oscar Freire 702, Jardins* ☎ *011/3068–6500* ⊕ *www.mariabonita.com.br.*

Mulher Elástica. Outfits built around leggings are no stretch for Mulher Elástica. Looks range from sporty to business casual. ⊠ *Rua Dr. Melo Alves 381, Jardins* ☎ *011/3060–8263* ⊕ *mulherelastica.com.br.*

Reinaldo Lourenço. Sophisticated, high-quality women's clothing is Reinaldo Lourenço's calling card. ⊠ *Rua Bela Cintra 2167, Jardins* ☎ *011/3085–8150* ⊕ *www.reinaldolourenco.com.br.*

Richards. The collections at Richards, one of Brazil's best sportswear lines, include outfits suitable for the beach or the mountains. ⊠ *JK Iguatemi, Av. Presidente Juscelino Kubitschek 2041, Vila Olímpia* ☎ *011/3073–1332* ⊕ *www.richards.com.br.*

HANDICRAFTS

Galeria de Arte Brasileira. Since 1920 Galeria de Arte Brasileira has specialized in art and handicrafts from all over Brazil. Look for objects made of pau-brasil wood, hammocks, jewelry, T-shirts, *marajoara* pottery (from the Amazon), and lace. ⊠ *Alameda Lorena 2163, Jardins* ☎ *011/3062–9452* ⊕ *www.galeriaartebrasileira.com.br.*

JEWELRY

H.Stern. An internationally known Brazilian brand for jewelry, H.Stern has shops in more than 30 countries. This one has designs made especially for the Brazilian stores. ⊠ *Rua Oscar Freire 652, Jardins* ☎ *011/3068–8082* ⊕ *www.hstern.com.br.*

LEATHER GOODS AND LUGGAGE

Le Postiche. One of the biggest brands for luggage and leather goods in Brazil, Le Postiche has 96 shops around the country. You can find one in almost any mall in São Paulo. ⊠ *R. Haddock Lobo, 1307, Jardins* ☎ *011/3081–9702* ⊕ *www.lepostiche.com.br.*

MOEMA

CLOTHING

Fil du Fil. The women's clothing brand Fil du Fil maintains three locations across Moema and Vila Olímpia. This address is dedicated to plus-size attire. Looks are casual with colorful blouses and dresses featuring prominently. ⊠ *Rua Canário 1253, Moema* ☎ *011/5561–2645* ⊕ *www.fildufil.com.br.*

Vila Romana Factory Store. The prices for suits, jackets, jeans, and some women's clothing (silk blouses, for example) at Vila Romana Factory Store are unbeatable. The store is a 40-minute drive from Centro. In-town mall branches are more convenient, but prices are higher. ⊠ *Via Anhanguera, Km 17.5, Rua Robert Bosch 1765, Osasco* ☎ *011/3604–5293* ⊕ *www.vilaromana.com.br* ⊠ *Shopping Ibirapuera, Piso Campo Belo, Av. Ibirapuera 3103, Moema* ☎ *011/5535–1808.*

HANDICRAFTS

Casa do Amazonas. As its name suggests, Casa do Amazonas has a wide selection of products from the Amazon. ⊠ *Alameda dos Jurupis 460, Moema* ☎ *011/5051–3098* ⊕ *www.arteindigena.com.br.*

MUSIC

Painel Musical. In shopping malls the best option is Painel Musical, a small record shop that carries CDs and DVDs. It usually has a good selection of instrumental Brazilian music and local rock. ⊠ *Shopping Ibirapuera, Av. Ibirapuera 3103, Moema* ☎ *011/5561–9981* ⊕ *www. painelmusical.com.br.*

MORUMBI

CENTERS AND MALLS

MorumbiShopping. MorumbiShopping, in the city's fastest-growing area, has taken a backseat to newer malls Cidade Jardim and JK Iguatemi. That said, it's still a slice of São Paulo's upper crust, seasoned with swank boutiques, record stores, bookstores, and restaurants. The atrium hosts art exhibits. ⊠ *Av. Roque Petroni Jr. 1089, Morumbi* ☎ *011/4003–4132* ⊕ *www.morumbishopping.com.br.*

Shopping Cidade Jardim. The feeling here is almost as though archaeologists have uncovered a lost jungle city's ancient temples—only they're to upscale shopping and gourmet dining, not deities and potentates. Trees outside sprout three stories high, and bevy of plants inside shrouds boutiques with names like Valentino, Omega, and Louis Vuitton. For resting, there's a huge open garden with splendid city views. ■**TIP**➔ **If you get hungry, head to the Argentine steakhouse Pobre Juan for a hearty meal or, for lighter fare, the French bakery and bistro Marie-Madeleine.** ⊠ *Av. Magalhães de Castro 12000, Morumbi* ☎ *011/3552–1000* ⊕ *www. shoppingcidadejardim.com.*

CLOTHING

FAMILY **Camu Camu.** Founded in 1974, Camu Camu sells stylish clothing for young girls and boys. ⊠ *Shopping Marketing Place, Av. Dr. Chucri Zaidan 902, Morumbi* ☎ *011/5181–1567* ⊕ *www.camucamu.com.br.*

PARAÍSO

HANDICRAFTS

Marcenaria Trancoso. The wooden products this shop sells are an elegant mixture of interior design and handicraft. ⊠ *Rua Mateus Grou 282, Pinheiros* ☎ *011/3816–1298* ⊕ *www.marcenariatrancoso.com.br* Ⓜ *Vila Madalena.*

LEATHER GOODS AND LUGGAGE

Arezzo. A leader in the leather game, with stores in most São Paulo shopping malls, Arezzo is best known for its footwear. The brand also has an extensive line of bags, wallets, and accessories. ⊠ *Shopping Paulista, Rua Treze de Maio 1947, Paraíso* ☎ *011/3171–1183* ⊕ *www.arezzo. com.br* Ⓜ *Brigadeiro.*

PINHEIROS

BOOKS

Fnac. You can buy maps and English-language books, magazines, and newspapers at Fnac. There are also locations in Paulista and Morumbi. ✉ *Praça dos Omaguás 34, Pinheiros* ☎ *011/3579–2000* ⊕ *www.fnac.com.br.*

VILA MADALENA

ART

Galeria Fortes Vilaça. This gallery promotes the works of up-and-coming Brazilian artists, and the curators have an eye for talent. ✉ *Rua Fradique Coutinho 1500, Vila Madalena* ☎ *011/3032–7066* ⊕ *www.fortesvilaca. com.br.*

CLOTHING

Uma. Young women are intrigued by the high-fashion designs of the swimsuits, dresses, shorts, shirts, and pants at Uma. ✉ *Rua Girassol 273, Vila Madalena* ☎ *011/3813–5559* ⊕ *www.uma.com.br.*

HANDICRAFTS

Ôoh de Casa. Souvenirs and presents, from vividly colored hammocks to papier-mâché piggy banks (cows, actually), are for sale here. ✉ *Rua Fradique Coutinho 899, Vila Madalena* ☎ *011/3812–4934, 011/3815–9577* ⊕ *www.oohdecasa.com.br.*

JEWELRY

Sou-Sou. Accessorize at Sou-Sou, a craft-jewelry workshop and store. The boutique also carries women's clothes. ✉ *Rua Aspicuelta 355, Vila Madalena* ☎ *011/3812–4076* ⊕ *loja.sou-sou.com.br/sou-sou.*

VILA MARIANA

ART

Galeria Jacques Ardies. If *art naïf* is your thing, Galeria Jacques Ardies is a must. As the name suggests, art naïf is simple, with a primitive and handcrafted look. ✉ *Rua Morgado de Mateus 579, Vila Mariana* ☎ *011/5539–7500* ⊕ *www.ardies.com* Ⓜ *Paraíso.*

SIDE TRIPS FROM SÃO PAULO

Updated by
Angelica Mari
Hillary

São Paulo's surroundings are perfect for all types of get-aways. The state has the best highways in the country, making it easy to travel by car or bus to its many small, beautiful beaches, and even beyond to neighboring states (Paraná, Rio de Janeiro, and Minas Gerais). Although most sandy stretches require one- or two-hour drives, good side trips from the city can be as close as the 30-minute trip to Embu.

Embu is famous for its furniture stores, and artisans from throughout Brazil sell their wares at its enormous weekend crafts fair; expect to see all the sights in one afternoon. Also less than an hour away, 1500s Santana de Parnaíba mixes historical settings and regional attractions with good restaurants.

For a weekend of relaxation, soak up the healing properties of Águas de São Pedro's spas and springs. If you like mountains, head up in another direction: Campos de Jordão, where cafés and clothing stores are often crowded with oh-so-chic *paulistanos* (natives of São Paulo city; inhabitants of São Paulo State are called *paulistas*). Serra Negra offers the mineral waters and an immersion in the coffee production history of Brazil, as well as several activities for families and couples looking for a romantic getaway. Favor the state's North Shore and Ilhabela (the name means "beautiful island") if you prefer the beach. The island is part of the Mata Atlântica (Atlantic Rain Forest) and has many waterfalls, trails, and diving spots.

ORIENTATION AND PLANNING

GETTING ORIENTED

Most of the towns in this chapter can be done as day trips from São Paulo. Trips by bus can take anywhere from one to four hours. It's even possible to take a taxi from the city to Embu das Artes and Santana do Parnaíba.

THE NORTH SHORE
The North Shore (about 210 km/130 miles from São Paulo) has beautiful beaches for every kind of sun or sports enthusiast. In the 1990s the area experienced a building boom, with condos popping up seemingly overnight. Luckily, the region still managed to maintain its pristine environment.

INLAND
Just a stone's throw from São Paulo, Embu das Artes is famous for its big handicraft fair with paintings, toys, and candles, as well as scrumptious pastries and breads. Campos do Jordão, known as the Switzerland of Brazil, attracts hordes of chill-seekers in winter, when temperatures drop below tepid. Serra Negra is the main city of São Paulo's Circuito das Águas (Water Circuit) and offers plenty of events and activities for families as well as a refuge for couples seeking romance.

PLANNING

WHEN TO GO

The area around São Paulo is lovely year-round. Most places have a steady stream of visitors, so it's always wise to book hotels well in advance. Summers are hot and humid, and it's the rainy season, so it's good to have some indoor plans in the back of your mind. In winter, temperatures drop into the 40s°F (5°C–10°C), so be sure to bring some warm clothing.

GETTING HERE AND AROUND

Bus travel to and from the towns around São Paulo can be a time-consuming affair since they don't run too frequently. A better option is renting a car or taking a taxi. The roads are good and traffic isn't too chaotic.

TOP REASONS TO GO

■ **Beach Paradises:** Bask on a range of beautiful beaches, from surfer paradises in Ubatuba to coastal islands and sandy rain-forest coves.

■ **Rich History:** Witness Brazil's colonial and rural history in Embu and Santana de Parnaíba.

■ **Gorgeous Landscapes:** Luxuriant forests in Campos de Jordão combine with impressive bodies of water and wildlife in Águas de São Pedro, Serra Negra and Ilhabela.

RESTAURANTS

Restaurants in coastal towns tend to be of the rustic beach-café sort, and predictably serve lots of seafood. For a change of taste, visit Ubatuba and these three neighborhoods in or near São Sebastião—Maresias, Boiçucanga, and Camburi—where you can find good pizzerias and Japanese restaurants. Some of the best restaurants in the state, outside of São Paulo, are in Campos do Jordão, a popular paulistano mountain retreat. In Serra Negra, you find countryside charm in a very compact town that can be explored by foot. Here you can try a Brazilian version of Swiss fondue (both the chocolate and the cheese varieties are delicious). *Prices in the reviews are the average cost of a main course at dinner or, if dinner is not served, at lunch.*

HOTELS

São Paulo has by far the best lodgings in the state. Elsewhere you can generally find basic *pousadas* (sort of like bed-and-breakfasts), with the occasional gems like Maison Joly and Pousada do Hibiscus in Ilhabela. Coastal towns are packed in summer (from December to March) and it's almost impossible to get anything without advance reservations. The same holds true for Campos do Jordão and Serra Negra in winter (June and September). *Prices in the reviews are the lowest cost of a standard double room in high season. For expanded reviews, facilities, and current deals, visit Fodors.com.*

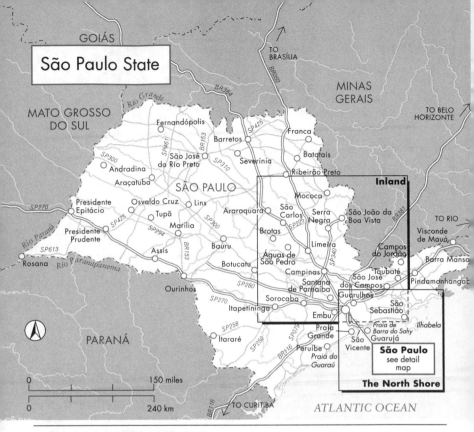

THE NORTH SHORE

The cleanest and best *praias* (beaches) in São Paulo State are along what is known as the Litoral Norte (North Shore). Mountains and bits of Atlantic Rain Forest hug numerous small, sandy coves. Some of the North Shore's most beautiful houses line the Rio-Santos Highway (SP 055) on the approach to Maresias. However, extra care is required when driving through the 055, as the road conditions and lighting are precarious, particularly past Maresias. On weekdays when school is in session, the beaches are gloriously deserted.

Beaches generally have restaurants nearby, or at least vendors selling sandwiches, soft drinks, and beer. They often don't have bathrooms or phones right on the sands, but several vendors rent beach umbrellas or chairs, especially in summer and on holidays and weekends. It is standard practice in Brazilian beaches to set up a *conta* with vendors, so you can order food and drinks during your stay and pay it all when you leave.

SÃO SEBASTIÃO

204 km (127 miles) southeast of São Paulo

São Sebastião stretches along 100 km (62 miles) of the North Shore. Its bays, islands, and beaches attract everyone from the youngsters who flock to Maresias and Camburi to the families who favor Barra do Sahy. Boating enthusiasts, hikers, and wildlife-seekers also come here, especially on weekends, when hotels are often crowded. Nightlife is good here—the main spots are in Maresias and Boiçucanga. The "beautiful island" of Ilhabela *(⇨ below)* is a 15-minute boat ride away from downtown São Sebastião.

GETTING HERE AND AROUND

Litorânea buses travel four times daily to São Sebastião (to the ferry dock) from São Paulo and take about 2½ hours.

The drive from São Paulo to São Sebastião is about 3½ hours if it is not raining. Take Rodovia Ayrton Senna–Carvalho Pinto (SP 070), followed by Rodovia Tamoios (SP 099) to Caraguatatuba, and then follow the signs, which lead all the way to the Ilhabela ferry landing.

ESSENTIALS

Bus Contacts Litorânea ☎ *0800/2853–047, 11/3775–3890* ⊕ *www.litoranea. com.br.* **Terminal Rodoviário** ⊠ *Praça Vereador Venino Fernandes Moreira, 10.*

Visitor Information Tourist Office Sectur. Tourist Office Sectur has trail maps that include descriptions of each trail's length and difficulty and, for the more popular routes, a listing of their unique features. Keep in mind that all trails require guides, which Sectur is happy to help arrange. ⊠ *Avenida Altino Arantes, 174, Centro* ☎ *012/3892–2620.*

BEACHES

FAMILY **Barra do Sahy.** Families with young children favor small, quiet Barra do Sahy. Its narrow strip of sand (with a bay and a river on one side and rocks on the other) is steep but smooth, and the water is clean and calm. Kayakers paddle about, and divers are drawn to the nearby Ilha das Couves. Area restaurants serve mostly basic fish dishes with rice and salad. Note that Barra do Sahy's entrance is atop a slope and appears suddenly—be on the lookout around marker Km 174. **Amenities:** food and drink, lifeguards, parking (no fee). **Best for:** sunrise, snorkeling. ⊠ *Rio-Santos Hwy., SP 055, 157 km/97 miles southeast of São Paulo.*

Camburizinho and Camburi. Wealthy paulistanos flock to Camburizinho and Camburi to sunbathe, surf, and party. While the first beach is more secluded and also where the families head to, the latter, on the other side of the river Camburi, is where the action is. At the center of the beaches is a cluster of cafés, ice-cream shops, bars, and restaurants, including Candeeiro, a fabulous Neapolitan-style pizzeria and Gelateria Parmalat, where you can find delicious ice cream. The two beaches are located just north of Barra do Sahy. If you're coming from the south, take the second entrance, which is usually in better shape than the first entrance, at Km 166. **Amenities:** food and drink, lifeguards, parking (fee). **Best for:** partiers, surfing, sunset. ⊠ *Rio-Santos Hwy., SP 055, 162 km/100 miles southeast of São Paulo.*

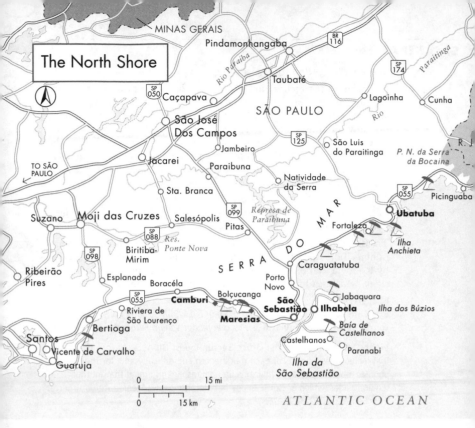

Maresias. Maresias is a 4-km (2-mile) stretch of white sand with clean, green waters that are good for swimming and surfing. Maresias is popular with a young crowd and compared with the other popular villages along the North Coast, it's a larger beach village with a better infrastructure, including bigger supermarkets, banks, and a wider choice of nightlife entertainment. **Amenities:** food and drink, toilets, parking (fee), lifeguards. **Best for:** partiers, surfing, windsurfing. ⊠ *Rio-Santos Hwy, Km 151, SP 055, 177 km/109 miles southeast of São Paulo.*

ILHABELA

7 km (5 miles)/15-minute boat ride from São Sebastião.

Fodor's Choice ★ Ilhabela is favored by those who like the beach and water sports; indeed, many sailing competitions are held here as well as scuba diving. This is the biggest sea island in the country, with 22 calm beaches along its western shore, which faces the mainland. The hotels are mostly at the north end, though the best sandy stretches are the 13 to the south, which face the open sea. Eighty percent of the island is in a state park area.

There are two small towns on the island: one is where the locals live; the other is where most visitors stay because of its hotels, restaurants, and stores. During the winter months most businesses that cater to tourists, including restaurants, are open only on weekends.

A BIT OF HISTORY

In the 19th century, farming, first of sugarcane, and then of coffee, was São Paulo's major industry and brought prosperity to the region.

At the beginning of the 20th century, São Paulo became the center for industry in Brazil, as factories were built at a rapid pace, mostly by an immigrant workforce. By mid-century, São Paulo was one of the largest industrialized centers in Latin America and the state with the highest population in Brazil, thanks in part to mass migration from within Brazil.

Today São Paulo is the richest and most multicultural state in the country. It has the largest Japanese community outside of Japan (an estimated 1 million people), about 1 million people of Middle Eastern descent, and about 6 million people of Italian descent.

5

Scuba divers have several 19th- and early-20th-century wrecks to explore—this region has the most wrecks of any area off Brazil's coast—and hikers can set off on the numerous inland trails, many of which lead to a waterfall (the island has more than 300). ■ TIP→ Mosquitoes are a problem; bring plenty of insect repellent.

GETTING HERE AND AROUND

Balsas (ferries) from São Sebastião to Ilhabela run every 30 minutes from 6 am to midnight and hourly during the night. The São Sebastião balsa transports vehicles as well as passengers. Fares range from R$11 (weekdays) to R$16,40 (weekends), including a car. To get to the ferry dock in São Sebastião, take Avenida São Sebastião from town to the coast. Make advance ferry reservations, particularly December through February.

The best way to get around Ilhabela is by car. There are no rental agencies on the island (or connecting bridges) so be sure to make arrangements beforehand. Public buses also cross the island from north to south daily.

ESSENTIALS

Ferry Information São Sebastião Balsa ☎ *012/3892–1576.*

Visitor Information Ilhabela Secretaria do Turismo ✉ *Praça Vereador José Leite dos Passos, 14* ☎ *012/3895–7492* ⊕ *www.ilhabela.sp.gov.br.* **Maremar Turismo** ✉ *Av. Princesa Isabel, 90* ☎ *012/3896–1418* ⊕ *www.maremar.tur.br* ☞ *Scuba diving, jeep, horseback riding, and hiking tours.*

BEACHES

Praia da Armação. The long strip of white sand, calm sea, and a large green area here attracts sailing, windsurfing, and kite-surfing aficionados. Busy during most of the year, Praia da Armação has an excellent infrastructure, with bars, restaurants, and kiosks serving various food and drinks and renting parasols and beach chairs. Bathrooms, baby changing facilities, and parking bays are available. There is a church on-site, which is said to be one of the oldest buildings on the island.

The beach was also once the site of a factory for processing blubber and other resources from whales caught in the waters around Ilhabela. **Amenities:** food and drink, toilets, parking (fee), lifeguards, water sports. **Best for:** surfing, snorkeling, sunset, walking. ✉ *14 km (9 miles) north of ferry dock.*

Praia do Curral. Curral is one of the most famous beaches of Ilhabela, one of the most popular destinations for tourists as well as young people. It has clear and slightly rough waters and also a large green area, which serves as a refuge for those wanting to take a break from sunbathing. The local vendors provide tables and chairs, fresh showers with clean water, bathrooms, and parking. At night people gather at the many restaurants and bars—some with live music—as well as places to camp. The wreck of the ship *Aymoré* (1921) can be found off the coast of this beach, near Ponta do Ribeirão, where you can also look for a waterfall trail. **Amenities:** food and drink, toilets, showers, lifeguards. **Best for:** partiers, sunset. ✉ *6 km (4 miles) south of Praia Grande.*

Praia Grande. It's busy, but some of the best infrastructure in Ilhabela can be found here: the kiosks have tables in the shade, you can rent a chair from most vendors along the long sandy strip, there are showers available free of charge and even a chapel. The beach is also sought for windsurfing, diving, and surfing. The sandy strip is rather inclined, with a tumble in the central part. The sands are thick and yellowish. On the far left there is a small river that ends in the sea. **Amenities:** food and drink, toilets, showers, lifeguards. **Best for:** walking, surfing, windsurfing, partiers. ✉ *13 km (8 miles) south of ferry dock.*

WHERE TO EAT AND STAY

$$ SEAFOOD

🍴 **Ilha Sul.** The best option on the menu at Ilha Sul is the grilled shrimp with vegetables. Fish and other seafood are also available. [$] *Average main: R$40* ✉ *Av. Riachuelo 287* ☎ *012/3894–9426* 🕒 *Closed Mon.–Thurs. Apr.–June and Aug.–Nov.*

$$$$ SEAFOOD FAMILY

🍴 **Viana.** *Camarão* (shrimp) is prepared in various ways at this traditional and petite restaurant with just a few tables. It's popular among locals, who come here to eat and enjoy the gorgeous view and sunsets. Grilled fish is also on the menu. Its open for breakfast Tuesday and on weekends. [$] *Average main: R$65* ✉ *Av. Leonardo Reale 2301* ☎ *012/3896–1089* ✍ *Reservations essential* 🕒 *Mon. and Thurs. no lunch. Closed Wed.*

$$$$ HOTEL Fodor's Choice ★

🏨 **Maison Joly.** Past guests of this exclusive hotel at the top of the Cantagalo Hill range from kings of Sweden to the Rolling Stones. **Pros:** beautiful surroundings; excellent restaurant. **Cons:** service a little erratic in busy seasons. [$] *Rooms from: R$575* ✉ *Rua Antônio Lisboa Alves 278* ☎ *012/3896–1201* 🌐 *www.maisonjoly.com.br* 🛏 *9 rooms* 🍽 *Breakfast.*

$ B&B/INN

🏨 **Pousada dos Hibiscos.** North of the ferry dock, this red house has midsize rooms, all at ground level. **Pros:** individualized rooms. **Cons:** couples looking for poolside relexation may be disturbed by large groups. [$] *Rooms from: R$220* ✉ *Av. Pedro de Paula Moraes 720* ☎ *012/3896–1375* 🌐 *www.pousadadoshibiscos.com.br* 🛏 *13 rooms* 🍽 *No meals.*

SPORTS AND THE OUTDOORS
BOATING AND SAILING
Because of its excellent winds and currents, Ilhabela is a sailor's mecca.

Iate Club de Ilhabela. For information on annual boating competitions that Ilhabela hosts, including a popular sailing week, contact Iate Club de Ilhabela. ⊠ *Av. Força Expedicionária Brasileira 187* ☎ *012/3896–2300.*

Ilha Sailing Ocean School. Sailing courses here run 12 hours and cost about R$500. ⊠ *Av. Pedro de Paula Moraes 578* ☎ *012/9766–6619* ⊕ *www.ilhasailing.com.br.*

HIKING
Cachoeira dos Três Tombos. This trail starts at Feiticeira Beach (a nude beach) and leads to three waterfalls.

Local Adventure. You can arrange guided hikes through local agencies such as Local Adventure. ⊠ *Av. Princesa Isabel 171* ☎ *012/3896–5777.*

Trilha da Água Branca. Trilha da Água Branca is an accessible, well-marked trail. Three of its paths go to waterfalls that have natural pools and picnic areas.

KITE- AND WINDSURFING
Many of the Brazilian windsurfing champions are based in Ilhabela and also train here. Savvy kite-surfers and windsurfers head to Ponta das Canas, at the island's northern tip. Side-by-side beaches Praia do Pinto and Armação, both located 12 km (7 miles) north of ferry dock, also have favorable wind conditions.

BL3. You can take kite-surfing, windsurfing, and sailing lessons at BL3, the biggest school in Ilhabela. Individual lessons are priced between R$160–200. ⊠ *Av. Pedro Paulo de Moraes 1166* ☎ *012/3285–1762* ⊕ *www.bl3.com.br* ⊠ *Armação Beach* ☎ *012/3896–1271.*

SCUBA DIVING
Diving is a popular activity for those visiting Ilhabela. In the calm, transparent waters, you can explore the marine wildlife as well as discover the mysteries surrounding the island's various shipwrecks. It is said that Ilhabela has more than 100 close to its shore. These vessels have formed huge submerged artificial reefs, and are now home to a wide variety of aquatic species such as turtles, octopuses, and the like. It is still possible to actually see the ships. Beginning divers should aim for the most popular wrecks, such as the Aymoré (1914; Curral beach; 3–7 meters) and the Darth (1894; Itaboca beach; 5–15 meters). There are numerous diving schools along nearly every beach, which also rent equipment if you are happy to go solo.

Colonial Diver. You can rent equipment, take diving classes, and arrange for a dive-boat trip through Colonial Diver. The basic course takes three to four days and costs around R$1000, which includes underwater videos and photographs, course material, and an international certificate. ⊠ *Av. Brasil 1751* ☎ *012/3894–9459* ⊕ *www.colonialdiver.com.br.*

Ilha das Cabras. The main attractions of this little piece of paradise—besides the white sand and clear water—are the tiny bars that serve delicious, fresh seafood and the Ecological Sanctuary of Ilha das Cabras.

The park, created in 1992, is a secluded reserve around the island and is also a great diving and fish-watching site. While most "baptisms" of diving beginners take place here, seasoned divers head off to their underwater adventures at the diving/snorkeling sanctuary off the shore of the isle, where a statue of Neptune can be found at the 22-foot depth. ⊠ *2 km (1 mile) south of ferry.*

Ilha de Búzios. A nearly two-hour boat trip separates Ilhabela from Ilha de Búzios, but the effort is totally worthwhile. Because it is located far from the coast, the water is very transparent, meaning divers will be able see plenty of colorful fish and other underwater fauna such as rays and sea turtles. The main stars, however, are the dolphins, which fearlessly approach boats. ⊠ *25 km (15 miles) offshore; take boat from São Sebastião.*

Itaboca. One of the best places for diving is Itaboca, where British ship *Darth* sank in 1884, leaving bottles of wine and porcelain dishes that can still be found. ⊠ *17 km (11 miles) south of ferry dock.*

SURFING

One of the best beaches to surf in Ilhabela is Baía de Castelhanos, which is located 22 km (14 miles) east of the ferry dock. To get there you'll need a four-wheel-drive vehicle, and if it rains even this won't be enough. Consider arriving by sailboat, which demands a 1½- to 3-hour trip that can be arranged through local tour operators. If you're lucky, you might spot a dolphin off the shore of this 2-km (1¼-mile) beach—the largest on the island. Pacuíba, which is located 20 km (12 miles) north of the ferry dock, also has decent wave action. The months of July and August are colder and much quieter. Boards can be rented in surf shops, ever-present on most beaches.

UBATUBA

234 km (145 miles) southeast of São Paulo

Many of the more than 70 beaches around Ubatuba are more than beautiful enough to merit the long drive from São Paulo. Young people, surfers, and couples with and without children hang out in the 90-km (56-mile) area, where waterfalls, boat rides, aquariums, diving, and trekking in the wild are major attractions. Downtown Ubatuba also has an active nightlife, especially in summer. Ubatuba can be reached from São Paulo via the Carvalho Pinto (SP 070) and Oswaldo Cruz (SP 125) highways.

GETTING HERE AND AROUND

Litorânea buses travel eight times a day to Ubatuba from São Paulo. The journey takes about four hours. By car from São Paulo, take Rodovia Ayrton Senna–Carvalho Pinto (SP 070), followed by Rodovia Tamoios (SP 099) to Caraguatatuba. Turn right and head north on SP 055.

ESSENTIALS

Bus Contacts Litorânea ☎ *011/6221–0244, 011/3775–3850* ⊕ *www.litoranea. com.br.* **Rodoviária Litorânea** ⊕ *www.rodoviariaubatuba.com.*

BEACHES

Praia Grande. For those seeking a party atmosphere, Praia Grande is a great option. It has bars and restaurants by the sea, with local samba and country music playing all day. Chairs and parasols can be hired from beach vendors. The waters here are clean and green, and the hard sands are ideal for football, volleyball, and racquetball; it's also a great place for hiking. Praia Grande is a major surf spot in Ubatuba, with very consistent and perfect waves. **Amenities:** food and drink, parking (fee), lifeguards. **Best for:** partiers, surfing, walking. ⊠ *Off Tamoios [SP 099] and Rio-Santos intersection.*

Praia do Prumirim. A small beach of coarse sands, turquoise calm waters, and surrounded by plenty of rain forest, Prumirim is lined with summer holiday mansions. However, this beach of exhuberant natural beauty is not very busy. A beautiful waterfall with a natural pool can be accessed by the Rio-Santos highway. The access to Prumirim is near Km 29 of BR–101 (Rio-Santos), past the entrance of a private condominium. Located 900 meters from the beach, Prumirim Island also has magnificent scenery and it is also a great place for diving. To reach the island you can hire one of the local fishermen or even swim. It has good waves for surfing, but the waves are generally smaller than Praia Grande. **Amenities:** food and drink. **Best for:** solitude, snorkeling, walking, sunrise. ⊠ *Near Km 29 of BR–101 (Rio-Santos).*

INLAND

São Paulo's inland region has beautiful mountains, springs, rivers, and waterfalls perfect for outdoor activities like hiking and rafting. Historic attractions are generally fewer than in other states. Save some time for clothing and crafts shopping, and for the lavish regional cuisine.

Highways that lead to inland towns are some of the best in the state. To get to Águas de São Pedro and Brotas, take Anhangüera–Bandeirantes (SP 330/SP 348); to Santana de Parnaíba, take Castelo Branco (SP 280); and to Campos de Jordão, take Ayrton Senna–Carvalho Pinto (SP 70). Embu is the exception—it's a 30-minute drive from the capital on the not-so-well-maintained Régis Bittencourt (BR 116). To go by bus, choose between the daily departures from the Tietê and Barra Funda terminals in São Paulo. Both are next to subway stations, making access fairly easy.

ÁGUAS DE SÃO PEDRO

180 km (112 miles) northwest of São Paulo.

Although Águas de São Pedro is one of the smallest cities in Brazil, at a mere 3.9 square km (1.5 square miles), its sulfurous waters made it famous countrywide in the 1940s and '50s. The healing hot springs were discovered by chance in the 1920s when technicians were drilling for oil.

Fonte Juventude is the richest in sulfur in the Americas and is often used to treat rheumatism, asthma, bronchitis, and skin ailments. The waters

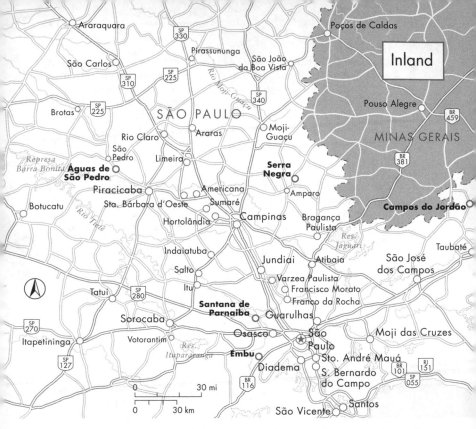

at Fonte Gioconda have minor radioactive elements (and, yes, they are reportedly good for you), whereas Fonte Almeida Salles's have chlorine bicarbonate and sodium (which are said to alleviate the symptoms of diabetes and upset stomach).

You can access the springs at the Balneário Publico (public bathhouse) or through some hotels. Though a number of illnesses respond to the water, most visitors are just healthy tourists soaking in relaxation. Águas de São Pedro is compact, so it's easy to get around on foot.

GETTING HERE AND AROUND
Águas de São Pedro is about a 2½-hour drive north of São Paulo on Anhangüera-Bandeirantes (SP 330/SP 348) and then SP 304.

ESSENTIALS
Visitor Information Águas de São Pedro Informações Turísticas.
This tourism office is open Monday through Friday from 9 am to 6 pm. On weekends and public holidays, a tourist information office operates at Avenida Carlos Mauro s/n, right next to the entrance of Parque Otavio de Moura Andrade, also from 9 to 6. ⊠ *Praça Pref Geraldo Azevedo, 153* ☎ *019/3482–1652* ⊕ *www.aguasdesaopedro.sp.gov.br.*

EXPLORING

Balneário Municipal Dr. Octávio Moura Andrade. Want immersion baths in sulfurous springwater? You can swim in the pool or sweat in the sauna while you wait for your private soak, massage, or beauty appointment. A snack bar and a gift shop round out the spa services. ✉ *Av. Carlos Mauro* ☎ *019/3482–1333* 🎟 *R$8–R$33* 🕒 *Mon.–Thurs. 7:30–noon, Fri.–Sat. 7–noon and 3–5:30, Sun. 7–noon.*

FAMILY **Bosque Municipal Dr. Octávio Moura Andrade.** A walk through the woods in Bosque Municipal Dr. Octávio Moura Andrade is a chance to relax. Horseback riding costs around R$10 for a half hour. It's part of the Balnéario complex *(⇨ below)*. Saunas, baths, and massages cost R$8–R$33. ✉ *Av. Carlos Mauro* ☎ *019/3482–1333* 🎟 *Free* 🕒 *Weekdays 7–noon, weekends 7–5.*

FAMILY **Thermas Water Park.** A good option if you have kids is Thermas Water Park. It has 11 pools, 8 waterslides, and a small working farm. Horseback rides are also available. ✉ *Km 189, SP 304* ☎ *019/3181–2111* 🎟 *R$60* 🕒 *Daily 8–6.*

WHERE TO STAY

$$ HOTEL ALL-INCLUSIVE 🏨 **Avenida Charme Hotel.** This hotel with an arcaded veranda resembles a large ranch house. **Pros:** excellent breakfast; friendly service. **Cons:** rooms are spacious but plain and sparsely decorated. [$] *Rooms from: R$300* ✉ *Av. Carlos Mauro 246* ☎ *019/3482–7900* 🌐 *www.hotelavenida.com.br* 🛏 *53 rooms* 💳 *No credit cards* 🍴 *All-inclusive.*

$$$$ HOTEL Fodor'sChoice ★ 🏨 **Grande Hotel São Pedro.** In the middle of a 300,000-square-meter (3.2 million-square-foot) park with more than 1 million trees and local wildlife, this hotel is in a beautiful art deco building that was a casino during the 1940s. **Pros:** beautiful location; excellent service. **Cons:** it often requires booking months in advance, especially during the winter season. [$] *Rooms from: R$700* ✉ *Parque Dr. Octávio de Moura Andrade* ☎ *019/3482–7600* 🌐 *www.grandehotelsenac.com.br* 🛏 *96 rooms, 16 suites* 🍴 *No meals.*

$ HOTEL 🏨 **Hotel Jerubiaçaba.** In a 17,000-square-meter (183,000-square-foot) green area with springs and a bathhouse, this hotel features rooms bathed in light colors. **Pros:** excellent location. **Cons:** rather simple furnishings; not very comfortable mattresses. [$] *Rooms from: R$200* ✉ *Av. Carlos Mauro 168* ☎ *0800/13–1411* 🌐 *www.hoteljerubiacaba.com.br* 🛏 *120 rooms, 8 suites* 🍴 *No meals.*

CAMPOS DO JORDÃO

184 km (114 miles) northeast of São Paulo.

In the Serra da Mantiqueira at an altitude of 5,525 feet, Campos do Jordão and its fresh mountain air are paulistanos' favorite winter attractions. In July temperatures drop as low as 32°F (0°C), though it never snows; in warmer months temperatures linger in the 13°C–16°C (55°F–60°F) range.

In the past some people came for their health (the town was once a tuberculosis treatment area), others for inspiration—including such Brazilian artists as writer Monteiro Lobato, dramatist Nelson Rodrigues, and painter Lasar Segall. Nowadays the arts continue to thrive, especially during July's Festival de Inverno (Winter Festival), which draws classical musicians from around the world.

Exploring Campos do Jordão without a car is difficult. The attractions are far-flung, except for those at Vila Capivari.

GETTING HERE AND AROUND

Six Passaro Marron buses leave São Paulo for Campos do Jordão daily. The journey takes three hours and costs R$38. To reach Campos do Jordão from São Paulo (a 2½-hour drive), take Rodovia Carvalho Pinto (SP 070) and SP 123.

ESSENTIALS

Bus Contacts Passaro Marron ☎ *0800/2853–047, 011/3775–3890* ⊕ *www. passaromarron.com.br.* **Terminal Rodoviário** ⊠ *Rua Benedito Lourenço, 285.*

Visitor Information Campos do Jordão Tourist Office ⊠ *At entrance to town* ☎ *012/3664–3525* ⊕ *www.camposdojordao.com.br.*

EXPLORING
TOP ATTRACTIONS

Amantikir Garden. Created in August 2007, the Amantikir Garden consists of 17 gardens that are inspired by famous international counterparts from around the world. On the grounds you can find a cafeteria and a learning center, where there are courses on gardening. Plans are in the works for expanding the area and building a bird-watching center. Reservations are mandatory, as the place receives a limited number of guests per day. An English-speaking guide is available if booked in advance. ⊠ *Rodovia Campos do Jordão/Eugênio Lefevre, 215* ☎ *012/3662–5044* ⊕ *www.amantikir.com.br* ⚏ *R$15, free on Tues.* ⊙ *Daily 8–5.*

Estação Ferroviária Emílio Ribas. A wonderful little train departs from Estação Ferroviária Emílio Ribas for tours of the city and its environs, including the 47-km (29-mile) trip to Reino das Águas Claras, where there's a park with waterfalls and models from Monteiro Lobato's characters (Lobato is a well-loved children's-book author). Be sure to book in advance. ⊠ *Av. Dr. Emílio Ribas, s/n, Vila Capivari.*

Horto Florestal. Horto Florestal is a natural playground for *macacosprego* (nail monkeys), squirrels, and parrots, as well as people. The park has a trout-filled river, waterfalls, and trails—all set among trees from around the world and one of the last *araucária* (Brazilian pine) forests in the state. ⊠ *Av. Pedro Paulo Km 13* ☎ *012/3663–3762* ⚏ *R$6–R$13* ⊙ *Daily 9–6.*

Morro do Elefante (*Elephant Hill*). Outside town a chairlift ride to the top of Morro do Elefante is a good way to enjoy the view from a 5,850-foot height. ⊠ *Av. José Oliveira Damas s/n* ☎ *012/3663–1530* ⚏ *R$7* ⊙ *Tues.–Fri. 1–5, weekends 9–5:30.*

Palácio Boa Vista. Palácio Boa Vista, the official winter residence of the state's governor, has paintings by such famous Brazilian modernists as Di Cavalcanti, Portinari, Volpi, Tarsila do Amaral, and Anita Malfatti. On the same property, the **Capela de São Pedro** (São Pedro Chapel) has sacred art from the 17th and 18th centuries. ⊠ *Av. Dr.*

Adhemar de Barros 3001 ☏ *012/3662–1122* ✉ *Free* ⊘ *Wed., Thurs., Sat.–Sun. 10–noon and 2–5.*

WORTH NOTING

Pedra do Baú. The athletically inclined can walk 3 km (2 miles) and climb the 300-step stone staircase to Pedra do Baú, a 6,400-foot trio of rocks inside an ecotourism park north of the city. A trail starts in nearby São Bento do Sapucaí, and it's recommended that you hire a guide. In the park you can also practice horseback riding, canopy walking, trekking, or mountain climbing, and spend the night in a dormlike room shared with other visitors. Some of the activities are only available on weekends. ⊠ *Km 25, Estrada São Bento do Sapucaí* ☏ *012/3662–1106* ✉ *R$7* ⊘ *Wed.–Sun. 8–6.*

WHERE TO EAT AND STAY

$$$
GERMAN
Fodor's Choice
★

✕ **Baden-Baden.** One of the specialties at this charming German restaurant and *chopperia* in the heart of town is sauerkraut *garni* (sour cabbage with German sausages), as well as some excellent cold draught beer. The typical dish serves two and is almost as popular as Baden-Baden's own brewery, which is open to visitors 10–5 on weekdays. $ *Average main: R$60* ⊠ *Rua Djalma Forjaz 93, Loja 10* ☏ *012/3663–3610.*

$
CAFÉ
✕ **Cyber Café.** Drink hot cocoa with crepes, fondue, or a slice of pie, while you browse the Internet at this downtown café. $ *Average main: R$10* ⊠ *Rua Djalma Forjaz 100, Loja 15* ☏ *012/3663–6351* ⊕ *www.cybercafeboulevard.com.br* ⊘ *Daily 9–6:20.*

$$$$
ITALIAN
✕ **Itália Cantina e Ristorante.** As its name suggests, this place specializes in Italian food. The pasta and the meat dishes are delicious, but you can also try trout, lamb, fondue, and even boar dishes. $ *Average main: R$70* ⊠ *Av. Macedo Soares 306* ☏ *012/3663–1140* ⊘ *Weekdays noon–4, 7–10; Sat. noon–10; Sun. noon–10:30.*

$$
HOTEL
▦ **Pousada Villa Capivary.** A stay at this cozy guesthouse puts you in the gastronomic and commercial center of Campos. **Pros:** friendly, helpful, and efficient staff; central location. **Cons:** often requires booking well in advance, particularly in the winter months. $ *Rooms from: R$330* ⊠ *Av. Victor Godinho 131* ☏ *012/3663–1746* ⊕ *www.capivari.com.br* ⤶ *15 rooms* ⫶⊙⫶ *Breakfast.*

SHOPPING

Baronesa Von Leithner. You can buy homemade jellies and jam at this working berry farm. There's also a cafeteria and restaurant if you're in the mood for a snack. ⊠ *Av. Fausto Arruda Camargo, 2.815, Alto da Boa Vista* ☏ *012/3662–1121* ⊕ *www.baronesavonleithner.com.br* ✉ *Free* ⊘ *Tues.–Sun. 9 am–10 pm.*

Boulevard Genéve. This mall in the busy Vila Capivari district is lined with cafés, bars, and restaurants, making it a nightlife hub. You can also find plenty of clothing stores, and candy shops selling chocolate, the town's specialty. ⊠ *Rua Doutor Djalma Forjas, 93, Vila Capivari* ☏ *012/3663–5060* ⊕ *www.boulevardgeneve.com.br.*

Chocolates Montanhês. Prices for goodies at this well-known chocolate shop start at R$48 per kilo. ⊠ *Praça São Benedito 45, Loja 6* ☏ *012/3663–1979* ⊕ *www.chocolatemontanhes.com.br.*

Os Bandeirantes

In the 16th and 17th centuries groups called *bandeiras* (literally meaning "flags" but also an archaic term for an assault force) set out on expeditions from São Paulo. Their objectives were far from noble. Their initial goal was to enslave Native Americans. Later, they were hired to capture escaped African slaves and destroy *quilombos* (communities the slaves created deep in the interior). Still, by heading inland at a time when most colonies were close to the shore, the *bandeirantes* (bandeira members) inadvertently did Brazil a great service.

A fierce breed, bandeirantes often adopted indigenous customs and voyaged for years at a time. Some went as far as the Amazon River; others only to what is today Minas Gerais, where gold and precious gems were found. In their travels they ignored the 1494 Treaty of Tordesilhas, which established a boundary between Spanish and Portuguese lands. (The boundary was a vague north–south line roughly 1,600 km (1,000 miles) west of the Cape Verde islands.) Other Brazilians followed the bandeirantes, and towns were founded, often in what was technically Spanish territory. These colonists eventually claimed full possession of the lands they settled, and thus Brazil's borders were greatly expanded.

Near Parque Ibirapuera in the city of São Paulo there's a monument, inaugurated in 1953, to honor the bandeirantes. It's a huge granite sculpture created by Victor Brecheret, a famous Brazilian artist. Protests are occasionally staged here by those who don't believe the bandeirantes deserve a monument.

Maison Geneve. The best handmade embroidered clothing in town is at Maison Geneve, open weekdays 10–7 and weekends 10–10. ⊠ *Rua Macedo Soares, 23, Lojas 1 a 3* ☎ *012/3663–5068* ⊕ *www.geneve.com.br.*

Paloma Malhas. For knits try Paloma Malhas, open weekdays 10–7 and weekends 10–10. ⊠ *Rua Djalma Forjaz 78, Loja 15* ☎ *012/3663–1218.*

SERRA NEGRA

142 km (88.2 miles) northeast of São Paulo.

At 4,265 feet above sea level in the Serra da Mantiqueira, Serra Negra's musical and cultural events that take place every month attract hordes of paulistanos and cruising motorbike fans looking for a bucolic weekend break in the mountains. In addition to various mineral water fountains, there is the Wine and Cheese Route, featuring dozens of artisan cheese and wine local producers and the Coffee Route, where you can drive though thousands of acres of coffee fields until you reach Cachoeira dos Sonhos (Dreams Waterfall), where it's possible to swim and have a snack. You can also head over to Alto da Serra, the town's highest point, where paragliding aficionados gather on the weekends. The town center is small enough to be explored by foot.

GETTING HERE AND AROUND

Seven Fênix buses leave São Paulo's Tietê bus terminal for Serra Negra daily. The journey takes 3½ hours and costs R$35. To reach Serra Negra from São Paulo (a 2½-hour drive), take Rodovia Fernão Dias (SP 381) to Atibaia, Rodovia Dom Pedro I (SP 065) toward Itatiba, then the SP 360.

ESSENTIALS

Bus Contacts **Rápido Fênix** ✉ *Praça Sesquicentenário, s/n* ☎ *019/3892–2098* 🌐 *www.rapidofenix.com.br.*

WHERE TO EAT AND STAY

$$$$ BRAZILIAN FAMILY Fodor's Choice ★ 🍴 **Cafe Boteco.** The best restaurant in Serra Negra and located by Joao Zelante square, Café Boteco incorporates some elements of the traditional Brazilian *boteco* (dive bar) in some of its recipes and decor, but the comparisons end here: bow-tied, friendly waiters serve excellent dishes, such as the *costelinha com polenta* (pork ribs with polenta chips) and the *escondidinho* (a type of cottage pie, with beef or chicken covered in creamy mash). Draught lager and a range of local beers are available. If you sit outside, bands often play live at the square on weekends. [$] *Average main: R$100* ✉ *Travessa Tenente Mário Dallari, 20* ☎ *019/3892–3481.*

$ BRAZILIAN FAMILY 🍴 **Padaria Serrana.** Located at the heart of Serra Negra, Serrana is a bakery that serves breakfast, light snacks, and also meals, as well as sharing platters. The *bolinhos de bacalhau* (cod fritters) are a popular choice, as is Ecobier, the local draught beer. Grab a *pao na chapa* (grilled bread) and coffee breakfast here on a Sunday morning and sit at one of the tables outside to watch the hordes of motorcycling aficionados—they flock to Serra Negra on weekends from other cities on their amazing touring bikes. [$] *Average main: R$20* ✉ *Rua Padre Joao Batista Lavello, 21* ☎ *019/3892–2289.*

$$ ALL-INCLUSIVE FAMILY Fodor's Choice ★ 🏨 **Hotel Firenze.** The choice of wealthy paulistanos, the Firenze is the smartest hotel in Serra Negra; its location, a stone's throw from the shopping area and the town main square, is the primary draw. **Pros:** excellent breakfast; comfortable rooms; unparalled service. **Cons:** the bar and games room close early. [$] *Rooms from: R$350* ✉ *Rua Sete de Setembro, 118* ☎ *019/3892–2899* 🌐 *www.hotelfirenzeserranegra.com.br* 🍽 *All-inclusive.*

EMBU

27 km (17 miles) west of São Paulo.

Founded in 1554, Embu, or Embu das Artes, is a tiny Portuguese colonial town of whitewashed houses, old churches, wood-carvers' studios, and antiques shops. It has a downtown handicrafts fair every weekend. On Sunday the streets sometimes get so crowded you can barely walk. Embu also has many stores that sell handicrafts and wooden furniture; most of these are close to where the street fair takes place.

GETTING HERE AND AROUND

EMTU runs an *executivo* (executive or first-class) bus from São Paulo to Embu–Engenho Velho on Line 179, which departs hourly from Anhangabaú. Regular (intermunicipal) buses travel more often: every 20 minutes, Line 033 leaves from Clínicas to Embu. The ride is less comfortable, though: you might have to stand up.

To make the 30-minute drive from São Paulo to Embu, drive from Avenida Professor Francisco Morato to Rodovia Régis Bittencourt (BR 116) and then follow the signs.

ESSENTIALS

Bus Contacts EMTU ☎ *0800/724-0555* 🌐 *www.emtu.sp.gov.br.*

Visitor Information Embu Secretaria de Turismo ✉ *Largo 21 de Abril 139* ☎ *011/4704-6565* 🌐 *www.embu.sp.gov.br.* **Gol Tour Viagens e Turismo** ☎ *011/3256-2388* 🌐 *www.goltour.com.br* ☞ *Day trips from São Paulo to Embu R$80–R$120.*

EXPLORING

FAMILY **Cidade das Abelhas** (*City of the Bees*). In the Mata Atlântica you can visit the Cidade das Abelhas, a farm with a small museum where you can watch bees at work. You can buy honey and other bee-related natural products while your kids climb the gigantic model of a bee. It's about 10 minutes from downtown; just follow the signs. ✉ *Km 7, Estrada da Ressaca* ☎ *011/4703-6460* 🎟 *R$12* 🕓 *Tues.–Sun. 8:30–5.*

Igreja Nossa Senhora do Rosário. Igreja Nossa Senhora do Rosário was built in 1690 and is a nice bet if you won't have a chance to visit the historic cities of Minas Gerais. The church contains baroque images of saints and is next to a 1730 monastery now turned into a sacred-art museum. ✉ *Largo dos Jesuítas 67* ☎ *011/4704-2654* 🎟 *R$2* 🕓 *Tues.–Sun. 9–5.*

WHERE TO EAT

$$ BRAZILIAN 🍴 **Casa do Barão.** In this colonial-style spot you find contemporary versions of country plates. Go for the exotic *picadinho jesuítico* (round-steak stew), served with corn, fried bananas, and farofa. Unlike most restaurants in the city, Casa do Barão serves single-person portions. Note that there are no salads or juices on the menu. [$] *Average main: R$40* ✉ *Rua Joaquim Santana 12* ☎ *011/4704-2053* 🕓 *Thurs.–Fri. 5–11, weekends noon–11.*

$$ ECLECTIC 🍴 **O Garimpo.** In a large room with a fireplace or around outdoor tables, choose between Brazilian regional dishes such as the house specialty, *moqueca de badejo* (spicy fish-and-coconut-milk stew), and German classics such as *eisbein* (pickled and roasted pork shank). There is live music on weekends, but note that it stops at 10:30 on the dot, regardless of how much patrons might be enjoying themselves. [$] *Average main: R$40* ✉ *Rua da Matriz 136* ☎ *011/4704-6344* 🕓 *Daily 11:30–10.*

$$ ECLECTIC 🍴 **Os Girassóis Restaurante e Choperia.** A great variety of dishes is served at this downtown restaurant next to an art gallery. The *picanha brasileira* (barbecued steak) with fries and *farofa* (cassava flour sautéed in butter) is recommended. [$] *Average main: R$30* ✉ *R. Nossa Senhora do Rosário, 3* ☎ *011/4781-6671* 🕓 *Closed Mon.*

SHOPPING

Cantão Móveis e Galeria. Cantão Móveis e Galeria is a good place to buy ceramics, paintings, sculptures, and antique decorations. Open on weekends 9–5. ⊠ *Largo dos Jesuítas 169* ☎ *011/4781–6671.*

Fenix Galeria de Artes. Fenix Galeria de Artes is a good place to find oil paintings as well as wood and stone sculptures. Open on weekends only 9–5. ⊠ *Rua Marechal Isidoro Lopes 10* ☎ *011/4704–5634.*

Galeria Jozan. Come here for lovely antiques. ⊠ *Rua Nossa Senhora do Rosarío 59* ☎ *011/4704–2600.*

Guarani Artesanato. Check out the handicrafts made of wood and stone, including sculptures carved from *pau-brasil* (brazilwood). Open weekdays 9 6 and weekends 8–6. ⊠ *Largo dos Jesuítas 153* ☎ *011/4704–3200.*

SANTANA DE PARNAÍBA

42 km (26 miles) northwest of São Paulo.

With more than 200 preserved houses from the 18th and 19th centuries, Santana de Parnaíba is considered the "Ouro Preto from São Paulo"—a town rich with history and colonial architecture. Santana was founded in 1580; by 1625 it was the most important point of departure for the bandeirantes.

In 1901 the first hydroelectric power station in South America was built here. Throughout the 20th century, Santana managed to retain its houses and charm while preserving a local tradition: a rural type of samba called "de bumbo," in which the pacing is marked by the *zabumba* (an instrument usually associated with rhythms from the northeastern states of Brazil). The proximity to a couple of São Paulo's finest suburbs explains the region's fine dining. Outdoors lovers feel at home with the canopy-walking and trekking options.

GETTING HERE AND AROUND

EMTU's *executivo* (executive or first-class) bus from Barra Funda in São Paulo to Pirapora do Bom Jesus (Line 385) stops in Santana de Parnaíba daily and takes one hour.

To reach Santana de Parnaíba from São Paulo—a 40-minute drive—take the express lane of Rodovia Castelo Branco (SP 280) and pay attention to the road signs. On weekends parking is scarce in Santana de Parnaíba, and parking lots can be expensive.

ESSENTIALS

Bus Contacts EMTU ☎ *0800/724–0555.*

Visitor Information Santana de Parnaíba Secretaria de Cultura e Turismo ⊠ *Largo da Matriz 19* ☎ *011/4154–1874, 011/4154–2377* ⊕ *www.santanadeparnaiba.sp.gov.br.*

EXPLORING

Centro Histórico. The best place to begin your trip to Santana de Parnaiba is in the Centro Histórico, where you'll be able to appreciate numerous examples of 17th- and 18th-century colonial architecture. The more than 200 well-preserved houses are concentrated around three streets: Suzana Dias, André Fernandes, and Bartolomeu Bueno—two of which are named after famous bandeirantes.

Igreja Matriz de Sant'Anna. Baroque Igreja Matriz de Sant'Anna was built in 1610 and restored in 1892. It has terra-cotta sculptures and an altar with gold-plated details. ✉ *Largo da Matriz* ☎ *011/4154–2401* 🎟 *Free* ⏲ *Daily 8–5.*

Museu Casa do Anhanguera. Museu Casa do Anhanguera provides a sharp picture of the bandeirantes era. In a 1600 house (the second-oldest in the state) where Bartolomeu Bueno—nicknamed Anhanguera, or "old devil," by the Indians—was born, the museum displays objects and furniture from the past four centuries. ✉ *Largo da Matriz 9* ☎ *011/4154–5042* 🎟 *R$1* ⏲ *Weekdays 8–4:30, weekends 11–5.*

WHERE TO EAT

$$ BRAZILIAN FAMILY 🍴 **Bartolomeu.** In a 1905 house, this restaurant serves regional specialties like *feijoada* and *picadinho* (steak stew served with rice and beans, farofa, fried banana, and fried egg). Salmon and boar ribs are some additional choices. [$] *Average main: R$40* ✉ *Praça 14 de Novembro 101* ☎ *011/4154–6566* ⏲ *Closed Mon.*

$$$ PORTUGUESE 🍴 **Dom Afonso de Vimioso.** A place like this would have reminded Portuguese colonists of the motherland. Options include fine wines and more than 10 dishes made with salt cod. Don't miss out on typical sweets such as *pastéis de Santa Clara* (yolk and sugar-filled pastries). [$] *Average main: R$60* ✉ *Km 36, Estrada dos Romeiros* ☎ *011/4151–1935.*

$$$ BRAZILIAN 🍴 **São Paulo Antigo.** In a century-old ranch-style house, taste *caipira* (rural) dishes such as *dobradinha com feijão branco* (intestines and white-bean stew) or *galinha atolada* (rural-style hen stew). [$] *Average main: R$60* ✉ *Rua Álvaro Luiz do Valle 66* ☎ *011/4154–2726* ⏲ *No dinner weeknights.*

SPORTS AND THE OUTDOORS

HIKING

Travessia do Caminho do Sol. This 240-km (150-mile) trail passes by 13 villages and crosses small rivers and cane plantations. The trail is considered the local version of the famous Camino de Santiago, in Spain. Call to join a group hike. ☎ *011/4154–2422.*

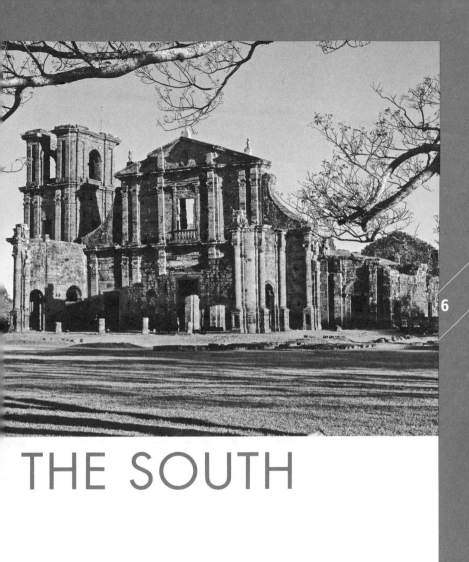

THE SOUTH

Updated by
Blake Schmidt

Expect the unexpected in the southern states of Paraná, Santa Catarina, and Rio Grande do Sul. The climate is remarkably cooler (the highest elevations even get a couple of inches of snow every year) and the topography more varied than in the rest of Brazil. You're also just as likely to find people of German and Italian ancestry as Portuguese. And as Brazil's breadbasket, the Região Sul (southern region) has a standard of living comparable to that of many developed nations.

The southern section of the Serra do Mar, a mountain range along the coast, stretches well into Rio Grande do Sul. It looks like one green wall—broken only by the occasional canyon or waterfall—separating the interior from the shore. Most mountainsides are still covered with the luxuriant Mata Atlântica (Atlantic Rain Forest), which is as diverse and impressive as the forest of the Amazon. The Serra do Mar gives way to hills that roll gently westward to the valleys of the *rios* (rivers) Paraná and Uruguay. Most of these lands were originally covered with dense subtropical forests interspersed with natural rangelands such as the Campos Gerais, in the north, and the Brazilian Pampas, in the south.

ORIENTATION AND PLANNING

GETTING ORIENTED

Touring the three states of this region—roughly the size of France—in a short time is a challenge, despite a relatively efficient transportation network. The South can be divided into two major areas: the coast and the interior. Coastal attractions, along a 700-km (450-mile) line from Curitiba south to Porto Alegre, include fantastic beaches, forested slopes, canyons, and the Serra do Mar mountains. Curitiba and Porto Alegre are updating infrastructure and soccer stadiums for the 2014 World Cup. In the interior, Foz do Iguaçu, far to the west, should not be missed.

PARANÁ

The state of Paraná has a very short coastline of about 100 km (62 miles), with islands and historical cities. Curitiba, the capital, known internationally as a green city for its innovative urban planning and many parks, is about 90 km (56 miles) from the coast, on a plateau. West of Curitiba lies the vast interior, which incorporates Vila Velha State Park, with its ancient sandstone formations, and stretches all the way to the Paraguayan border and Foz do Iguaçu.

FOZ DO IGUAÇU

The grandeur of this vast sheet of white water cascading in constant cymbal-banging cacophony makes Niagara Falls and Victoria Falls seem sedate. Allow at least two full days to take in this magnificent sight, and be sure to see it from both the Argentine and Brazilian sides.

SANTA CATARINA

Geographically, Santa Catarina is the opposite of Paraná: a long coastline of about 500 km (310 miles) and narrow interior. Most of the attractions are on or near the coast. Santa Catarina has some of the best beaches in South Atlantic. The capital, Florianópolis, an ideal hub for exploring the state's attractions, is on the Ilha de Santa Catarina (Santa Catarina Island).

RIO GRANDE DO SUL

Most tourist attractions in this state, with equal parts coast and interior, are in the heavily populated northeastern corner, including the capital, Porto Alegre, about 100 km (62 miles) from the coast. One highlight in the west is the Jesuit mission ruins in São Miguel.

> ### TOP REASONS TO GO
>
> ■ **Waterfalls and More Waterfalls:** Witness the mighty Iguaçu Falls.
>
> ■ **Rain Forest:** Take a train through Paraná coast's virgin rain forest.
>
> ■ **Lovely Beaches:** Soak up the sun on the beaches of Santa Catarina.
>
> ■ **Brazilian Vineyards:** Sip wine on the slopes of Vale dos Vinhedo.
>
> ■ **Outdoor Adventures:** Hike through the impressive green-clad canyons in northeastern Rio Grande do Sul.

6

PLANNING

WHEN TO GO

November through March is normally hot and humid. Rainfall is quite frequent, but less intense than in northern Brazil. Some years might have extremely rainy El Niño–related summers or, conversely, quite dry La Niña–affected years. January and February are top vacation months, so expect crowded beaches, busy highways, and higher prices. Winter (April–November) brings much cooler temperatures, sometimes as low as the upper 20s in the higher elevations at night. Major cold fronts blowing in from Patagonia can bring some gray, blustery days, usually followed by chilly days with deep blue skies.

GETTING HERE AND AROUND

You'd need at least 20 days to visit all of the South's main attractions, but if you only have about a week, fly to Florianópolis and make it your hub to the South. From there visit the attractions in Ilha de Santa Catarina and choose one of the beaches up or down the coast (Garopaba or Porto Belo). You can get a rental car or take regular bus lines. One side trip you shouldn't miss is to Foz do Iguaçu, on the Argentina border. Either join an organized (three-day) bus tour or fly on your own to the falls.

If you have a few more days, choose either Porto Alegre or Curitiba as a secondary hub. Fly or take a bus to these cities. Set aside at least two days to visit local sights and, depending on your interests, take quick jaunts to other attractions. If you have an interest in nature, take a tour of the Aparados da Serra region in Rio Grande do Sul or Vila Velha State Park in Paraná, or take the train to Paranaguá in Paraná. If you're more interested in history, join a tour to the missions in Rio Grande do Sul, perhaps extending the trip to the mission site in Argentina.

Avoid long trips in rental cars, as roads are busy with heavy truck traffic and the pavement isn't always in good condition; take flights or bus trips instead. You can always rent a car or take taxis or local buses when you arrive. Organized tours are highly recommended for visiting remote attractions.

BORDER CROSSINGS AT FOZ DO IGUAÇU

U.S., Canadian, and British citizens need only a valid passport for stays of up to 90 days in Argentina, so crossing the border at Iguaçu isn't a problem. Crossing back into Brazil from Argentina, however, is a thorny issue. In theory, *all* U.S. citizens need a visa to enter Brazil, so make sure your paperwork is in order before you depart.

Many local taxis (both Argentine and Brazilian) have "arrangements" with border control and can also get you across with no visa. Most charge 150–200 pesos for the return trip. Though the practice is well-established (most hotels and travel agents in Puerto Iguazú have deals with Brazilian companies and can arrange a visa-less visit), it *is* illegal. Enforcement of the law is generally lax, but sudden crackdowns and on-the-spot fines of hundreds of dollars have been reported.

RESTAURANTS

Churrasco (slow-grilled and roasted meat), one of the most famous foods of Brazil, originated in Rio Grande do Sul. But the cuisine is eclectic here in cowboy country, and rice and beans sit on southern tables beside Italian and German dishes, thanks to the South's many European immigrants. Look for *barreado,* a dish from coastal Paraná made by stewing beef, bacon, potatoes, and spices for hours in a clay pot made airtight with moistened manioc flour. *Café colonial* is the elaborate 5 pm tea—with breads, pies, and German kuchen—popular among the Germans in the South. *Prices in the reviews are the average cost of a main course at dinner or, if dinner is not served, at lunch.*

HOTELS

The south has a great variety of hotels and inns. Except for in the smallest towns and most remote areas, however, you shouldn't have a problem finding comfortable accommodations. Pousadas in historic buildings are common, particularly in beach towns. Hotel-fazendas are popular in rural areas. Southern beaches attract many South American tourists, and seaside cities might become crowded and highway traffic nightmarish from December through March. Make advance reservations. *Prices in the reviews are the lowest cost of a standard double room in high season. For expanded reviews, facilities, and current deals, visit Fodors.com.*

FIFA WORLD CUP FEVER

Soccer, or *o jogo bonito* (the beautiful game), is a passion and an art form in Brazil. No trip here is complete without taking in at least one soccer match. Watching a rivalry unfold from the bleachers of Rio de Janeiro's intimate São Januário stadium or being part of mass euphoria in the iconic Maracanã Stadium is an exhilarating immersion into a uniquely Brazilian experience.

All the excitement that accompanies soccer matches in Brazil will be intensified when the country hosts the 64 matches of the FIFA World Cup from June 12 to July 13, 2014. Straight through the championship match in the fully refurbished Maracanã Stadium in Rio de Janeiro, Brazilians all across the country, along with the 600,000 international visitors expected to make the journey for the event, will cheer, chant, and do whatever it takes to spur their national teams to victory.

PLANNING YOUR WORLD CUP EXPERIENCE

Brazilian fans rooting for their national team.

Anticipation is building for the World Cup. After the qualifying draw in December 2013, it's time to start planning: logistics, lodging, and tickets. The matches take place in 12 cities spread across this continent-size nation.

If you plan to crisscross the country while following your national team, you can make travel arrangements through sports-events trip organizers such as Roadtrips (*www.roadtrips.com*), or through national team fan clubs such as Sam's Army (*sams-army.com*), which follows the U.S. team. Purchasing pre-set packages with organizations like these allows you to buy hotel rooms and airline tickets in bulk, likely giving you a better deal than you'd get on your own.

But if you intend to pick a city or part of the country to catch a few matches and soak up the atmosphere—or if you're set on booking your own travel—a little early thinking will save you some headaches and travel dollars.

LODGING

One of your biggest concerns will be where to stay. In spite of the 147 new hotels erected for this event, finding a room will be tough. Book as soon as you know the cities you plan to visit.

In addition to hotels and *pousadas*—smaller, often family-run establishments—it's worthwhile to look into room rentals. The idea of hosting foreigners has started to catch on in Brazil over the past few years, and a number of sites offer accommodations throughout the country: *airbnb.com*, *camaecafe.com.br*, and *bedandbreakfast.com*, to name a few. With these, it always pays to read the comments of previous guests and make sure your hosts are well reviewed.

TRAVEL

Because of the vastness of Brazil, travel between most localities will be possible only by air, although a handful of cities—Rio de Janeiro, Belo Horizonte, and São Paulo in the southeast, or Fortaleza, Natal, and Recife in the northeast—are within 3–7 hours of each other and accessible by bus.

If you choose to travel by bus, you can purchase tickets in the bus stations, or online from sites such as *rodoviaria online.com.br* or *passagemrapida.com.br*. A major drawback of using online services to buy anything in Brazil, including bus or airline tickets, is that they usually require you to enter a CPF number—the Brazilian equivalent of a social security number—and often will only accept Brazilian credit cards. International travelers should instead book travel through travel agencies or use non-Brazilian websites even when buying tickets for internal flights.

Of course, bus tickets can always be purchased in the bus stations themselves, but keep in mind that bus travel is popular among Brazilians, and tickets sell out on dates when there is high demand. It is a good idea to buy these as early as possible.

TICKETS TO THE MATCHES

Tickets are available through the FIFA website (*www.fifa.com*) or through travel agencies. The cost will vary according to where you're sitting and how far along the match is in the championship. Tickets will not be released all at once, and some countries will have more tickets allotted to them than others. Check with your national soccer federation for more information (i.e., the United States Soccer Federation or the English Football Association).

You're never too young to enjoy a World Cup match.

TIPS FOR ATTENDING A MATCH

■ Get there early—one or two hours before the match—to mingle with other fans, have a drink, and let expectations build.

■ No outside food or drink will be allowed into stadiums.

■ Bring cash, preferably small bills, and do not carry backpacks or valuables.

■ Never underestimate traffic and the long lines generated at World Cup games. In South Africa, many fans missed the first half of matches because they couldn't get into the stadium on time.

■ Wear comfortable clothing, as it will be a long day.

■ The matches will happen during Brazil's winter, so a light jacket is a good idea, particularly in the South.

■ Do not expect to find a taxi to or from the stadium; plan to walk to the nearest public transportation option.

■ Think of it as a pilgrimage, and enjoy the experience, hassles and all.

WORLD CUP CITIES: June 12–July 13, 2014

BRAZIL

Fortaleza
Natal
Manaus
Recife
Brasília
Salvador
Cuiabá
Belo Horizonte
São Paulo
Rio de Janeiro
Curitiba
Porto Alegre

PACIFIC OCEAN

ATLANTIC OCEAN

in the atmosphere during the World Cup. Enjoy it at beaches like Ipanema or Copacabana, where giant screens will be set up. At night, head to bohemian Lapa, where bars will be playing the matches on television amid samba beats and rounds of *chopp*—the light draft beer that fuels Brazilians day and night.

SÃO PAULO

This city is home to three first-division soccer teams: São Paulo F.C., Palmeiras, and Corinthians. Of these big leaguers, the only team without its own stadium is the one with the largest following across Brazil: Corinthians. It has traditionally played at the Pacaembu, a city-owned arena that is

RIO DE JANEIRO

Rio is home to the **Maracanã Stadium**, the beating heart of Brazilian soccer, and will host seven matches, including the Cup's final match. The stadium and the surrounding area are being deeply transformed for the event: the playing field was lowered, its roof was replaced, and the capacity reduced by 10,000 seats to 76,000.

The arena will not be the only place in town to take

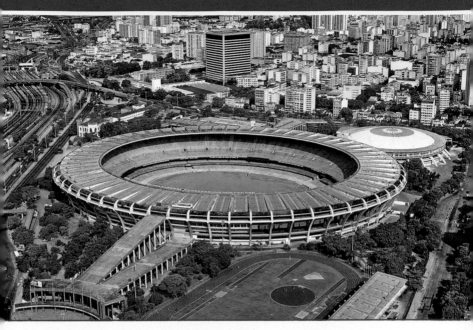

also home to the **Museu do Futebol**, or Soccer Museum. With the World Cup around the corner, Corinthians is finally getting its own stadium. The **Arena de São Paulo** is planned for the Corintiano stronghold of Itaquera, a working-class neighborhood that is seeing new jobs and revitalization as a result. This brand-new arena will host the Cup's opening match and five others, including a semifinal.

Those without tickets can congregate at the city's bars entirely dedicated to soccer, such as the São Cristovão in Vila Madalena. Thousands of spectators will also gather in Vale do Anhangabaú downtown for the FIFA fan fest.

BELO HORIZONTE

The **Mineirão**, Belo Horizonte's stadium, is undergoing vast refurbishing in preparation for the World Cup. It'll remain the raucous heart of soccer in the state of Minas Gerais, and will host six matches.

SALVADOR

This coastal city's main soccer stadium was razed to make way for the new **Arena Fonte Nova**, which will include a shopping and entertainment complex with a museum of soccer, restaurants, and a hotel. The city, known for over-the-top street Carnival celebrations and strong Afro-Brazilian roots, will host six World Cup matches.

RECIFE

The **Arena Pernambuco** is being built from scratch in a nearby suburban town, São Lourenço da Mata, part of a huge real-estate development called Cidade da Copa, or the World Cup City. Recife, which will host five matches, has a strong soccer culture. The city is also investing in new transportation—a Bus Rapid Transit system and light rail—to link the suburban stadium with Recife's tourist district, 11 miles away.

(clockwise from bottom left) Museu do Futebol; Model of Arena de São Paulo; André Santos, Neymar, and Ramires celebrate Neymar's goal; Maracanã Stadium.

BRASÍLIA

The country's capital, Brasília was raised from the dust in the 1950s in a huge urban development experiment that later earned it UNESCO World Heritage status. It is home to the second-largest World Cup venue: the refurbished **Estádio Nacional**, better known by its nickname, Mané Garrincha, after Brazil's star player in the 1958 and 1962 World Cups. It'll host seven World Cup matches.

(clockwise from bottom left) Brazilian fans; Tickets to the FIFA Confederations Cup; Dani Alves of Brazil in action during the FIFA World Cup in Johannesburg, 2010; Fuleco, the 2014 World Cup mascot; Model of Arena Amazonia, Manaus.

NATAL

Perennially sunny Natal is known for its vast beaches of white sand and cobalt-blue water. Its newly constructed **Estádio das Dunas**, named in honor of the region's towering white dunes, lies outside the central city and will welcome four World Cup matches.

CURITIBA

This southern city has one of only two private stadiums to be used in the Cup, the **Estádio Joaquim Américo Guimarães**, owned by the Clube Atlético Paranaense team. Like stadiums all over Brazil, it has always been known by its nickname, Arena da Baixada. Curitiba will host four World Cup matches.

FORTALEZA

On Brazil's stunning northernmost coast, Fortaleza has warm waters and sunshine nearly year-round. Its stadium, popularly known as **Castelão**, or Big Castle, was refurbished and the first to be ready for the World Cup. The city will host six matches.

PORTO ALEGRE

Brazil's southernmost capital has a different feel and culture than the rest of the country, sharing much with neighboring Argentina and Uruguay. With a 51,300-seat capacity, Porto Alegre's stadium, the **Beira-Rio**, is one of the largest arenas in the region. Five of the Cup's matches will be held here.

Brazilians love big communal bashes, and each host city will have a fan-fest location: a designated beach, public square, or park where crowds will be able to follow all World Cup matches on massive screens, while also enjoying live music, drinks, and other festivities. Get there early—two hours before the game if possible—and stake out a spot close to the screen. No tickets are necessary and it is first-come, first-served. The areas will be closed after a certain number of spectators gather to avoid overcrowding, but be prepared for Brazilians' limited need for personal space.

Belo Horizonte: Praça da Estação

Brasília: Esplanada dos Ministérios

Cuiabá: Parque de Exposições Acrimat

Curitiba: Parque Barigui

Fortaleza: Praia de Iracema (Aterrão)

Manaus: Memorial Encontro das Águas

Natal: Praia do Forte

Porto Alegre: Largo Glênio Peres

Recife: Marco Zero

Rio de Janeiro: Praia de Copacabana

Salvador: Jardim de Alah

São Paulo: Vale do Anhangabaú

CUIABÁ

Known as a jumping-off point for exploring the Pantanal region, western Cuiabá is undergoing extensive renovations to host four Cup matches. Its stadium, popularly known as "Verdão" or the Big Green, was torn down to make way for the 43,000-seat **Arena Pantanal**. Hundreds of millions of dollars are also being poured into remodeling the airport, creating an exclusive bus transport lane and a light rail system that promise to improve congestion in the city.

MANAUS

The playing field and bleachers at the 47,000-seat **Arena Amazonia** in Manaus are enclosed in metal gridwork meant to resemble a straw

FAST FACTS

Dates: June 12–July 13, 2014

Total Matches: 64

Ticket Prices: $90–$175

Where to Purchase: www.fifa.com

basket, a traditional indigenous craft. It also includes a retractable roof, which is useful in the blistering sun and torrential downpours that are near daily occurrences in the Amazon. Manaus is a great spot to catch a few matches—four will be played here—and then set off on a jungle tour.

The newly refurbished Maracanã Stadium will host the championship match of the 2014 FIFA World Cup.

Brazil is the only nation to have claimed five World Cup trophies, and it's no exaggeration to say that soccer is a pillar of national identity, the glue that binds the nation. During times when the country was struggling and there was little cause for patriotism, soccer spurred the wealthiest and the most downtrodden to set aside their worries and wave the country's flamboyant green and yellow colors.

Rooting for a favorite team in soccer stadiums across the country leads to unbridled displays of emotion that make being a spectator at a contested match fascinating, even if you have no rooting interest. The audience puts on a show of its own, singing their team's songs, exploding in glee with each goal, spewing encouragement and abuse at the players and refs, waving massive flags, and laughing and crying over the results.

The *torcidas organizadas*—tightly knit groups of fans who wear uniforms, carry giant banners, and lead chants—are the most fun to watch. Get in on the action by buying tickets to the bleachers and getting as close as you're comfortable with to the crazed fans blowing horns and waving flags.

That said, you can avoid the crowd and the hassle—public transportation is paltry and easily overwhelmed by game-day crowds—and have a fantastic time simply by pulling up a chair in any corner bar and sharing a game and a beer with whoever gathers. An easy camaraderie develops as random passersby join in the communal rooting and yelling at the television.

USEFUL WEBSITES

The official FIFA website: www.fifa.com

The official Brazilian World Cup website: www.copa2014.gov.br/en

Brazil Tourism Board World Cup website: www.braziltour360.com

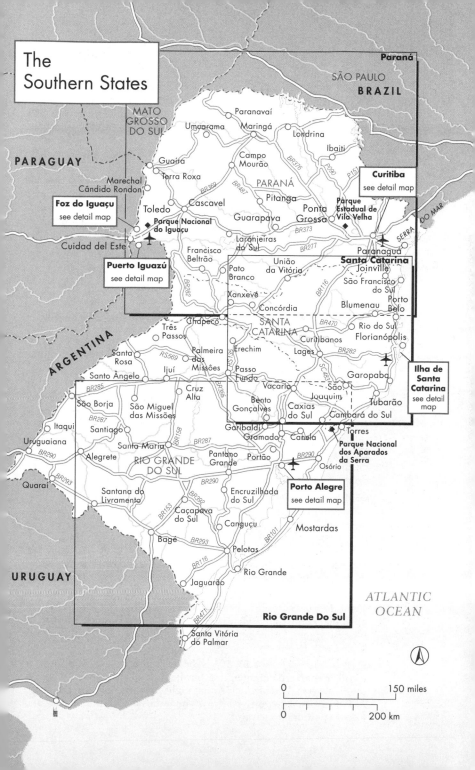

The Southern States

Paraná

SÃO PAULO
BRAZIL

MATO GROSSO DO SUL

PARAGUAY

Paranavaí
Umuarama
Maringá
Londrina
Ibaiti

Guaíra
Campo Mourão
PARANÁ

BR376
BR090
P151

Marechal Cândido Rondon
Terra Roxa
Pitanga

Curitiba
see detail map

Foz do Iguaçu
see detail map

Toledo
Cascavel
Guarapava
Ponta Grossa
Parque Estadual de Vila Velha
BR373

BR369
BR467

Parque Nacional do Iguaçu
Larânjeiras do Sul
BR277

Cuidad del Este

SERRA DO MAR

Paranaguá

Puerto Iguazú
see detail map

Francisco Beltrão

União da Vitória
Santa Catarina
Joinville

Pato Branco
São Francisco do Sul
Porto Belo

BR282

Xanxevê
Concórdia
Blumenau

BR116

Três Passos
Chapecó
SANTA CATARINA
BR470
Rio do Sul
Florianópolis

ARGENTINA

Palmeira das Missões
Erechim
Curitibanos
Lages
BR282

Santa Rosa
Ijuí
Passo Fundo
SC483

RS569
BR386
Vacaria
São Joaquim
Garopaba

Santo Ângelo
Cruz Alta
Bento Gonçalves
Caxias do Sul
Tubarão

Ilha de Santa Catarina
see detail map

São Borja
São Miguel das Missões
Santiago
BR287
Garibaldi
Gramado
Canela
Cambará do Sul
Torres

BR285
BR287

Itaqui
Santa Maria
Pantano Grande
Portão
Parque Nacional dos Aparados da Serra

Uruguaiana
Alegrete
RIO GRANDE DO SUL
BR290
Osório

BR290
BR153
BR392

BR290

BR293
Quaraí
Santana do Livramento
Caçapava do Sul
Encruzilhada do Sul
Porto Alegre
see detail map

Bagé
Canguçu
Mostardas

BR293
Pelotas
BR101

BR116
Rio Grande

URUGUAY
Jaguarão

Rio Grande Do Sul

ATLANTIC OCEAN

Santa Vitória do Palmar

0   150 miles

0   200 km

PARANÁ

The state of Paraná is best known for the Foz do Iguaçu, a natural wonder, and the Itaipú Dam, an engineering marvel. But also worth a visit is Vila Velha, a series of strange sandstone formations in the center of Paraná that might remind you of the eerily moving landscapes of the western United States. At one time the rolling hills of the state's plateau were covered with forests dominated by the highly prized Paraná pine, an umbrella-shape conifer. Most of these pine forests were logged by immigrants half a century ago, and the cleared land of the immense interior is now where soybeans, wheat, and coffee are grown. (Still, be on the lookout for the occasional Paraná pine.) The state has a very short coastline, but the beaches are spectacular, as is the Serra do Mar, which still has pristine Atlantic forest and coastal ecosystems. Curitiba, the upbeat capital, ranks as a top Brazilian city in efficiency, innovative urban planning, and quality of life.

CURITIBA

408 km (254 miles) south of São Paulo, 710 km (441 miles) north of Porto Alegre.

A 300-year-old city, Curitiba is on the Paraná plateau, at an elevation of 2,800 feet. It owes its name to the Paraná pinecones, which were called *kur-ity-ba* by the native Guaranis. In a region that already differs considerably from the rest of the country, this city of 1.7 million is unique for its temperate climate (with a mean temperature of 16°C/61°F) and the 50% of its population that is of non-Iberian European ancestry.

With one of the highest densities of urban green space in the world, Curitiba is known as the environmental capital of Brazil. This is not only because of its array of parks but also because since the 1980s it has had progressive city governments that have been innovative in their urban planning. The emphasis on protecting the environment has produced an efficient public transportation system and a comprehensive recycling program that are being used as models for cities around the globe.

GETTING HERE AND AROUND

The flight from São Paulo to Curitiba is about an hour. A bus takes six hours. Curitiba's Aeroporto Internacional Afonso Pena is 21 km (13 miles) east of downtown. A cab ride to downtown is around R$50. A minibus service (R$8) provides transportation between Rua 24 Horas and Estação Rodoferroviária, passing by several downtown hotels on its way to the airport.

You can drive from Curitiba to Foz do Iguaçu on BR 277, which traverses Paraná State. It's a long drive, but this toll highway is kept in good shape. To visit the picturesque seaside around historic Paranaguá, it's best to join a tour, especially one that includes a train ride on the Serra Verde Express.

The coastal, single-lane BR 101 is the most direct route from Curitiba to other southern communities, but it's one of the country's busiest roads—there's lots of truck traffic night and day. The stretch south of Florianópolis to Porto Alegre is dangerous during the January and February vacation months.

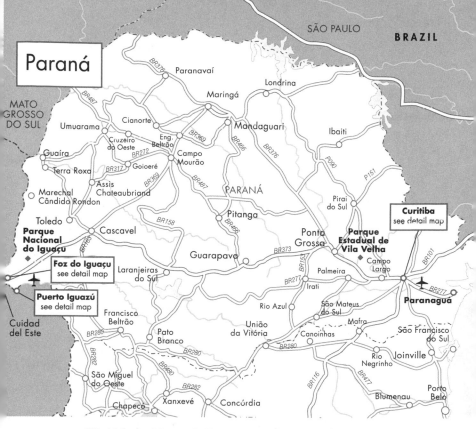

BR 116, the Mountain Route, runs from Curitiba to Porto Alegre. Although it's scenic for much of the way—and a little shorter than other routes—it's also narrow, with many curves and many trucks.

Curitiba is internationally renowned for its modern and efficient public transportation system. Buses take you quickly to any place in the city. There are regular lines (R$1.90) and *ligeirinho* express lines (R$3.50). Moreover, tourists have a special service to get to the attractions, the 2½-hour Linha Turismo tour. Taxis are easy to find in Curitiba. A ride from downtown to the Jardim Botânico costs about R$30.

ESSENTIALS

Airport Aeroporto Internacional Afonso Pena (*CWB*) ⊠ *Av. Rocha Pombo, s/n, Águas Belas, São José dos Pinhais* ☎ *041/3381 1515.*

Bus Contacts Estação Rodoferroviária (Bus Station) ⊠ *Av. Pres. Affonso Camargo 330, Jardim Botânico* ☎ *041/3320–3000.* **Linha Turismo.** This bus line maintained by the city follows a 2½-hour circular route, allowing five stops along the way for one fare. Buses depart every 30 minutes from 9 to 5:30 (Tuesday–Sunday) from the Praça Tiradentes, stopping at 25 attractions. Plan to spend an entire day on this route. There are taped descriptions of the sights (available in English), and the fare is R$29. ⊠ *Praca Tiradentes* ☎ *041/3320–3232* ⊙ *www.urbs.curitiba.pr.gov.br/transporte/linha-turismo.*

Emergencies and Medical Assistance ■ TIP➔ For any emergency in Curitiba, dial ☎ 100.

Taxi Contacts Radio taxi ☎ *0800/600–6666, 0800/41–4646.*

Visitor and Tour Information BWT ✉ *Av. Pres. Affonso Camargo 330, Estação Rodoferroviária, Centro* ☎ *041/3888–3499* ⊕ *www.bwtoperadora.com. br* ✆ *Tours include: city of Curitiba, Paranaguá-Ilha do Mel, Parque Nacional Superaguí, Serre Verde Express train (to Morretes and Paranaguá).* **Paraná Turismo** (*State Tourism Board*) ✉ *Rua Dep. Mário de Barros 1290, 3rd fl., Centro Cívico* ☎ *041/3313–3500, 041/3254–1516 hotline* ⊕ *www.turismo.pr.gov.br/ modules/turista-pt* ⊙ *Weekdays 8:30–6.*

EXPLORING

Much as in other Brazilian cities, the history of the downtown district of Curitiba revolves around the first church built in the city, Igreja de São Francisco. In the early days it was the focal point where roads and streets converged, businesses set up shop, the government established its representation, and urban sprawl unfolded. Development in the last 50 years moved the administrative and commercial district away from the original center, where symbols of early days are preserved. As of this writing, the city's airport, bus terminal, roads, and main soccer stadium are being expanded in anticipation of the 2014 World Cup.

It would be a shame to visit Brazil's environmental capital without seeing one of its many parks, especially the Jardim Botânico, east of downtown.

TOP ATTRACTIONS

Jardim Botânico. Although not as old and renowned as its counterpart in Rio, the Botanical Garden has become a Curitiba showplace. Its most outstanding feature is the tropical flora in the two-story steel greenhouse that resembles a castle. The Municipal Botanical Museum, with its library and remarkable collection of rare Brazilian plants, is also worth visiting. There are several paths for jogging or just wandering. ✉ *Rua Eng. Ostoja Roguski s/n, Jardim Botânico* ☎ *041/3264–6994* 🎟 *Free* ⊙ *Daily 6 am–8 pm in winter, 6 am–9 pm in summer.*

Museu Oscar Niemeyer. Pictures of Oscar Niemeyer's projects throughout the world are on display at this museum designed by the architect himself. Museu Oscar Niemeyer also incorporates a collection of the works of Paraná's artists from the former Museu de Arte do Paraná with temporary modern art exhibits. Niemeyer's futuristic design includes a long rectangular building, formerly a school. The main building, a suspended eye-shape structure overlooking the adjacent John Paul II Woods, contains the major modern art exhibit. ✉ *Rua Marechal Hermes 999, Centro Cívico* ☎ *041/3350–4400* ⊕ *www. museuoscarniemeyer.org.br* 🎟 *R$6* ⊙ *Tue.–Sun. 10–6.*

Museu Paranaense. Founded in 1876, the State Museum of Paraná moved several times before installing its collections in this imposing art nouveau building, which served as city hall from 1916 to 1969. The permanent displays contain official documents, ethnographic materials of the native Guaraní and Kaigang peoples, coins and photographs, and archaeological pieces related to the state's history. ⊠ *Rua Kellers 289, Centro Histórico* ☎ *041/3304–3300* ⊕ *www.museuparanaense.pr.gov. br* ☞ *R$4* ⊙ *Weekdays 9–6, weekends 10–4.*

Parque das Pedreiras. This cultural complex was built in the abandoned João Gava quarry and adjacent wooded lot. The quarry itself was converted to an amphitheater that can accommodate 60,000 people. The 2,400-seat **Opera de Arame** (Wire Opera House), also on the grounds here, was constructed from tubular steel and wire mesh above a water–field quarry pit. National and international musical events have given this facility world renown. ⊠ *Rua João Gava s/n, Pilarzinho* ☎ *041/3355–6071* ☞ *Free* ⊙ *Tues.–Sun. 8–10.*

OFF THE BEATEN PATH

Santa Felicidade. What was once an Italian settlement, dating from 1878, is now one of the city's most popular neighborhoods. It has been officially designated as Curitiba's "gastronomic district," and, indeed, you'll find some fantastic restaurants—as well as wine, antiques, and handicrafts shops—along Via Veneto and Avenida Manuel Elias. The area also has some colonial buildings, such as the Igreja Matriz de São José (St. Joseph's Church).

WORTH NOTING

FAMILY **Bosque Alemão.** The 8-acre German Woods, a park honoring German immigration, is on a hill in the Jardim Schaffer neighborhood. On its upper side is the Bach Oratorium, a small concert hall that looks like a chapel; it's the site of classical music performances. The park also has a viewpoint with a balcony overlooking downtown, a library with children's books, and a path through the woods called Hans and Gretel Trail, which depicts the Grimm Brothers' tale in 12 paintings along the way. The trail ends at the Mural de Fausto, where there's a stage for music shows. ⊠ *Rua Nicolo Paganini at Rua Francisco Schaffer, Jardim Schaffer* ☎ *041/3338–6012, 041/3350–9183* ☞ *Free* ⊙ *Park daily dawn–dusk. Library Mon.–Sat. 9–5.*

Igreja de São Francisco. Curitiba's oldest church, St. Francis was built in 1737 and fully restored in 1981. Check out its gold-plated altar before ducking into the attached **Museu de Arte Sacra** (Sacred Art Museum), with its baroque religious sculptures made of wood and terra-cotta. ⊠ *Largo da Ordem s/n, Curittiba* ☎ *041/3223–7545 church, 041/3321–3265 museum* ☞ *Free* ⊙ *Tues.–Fri. 9–6, weekends 9–2.*

NEED A BREAK?

Rua 24 Horas. To satisfy your hunger, head for Rua 24 Horas. In this downtown alley sheltered by a glass roof, you'll find souvenir shops and newsstands as well as coffeehouses and bars whose tables spill out onto the walkway. Most are open 24 hours a day, seven days a week. ⊠ *Rua Coronel Mena Barreto, between Rua Visconde de Rio Branco and Rua Visconde de Nacar, Centro* ☎ *041/3225–1732* ⊕ *www.rua24horascuritiba.com.br.*

Parque Tangüá. The most-visited park in the city, Tangüá shows creative landscaping in an abandoned quarry with its pond, tunnel (dug 160 feet into the rock wall), artificial waterfall, and walkway over the water, all surrounded by woods, with many imposing Brazilian pines. ⊠ *Rua Dr. Bemben s/n, Pilarzinho* ☎ *041/3352–7607* ☞ *Free* ⊙ *Daily dawn–dusk.*

6

Catedral Basílica Menor 2
Igreja de São Francisco ... 3
Museu Oscar Niemeyer 5
Museu Paranaense 1
Passeio Público 4

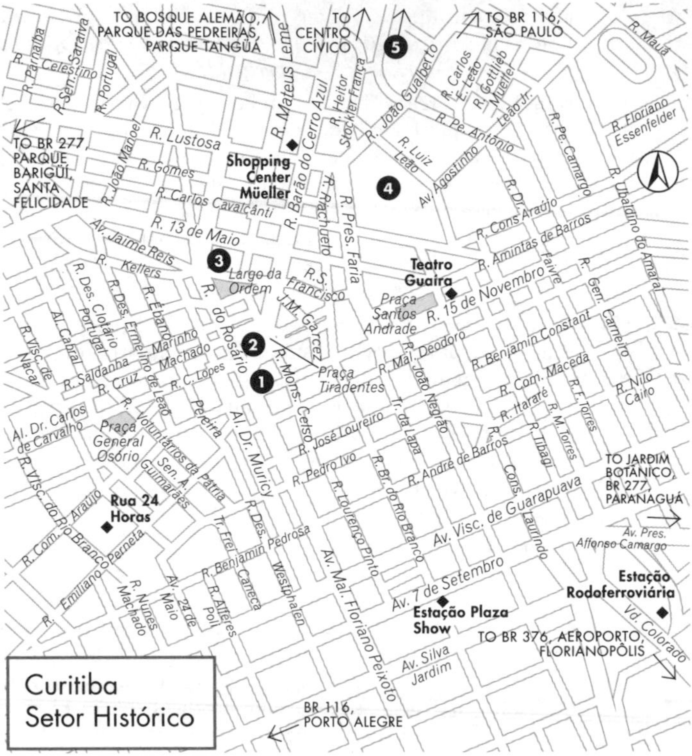

Curitiba Setor Histórico

Passeio Público. Opened in 1886, the Public Thoroughfare was designed as a botanical and zoological garden and soon became a favorite place for the affluent to spend their weekend afternoons. The main gate is a replica of that at the Cimetière des Chiens in Paris. Although it's no longer the official city zoo, you can observe several Brazilian primates and birds still kept in the park, as well as majestic sycamores, oaks, and the *ipê amarelo*, a striking Brazilian tree with vibrant yellow flowers. ✉ *Main Gate:, Rua Pres. Faria at Pres. Carlos Cavalcanti, Setor Histórico* ☎ *041/3222–2742, 041/3350–9920* 🎫 *Free* ⏲ *Tues.–Sun. 6 am–8 pm.*

WHERE TO EAT

As one of the major centers of industry, commerce, and tourism in Brazil, Curitiba has wide a variety of dining and lodging options that caters to hurried and demanding business travelers. The Santa Felicidade neighborhood carved a name for affordable restaurants that serve locally influenced Italian cuisine.

$$$ SEAFOOD ✕ **Bombordo.** This small but highly regarded restaurant serves the best seafood in town. The nautical decor, with model boats, ships' wheels, and fish figurines, creates the perfect ambience. Try the *congrio grelhado com molho de camarão* (grilled conger eel in shrimp sauce). At lunchtime a prix-fixe seafood buffet is served. [$] *Average main: R$55* ✉ *Shopping Estação, Av. 7 de Setembro 2275, Centro* ☎ *041/3233–2350* ⏲ *Daily 10–11.*

CLOSE UP

The Mata Atlântica

The Amazonian rain forest is so famous that most tourists are amazed to learn that Brazil's southern states were once covered by an equally lush humid forest, teeming with animal and plant biodiversity. The Mata Atlântica (Atlantic Forest), really a series of forests, originally covered about a fourth of Brazil, mostly along the southeastern seaboard. One of the most complex ecosystems on earth, these evergreen forests contained about 7% of all known vertebrates and more than 20,000 plant species.

The major difference between the Amazon and the Mata Atlântica is the flora. In the Amazon plants are essentially lowland types adapted to the humid climate; those in the Atlantic forests have adapted to mountainous terrain, less rainfall, and lower mean annual temperatures. Unique Mata Atlântica fauna includes primates like the *mico-leão dourado* (golden-lion tamarin) and the *muriqui* (spider monkey), parrots, toucans, *arapongas* (bell birds), and the *anta* (tapir).

The flora includes rich *pau-brasil* (brazilwood) and, at higher elevations, *araucária* (Brazilian pine). The hundreds of orchid species, the yellow flowers of the *ipê* (Brazil's national flower), and the flowers of the *manacá* (princess flower tree) that turn from white to purple to violet within days, compose a colorful spectacle.

The Mata Atlântica has been seriously overexploited since the 16th century, and is threatened by human encroachment and agricultural land conversion. Recent estimates indicate that only 8% of the original remains. Preservation, conservation, and recovery efforts by the national government and private organizations are ongoing. "Bright spots" include Foz do Iguaçu, Superagüí National Park (near Paranaguá), a golden tamarin reserve in southern Bahia State, and organizations that train farmers in sustainable agriculture practices.

6

$$$$ FRENCH 🍴 **Boulevard.** A sophisticated restaurant with an excellent wine selection (including a long list of imports), Boulevard has a sober decor, with impeccably white linen table cloths and dark wood. The fare by renowned chef Celso Freire doesn't fail to impress. Try the wild boar ribs with herbs, truffles, and mustard sauce or the chef's take on grilled tenderloin with mustard sauce. [$] *Average main: R$80* ✉ *Rua Voluntários da Pátria 539, Centro* ☎ *041/3023–8244* 🕒 *Closed Sun.*

$$$$ ECLECTIC Fodors Choice ★ 🍴 **Durski.** This family-run restaurant has brought traditional Polish and Ukrainian food center stage. Occupying a renovated house in the historical district, Durski has a rustic yet sleek look with tile floors and exposed-brick walls. The impeccable service by staff in traditional attire, as well as the borscht, pierogi, and *bigos* (a round loaf of bread stuffed with sausages and sauerkraut), transport you to central Europe. There's also an alternative international menu that has many pasta, beef, and fish options. [$] *Average main: R$80* ✉ *Rua Jaime Reis 254, São Francisco* ☎ *041/3225–7893* 🌐 *www.durski.com.br* ✍ *Reservations essential* 🕒 *Lunch only* 🕒 *Closed Mon. and Sun.*

$$ ✕**Estrela da Terra.** On weekends this restaurant in a grand colonial
BRAZILIAN house is *the* place to try the local *barreado* (a long-simmered stew of
beef, bacon, potatoes, and spices). On weekdays a buffet is served with
several other regional choices, including *frango com pinhão* (grilled
chicken breast with cream sauce and Brazilian pine nuts). $ *Average
main: R$32 ✉ Rua Jaime Reis 176, Largo da Ordem* ☎ *041/3222–5007*
◷ *Lunch only* ◷ *Closed Mon.*

$$$ ✕**Madalosso.** One of the best-known establishments for Italian cuisine
ITALIAN in Curitiba, Madalosso is also possibly the largest restaurant in Brazil:
the hangarlike building seats 4,600 diners. The prix-fixe menu includes
a huge selection of pastas and sauces, chicken dishes, and salads. The
gnocchi and lasagna are particularly noteworthy. The restaurant keeps
a large wine cellar, with many renowned Brazilian and international
wines, as well as a house wine, made for the restaurant in the vineyards
of Rio Grande do Sul. $ *Average main: R$50 ✉ Av. Manoel Ribas
5875, Santa Felicidade* ☎ *041/3372–2121* ◷ *No dinner Sun.*

$$ ✕**Schwarzwald (Bar do Alemão).** The city's most popular German bar–res-
GERMAN taurant, Schwarzwald has carved a name for itself with great draft beer,
including some imported brands and local bocks (German-style dark
beers), which are hard to find in Brazil. Highly recommended entrées
are the house version of *eisbein* (pig's leg served with mashed potatoes),
kassler (beef fillet with a cream sauce), and duck with red cabbage.
The restaurant is somewhat small and packed with tables, but there's
plenty of space on the sidewalk in front. $ *Average main: R$40 ✉ Rua
Claudino dos Santos 63, Setor Histórico* ☎ *041/3223–2585* ⊕ *www.
bardoalemaocuritiba.com.br.*

WHERE TO STAY

$ ⊞**Duomo Park Hotel.** At this small, comfortable hotel, the rooms and
HOTEL suites are unusually spacious and come with large beds, blond-wood
furniture, and carpeting. **Pros:** great service and location. **Cons:** fur-
niture needs updating; small commons area. $ *Rooms from: R$165
✉ Rua Visconde de Rio Branco 1710, Centro* ☎ *041/3321–1900*
⊕ *www.hotelduomo.com.br* ➳ *40 rooms, 8 suites* ❑| *Breakfast.*

$$ ⊞**Four Points by Sheraton.** Widely regarded as Curitiba's finest hotel, the
HOTEL Four Points is geared toward the discriminating business traveler. **Pros:**
great business facilities; central location. **Cons:** expensive; few amenities for leisure travelers. $ *Rooms from: R$375 ✉ Av. Sete de Setembro
4211, Água Verde* ☎ *041/3340–4000, 0800/368–7764 toll free* ⊕ *www.
fourpoints.com/curitiba* ➳ *165 rooms* ❑| *Breakfast.*

$ ⊞**Slaviero Slim Centro Hotel.** In a landmark building overlooking the Rua
HOTEL das Flores walkway, Slaviero Braz has large rooms with wood paneling
and matching furniture. **Pros:** central location; good value for the better rooms. **Cons:** some rooms are small; few amenities. $ *Rooms from:
R$155 ✉ Av. Luiz Xavier 67, Centro* ☎ *041/3322-2829, 0800/704–
3311* ⊕ *www.hotelslaviero.com.br* ➳ *89 rooms, 2 suites* ❑| *Breakfast.*

NIGHTLIFE AND THE ARTS
Curitiba has a bustling cultural scene, a reflection of the European background of many of its citizens. Complete listings of events are published
in the *Gazeta do Povo*, the major daily newspaper.

NIGHTLIFE

Aos Democratas. A traditional *boteco* (small bar) that caters to soccer fans, Aos Democratas is a great place to watch games and hear the fans. It's rumored to have "the best draft beer in town." ✉ *Rua Dr. Pedrosa 485, Centro* ☎ *041/3024–4496* ⊕ *www.aosdemocratas.com.br.*

THE ARTS

Teatro Guaíra. Formerly the Teatro São Teodoro (circa 1884), the Teatro Guaíra was rebuilt in its present location and reopened in 1974. It has a modern, well-equipped 2,000-seat auditorium, as well as two smaller rooms. Shows include plays, popular music concerts, and the occasional full-fledged opera. ✉ *Rua 15 de Novembro 971, Centro* ☎ *041/3322–8191* ⊕ *www.tguaira.pr.gov.br.*

SPORTS AND THE OUTDOORS

Curitiba has three professional soccer clubs: Coritiba, Atlético Paranaense, and Paraná Clube. Check local newspaper listings for upcoming game times and locations. Many of the area's parks have paths for jogging and bicycling.

HIKING

Parque Barigüí. This park contains soccer fields, volleyball courts, and paths spread across 310 acres. ✉ *Av. Candido Hartmann at Av. Gen. Tourinho, off Km 1, BR 277, Cascatinha* ☎ *041/3339–8975.*

SOCCER

Arena da Baixada. Also known as Estadio Joaquim Americo Guimaraes, the Arena da Baixada is home to the Atlético Paranaense Club. Long considered the most modern sports facility in the country, the stadium is one of the 12 stadiums receiving a makeover for the 2014 FIFA World Cup. The 234-million-reais expansion will boost capacity to 41,000. ✉ *R. Madre Maria dos Anjos, 1071, Água Verde* ☎ *041/2105–5616.*

SHOPPING

Feira de Artesanato. Interact directly with the artisans every Sunday from 9 to 3 at the Feira de Artesanato do Largo da Ordem, a popular fair with paintings from local artists, pottery, tapestry, handicrafts, and antiques. ✉ *Largo da Ordem and Praça Garibaldi, Setor Histórico* ⊕ *www.feiradolargo.com.br.*

Shopping Center Mueller. One of the city's prime shopping destinations, Shopping Center Mueller includes branches of national chains, upscale fashion and jewelry stores, as well as some small handicraft shops, restaurants and cafés, bookstores, and movie theaters. ✉ *Rua Candido de Abreu 127, São Francisco* ☎ *041/3074–1000* ⊕ *www. shoppingmueller.com.br.*

FAMILY **Shopping Estação.** In what was once a railway terminal, the Shopping Estação is a 700,000-square-foot covered area with a colorful and noisy collection of bars and restaurants, amusement parks, exhibits, a railway museum, a cineplex, daily live music shows, and more than 100 shops. The complex is open daily 10–10. ✉ *Av. 7 de Setembro 2775, Centro* ☎ *041/3094–5300.*

PARANAGUÁ

90 km (56 miles) east of Curitiba.

Most of Brazil's coffee and soybeans are shipped out of Paranaguá, the nation's second-largest port, which also serves as chief port for land-locked Paraguay. Downtown holds many examples of colonial architecture and has been designated an official historic area. The city, founded in 1565 by Portuguese explorers, is 30 km (18 miles) from the Atlantic on the Baía de Paranaguá. The bay area is surrounded by the Mata Atlântica, of which a great swatch on the northern side is protected; several islands in the bay also have rain forests as well as great beaches. You'll find other less scenic but popular sandy stretches farther south, toward the Santa Catarina border.

GETTING HERE AND AROUND

Although you can reach Paranaguá from Curitiba on BR 277, consider taking the more scenic Estrada da Graciosa, which follows the route taken by 17th-century traders up the Serra do Mar. This narrow, winding route—paved with rocks slabs in some stretches—is some 30 km (18 miles) longer than BR 277, but the breathtaking peaks and slopes covered with rain forest make the extra travel time worthwhile. You can drive or take a Viação Graciosa bus (75 minutes; R$23), but most tourists take the scenic train as part of an organized tour.

ESSENTIALS

Currency exchange is difficult in the Paranaguá area. Exchange reais in Curitiba.

Bus Contacts Terminal Municipal Rodoviário (Municipal Bus Station)
✉ *Rua João Estevam at Rua João Regis, Centro.*

Taxi Contacts Ponto de Taxi ☎ *041/3423–4548 in Centro Histórico.*

Visitor Information Informações Turísticas ✉ *Rua Gen. Carneiro 258, Setor Histórico* ☎ *041/3425–4542* ☉ *Tues.–Sat. 9–5.* **Serra Verde Express.** This tourist rail line runs from Curitiba to Paranaguá—a fabulous 69-mile trip along the Serra do Mar slope descending from 3,300 feet to 17 feet, with views of peaks, waterfalls, and Atlantic rain forest, and stops in historic towns. The regular train to Morretes, the end of the scenic route (3 hours; R$65–R$123) departs at 8:15 am daily, returning at 3 pm from Monday to Saturday and 4 pm on Sunday. The full route to Paranagua is Sundays only on the more luxurious *litorina* train (5 hours; R$270), which departs at 7:30 am Sundays and returns at 1:30 pm. You can return from Morretes on a van along the Serra da Graciosa scenic road. ✉ *Av. Pres. Affonso Camargo, 330, Curitiba* ☎ *041/3888–3488* ⊕ *www.serraverdeexpress.com.br.*

SAFETY AND PRECAUTIONS

Paranaguá has some difficult neighborhoods, but the historic district downtown, where most attractions are, is fairly safe. All the same, be extra careful with valuables.

EXPLORING

TOP ATTRACTIONS

Fodor'sChoice **Ilha do Mel** (*Honey Island*). The 10-km-long (6-mile-long) Ilha do Mel,
★ a state park in the Baía de Paranaguá, is the most popular destination on Paraná's coast. It's crisscrossed by hiking trails—cars aren't
allowed, and the number of visitors is limited to 5,000 at any one
time—and has two villages, Encantadas and Nova Brasília, and several pristine beaches. Local lore has it that the east shore's Gruta das
Encantadas (Enchanted Grotto) is frequented by mermaids. On the
south shore check out the sights around Farol das Conchas (Lighthouse of the Shells) and its beach. From Forte de Nossa Senhora dos
Prazeres (Our Lady of Pleasures Fort), built in 1767 on the east shore,
take advantage of the great views of the forest-clad northern bay
islands. The most scenic ferry rides leave from Paranaguá between
8 am and 1 pm (2 hours; R$32). More convenient are the ferries
that depart from Pontal do Sul, 30 miles east of Paranaguá, every 30
minutes. Prices start at R$27. To ensure admission in the high season
(December–March), book an island tour before you leave Curitiba.
✉ *Trapiche (Pier), Rua da Praia, Centro* ☎ *041/3455–1129 ABALINE
(ferry operators) in Paranaguá, 041/3455–2616.*

Parque Nacional de Superagüí. The northern shore of Baía de Paranaguá is
home to the 54,000-acre Parque Nacional de Superagüí and its complex
system of coves, saltwater marshes, and forested islands—including Ilha
Superagüí and Ilha das Peças. Most of these pristine settings containing animal and bird species unique to the Mata Atlântica are closed to
visitors. You can, however, see many bird and animal species by basing
yourself in the fishing village of Barra do Superagüí—reached by a three-
hour ferry ride from Paranaguá's harbor—and then touring the bay and
trails around the park. Your best bet for viewing wildlife is to explore
the islands on a guided boat tour. Ask for local boat operators and
guides in the Paranaguá ferry dock or at the park headquarters. ✉ *Park
administration: 2 km (1 mile) north of Guaraqueçaba. Ferry Dock: Rua
da Praia s/n, Barra do Superagüí, Guaraqueçaba, PR* ☎ *041/3482–7146
park adminstration, 041/3482–7150 ferry information: Capitão Jacó*
✉ *Park free, ferry R$25* ☉ *Park daily 9–6.*

WORTH NOTING

Museu de Arqueologia e Etnologia (*Archaeology and Ethnology Museum*).
Built in 1755 and recently renovated, the Museu de Arqueologia e Etnologia (MAE) occupies a building that was once part of a Jesuit school.
The collection here includes pieces found in excavations in the area,
most belonging to the Sambaqui, a coastal dwelling native people, as
well as other native peoples of Paraná such as the Kaigang and Guaraní. The museum also hosts many temporary art exhibits. ✉ *Rua XV de
Novembro, 575, Setor Histórico* ☎ *041/3423–2511* ✉ *R$10* ☉ *Tues.–
Fri. 9–6, weekends 12–6.*

WHERE TO EAT AND STAY

$$$ ✕**Casa do Barreado.** This small, family-run, buffet-style restaurant
BRAZILIAN specializes in the traditional dish most associated with Paraná State:
the *barreado* (meat stew simmered in a sealed clay pot). Because *bar-
reado* takes 24 hours to cook, you must order it a day in advance. The

6

prix-fixe menu includes *galinha na púcara* (chicken cooked in wine, tomato, and bacon sauce), several salads, and *cachaças* (Brazilian liquor distilled from sugarcane). Although the restaurant is officially open only on weekends, you can call ahead to arrange a dinner during the week. [$] *Average main: R$50* ✉ *Rua José Antônio Cruz 78, Ponta do Cajú* ☎ *041/3423–1830* ✍ *Reservations essential* ⏲ *Lunch only* ⏲ *Closed weekdays.*

$$ RESORT 🏨 **Camboa Resort.** Right in the historic district, Camboa Resort has comfortable facilities, a long roster of activities, and a dedicated staff that can arrange tours in the region. **Pros:** close to historic district; many amenities. **Cons:** very busy in summer months; poor Internet connection. [$] *Rooms from: R$270* ✉ *Rua João Estevão s/n, Ponta do Cajú* ☎ *041/3420–5200 lobby, 041/3323–5546 reservations* 🌐 *www.hotelcamboa.com.br* 🛏 *134 rooms* 🍴 *Breakfast.*

IGUAÇU FALLS

637 km (396 miles) west of Curitiba, 544 (338 miles) west of Vila Velha; 1,358 km (843 miles) north of Buenos Aires.

Iguaçu consists of some 275 separate waterfalls—in the rainy season there are as many as 350—that plunge more than 200 feet onto the rocks below. They cascade in a deafening roar at a bend in the Iguazú River (Río Iguazú/Rio Iguaçu) where the borders of Argentina, Brazil, and Paraguay meet. Dense, lush jungle surrounds the falls: here the tropical sun and the omnipresent moisture make the jungle grow at a pace that produces a towering pine tree in two decades instead of the seven it takes in, say, Scandinavia. By the falls and along the roadside, rainbows and butterflies are set off against vast walls of red earth, which is so ubiquitous that eventually even paper currency in the area turns red from exposure to the stuff.

The falls and the lands around them are protected by Brazil's Parque Nacional do Iguaçu (where the falls go by the Portuguese name of Foz do Iguaçu) and Argentina's Parque Nacional Iguazú (where the falls are referred to by their Spanish name, the Cataratas de Iguazú). The Brazilian town of Foz do Iguaçu and the Argentine town of Puerto Iguazú are the hubs for exploring the falls (the Paraguayan town of Ciudad del Este is also nearby).

GETTING HERE AND AROUND

BRAZIL INFO

There are direct flights between Foz do Iguaçu and São Paulo (1½ hours; R$380), Rio de Janeiro (2 hours; R$440), and Curitiba (1 hour; R$250) on TAM, which also has connecting flights to Salvador, Recife, Brasília, other Brazilian cities, and Buenos Aires. Low-cost airline Gol operates slightly cheaper direct flights on the same three routes.

The Aeroporto Internacional Foz do Iguaçu is 13 km (8 miles) southeast of downtown Foz. The 20-minute taxi ride should cost R$40; the 45-minute regular bus ride about R$3. Note that several major hotels are on the highway to downtown, so a cab ride from the airport to these may be less than R$30. A cab ride from downtown hotels directly to the Parque Nacional in Brazil costs about R$90.

Via bus, the trip between Curitiba and Foz do Iguaçu takes 9–10 hours with Catarinense (R$90; R$180 for sleeper service). The same company operates the 17-hour route to Florianópolis (R$120). Pluma travels to Rio de Janeiro, which takes 11½ hours (R$130), and São Paolo, which takes 14 hours (R$130; R$205 for sleeper). The Terminal Rodoviário in Foz do Iguaçu is 5 km (3 miles) northeast of downtown. There are regular buses into town, which stop at the Terminal de Transportes Urbano (local bus station, often shortened to TTU) at Avenida Juscelino Kubitschek and Rua Mem de Sá. From here, buses labeled Parque Nacional also depart every 15 minutes (7–7) to the visitor center at the park entrance; the fare is R$6. The buses run along Avenida Juscelino Kubitschek and Avenida Jorge Schimmelpfeng, where you can also flag them down.

There's no real reason to rent a car in Foz do Iguaçu: it's cheaper and easier to use taxis or local tour companies to visit the falls, especially as you can't cross the border in a rental car. There are taxi stands (*pontos de taxi*) at intersections all over town, each with its own phone number. Hotels and restaurants can call you a cab, but you can also hail them on the street.

BRAZIL ESSENTIALS

Airline Contacts Aeropuerto Internacional de Foz do Iguaçu/Cataratas ⊠ *BR 469, Km 16.5, Foz do Iguaçu* ☎ *45/3521-4200.* **GOL** ☎ *300/115-2121 toll-free, 45/3521-4230 in Foz do Iguaçu* ⊕ *www.voegol.com.br.* **TAM** ☎ *800/570-5700 toll-free, 45/3521-7500 in Foz do Iguaçu* ⊕ *www.tam.com.br.*

Bus Contacts Catarinense ☎ *300/147-0470 toll-free, 45/3522-2050 in Foz do Iguaçu* ⊕ *www.catarinense.net.* **Pluma** ☎ *800/646-0300 toll-free, 045/3522-2515 in Foz do Iguaçu* ⊕ *www.pluma.com.br.* **Terminal Rodoviário** ⊠ *Av. Costa e Silva 1601, Jardim Polo, Foz do Iguaçu* ☎ *45/3522-2590.* **Terminal de Transportes Urbano (TTU)** ⊠ *Av. Juscelino Kubitschek s/n at Rua Mem de Sá, across from army barracks, Centro, Foz do Iguaçu* ☎ *0800/45-1516.* **Tres Fronteras.** This bus line runs an hourly cross-border public bus service between the centers of Puerto Iguazú and Foz do Iguaçu. Locals don't have to get on and off for immigration but be sure you do so. To reach the Argentine falls, change to a local bus at the intersection with RN 12 on the Argentine side. For the Brazilian park, change to a local bus at the Avenida Cataratas roundabout. ☎ *3757/3523-4625 in Puerto Iguazú.*

Taxi Contacts Ponto de Taxi 20 ☎ *45/3523-4625.*

Visitor Information Foz do Iguaçu Tourist Office ⊠ *Praça Getúlio Vargas 69, Centro, Foz do Iguaçu* ☎ *45/3521-1455* ⊕ *www.iguassu.tur.br* ⊗ *7 am–11 pm.*

ARGENTINA INFO

Aerolíneas Argentinas flies four to six times daily between Aeroparque Jorge Newbery in Buenos Aires and the Aeropuerto Internacional de Puerto Iguazú (20 km/12 miles southeast of Puerto Iguazú); the trip takes 1¾ hours. Four Tourist Travel runs shuttle buses from the airport to hotels in Puerto Iguazú. Services leave after every flight lands and cost 12 pesos. Taxis to Puerto Iguazú cost 80 pesos.

Vía Bariloche operates several daily bus services between Retiro bus station in Buenos Aires and the Puerto Iguazú Terminal de Omnibus in the center of town. The trip takes 16–18 hours, so it's worth paying the little extra for *coche cama* (sleeper) or *cama ejecutivo* (deluxe sleeper) services, which cost 300 pesos one-way (regular semicama services cost around 250 pesos). You can travel direct to Rio de Janeiro (22 hours) and São Paolo (15 hours) with Crucero del Norte; the trips cost 250 and 200 pesos, respectively.

From Puerto Iguazú to the falls or the hotels along RN 12, take El Práctico from the terminal or along Avenida Victoria Aguirre. Buses leave every 15 minutes 7–7 and cost 20 pesos round-trip.

There's little point in renting a car around Puerto Iguazú: daily rentals start at 300 pesos, more than twice what you pay for a taxi between the town and the falls. A rental car is useful for visiting the Jesuit ruins at San Ignacio, 256 km south of Puerto Iguazú on RN 12, a two-lane highway in excellent condition.

ARGENTINA ESSENTIALS
Airline Contacts Aerolíneas Argentinas ☎ *800/222–86527* ⊕ *www. aerolineas.com.ar.* **Aeropuerto Internacional de Puerto Iguazú** ⊠ *Ruta Provincial 101, Aeropuerto, Puerto Iguazú, Misiones, Argentina* ☎ *3757/421–996* ⊕ *www.aa2000.com.ar* ☞ *IATA Code: IGR.*

Bus Contacts Crucero del Norte ☎ *11/5258–5000 in Buenos Aires, 3757/42–1916 in Puerto Iguazú* ⊕ *www.crucerodelnorte.com.ar.* **El Práctico** ☎ *3757/42–0742 in Puerto Iguazú.* **Puerto Iguazú Terminal de Ómnibus** ⊠ *Avs. Córdoba and Misiones, Puerto Iguazú, Misiones, Argentina* ☎ *3757/42–2730.* **Vía Bariloche** ☎ *11/4315–7700 in Buenos Aires, 3757/42–0854 in Puerto Iguazú* ⊕ *www.viabariloche.com.ar.*

Taxis Contacts Remises Iguazú ⊠ *Puerto Iguazú, Misiones, Argentina* ☎ *3757/42–2008.*

Visitor Information Cataratas del Iguazú Visitors Center ⊠ *Park entrance, Parque Nacional, Puerto Iguazú, Misiones, Argentina* ☎ *3757/42–0722* ⊕ *www.parquesnacionales.gov.ar* 💲 *170 pesos* ◷ *Daily 8–6.* **Puerto Iguazú Tourist Office** ⊠ *Av. Victoria Aguirre 311, Puerto Iguazú, Misiones, Argentina* ☎ *3757/42–0800, 3757/42–2938.*

EXPLORING

To visit the falls, you can base yourself in the small Argentine city of Puerto Iguazú, or its sprawling Brazilian counterpart, the city of Foz do Iguaçu. The two cities are 18 km (11 miles) and 25 km (15 miles) northwest of the falls, respectively, and are connected by an international bridge, the Puente Presidente Tancredo Neves. Another bridge links Foz do Iguaçu with Ciudad del Este in Paraguay. Together, the three cities form the *Triple Frontera* (Tri Border).

Originally a port for shipping wood from the region, Puerto Iguazú now revolves around tourism. This was made possible in the early 20th century when Victoria Aguirre, a high-society porteña, funded the building of a road to the falls to make it easier for people to

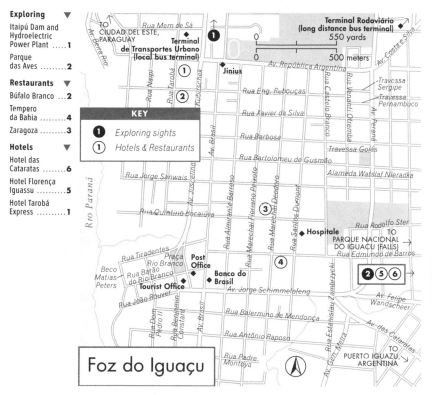

KEY

① Exploring sights
① Hotels & Restaurants

Foz do Iguaçu

visit them. Despite the constant stream of visitors from Argentina and abroad, Puerto Iguazú is still a somewhat sleepy small city of 82,000 inhabitants.

The same was once true of Foz de Iguaçu, but the construction of the Itaipú dam (now the second largest in the world) in 1975 transformed it into a bustling city with three times more people than Puerto Iguazú. Many have jobs connected with the hydroelectric power station at the dam, while others are involved with trade (both legal and illegal) with the duty-free zone of Ciudad del Este, in Paraguay.

In general it makes more sense to stay in tourism-oriented Puerto Iguazú: hotels and restaurants are better, peso prices are lower, and it's safer than Foz do Iguaçu, which has a bad reputation for violent street crime. There's also more to do and see on the Argentine side of the falls, which take up to two days to visit. The Brazilian side, though impressive, only warrants half a day.

Many travel agencies offer packages from Buenos Aires, São Paulo, or Curitiba that include flights or bus tickets, transfers, accommodation, and transport to the falls. These packages are usually more expensive than booking everything yourself, but you do get round-the-clock support.

If you're staying in town, rather than at the hotels in the parks, you can easily reach the falls on your side of the border by public bus, private shuttle (most hotels work with a shuttle company), or taxi. Travel agencies and tour operators in Puerto Iguazú and Foz de Iguaçu also offer day trips to the opposite sides of the border. Most are glorified shuttle services that save you the hassle of changing buses and get you through immigration formalities quickly. Use them to facilitate getting to the park, but avoid those that include in-park tours: most drag you around with a huge group of people and a megaphone, which rather ruins the fabulous natural surroundings.

Both parks are incredibly well organized and clearly signposted, so most visitors have no trouble exploring independently. Once in the park, be sure to go on a boat trip, an unmissable—though drenching—experience that gets you almost under the falls. You can reserve these through tour operators or hotels, or at booths inside the parks.

WORTH NOTING

Surprisingly, Iguaçu is not the only site to see in these parts, though few people actually have time (or make time) to go to see them.

IN BRAZIL

Itaipú Dam and Hydroelectric Power Plant. It took more than 30,000 workers eight years to build this 8-km (5-mile) dam, voted one of the Seven Wonders of the Modern World by the American Society of Civil Engineers. The monumental structure produces 25% of Brazil's electricity and 78% of Paraguay's, and was the largest hydroelectric power plant in the world until China's Three Gorges (Yangtze) Dam was completed.

You get plenty of insight into how proud this makes the Brazilian government—and some idea of how the dam was built—during the 30-minute video that precedes hour-long guided panoramic bus tours of the complex. Although commentaries are humdrum, the sheer size of the dam is an impressive sight. To see more than a view over the spillways, consider the special tours, which take you inside the cavernous structure and include a visit to the control room. Night tours—which include a light-and-sound show—begin at 8 on Friday and Saturday, 9 during the summer months (reserve ahead). ⊠ *Av. Tancredo Neves 6702, Foz do Iguaçu* ☎ *0800/645–4645* ⊕ *www. turismoitaipu.com.br* ✆ *Panoramic tour R$24, special tour R$60* ⊙ *Regular tours daily 8–4 (hourly on the hour). Special tours daily 8, 8:30, 10, 10:30, 1:30, 2, 3:30, and 4.*

Ecomuseu de Itaipú (*Itaipú Eco-Museum*). At the Ecomuseu de Itaipú you can learn about the geology, archaeology, and efforts to preserve the flora and fauna of the area since the Itaipú Dam and Hydroelectric Power Plant was built. Note, however, that this museum is funded by the dam's operator, Itaipú Binacional, so the information isn't necessarily objective. ⊠ *Av. Tancredo Neves 6001, Foz do Iguaçu* ☎ *045/3520–6398* ⊕ *www.turismoitaipu.com.br* ✆ *R$10* ⊙ *Tues.–Sun. 8–4:30.*

Parque das Aves (*Bird Park*). Flamingos, parrots, and toucans are some of the more colorful inhabitants of this privately run park. Right outside the Parque Nacional Foz do Iguaçu, it's an interesting complement to a visit to the falls. A winding path leads you through untouched tropical forest and walk-through aviaries containing hundreds of species of birds. Iguanas, alligators, and other nonfeathered friends have their own pens. ⊠ *Km 17.1, Rodovia das Cataratas, Foz do Iguaçu* ☏ *045/3529–8282* ⊕ *www.parquedasaves.com.br* 💲 *US$15* ☉ *Daily 8:30–5.*

IN ARGENTINA

GüiraOga. Although Iguazú is home to around 450 bird species, the parks are so busy these days that you'd be lucky to see so much as a feather. It's another story at GüiraOga, which means "house of the birds" in Guaraní, although "bird rehab" might be more appropriate. Injured birds, birds displaced by deforestation, and birds confiscated from traffickers are brought here for treatment. The large cages also contain many species on the verge of extinction, including the harpy eagle and the red macaw, a gorgeous parrot. The sanctuary is in a forested plot just off RN 12, halfway between Puerto Iguazú and the falls. ⊠ *RN 12, Km 5, Puerto Iguazú, Misiones, Argentina* ☏ *3757/42–3980* ⊕ *www.guiraoga.com.ar* 💲 *Free* ☉ *Daily.*

La Aripuca. It looks like a cross between a log cabin and the Pentagon, but this massive wooden structure—which weighs 551 tons—is a large-scale replica of a Guaraní bird trap. La Aripuca officially showcases different local woods, supposedly for conservation purposes—ironic, given the huge trunks used to build it, and the overpriced wooden furniture that fills the gift shop. ⊠ *RN 12 Km 5, Puerto Iguazú, Misiones, Argentina* ☏ *3757/42–3488* ⊕ *www.aripuca.com.ar* 💲 *20 pesos* ☉ *Daily 9–6.*

Hito Tres Fronteras. This viewpoint west of the town center stands high above the turbulent reddish-brown confluence of the Iguaçú and Paraná rivers, which also form the *Triple Frontera,* or Tri Border. A mini pale-blue-and-white obelisk reminds you that you're in Argentina; across the Iguazú river is Brazil's green-and-yellow equivalent; farther away, across the Paraná, is Paraguay's, painted red, white, and blue. A row of overpriced souvenir stalls stands alongside it. ⊠ *Av. Tres Fronteras, Puerto Iguazú, Misiones, Argentina.*

WHERE TO EAT

Booming tourism is kindling the restaurant scenes of Puerto Iguazú and Foz do Iguaçu, and each has enough reasonably priced, reliable choices to get most visitors through the two or three days they spend there. Neither border town has much of a culinary tradition to speak of, though most restaurants at least advertise some form of the local specialty *surubí* (a kind of catfish). Instead, parrillas or churrascarias abound, as do pizza and pasta joints.

FOZ DO IGUAÇU

$$$
BRAZILIAN

✗**Búfalo Branco.** The city's finest and largest churrascaria does a killer *rodízio* (all-you-can-eat meat buffet). The *picanha* (beef rump cap) stands out among the 25 meat choices, but pork, lamb, chicken, and even—yum—bull testicles find their way onto the metal skewers they use to grill the meat. Never fear, vegetarians—the salad bar is also well stocked. 💲 *Average main: R$50* ⊠ *Av. Rebouças 530* ☏ *45/3523-9744* ⊕ *www.bufalobranco.com.br* ☉ *Daily noon–11.*

Exploring ▼

La Aripuca **2**

Gúira Oga **3**

Hito Tres Fronteras **1**

Restaurants ▼

Aqva **2**

El Quincho del Tio Querido .. **5**

La Rueda 1975 Restaurant . **3**

Hotels ▼

Panoramic Hotel Iguazú **1**

Secret Garden Iguazú **4**

Sheraton International Iguazú **6**

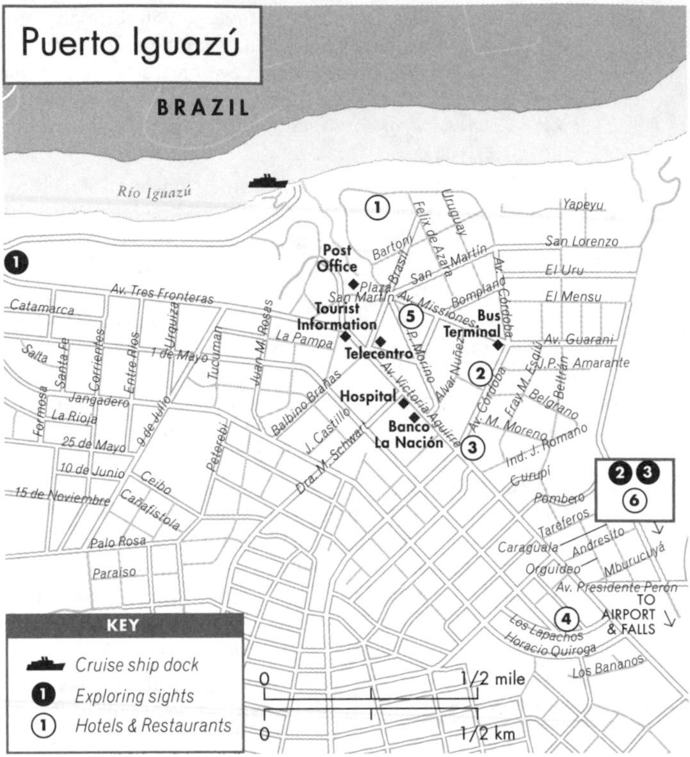

Puerto Iguazú
BRAZIL
Río Iguazú
Post Office
Plaza San Martín
Tourist Information
Telecentro
Hospital
Banco La Nación
Bus Terminal
Catamarca
Av. Tres Fronteras
Salta
Formosa
Santa Fe
Corrientes
Entre Ríos
Urquiza
Tucumán
Juan M. Rosas
La Pampa
1 de Mayo
Jangadero
La Rioja
25 de Mayo
10 de Junio
15 de Noviembre
9 de Julio
Ceibo
Cañafistola
Palo Rosa
Paraíso
Peterebi
Balbino Brañas
J. Castillo
Dra. M. Schwarz
Bartoni
Brasil
Félix de Azara
Uruguay
San Martín
Av. Misiones
Bompland
Av. Córdoba
P. Moreno
Alvar Nuñez
Av. Victoria Aguirre
Yapeyu
San Lorenzo
El Uru
El Mensu
Av. Guaraní
J.P. Amarante
Fray M. Esquiú
Beltrán
Belgrano
M. Moreno
Ind. J. Romano
Curupí
Pombero
Tareferos
Caraguata
Andresito
Orquídeo
Mburucuyá
Av. Presidente Perón
TO AIRPORT & FALLS
Los Lapachos
Horacio Quiroga
Los Bananos
KEY
Cruise ship dock
Exploring sights
Hotels & Restaurants
0
1/2 mile
0
1/2 km

$$$ SEAFOOD 🍴 **Tempero da Bahia.** If you're unable to venture up to Bahia on your trip, you can at least savor some of its flavors at this busy, tangerine-painted restaurant. Tempero de Bahia specializes in northeastern fare like *moquecas* (a rich seafood stew made with coconut milk and palm oil), but their delicious versions are unusual for mixing prawns with local river fish. Spicy panfried sole and salmon are lighter options. The flavors aren't quite as subtle at the all-out seafood (and riverfood) buffets they hold several times a week, but the offerings are tasty and cheap enough to pull in crowds. [$] *Average main: R$58* ✉ *Rua Marechal Deodoro 1228* ☎ *045/3025–1144* 🌐 *www.restaurantetemperodabahia.com* ⏰ *No dinner Sun.*

$$$ SPANISH 🍴 **Zaragoza.** On a tree-lined street in a quiet neighborhood, this traditional restaurant's Spanish owner is an expert at matching Iguaçu's fresh river fish to authentic Spanish seafood recipes. Brazilian ingredients sneak into some dishes—the *surubi à Goya* (catfish in a tomato-and-coconut-milk sauce) definitely merits a try. [$] *Average main: R$50* ✉ *Rua Quintino Bocaiúva 882, Foz do Iguaçu* ☎ *045/3028–8084* 🌐 *www.restaurantezaragoza.com.br* ⏰ *Daily 11:30–3 and 7–midnight.*

Continued on page 258

IGUAZÚ FALLS

By Victoria Patience

Big water. That's what *y-guasu*—the name given to the falls by the indigenous Guaraní people—means. As you approach, a thundering fills the air and steam rises above the trees. Then the jungle parts. Spray-soaked and speechless, you face the Devil's Throat, and it's clear that "big" doesn't come close to describing this wall of water.

Taller than Niagara, wider than Victoria, Iguazú's raging, monumental beauty is one of nature's most awe-inspiring sights. The Iguazú River, on the border between Argentina and Brazil, plummets 200 feet to form the Cataratas de Iguazú (as the falls are known in Spanish) or Foz do Iguaçu (their Portuguese name). Considered to be one waterfall, Iguazú is actually made up of around 275 individual drops, that stretch along 2.7 km (1.7 miles) of cliff-face. Ranging from picturesque cascades to immense cataracts, this incredible variety is what makes Iguazú so special. National parks in Brazil and Argentina protect the falls and the flora and fauna that surround them. Exploring their jungle-fringed trails can take two or three days: you get right alongside some falls, gaze down dizzily into others, and can take in the whole spectacle from afar. You're sure to come across lizards, emerald- and sapphire-colored hummingbirds, clouds of butterflies, and scavenging raccoon-like coatis. You'll also glimpse monkeys and toucans, if you're lucky.

GEOLOGY 101

Over 100 million years ago, lava surged up through cracks in the earth's crust near Iguazú. It spread out over the surrounding area, forming three layers of basalt (a dark, fine-grained rock) tens of meters high. The Iguazú River, which starts 1,200 km (745 miles) east, flowed over this. Later, the movement of tectonic plates raised parts of the surface, which became stepped. As the river flowed over these steps it eroded the rock surface it fell on even more, and over the next few million years, the waters carved out what are now the falls.

WHEN TO GO

Time of year	Advantages	Disadvantages
Nov.—Feb.	High rainfall in December and January, so expect lots of water.	Hot and sticky. December and January are popular with local visitors. High water levels stop Zodiac rides.
Mar.—Jun.	Increasingly cooler weather. Fewer local tourists. Water levels are usually good.	Too cold for some people, especially when you get wet. Occasional freak water shortages.
Jul.—Oct.	Cool weather.	Low rainfall in July and August—water levels can be low. July is peak season for local visitors.

WHERE TO GO: ARGENTINA VS. BRAZIL

Argentines and Brazilians can fight all day about who has the best angle on the falls. But the two sides are so different that comparisons are academic. To really say you've done Iguazú (or Iguaçu), you need to visit both. If you twist our arm, we'll say the Argentine side is a better experience with lots more to do, but (and this is a big "but") the Brazilian side gives you a tick in the box and the best been-there-done-that photos. It's also got more non-falls-related activities (but you have to pay extra for them).

	ARGENTINA	BRAZIL
Park Name	Parque Nacional Iguazú	Parque Nacional do Iguaçu
The experience	Up close and personal (you're going to get wet).	What a view!
The falls	Two-thirds are in Argentina including Garganta del Diablo, the star attraction.	The fabulous panoramic perspective of the Garganta do Diablo is what people really come for.
Timing	One day to blitz the main attractions. Two days to explore fully.	Half a day to see the falls; all day if you do other activities.
Other activities	Extensive self-guided hiking and Zodiac rides.	Organized hikes, Zodiac rides, boat rides, helicopter rides, rafting, abseiling.
Park size	67,620 hectares (167,092 acres)	182,262 hectares (450,370 acres)
Animal species	80 mammals/450 birds	50 mammals/200 birds

VITAL STATISTICS

Number of falls: 160—275*	Total length: 2.7 km (1.7 miles)	Average Flow: 396,258 gallons per second Peak Flow: 1,717,118 gallons per second
Major falls: 19	Height of Garganta del Diablo: 82 m (270 feet)	Age: 120—150 million years

*Depending on water levels

IGUAZÚ ITINERARIES

LIGHTNING VISIT. If you only have one day, limit your visit to the Argentine park. Arrive when it opens, and get your first look at the falls aboard one of Iguazú Jungle Explorer's Zodiacs. The rides finish at the Circuito Inferior: take a couple of hours to explore this. (Longer summer opening hours give you time to squeeze in the **Isla San Martín**.) Grab a quick lunch at the Dos Hermanas snack bar, then blitz the shorter Circuito Superior. You've kept the best for last: catch the train from **Estación Cataratas** to **Estación Garganta del Diablo**, where the trail to the viewing platform starts (allow at least two hours for this).

BEST OF BOTH SIDES. Two days gives you enough time to see both sides of the falls. Visit the Brazilian park on your second day to get the panoramic take on what you've experienced up-close in Argentina. If you arrive at 9 am, you've got time to walk the entire trail, take photos, have lunch in the Porto Canoas service area, and be back at the park entrance by 1 pm. You could spend the afternoon doing excursions and activities from Macuco Safari

and Macuco EcoAventura, or visiting the Itaipú dam. Alternatively, you could keep the visit to Brazil for the afternoon of the second day, and start off with a lightning return visit to the Argentine park (half-price entrance on second visit) and see the **Garganta del Diablo** (left) with the sun rising behind it.

SEE IT ALL. With three days you can explore both parks at a leisurely pace. Follow the one-day itinerary, then return to the Argentine park on your second day. Make a beeline for the Garganta del Diablo, which looks different in the mornings, then spend the afternoon exploring the **Sendero Macuco** (and Isla San Martín, if you didn't have time on the first day). You'll also have time to visit Güira Oga bird sanctuary or La Aripuca (both on RN 12) afterwards. You could spend all of your third day in the Brazilian park, or just the morning, giving you time to catch an afternoon flight or bus.

IGUAZÚ FALLS

6

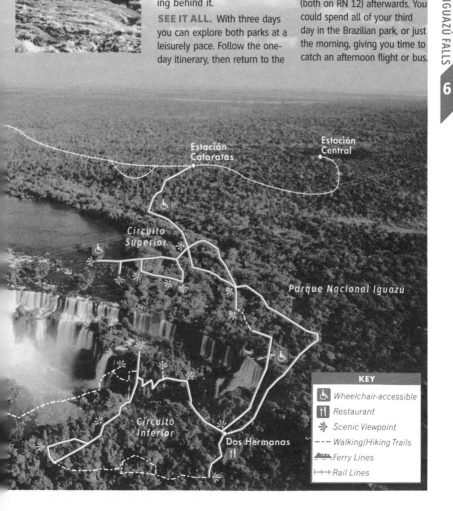

Estación Cataratas

Estación Central

Circuito Superior

Parque Nacional Iguazú

Circuito Inferior

Dos Hermanas

KEY

♿ *Wheelchair-accessible*

🍴 *Restaurant*

⚶ *Scenic Viewpoint*

--- *Walking/Hiking Trails*

⛴ *Ferry Lines*

╪╪╪ *Rail Lines*

VISITING THE PARKS

Visitors gaze at the falls in Parque Nacional Iguazú.

Argentina's side of the falls is in the **Parque Nacional Iguazú**, which was founded in 1934 and declared a World Heritage Site in 1984. The park is divided into two areas, each of which is organized around a train station: Estación Cataratas or the Estación Garganta del Diablo. (A third, Estación Central, is near the park entrance.)

Paved walkways lead from the main entrance past the **Visitor Center,** called *Yvyrá Retá*— "country of the trees" in Guaraní (☎3757/ 49–1469 ⊕ www.iguazuargentina.com ☑170 pesos; 85 pesos on second day ⊙ 8–6). Colorful visual displays provide a good explanation of the region's ecology and human history. To reach the park proper, you cross through a small plaza containing a food court, gift shops, and ATM. From the nearby Estación Central, the gas-propelled Tren de la Selva (Jungle Train) departs every 20 minutes.

In Brazil, the falls can be seen from the **Parque Nacional Foz do Iguaçu** (☎45/ 3521–4400 ⊕ www.cataratasdoiguacu.com. br ☑R$41.60 ⊙ 9–5). Much of the park is protected rain forest—off-limits to visitors and home to the last viable populations of panthers as well as rare flora. Buses and taxis drop you off at a vast plaza alongside the park entrance building. As well as ticket booths, there's an ATM, a snack bar, gift shop, and information and currency exchange. Next to the entrance turnstiles is the small **Visitor Center,** where helpful geological models explain how the falls were formed. Double-decker buses run every 15 minutes between the entrance and the trailhead to the falls, 11 km (7 miles) away; the buses stop at the entrances to excursions run by private operators Macuco Safari and Macuco Ecoaventura (these aren't included in your ticket). The trail ends in the **Porto Canoas** service area. There's a posh linen-service restaurant with river views, and two fast-food counters the with tables overlooking the rapids leading to the falls.

VISAS

U.S. citizens don't need a visa to visit Argentina as tourists, but the situation is more complicated in Brazil. ⇨ See the planning section at the beginning of the chapter.

EXCURSIONS IN AND AROUND THE PARKS

A Zodiac trip to the falls.

Iguazú Jungle Explorer (☎ 3757/42–1696 ⊕ www.iguazujungle.com) runs trips within the Argentine park. Their standard trip, the Gran Aventura, costs 310 pesos and includes a truck ride through the forest and a Zodiac ride to San Martín, Bossetti, and the Salto Tres Mosqueteros (be ready to get soaked). The truck carries so many people that most animals are scared away: you're better off buying the 150 peso boat trip—Aventura Nautica—separately.

You can take to the water on the Brazilian side with **Macuco Safari** (☎ 045/3574–4244 ⊕ www.macucosafari.com.br). Their signature trip is a Zodiac ride around (and under) the Salto Tres Mosqueteros. You get a more sedate ride on the Iguaçu Explorer, a 3½ hour trip up the river.

It's all about adrenaline with **Iguazú Forest** (☎ 3757/42–1140 ⊕ www.iguazuforest.com). Their full day expedition involves kayaking, abseiling, waterfall-climbing, mountain-biking, and canopying all within the Argentine park.

In Brazil, **Cânion Iguaçu** (☎ 045/3529–6040 ⊕ www.campodedesafios.com.br) offers rafting and canopying, as well as abseiling over the river from the Salto San Martín. They also offer wheelchair-compatible equipment.

Argentine park ranger Daniel Somay organizes two-hour Jeep tours with an ecological focus through his Puerto Iguazú–based **Explorador Expediciones** (☎ 3757/42–1632 ⊕ www.rainforestevt.com). The tours cost 50 pesos and include detailed explanations of the Iguazú ecosystem and lots of photo ops. A specialist leads the birdwatching trips, which include the use of binoculars.

Macuco Ecoaventura (☎ 045/3529–9665 ⊕ www.macucoecoaventura.com.br) is one of the official tour operators within the Brazilian park. Their Trilha do Pozo Negro combines a 9-km guided hike or bike ride with a scary boat trip along the upper river (the bit before the falls). The aptly-named Floating trip is more leisurely; shorter jungle hikes are also offered.

ON THE CATWALK

You spend most of your visit to the falls walking the many trails and catwalks, so be sure to wear comfortable shoes.

PUERTO IGUAZÚ

$$ ✕ **Aqva.** Locals are thrilled: finally, a date-night restaurant in Puerto
SEAFOOD Iguazú. Although this high-ceilinged, split-level cabin seats too many to
be truly intimate, it makes up for it with well-spaced tables, discreet ser-
vice, and low lighting. Softly gleaming timber from various native trees
lines the walls, roof, and floor. Local river fish like *surubí* and *dorado*
are the specialty: have them panfried, or, more unusually, as empanada
fillings. Forget being romantic at dessert time: the chef's signature des-
sert, fresh mango and pineapple with a *torrontés sabayon,* is definitely
worth keeping to yourself. $ *Average main: 100 pesos* ✉ *Av. Córdoba
and Carlos Thays, Puerto Iguazú, Misiones, Argentina* ☎ *03757/42–
2064* ⊕ *www.aqvarestaurant.com* ☯ *Daily noon–midnight.*

$$$$ ✕ **El Quincho del Tio Querido.** Enjoy a hearty churrasco and a glass
ARGENTINE of Argentine malbec while watching a live tango show at the best
churrascaria in town. Argentina bolero and folklore music are played
nightly after 8:30, and there's a live tango show every Thursday and
Friday. Pick the *bife de chorizo* for an exquisite cut of meat at a fair
price. $ *Average main: 90 pesos* ✉ *Av. Peron y Caraguatá, Puerto
Iguazú, Misiones, Argentina* ☎ *3757/420–151* ⊕ *eltioquerido.com.ar*
☯ *Tues.–Sun. 11:30–2:30 and 6:30–11:30; Mon. 6:30–11:30* ☯ *No
lunch Mon.*

$$ ✕ **La Rueda 1975 Restaurant.** This parrilla is so popular with visitors that
ARGENTINE they start serving dinner as early as 7:30 pm—teatime by Argentine
standards. The local beef isn't quite up to Buenos Aires standards, but
La Rueda's *bife de chorizo* (sirloin strip steak) is one of the best in town.
Surubí is another house specialty, but skip the traditional Roquefort
sauce, which eclipses the river fish's flavor. The restaurant has stayed
true to its rustic roots: hefty tree trunks hold up the bamboo-lined
roof, and the walls are adorned by a curious wooden frieze carved by
a local artist. $ *Average main: 100 pesos* ✉ *Av. Córdoba 28, Puerto
Iguazú, Misiones, Argentina* ☎ *3757/42–2531* ⊕ *www.larueda1975.
com* ✍ *Reservations essential.*

WHERE TO STAY

Once you've decided which country to base yourself in, the next big
decision is whether to stay in town or at the five-star hotel inside each
park. If you're on a lightning one-night visit and you only want to see
one side of the falls, the convenience of staying inside the park might
offset the otherwise unreasonably high prices for mediocre levels of
luxury. Otherwise, you get much better value for money at the establishments in town or on highways BR 489 (Rodavia das Cataratas)
in Brazil, or RN 12 in Argentina. During the day you're a 20-minute
bus ride from the falls and the border, and at night you're closer to
restaurants and nightlife (buses stop running to the park after 7 or
8; after that, it's a 70-peso taxi ride into town from the park). Hotels
in Argentina are generally cheaper than in Brazil. During low season
(late September–early November and February–May, excluding Easter),
rooms are often heavily discounted.

⚠ **Staying on the Brazilian side (apart from at the Hotel das Cataratas in the park) is not recommended. It's dangerous, especially after dark, more expensive, and the hotels are worse.**

FOZ DO IGUAÇU

$$$$
RESORT
Fodor's Choice
★

🔲 **Hotel das Cataratas.** Not only is this stately hotel *in* the national park, with views of the smaller falls from the front-side suites, but it also provides the traditional comforts of a colonial-style establishment: large rooms, terraces, vintage furniture, and hammocks. **Pros:** right inside the park, a short walk from the falls; serious colonial-style charm; friendly, helpful staff. **Cons:** rooms aren't as luxurious as the price promises; far from Foz do Iguaçu so you're limited to the on-site restaurants; only the most-expensive suites have views of the falls. $ *Rooms from: R$900* ✉ *Km 28, Rodovia das Cataratas, Foz do Iguaçu* ☎ *045/2102–7000, 0800/726–4545* ⊕ *www.hoteldascataratas.com.br* ⇆ *198 rooms, 5 suites* ⌖ *Breakfast.*

$
HOTEL

🔲 **Hotel Florença Iguassu.** In a sprawling wooded lot on the road to the national park, Florença combines budget rates with excellent service. **Pros:** peaceful, natural surroundings; close to Brazilian park and to the border with Argentina; good value for money. **Cons:** far from town center and restaurants; bland on-site restaurant; dead zone at night. $ *Rooms from: R$180* ✉ *Km 16.7, Rodovia das Cataratas, Cataratas* ☎ *045/3529–7755* ⊕ *www.hotelflorenca.com* ⇆ *63 rooms* ⌖ *Breakfast.*

$
HOTEL

🔲 **Hotel Tarobá Express.** Bright, modern-looking rooms set this hotel apart from most of the budget offerings in downtown Foz. **Pros:** clean and cheerful rooms; relaxing pool area; good value for money. **Cons:** street noise; area can be dangerous after dark; not particularly convenient for visiting either park. $ *Rooms from: R$200* ✉ *Rua Tarobá 1048* ☎ *045/2102–7770* ⇆ *82 rooms* ⌖ *Breakfast.*

PUERTO IGUAZÚ

$
HOTEL

🔲 **Panoramic Hotel Iguazú.** The falls aren't the only good views in Iguazú: half the rooms of this chic hotel look onto the churning, jungle-framed waters of the Iguazú and Paraná rivers. **Pros:** river views; great attention to detail in the beautifully designed rooms; the gorgeous pool. **Cons:** the in-house casino can make the lobby noisy; indifferent staff aren't up to the price tag; it's a short taxi ride to the town center and in-house transport is overpriced. $ *Rooms from: $200* ✉ *Paraguay 372, Puerto Iguazú, Misiones, Argentina* ☎ *3757/498–050* ⊕ *www.panoramic-hoteliguazu.com* ⇆ *91 rooms* ⌖ *Breakfast.*

$$$$
B&B/INN

🔲 **Secret Garden Iguazú.** Dense tropical vegetation overhangs the wooden walkway that leads to this tiny guesthouse's three rooms, tucked away in a pale-blue clapboard house. **Pros:** wooden deck overlooking the back-to-nature garden; knowledgeable owner's charm and expert mixology; home-from-home vibe. **Cons:** the three rooms book up fast; no pool; comfortable but not luxurious. $ *Rooms from: 1300 pesos* ✉ *Los Lapachos 623, Puerto Iguazú, Misiones, Argentina* ☎ *3757/42–3099* ⊕ *www.secretgardeniguazu.com* ⇆ *3 rooms* ⊟ *No credit cards* ⌖ *Breakfast.*

$$$$ 🏨 **Sheraton International Iguazú.** That thundering you hear in the dis-
HOTEL   tance lets you know how close this hotel is to the falls. **Pros:** the falls
are on your doorstep; great buffet breakfasts; well-designed spa. **Cons:**
rooms are in need of a complete makeover; mediocre food and service
at dinner; other restaurants are an expensive taxi-ride away. 💲 *Rooms
from: 1580 pesos* ✉ *Parque Nacional Iguazú, Puerto Iguazú, Misiones, Argentina* ☎ *3757/491–800* ⊕ *www.sheraton.com* ⟿ *176 rooms,
4 suites* ❢◎❢ *Breakfast.*

SANTA CATARINA

The state of Santa Catarina, the South's smallest state, has almost 485
km (300 miles) of coastline (with many gorgeous beaches). The capital,
Florianópolis, is on Ilha de Santa Catarina, an island with 42 beaches
and many world-class hotels and resorts that has become a major travel
destination in Brazil. North and south of Florianópolis along the coast
are other great destinations, where thousands of Brazilian and foreign
tourists flock every summer. Santa Catarina is also home to the German settlements of Blumenau and Joinville, in the northern valleys.
These highly industrialized cities still retain some of their German flavor,
including a popular Oktoberfest.

ILHA DE SANTA CATARINA

*300 km (187 miles) southeast of Curitiba, 476 km (296 miles) north-
east of Porto Alegre.*

Its nickname is "Magic Island," which is an appropriate moniker for
this island with breathtaking shoreline, easy-to-reach beaches—some
with warm waters—and seemingly endless vacation activities. Every
summer (December–March), thousands of Argentines arrive here, adding to the constant influx of Brazilians, making this one of the country's top tourist destinations. The island's northern *praias* (beaches) are
considered the best—because of their warm waters—and are therefore
the busiest. Impressive seascapes dominate the Atlantic beaches, and
southern beaches have fewer sun worshippers and a more laid-back
atmosphere. Scuba diving, surfing, sailing, and parasailing are among
the many water sports. You can also go for nature walks along trails
with the ocean as backdrop.

The city of **Florianópolis** played an important part in the history of the
island of Santa Catarina. Settled by colonists from the Azore Islands, it
was the southernmost post of the Portuguese empire for some time, and
it was the site of several skirmishes with the Spanish before the border
disputes were settled. You might be lured by the beaches—which rank
among the most beautiful in Brazil—but downtown Florianópolis also
has worthwhile attractions.

▪**TIP**→ Note that Brazilians tend to refer to all of Santa Catarina island as
"Florianópolis," and all the beaches and forts on the island are under the
city's jurisdiction.

GETTING HERE AND AROUND

Flights from São Paulo to Florianópolis are about an hour in length. The Aeroporto Internacional Hercílio Luz is 12 km (8 miles) south of downtown Florianópolis. Taking a cab into town costs about R$45. In addition, there's *amarelinho* (minibus) service for R$10.

Several bus companies have regular service to and from Florianópolis's Terminal Rodoviário Rita Maria. For the 12-hour journey to São Paulo, the 2-hour trip to Blumenau, or the 14-hour trip to Foz do Iguaçu, use Catarinense. Pluma buses travel to Curitiba (5 hours). União Cascavel/ Eucatur and Catarinense travel to Porto Alegre (6 hours).

To drive to Ilha de Santa Catarina from the mainland, take the BR 262 exit off BR 101. Downtown Florianópolis is 7 km (4½ miles) from the exit. The island is joined to the mainland by two bridges: the modern, multilane Ponte Colombo Sales and the now condemned 60-year-old Ponte Hercilio Luz.

Attractions are spread about the island, so a rental car is recommended. A quick, convenient way to visit the beaches is by *amarelinho* (also called *executivo*), express minibuses that cost about R$8. They leave regularly from designated places around Praça XV and are convenient if you plan to spend the day in one beach. If you want to move about and see different beaches and attractions in one day, a car is your only viable option.

ESSENTIALS

Airport Information Aeroporto Internacional Hercílio Luz *(FLN)* ⊠ *Km 12, Av. Deomício Freitas 3393, Carianos* ☎ *048/3331–4000.*

Bus Contacts Catarinense ☎ *048/4002-4700.* **Pluma** ☎ *0800/646-0300.* **Terminal Rodoviário (Bus Terminal) Rita Maria** ⊠ *Av. Paulo Fontes 1101, Centro* ☎ *048/3212-3100.* **Eucatur** ☎ *0800/45-5050.*

Taxi Contact Radio Taxi ☎ *048/3240–6009.*

Visitor and Tour Information Amplestur ⊠ *Rua Jerônimo Coelho 293, Loja 01, Centro* ☎ *048/2108–9422* ⊕ *www.amplestur.com.br* ☞ *Van tours of city, beaches, and more.* **SanTur** *(State Tourism Authority)* ⊠ *Rua Felipe Schmidt 249, 9th fl., Centro* ☎ *048/3212–6300, 048/3212–6315* ⊕ *www.santur.sc.gov.br.*

SAFETY AND PRECAUTIONS

Florianópolis is essentially a safe city and the beaches around the island even more so. Theft is occasionally a problem on beaches and during the crowded New Year's and Carnaval celebrations.

EXPLORING

TOP ATTRACTIONS

Museu Histórico de Santa Catarina. This museum is in the 18th-century baroque-and-neoclassical Palácio Cruz e Souza; its stairways are lined with Carrara marble. The sidewalks around the building are still paved with the original stones brought from Portugal. Exhibits revolve around state history: documents, personal items, and artwork that belonged to former governors (this used to be the governor's home). ⊠ *Praça 15 de Novembro 227, Centro* ☎ *048/3228–8091* ▧ *R$2* ☉ *Tues.–Fri. 10–6, weekends 10–4.*

WORTH NOTING

Box 32. Although small and somewhat cramped, Box 32 relives its tradition of being the meeting place for everyone from businesspeople to students. It has more than 800 kinds of liquor, including *cachaça*. Try the house specialty, *bolinho de bacalhau* (minced cod, formed into balls and fried) and the salmon carpaccio. ⊠ *Mercado Público, Rua Cons. Mafra 255, Centro* ☎ *048/3224–5588* ⊕ *www.box32.com.br.*

Mercado Público (*Public Market*). Beyond the Museu Histórico de Santa Catarina is the picturesque Mercado Público, a Portuguese colonial structure with a large central patio. Even though the original market was destroyed in a fire in 2005, the recently renovated market—filled with stalls selling fish, fruit, and vegetables—preserves its Arabian-bazaar atmosphere. ⊠ *Rua Conselheiro Mafra 255, Centro* ☎ *048/3225–8464* ⊠ *Free* ⊙ *Weekdays 7 am–9 pm; Sat. 8 am–4 pm.*

BEACHES

Praia da Joaquina. Surfers have staked claims to this beach, the site of several surfing events, including one round of the world professional circuit. **Amenities:** food and drink; lifeguards; parking; water sports. **Best for:** surfing. ⊠ *15 km (9 miles) east of Florianópolis, SC-406, Lagoa da Conceição.*

Praia da Lagoinha do Leste. This secluded mile-long beach is surrounded by hills covered with lush tropical vegetation (now mostly protected by a municipal park) and offers breathtaking views of the Atlantic. It can only be reached by boat or by a steep, 5-km (3-mile) path that starts at the entrance of the Pântano do Sul village. **Amenities:** none. **Best for:** solitude. ⊠ *18 km (11 miles) south of Florianópolis, SC-406, Pantano do Sul.*

Praia do Canasvieiras. This sophisticated beach has calm, warm waters, and great services and facilities. **Amenities:** food and drink; parking; water sports. **Best for:** swimming. ⊠ *27 km (17 miles) north of Florianópolis, SC-401, Canasvieiras.*

Praia do Pântano do Sul. This small beach community is surrounded by hills and has good restaurants and fishing-boat rides to other beaches and smaller islands nearby. **Amenities:** food and drink; water sports. **Best for:** walking. ⊠ *24 km (15 miles) south of Florianópolis, SC 406, Pantano do Sul.*

Praia dos Ingleses (*Englishmen Beach*). Named for a British sailboat that sank here in 1700, this narrow beach has an unparalleled lineup of hotels and restaurants for all budgets, making it one of the most popular beaches on the island. In summer Spanish with an Argentine accent is the local language. **Amenities:** food and drink; lifeguards; parking; showers; toilets; water sports. **Best for:** swimming. ⊠ *34 km (21 miles) northeast of Florianópolis, SC-403, Ingleses.*

Praia Jurerê. Located about 15 miles north of Florianópolis city center and home to an upscale resort and condominiums, Jurerê normally has bigger waves than its neighbors. The increased development of beachfront hotels, restaurants, and shops has attracted many out-of-state visitors. **Amenities:** food and drink; parking; toilets. **Best for:** walking. ⊠ *Km 24 SC 400, Jurerê.*

Praia Mole. Nudism is tolerated at this white-sand beach that mostly attracts surfers and foreign tourists. You can paraglide here, and there are a number of beachfront bars. **Amenities:** food and drink; water sports. **Best for:** nudists; surfing. ✉ *14 km (8½ miles) east of Florianópolis, SC 406, Lagoa da Conceição.*

SCHOONER TOURS

Scuna Sul. This company operates several schooner tours that visit some of the historic forts and various islands. They also traverse the Baía dos Golfinhos (Dolphin Bay), home to dozens of gray dolphins. Tours depart from the downtown harbor (near Hercilio Luz bridge) or Canasvieiras pier, last about five hours, and cost R$50 (cash only). English-speaking staff is sometimes on hand to take reservations; otherwise, make arrangements through your hotel. ✉ *Albatross Bldg., Rua Antonio Heil 605, Suite 01, Canasvieiras* ☎ *048/3225–1806* 🌐 *www.scunasul.com.br.*

WHERE TO EAT

$$$ ECLECTIC Fodor's Choice ★

🍴 **Chef Fedoca.** On the second floor of the Marina Ponta da Areia complex, this restaurant has a grand view of the Lagoa da Conceição, with surrounding green hills as the backdrop. The fare, carefully created by Chef Fedoca, a diver himself, includes a wide variety of seafood and pasta options. Fedoca's *moqueca* (a fish, shrimp, octopus, and mussel stew), inspired by the famed Bahian dish, is the house specialty, as are the lobster dishes. [$] *Average main: R$57* ✉ *Rua Sen. Ivo D'Aquino Neto 133, Marina Ponta da Areia, Lagoa da Conceição* ☎ *048/3232–0759* ⏲ *Daily 11–11.*

$$$ SEAFOOD

🍴 **Gugu.** This off-the-beaten-path restaurant combines no-frills service and undistinguished decor with an outstanding seafood menu. Start with the steamed oysters and then move on to the seafood stew or fish fillet with shrimp sauce. [$] *Average main: R$50* ✉ *Rua Fernando José de Andrade 147, Sambaqui* ☎ *048/3335–0288* ⏲ *No lunch Mon.*

WHERE TO STAY

$$$$ RESORT Fodor's Choice ★

🏨 **Costão do Santinho Resort.** The ocean view from the north-facing rooms is one reason to stay at the island's most sophisticated resort; the surrounding 100-acre Atlantic Forest is another (there are several trails, including one that leads to petroglyphs on the hill). **Pros:** many amenities; large and comfortable rooms. **Cons:** hectic when hosting conventions; service not as attentive in high season. [$] *Rooms from: R$700* ✉ *Rua Ver. Onildo Lemos 2505, Praia do Santinho* ☎ *048/3261–1000, 0800/48–1000* 🌐 *www.costao.com.br* 🛏 *696 rooms* 🍽 *Some meals* ☞ *3-day minimum stay.*

$$ HOTEL

🏨 **Hotel Plaza Baía Norte.** Lush, meticulously furnished suites with hot tubs await discerning guests at this popular hotel. **Pros:** great service; great views. **Cons:** cramped rooms; small bathrooms. [$] *Rooms from: R$250* ✉ *Av. Beira-Mar Norte 220, Centro* ☎ *048/3229–3144, 0800/702–2021* 🌐 *www.baianorte.com.br* 🛏 *99 rooms, 9 suites* 🍽 *Breakfast.*

$$$ HOTEL FAMILY

🏨 **Hotel Ponta das Canas.** Cozy up in the poolside Jacuzzi to watch an epic sunset over the mainland at this hotel on the northern tip of Santa Catarina Island. **Pros:** the best sunset view on the island; excellent service. **Cons:** nearby beaches crowded in high season. [$] *Rooms from: R$469* ✉ *R. Dep. Fernando Viegas, 560* ☎ *048/3261–0800* 🌐 *hoteiscostanorte.com.br* 🍽 *Some meals.*

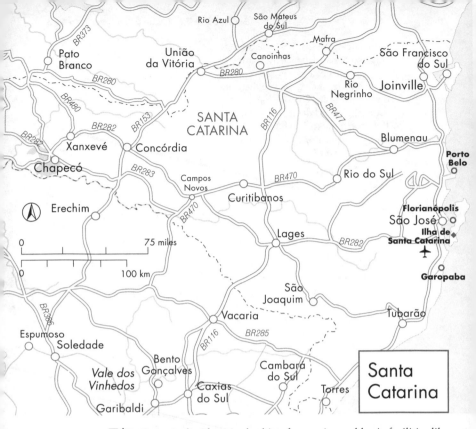

$ ▦ **Íbis Florianópolis.** If you're looking for service and basic facilities like

HOTEL   those you can find back home, Íbis is a welcome retreat. **Pros:** modern facilities; convenient location for business travelers; bargain price. **Cons:** far from beaches; small common area. $ *Rooms from: R$150* ✉ *Av. Rio Branco 37, Centro* ☎ *048/3216–0000, 0800/703-7000* ⊕ *www. ibishotel.ibis.com.br* ⬳ *198 rooms.*

$$$$ ▦ **Jurerê Beach Village.** This renowned hotel has lush rooms with veran-

RESORT das, most of which give ample view of the beach; some are apartments

ALL-INCLUSIVE with a small kitchen, perfect for longer stays. **Pros:** many amenities and

Fodor's Choice sports; friendly staff. **Cons:** expensive; some rooms small and cramped.

★ $ *Rooms from: R$650* ✉ *Alameda César Nascimento 646, Praia de Jurerê* ☎ *048/3261–5100, 0800/48–0110* ⊕ *www.jurere.com.br* ⬳ *222 apartments* ⦿ *All-inclusive.*

$$$ ▦ **Lexus Internacional Ingleses.** Although it has much to offer, this mid-

RESORT size hotel's main attraction is its location on the popular (and therefore crowded in high season) Praia dos Ingleses. **Pros:** great for extended stays; prime location. **Cons:** crowded beach in summer; rooms opposite the beach are noisy. $ *Rooms from: R$390* ✉ *Rua Dom João Becker 859, Praia dos Ingleses* ☎ *048/3266–0883* ⊕ *www.lexushotel.com.br* ⬳ *63 rooms* ⦿ *Breakfast.*

$ ▦ **Praia Mole EcoVillage.** Bordered by a lagoon on one side and a beach

B&B/INN on the other, this hotel has neatly decorated rooms in light colors that enhance the green exterior. **Pros:** many amenities; quiet and scenic location. **Cons:** far from commercial neighborhoods and most city services. [$] *Rooms from: R$200* ✉ *Rua Jornalista Manoel de Menezes 2001(Estrada da Lagoa), Praia Mole* ☎ *048/3239–7500* 🌐 *www.praiamole.com.br* 🛏 *74 rooms, 18 chalets* 🍴 *Breakfast.*

NIGHTLIFE

Florianópolis has an active night life, especially in summer. Listings of entertainment and cultural events can be found in the daily paper *Diario Catarinense.* Just east of the city proper, the lively Lagoa da Conceição has popular bars and live-music venues. In summer expect heavy car and pedestrian traffic.

Cachaçaria da Ilha. A popular bar at happy hour and a favorite meeting place for visitors, Cachaçaria da Ilha features live-music performances (Brazilian and rock and roll) on weekends later in the evening. ✉ *Rua Osmar Cunha 164, Centro* ☎ *048/3224–0051.*

John Bull Pub. This popular pub is *the* place for live music on the island. A roster of local and nationally known bands performs everything from blues, rock and roll, and reggae to Brazilian popular music. It's also a great place for drinks and snacks. ✉ *Av. das Rendeiras 1046, Lagoa da Conceição* ☎ *048/3232–8535* 🌐 *www.johnbullfloripa.com.br.*

6

SPORTS AND THE OUTDOORS

Sports lovers have much to keep them occupied on the island. Sandboarding, which is essentially snowboarding on sand, is practiced on the gigantic dunes at Praia da Joaquina. Windsurfing and jet skiing are popular on Lagoa da Conceição, but strict zoning rules are enforced and you must obtain a license by taking a course at an accredited outfitter or school—something most visitors won't have the time for.

BOATING

Marina Ponta da Areia. This is the place to go for boat rentals on Florianópolis. ✉ *Rua Sen. Ivo D'Aquino Neto 133, Lagoa da Conceição* ☎ *048/3232–0759.*

KITE-SURFING

OpenWinds. This company gives kite-surfing lessons. A full course costs about R$1,000. Surfing and windsurfing lessons can be arranged here and they also sell and rent gear. ✉ *Servidão dos Coroas 41, Lagoa da Conceição* ☎ *048/9962–3778* 🌐 *www.openwinds.com.br.*

PARASAILING

Parapente Sul. A center for parasailing—a popular sport on this mountainous, windy coast of Santa Catarina— Parapente Sul leads tandem flights with an instructor for about R$200. For enthusiasts, a full course is available as well as equipment rental. ✉ *Rua João Antônio da Silveira 201, Lagoa da Conceição* ☎ *048/3232–0791* 🌐 *www.parapentesul.com.br.*

SNORKELING AND SCUBA DIVING

Parcel Dive Center. Snorkeling and scuba diving are very popular on the northern beaches; check out Parcel Dive Center for internationally accredited diving lessons, diver's certification, and for equipment sale and rentals. The cost to rent basic gear is about R$275 a day. ✉ *Av. Luiz B. Piazza 3257, Cachoeira do Bom Jesus* ☎ *048/3284–5564* 🌐 *www.parcel.com.br.*

GAROPABA

Fodor's Choice ★ *91 km (57 miles) south of Florianópolis, 380 km (238 miles) northwest of Porto Alegre.*

Around Garopaba you can find great beaches and sand dunes, green hills, and rocky cliffs that end right in the ocean. Praia do Rosa and Praia da Ferrugem have acquired national recognition for their awesome beauty and laid-back atmosphere. This is also prime sandboarding and surfing territory, but watching the *baleia-franca* (right whales) breeding grounds off the coast—a protected area—is quickly becoming popular. The warm waters here attract whales from Patagonia (especially from Peninsula Valdéz) July through November.

GETTING HERE AND AROUND

To reach Garopaba, fly to Florianópolis and either drive or take a bus. PauloTur bus lines offers hourly service both ways, from 6 am to 8 pm.

ESSENTIALS

Bus Contacts Estação Rodoviária (Bus Station) ✉ *Praça Ivo Silveira 64, Centro* ☎ *48/3254–3169.* **PauloTur** ☎ *048/3244–2777.*

Taxi Contacts Ponto de Taxi ✉ *Praça Ivo Silveira s/n, Centro* ☎ *048/3254–3366.*

EXPLORING

OFF THE BEATEN PATH

Laguna. The city of Laguna is the second-oldest Portuguese settlement in the state of Santa Catarina. Most downtown buildings reflect the early colonial days. Known for its many beaches, Laguna has one of the liveliest Carnival festivities of southern Brazil. Part of the city faces Laguna Imaruí (Imaruí Lagoon), which connects to the Atlantic 5 km (3 miles) farther east. You can drive or hire a boat on the beaches to get to the Imaruí Lake delta, where exploring the imposing Santa Marta Lighthouse and nearby beaches is well worth a day's outing. ✉ *62 km (38 miles) south of Garopaba on BR 101, Laguna, SC.*

WHERE TO STAY

$$$ HOTEL 🏨 **Vida, Sol e Mar Beach Village.** This pousada offers easy access to the beach and several amenities, with comfortable but rustic rooms in the main building and chalets with grand views of the sea scattered on the property, among palm trees and shrubbery. **Pros:** great setting; close to beach; great for outdoor activities. **Cons:** some bathrooms are small; far from city. [$] *Rooms from: R$450* ✉ *Km 6 Estrada Geral do Rosa, Ibiraquera, Imbituba* ☎ *048/3355–6111, 048/3254–4198 whale-watching* 🌐 *www.vidasolemar.com.br* 🛏 *26 rooms, 17 chalets* 🍴 *Breakfast.*

SPORTS AND THE OUTDOORS

WHALE-WATCHING

Instituto Baleia Franca (*Right Whale Institute*). This not-for-profit organization provides whale-watching tours on Zodiacs from July to November, right when whales from Antarctica come to the warmer waters near Garopaba. ✉ *Rua Manuel Álvaro de Araújo 200, Centro* ☎ *048/3254–4198* 🌐 *www.baleiafranca.org.br.*

RIO GRANDE DO SUL

The state of Rio Grande do Sul is almost synonymous with the *gaúcho*, the South American cowboy who is glamorized as much as his North American counterpart. There's more to this state, however, than the idyllic cattle-country lifestyle of the early days. As it's one of Brazil's leading industrial areas, its infrastructure rivals that of any country in the northern hemisphere. Its mix of Portuguese, German, and Italian cultures is evident in the food and architecture. Indeed, to be gaúcho (which is a term for all people and things from this state) may mean to be a vintner of Italian heritage from Caxias do Sul or an entrepreneur of German descent from Gramado as much as a cattle rancher with Portuguese lineage out on the plains.

The state capital, Porto Alegre, is a sophisticated metropolis of 1.5 million that rivals Curitiba in quality of life. This important industrial and business center has universities, museums, and convention centers. It's also one of the greenest cities in Brazil, with many parks and nature preserves. The slopes of the Serra Gaúcha were settled by Italian immigrants; thanks to their wine-making skills, the state now produces quality wines, particularly in the Caxias do Sul and Bento Gonçalves areas. Along the coast, basaltic cliffs drop into a raging Atlantic and provide an impressive backdrop for the sophisticated seaside resort of Torres. Farther inland, straddling the state's highest elevations, is the Aparados da Serra National Park, whose gargantuan canyons are the result of millions of years of erosion.

> ## DOUBLE-DECKER CITY TOUR
>
> **Linha Turismo.** A double-decker bus tour, the Linha Turismo departs from the Cidade Baixa SAT location. One ticket for the 80-minute ride costs about R$15. Service is available Tuesday through Friday, departing hourly between 9–12 and 1:30–4:30. The schedule is reduced in winter (May–September). Passengers can get on and off at four other stops: Av. 24 de Outubro with Rua Comendador Caminha, Av. Borges de Medeiros near the Mercado Publico, in front of Fundação Iberê Camargo Museum, and, on weekends, Av. Osvaldo Aranha near Mercado do Bom Fim and Parque da Redenção.

PORTO ALEGRE

476 km (296 miles) southwest of Florianópolis, 760 km (472 miles) southwest of Curitiba, 1,109 km (690 miles) southwest of São Paulo.

Porto Alegre's hallmark is the hospitality of its people, a trait that has been acknowledged over and over by visitors, earning it the nickname "Smile City." The capital of one of Brazil's wealthiest states, it has many streets lined with jacaranda trees that create violet tunnels when in full spring bloom.

The city was founded on the banks of the Rio Guaíba in 1772 by immigrants from the Azores. The Guaíba is actually a 50-km-long (31-mile-long) lagoon formed by four rivers that merge a few miles upstream from the city. The city has an important port, connected to the Atlantic by the Lagoa dos Patos.

GETTING HERE AND AROUND

It takes about 90 minutes to fly from São Paulo to Porto Alegre. The Aeroporto Internacional Salgado Filho is one of Brazil's most modern air terminals. It's only 8 km (5 miles) northeast of downtown. The cost of a cab ride is around R$30. At a booth near the arrivals gate you can prepay your cab ride. There's also a minibus shuttle into town for about R$5.

Penha bus has service to São Paulo (19 hours); Pluma buses travel to Curitiba (12 hours); Florianópolis (6 hours) is served by Eucatur or Catarinense. To reach Foz do Iguaçu (14 hours), Unesul is the only option. Public bus service to São Miguel das Missões is painfully slow; instead, book a tour from Porto Alegre via a flight or charter bus.

> **BEAUTIFUL VIEWS**
>
> From Morro de Santa Teresa (Santa Teresa Hill), you get a grand view of the skyline as it confronts the expanse of the Rio Guaíba. From this spot and the numerous riverfront parks, the great spectacle of Porto Alegre's sunset is inspirational. As local poet Mário Quintana put it: "Skies of Porto Alegre, how could I ever take you to heaven?" For another great perspective of Centro, consider taking a riverboat tour of the Rio Guaíba and its islands (Galápagos Tur and Noiva do Caí do these tours), which are part of a state park.

Ask your hotel reception which lines to take. Alternatively, the Linha Turismo bus (⇨ *"Double Decker City Tour"*) stops at most tourist attractions. Another option is to take a cab downtown, where most sights are within walking distance of each other.

ESSENTIALS

Airport Aeroporto Internacional Salgado Filho (*POA*) ⊠ *Av. Severo Dulius 90010, São João* ☎ *051/3358–2000.*

Bus Contacts Catarinense ☎ *051/3228–8900, 0800/470–470.* **Estação Rodoviária (Bus Station)** ⊠ *Largo Vespasiano Veppo 70* ☎ *051/3228–0699* ⊕ *www.rodoviaria-poa.com.br.* **Penha** ☎ *051/3374–3700.* **Pluma** ☎ *051/3228–5112.* **Unesul** ☎ *051/3375–9000.* **Eucatur** ☎ *051/3901–5920.*

Taxi Contacts Radio taxi ☎ *051/3472–3448.*

Visitor and Tour Information Cisne Branco ⊠ *Port of Porto Alegre, Main Gate, Av. Mauá 1050, Centro* ☎ *051/3224–5222* ⊕ *www.barcocisnebranco.com.br* ☞ *Day and night boat trips on Guaíba.* **Galápagos Tour** ⊠ *R. Siqueira Campos, 1184, Centro* ☎ *051/3286–7094* ⊕ *www.galapagostour.com.br* ☞ *Tours of city, Serra Gaúcha, and off coast.* **Noiva do Caí** ⊠ *Usina do Gasômetro, Av. João Goulart 551, Centro* ☎ *051/3211–7662* ☞ *Day boat trips on the Guaíba lake.* **Secretaria de Turismo** (*State Tourism Authority, Serviço de Apoio ao Turista*). ⊠ *Rua General Câmara 156, 4th fl., Centro* ☎ *051/3288–5400* ⊕ *www.turismo. rs.gov.br.* **Serviço de Atenção ao Turista** (*SAT*). ⊠ *Travessa do Carmo, 84, Cidade Baixa* ☎ *0800/51–7686, 051/3289–6700* ⊕ *www.portoalegre.rs.gov.br/ turismo* ☞ *Open daily 9–6.*

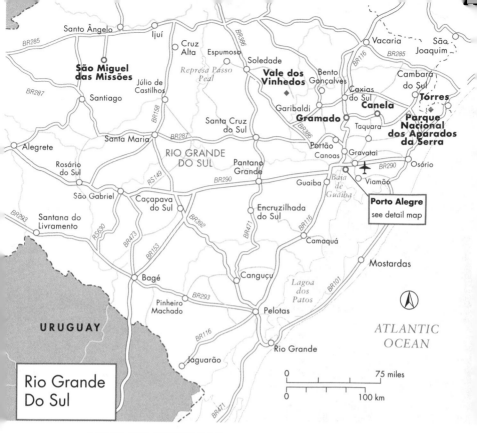

Rio Grande
Do Sul

SAFETY AND PRECAUTIONS

Some neighborhoods of Porto Alegre, such as the central district, are sketchy at night. Ask your hotel reception about the safety of your destination. During the day, pickpockets are generally the only concern.

EXPLORING

The heart of Porto Alegre lies within a triangle formed by Praça da Alfândega, the Mercado Público, and the Praça da Matriz. Not only is this the main business district, it's also the site of many cultural and historical attractions. Outside this area, Casa de Cultura Mário Quintana and Usina do Gasômetro are very active cultural centers, with movies, live performances, art exhibits, and cafés.

TOP ATTRACTIONS

Memorial do Rio Grande do Sul. Built to house the post-office headquarters at the turn of the 20th century, this building was declared a national architectural landmark in 1981. It now houses a state museum. Although the overall style is neoclassical, German baroque influences are strong; the asymmetrical corner towers with their bronze rotundas are said to resemble Prussian army helmets. A permanent exhibit focuses on the state's history and the lives of important gaúchos, and the second floor houses one of the country's largest collections of documents and manuscripts about Brazilian society. ⊠ *Rua*

Sete de Setembro 1020, Praça da Alfândega, Centro ☎ *051/3224–7210* ⊕ *www.memorial.rs.gov.br* ✉ *Free* ☾ *Tues.–Sat. 10–6.*

Mercado Público. Constructed in 1869, the neoclassical Public Market has undergone repeated renovations, the last of which added the glass roof that now covers the central inner plaza. With these changes, some of the produce stalls have been replaced by souvenir shops, cafés, and restaurants, taking away a bit of the boisterous bazaar ambience but increasing the options for the visitor. One of the best restaurants in the city, Gambrinus, is here. ⊠ *Largo Glenio Peres s/n, Centro* ⊕ *www.portoalegre.rs.gov.br/mercadopublico* ☾ *Weekdays 7 am–7:30 pm, Sat. 7:30 am–6:30 pm.*

Museu de Arte do Rio Grande do Sul. At this art museum housed in the old, neoclassical customs building you can also see paintings, sculptures, and drawings by gaúcho and other Brazilian artists from several periods. Two works of Di Cavalcanti—one of the country's most renowned painters—are exhibited as well as several pieces by local sculptor Xico Stockinger. ⊠ *Praça da Alfândega s/n, Centro* ☎ *051/3227–2311* ⊕ *www.margs.rs.gov.br* ✉ *Free* ☾ *Tues.–Sun. 10–7.*

Museu Júlio de Castilhos. The small Júlio de Castilhos Museum is the oldest in the state. On display is an impressive collection of gaúcho documents, firearms, clothing, and household utensils. The home belonged to Governor Julio de Castilhos, who lived here at the turn of the 20th century, before the Palácio Piratini was built. ⊠ *Rua Duque de Caxias 1231, Centro* ☎ *051/3221–3959* ⊕ *museujuliodecastilhos.blogspot.com.br* ✉ *Free* ☾ *Tues.–Sat. 10–5.*

WORTH NOTING

Centro Cultural Santander. This stately building, constructed in 1927–32 and the former headquarters of various banks, is now owned by Banco Santander of Spain, which has transformed it into a cultural center and gallery (it's no longer a working bank). Guided tours (Portuguese only) show the intricate ironwork of the entrance door and second-floor balcony as well as the ceiling's neoclassical paintings. The massive bank vault now houses a café. ⊠ *Rua Sete de Setembro 1028, Centro* ☎ *051/3287–5940* ✉ *Free* ☾ *Tues.–Sat. 10–7, Sun. 1–7.*

Palácio Piratini. The Roman columns of the stately governor's mansion convey a solidity and permanence uncommon in official Brazilian buildings. In the main room murals by Aldo Locatelli depict gaúcho folktales. Guided 20-minute tours (Portuguese only) are given by appointment. ⊠ *Praça da Matriz s/n, Centro* ☎ *051/3210–4170* ✉ *Free* ☾ *Weekdays 9–5.*

Parque Estadual de Itapoã. Where the Rio Guaíba flows into Lagoa dos Patos, 57 km (35 miles) south of Porto Alegre, Itapoã State Park protects 12,000 acres of granitic hills and sandy beaches. Although the infrastructure is minimal, visitors can bathe in the river, walk along marked trails, and watch magnificent sunsets. Rare cacti, bands of *bugios* (howler monkeys), and a century-old lighthouse round out the list of park highlights. Check with travel agencies in Porto Alegre for boat tours to the park's beaches and lighthouse. ⊠ *Park entrance:, Km 1, Estrada das Pombas, Itapoã, Viamão* ☎ *051/3494–8083* ✉ *R$12* ☾ *Wed.–Sun. 9–6.*

Centro Cultural Santander **3**
Memorial do Rio Grande do Sul **2**
Mercado Público **4**
Museu de Arte do Rio Grande do Sul **1**
Museu Júlio de Castilhos **5**
Palácio Piratini **6**

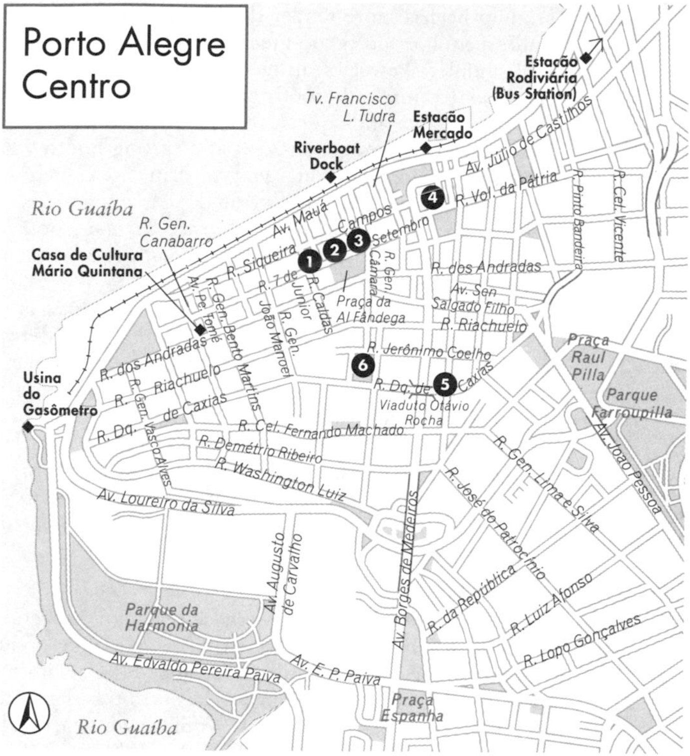

WHERE TO EAT

$$$ NORTHERN ITALIAN Fodor's Choice ★ 🍴 **Al Dente Ristorante.** You may be surprised at the quality and authenticity of the northern Italian cuisine at this small restaurant in Porto Alegre. Among many excellent choices are *garganelli* (a variety of pasta from Emilia-Romagna) with salmon in wine sauce and fettuccine *nere* (fettuccine with a black tinge from squid's ink) with caviar sauce. A house novelty is the Italian-gaúcho risotto, made with sun-dried meat, tomatoes, and squash. The decor is sober, with candlelit tables and cream drapes covering most of the walls. [$] *Average main: R$55* ✉ *Rua Mata Bacelar 210, Auxiliadora* ☎ *051/3237–3695* 🌐 *www.aldenteristorante.com.br* 🕒 *Closed Sun. No lunch weekdays.*

$$ CAFÉ 🍴 **Café do Porto.** One of the trendiest cafés in town, Porto serves several types of coffee, plus drinks, sandwiches, pies, and pastries. Try the *espetinho* (little skewer of meats and vegetables) combined with a glass of Chardonnay or the house cappuccino. All coffee is Brazil's finest, from the Mogiana region in São Paulo. [$] *Average main: R$33* ✉ *Rua Padre Chagas 293, Moinhos de Vento* ☎ *051/3346–8385* 🌐 *www.cafedoporto.com.br.*

$$ BRAZILIAN 🍴 **Galpão Crioulo.** One of Porto Alegre's largest churrascarias, Galpão Crioulu serves traditional *espeto-corrido*—a prix-fixe, never-ending rotation of roasted and grilled meats brought to the table, called *rodízio* elsewhere in Brazil—accompanied by a salad buffet. Its

premium beef is more tender than nearly all of its competitors'. If a full espeto-corrido is too much for you, ask for the *miniespeto* (a small sampler skewer of all meats). Another option is the *comidas campeiras* (countryside food) buffet, which includes many recipes with rice, beans, and squash traditional to the South. Have a cup of *chimarrão* (an indigenous tea) at a tasting booth where the staff demonstrates the traditional way to drink it. Gaúcho musical performances take place in the evening. [$] *Average main: R$42* ✉ *Rua Loureiro da Silva s/n, Parque Maurício Sirotsky Sobrinho, Centro* ☎ *051/3226–8194* 🌐 *www.churrascariagalpaocrioulo.com.br* ⏲ *Daily 11:30–3 and 7:30–midnight.*

$$$ BRAZILIAN Fodor's Choice ★ 🍴 **Gambrinus.** Porto Alegre's best-known restaurant has been in business at the same spot, steps from city hall at the Mercado Público, since 1889. Walls are covered with azulejo tiles, antiques, and period photographs exalting those early days. The restaurant is a popular happy-hour spot for politicians and businesspeople. The menu varies daily from beef to fish dishes. One of the highlights is the large Brazilian grey mullet stuffed with shrimp (served Friday and Saturday). [$] *Average main: R$47* ✉ *Rua Borges de Medeiros 85, Centro* ☎ *051/3226–6914* 🌐 *www.gambrinus.com.br* ⏲ *No dinner weekends. Closes at 9 pm weekdays. Closed Sun.*

WHERE TO STAY

$$ HOTEL 🏨 **Blue Tree Towers.** A haven for those seeking a peaceful night's rest, the Blue Tree Towers is in the safe, scenic, and quiet residential Mont Serrat neighborhood, and boasts spacious rooms with modern decor and king-size beds. **Pros:** great for business travelers; attentive staff; spacious common area. **Cons:** far from downtown; small restaurant. [$] *Rooms from: R$350* ✉ *Rua Lucas de Oliveira 995, Mont Serrat* ☎ *051/3019–8000, 0300/150–5000* 🌐 *www.bluetree.com.br* 🛏 *130 rooms, 2 suites* 🍽 *Breakfast.*

$$$ HOTEL 🏨 **Plaza San Rafael.** Long one of the city's most sophisticated hotels, the Plaza San Rafael features a lobby and commons clad in white marble and dark-wood paneling, along with comfortable, tastefully furnished rooms painted in light colors. **Pros:** excellent restaurant; spacious common area; close to downtown. **Cons:** very busy during conventions; neighborhood sketchy at night. [$] *Rooms from: R$375* ✉ *Rua Alberto Bins 514, Centro* ☎ *051/3220–7000, 0800/707–5292* 🌐 *www.plazahoteis.com.br* 🛏 *260 rooms, 24 suites* 🍽 *Breakfast.*

$$$ HOTEL Fodor's Choice ★ 🏨 **Sheraton Porto Alegre.** In the fashionable neighborhood of Moinhos de Vento, the Sheraton sets the city's standard of luxury; the level of comfort is outstanding, from the lobby to the top-floor rooms. **Pros:** top-notch service; prime location; many amenities. **Cons:** can be hectic during business conferences. [$] *Rooms from: R$490* ✉ *Rua Olavo Barreto Viana 18, Moinhos de Vento* ☎ *051/2121–6000* 🌐 *www.sheratonpoa.com.br* 🛏 *156 rooms, 22 suites* 🍽 *Breakfast.*

NIGHTLIFE AND THE ARTS

Porto Alegre has a very active cultural life. Rua Padre Chagas (and adjacent streets in the Moinhos de Vento neighborhood) is a good place to find sophisticated cafés, bars, and restaurants.

THE ARTS

Casa de Cultura Mário Quintana. Occupying what was Porto Alegre's finest hotel at the turn of the 20th century, the Casa de Cultura Mário Quintana has two art-film cinemas, one theater, and several exhibit rooms. The popular Café Santo da Casa, on the seventh floor, has regular jazz and classical music performances and is popular during happy hour. ✉ *Rua dos Andradas 736, Centro* ☎ *051/3221–7147* ⊕ *www.ccmq.rs.gov.br.*

Centro Cultural Usina do Gasômetro. With its conspicuous 350-foot brick smokestack, the Centro Cultural Usina do Gasômetro was the city's first coal-fired power plant—built in the early 1920s, when the city experienced rapid growth. Today it holds theaters, meeting rooms, and exhibit spaces on the banks of the Rio Guaíba. A terrace café overlooking the river is the perfect place to take in a sunset. The center is open Tuesday–Sunday 9–9. ✉ *Av. João Goulart 551, Centro* ☎ *051/3289–8600.*

NIGHTLIFE

Barbazul. This club attracts the young and trendy for live music performances (mostly rock and roll) and dance. ✉ *Av. Itaqui, 57, Petrópolis* ☎ *051/3331–6180* ⊕ *www.barbazul.com.br.*

Dado Bier Bourbon Country. The city's first microbrewery, Dado Bier has expanded into a full-fledged restaurant serving international fare by renowned chef Edevaldo Nunes. ✉ *Bourbon Country Center, Av. Túlio de Rose 100, Três Figueiras* ☎ *051/3378–3000* ⊕ *www.dadobier.com. br* ⊘ *No dinner Sun.*

SPORTS AND THE OUTDOORS
SOCCER

Estádio Beira-Rio. The home of Internacional—one of the Porto Alegre's major *futebol* (soccer) clubs—Estádio Beira-Rio will host several 2014 FIFA World Cup soccer games. A major renovation before the tournament will expand the current seating capacity to roughly 65,000. ✉ *Av. Padre Cacique 891, Praia de Belas* ☎ *051/3230–4600.*

SHOPPING

Brique da Redenção. Originally a flea market that took place on the sidewalks of Parque Farroupilha, Brique da Redenção has expanded into a full-blown antiques, crafts, and arts fair that spills over the full length of Rua José Bonifácio on the southeast side. ✉ *Rua José Bonifácio, Bom Fim.*

Shopping Center Iguatemi. The city's largest mall, Shopping Center Iguatemi includes branches of large chain stores as well as high-end specialty shops. ✉ *Rua João Wallig 1831, Três Figueiras* ☎ *051/3131–2000.*

Vinhos do Mundo. If you don't have the time to venture into Brazilian wine country, look for a sample to buy at Vinhos do Mundo. ✉ *Rua Cristóvão Colombo 1493, Floresta* ☎ *051/3228–1998.*

6

VALE DOS VINHEDOS

124 km (77 miles) north of Porto Alegre

The Serra Gaúcha—the mountainous region of Rio Grande do Sul—produces 90% of Brazilian wine. Grapevines grow throughout the hilly terrain, but the heart of the winemaking country is within the municipality of Bento Gonçalves, settled by Italian immigrants in the late 19th century. Because the best-known Brazilian wineries are within a few miles in this region, the name Vale dos Vinhedos (Vineyard Valley) has become synonymous with quality wines.

GETTING HERE AND AROUND

To visit Vale dos Vinhedos, either rent a car or join an organized tour. From Porto Alegre, Bento Gonçalves is accessible by RS 240 and then RS 470 (exit in São Vendelino). The wineries on Vale dos Vinhedos are on RS 444, which intersects with RS 470 at Km 217.

ESSENTIALS

Make sure you have reais or credit cards when coming to Bento Gonçalves, as currency exchange is not readily available. All hotels and pousadas have business center access, and most are adopting Wi-Fi connection.

Tour Information Valle Verde. This travel agency can arrange two- to-three-day tours in the Vale dos Vinhedos departing from Porto Alegre, including the major wineries, restaurants, and other attractions. ⊠ *Rua 13 de Maio 800, Centro* ☎ *054/3451–4775.*

WINERIES

Casa Valduga. Run by Luiz Valduga and his sons, Casa Valduga produces several lines of premium wines; the Cabernets and sparkling wines in particular are highly regarded. In summer you can take a tour of the family-owned vineyards and purchase other house products such as grape juice and fruit jellies. ⊠ *Vale dos Vinhedos, Km 6, RS 444, Linha Leopoldina* ☎ *054/2105–3122, 054/2015–3154* ⊕ *www.casavalduga.com.br* ☒ *Free* ☉ *Tours Dec.–Feb. by appointment; wine tastings weekdays 9:30–1:30; pairings course 6:15 pm; wine and cheese course twice a month.*

Vinícola Miolo. The Miolo family made a name for itself in the Brazilian wine industry with Vinícola Miolo and now they own a handful of other wineries throughout Brazil's grape-growing regions. One of Brazil's largest wine exporters, the company produces wines under 100 different labels on seven vineyards in southern Brazil. A visit to the vineyard gives a glimpse of the Miolo family's wine-making tradition that goes back to the 19th century. Tours of the vineyards and tastings of Chardonnays, Cabernet Sauvignons, Sauvignon Blancs, and sparkling wines are run daily. ⊠ *Km 9, RS 444, Vale dos Vinhedos* ☎ *054/2102–1500, 0800/9704–165* ⊕ *www.miolo.com.br* ☒ *R$10* ☉ *Tours daily 9–5.*

WHERE TO EAT AND STAY

$$

ITALIAN

✕ **Giuseppe.** Be ready for a hearty luncheon: this highly regarded restaurant serves a prix-fixe Italian menu with *galeto al primo canto* (crispy grilled chicken) and a large selection of pasta dishes. Accompaniments

Brazilian Wine

The first grapevines were brought to Brazil in 1532 by early Portuguese colonists, but it was the Jesuits, who settled in the South decades later, who were the first to establish true vineyards and wineries (to produce wine for the Catholic mass). Viticulture didn't gain importance in Brazil until Italian immigrants arrived, with the blessing of Italian-born empress Teresa Cristina, wife of Dom Pedro II, in 1875. In the next decades at least 150,000 Italians came to settle the Serra Gaúcha. They were the first to produce significant quantities of wine.

Although the South is suitable for growing grapes, the rainfall is often excessive from January to March—when the grapes reach maturity. This has traditionally made local wine-growers true heroes for being able to produce decent wines despite difficult conditions. Traditional grapes such as Merlot and Cabernet were grown to some extent, but most of the wine produced originated from less impressive American stock—Concord and Niagara grapes. These average wines are still produced for local markets.

New agricultural techniques and hybridization of grapes have brought

modern viticulture to the area and allowed a dramatic expansion of higher-quality grapes. This has significantly improved wine quality and attracted such international industry heavyweights as Almadén, Moët et Chandon, and Heublein. In 1992 Almadén broke new ground and established vineyards in the hills near the city of Santana do Livramento—about 480 km (300 miles) southwest of Porto Alegre, on the Uruguay border—where, according to current agricultural knowledge, climate and soils are more apt to produce quality grapes.

Other wineries are following its steps. Today there are more than 100 *cantinas* (winemakers) in Rio Grande do Sul, primarily in the Vale dos Vinhedos (Vineyard Valley) near Bento Gonçalves. The wine producers' association of the Vale dos Vinhedos, IBRAVIN (⊕ *www.ibravin.com.br*), has registered a government-certified system similar to that used in European countries for controlled-origin wines to promote and warrant the quality of their products. A recent trend in the local wine industry is to focus on sparkling wines, which are considered outstanding due to the environmental conditions and grape varieties grown.

6

include cappelletti soup, polenta, and *radicci* (a green-leaf salad). $ *Average main: R$35* ⊠ *Km 221, RS 470, Centro* ☎ *054/3463–8505* ☉ *Lunch only.*

$$ ⛺ **Villa Valduga.** The Valduga winery maintains four redbrick houses
B&B/INN with large, comfortable rooms overlooking the vineyards. **Pros:** great services; large and comfortable rooms. **Cons:** few amenities; no children allowed. $ *Rooms from: R$320* ⊠ *Km 6, RS 444, Vale dos Vinhedos* ☎ *054/2105–3154* ⊕ *www.villavalduga.com.br* ⇆ *24 rooms* ⦿ *Breakfast.*

GRAMADO

115 km (72 miles) northeast of Porto Alegre.

No doubt it was Gramado's mild mountain climate that attracted German settlers to the area in the late 1800s. They left a legacy of German-style architecture and traditions that attract today's travelers. Ample lodging options and a seemingly endless choice of restaurants have given this city a reputation with conventioneers and honeymooners. Every August the city hosts the Festival de Cinema da Gramado, one of Latin America's most prestigious film festivals. At Christmastime the city is aglow with seasonal decorations and musical performances of the Natal Luz (Christmas lights) festivities. During peak periods around Christmas and in July it can be difficult to find lodgings without a reservation.

GETTING HERE AND AROUND

Gramado is easily reached from Porto Alegre by car. Take BR 116 north for about 40 km to the intersection with RS 115. Then it's 97 km (60 miles) northeast to Gramado. Regular buses run by Citral depart from Porto Alegre every other hour during the day; the trip is 90 minutes and costs R$28. Although you might appreciate the independence of a rental car, most attractions are not too far apart and taxiing about is convenient.

ESSENTIALS

Bus Contacts Estaçao Rodoviária (Bus Station) ✉ *Av. Borges de Medeiros 2100, Centro* ☎ *054/3286–4762.*

Taxi Contact Taxi Rodoviária ☎ *054/3286–1230.*

Visitor and Tour InformationCentro de Informações Turísticas ✉ *Rua Borges de Medeiros 1667, Centro* ☎ *054/3286–1475* 🌐 *www.gramado.rs.gov.br* ⏲ *Daily 9–6.*

WHERE TO EAT AND STAY

$$ ITALIAN 🍴 **Casa di Pietro.** This Italian cantina–style restaurant has an excellent prix-fixe salad-and-soup buffet at dinner. Surefire soup choices include the cappelletti—best topped with grated Parmesan cheese—and the Serrano (a local vegetable soup). If this light fare doesn't suit you, opt for the grilled beef directly from the grill. [$] *Average main: R$39* ✉ *Rua Pedro Benetti 05, Centro* ☎ *054/3286–4077* 🌐 *www.dipietro.com.br* ⏲ *Closed Tues.*

$$$$ GERMAN 🍴 **Gasthof Edelweiss.** With a veranda that overlooks nearby pine trees and gardens, this German restaurant creates a relaxing ambience that perfectly complements its traditional offerings such as duck *à la viennese* (with an orange-flavor cream sauce)—the house specialty. Some tables are in the wine cellar, which has more than 1,000 bottles. [$] *Average main: R$65* ✉ *Rua da Carriere 1119, Lago Negro, Lago Negro* ☎ *054/3286–1861.*

$ HOTEL 🏨 **Pousada Zermatt.** This charming inn has a homey atmosphere, especially in the rooms with Brazilian-pine floors and wall panels, fireplaces, and colorful, locally made bedspreads. **Pros:** good service; great price. **Cons:** no restaurant; small rooms; few amenities. [$] *Rooms from: R$120*

✉ *Rua da Fé 187, Bavaria* ☎ *054/3286–2426* ⊕ *www.pousadazermatt. com.br* ⦿ *No meals.*

$$$
HOTEL
FAMILY

🏨 **Serra Azul.** This prestigious downtown hotel is synonymous with fine lodging in the region. **Pros:** downtown location; great service. **Cons:** hectic when hosting business meetings; small bathrooms. $ *Rooms from: R$450* ✉ *Rua Garibaldi 152, Centro* ☎ *054/3295–7200* ⊕ *www. serraazul.com.br* ⤴ *152 rooms, 18 suites* ⦿ *Breakfast.*

$$$
RESORT
Fodor's Choice
★

🏨 **Serrano Resort.** Everything at the Serrano is designed to make your stay enjoyable and unforgettable: superb restaurants, plenty of sports and leisure options, and a can't-beat location, just a few blocks from downtown Gramado. **Pros:** excellent facilities; great services; multiple dining options. **Cons:** expensive; hectic when hosting conventions. $ *Rooms from: R$490* ✉ *Av. das Hortensias 1480* ☎ *054/3295–8000, 0800/600–8088* ⊕ *www.serranoresort.com.br* ⤴ *244 rooms, 28 suites* ⦿ *Breakfast.*

SHOPPING

Gramado is well known for high-quality leather, cotton, and wool-knit clothing. There are dozens of shops throughout the city. Shops vie for customers with frequent promotions, so shopping around can net bargains.

Kouro Arte. This local store has a great variety of leather apparel. ✉ *Largo Claudio Pasqual 65, Centro* ☎ *054/3286–1835* ⊕ *www. kouroartegramado.com.br.*

CANELA

8 km (5 miles) east of Gramado, 137 km (85 miles) north of Porto Alegre.

Gramado's "smaller sister" is quieter and more low-profile. Brazilians immediately associate this city with the beautiful Caracol Waterfall, but it also has great shopping, for cotton and wool-knit apparel, handmade embroidered items, and handicrafts. The impressive views of the forest-clad valleys with meandering rivers also bring many tourists.

Most visitors stay in Gramado, which has many more accommodations, and visit the attractions in Canela as a day trip.

GETTING HERE AND AROUND

The route from Porto Alegre to Canela is the same to Gramado; from there drive or a take a taxi via RS 235 east for about 20 minutes to Canela.

EXPLORING

Fodor's Choice
★

Parque Estadual do Caracol (*Caracol State Park*). The Parque Estadual do Caracol is renowned for its breathtaking 400-foot waterfall that cascades straight down into a horseshoe-shape valley carved out of the basaltic plateau. The park also includes 50 acres of native forests with several well-marked paths, dominated by Paraná pine and an environmental education center for children. The entrance area is somewhat overcrowded with souvenir shops and snack tents and the river water smells a bit polluted, but the tranquil hikes and stunning waterfall more than make up for this. ✉ *Km 9, Estrada do Caracol* ☎ *054/3278–3035* 🎫 *Park R$12, elevator to lookout tower R$16* ⊙ *Daily 8:45–5:45.*

6

Parque da Ferradura. This private nature preserve has three lookouts to the Vale da Ferradura (Horseshoe Valley), formed by Rio Santa Cruz. You can hike across trails in more than 500 acres of pine forests through hilly countryside. A strenuous but rewarding two-hour trek reaches Rio Caí near its source. Make sure you remain alert while hiking: it's quite common to spot a variety of wildlife here, such as deer, anteaters, and badgers. ✉ *Km 15, Estrada do Caracol* ☎ *054/9969–6785* 🌐 *www.valedaferradura.com.br* 🎫 *R$7* ⏲ *Daily 8:30–5:30.*

WHERE TO EAT AND STAY

$$$ CONTEMPORARY 🍴 **Emporio Dona Fillipa.** Named after the English princess who became a Portuguese queen, this bistro and café boasts service that is fit for royalty. Ask for a table next to the ample wine cellar, which includes bottles from Bordeaux to the nearby Vale de Vinhos. You can't go wrong with the smoked salmon with yogurt and honey sauce, or the bistro's impressive array of risotto dishes. You can eat outside on the patio on a warm day. The café pours an aromatic selection of Brazil's finest coffees. [$] *Average main: R$60* ✉ *Rua Don Luiz Guanela 53, Centro* ☎ *054/3282–1196.*

$ HOTEL FAMILY 🏨 **Laje de Pedra Hotel.** This family-friendly hotel in a resort complex allows guests to sit around the lounge fireplace and enjoy panoramic views of the Quilombo Valley. **Pros:** family-oriented; nice views. **Cons:** location inside of a complex that also houses vacation homes can feel a bit guarded. [$] *Rooms from: R$200* ✉ *Rua das Flores 222* ☎ *054/3278–9900, 0800/644–3311 reservations* 🌐 *www.lajedepedra.com.br* 🛏 *250 rooms* 🍽 *No meals.*

PARQUE NACIONAL DOS APARADOS DA SERRA

47 km (29 miles) north of Gramado, 145 km (91 miles) north of Porto Alegre.

GETTING HERE AND AROUND

Cambará can be reached by car via RS 020. About half of the route is steep, winding single-lane road. The green mountain scenery, good pavement, and signage recommend it.

ESSENTIALS

Visitor and Tour Information Caá-Etê Ecoturismo & Aventura ✉ *Av. Protásio Alves 2715, Suite 905, Petrópolis, Porto Alegre* ☎ *051/3338–3323* 🌐 *www.caa-ete.com.br* ☞ *Guided tours or hiking expeditions to the canyons in and around Aparados da Serra national park (Rio Grande do Sul).* **Serviço Informação ao Turista** (*Municipal Tourist Information Service*) ✉ *Rua Adail de Lima Valim 31, Centro, Cambará do Sul* ☎ *054/3251–1320* ☞ *Daily 8–6.*

EXPLORING

Fodor's Choice ★ **Parque Nacional dos Aparados da Serra.** One of Brazil's first national parks, Aparados da Serra was created to protect Itaimbezinho, one of the most impressive canyons dissecting the plateau in the north of Rio Grande do Sul State. In 1992 the Parque Nacional da Serra Geral was established to protect the other great canyons farther north, the Malacara, Churriado, and Fortaleza. Winter (June–August) is the best time to take in the spectacular canyon views, as there's less chance of fog. The main entrance to the park, the Portaria Gralha Azul, is 20 km (13 miles) southeast of Cambará do Sul, the small town that serves as the park's hub. A visitor center provides information on regional flora and fauna, as well as the region's geology and history. Beyond the entrance you come to grassy meadows that belie the gargantuan depression ahead. A short path (a 45-minute walk, no guide necessary) takes you to the awesome Itaimbezinho Canyon rim, cut deep into the basalt bedrock to create the valley 2,379 feet below. The longest path requires a hired guide and trekking gear to traverse the strenuous descent into the canyon's interior. The local tourist office can also make arrangements for other trekking tours in the region.

■ **TIP→ The best way to visit the park is to join an organized tour in Porto Alegre** that includes an overnight stay in one of the region's pousadas. Those visiting Gramado can join a day tour to visit the canyons *(⇨ Visitor and Tour Info in Gramado).* ✉ *18 km (11 miles) on RS 429 (unpaved road), southeast of Cambará do Sul* ☎ *051/3251–1262, 051/3251–1277 for tour guides (Cambará Ecotourism Guides Association)* 🎟 *R$6 per person, R$5 parking ticket* ⏲ *Tues.–Sun. 8–5.*

WHERE TO EAT AND STAY

$$ BRAZILIAN 🍴 **Galpão Costaneira.** This churrascaria in a picturesque wooden bungalow is your best bet for experiencing the ubiquitous southern Brazilian *espeto-corrido* (a continuous service of grilled meats). They also serve a fixed-price buffet with less advertised gaúcho dishes such as *arroz de carreteiro* (rice with dried beef), *farofa* (sautéed cassava flour), and cooked cassava. Traditional-music performances take place on Friday and Saturday. [$] *Average main: R$30* ✉ *R. Da Úrsula, 861, Centro, Cambará do Sul* ☎ *054/3251–1005* 💳 *No credit cards* ⏲ *Closed Mon.*

$$$ HOTEL 🏨 **Pedra Afiada Refúgio.** The most comfortable lodging at the end of the canyon valleys, this pousada has established its niche among adventure tourists, who depart from here to explore the Malacara and other canyons beyond. **Pros:** unique location; great for adventure tourism. **Cons:** basic amenities; far from city. [$] *Rooms from: R$380* ✉ *Estrada da Vila Rosa s/n, Praia Grande* ☎ *048/532–1059, 051/3338–3323* 🌐 *www.pedraafiada.com.br* 🛏 *11 rooms* 🍽 *Some meals.*

$ B&B/INN 🏨 **Pousada das Corucacas.** Immerse yourself in the region's rugged landscapes by staying at this inn on a working gaúcho horse-and-cattle farm: the 1,200-acre Fazenda Baio Ruano. **Pros:** great for experiencing local traditions; bargain price. **Cons:** small bathrooms. [$] *Rooms from: R$155* ✉ *Km 1, RS 020 (Estrada do Ouro Verde), Cambará do Sul* ☎ *054/3251–1123* 🌐 *www.corucacas.com* 🛏 *11 rooms* 🍽 *Some meals.*

TORRES

205 km (128 miles) northeast of Porto Alegre.

The beaches around the city of Torres are Rio Grande do Sul's most exciting. The sophistication of the seaside areas attracts international travelers, particularly Argentines and Uruguayans. Some of the best beaches are Praia da Cal, Praia da Guarita, and Praia Grande. The Parque Estadual da Guarita (Watchtower State Park), 3 km (2 miles) south of downtown, was set aside to protect the area's unique vegetation as well as the basalt hills that end abruptly in the Atlantic. Locals like to fish from these cliffs. South of Torres, and extending well into Uruguay, the coastline is a 650-km-long (400-mile-long) sandy stretch interrupted only by a few river deltas and lagoons.

GETTING HERE AND AROUND

In the northeastern corner of Rio Grande do Sul, right on the border with Santa Catarina, Torres is easily reached by car or bus via the roads to the coast of Rio Grande do Sul (BR 290 to Osório and then North BR 101 or RS 389). The bus trip, with Unesul lines, takes about 2½ hrs and costs R$40. From Florianópolis, drive about 280 km (175 miles) south on BR 101.

ESSENTIALS

Bus Contacts Estação Rodoviária (Bus Station) ⊠ *Av. José Bonifácio 524, Centro.* **Unesul** ⊠ *Largo Vespasiano Julioveppo, 9, Centro* ☏ *051/3375–9000.*

Taxi Contacts Ponto de Taxi Central ⊠ *Rua Jose Luiz de Freitas 824, Centro* ☏ *051/3626–2441.*

Visitor and Tour Information Casa do Turista (*Municipal Tourist Ofice*). ⊠ *Av. Barão do Rio Branco, 315, Centro* ☏ *051/3364–1411* ⊙ *Daily 8–8.*

WHERE TO EAT AND STAY

$$

SEAFOOD

✕**Anzol.** The decor may not be distinguished at this restaurant, but the ample windows overlooking Rio Mampituba create the perfect setting for a fine dinner. Seafood, either grilled or stewed, is the specialty here. Try the *camarão na moranga* (shrimp in a squash puree). $ *Average main: R$37* ⊠ *Rua Cristovão Colombo 265, Centro* ☏ *051/3664–2427* ⊕ *www.restauranteanzol.com.br.*

$$

HOTEL

Guarita Park. Considered one of the finest lodging options on the shores of Rio Grande do Sul, this hotel is within walking distance of Watchtower State Park and its beaches. **Pros:** prime location; great views; good service. **Cons:** far from downtown; sometimes hectic with corporate meetings. $ *Rooms from: R$350* ⊠ *Rua Alfiero Zanardi 1017, Parque da Guarita* ☏ *051/3664–5200* ⊕ *www.guaritaparkhotel.com.br* ⇋ *67 rooms* |○| *Breakfast.*

SÃO MIGUEL DAS MISSÕES

482 km (300 miles) northwest of Porto Alegre.

Of seven large missions in the area dating from the late 1600s to mid-1700s, São Miguel is the best preserved and the only one that has tourism infrastructure and allows visitors. The 120-acre Parque Histórico de São Miguel was created around the mission, which is a UNESCO World Heritage site. A nondescript town of about 7,000 has grown around the mission site and shares its name. Joining an organized, Porto Alegre–based tour with an English-speaking guide is the recommended option for visiting the mission.

GETTING HERE AND AROUND

Most of the 482-km (300-mile) route from Porto Alegre to São Miguel das Missões is via toll roads (BR 386 and BR 285), which are single-lane but generally in good condition. Expect heavy truck traffic. São Miguel is 11 km (7 miles) off BR 285, via BR 466.

Ouro e Prata bus lines runs daily service to São Miguel (6 hours; R$85) from Porto Alegre. The closest airport to São Miguel das Missões is 60 km (38 miles) away, in Santo Angelo. It's served daily by NHT, with daily flights from Porto Alegre.

ESSENTIALS

Airport Aeroporto Municipal de Santo Angelo ⊠ *Km 13, RS 218, Santo Angelo* ☎ *055/3312–9779.*

Bus Contacts Estação Rodoviária (Bus Station) ⊠ *Av. Antunes Ribas 1525, Centro, São Miguel das Missões.* **Ouro e Prata** ⊠ *Rua Frederico Mentz 1419, Anchieta, Porto Alegre* ☎ *0800/051–6216.*

Tour Information Galápagos ⊠ *Av. Senador Salgado Filho, 135, Room 202, Centro, Porto Alegre* ☎ *051/3286–7094* ⊕ *www.galapagostour.com.br* ☞ *Package tours to the São Miguel mission, and other mission sites in Brazil, Argentina, and Paraguay.*

EXPLORING

São Miguel das Missões. The best-preserved and best-organized Jesuit mission in Brazil, São Miguel das Missões is an impressive, circa-1745 church built with reddish basalt slabs brought by the Guaranís from quarries miles away. The ruins are now a UNESCO World Heritage Site.

Jesuit missionaries moved into the upper Uruguay River basin around 1700. In the following decades the local Guaraní peoples were converted to Christianity, leading them to abandon their seminomadic lifestyle and congregate around the new missions—locally known as *reduções* (missionary communities). Seven of these existed in what is now Brazil, and several more were in Argentina and Paraguay—all linked by a closely knit trade and communication route. Historians have claimed that at the peak of their influence, the Jesuits actually created the first de facto country in the Americas, complete with a court system and elections. After the Treaty of Madrid granted rights over the lands and native peoples in the area to the Portuguese crown, the Jesuits were under pressure to leave. Recurrent clashes with Portuguese militia precipitated the breakdown of the mission system, but the final blow came with the decree of expulsion of the Jesuit order from Portuguese territory. Most of the Guaranís dispersed back into unexplored country. This important historical period was depicted in the movie *The Mission,* starring Robert DeNiro, with several scenes shot at Iguaçu Falls.

A small museum on the grounds, designed by Lucío Costa (who was instrumental in the development of Brasília), holds religious statues carved by the Guaranís, as well as other pieces recovered from archaeological digs. Guided tours (in Portuguese) are given by appointment. Admission to the site includes a sound-and-light show that tells the mission's story, at 9 pm in summer and 7 pm in winter.

Other mission sites with ruins are **São Lourenço** and **São Nicolau,** about 70 km (43 miles) from São Miguel, but there's much less to be seen at these sites, which are not normally in tours. Across the border in Argentina, there's a larger and better preserved mission site, **San Ignácio Mini.** Tours of these missions and of São Miguel das Missões can be booked through Galápagos *(⇨ Tour Information).* *✉ Parque Histórico São Miguel Arcanjo, Rua São Miguel s/n, Centro, São Miguel das Missões ☎ 055/3381–1399 🎫 R$8 ⏲ Museum and grounds daily 9–12; 2–6.*

WHERE TO EAT AND STAY

$$ BRAZILIAN 🍴 **Churrascaria Barrichello.** This simple, typical gaúcho restaurant is the best option in town. Savor the espeto-corrido, with more than a dozen cuts of beef, pork, and poultry. *[$] Average main: R$32 ✉ Av. Borges do Canto 1567, Centro, São Miguel das Missões ☎ 055/3381–1272.*

$ HOTEL 🏨 **Wilson Park Hotel Missões.** Not only the nicest accommodations in the region, the Wilson Park is a fine hotel by any standards; the large rooms have colonial-style furnishings and arched doorways that echo the design of the mission a few blocks away. **Pros:** attentive staff; great service; close to the mission. **Cons:** some rooms need updating. *[$] Rooms from: R$125 ✉ Rua São Miguel 664, Centro, São Miguel das Missões ☎ 055/3381–2000, 0800/510–2909 🌐 www.wilsonparkhotel.com.br 🛏 78 rooms 🍽 Breakfast.*

MINAS GERAIS

Updated by
Angelica Mari
Hillary

Though it's far from the circuit of Brazil's most visited places, the state of Minas Gerais holds unforgettable historical, architectural, and ecological riches. Minas has more UNESCO World Heritage sites that any other state in Brazil. This mountainous state's name, which means "general mines," was inspired by the area's great mineral wealth.

Prior to the 18th century the region was unexplored due to its difficult terrain, but in the late 17th century *bandeirantes,* or adventurers, forged into the interior, eventually discovering vast precious-metal reserves. As a result, the state, and particularly the city of Ouro Preto, became the de facto capital of the Portuguese colony. That period of gold, diamond, and semiprecious-stone trading is memorialized in the historic towns scattered across the jagged blue mountain ridges. It remains a tremendous source of pride for *mineiros* (inhabitants of the state).

Though the Gold Towns—Ouro Preto, Mariana, Tiradentes, and Congonhas—are awe-inspiring, Minas Gerais has other attractions. Roughly six hours south of the state capital of Belo Horizonte, several mineral-spa towns form the Circuito das Águas (Water Circuit). Thought to have healing powers, the natural springs of places such as São Lourenço and Caxambu have attracted the Brazilian elite for more than a century. Close by is the unusual town of São Tomé das Letras—a place where UFOs are said to visit and where mystics and bohemians wait for the dawn of a new world.

ORIENTATION AND PLANNING

GETTING ORIENTED

A landlocked state in southeastern Brazil that encompasses 588,384 square km (227,176 square miles), Minas is approximately the size of France. It shares borders with six other Brazilian states. The Serra da Mantiqueira range creates a natural boundary between Minas and Rio de Janeiro. It encircles to the south the Paraíba Valley, an area between the states of São Paulo, Rio de Janeiro, and Minas Gerais. The Serra da Canastra mountain range is a source of the São Francisco River. The longest river in the country, the São Francisco flows down from the mountains through most of Minas Gerais and Bahia and enters the ocean between the states of Sergipe and Alagoas. With a population of 19.4 million, Minas is one of Brazil's most populous states, and with approximately 16% of the country's paved roads, it's one of the easiest to navigate. Although Minas is large, its major attractions, including Belo Horizonte, Ouro Preto, and the mineral-spa towns, are in the state's southeastern portion, within driving distance of one another.

TOP REASONS TO GO

■ **Colonial Towns:** Walk on the *paralelepípedos* (cobblestones) in Ouro Preto, Diamantina, and Tiradentes, all magnificently preserved baroque towns of white and pastel houses and churches.

■ **Stunning Architecture:** Seeing the baroque gems of architect and sculptor Aleijadinho, whom an ex-curator of the Louvre called the "Michelangelo of the Tropics."

■ **Traditional Cuisine:** Indulge your taste buds in every Brazilian's favorite culinary state—if only for the *pão de queijo* (cheese bread) and the *doce de leite* ("sweet of the milk"), a boiled version of condensed milk.

■ **Shimming Gems:** Check out the colored gemstones (Minas Gerais produces the most in the world), including amethysts, aquamarines, tourmalines, and emeralds—and the imperial topaz, which can only be found in Ouro Preto and in the Ural mountains in Russia.

■ **Parks and Spas:** Hike, horseback ride, and swim in and around the beautiful national parks and natural springs tapped by numerous spa towns.

BELO HORIZONTE

Belo Horizonte is Brazil's third-largest city, with more than 2½ million inhabitants. At an elevation of 2,815 feet, the city lies in a valley encircled by a ring of mountains, the Serra do Curral. The city center was planned for carriages, and the streets crisscross each other at 45-degree angles, hardly efficient for modern-day traffic. Social and cultural activity is concentrated along three main plazas in the center: Praça Sete, Praça da Liberdade, and Praça da Savassi.

THE COLONIAL AND GOLD TOWNS

The historic cities of Ouro Preto, Tiradentes, and Diamantina lie in the Serra do Espinhaço range, with Ouro Preto at 4,000 feet. This central region of Minas Gerais is the most populous, with more than 7 million inhabitants. The towns are typically very hilly, with narrow, winding streets that are more easily navigated on foot than in a car.

THE MINERAL SPA TOWNS

The Circuito das Águas (Water Circuit) of Minas Gerais is concentrated in the southeastern regions (essentially counties) of Sul de Minas (2.6 million inhabitants) and Mata (population 2.2 million). The small cities of Caxambu and São Lourenço sit at an elevation of about 4,000 feet and have less than 50,000 inhabitants each. They're equidistant from the cities of São Paulo, Rio de Janeiro, and Belo Horizonte (400 km/250 miles).

PLANNING

WHEN TO GO

The busiest and most expensive time to travel is during Christmas, Easter, Carnival, and the month of July—because most Brazilians take their vacations at this time. The most exciting time to be in the colonial towns is during the Semana Santa (the Holy Week of Easter), when there

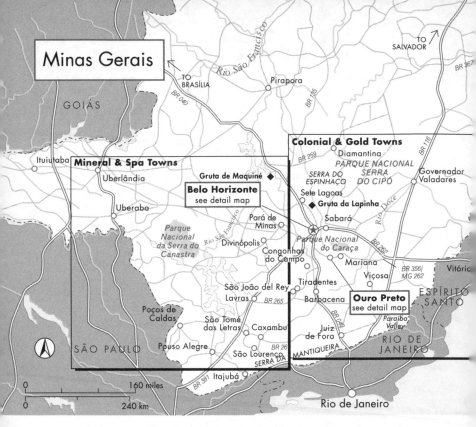

are colorful processions of joyous locals in the streets, and everyone celebrates. Temperatures are usually around 24°C (75°F) in summer and 17°C (63°F) in winter. Summer is the rainy season, winter is dry but cooler; sturdy shoes and jackets are highly recommended at all times. To avoid crowds and rain, travel from April to June or August to November. Discounts may be available during these months, although fewer services will be offered.

YELLOW-FEVER VACCINATIONS

Yellow fever has subsided after a major outbreak in Brazil's interior in early 2008. However, Belo Horizonte as well as the rest of Minas Gerais are still in the medium-risk category, so a yellow-fever vaccine, administered at least 10 days before your trip, is advisable.

GETTING HERE AND AROUND

Aeroporto Internacional Tancredo Neves, near Belo Horizonte, is the main point of entry to Minas Gerais. The domestic airport of Pampulha is more centrally located and closer to Belo Horizonte's main bus station, where connections to other parts of Minas and the country can be made. Bus travel between São Paulo and Rio de Janeiro is feasible, but it is advisable to take *leito* (bed) bus service late at night and arrive in early in the morning.

A Bit of History

Exploration of Minas began in the 17th century, when *bandeirantes* (bands of adventurers) from the coastal areas came in search of slaves and gold. What they found in the area was a black stone that was later verified to be gold (the coloring came from the iron oxide in the soil). In 1698 the first capital of Minas was founded and called Vila Rica de Ouro Preto (Rich Town of Black Gold), and some 13 years later Brazil's first gold rush began. Along with the fortune seekers came Jesuit priests, who were later exiled by the Portuguese (for fear they would try to manipulate the mineral trade) and replaced by *ordens terceiras* (third, or lay, orders). By the middle of the century the Gold Towns of Minas were gleaming with new churches built first in the baroque-rococo style of Europe and later in a baroque style unique to the region.

By the end of the 18th century the gold had begun to run out, and Ouro Preto's population and importance decreased. The baroque period ended at the start of the 19th century, when the Portuguese royal family, in flight from the conquering army of Napoléon Bonaparte, arrived in Brazil, bringing with them architects and sculptors with different ideas and artistic styles. Ornate twisted columns and walls adorned with lavish carvings gave way to simple straight columns and walls painted with murals or simply washed in white.

Today Minas Gerais is Brazil's second most industrialized state, after São Paulo. The iron that darkened the gold of Ouro Preto remains an important source of state income, along with steel, coffee, and auto manufacturing. The traffic that the mines brought here in the 17th century thrust Brazil into civilization, and now, well into the wake of the gold rush, a steady sense of progress and a compassion for the land remain.

It's possible to take in all the Minas highlights on a two-week vacation. If you have a week, you could spend three days in Ouro Preto, two in Tiradentes, and two in Belo Horizonte. If you only have three days, focus on culturally rich Ouro Preto. Buses throughout Minas are comfortable and inexpensive, and travel regularly between Belo Horizonte, Diamantina, Ouro Preto, Tiradentes, and other historic towns. The only reason to rent a car is to take in some of the national and state parks not easily accessed by bus. Sabara and Congonhas are comfortable day trips from the capital, while Mariana and Ouro Preto deserve at least two full days of exploring. With more time you can head 380 km (236 miles) north to Diamantina or 210 km (130 miles) south to the charming town of Tiradentes. From Tiradentes you can drive down to towns that are hailed for their healing waters, among them São Lourenço, and Caxambu.

RESTAURANTS

Probably the most popular cuisine in the country, Mineiran food is a mixture of Portuguese, Indian, and African flavors. Famous foods include *lombo de porco* (pork loin) often served with sausage on the side, and for dessert, *goiabada* (guava paste). *Pão de queijo*, chewy cheese bread in roll form, is the state's culinary hallmark—mineiro bakeries get the consistency just right. The *cachaça* (sugarcane rum) from the northern region of Salinas is considered the best in the country. Mineiros tend to eat dinner after 8. Many restaurants close on Monday. Reservations may be required, especially on weekends. *Prices in the reviews are the average cost of a main course at dinner or, if dinner is not served, at lunch.*

HOTELS

In the interior of Minas Gerais, especially in the historic cities and state parks, there are two types of traditional accommodations for tourists: *pousadas* (inns), with simple rooms, and *fazendas* (Texan-ranch-style farms), which can be a fun option. Most hotels outside of Belo Horizonte are small, lack English-speaking staff, and have few of the amenities common in American and European chains. In Belo Horizonte you can find large hotels and chain hotels equivalent to those found in U.S. cities that cater to the regular and business traveler. When you book, you'll likely be given a choice between an *apartamento standard* (standard room) and an *apartamento de luxo* (luxury room), which may be slightly larger, with air-conditioning and a nicer bathroom. Significant weekend discounts are common in Belo Horizonte. *Prices in the reviews are the lowest cost of a standard double room in high season. For expanded reviews, facilities, and current deals, visit Fodors.com.*

BELO HORIZONTE

444 km (276 miles) northwest of Rio, 586 km (364 miles) northeast of São Paulo, 741 km (460 miles) southeast of Brasília.

The Cidade de Minas (city of Minas), now Belo Horizonte, was established in 1897, when Ouro Preto, because of its mountainous geography, could no longer afford a population expansion. Since the planned uprising of the Inconfidentes in 1789, however, the residents of Minas Gerais had dreamed of a state capital, free of Portuguese influence, that would open a new historical chapter. The first planned modern city in Brazil (its design was overseen by the engineer Aarão Reis) modeled its streets on the wide avenues of Paris and Washington, and on their circular city centers.

In 1906 the city assumed its current name of Belo Horizonte. It earned its nickname, "the Garden City," during the 1940s and 1950s, when the main avenue, Afonso Pena, was lined with huge trees. (As head of state in the 1890s, Pena proclaimed this the site of Minas Gerais's new capital.) These days the city can look both like a metropolis—with traffic jams, tall buildings, and urban noise—and, in its tranquil downtown neighborhoods, like a simple country town. Because it's in a valley surrounded by mountains, traffic and industrial pollution is concentrated in the city center and sometimes the surrounding mountains get smogged in.

Today Belo Horizonte, the third-largest city in Brazil after Rio and São Paulo, is distinguished by its politics and its contributions to the arts. In the early 20th century, Brazil's political system was referred to as Café com Leite ("coffee with milk") because the presidency was alternately held by natives of São Paulo (where much of Brazil's coffee is produced) and natives of Minas Gerais (the milk-producing state). The current system is more diverse, but mineiros are still influential in national politics. Minas Gerais is home to respected theater and dance companies and some of Brazil's most famous pop bands. The artistic tradition is emphasized by the many festivals dedicated to all forms of art, from comic books to puppet theater and short movies to electronic music. The arts and nightlife scene, along with the stunning modern architecture, are reasons to visit Belo Horizonte

BEAUTIFUL HORIZONS

Belo Horizonte assumed its name in 1906. Its name means "beautiful horizons," so called because of the striking panoramic view of the mountains that used to dominate the city when it was just a village. The horizon is no longer visible because of pollution and skyscrapers. Brazilians will be impressed if you refer to the city as BH, (pronounced bei ah-*gah*), its affectionate nickname.

before or after traversing Minas Gerais's peaceful countryside.

GETTING HERE AND AROUND

Flights from Rio de Janeiro or São Paulo to Belo Horizonte take less than an hour and can be quite inexpensive. The same trip by bus or car takes approximately six to eight hours. Roads can be bad and truck traffic is constant—flying is by far the easiest option.

AIR TRAVEL

Belo Horizonte's main airport—officially Aeroporto Internacional Tancredo Neves, but also called Confins airport (for the town it's in)—receives domestic and international flights. It's a half-hour taxi ride (about R$90) north of the downtown. *Executivo* (air-conditioned) buses leave every 45 minutes and cost R$10–R$15. Aeroporto Pampulha is 9 km (5 miles) northwest of downtown and serves some domestic flights. Taxis from here to downtown cost about R$40.

Airports **Aeroporto Internacional Tancredo Neves** (*Aeroporto de Confins*). ✉ *Rodovia MG 10, 38 km (24 miles) north of Belo Horizonte, Confins* ☎ *031/3689–2557* ⊕ *www.infraero.gov.br.* **Aeroporto Pampulha** ✉ *Praça Bagatelle 204, Pampulha* ☎ *031/3490–2001* ⊕ *www.infraero.gov.br.*

BUS TRAVEL

Frequent buses connect Belo Horizonte with Rio (R$75–R$115; 7 hours), São Paulo (R$95–R$160; 8 hours), and Brasília (R$117–R$123; 12 hours). Most buses have air-conditioning. It's advisable to use leito services. These buses, with wide, reclinable seats, are the closest to a bed you can get for long journeys. Buy tickets in advance at holiday times. All buses arrive at and depart (punctually) from the Terminal Rodoviário Israel Pinheiro da Silva. Bus companies include Cometa, for Rio and São Paulo; Gontijo, for São Paulo; Itapemirim, for Brasília, Rio, and São Paulo; and Útil, for Rio.

The central and original section of Belo Horizonte, planned in the 19th century, is surrounded by Avenida do Contorno. The city's main attractions are downtown (the center) and in the southern zone. On a map the center looks easily walkable, but the blocks are a lot larger than they seem and sometimes taking a bus is advisable.

Belo Horizonte

City buses in Belo Horizonte are safe and easy to use, though buses are crowded during rush hour. Bhtrans, the city's transit authority, has route information. Fares depend on the distance traveled but are always less than R$4.

Bus Contacts BH Trans. The public transport authority of Belo Horizonte, offers information on bus timetables, maps, and traffic. ⊠ *Av. Eng. Carlos Goulart 900, Buritis* ☎ *031/3429–0405* ⊕ *www.bhtrans.pbh.gov.br.* **Terminal Rodoviário Governador Israel Pinheiro** ⊠ *Av. Afonso Pena at Praça Rio Branco s/n, Centro* ☎ *031/3271–3000, 031/3271–8933* ⊕ *www.pbh.gov.br/rodoviaria.* **Viação Cometa** ☎ *031/3201–5520* ⊕ *www.viacaocometa.com.br.* **Viação Gontijo** ☎ *031/2102–6000* ⊕ *www.gontijo.com.br.* **Viação Itapemirim** ☎ *031/3429–2700* ⊕ *www.itapemirim.com.br.* **Viação Útil** ☎ *031/3271–6115, 031/3907–9000* ⊕ *www.util.com.br.*

CAR TRAVEL

Driving to BH from major cities is safe; the roads are in good condition, although exits aren't always clearly marked. BR 040 connects Belo Horizonte with Rio (6½ hours) to the southeast, and Brasília (10 hours) to the northwest. BR 381 links the city with São Paulo (7½ hours).

Belo Horizonte's rush-hour traffic can be heavy, and parking can be difficult. For on-street parking you must buy a card at a newsstand or bookshop. Taking the bus in Belo Horizonte is recommended over driving because of the traffic and the city's diagonal grid, which is hard to navigate.

TAXI TRAVEL

To get to neighborhoods away from downtown, such as Pampulha, taking a bus or a taxi is advisable. When taking taxis, aim for taxi stands or hotels, where taxis can often be found. Most taxis in Belo Horizonte are white (*taxi comum*); there are also special black taxis that can be hailed or called. Both are metered. The meter starts at about R$4; with about R$2.30 added for every kilometer traveled (slightly higher at night and on weekends).

Taxi Contacts BH Taxi ☎ *031/3418–2000* ⊕ *www.bhtaxi.com.br.* **Unitaxi** ☎ *031/3418–2233.*

VISITOR INFORMATION

AMO-TE, the Ecotourism Association of Minas Gerais, focuses on adventure/ecotourism. Belotur, Belo Horizonte's official tourism agency, has a website with pages in Portuguese and English and operates several information kiosks throughout the city. The state-run Setur has information about historic cities and attractions. Y TUR Turismo arranges tours of Belo Horizonte and beyond and helps with hotels and bookings.

Visitor Information AMO-TE ⊠ *Rua Monte Verde 125, São Salvador* ☎ *031/3477–7757* ⊕ *www.amote.org.br.* **Belotur** ⊠ *Rua Aimorés 981, 6th fl., Funcionários* ☎ *031/3277–9777* ⊕ *www.belohorizonte.mg.gov.br/visit/en* (English), *www.belotur.com.br* (Portuguese) ⊠ *Mercado das Flores, Av. Afonso Pena 1055, Centro* ☎ *031/3277–7666* ⊘ *Weekdays 8:30–6:30, weekends and public holidays 8:30–3* ⊠ *Rodoviária (Bus Station), Praça Rio Branco, near Av. Afonso Pena, Centro* ☎ *031/3277–6907* ⊘ *Daily 8–6* ⊠ *Mercado Central, Av.*

Augusto de Lima 744, Centro ☎ 031/3277-4691 ⊘ Weekdays 8–6:30, weekends and public holidays 8–3 ✉ Aeroporto Internacional Tancredo Neves, Rodovia MG-10, Confins ☎ 031/3689-2557 ⊘ Daily 8 am–10 pm. **Setur** ✉ *Praça da Liberdade s/n, 2nd fl., Funcionários ☎ 031/3270-8501, 031/3207-8502 ⊕ www. turismo.mg.gov.br ⊘ Weekdays 8–6.* **YTUR Turismo** ✉ *Av. do Contorno 8000, Loja 2, Lourdes ☎ 031/2111-8000 ⊕ www.ytur.com.br.*

EXPLORING

TOP ATTRACTIONS

Fodor'sChoice **Conjunto Arquitetônico da Pampulha.** Oscar Niemeyer designed this mod-
★ ern 1940s complex, one of Belo Horizonte's don't-miss sights. On the
banks of Lagoa da Pampulha, the Conjunto Arquitetônico encompasses
the **Museu de Arte da Pampulha,** the **Casa do Baile** (under renovation),
and the **Igreja de São Francisco de Assis.**

The museum, one of Niemeyer's first projects, shows the influence
of the European architect Le Corbusier on the young Brazilian.
The glass and concrete structure, whose landscape gardens were
designed by Richard Burle Marx, served as the city's casino until
1946, when gambling was prohibited in Brazil, and was converted
into a museum in 1957. ■**TIP**➔ **The museum is open only for guided
visits that are worth scheduling.**

The glass and stucco church's 14 exterior mosaic panels, which describe
the life and activities of its namesake, St. Francis of Assisi, are moving
riffs off the *azulejos* (decorative blue Portuguese tiles) found in many
colonial churches in Brazil. Though the church is regarded these days as
a national treasure, the local archbishop, in part because of Niemeyer's
communist beliefs, wanted it destroyed. ✉ *Av. Otacílio Negrão de Lima,
Pampulha ☎ 031/3277-7946 museum, 031/3427-1644 church ⊠ Museum free, church R$2 ⊘ Museum Tues.–Sun. 9–9; church Tues.–Sat.
9–5, Sun. 9:30 (mass) and noon–5.*

Mercado Central (*Central Market*). In the more than 400 stores in this
beautiful old market dating from 1929 you can find typical products
from Minas Gerais such as cheese, guava and milk sweets, arts and
crafts, and medicinal herbs and roots. ■**TIP**➔ **Many people, including
local celebrities, stop by the popular bars inside the market to drink beer
and sample the famous appetizers, such as liver with onions.** ✉ *Av. Augusto
de Lima 744, Centro ☎ 031/3274-9434 ⊕ www.mercadocentral.com.
br ⊠ Free ⊘ Mon.–Sat. 7–6, Sun. 7–1.*

Fodor'sChoice **Palácio das Artes.** Designed by Oscar Niemeyer and built in 1970, the
★ Palace of the Arts is the most important cultural center in Belo Horizonte, comprising three theaters, three art galleries, a movie theater,
a bookstore, a coffee shop, and the Centro de Artesanato Mineiro
(Mineiro Artisan Center), where contemporary Minas handicrafts—
among them wood and soapstone carvings, pottery, and tapestries—
are for sale. The main theater, Grande Teatro, stages music concerts,
plays, operas, ballets, and other productions by Brazilian and foreign
artists. ✉ *Av. Afonso Pena 1537, Centro ☎ 031/3236-7400 ⊕ www.
palaciodasartes.com.br ⊠ Free ⊘ Tues.–Sat. 10–9, Sun. 2–8.*

FAMILY **Parque Municipal Américo Renée Giannetti.** With 45 acres of luscious tropical plants and magical winding walkways, the Parque Municipal (municipal park) was inspired by the landscaping of French gardens and inaugurated in 1897. It shelters an orchid house, a school, a playground, and the Francisco Nunes Theater, a beautiful modern building designed by the architect Luiz Signorelli in the 1940s that still presents theatrical plays and musical performances. With more than 50 tree species, the Municipal Park is highly recommended for walks. ⊠ *Av. Afonso Pena s/n, Centro* ☎ *031/3273–4161 park, 031/3277–6325 theater* ⊠ *Free* ⊙ *Tues.–Sun. 6–6.*

FAMILY **Praça da Liberdade** (*Liberty Square*). When the city was founded, this square was created to house public administration offices. Today, in addition to centenarian palm trees, fountains, and a bandstand, the square also has neoclassical, art deco, modern, and postmodern buildings. ⊠ *Between Avs. João Pinheiro and Cristóvão Colombo, Funcionários.*

> ### NIEMEYER AND PORTINARI
>
> Two great Brazilian artists, both renowned communists, Oscar Niemeyer and Candido Portinari collaborated on the Pampulha complex. Portinari grew up in São Paulo, the son of Italian immigrants, and was famous for his neorealistic style. He died at the age of 34 from lead poisoning from his paints. Niemeyer, who died in 2012 at the age of 104, ranks among the world's most important architects for his singular designs employing reinforced concrete. Many of his works can be found in Minas.

WORTH NOTING

Basílica de Lourdes. Conceived when the capital was founded but only inaugurated in 1923, Our Lady of Lourdes Church was elevated to the category of basilica by Pope Pius XII in 1958. Its Gothic architecture has undergone some adaptations, but it's still a magnificent building. ⊠ *Rua da Bahia 1596, Lourdes* ☎ *031/3213–4656* ⊕ *www.basilicadelourdes. com.br* ⊠ *Free* ⊙ *Weekdays 7 am–7:30 pm, Sun. and public holidays 7:30 am–8 pm.*

Centro de Cultura de Belo Horizonte. The city's only example of the neo-Gothic style of Portuguese inspiration, this building was erected in 1914 to house the first legislative assembly of the capital as well as the public library. Belo Horizonte's first radio station also operated out of the structure, which in 1997 was transformed into a cultural space. Local art art exhibitions often take place, and the Centro de Referência da Moda (Fashion Reference Center) is located here. ⊠ *Rua da Bahia 1149, Centro* ☎ *031/3277–9248, 031/3277–4384* ⊠ *Free* ⊙ *Weekdays 10–7, Sat. 10–4.*

FAMILY **Museu de História Natural e Jardim Botânico.** Although it has an area of nearly 150 acres with Brazilian fauna, flora, archaeology, and mineralogy, the museum's main attraction is the Presépio do Pipiripau (Pipiripau Crèche). This ingenious work of art narrates Christ's life in 45 scenes, with 580 moving figures. It was built by Raimundo Machado de Azevedo, who began assembling it in 1906 and finished in 1984. ⊠ *Rua Gustavo da Silveira 1035, Santa Inês* ☎ *031/3409–7600, 031/3482–9723* ⊕ *www. ufmg.br/museu* ⊠ *R$4* ⊙ *Tues.–Fri. 8–noon and 1–4, weekends 10–5.*

7

ARTISAN MARKET

Sunday morning the Avenida Afonso Pena is crowded with tents for the Feira de Artesanato (Artisans Fair). This is a meeting point for locals, who then head off to the neighboring bars along Rua da Bahia to resume drinking and to watch a Sunday football match. Here you can also taste some delicious Brazilian street food. We like a refreshing *coco gelado*, a large green coconut filled with sweet water, or *acarajé*, a deep-fried pastry stuffed with shrimps, ground cashews, and spices. The fair is famous for nice leather shoes and wallets, beautiful knitted shirts and skirts, handmade home accessories and jewelry made from beads and seashells. It is advisable to get there early, just before 8 am, or after 1 pm, one hour before the vendors start packing up and when you can get the best bargains.

FAMILY **Museu de Mineralogia Professor Djalma Guimarães.** More than 3,000 pieces extracted from sites all over the world are on display in the mineralogy museum, which is housed in a postmodern steel-and-glass building. ✉ *Av. Bias Fortes 50, Funcionários* ☎ *031/3271–3415* 🌐 *www.pbh.gov.br* 🎟 *Free* 🕐 *Tues.–Fri. 8–5, Sat. 9–5, Sun. 10–5.*

Museu Histórico Abílio Barreto. Attached to an old colonial mansion, the Abílio Barreto Historical Museum (MHAB) presents permanent and temporary exhibitions about the city of Belo Horizonte. Outdoors are lush, pleasant gardens and a stage where concerts occasionally take place. ■ **TIP→ The comfortable coffee shop here is open until midnight.** ✉ *Av. Prudente de Morais 202, Cidade Jardim* ☎ *031/3277–8573* 🎟 *Free* 🕐 *Museum Tues. and Fri.–Sun. 10–5, Wed. and Thurs. 10–9. Gardens Tues.–Sun. 7–6.*

Palácio da Liberdade. Built in 1898, the French-style Liberdade Palace is the headquarters of the Minas Gerais government and is the official residence of the governor. Of note are the gardens by Paul Villon, the Louis XV–style banquet room, the paintings in Noble Hall, and a panel by Antônio Pereira. ✉ *Praça da Liberdade s/n, Funcionários* ☎ *031/3217–9543* 🎟 *Free* 🕐 *Sun. 9 am–12:30 pm.*

WHERE TO EAT

$$$$ ECLECTIC 🍴 **Casa dos Contos.** A popular gathering place for local journalists, artists, and intellectuals, the old-school House of Tales has an unpretentious and varied menu that includes fish, pasta, and typical mineiro dishes. In tune with its bohemian clientele, Casa serves well past midnight. [$] *Average main: R$75* ✉ *Rua Rio Grande do Norte 1065, Funcionários* ☎ *031/3261–5853* 🌐 *www.restaurantecasadoscontos.com.br.*

$$$ BRAZILIAN 🍴 **Dona Lucinha.** Roughly 32 traditional Minas dishes, like feijão tropeiro, frango com quiabo, and frango ao molho pardo, are available at this reasonably priced buffet restaurant. The food is the only reason to go, as the place—in an old house devoid of taste—lacks charm.

Eating Like a Mineiro

Some gastronomic critics say there are only three native Brazilian cuisines: the cuisine from the North (particularly from Pará); the Capixaba cuisine from Espírito Santo; and *comida mineira,* the cuisine from Minas Gerais. Purportedly, all other Brazilian cuisines are originally from outside Brazil. Since Minas Gerais is one of the few states without access to the sea, its cuisine is strongly based on pork and chicken, and legumes and cereals (most notably beans and corn).

The mainstay of comida mineira is *tutu,* a tasty mash of beans with roast pork loin, pork sausage, chopped collard greens, manioc meal, and boiled egg served with meat dishes. Another favorite is *feijão tropeiro,* a combination of beans, manioc meal, roast pork loin, fried egg, chopped collard greens, and thick pork sausage. Among meat dishes, pork is the most common, in particular the famed *lingüiça* (Minas pork sausage) and *lombo* (pork tenderloin), which is often served with white rice and/or corn porridge. The most typical chicken dish is *frango ao molho pardo,* broiled chicken served in a sauce made with its own blood. Another specialty is *frango com quiabo,* chicken cooked in broth with chopped okra. The region's very mild white cheese is known throughout Brazil simply as *queijo Minas* (Minas cheese). Pão de queijo (bread baked with Minas cheese) is irresistible, and popular throughout Brazil. You'll realize very quickly that Minas Gerais isn't the place to start a diet.

Children get significant discounts. $ *Average main: R$55* ⊠ *Rua Padre Odorico 38, São Pedro* ☎ *031/3227–0562* ⊕ *www.donalucinha.com.br* ⊗ *No dinner on weekends* $ *Average main: R$55* ⊠ *Rua Sergipe 811, Funcionários* ☎ *031/3261–5930* ⊗ *No dinner Sun.*

$$$ ✕**Memmo Pasta & Pizza.** This casual Italian eatery is popular with Brazil-
ITALIAN ians celebrating the end of the workday with appetizers like the *champignon Recheado* (mushroom stuffed with shrimp and prosciutto), and entrées like *tourneado Amici Miei* (filet mignon wrapped in bacon and marinated in garlic and olive oil). The pizza is arguably the best in town. The restaurant is often packed both inside and on the large outdoor patio; you may need to wait for the staff to find you a table. $ *Average main: R$60* ⊠ *Rua Tome de Souza 1331, Funcionários* ☎ *031/3282–4992* ⊗ *Closed Mon. No dinner Sun.*

$$$ ✕**Restaurante Varandão.** On the 25th floor of the Othon Palace hotel,
ECLECTIC this romantic restaurant has spectacular urban vistas. Start off with a cocktail at one of the outdoor candlelighted tables by the pool before coming inside for dinner, where a generous buffet serves as the dining room's centerpiece. Feijoada, pastas, salads, and various meats are on the buffet daily and are available as à la carte options. The feijoada on Saturday is a special meal that centers mainly on the pork and beans component of the usual buffet and is accompanied by live music. $ *Average main: R$50* ⊠ *Av. Afonso Pena 1050, Centro* ☎ *031/2126–0000, 031/2126–0090* ⊕ *www.othon.com.br.*

$$$$ ✕ **Splêndido Ristorante.** The food and the service at this cosmopolitan
ECLECTIC restaurant are exceptional. The kitchen blends French and northern Italian cuisines to produce a menu with a mix of pasta, seafood, and meat dishes. It's assured that anyone who's anyone will show up here at some point during a visit to Belo Horizonte. The restaurant has the best wine cellar in town, with about 200 labels on the menu. $ *Average main: R$100* ✉ *Rua Levindo Lopes 251, Funcionários* ☎ *031/3227–6446* ⊘ *No lunch Sat. No dinner Sun.*

$$$$ ✕ **Vecchio Sogno.** What is widely considered Belo Horizonte's best Italian restaurant attracts a well-heeled clientele. Tuxedo-clad waiters
ITALIAN serve selections from the extensive wine list as well as steak, seafood, and pasta dishes. Consider the grilled fillet of lamb with saffron risotto in a mushroom-and-garlic sauce; the gnocchi *di mare,* with spinach and potatoes, topped with a white clam and scallop sauce; or the *badejo,* a local white fish baked and dressed in a seafood sauce. The restaurant allows its diners into its kitchen to see the preparation of food. With its beautiful wood paneling and an extensive bar, Vecchio Sogno has the feel of a 1940s jazz club. $ *Average main: R$100* ✉ *Rua Martim de Carvalho 75, Santo Agostinho* ☎ *031/3292–5251* ⊕ *www.vecchiosogno.com.br* ⌃ *Reservations essential* ⊘ *No lunch Sat. No dinner Sun.*

WHERE TO STAY

Given Belo Horizonte's hills and the long walking distances between key places of interest, the location of your hotel is crucial. To capture a glimpse of everyday life here, the city center is the best place to be—particularly the region around Avenida Afonso Pena, where the main shopping district, the Municipal Park, the Palace of Arts theater, and noteworthy churches are located. This is also where the Sunday craft market takes place. On the other hand, while the city center pulses during the day, it's somewhat gritty at night. Most bars and restaurants close at about 7 pm. For an upmarket area with sophisticated evening entertainment, consider the Lourdes neighborhood, around Avenida do Contorno. This is the destination of well-off *belo-horizontinos* and home to top restaurants and bars serving local and international food. In this neighborhood you'll be nearer to the museums and churches around Liberty Square and Savassi. The drawback to staying here, though, is the uphill climb from the main tourist destinations in the city center.

$ ⊞ **Hotel Amazonas Palace.** The clean, simple rooms at this downtown
HOTEL hotel are reasonably priced, and the 11th-floor restaurant affords fine city views. **Pros:** solarium good for tanning; quiet rooms despite the central location. **Cons:** lacks character; basic breakfast; conventions often held here. $ *Rooms from: R$170* ✉ *Av. Amazonas 120, Centro* ☎ *031/3207–4644, 031/3207–4600* ⊕ *www.amazonaspalace.com.br* ⮐ *76 rooms* ⃝ *Breakfast.*

$ ⊞ **Hotel Wimbledon.** Its central location, elegance, and warmth place this
HOTEL hotel above others in its price range. **Pros:** charming setting; attentive service that makes this feel like a bed-and-breakfast. **Cons:** only luxury

(*apartamentos luxo*) rooms have whirlpool baths. [$] *Rooms from: R$241* ✉ *Av. Afonso Pena 772, Centro* ☎ *031/3222–6160* 🌐 *www.wimbledon.com.br* 🛏 *69 rooms, 2 suites* 🍴 *Breakfast.*

$ HOTEL 🏨 **Ibis.** A neat and comfortable budget option, the Ibis has spacious rooms with white oak furniture and large beds. **Pros:** in the best part of the city; good choice for disabled visitors. **Cons:** sparse furnishings for a hotel in this price range; basic breakfast. [$] *Rooms from: R$169* ✉ *Rua João Pinheiro 602, Lourdes* ☎ *031/2111–1500* 🌐 *www.accorhotels.com.br* 🛏 *130 rooms* 🍴 *No meals.*

$$ HOTEL 🏨 **Mercure Lourdes.** On a main city avenue, close to Savassi and not far from central Belo Horizonte, the Mercure is popular with executives, artists, and athletes. **Pros:** central location near restaurants and bars; rooms on higher floors have wonderful city views. **Cons:** Internet not free in standard apartments; small swimming pool. [$] *Rooms from: R$364* ✉ *Av. do Contorno 7315, Lourdes* ☎ *031/3298–4100* 🌐 *www.accorhotels.com.br* 🛏 *379 rooms* 🍴 *Breakfast.*

$$$ HOTEL 🏨 **Minas Hotel.** The lobby of this centrally located hotel, one of the city's oldest, is often crowded with conventioneers. **Pros:** many rooms have the same view of the city and surrounding mountains that you'll find from the small rooftop pool and bar. **Cons:** rooms that don't have this view tend to be dark. [$] *Rooms from: R$380* ✉ *Rua Espírito Santo 901, Centro* ☎ *031/3248–1000* 🌐 *www.dayrell.com.br* 🛏 *240 rooms* 🍴 *Breakfast.*

$ HOTEL 🏨 **Othon Palace.** Across from beautiful and exotic Parque Municipal, the Othon has comfortable rooms with incredible city and park views. **Pros:** superb location; great rooftop pool and bar; stellar restaurant. **Cons:** dated room decor. [$] *Rooms from: R$200* ✉ *Av. Afonso Pena 1050, Centro* ☎ *031/2126–0000, 0800/762–1296* 🛏 *266 rooms, 19 suites* 🍴 *Breakfast.*

$$ HOTEL Fodor's Choice ★ 🏨 **Ouro Minas Palace Hotel.** The palatial Ouro Minas, which underwent an extensive renovation to retain its five-star rating, has rooms with large beds and well-appointed bathrooms. **Pros:** great breakfast and bar; good leisure center, including a well-equipped gym. **Cons:** not centrally located. [$] *Rooms from: R$280* ✉ *Av. Cristiano Machado 4001, Ipiranga* ☎ *031/3429–4001, 031/3429–4000* 🌐 *www.ourominas.com.br* 🛏 *301 rooms, 45 suites* 🍴 *Breakfast.*

NIGHTLIFE AND THE ARTS

NIGHTLIFE

"Se não tem mar, vamos pro bar!" (We haven't got the sea, so we'll go to the bar) is a mineiro catchphrase that epitomizes the Belo Horizonte lifestyle. No other city in Brazil has as many bars and coffee shops as Belo Horizonte—there are 14,000, or one for every 150 inhabitants. This isn't a recent trend: the first bar appeared in 1893, four years before the city was founded. The bar culture is the core of the city's nightlife. There's even a contest every year in April, the Comida di Buteco, or Bar Food Contest (🌐 *www.comidadibuteco.com.br*), to reward the bar with the best appetizers (*tira-gosto,* as the locals say) and the coldest beer.

BARS

Fodor's Choice ★ **Alambique Cachaçaria e Armazém.** For fabulous city views and some of Brazil's best cachaças, head to this bar where musicians perform daily except Mondays. You can party all night here: Alambique opens at 10 and closes at dawn. ✉ *Av. Raja Gabáglia 3200, Chalé 1D, Estoril* ☎ *031/3296–7188* ⊕ *www.alambique.com.br.*

Arrumação. A traditional bar in a colonial building owned by Brazilian comedian and actor Saulo Laranjeira, Arrumação specializes in cachaças and serves excellent appetizers. It often hosts performances and concerts. ✉ *Av. Assis Chateaubriand 524, Floresta* ☎ *031/3222–9794* ⊕ *www.saulolaranjeira.com.br.*

Bar do Bolão. Bohemians, musicians, and poets hang out at this bar and restaurant in Santa Tereza, a neighborhood worth wandering itself. Members of the bands Sepultura and Skank have been known to drop by. ■**TIP➔Grab a seat outside and order a cold lager and the rochedão (the big rock), a hearty dish of steak, eggs, potatoes, rice, and beans.** ✉ *Rua Mármore 689, Santa Tereza* ☎ *031/3463–0719.*

Cantina do Lucas. Established in 1962, the cantina is a cultural landmark beloved by middle-aged locals, who flock here on weekends for its honest Italian fare. The portions are enormous—and cheap—and the service is efficient and courteous. This could be a good option for the start of your evening: order a *porção* (sharing snack platter) and a glass of cold lager. ✉ *Av. Augusto de Lima 233, Loja 18, Centro* ☎ *031/3226–7153.*

Choperia Maria de Lourdes. This bar serves an excellent feijoada on Saturdays and good house draft beer all week long. ✉ *Rua Bárbara Heliodora 141, Lourdes* ☎ *031/3292–7203* ⊕ *www.mariadelourdes.com.br.*

Mercearia do Lili. One of BH's best bars operates out of a small grocery store in a bohemian enclave. By day the owner sells eggs, cereal, and soap. In the evening, tables are placed on the sidewalk, and he serves iced beer and incomparable appetizers. ✉ *Rua São João Evangelista 696, Santo Antônio* ☎ *031/3293–3469.*

CAFÉS

Fodor's Choice ★ **Café com Letras.** Belo Horizonte's intellectual beau monde collects at this café to eat dainty salads and drink imported wine in a beautiful interior surrounded by books and art. DJs spin music on most nights, and there's sometimes live jazz. ✉ *Rua Antônio de Albuquerque 781, Savassi* ☎ *031/3225–9973* ⊕ *www.cafecomletras.com.br.*

Status Café Cultura e Arte. A great spot to hear live music, the Status is the perfect place to wait out a rain shower. The large, warm space houses a café/bar and a bookstore. ✉ *Rua Pernambuco 1150, Funcionários* ☎ *031/3261–6045.*

DANCE CLUBS

Fodor's Choice ★ **A Obra.** A hip and young crowd ranging in age from 18 to mid-30s gathers at A Obra, a basement-level pub with a dance floor. Music styles vary from indie rock to classic rock and more, but this is always a good place to go for something other than mainstream music. ✉ *Rua Rio Grande do Norte 1168, Funcionários* ☎ *031/3261–9431* ⊕ *www. aobra.com.br.*

Josefine. The dance club Josefine is popular with the GLS crowd—*gays, lésbicas, e simpatizantes* (gays, lesbians, and sympathizers). ⊠ *Rua Antônio de Albuquerque 729, Savassi* ☎ *031/3269–4405* ⊕ *www.josefine.com.br.*

Na Sala. BH's most modern and well-equipped nightclub is also its premier house-music venue. ⊠ *Ponteio Lar Shopping mall, BR 356 no. 2500, Santa Lúcia* ☎ *031/3286–4705* ⊕ *www.nasala.com.br* ⊘ *Closed Sun.–Wed.*

LIVE MUSIC

Lapa Multshow. The crowd here comes to experience typical Brazilian musical styles such as samba and ones associated with forró. ⊠ *Rua Álvares Maciel 312, Santa Efigênia* ☎ *031/3241–2074.*

Pedacinhos do Céu. Belo Horizonte's best and most authentic live-music venue is Pedacinhos do Céu, literally, "little pieces of heaven." This small bar is known mostly for *choro,* an instrumental version of samba, for which guitars dominate the sound. Groups of musicians gather here with their *cavaquinhos* (small four-string guitars), *violões* (guitars), and flutes for jam sessions that last late into the night. The bar is named after a song by composer Waldir Azevedo (1923–80) and provides access to his archive. ⊠ *Rua Belmiro Braga 774, Caiçara Adelaide* ☎ *031/3462–2260* ⊕ *www.pedacinhosdoceu.com.br.*

Utópica Marcenaria. By day a furniture store and an architecture office, this space transforms at night into a venue for jazz, blues, and Brazilian and Cuban rhythms. ⊠ *Av. Raja Gabáglia 4700, Santa Lúcia* ☎ *031/3296–2868* ⊕ *www.utopica.com.br* ⊘ *Closed Sun. and Mon.*

THE ARTS

Belo Horizonte has produced some of the most creative artists in the country. One of the 20th century's most literary writers, João Guimarães Rosa (1908–67) was born near BH and attended high school and college here. As a young architect, Oscar Niemeyer was chosen to design parts of the city, and his designs dominate the Pampulha district and the Praça da Liberdade. Rock and metal groups like Skank, Pato Fu, Jota Quest, and Sepultura all started their musical careers in BH. Numerous art festivals take place here year-round, including the Savassi Jazz Festival. One of Brazil's famous theater groups, Grupo Galpão, is based in BH, as are other theaters and a dozen children's-theater companies.

The daily newspaper *Estado de Minas* (⊕ *www.estaminas.com.br*) has information about cultural programs in print and online. *Jornal Pampulha*, another good source, comes out on Saturday.

CONCERT HALLS

Chevrolet Hall. The 3,700-seat hall presents concerts by famous Brazilian and foreign musical artists and is a venue for volleyball and basketball games. ⊠ *Av. Nossa Senhora do Carmo 230, Savassi* ☎ *031/4003–5588* ⊕ *www.chevrolethallbh.com.br.*

Palácio das Artes. The center of cultural life in Belo Horizonte, this intimate concert hall hosts symphony orchestras; ballet, opera, and theater companies; and famous Brazilian acts such as singer Caetano Veloso. ⊠ *Av. Afonso Pena 1537, Centro* ☎ *031/3236–7400* ⊕ *www.fcs.mg.gov.br.*

7

FILM

Espaço Usiminas Belas Artes Liberdade. This cinema screens art-house films. Also here are a coffee shop, a bookstore, and a small store that sells aboriginal arts and crafts. ⊠ *Rua Gonçalves Dias 1581, Lourdes* ☎ *031/3252-7232* ⊕ *www.usiminasbelasartes.com.br.*

Usina Unibanco de Cinema. Art and European films are screened here. ⊠ *R. Gonçalves Dias, 1581, Lourdes* ☎ *031/3252–7232.*

SPORTS AND THE OUTDOORS

The daily newspaper *Estado de Minas* (⊕ *www.estaminas.com.br*) has information about sports events and tickets, as does the *Jornal Pampulha*, which comes out on Saturday. Most city parks have short jogging paths, and running is common during the day. As elsewhere in Brazil, soccer is a big deal in Belo Horizonte. For amateur spelunkers, the mountains of Minas are replete with caves to be explored, though they must be seen with a tour guide (look for one at any cave's entrance booth). *For outdoor activities near the city, see Side Trips from Belo Horizonte.*

JOGGING

FAMILY **Parque das Mangabeiras.** This 568-acre open space in the mountains surrounding BH is one of Brazil's largest urban parks. Along its jogging paths and hiking trails you might spot monkeys, squirrels, and other local fauna. There are playgrounds, sports courts and fields, and a stage for concerts. ⊠ *Av. José do Patrocínio Pontes 580, Mangabeiras* ☎ *031/3277–8277* ⊗ *Closed Mon.*

SOCCER

Estádio Mineirão. The 75,000-seat Estádio Mineirão is Brazil's third-largest stadium and the home field of BH's two professional *futebol* (soccer) teams: Atlético Mineiro and Cruzeiro. For R$2 you can look around the stadium (there are no guided tours). It's open daily from 8 to 5, except during matches. Expect to pay from R$15 to R$40 or more for tickets to a big game. ⊠ *Av. Antônio Abrahão Caram 1001, Pampulha* ☎ *031/3916–0488* ⊕ *www.ademg.mg.gov.br.*

SPELUNKING

Gruta da Lapinha. This cave is 36 km (22 miles) north of BH, near the city of Lagoa Santa, on the road leading from Tancredo Neves airport. ☎ *031/3689–8422* ⊕ *www.lagoasanta.mg.gov.br* ⊠ *R$10* ⊗ *Tues.–Sun. 8:30–4:30.*

Gruta do Maquiné. The most popular cavern around BH, with six large chambers, the Gruta do Maquiné lies 113 km (70 miles) northwest of the capital, near Cordisburgo. ⊠ *Village Alberto Ramos, MG 231, km 7* ☎ *031/3715–1425* ⊕ *www.grutadomaquine.tur.br* ⊠ *R$16* ⊗ *Daily 8–5.*

SHOPPING

The fashionable Savassi and Lourdes neighborhoods have the city's best antiques, handicrafts, and jewelry stores. For clothing, head to one of the major shopping centers such as BH Shopping. On Saturday between 10 am and 6 pm, an antiques fair and food market takes place on the Avenida Bernardo Monteiro between Avenida Brasil and Rua dos Otoni. Bands often play, and you can sample mineiro cuisine. On Sunday between 8 am and 2 pm, nearly 3,000 vendors show up for the arts-and-crafts fair in front of the Othon Palace hotel, on Avenida Afonso Pena. For a range of fashions, hit the malls and shopping centers *(below)*.

> ### MAGICAL REALISM FROM MINAS
>
> João Guimarães Rosa's oeuvre is unlike anything else written in Brazil. It could be compared to Gabriel García Márquez in his use of magic and spiritualism to weave stories in rural settings. Rosa infused readers with the sounds and legends of Minas Gerais, creating a mystical and linguistic landscape not unlike Faulkner's South. During the Second World War, Rosa assumed a diplomatic post in Europe and was instrumental in helping many people fleeing the Holocaust with visas to Brazil.

ANTIQUES

Arte Sacra Antiguidades. Fine Minas antiques are the specialty of Arte Sacra Antiguidades. ✉ *Rua Alagoas 785, Funcionários* ☎ *031/3261–7256.*

CLOTHING

Ronaldo Fraga. Minas Gerais culture influences the fashions that designer Ronaldo Fraga creates. ✉ *Rua Fernandes Tourinho 81, Savassi* ☎ *031/3282–5379* ⊕ *www.ronaldofraga.com.*

HANDICRAFTS

Centro de Artesanato Mineiro. The wide range of crafts by regional artisans makes a visit to this center with the Palácio das Artes complex well worth a visit. ✉ *Palácio das Artes, Av. Afonso Pena 1537, Centro* ☎ *031/3272–9513.*

MALLS AND CENTERS

BH Shopping. Many shops in Belo Horizonte's most exclusive mall sell designer togs for men and women. ✉ *BR 356 no. 3049, Belvedere* ☎ *031/4003–4135.*

Shopping Cidade. The shops at this popular downtown mall carry clothes, electronics, and just about everything else you could want. ✉ *Rua Tupis 337, Centro* ☎ *031/3279–1200* ⊕ *www.shoppingcidade.com.br.*

SIDE TRIP TO SABARÁ

19 km (12 miles) east of Belo Horizonte.

The grandeur of Sabará's baroque churches, their interiors rich with gold-leaf paneling, makes clear how enormously wealthy Minas Gerais was during the gold-rush days. This former colonial town, now a sprawling Belo Horizonte suburb of 140,000 people, makes for a fun half-day trip. Sabará's historic sites are scattered about, but signs at Praça Santa Rita point to all the major ones. As in most colonial towns, the churches are closed on Mondays.

GETTING HERE AND AROUND

Buses for Sabará (Viação Cisne No. 5509) depart from behind the BH bus station (the local part of the station). Buses are frequent, and the ride takes less than 30 minutes. To get here by car, take BR 262 from BH; the drive takes 30 minutes.

EXPLORING

Fodor'sChoice ★ **Igreja de Nossa Senhora da Conceição.** The ornate Church of Our Lady of the Immaculate Conception, though small, is Sabará's main church and an outstanding example of Portuguese baroque architecture with Asian influences. Its simple exterior gives no indication of the wealth inside, typified by the luxurious gold altar and the lavishly decorated ceiling. ⊠ *Praça Getúlio Vargas 5* ☎ *031/3671–1724* ⊕ *www.nsconceicao.com* ⊡ *R$2* ⊗ *Weekdays 9–noon and 2–5.*

Igreja de Nossa Senhora do Ó. Our Lady of Ó Church, one of Brazil's oldest and smallest churches, contains paintings said to have been completed by 23 Chinese artists brought from the former Portuguese colony of Macau. Other signs of Asian influence include the Chinese tower and the gilded arches. ⊠ *Largo de Nossa Senhora do Ó s/n, Sabará* ☎ *031/3671–1724* ⊡ *R$2* ⊗ *Weekends 9–noon and 2–5.*

THE COLONIAL AND GOLD TOWNS

Two hours southeast of Belo Horizonte is Ouro Preto, a UNESCO World Heritage Site. The country's de facto capital during the gold-boom years, it was also the birthplace of Brazil's first independence movement, the Inconfidência Mineira. Today a vibrant student population ensures plenty of year-round activity, and lodging, dining, and shopping options abound.

All the Gold Towns—Ouro Preto, Mariana, Tiradentes, and Congonhas—are characterized by winding cobblestone streets, brilliant baroque churches, impressive mansions and museums, and colorful markets. Tiradentes is smaller than Ouro Preto but no less charming; this town truly seems to have stopped in time about midway through the 18th century. Between Ouro Preto and Tiradentes lies Congonhas, whose Basilica do Bom Jesus de Matosinhos and its famous Prophets, sculpted by Aleijadinho, are UNESCO World Heritage Sites. Diamantina rivals Ouro Preto in its scope and the beautiful scenery of the mountains around it; the rich cultural history here sheds considerable light on colonial Brazil.

DIAMANTINA

290 km (180 miles) northeast of Belo Horizonte.

Diamantina took its name from the diamonds that were extracted in great quantities here in the 18th century. Perhaps because of its remote setting in the barren mountains close to the *sertão* (a remote arid region), Diamantina is extremely well preserved, although its churches

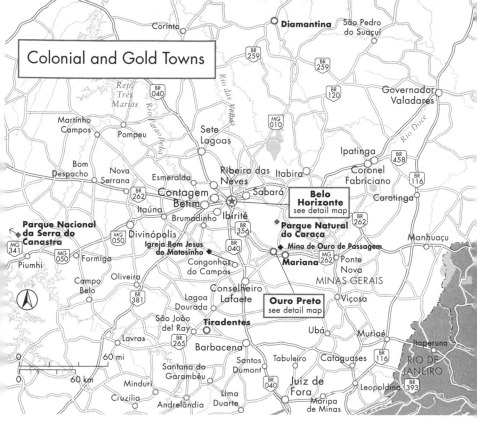

Colonial and Gold Towns

lack the grandeur of those in other historic towns. Its white-wall structures stand in pristine contrast to the iron red of the surrounding mountains. The principal attraction in Diamantina is the simple pleasure of walking along the clean-swept cobblestone streets lined with colonial houses—note the overhanging roofs with their elaborate brackets.

The city was the home of two legendary figures of the colonial period: diamond contractor João Fernandes de Oliveira and his slave mistress, Chica da Silva, one of Brazilian history's first powerful Afro-Brazilian women. Two area attractions are linked with her; to see them, you should contact the Casa da Cultura to arrange a guided tour.

GETTING HERE AND AROUND

Twelve daily Pássaro Verde buses leave the rodoviária in Belo Horizonte for Diamantina. The trip takes five hours and costs about R$76. By car, there's no ideal direct route; your best bet is to drive north on BR 040 and then east on BR 259 (5 hours).

ESSENTIALS

Bus Contacts Pássaro Verde ☎ 038/3531–1758, 0800/724–4400 ⊕ www.passaroverde.com.br. **Rodoviária de Diamantina** ⊠ Largo Dom João 134 ☎ 038/3531–9176.

Taxi Contacts Ponto de Taxi Largo Dom João ☎ 038/3531–1413.

Visitor and Tour Information

Secretaria Municipal de Cultura e Turismo ✉ *Praça Antônio Eulálio 53* ☎ *038/3531-9530* 🕒 *Weekdays noon–6, Sat. 9–5, Sun. 9–noon.*

EXPLORING

TOP ATTRACTIONS

Casa de Chica da Silva. One of Brazil's wealthiest and most famous former slaves, Chica da Silva (also spelled Xica da Silva), lived in this house with her Portuguese partner, João Fernandes de Oliveira, from 1763 to 1771. The house contains colonial furniture and Chica's private chapel. A permanent art exhibit shows Chica in torrid poses and tawdry clothes as a personification of the Seven Deadly Sins. ✉ *Praça Lobo de Mesquita 266* ☎ *038/3531–2491* 🎟 *Free* 🕒 *Tues.–Sat. noon–5, Sun. 9–1.*

> **THE SERENADE TOWN**
>
> Diamantina has the distinction of being Brazil's center of serenading. At night, particularly on weekends, romantics gather in a downtown alley called Beco da Mota, the former red-light district and now home to several popular bars. Strolling guitarists also gather on Rua Direita and Rua Quitanda.

Fodor's Choice ★ **Igreja Nossa Senhora do Carmo.** João Fernandes de Oliveira had the Church of Our Lady of Mount Carmel built as a gift to his mistress. Supposedly, Chica da Silva ordered that the bell tower be built at the back of the 1751 structure so the ringing wouldn't disturb her. The altar has gold-leaf paneling, and the organ has 514 pipes. ✉ *Rua do Carmo s/n* 🎟 *R$2* 🕒 *Tues.–Sat. 8–12 and 2–6, Sun. 8–noon.*

FAMILY **Museu do Diamante.** The city's Diamond Museum, in a building that dates from 1789, displays equipment used in colonial-period mines. The museum occupies the former house of Padre Rolim, one of the Inconfidentes (supposedly Chica da Silva once belonged to Rolim as well). The items on exhibit here include instruments made to torture slaves and sacred art from the 16th to the 19th century. There are guided tours of the rooms where diamonds were classified and separated. ✉ *Rua Direita 14* ☎ *038/3531–1382* 🎟 *R$1* 🕒 *Tue.–Sat. 10–5, Sun. and public holidays 9–1.*

WORTH NOTING

Casa de Juscelino Kubitschek. The childhood home of one of Brazil's most important 20th-century presidents—he was responsible for the construction of Brasília—is now a small museum. ✉ *Rua São Francisco 241* ☎ *038/3531–3607* 🎟 *R$2* 🕒 *Tues.–Sat. 8–7, Sun. 8–1.*

WHERE TO EAT AND STAY

$$$ BRAZILIAN 🍴 **Cantina do Marinho.** This well-respected restaurant specializes in comida mineira. Diners' favorites include pork steak with tutu and pork tenderloin with feijão tropeiro. You can order à la carte from the menu or head over to the self-service buffet. [$] *Average main: R$55* ✉ *Rua Direita 113* ☎ *038/3531–1686.*

$ HOTEL 🏨 **Hotel Tijuco.** Oscar Niemeyer designed the sleek structure that houses this historic-district inn. **Pros:** considered the best hotel in town; amazing views of the hills from some rooms. **Cons:** few facilities; 1950s-modern structure seems out of place in historic Diamantina. [$] *Rooms from: R$130* ✉ *Rua Macau do Meio 211* ☎ *038/3531–1022* 🌐 *www.hoteltijuco.com.br* 🛏 *27 rooms* 🍽 *Breakfast.*

OURO PRETO

97 km (60 miles) southeast of Belo Horizonte.

The former gold-rush capital is the best place to see the legendary Aleijadinho's artistry. Now a lively university town, it's been preserved as a national monument and a World Heritage site. The surrounding mountains, geometric rows of whitewashed buildings, cobblestone streets, red-tile roofs that climb the hillsides, morning mist and evening fog—all give Ouro Preto a singular beauty.

In its heyday Ouro Preto (also seen as Ouro Prêto, an archaic spelling) was one of Brazil's most progressive cities and the birthplace of the colony's first stirrings of independence. Toward the end of the 18th century the mines were running out, with all of the gold and jewels being sent to Portugal. The residents were unhappy with the corruption of the governor, and the Inconfidência Mineira was organized to overthrow the Portuguese rulers and establish an independent Brazilian republic. It was to have been led by a resident of Ouro Preto, Joaquim José da Silva Xavier, a dentist nicknamed Tiradentes ("tooth-puller").

Walk down the hill from the bus station on the beautiful cobblestone street and you'll come to the former prison or the Museu de Inconfidência. Praça Tiradentes, the town's central square, teems with gossiping students, eager merchants, and curious visitors. Ouro Preto has several museums, as well as 13 colonial *igrejas* (churches) that are highly representative of mineiro baroque architecture. The Minas style is marked by elaborately carved doorways and curving lines. Most distinctive, though, are the interiors, richly painted and decorated lavishly with cedarwood and soapstone sculptures. Many interiors are unabashedly rococo, with an ostentatious use of gold leaf, a by-product of the region's mineral wealth. Note that many museums and churches are closed on Mondays.

THE PRICE OF BETRAYAL

The Inconfidência Mineira, a 1789 attempt to gain independence from Portugal, was to have been led by Joaquim José da Silva Xavier, better known as Tiradentes, and 11 followers. But Joaquim Silvério dos Reis, a Mineiran who was in on the conspiracy, betrayed the movement in exchange for the pardon of his debt to the crown. Tiradentes assumed responsibility for the planned uprising and was sentenced to death. The Empress Dona Maria I documented how he was to be killed: drawn and quartered, with his body parts hung around Ouro Preto. The date of Tiradentes's execution, April 21st, is a national holiday.

GETTING HERE AND AROUND

Pássaro Verde buses connect Belo Horizonte with Ouro Preto (R$26; 2 hours). Útil serves Ouro Preto from Rio (R$78–R$120; 8 hours). By car from Belo Horizonte you can take BR 040 south and BR 356 (it becomes MG 262) east to Ouro Preto (1½–2 hours).

All of the town's sights are within easy walking distance of the central square, Praça Tiradentes, which is a seven-minute walk from the bus station. A taxi from the bus station to the center costs R$15. A small bus travels around town every 10 to 15 minutes.

The main streets of Ouro Preto have two names: one from the 18th century, still used by the city's inhabitants, and the other an official name, used on maps but not very popular. Therefore, Rua Conde de Bobadela is better known as Rua Direita, Rua Senador Rocha Lagoa as Rua das Flores, and Rua Cláudio Manoel as Rua do Ouvidor. Street signs sometimes use the official name and sometimes both. We use the official names in this guide.

The steep hills in Ouro Preto are very hard on cars—and legs. And when it rains, cobblestones are very slippery; sturdy footwear and warm clothing are recommended year-round.

VISITOR INFORMATION

The professional tour guides of the Associação de Guias conduct excellent six-hour historic walking tours in English, and the group provides general information about Ouro Preto. Posto de Informações Turísticas dispenses information at the bus station, but its main location is at Praça Tiradentes, where there's an art gallery, a beautiful café, and a bookstore.

ESSENTIALS

Bus Contacts Viação Pássaro Verde ⊠ *Rua Padre Rolim 661* ☎ *031/3551–1081* ⊕ *www.passaroverde.com.br.* **Rodoviária Ouro Preto** ⊠ *Rua Padre Rolim 661, São Cristóvão* ☎ *031/3559–3252.* **Viação Útil** ☎ *031/3551–3166* ⊕ *www.util.com.br.*

Taxi Contacts Ponto de Táxi ☎ *031/3551–2123, 031/3551–1977.*

Visitor and Tour Information Associação de Guias de Ouro Preto ⊠ *Rua Padre Rolim s/n, São Cristóvão* ☎ *031/3551–2655* ⊗ *Weekdays 8–6.* **Posto de Informações Turísticas** ⊠ *Praça Tiradentes, 4, Centro* ☎ *031/3559–3269* ⊗ *Daily 8–5 (also at bus station weekdays 7–1).*

EXPLORING

TOP ATTRACTIONS

Fodor's Choice ★ **Igreja de Nossa Senhora do Carmo.** The impressive Our Lady of Carmel Church, completed in 1776, contains the last works of Aleijadinho. It was originally designed by Aleijadinho's father, an architect, but was later modified by Aleijadinho, who added additional rococo elements, including the soapstone sculptures of angels above the entrance. Frequented by the high society of Ouro Preto at the time it was inaugurated, the church contains the only examples of *azulejos* (decorative Portuguese tiles) from this period in Minas Gerais. ⊠ *Praça Brigadeiro Musqueira s/n, Centro* ☎ *031/3551–2601* ⊠ *R$2* ⊗ *Tues.–Sun. 9–11 and 1–4:45.*

Fodor's Choice ★ **Igreja de Nossa Senhora da Conceição.** The charming Our Lady of the Conception church, decorated in unique rose and blue pastels, was completed in 1760. It contains the tomb of Aleijadinho as well as a small museum dedicated to him. On the same street is the artist's house, now in private hands. ⊠ *Praça Antônio Dias s/n, Centro* ☎ *031/3551–3282* ⊠ *R$6 (includes admission to Aleijadinho Museum)* ⊗ *Tues.–Sun. 8–noon and 1:30–5.*

Igreja de Nossa Senhora do Pilar. Local lore has it that 400 pounds of gold and silver leaf were used to cover the interior of Ouro Preto's most richly decorated church, built on the site of an earlier chapel and consecrated in 1733. The church building also houses the Museu de Arte Sacra (Museum of Sacred Art). ✉ *Praça Monsenhor João Castilho Barbosa s/n, Centro* ☎ *031/3551–4736* ⌨ *R$7* ☾ *Tues.–Sun. 9–10:45 and noon–4:45.*

Igreja de Santa Efigênia. On a hill east of Praça Tiradentes, this interesting slave church was built over the course of 60 years (1730–90) and was funded by Chico-Rei. This

> **THE ROYAL ROAD**
>
> The *Estrada Real* Royal Road was constructed by slaves, linking the colonial towns with the port of Paraty and the ships waiting to transport the mineral wealth to Portugal. Huge stone slabs are still present in parts of this historical trail. Thousands of slaves died building this road and taking the wealth to the coast. Parts of the road can be traversed by horse, on foot, and by car. Set up trips through the Instituto Estrada Real. ☎ *031/3241–7166.*

African ruler was captured during Brazil's gold rush and sold to a mine owner in Minas Gerais. Chico eventually earned enough money to buy his freedom—in the days before the Portuguese prohibited such acts—and became a hero among slaves. The clocks on the facade are the city's oldest, and the interior contains cedar sculptures by Francisco Xavier de Brito, Aleijadinho's teacher. ✉ *Rua de Santa Efigênia s/n, Centro* ☎ *031/3551–5047* ⌨ *R$2* ☾ *Tues.–Sun. 8:30–4:30.*

Fodor's Choice ★ **Igreja de São Francisco de Assis.** Considered Aleijadinho's masterpiece, this church was begun in 1766 by the Franciscan Third Order but wasn't completed until 1810. Aleijadinho designed the structure and was responsible for the wood and soapstone sculptures on the portal, high altar, side altars, pulpits, and crossing arch. Manuel da Costa Ataíde, a brilliant artist in his own right, painted the panel on the nave ceiling representing the Virgin's glorification. Cherubic faces, garlands of tropical fruits, and allegorical characters carved into the main altar are still covered with their original paint. ✉ *Largo de Coimbra s/n, Centro* ⌨ *R$6* ☾ *Tues.–Sun. 8:30–noon and 1:30–5.*

Fodor's Choice ★ **Museu da Inconfidência.** One of the best historical museums in Brazil, this former 18th-century prison and onetime city hall has great interactive computer and television screen displays devoted to the history of the failed uprising of the Inconfidêntes, life in colonial Tiradentes, slavery, and a number of other interesting topics. Other displays include period furniture, clothing, slaves' manacles, firearms, books, and gravestones, as well as works by Aleijadinho and Ataíde. The museum also holds the remains of revolutionaries, some brought back from exile in Portugal's African colonies, and the document in which Maria I details the fate of Tiradentes's body parts. ✉ *Praça Tiradentes 139, Centro* ☎ *031/3551–1121* ⌨ *R$6* ☾ *Tues.–Sun. noon–6.*

Museu de Ciência e Técnica. Opposite the Museu da Inconfidência in the former governor's palace, the Museum of Science and Technology contains an enormous collection of stunning precious and semiprecious

7

gems, along with gold and crystals. Exhibits also survey the geology of Minas Gerais and explain the mining process. An entire floor is devoted to gems organized according to their chemical families. ✉ *Praça Tiradentes 20, Centro* ☎ *031/3559–3119* 🌐 *www.museu.em.ufop.br* 🎫 *R$5* 🕒 *Tues.–Sun. noon–5.*

Museu do Oratório. Established in the historic house of the St. Carmel novitiate, once a home to Aleijadinho, this museum celebrates 18th- and 19th-century sacred art. Some of the oratories, which reflect ideas of religious beauty from the period, have been displayed at the Louvre. ✉ *N. Sra. do Carmo 28, Centro* ☎ *031/3551–5369* 🌐 *www.oratorio.com.br* 🎫 *R$10* 🕒 *Daily 9:30–5:30.*

ALEIJADINHO

Brazil's most famous baroque artist was the son of a Portuguese architect and a former slave. Antônio Francisco Lisboa was born in 1738 in the vicinity of present-day Ouro Preto. In adulthood, a disease left his arms and feet deformed. Unable to hold his instruments Aleijadinho ("little cripple") worked with chisel and hammer strapped to his wrists. His work, primarily in cedarwood and soapstone, is profoundly moving. His sculptures have a singular look, many of his angels have curly hair, and enormous, humble eyes.

WORTH NOTING

Casa dos Contos. This colonial coinage house dating from the 1780s had many uses, one as a prison for some of the Inconfidentes, two of whom—Padre Rolim and Claudio Manuel da Costa—died here. It contains the foundry that minted coins of the gold-rush period and has exhibits of coins and period furniture. The building is considered one of the best examples of Brazilian colonial architecture. The beautiful park at the back of the building snakes past a waterfall and alongside a river to the other side of town. ✉ *Rua São José 12, Centro* ☎ *031/3551–1444* 🎫 *R$3* 🕒 *Mon. 2–6, Tues.–Sat. 10–6, Sun. 10–4.*

Igreja de Nossa Senhora do Rosário dos Pretos. The small, intriguing Church of Our Lady of the Rosary of the Blacks was inaugurated by slaves in 1785, some of whom bought their freedom with the gold they found in Ouro Preto. According to legend, the church's interior is bare because the slaves ran out of gold after erecting the baroque building. In the unusual oval interior the church houses sculptures of Santa Helena, Santo Antônio, and São Benedito. ✉ *Largo do Rosário s/n, Centro* ☎ *031/3551–4736* 🎫 *Free* 🕒 *Tues.–Sat. noon–4:45.*

WHERE TO EAT

$ CAFÉ FAMILY 🍴 **Café Cultural.** Within the same building as the Tourist Information Office of Praça Tiradentes, Café Cultural is the perfect place to rest a bit and enjoy a cold drink and a quick bite. Quiches, little appetizers, and cakes are served, and the extensive beer list includes local gems such as the Backer beer. Ambient music and comfortable sofas allow you to sit back and watch the world pass by the café's large windows. [$] *Average main: R$20* ✉ *Rua Claudio Manoel 15, Centro* ☎ *031/3551–1361.*

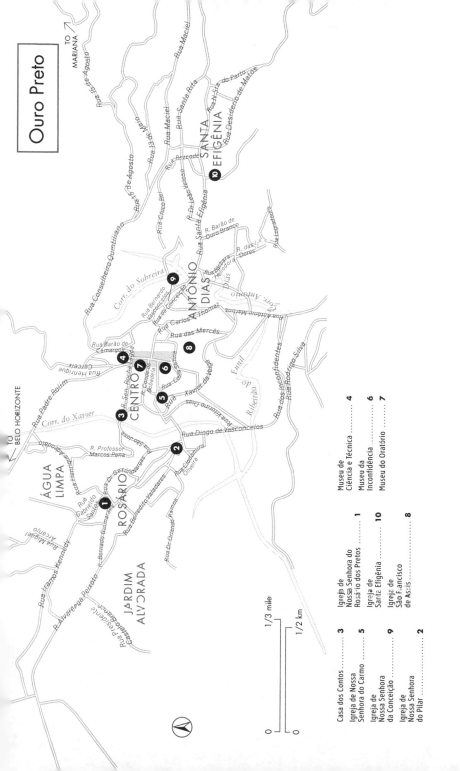

Ouro Preto

TO MARIANA

TO
BELO HORIZONTE

SANTA EFIGÉNIA

ANTÔNIO DIAS

CENTRO

ÁGUA LIMPA

ROSÁRIO

JARDIM ALVORADA

0
1/3 mile

0
1/2 km

Casa dos Contos 3

Igreja de Nossa
Senhora do Carmo 5

Igreja de
Nossa Senhora
da Conceição 9

Igreja de
Nossa Senhora
do Pilar 2

Igreja de
Nossa Senhora do
Rosário dos Pretos 1

Igreja de
Santa Efigénia 10

Igreja de
São Francisco
de Assis 8

Museu de
Ciência e Técnica 4

Museu da
Inconfidência 6

Museu do Oratório 7

$$ BRAZILIAN 🍴 **Café Geraes/Escadabaixo.** A Parisian-like café and restaurant in an 18th-century building, this beautiful establishment serves delicious sandwiches, soups, and pastries, as well as full entrées. It's especially appealing on a rainy day to sip a cup of coffee or a glass of wine here to the accompaniment of a good novel. The happy hour bar downstairs, Escadabaixo, is the town's most popular hangout for wealthier *ouropretanos* and tourists. [$] *Average main: R$44* ✉ *Rua Conde de Bobadela 122, Centro* ☎ *031/3551–5097.*

ELIZABETH BISHOP

One of America's greatest poets, U.S. poet laureate Elizabeth Bishop (1911–79) lived in Ouro Preto for many years with her female partner Lota de Macedo Soares. She bought a house here in 1965 and called it Casa da Mariana, a tribute to the poet Marianne Moore. Ouro Preto is the subject of a number of Bishop's paintings and poems.

$$$ BRAZILIAN Fodor's Choice ★ 🍴 **Casa do Ouvidor.** A large and welcoming restaurant above a jewelry store, Casa do Ouvidor has won numerous awards for regional dishes such as tutu, feijão tropeiro, and frango com quiabo. The portions are generous. Since the restaurant's opening in 1972, it has hosted former President of France François Mitterand, actor Richard Dreyfuss, diplomat Henry Kissinger, author John Updike, and many other luminaries. **■ TIP→ Try to sit by the windows, which look out on the street below.** [$] *Average main: R$50* ✉ *Rua Conde de Bobadela 42, Centro* ☎ *031/3551–2141* 🌐 *www.casadoouvidor.com.br.*

$$$ BRAZILIAN 🍴 **Chafariz.** The best place for a mineiran buffet in Ouro Preto is in this vividly decorated eatery near the Casa dos Contos. The large dining room has beautiful furniture designed by Oscar Niemeyer, and the cupboards are decorated with antiques and candles. On the gorgeous balcony in the back you can sip *jaboticaba* (a purple grapelike fruit) drinks as you peruse the countryside. [$] *Average main: R$50* ✉ *Rua São José 167, Centro* ☎ *031/3551–2828* ⏲ *No dinner.*

$$$$ PIZZA FAMILY 🍴 **O Passo Pizza Jazz.** An excellent restaurant just oozing with charm, O Passo serves local meat and seafood dishes in addition to pizza. Large bay windows, subtle colors, and candlelight—as well as jazz and Brazilian popular music (MPB) played live on weekends—create a sophisticated but accessible atmosphere that attracts young couples and families. Among the many tantalizing pizzas worth a try, the *calabresa with azeitona* (wafer thin slices of cured pork sausage sprinkled with black olives) and the *quatro funghi* (with four types of mushrooms) stand out. [$] *Average main: R$80* ✉ *Rua São José 56, Centro* ☎ *031/3552–5089* ✍ *Reservations essential.*

$$$$ ITALIAN 🍴 **Oro Nero Trattoria.** Couples seeking a hearty meal seek out this trattoria in a beautifully decorated house next to the Sanctuary of the Immaculate Conception. The restaurant serves large pasta portions, often flavored with its signature and flawless arrabiata sauce; another good choice is the polenta with a sweet-and-spicy pork-sausage ragout. The wine list showcases Italian vintages. **■ TIP→ Save room for the lush yet light tiramisu: days later, you'll still have pleasant memories of it.** [$] *Average main: R$80* ✉ *Rua Bernardo de Vasconcelos 98, Antônio Dias* ☎ *031/3552–2930* 🌐 *www.trattoriaoronero.com.br* ⏲ *Closed Mon. and Tues.*

$$$$ ✕ **Senhora do Rosário.** Ouro Preto's finest restaurant is in the Solar Nossa
MODERN FRENCH Senhora do Rosário hotel. An elegant atmosphere with formal place
Fodor's Choice settings, attentive service, and soft Brazilian music makes this the ideal
★ spot for a quiet, romantic dinner. The chef, whose menu changes frequently, focuses on Italian and French fare with a mineiran accent: you
might find intriguing, perfectly prepared dishes such as *carne seca* (beef
jerky) risotto with Gorgonzola cheese. The dessert options include *doce
de leite* (caramel), a Minas specialty, as well as international options
like petit gâteau. Argentina, France, Italy, and Brazil itself are among
the nations whose wines are represented on the excellent list. $ *Average
main: R$100* ⊠ *Rua Getúlio Vargas 270, Rosário* ☎ *031/3551–5200*
⊕ *www.hotelsolardorosario.com* ⚘ *Reservations essential.*

WHERE TO STAY
Some families in Ouro Preto rent rooms in their homes, although
usually only during Carnival and Easter, when the city's hotels fill up.
For a list of rooms to rent, contact the Associação de Guias *(⇨ Essentials, above).*

$$ 🏨 **Estalagem das Minas Gerais.** Near a nature preserve and perfect for
B&B/INN those who love a walk in the woods, this lodging has clean, modern
rooms. **Pros:** beautiful setting; rooms in front have wonderful valley
views; chalets good for large groups. **Cons:** away from town center.
$ *Rooms from: R$260* ⊠ *Rod. dos Inconfidentes Km 88, Centro*
☎ *031/3551–2122* ⬎ *114 rooms, 32 chalets* ⦿| *Breakfast.*

$ 🏨 **Grande Hotel de Ouro Preto.** Designed by the famous architect Oscar
HOTEL Niemeyer and Ouro Preto's premier modernist structure, the Grande
FAMILY is, as its name suggests, one of the city's largest hotels by overall size.
Pros: central location; historic building. **Cons:** steep hill from street level
to hotel; late-night music from neighboring restaurants can be heard
in some rooms. $ *Rooms from: R$230* ⊠ *Rua Senador Rocha Lagoa
162, Centro* ☎ *031/3551–1488* ⊕ *www.grandehotelouropreto.com.br*
⬎ *35 rooms* ⦿| *Breakfast.*

$ 🏨 **Hotel Colonial.** Close to the main square, this is a typical mid-range
B&B/INN inn with basic rooms. **Pros:** clean rooms; low price; hearty breakfast;
room with loft sleeps five. **Cons:** small; no frills. $ *Rooms from: R$140*
⊠ *Rua Padre Camilo Veloso 26, Centro* ☎ *031/3551–3133* ⬎ *18 rooms*
⦿| *Breakfast.*

$ 🏨 **Luxor Ouro Preto Pousada.** With dark wooden floors, antique furnish-
B&B/INN ings, and stone walls dating back two centuries, this friendly hotel
has the feeling of a rustic 19th-century lodge. **Pros:** gorgeous hotel;
unparalleled service; rooms have incredible city views. **Cons:** potentially
romantic restaurant often packed with hotel guests. $ *Rooms from:
R$190* ⊠ *Rua Dr. Alfredo Baeta 16, Antônio Dias* ☎ *031/3551–2244*
⊕ *www.luxorhoteis.com.br* ⬎ *19 rooms* ⦿| *Breakfast.*

$$ 🏨 **Pousada Clássica.** Near the main churches and museums and the prime
HOTEL shopping area, this pousada occupies an elegant house. **Pros:** spectacu-
lar city view from balconies; stylish reception area and breakfast room.
Cons: boring room decor and furniture; noise from Rua Direita's bars;
quietest rooms have lesser views. $ *Rooms from: R$326* ⊠ *Rua Conde
de Bobadela 96, Centro* ☎ *031/3551–3663* ⊕ *www.pousadaclassica.
com.br* ⬎ *25 rooms, 2 suites* ⦿| *Breakfast.*

7

$$ **Pousada do Mondego.** This intimate hotel in a 1747 merchant's man-
HOTEL sion sits next to the Igreja de São Francisco de Assis and opposite
Fodor's Choice the soapstone market. **Pros:** good mix of modern amenities (marble
★ bathrooms, TVs) and 18th-century charm. **Cons:** low ceilings in some
areas may annoy tall guests. $ *Rooms from: R$350* ⊠ *Largo de Coim-
bra 38, Centro* ☎ *031/3551-2040, 021/2287-1592 reservations in
Rio* ⊕ *www.roteirosdecharme.com.br/hotel.php?hotel=6* ⇨ *24 rooms*
|○| *Breakfast.*

$$ **Pousada Minas Gerais.** The wonderful Pousada Minas Gerais occupies
HOTEL a new building that replicates Ouro Preto's colonial exteriors. **Pros:** safe,
FAMILY quiet street; family friendly; good business facilities; off-street parking area. **Cons:** location is away from churches and restaurants; no
leisure area or swimming pool. $ *Rooms from: R$270* ⊠ *Rua Xavier
da Veiga 303, Centro* ☎ *031/3551-5506* ⊕ *www.pousadaminasgerais.
com.br* ⇨ *18 rooms* |○| *Breakfast.*

$ **Pouso com Arte.** The hospitality at this family-run bed-and-breakfast
B&B/INN will make you feel like you're visiting a friend's house. **Pros:** traditional
mineiran decor; great breakfast; central location. **Cons:** few amenities;
no room service. $ *Rooms from: R$200* ⊠ *Rua das Mercês 45, Centro*
☎ *031/3552-2671* ⇨ *5 rooms* |○| *Breakfast.*

$$$ **Solar Nossa Senhora do Rosário.** An intimate atmosphere and the world-
HOTEL class Senhora do Rosário restaurant are among this hotel's draws. **Pros:**
Fodor's Choice very comfortable rooms; excellent mineiran breakfast. **Cons:** service can
★ be slow and isn't always friendly. $ *Rooms from: R$450* ⊠ *Rua Getúlio
Vargas 270, Rosário* ☎ *031/3551-5200* ⊕ *www.hotelsolardorosario.
com.br* ⇨ *41 rooms* |○| *Breakfast.*

NIGHTLIFE AND THE ARTS
NIGHTLIFE
Fodor's Choice **Acaso 85 Scotch Bar e Restaurante.** With its high ceilings, stone walls, 18th-
★ century fountain, and gorgeous garden with tropical plants, Acaso 85 is
an impressive stop for an evening cocktail, though the food and service
can be hit or miss. ⊠ *Largo do Rosário 85, Rosário* ☎ *031/3551-2397*
⊕ *www.acaso85.com.br* ⊗ *Closed Mon.*

À Direita. From midafternoon until midnight this bar serves delicious
porções (appetizers) you can wash down with one of the many tasty
beers on offer. The service here is unfailingly friendly. ⊠ *Rua Direita
75, Centro* ☎ *031/3551-6844.*

THE ARTS
Fundação de Artes de Ouro Preto. FAOP, the local arts foundation, hosts
art and photographic exhibitions throughout the year. ⊠ *Rua Alvarenga
794, Cabeças* ☎ *031/3551-2014* ⊕ *www.faop.mg.gov.br.*

SHOPPING
HANDICRAFTS
There are numerous handicrafts stores on Praça Tiradentes and its sur-
rounding streets.

Bié. This shop on Praça Professor Amadeu Barbosa specializes in sculp-
ture. ⊠ *Praça Professor Amadeu Barbosa 129* ☎ *031/3551-2309.*

Caixa de Luz. This shop sells photographs of Ouro Preto, cosmetics of traditional Brazilian perfumeries, and fine objects and books. ⊠ *Rua Getúlio Vargas, 269, Rosário* ☎ *031/3552–2262* ☉ *Closed Sun.*

Fodor's Choice **Gomides.** This shop in the Barra neighborhood carries unique sculptures.
★ ⊠ *Beco da Mãe Chica 29, Barra* ☎ *031/3551–2511.*

Handicrafts Fair. At the daily handicrafts fair in front of the Igreja de São Francisco de Assis, vendors sell soapstone and wood carvings, paintings, and other objects. ⊠ *Largo de Coimbra s/n, Centro.*

JEWELRY

Ouro Preto has a reputation for the best selection and prices in Brazil, but keep in mind that gems vary widely in quality and value. Don't buy them on the streets, and be wary about buying them from smaller shops. Gemstones can be fakes—glass colored to look like gemstones—and if real they're apt to be overpriced. Do your research, and get references for a jeweler before you buy.

Know that gold topaz, smoky topaz, and some other types of "topaz" are really quartz, and that it's difficult to tell the difference between well-crafted synthetic lookalikes and the real deal. Imperial topaz, sometimes called precious topaz, comes in shades of pink and tangerine. In general, the clearer the stone, the better the quality. Imperial topaz can, at first glance, easily be confused with citrine quartz, found elsewhere in Brazil, but is harder, denser, and more brilliant.

Brasil Gemas. Here you can visit the stone-cutting and -setting workshop. ⊠ *Praça Tiradentes 74* ☎ *031/3551–4448.*

Ita Gemas. This is one of the best gem shops in town, especially for the rare imperial topaz. ⊠ *Rua Conde de Bobadela 40, Centro* ☎ *031/3551–4895.*

SIDE TRIP TO MARIANA

11 km (7 miles) east of Ouro Preto, 110 km (68 miles) southeast of Belo Horizonte.

The oldest city in Minas Gerais (founded in 1696) is also the birthplace of Aleijadinho's favorite painter, Manuel da Costa Ataíde. Mariana, like Ouro Preto, has preserved much of the appearance of an 18th-century gold-mining town. Its three principal churches showcase examples of the art of Ataíde, who intertwined sensual romanticism with religious themes. The faces of his saints and other figures often have mulatto features, reflecting the composition of the area's population at the time. Today Mariana is most visited for the weekly organ concerts at its cathedral.

GETTING HERE AND AROUND

The most enjoyable way to get to Mariana is by train. From Friday to Sunday, vintage trains leave from Ouro Preto train station. Make sure to sit on the right-hand side to get the best views, including one (halfway to Mariana) of a waterfall. One train departs from Ouro Preto in the morning and another in the afternoon, and two trains return from Mariana in the afternoon. The cost for the 30-minute ride is R$50 each way. Credit cards are accepted at the ticket office, and tickets can be purchased with cash on board. (The credit-card system here has been known to fail, so it's advisable to have sufficient cash just in case.) Buses from Ouro Preto to Mariana depart every 30 minutes (R$3; 30 minutes). If you're driving, take BR 040 south and BR 356 (it becomes MG 262) east to Ouro Preto and continue 11 km (7 miles) to Mariana (30 minutes).

EN ROUTE

Mina de Ouro de Passagem. Between Ouro Preto and Mariana lies Brazil's oldest gold mine. During the gold rush thousands of slaves perished at Mina de Ouro de Passagem because of its dangerous, backbreaking conditions. Although the mine is no longer in operation, you can ride an old mining car through 11 km (7 miles) of tunnels and see exposed quartz, graphite, and black tourmaline. Buses travel here from Ouro Preto (catch them beside the Escola de Minas) and cost about R$3; a taxi ride costs about R$30. ⊠ *Road to Mariana, 4 km (3 miles) east of Ouro Preto* ☎ *031/3557–5001* ⊕ *www.minasdapassagem.com.br* ⊠ *R$25* ☉ *Mon. and Tues. 9–5, Wed.–Sun. 9–5:30.*

EXPLORING

Catedral Basílica da Sé. The cathedral, completed in 1760, contains paintings by Ataíde, but it's best known for its 1701 German organ, built by Arp Schnitger. Transported by mule from Rio de Janeiro in 1720, the instrument was a gift from the Portuguese court to the first diocese in Brazil. This is the only Schnitger organ outside Europe, and one of the best preserved in the world. Concerts take place on Fridays at 11 am and Sundays at 12:15 pm. ■**TIP**→ **To get a place near the organ, try to arrive at least 30 minutes early.** ⊠ *Praça Cláudio Manoel s/n* ☎ *031/3557–1216* ⊠ *R$2 donation, R$15 concerts* ☉ *Tues.–Sun. 8–noon and 2–6:30.*

Fodor's Choice
★

Igreja da Nossa Senhora do Carmo (*Our Lady of Carmel Church*). Our Lady of Carmel Church, with works by Ataíde and Aleijadinho, is noteworthy for its impressive facade and sculpted soapstone designs. Ataíde is buried at the rear of the church, built in the late 1700s. A fire in 1999 during renovation nearly destroyed the site, sparing only the rococo-style altar. ⊠ *Praça Minas Gerais* ☎ *031/3558–1979* ⊕ *www. mariana.mg.gov.br* ☉ *Tues.–Sun. 9–noon and 1–4.*

Igreja de São Francisco de Assis (*Church of St. Francis of Assisi*). Although the 1793 Igreja de São Francisco de Assis has soapstone pulpits and altars by Aleijadinho, its most impressive works are the sacristy's ceiling panels, which were painted by Ataíde. They depict, in somber tones, the life and death of St. Francis of Assisi and are considered by many to be the artist's masterpiece. Sadly, they've been damaged by termites and water. ⊠ *Praça Minas Gerais* ☎ *031/3557–1023* ⊠ *R$2* ☉ *Tues.– Sun. 8–noon and 1–4.*

Museu Arquidiocesano de Arte Sacra de Mariana (Museu Aleijadinho). Wood and soapstone carvings by Aleijadinho and paintings by Ataíde are among the noteworthy items on exhibit at the Archdiocesan Museum of Sacred Art, also known as the Aleijadinho Museum. Located behind the Catedral Basílica da Sé in a well-composed rococo structure, the museum claims to have the state's largest collection of baroque painting and sculpture. ⊠ *Rua Frei Durão 49* ☎ *031/3557–2581* ⊠ *R$5* ☉ *Tues.–Sun. 8:30–noon and 1:30–5.*

**EN
ROUTE**

Basílica Bom Jesus do Matosinho. Dominating the small Gold Town of Congonhas do Campo is Aleijadinho's crowning effort, the hilltop pilgrimage church Basílica Bom Jesus do Matosinho. Built in 1757, it's the focus of great processions during Holy Week. At the churchyard entrance are Aleijadinho's 12 life-size Old Testament prophets carved in soapstone, one of the greatest works of art from the baroque period. The prophets appear caught in movement, and every facial expression is unforgettable. Leading up to the church on the sloping hillside are six chapels, each containing a scene of the stations of the cross. The 66 figures in this remarkable procession were carved in cedar by Aleijadinho and painted by Manuel da Costa Ataíde and Francisco Xavier Carneiro. ■ **TIP→** Congonhas is about 50 km (31 miles) west of Mariana; take BR 356 to MG 440 to MG 030, then go north on BR 040. This is also a fairly easy trip by bus or car from Belo Horizonte (94 km/58 miles) or Tiradentes (130 km/81 miles). ⊠ *Praça da Basílica 180, Congonhas do Campo* ☎ *031/3731–1591* 🎫 *Free* ⊙ *Tues.–Sun. 8–6.*

TIRADENTES

210 km (130 miles) southwest of Belo Horizonte.

Probably the best historic city to visit after Ouro Preto and Diamantina, Tiradentes was the birthplace of a martyr who gave the city its name (it was formerly called São José del Rei) and retains much of its 18th-century charm. Life in this small town—nine streets with eight churches set against the backdrop of the Serra de São José—moves slowly. About two-dozen shops selling excellent handicrafts line Rua Direita in the town center. At the tourist office Secretaria de Turismo de Tiradentes, you can learn about horseback and hiking trips in the area.

7

GETTING HERE AND AROUND

From Belo Horizonte there are six buses every day. You must first travel to São João del Rei on the Viação Sandra bus line (R$35; 3½ hours), then to Tiradentes on a Vale do Ouro bus. From São João del Rei, buses run every 1½ hours, and the trip costs about R$3.

To reach Tiradentes from Belo by car, take BR 040 south (Congonhas do Campo, with its Igreja Bom Jesus do Matosinho, is on this route) and then BR 265 west. The drive takes approximately 3½ hours.

ESSENTIALS

Bus Contacts Rodoviária (Terminal Turístico) ⊠ *Praça Silva Jardim, near Igreja São Francisco de Paula* ☎ *032/3355–1100.* **Viação Vale do Ouro** ☎ *032/3371–5119, 031/3557–9200.* **Viação Sandra** ☎ *031/3201–2927.*

Visitor and Tour Information Secretaria de Turismo de Tiradentes ⊠ *Rua Resende Costa 71* ☎ *032/3355–1212* ⊙ *Daily 8–5.*

EXPLORING

Matriz de Santo Antônio. A celebration of baroque architecture, the Church of Santo Antônio is the one not to miss in Tiradentes. Built in 1710, it contains well-preserved gilded carvings of saints, cherubs, and biblical scenes. The soapstone frontispiece is attributed to Aleijadinho. ■ **TIP→** Organ concerts take place here on Friday evenings; if you can time your visit to attend one, by all means do so. ⊠ *Rua Padre Toledo s/n*

📞 *032/3355–1212* 💳 *R$2; concerts R$15* 🕐 *Daily 9–5, concerts Fri. 8:30 pm.*

WHERE TO EAT

$$
BRAZILIAN

✕ **Estalagem do Sabor.** Patrons of the Estalagem rave about the feijão tropeiro and frango ao molho pardo, just two of the Brazilian dishes prepared by chef Beth. Although the restaurant is small, the atmosphere is elegant. Light music and an attentive staff make this an appealing place to dine. 💲 *Average main: R$45* ✉ *Rua Ministro Gabriel Passos 280, Centro* 📞 *032/3355–1144* 💳 *No credit cards* 🕐 *No dinner on Sun.*

$$$$
ECLECTIC

✕ **Tragaluz.** This combined store, coffee shop, and restaurant serves unusual dishes such as jaboticaba ice cream. Caetano Veloso, Brazil's top musical export, once popped in to play for an hour and eat the amazing chorizo beef. The gnocchi, Argentine meat, and *frango de Angola* (marinated chicken), are all worth a try, as is, for dessert, the *goiabada frita* (fried goiaba fruit jam). Reservations are essential on weekends. 💲 *Average main: R$75* ✉ *Rua Direita 52* 📞 *032/3355–1424, 032/9968–4837* 🌐 *www.tragaluztiradentes.com* 🕐 *Closed Tues.*

$$
BRAZILIAN
FAMILY
Fodor's Choice
★

✕ **Viradas do Largo.** One of Brazil's best restaurants for comida mineira, the Viradas do Largo (also known as Restaurante da Beth) serves dishes such as chicken with *ora pro nobis* (a Brazilian cabbage) and feijão tropeiro with pork chops. Some of the ingredients, such as the *borecole* (kale), are cultivated in the restaurant's backyard. The portions are generous, enough for three or four people, but you can ask for a half order of any dish. The restaurant is also a market, with typical arts and crafts from Minas Gerais. Reservations are essential on weekends. 💲 *Average main: R$40* ✉ *Rua do Moinho 11* 📞 *032/3355–1111, 032/3355–1110.*

WHERE TO STAY

$$
B&B/INN

🏨 **Pousada Três Portas.** Locally made furniture and artworks decorate this pousada inside an adapted colonial house in Tiradentes's historic center. **Pros:** central location; clean, modern rooms. **Cons:** prices jump dramatically on weekends. 💲 *Rooms from: R$330* ✉ *Rua Direita 280A* 📞 *032/3355–1444* 🌐 *www.pousadatresportas.com.br* 🛏 *8 rooms, 1 suite* 🍴 *Breakfast.*

$
B&B/INN

🏨 **Pouso Alforria.** The many return guests to Alforria appreciate its peaceful location and fabulous view of the São José Mountains. **Pros:** light-filled rooms; modern bathrooms; faultless service; that view. **Cons:** with so few rooms, it's necessary to make reservations well ahead of time. 💲 *Rooms from: R$280* ✉ *Rua Custódio Gomes 286* 📞 *032/3355–1536* 🌐 *www.pousoalforria.com.br* 🛏 *8 rooms* 🍴 *Breakfast.*

SMOKING MARY

Maria Fumaça (Smoking Mary), a little red steam train in operation since the 19th century, is an authentic and fun way to get from São João del Rei to Tiradentes. The 13-km (8-mile) ride goes up the valley and through the oldest mining area in the state in 35 minutes (round-trip R$25, one-way R$15; twice daily from Friday to Sunday and on holidays). The train leaves from São João del Rei's Estação Ferroviária (Av. Hermilio Alves); tickets do not need to be bought in advance. The train leaves São João del Rei at 10 am and 3 pm and returns from Tiradentes at 1 pm and 5 pm.

CLOSE UP

Brazilian Baroque

When gold was discovered in Minas Gerais in the 17th century, the Portuguese, to ensure their control of the mining industry, exiled the traditional religious orders, which led to the formation of third orders. Attempts by these lay brothers to build churches based on European models resulted in improvisations (they had little experience with or guidance on such matters) and, hence, a uniquely Brazilian style of baroque that extended into the early 19th century. Many churches from this period have simple exteriors that belie interiors whose gold-leaf-encrusted carvings are so intricate they seem like filigree.

As the gold supply diminished, facades became more elaborate—with more sophisticated lines, elegant curves, and large round towers—and their interiors less so, as murals were used more than carvings and gold leaf. Many sculptures were carved from wood or soapstone. Today Minas Gerais has the largest concentration of baroque architecture and art of any state in Brazil. You can see several outstanding examples of baroque architecture, many of them attributed to the legendary Aleijadinho, in Ouro Preto (where there are 13 such churches) and the other Gold Towns of Minas: Mariana, Tiradentes, and Congonhas.

7

$$$$ HOTEL Fodor's Choice ★ 🏨 **Solar da Ponte.** In every respect—from the stunning antiques to the comfortable beds to the elegant place settings—this inn is a faithful example of regional style. **Pros:** breakfast and afternoon tea (included in the rate) are served in the dining room, overlooking well-tended gardens. **Cons:** two-night minimum stay in high season. [$] *Rooms from: R$615* ✉ *Praça das Mercês s/n* ☎ *032/3355–1255* 🌐 *www.solardaponte.com.br* 🛏 *18 rooms* 🍴 *Breakfast.*

THE ARTS

Centro Cultural Yves Alves. Cultural life in Tiradentes revolves around this arts center that hosts theatrical performances, films, concerts, and art exhibitions. ✉ *Rua Direita 168* ☎ *032/3355–1503.*

Fodor's Choice ★ **Theatro da Villa.** A triple-threat bar, restaurant, and late-night entertainment venue, the Theatro da Villa occupies an 1850 theater in the historic center of Tiradentes. On weekends, musical shows accompany dinner, whose preparation is overseen (all week) by chef Carlos Eduardo, a disciple of the slow-food movement. The wine list is excellent, and the service, directed by the chef's twin brother, Carlos Fernando, is impeccable. ✉ *Rua Padre Toledo 157* ☎ *032/3355–1275* 🌐 *www.theatrodavilla.com.br.*

SHOPPING

Local artwork is the biggest draw here, with painters and sculptors famous throughout Brazil working in their gallerylike studios. The main street for galleries and antiques shops is Rua Direita.

Artstones. Although not as upscale as the stores in Ouro Preto, Artstones carries imperial topazes, emeralds, quartz, and tourmalines and has some finished jewelry. ⊠ *Rua Ministro Gabriel Passos 22* ☎ *032/3355-1730.*

Bichinho. The small, quiet village of Bichinho is recognized in the region for the quality of its arts and crafts. It's a good option for a day trip. ⊠ *8 km/5 miles northeast of Tiradentes* ⊕ *www.bichinho.net.*

MINAS'S PARKS

Less than three hours from Belo Horizonte are some wild, wonderful national parks—worth a day or an overnight trip if you have the time. Though it's not a national park, at the Parque Natural do Caraça you can stay at a lovely monastery and have monks cook for you, while during the day you hike the peaks surrounding it. The parks only take cash, so be sure to bring enough with you.

PARQUE NATURAL DO CARAÇA

123 km (76 miles) southeast of Belo Horizonte.

GETTING HERE AND AROUND

From Belo Horizonte you can either drive or take a bus to Santa Barbara. Pássaro Verde buses (R$30) serve Santa Barbara (2½ hours) a dozen or so times daily; from there it's a 25-minute taxi ride (R$70) to the park. If you're driving from Belo Horizonte, take BR 262 to Santa Barbara (follow signs for Vitória); at Barão de Cocais, continue on BR 262 toward Santa Barbara for 5 km (3 miles) more, until you see a sign on your right for Caraça. The road here leads about 20 km (12 miles) to the park entrance.

ESSENTIALS

Bus Contact Viação Pássaro Verde ⊠ *Rua Itapetinga 200* ☎ *031/3073-7000* ⊕ *www.passaroverde.com.br.*

EXPLORING

FAMILY

Fodor'sChoice

★

Parque Natural do Caraça. Waterfalls, natural pools, and caves—among them Gruta do Centenário, one of the world's largest quartzite caves—fill this rugged park whose name means "big face," in homage to its main mountain. The park's most famous inhabitant is the *lobo guará,* a beautiful orange wolf threatened by extinction. Historic buildings here include an 18th-century convent and the Igreja de Nossa Senhora Mãe dos Homens (Church of Our Lady, Mother of Men), built at the end of the 19th century. The church's French stained-glass windows, rare organ, baroque altars, and painting of the Last Supper by Ataíde make it well worth a stop. There was once a seminary here as well, but it caught fire in 1968. After the accident, the building was transformed into an inn and small museum.

Guided tours—walking, spelunking, and other activities—can be arranged at the administration office, run by Catholic priests, once you arrive. ■TIP➜ **You can hike in the lower elevations on your own, but to visit the tallest peaks, some of which rise to about 6,000 feet,**

you're required to go with a guide. The park's website has information about guides. ☎ *031/3837–2698* 🌐 *www.santuariodocaraca.com.br* 🎟 *R$5 per person, guided tours extra* 🕓 *Daily 8–5; 7 am–9 pm for inn guests.*

WHERE TO STAY

$ B&B/INN Fodor'sChoice ★ 🏨 **Pousada do Caraça.** The park's hotel and restaurant are in an old school that was destroyed in a 1968 fire. **Pros:** delicious food; generous breakfasts; some rooms can accommodate five people. **Cons:** tight meal schedule; hotel often books large groups, so reservations need to be made at least three weeks in advance. [$] *Rooms from: R$180* ✉ *Km 25, Parque Natural do Caraça* ☎ *031/3837–2698* 🌐 *www.santuariodocaraca.com.br* 🛏 *51 rooms* 🍴 *All meals.*

> **THE LEGEND OF CARAÇA**
>
> There are many legends about the founder of what's now the Parque Natural do Caraça, Carlos Mendonça. The most famous is that he belonged to a prominent Jesuit family in 18th-century Portugal, at a time when the royal family was persecuting Jesuits. In 1758 there was an assassination attempt against King D. Jose. When suspicion fell on his family, Carlos Mendonça fled to Brazil and joined the Franciscan Order, using the name Father Lourenço. He later founded the sanctuary of Caraça.

PARQUE NACIONAL DA SERRA DA CANASTRA

320 km (199 miles) southwest of Belo Horizonte.

GETTING HERE AND AROUND

From Belo Horizonte take the MG 050 southwest to Piumhi, then take the road to São Roque de Minas. The entrance to the park is 35 km (21 miles) west of São Roque de Minas (320 km from Belo Horizonte). By bus, take the Gardenia line from Belo to Piumhi—there are six buses daily (R$50; 5 hours)—then take the Transunião bus to São Roque de Minas (1½ hours). Canastra Aventura, an adventure-tour company, leads quad bike tours through the park.

ESSENTIALS

Bus Contact Viação Gardênia ✉ *Rodoviaria de Piumhi* ☎ *037/3371–1310* 🌐 *www.expressogardenia.com.br.*

Tour Information Canastra Aventura ☎ *035/9840–8553* 🌐 *canastraaventura.com.br.*

EXPLORING

Parque Nacional da Serra do Canastra. Serra do Canastra National Park was created to preserve the springs of Rio São Francisco, one of the most important rivers in South America, which cuts through five Brazilian states. Its main attractions are its waterfalls, including the 610-foot Casca D'Anta. The park is in the city of São Roque de Minas, almost to Minas Gerais's border with São Paulo State. The Brazilian Institute of the Environment (IBAMA) manages the park from its headquarters in São Roque de Minas. ✉ *Off road to São Roque de Minas* ☎ *037/3433–1195 for IBAMA* 🎟 *R$6.50 Brazilians, R$13 foreigners* 🕓 *Daily 8–6.*

7

THE MINERAL SPA TOWNS

Known for the curative properties of their natural springs, a collection of mineral-spa towns in southern Minas Gerais forms the Circuito das Águas (Water Circuit). For more than a century people have flocked to these mystical towns, bathing in the pristine water parks and drinking from the bubbling fountains. Today the towns are especially popular among older, wealthier Brazilians.

⚠ Despite the purported curative properties of the mineral waters in the spa towns, don't drink too much when you first arrive unless you want to cleanse your system thoroughly.

SÃO LOURENÇO

387 km (240 miles) south of Belo Horizonte.

This most modern of the mineral-spa towns is a good base from which to visit the other Circuito das Águas communities. From here taxis and tour operators happily negotiate a day rate for the circuit, usually around R$50.

GETTING HERE AND AROUND

From Belo Horizonte, there are three buses a day to São Lourenço. The journey takes roughly seven hours and costs about R$100. The bus line is Gardênia. If you're driving, take BR 381 south of Belo Horizonte. You can also take BR 040 south to BR 267 west. For R$80 you can take a taxi from São Lourenço to Caxambu (26 km/16 miles) or São Tomé das Letras R$150 (80 km/50 miles).

ESSENTIALS

Bus Contacts Viação Gardênia ☎ *0300/313–2020, 031/3495–1010, 035/3423–3272* ⊕ *www.expressogardenia.com.br.* **Rodoviária-São Lourenço** ✉ *Rua Manoel Carlos 130, Centro* ☎ *035/3332–4476.*

EXPLORING

Parque das Águas São Lourenço. São Lourenço's Water Park includes a picturesque lake with art deco pavilions, fountains, and gorgeous landscaping. The center of activity is its *balneário,* a hydrotherapy spa where you can immerse yourself in bubbling mineral baths and marble surroundings. There are separate bath and sauna facilities for men and women, and you can also get a massage at an extra cost. ✉ *Praça Brasil s/n* ☎ *035/3332–3066* 🗊 *R$5* ☉ *Park daily 8–6; Balneário Tues. 8–noon, Wed.–Sat. 8–noon and 2–4:50, Sun. 8:30–noon.*

Templo da Eubiose. If your experience at the Parque das Águas fails to rid you of all ailments, head to the Templo da Eubiose, the temple of a spiritual organization dedicated to wisdom and perfection through yoga. The Eubiose, a group of New Age spiritualists, similar to European Theosophists, believe in living in harmony with nature. They also believe this will be the only place to survive the end of the world. ✉ *Praça da Vitória s/n* ☎ *035/3332–6477* ⊕ *www.eubiose.org.br* 🗊 *Donations accepted* ☉ *Weekends 2–4.*

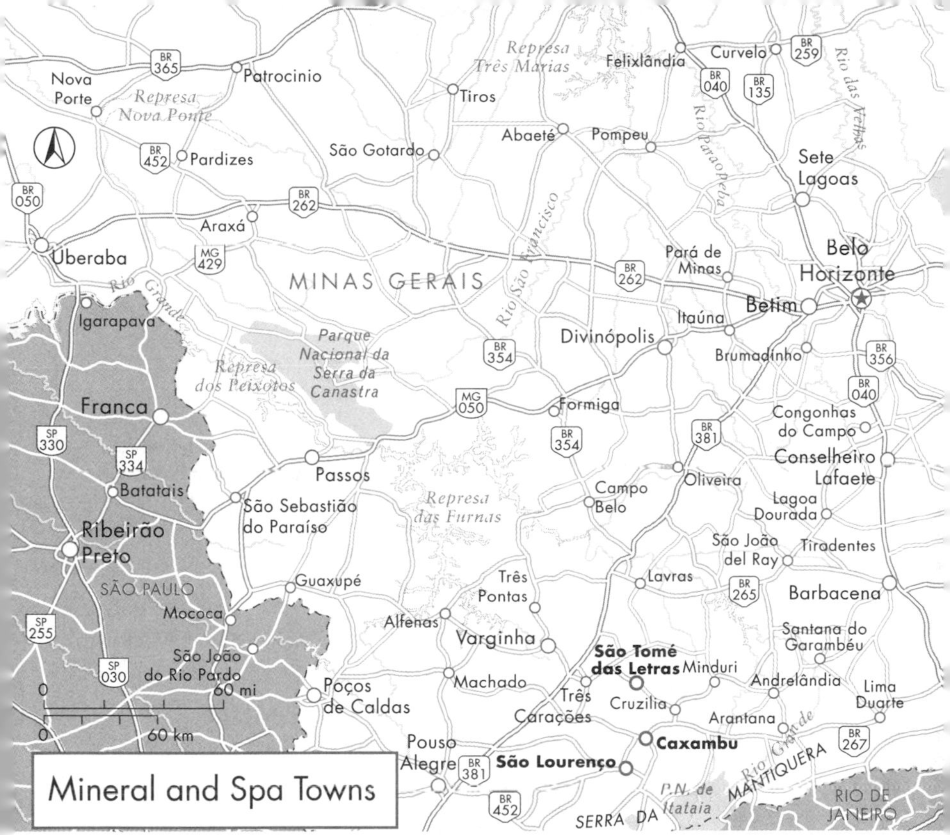

Mineral and Spa Towns

WHERE TO STAY

$$ ALL-INCLUSIVE FAMILY

🏨 **Emboabas Hotel.** This gracious fazenda is more like a private estate than a rural farm. **Pros:** beautiful farm with nice rooms; occasional performances in the fazenda's theater. **Cons:** about a half-hour walk from the Parque das Águas. [$] *Rooms from: R$335* ✉ *Alameda Jorge Amado 350, Solar dos Lagos* ☎ *035/3332–4600* 🌐 *www.emboabashotel.com.br* 🛏 *60 rooms* 🍴 *All-inclusive.*

$$ ALL-INCLUSIVE FAMILY

🏨 **Hotel Brasil.** This luxury hotel just across from the Parque das Águas has its own pools, fountains, and mineral waters, as well as games rooms and tennis courts. **Pros:** excellent facilities; good prix-fixe regional cuisine. **Cons:** rooms look dated and lack sophistication and charm. [$] *Rooms from: R$280* ✉ *Praça Duque de Caxias, Alameda João Lage 87* ☎ *035/3332–2000* 🌐 *www.hotelbrasil.com.br* 🛏 *150 rooms* 🍴 *All-inclusive.*

$$ RESORT FAMILY

🏨 **Hotel Fazenda Vista Alegre.** The many activities and the low price of accommodations compensate for the lack of proximity to the water park. **Pros:** lots of facilities; good range of rooms. **Cons:** around 4 km (3 miles) from the water park. [$] *Rooms from: R$250* ✉ *Estrada São Lourenço-Soledade, Km 1* ☎ *035/3331–2920* 🌐 *www.hfvistaalegre.com.br* 🛏 *9 chalets, 35 suites* 🍴 *All meals.*

CAXAMBU

30 km (19 miles) northeast of São Lourenço.

A 19th-century town once frequented by Brazilian royalty, Caxambu remains a favorite getaway for wealthy and retired *cariocas* (residents of Rio). Although most people spend their time here relaxing in bathhouses and drinking curative waters, you can also browse in the markets where local sweets are sold or take a horse-and-buggy ride to a fazenda.

THE MINEIRAN BADEN-BADEN

While soaking in curative waters was a huge fad in early 19th-century Europe, Brazilians did not catch on until Princess Isabel came to partake of the waters in 1868 to find a cure for infertility. The Caxambu Water Company was founded in 1886, and other spa towns sprang up rapidly to form what is now one of the most extensive natural-spa regions in the world.

GETTING HERE AND AROUND

Gardênia buses connect Belo Horizonte with Caxambu twice daily (7 hours; R$95). Caxambu is south of BH off BR 381, parts of which are under construction. As an alternative, you can take BR 040 south to BR 267 west. A taxi between São Lourenço and Caxambu runs about R$80.

ESSENTIALS

Bus Contacts Viação Gardênia ☎ *031/3491–3300, 031/3495–1010, 035/3231–3844.* **Rodoviária** ✉ *Praça Cônego José de Castilho Moreira s/n.*

Taxi Contact Ponto de Táxi ☎ *035/3341–1730.*

Visitor and Tour Information Caxambu Tourist Desk ✉ *Rua João Carlos 100* ☎ *035/3341–1298* ⊕ *www.caxambu.mg.gov.br* ⊗ *Weekdays 8–6.*

EXPLORING

Cristo Redentor. A chairlift (daily 9–5; R$10) accessed near the bus station heads to the peak of the Cristo Redentor, a smaller version of the one in Rio. The summit has a small restaurant and an impressive city view. ☎ *035/9983–2223.*

Horse-and-buggy rides. A delightful way to explore the streets of Caxambu, as well as old farms in the surrounding area, is by horse and buggy. Rides are arranged on a first-come, first-served basis near the entrance to Parque das Águas. ☎ *035/3332–1936* 🎫 *R$10–R$45.*

Igreja Santa Isabel da Hungria. After suffering from infertility for many years, in 1868 Princess Isabel, daughter of Dom Pedro II, took to the springs of the Parque das Águas; convinced that they restored her fertility, she built the Church of Saint Elizabeth of Hungary overlooking them. She first gave birth to a stillborn baby, but ultimately bore three boys. ✉ *Rua Princesa Isabel s/n* ☎ *035/3341–1582* 🎫 *Donations accepted* ⊗ *Daily 8–11 am.*

Fodor's Choice ★ **Parque das Águas.** Towering trees, shimmering ponds, and fountains containing various minerals—each believed to cure a different ailment—fill the Parque das Águas. Lavish pavilions protect the springs, and the balneário, a beautiful Turkish-style bathhouse, offers saunas and massages.

Hundreds of thousands of liters of mineral water are bottled here daily and distributed throughout Brazil. ✉ *Town center* ☎ *035/3341–3266* ⊕ *www.descubracaxambu.com.br/parquedasaguas* 🎟 *Park R$4, balneário R$12* ⊘ *Park daily 7–6, balneário Tues.–Sun. 2–5.*

WHERE TO EAT AND STAY

$$$
SCANDINAVIAN
Fodor'sChoice
★

✕ **La Forelle.** Caxambu's best restaurant is inside the Hotel Fazenda Vale Formoso. Along with typical Minas Gerais fare, it also serves Danish cuisine. The filet mignon, the salmon, and the shrimp are among the many fine entrées; the specialty of the house is baked trout with potatoes. The fondues here are delicious, and so are the freshly made breads. 🖫 *Average main: R$60* ✉ *Estrada do Vale Formoso, Km 8. Access via BR-267 to Cambuquira (8 km/5 miles on unpaved roads)* ☎ *035/3343–1900, 035/9140–0590* 🍴 *Reservations essential* ⊘ *Open weekends only.*

$$
RESORT
FAMILY

🏨 **Hotel Fazenda Vale Formoso.** A 19th-century coffee plantation transformed into a hotel 13 km (8 miles) from the center of Caxambu, this fazenda sits on more than 740 acres and is surrounded by mountains, lakes, and virgin forest. **Pros:** beautiful environs; walking and riding trails. **Cons:** rooms are comfortable but not luxurious. 🖫 *Rooms from: R$250* ✉ *Estrada do Vale Formoso, Km 8. Access via BR 267 to Cambuquira (8 km/5 miles on unpaved roads)* ☎ *035/3343–1900* ⊕ *www.hotelvaleformoso.com.br* 🛏 *17 rooms* 🍽 *All meals.*

$$$
RESORT
Fodor'sChoice
★

🏨 **Hotel Glória.** Although it's just across from Caxambu's Parque das Águas, this luxury resort has its own rehabilitation pool and sauna as well as numerous sports amenities. **Pros:** gorgeous resort; meals served in an antiques-filled dining room. **Cons:** full-size beds only in luxury rooms. 🖫 *Rooms from: R$400* ✉ *Av. Camilo Soares 590* ☎ *035/3341–9200* ⊕ *www.hotelgloriacaxambu.com.br* 🛏 *145 rooms* 🍽 *All meals.*

SÃO TOMÉ DAS LETRAS

54 km (34 miles) northwest of Caxambu.

With its tales of flying saucers, its eerie stone houses that resemble architecture from outer space, and its 7,500 inhabitants who swear to years of friendship with extraterrestrials, São Tomé das Letras may be one of the oddest towns on earth. In a stunning mountain setting, it attracts mystics, psychics, and flower children who believe they've been spiritually drawn here to await the founding of a new world. Most visitors make São Tomé a day trip from Caxambu, smartly escaping nightfall's visiting UFOs.

GETTING HERE AND AROUND

To reach São Tomé das Letras by bus from Belo Horizonte (eight buses per day), take the Expresso Gardênia to Três Corações; from there, take the Viação Trectur (five buses daily). The entire journey from Belo Horizonte takes 5½ hours and costs about R$90. São Tomé das

Letras can be reached from Belo via BR 381 south or BR 040 south to BR 267 west. A taxi between São Lourenço and São Tomé das Letras costs about R$100.

ESSENTIALS

Bus Contacts Rodoviária ✉ *Av. Tomé Mendes Peixoto s/n* ☎ *035/3237–1530.* **Viação Trectur** ✉ *Av. Tomé Mendes Peixoto s/n* ☎ *035/9901–4889.*

EXPLORING

Caverns and Waterfalls. Just 3 km (2 miles) from São Tomé, two caverns, Carimbado and Chico Taquara, both display hieroglyphs. A short walk from the caves puts you in view of Véu da Noiva and Véu da Eubiose, two powerful waterfalls.

Gruta de São Tomé. Next to the Igreja Matriz is the Gruta de São Tomé, a small cave that, in addition to its shrine to São Tomé, features some of the mysterious inscriptions for which the town is famous.

Igreja Matriz. A center of religious activity and one of the few non-stone buildings in São Tomé, Igreja Matriz is in São Tomé's main square and contains frescoes by Brazilian artist Joaquim José de Natividade. ⊕ *Daily 8–5.*

BRASÍLIA AND THE WEST

Updated
by Mark
Beresford

Visiting Brasília is like leaping into the future, or at least the future as imagined in the early 1960s. Rising from the red earth of the 3,000-foot *Planalto Central* (Central Plateau) is one of the world's most singular cities. Its structures crawl and coil along the flat landscape and then shoot up in shafts of concrete and glass that capture the sun's rays.

All around this icon of modernity nestles the old and present Brazil—the *cerrado* (Brazilian savanna), intersected by sluggish rivers, now the land of soybean and sugarcane plantations and cattle ranches. Nevertheless, those who flock to the rugged yet beautiful west have their eyes on the future. The surreal collection of migrants includes opportunists with get-rich-quick schemes; frontier folk with hopes of a solid, stable tomorrow; mystics and prophets who swear by the region's spiritual energy; and dreamers who are convinced that extraterrestrials visit here regularly. For most earthly visitors, however, the high point of the west is the Pantanal, a flood plain the size of Great Britain that's home to an amazing array of wildlife and the ever-present possibilities for adventure.

ORIENTATION AND PLANNING

GETTING ORIENTED

The states that make up the western part of Brazil cover an area larger than Alaska, extending from the heart of the country—where Brasília is located—to the borders of Paraguay and Bolivia. Brasília, Cuiabá, and Campo Grande (the latter two the capitals of Mato Grosso and Mato Grosso do Sul states), form a massive triangle with roughly equal sides of about 700 miles. These large distances through agricultural areas mean that the best way to explore this region is by air.

BRASÍLIA
Brasília sits on the flat plateau known as the Planalto Central. The capital is actually part of the *Distrito Federal* (Federal District), a 55,000-square-km (21,000-square-mile) administrative region. Also within this district are the *cidades-satélite* (satellite cities), which originated as residential areas for Brasília workers but are now communities in their own right.

THE PANTANAL
Several rivers in the west of Brazil and from neighboring Bolivia and Paraguay run through the sprawling lowlands in the area known as the Pantanal. The region is a vast alluvial plain that covers most of the southwest of the state of Mato Grosso and northwest of Mato Grosso do Sul. The Paraguay River, which runs roughly north–south, is the backbone of the Pantanal, providing the one outlet to the enormous amounts of water that fall during the rainy season. The city of Corumbá, at its southern edge, is about 1,300 km (800 miles) from the Atlantic.

PLANNING

WHEN TO GO

In Brasília and much of the west you can count on clear days and comfortable temperatures from March to July (the mean temperature is 22°C/75°F). The rainy season runs from November to February; in August and September the mercury often rises to 38°C (100°F). When congress adjourns (July, January, and February), the city's pulse slows noticeably, and hotel rooms are easier to come by. It's nearly impossible to get a room during major political events. On the other hand, popular holidays such as New Year's and Carnival are much less hectic than in other cities.

TOP REASONS TO GO

■ **Incredible Architecture:** Brasília's remarkable architectural style is unique even among the world's other planned cities.

■ **Amazing Wildlife:** The wildlife of the Pantanal, the immense wetlands in the heart of South America, is amazing.

■ **Lovely Parks:** The mountains, valleys, and waterfalls of Chapada dos Veadeiros or Chapada dos Guimarães highlands stand out against the plains.

The best season to visit the Pantanal depends on what you intend to do. If the plan is to take photos of wildlife, the ideal time is the dry season running from June to October. As the waters dwindle, animals are concentrated in a smaller area, making them easier to spot. For fishing, the best time to visit is from August to October, before the onset of the rainy season, when most fish move upstream to spawn.

GETTING HERE AND AROUND

Exploring this region is no small feat. Given the great distances, you should fly among the large cities of Brasília, Cuiabá, and Campo Grande. To visit the interior you must either drive, take a bus, or join a tour. If you only have a week or so, it's best to concentrate on Brasília and the surrounding area. The mighty Pantanal and its many natural wonders justify an extended trip.

RESTAURANTS

As the capital, Brasília attracts citizens from throughout the country as well as dignitaries from around the world. You can find a variety of regional cuisines as well as international fare. Brasília also has plenty of "per kilo" restaurants, usually decently priced cafeteria-like places where you pay according to the weight of your plate. Except for fish dishes in the Pantanal, the food here is neither as interesting nor as flavorful as that found elsewhere in the country. That said, the food is hearty, and the meals are large; affordable all-you-can-eat buffets are everywhere. *Prices in the reviews are the average cost of a main course at dinner or, if dinner is not served, at lunch.*

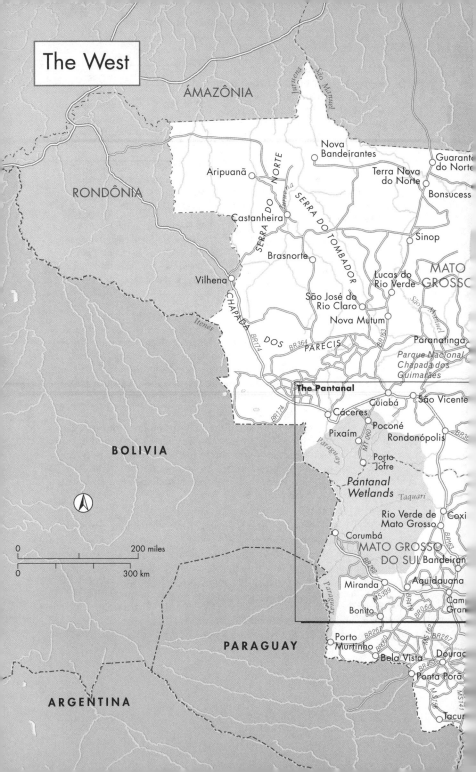

The West

ÁMAZÔNIA

RONDÔNIA

BOLIVIA

PARAGUAY

ARGENTINA

Nova
Bandeirantes

Aripuanã

Castanheira

Serra do Norte

Serra do Tombador

Terra Nova
do Norte

Guarant
do Norte

Bonsucess

Sinop

MATO
GROSSO

Brasnorte

Vilhena

Itenes

Chapada Dos Parecis

BR174

BR364

Lucas do
Rio Verde

São José do
Rio Claro

Nova Mutum

Páranatinga

São Manuel

Páranatinga

BR163

Parque Nacional
Chapada dos
Guimarães

The Pantanal

Cáceres

Cuiabá

São Vicente

BR174

Pixaím

Poconé

Rondonópolis

BR

MT 060

Porto
Jofre

Paraguay

*Pantanal
Wetlands*

Taquari

Rio Verde de
Mato Grosso

Coxi

Corumbá

BR262

MATO GROSSO
DO SUL

Bandeiran

Miranda

Aquidauana

Cam
Gran

MS339

BR419

BR060

Bonito

Paraguay

Porto
Murtinho

BR267

Bela Vista

Dourac

Ponta Porã

Tacur

0   200 miles
0   300 km

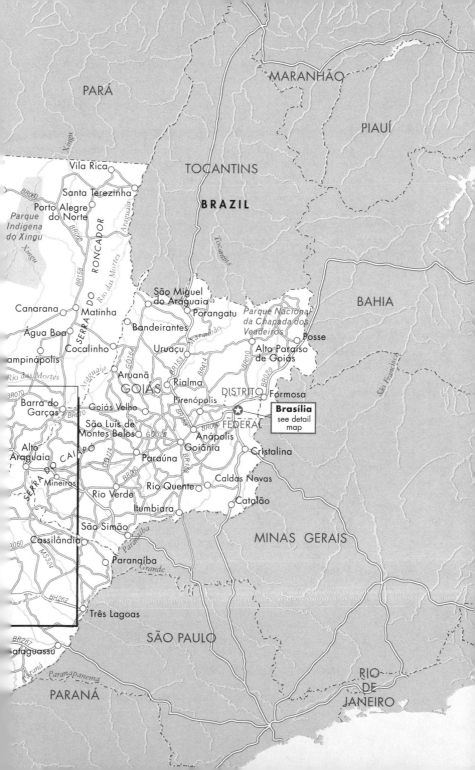

HOTELS

Brasília's hotels cater primarily to business executives and government officials. Most hotels, from the upscale resorts to the budget inns, are found in the Hotel Sectors and along Lago Paranoá. For ease in exploring the city, try to stay in Plano Piloto, close to most architectural landmarks, shopping malls, and a number of good restaurants.

West of Brasília, deluxe accommodations are scarcer. In the Pantanal, the *fazendas* (farms) are quite spartan. But there are a few extremely comfortable jungle lodges with nearly everything you could need.

When you book a room, note that a 10% service charge will be added.

Prices in the reviews are the lowest cost of a standard double room in high season. For expanded reviews, facilities, and current deals, visit Fodors.com.

BRASÍLIA

1,015 km (632 miles) north of São Paulo, 1,200 km (750 miles) northwest of Rio de Janeiro.

The idea of moving Brazil's capital to the interior dates from the early days of the country's independence, but it wasn't until 1955 that the scheme became more than a pipe dream. Many said Brasília couldn't be built; others simply went ahead and did it. The resolute Juscelino Kubitschek made it part of his presidential campaign platform. On taking office, he organized an international contest for the city's master plan. A design submitted by urban planner Lúcio Costa was selected, and he and his contemporaries—including architect Oscar Niemeyer and landscape artist Roberto Burle Marx—went to work. The new capital was built less than five years later, quite literally in the middle of nowhere.

Costa once mused, "The sky is the sea of Brasília." He made sure that the city had an unhindered view of the horizon, with buildings whose heights are restricted, wide streets and avenues, and immense green spaces. The sky here is an incredible blue that's cut only by occasional clusters of fleecy clouds. The earth is such an amazing shade of red that it seems to have been put here just for contrast. At night it's hard to tell where the city lights end and the stars begin. The renowned contemporary architect Frank O. Gehry said of Brasília, "It's a different city. I call it holy land, an untouchable icon of architecture."

Brasília is a great place for those interested in architecture and in a different city experience from Rio, Salvador, or São Paulo. Everything is divided into sectors (hotels, residences, swimming places, etc.), and the streets were designed without sidewalks—it's said that Brasília is a driver's paradise, but a pedestrian's nightmare. Because of this, Brasília has long been known as "the city without corners."

GETTING HERE AND AROUND

Brasília's international airport, Aeroporto Juscelino Kubitschek (BSB), is one of the busiest in Brazil. To get to the city center, taxis are your only real option. Trips to the hotel sectors along the Eixo Monumental

A Bit of History

The occupation of the center-west of Brazil did not keep up with the pace of occupation in the other regions. It was not until the discovery of gold in the mid-18th century in the states of Mato Grosso and Goiás that the first prominent urban centers were established in the region: Cuiabá (1727), Vila Boa (1739), and Santíssima Trindade (1752). The roads opened by the first *bandeirantes* (explorers) in the 1820s—probably following the trails of the Indian tribes who lived in the area, the Macro-jê or Tapuias—were used by approximately 6,000 people at the time. The region was an important economic hub 250 years before the construction of Brasília.

Between 1906 and 1910 the government-sponsored Rondon Expedition set out to explore and map an area the size of France. Explorers faced some indigenous Xavantes tribes in the area of the Araguaia River, who attacked to defend their territory. Colonization of the center-west was intensified in the '50s, with the construction of Brasília and the new integration roads, together with the increase in agricultural practices in the region.

The creation of Brasília began long before its construction in 1956. The idea of moving the capital to the countryside was first voiced in the 18th century, allegedly by the

Portuguese Marquis of Pombal. Several sites were proposed, in different central states. A team was commissioned to study the climatic conditions of inland Brazil and demarcate an area for the future capital. The team's final report was submitted in 1894, but it wasn't until 1946 that the plan of moving the capital to the Central Plateau became a reality with the advent of a new Constitution. President Juscelino Kubitschek ordered the construction of Brasília in 1956.

The mystic part of the history of Brasília revolves around bishop Dom Bosco and the prophetic dream he had in the 19th century, 75 years before the construction of the city. Dom Bosco dreamed about Brasília being the "promised land, flowing with milk and honey and inconceivable riches" between parallels 15 and 20. Dom Bosco's dream was used as one of the mottos to justify the moving of the capital to the interior of the country.

Brasília was unveiled in 1960. In 1987 UNESCO declared the city a World Heritage Site. Since its founding, Brasília has seen important political and social changes, such as the enactment of the current Brazilian Constitution in 1988 (the first after the military dictatorship stepped down) and rallies against former President Fernando Collor de Mello, the only Brazilian president to be impeached, in 1992.

8

take roughly 15 minutes and cost about R$40. City buses, which cost about R$3, make many stops and don't have space for luggage.

Interstate buses arrive and depart from the Estação Rodoviária. Real makes the 15-hour trip between Brasília and São Paulo. Itapemirim buses run to and from Rio de Janeiro (17 hours). As in most cities in Brazil, the public transportation system is based on commuter buses. Most bus lines depart from Estação Rodoviária, and from there you can go to virtually any part of the city. Rides within the Plano Piloto cost

Brasília

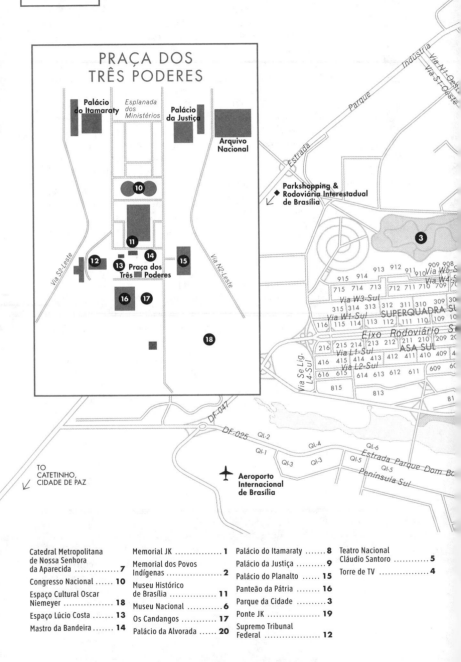

PRAÇA DOS TRÊS PODERES

Palácio do Itamaraty
Esplanada dos Ministérios
Palácio da Justiça
Arquivo Nacional

Parkshopping & Rodoviária Interestadual de Brasília

Praça dos Três Poderes

Via S2-Leste
Via N2-Leste
Via Se Lig. L4-Sul

SUPERQUADRA SUL
Via W5-S
Via W4-S
Via W3-Sul
Via W1-Sul
Eixo Rodoviário S
ASA SUL
Via L1-Sul
Via L2-Sul

Parque
Indústria
Via N1-Oeste
Via S1-Oeste
Estrada

DF-047
DF-025
QI-2
QI-1
QI-3
QI-3
QI-4
QI-5
QI-5
QI-6
Estrada Parque Dom Bo
Península Sul

TO CATETINHO, CIDADE DE PAZ

✈ Aeroporto Internacional de Brasília

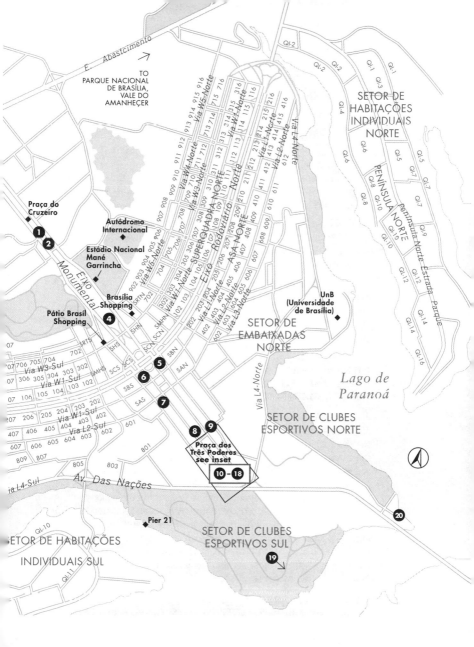

about R$3. Although Brasília does have a subway, it is mainly useful for commuters from suburbs, such as Taguatinga and Samambaia. The regional government has also announced plans to construct a tramway linking the airport with the Eixo Monumental.

The best way to get around is by car—either taxi or rental car. Taxi fares in Brasília are a bit lower than in the rest of the country, and most cabs are organized as cooperatives with dispatchers ("radio taxis"). It's best to tackle the Eixo Monumental and then to visit the Praça dos Três Poderes first, and then choose other sights farther away. For this, hire a cab or join an organized tour. Alternatively, combine walking and bus rides with lines 104 and 108, which run by the Eixo Monumental.

ESSENTIALS

Airport Aeroporto Internacional Juscelino Kubitschek (*BSB*)
⊠ *Aeroporto Internacional de Brasília s/n, Área Especial* ☎ *061/3364–9000* ⊕ *www.aeroportobrasilia.net.*

Bus Contacts Estação Rodoviária ⊠ *Eixo Monumental, at intersection of Asa Norte and Asa Sul* ☎ *61/3327–4631.* **Itapemirim** ☎ *61/3361–4505, 0800/723–2121* ⊕ *www.itapemirim.com.br.* **Real Expresso** ☎ *0800/280–7325* ⊕ *www.realexpresso.com.br.* **Rodoviária Interestadual de Brasília** ⊠ *SMAS, Trecho 4, Cj. 5/6, Asa Sul* ☎ *061/3234–2185* ⊕ *www.socicam.com.br/terminais-rodoviarios.php.* **Util** ☎ *061/3361–4342* ⊕ *www.util.com.br.*

Taxi Contacts Radio Táxi Alvorada ☎ *061/3321–3030* ⊕ *www.radiotaxi33213030.com.br.* **Rádio Táxi Maranata** ☎ *61/3323–3900.* **Unitáxi** ☎ *061/3323–3030.*

Visitor and Tour Information Brasília City Tour. Tours of the city on double-decker buses, in English, are available from this operator for R$25 per person. The tours, which last 2½ hours, take in the main sights of the city, have three short stops, and depart from Brasília Shopping three times daily on weekdays, and four times daily on weekends. ⊠ *Brasilia Shopping, side entrance, SCN Q. 05 Bl. A, Asa Sul* ☎ *061/9298–9416.* **BSB Tour.** This company offers city tours, boat trips on Lago Paranoá, and excursions into the countryside around Brasília. ⊠ *Q. 2, Bl. J, Sala 175, Ed. Garvey Park Hotel, Setor Hoteleiro Norte* ☎ *061/3039–2011* ⊕ *www.bsbtour.com.br.* **SETUR.** SETUR, the Brasília Tourism Agency, is open weekdays 9 to 5. A branch at the airport is open weekdays 7 to 10, and a branch at the Eixo Monumental is open daily 8 to 6. ⊠ *Centro de Convenções Ulysses Guimarães, Eixo Monumental, Lote 5, Asa Sul* ☎ *61/3214–2744* ⊕ *www.setur.df.gov.br.*

SAFETY AND PRECAUTIONS

Brasília, especially the Plano Piloto, is safe. In the residential blocks and their commercial subsectors you can wander in the evening without much concern. One exception is the commercial area around Estação Rodoviária, which can be sketchy at night. Watch out for pickpocketing, counterfeit items, and con artists.

The Method to the Madness

Addresses in Brasília's Plano Piloto can make even surveyors scratch their heads. Although the original layout of the city is very logical, it can be hard to get chapter-and-verse addresses, making them seem illogical. Some necessary vocabulary, with abbreviations:

Superquadras (SQ): Supersquares

Setores (S.): Sectors

Quadra (Q.) Block within a Supersquare or Sector

Quadra Interna (QI.) Internal block

Bloco (BL.): A large building within a *superquadra* or *setor*

Lote (Lt.): Lot, subdivision of a block

Conjunto (Cj.): A building subdivision

Loja (Lj.): Part of a larger building.

The Eixo Rodoviário has a line of superquadras made up of two (usually) quadras numbered from 100 to 116, 200 to 216, or 300 to 316 and consisting of six-story blocos. Quadras numbered 400 and above have been added outside the initial plan.

In addresses, compass points are sometimes added: *norte* (north), *sul* (south), *leste* (east), *oeste* (west). So an address might include SQN, meaning "superquadra norte." The Lago (Lake) region of the city is divided into the Lago Sul and Lago Norte districts. The residental areas on the shores of the lake include the Setores de Habitações Individuais (SHI) and the Setores de Mansões (SM).

Some important neighborhoods are:

Setor Comercial Local (SCL): for commercial areas within the Superquadras.

Setor Hoteleiro Norte (SHN): for hotels in the northern part of the city.

Setor Hoteleiro Sul (SHS): for hotels in the southern part of Brasília.

Setor de Diversões Sul (SDS): where the malls are located

EXPLORING

Shaped like an airplane when seen from above, the Plano Piloto (Pilot Plan) is the name of the original design for the city conceived by Lúcio Costa. The plan had four basic features: well-ventilated housing near green spaces; work spaces that were separate from housing; spaces for cultural activities near residential space; and the separation of vehicle and pedestrian pathways.

The Eixo (pronounced *eye*-shoo) Monumental, the "fuselage" portion of the plan, is lined with government buildings, museums, monuments, banks, hotels, and shops. It runs roughly from the Praça do Cruzeiro to the "cockpit," or the Praça dos Três Poderes. Intersecting the Eixo Monumental to form the Plano Piloto's "wings" is the Eixo Rodoviário. In and around the two main axes are streets and avenues that connect still more residential and commercial areas, parks and gardens, and the Lago Paranoá, formed by a dam built about 16 km (10 miles) southeast of the Plano Piloto. Along the outer shores of this lake, new neighborhoods are sprouting at a fast pace.

EIXO MONUMENTAL

Most of the Plano Piloto's major sights are along or just off the grand 8-km-long (5-mile-long) Eixo Monumental and its multilane boulevards. The distances are quite long, so if you want to explore on your own rather than as part of an organized tour, combine walking with riding the buses or taking taxis.

TOP ATTRACTIONS

Fodor's Choice ★ **Catedral Metropolitana de Nossa Senhora da Aparecida.** The city's cathedral, considered one of Niemeyer's masterpieces, was finished in 1967. From outside, what is visible is a circular structure—a bundle of 16 concrete "fingers" arching skyward. For some, it resembles a crown of thorns. Large panes of stained glass supported by the concrete structure shelter the nave, leaving it awash in natural light. Inside, *Os Anjos (The Angels)*—an aluminum sculpture by Brazilian artist Alfredo Ceschiatti—hovers above the altar. The city's first mass was held at the Praça do Cruzeiro, on May 3, 1957; the *cruz* (cross) used is now here at the cathedral. The building's entrance is guarded by four majestic bronze statues, also by Ceschiatti, *Os Evangelistas (The Evangelists)*. The outdoor carillon is a gift of the Spanish government. ⊠ *Esplanada dos Ministérios S/N, Eixo Monumental Leste* ☎ *61/3224–4073* 🎫 *Free* ⊙ *Daily 8–6.*

Fodor's Choice ★ **Memorial JK.** This Niemeyer structure is a truncated pyramid and has a function similar to its Egyptian counterpart: it's the final resting place of former president Juscelino Kubitschek, the city's founding father, who died in 1981. The mortuary chamber has a lovely stained-glass roof by local artist Marianne Peretti. JK's office and library from his apartment in Rio have been moved to the memorial's north wing. The bronze statue of JK—his hand raised as if in blessing—surrounded by a half-shell (a trademark of Brasília) looks down upon the Eixo Monumental and makes this one of the capital's most iconic and moving monuments. Permanent and changing exhibits here document the city's construction. The most recent addition is JK's lovingly restored Ford Galaxie. ⊠ *Praça do Cruzeiro, at Eixo Monumental Oeste, Zona Cívico-Administrativa* ☎ *61/3225–9451* 🎫 *R$10* ⊙ *Tues.–Sun. 9–6.*

Palácio da Justiça. The front and back facades of Niemeyer's Justice Ministry have waterfalls that cascade between its arched columns. Besides the administrative offices, there's a library with more than 80,000 books. On the third floor there's a garden by Burle Marx. ⊠ *Esplanada dos Ministérios, Zona Cívico-Administrativa* ☎ *61/3429–3401* 🎫 *Free* ⊙ *Tours weekdays 9–11 and 3–5.*

Palácio do Itamaraty. For the home of the Foreign Ministry, Niemeyer designed a glass-enclosed rectangular structure with a series of elegant arches on the facade. A reflecting pool augments the sense of spaciousness. The building and the water create a perfect backdrop for the *Meteoro (Meteor)*, a round, abstract Carrara-marble sculpture by Brazilian-Italian artist Bruno Giorgi. A guided tour shows a collection of art—including paintings by Brazilian artists like Cândido Portinari—and the impressive tropical gardens by Brazilian landscape designer Burle Marx. Reserve ahead for a tour in English. ⊠ *Esplanada* *dos Ministérios, Zona Cívico-Administrativa* ☎ *61/3411–6159* ⊕ *www.itamaraty.gov.br* ✉ *Free* ⊙ *Weekdays 2–5, weekends 10–3.*

WORTH NOTING

Memorial dos Povos Indígenas. Another Niemeyer project, this cylindrical structure was inspired by the huts built by the Yanomami people. A spiraling ramp leads to a central plaza where collections of indigenous crafts are displayed. Highlights among the main collection: pottery, headdresses, and feather ornaments made by the

Kayapó, the Xavante, and other indigenous peoples. The space often houses temporary exhibits from other collections. ⊠ *Palácio do Buriti, Eixo Monumental Oeste, Zona Cívico-Administrativa* ☎ *61/3342–1157* ✉ *Free* ⊙ *Tues.–Fri. 9–5, weekends 10–5.*

Museu Nacional. After more than 40 years in the planning stages, the National Museum opened in late 2006, on architect Oscar Niemeyer's 99th birthday. The sweeping, circular design was inspired by the *oca*, the round palm-covered hut of the country's native peoples. The space is mainly used to display frequently changing exhibits, often of works by international artists. ⊠ *Setor Cultural Sul, at Eixo Monumental Leste* ☎ *61/3225–6410* ✉ *Free* ⊙ *Tues.–Sun. 9–6.*

Fodor's Choice
★

Museu de Valores. Located on the second floor of the imposing headquarters of Brazil's central bank, this exhibition explores the often turbulent history of the nation's notes and coins, providing a detailed history of Brazil along the way. Look out for the highest-denomination note ever issued in Brazil. There is also a well-designed and informative section devoted to gold and gold mining. On the eighth floor, don't miss the bank's art gallery, home to one of the finest collections of modernist Brazilian art in the country. ⊠ *SBS, Q. 3, Bl. B* ☎ *061/3414–2093* ⊕ *www.bcb.gov.br* ✉ *Free* ⊙ *Tues.–Sun. 10–5.*

Parque da Cidade. A few blocks from the Instituto Histórico and Geográfico is City Park or Parque da Cidade Dona Sarah Kubitschek, a collaborative effort by Costa, Niemeyer, and Burle Marx. Locals say the park is the largest city park in the world. Bright lights and the reassuring presence of security guards make an evening walk, run, or bike ride along a path more agreeable than ever. There are also playgrounds and fair rides for the young. ⊠ *Entrances at Q. 901 S and Q. 912 S, Asa Sul* ☎ *61/3225–2451* ⊙ *Daily 5 am–midnight.*

Torre de TV. From the *Salão Panorâmico* (Observation Deck) of this 670-foot TV tower, you'll have a 360-degree view of the city. At night the view of the Congress building is spectacular. ⊠ *Eixo Monumental Oeste, Zona Cívico-Administrativa* ☎ *061/3321–7944* ✉ *Free* ⊙ *Mon. 2–9, Tues.–Sun. 9–9.*

8

PRAÇA DOS TRÊS PODERES

The buildings housing the government's three branches symbolically face each other in the Plaza of the Three Powers, the heart of the Brazilian republic. Here both power and architecture have been given balance as well as a view of Brasília and beyond. Indeed, the cityscape combined with the Planalto's endless sky have made the plaza so unusual that Russian cosmonaut Yuri Gagarin once remarked, "I have the impression of landing on a different planet, not on Earth!"

TOP ATTRACTIONS

Congresso Nacional. One of Niemeyer's most daring projects consists of two 28-story office towers for the 500 representatives of the Câmara dos Deputados (House of Representatives) and the 80 members of the Senado (Senate). The convex dome is where the Câmara meets, and the concave bowl-like structure is where the Senado convenes. The main building is connected by tunnels to several *anexos* (annexes) located at the sides of Eixo Monumental. The complex contains works by such Brazilian artists as Di Cavalcanti, Bulcão, and Ceschiatti. A guided tour takes you through major sites within the building. Tours in English are available by request. No shorts or sandals allowed. ⊠ *Praça dos Três Poderes* ☎ *61/3216–1771 tours* 🖭 *Free* ☉ *Daily 9:30–5.*

Espaço Cultural Oscar Niemeyer. This branch of the Oscar Niemeyer Foundation—which is based in Rio and was created to preserve and present the architect's work—houses a collection of sketches and drafts as well as a database with texts and images from Niemeyer's archives. ⊠ *Praça dos Três Poderes, Lote J, Asa Sul* ☎ *61/3226–6797* ⊕ *www.niemeyer. org.br* 🖭 *Free* ☉ *Weekdays 10–5.*

Espaço Lúcio Costa. As a tribute to the urban planner who masterminded Brasília, this underground complex was added to the plaza and inaugurated in 1992. It has a 1,500-square-foot display of the city's blueprint, and you can read Costa's original ideas for the project (the text is in Portuguese and English). ⊠ *Praça dos Três Poderes* ☎ *61/3325–6163* ⊕ *www.sc.df.gov.br/espaco-lucio-costa.html* 🖭 *Free* ☉ *Tues.–Sun. 9–6.*

Mastro da Bandeira. This 300-foot steel flagpole supporting a 242-square-foot Brazilian flag is the only element of Praça dos Três Poderes not designed by Niemeyer. At 4 pm on the first Sunday of the month, members of the armed forces take part in a *troca da bandeira* (flag changing) ceremony, to the sound of the Brazilian Army band. ⊠ *Praça dos Três Poderes, Esplanada dos Ministérios, Plano Piloto.*

THE BRAZILIAN FLAG

The Brazilian flag's green background symbolizes the forests that once spanned much of the country. The yellow diamond represents the gold-mining period that so influenced the nation's history. The blue circle in the center is homage to the great blue skies that dominate the territory; inside it are 27 stars, one for each state and the Federal District. The white band curving across the circle displays the national motto, *"Ordem e Progresso"* ("Order and Progress").

OSCAR NIEMEYER: THE ARCHITECT OF BRAZIL

If you're in Brasília and looking for a monument to Oscar Niemeyer, who died in 2012 at the age of 104, just look around you. The center of the city is a living museum to the legacy of the modernist architect, who has been acclaimed as Brazil's most outstanding figure in any of the arts.

Much of Niemeyer's work molds humble concrete into sweeping lines and graceful, alluring curves, resulting in structures that can appear almost to be visual poems more than just buildings. "What attracts me are free and sensual curves. The curves we find in mountains, in the waves of the sea, in the body of the woman we love," he wrote.

Niemeyer's buildings can be seen all over the world, but Brasília is home to a unique array of celebrated masterpieces, including Congress, the Palácio do Planalto, the Palácio do Itamaraty, and the Cathedral. If you're in the city on a Wednesday afternoon, a visit to the recently reopened Palácio da Alvorada, the official residence of the President, is a must.

Further afield, architecture buffs should not miss out on the St. Francis of Assisi church in Belo Horizonte, the Museum of Contemporary Art in Niterói, and the Capanema Palace in Rio.

But it is fitting that Niemeyer's final design, Brasília's striking 590-foot Digital TV tower, is visible on the horizon from all over the city that he shaped.

Museu Histórico de Brasília. Brasília's first museum has a small collection of pictures of the city and writings about it by such luminaries as Pope Pius XII, Kubitschek, and Niemeyer. The statue of Kubitschek on its facade is a 1960 work of Brazilian sculptor José Pedrosa. ⊠ *Praça dos Três Poderes, Zona Cívico-Administrativa* ☎ *61/3325–5220* 🖃 *Free* ⊙ *Tues.–Sun. 9–6.*

Os Candangos. This 25-foot-tall bronze sculpture by Giorgi has become the symbol of Brasília. It pays homage to the *candangos*, the workers who built the city from scratch. The statue, depicting two gracefully elongated figures holding poles, is across from the Palácio do Planalto. ⊠ *Praça dos Três Poderes, Esplanada dos Ministérios.*

Panteão da Pátria. Niemeyer designed this building to resemble a dove taking flight. Opened in 1986, the building honors such national heroes as Tancredo Neves, whose untimely death prevented him from being sworn in as Brazil's first democratically elected president after years of military dictatorship. Inside the curved structure are murals and stained-glass panels by Athos Bulcão, Marianne Peretti, and João Camara. One set of panels, *Os Inconfidentes*, depicts the martyrs of the 18th-century republican movement. It's extremely dark inside, so watch your step. ⊠ *Praça dos Três Poderes, Zona Cívico-Administrativa* ☎ *61/3325–6244* 🖃 *Free* ⊙ *Tues.–Sun. 9–6.*

Palácio do Planalto. Niemeyer gave this highly acclaimed structure, the office of the President, an unusual combination of straight and slanting lines, a variation of the design of Palácio da Alvorada. The access ramp to the main entrance is part of the national political folklore, because it represents the rise to power (presidents go up the ramp when inaugurated). ⊠ *Praça dos Três Poderes, Esplanada dos MinistériosEixo Monumental, Zona Cívico-Administrativa* ☎ *61/3411–2317* 💷 *Free* ☉ *Sun. 9:30–2:30.*

Supremo Tribunal Federal. The Brazilian Supreme Court building is classic Niemeyer—an otherwise ponderous structure seems lighter than air because of the curving lines of the columns that support the roof. In front of the building is one of the city's best-known monuments, the 10-foot granite statue *Justice,* by Alfredo Ceschiatti. ⊠ *Praça dos Três Poderes, Zona Cívico-Administrativa* ☎ *61/3217–3601* 💷 *Free* ☉ *Weekends 10–5:30.*

WORTH NOTING

Palácio da Alvorada. Open to the public on Wednesdays, the president's official residence was Niemeyer's first project in the new capital and is located at the edge of Lago Paranoá. Niemeyer used delicate slanting support columns, here clad in white marble. The name of the building translates as Palace of the Dawn, and its design is suitably inspired. Get here early to avoid a long wait for a guided tour (Portuguese only). ⊠ *SHTN, Via Presidencial s/n, Zona Cívico-Administrativa* ☉ *Wed. 3–5:30.*

BEYOND THE PLANO PILOTO

If you have the time, head beyond the Plano Piloto and explore Lago Paranoá's outer perimeter, which has parks, gardens, and residential neighborhoods. Since its inception, the city has attracted a variety of religious groups; several of these "cult communities" have headquarters here. They reflect Brasília's mystical side, the origin of which can be traced to a vision by an Italian priest named Dom Bosco. In 1883 he dreamed of a new civilization rising around a lake between the 15th and 20th parallels. Many believe the city is "the promised land" in Bosco's vision. (Bosco never actually set foot in Brazil, making his vision seem even more mysterious.)

TOP ATTRACTIONS

Catetinho. While the new capital was being built, the president's temporary quarters was called the *Catetinho,* meaning a smaller version of the grand Palácio do Catete in Rio. The wooden edifice was built in 10 days during the summer of 1956. A nearby landing strip allowed the president to fly in from Rio for his frequent inspections. The recently restored building is a must-see museum for those interested in the city's history. It's surrounded by woods with a small spring where the president and his entourage once bathed. ⊠ *Km 0, BR 040, 16 km (10 miles) southeast of Estação Rodoviária* ☎ *61/3338–8694* 💷 *Free* ☉ *Tues.–Sun. 9–5.*

FAMILY **Dom Bosco Shrine.** To view the best sunset in town, head to the Ermida Dom Bosco, in a peaceful setting by the southern shores of Lake Paranoá. There's a small shrine to Dom Bosco, but most people come here to walk, run, swim in the lake, or just watch the sunset with friends. ⊠ *SHIS, QI. 29, Lago Sul* ☎ *061/3367–4505* ☉ *Daily 8 am–10 pm.*

The Making of a Capital

As far back as 1808 Brazilian newspapers ran articles discussing Rio's inadequacies as a capital (Rio became the capital in 1763, following Brazil's first capital, Salvador), the argument being that contact with Pará and other states far from Rio was difficult. Also, Rio was right on the water, and an easy target for enemy invasion. In 1892 congress authorized an overland expedition to find a central locale where "a city could be constructed next to the headwaters of big rivers" and where "roads could be opened to all seaports." Within three months the expedition leaders had chosen a plateau in the southeastern Goiás region.

But it was not until the mid-1950s that Juscelino Kubitschek made the new capital part of his presidential campaign agenda, which was summarized in the motto "Fifty Years in Five." When he was elected in 1956, he quickly set the wheels in motion. Within a few days the site was selected (in Goiás, as proposed by the 1892 expedition), work committees were set up, and Niemeyer was put in charge of architectural and urban development. The design, called the Plano Piloto (Pilot, or Master, Plan), was the work of Lúcio Costa, chosen from an international contest. The concept was simple and original: "Brasília was conceived by the gesture of those who mark a place on a map: two axes intersecting at a right angle, that is, the sign of a cross mark." The Plano Piloto's most important gardens were to be created by famed landscape designer Roberto Burle Marx.

Among Costa's objectives were to do away with a central downtown, design highways that were as accident-free as possible, and ensure that the vast horizon would always be visible. Construction officially began in February 1957—with 3,000 workers on-site.

Building a modern seat of power for Latin America's largest nation was a monumental undertaking. Before paved roads were built, supplies had to be flown in from the eastern cities. The majority of the workers were immigrants from the Northeast, and unskilled. They learned fast and worked hard, however. Settlements of shacks and tents sprang up around the construction site. The largest, Freetown (now the suburb Nucleo Bandeirante), was home to close to 15,000 workers and their families.

In Rio, opposition to the new capital was heated. Debates in the senate turned into fistfights. Government employees feared that Rio's business would decline and its real-estate values would drop, and were reluctant to leave Rio's comforts and beaches. Kubitschek's government induced them with 100% salary increases, tax breaks, early retirement options, ridiculously low rents, and even discounts on home furnishings.

On April 21, 1960, the city was inaugurated. The day began with mass in the uncompleted cathedral and ended with a fireworks display, where the president's name burned in 15 foot high letters. A new era of pioneering and colonization followed the realization of Kubitschek's vision of a "nation of the future," looking westward from the coast.

8

Parque Nacional de Brasília. Because of its many springs, locals refer to the 60,000-acre Brasília National Park as Água Mineral (Mineral Water). There are two spring-fed pools where people can cool off, dressing rooms, and picnic areas. Created to protect the water supply of Lago Paranoá, the park also preserves a bit of the region's *cerrado,* or grassy plains interspersed with thickets and woods. An informative trail that runs through mostly flat terrain starts at the visitor center, where you can pick up maps and brochures. ✉ *Rodovia DF 003, Km 8.5, 9 km (6 miles) from Eixo Monumental, Zona Industrial* ☎ *61/3233–4553* 🎫 *R$13* 🕒 *Daily 8–4.*

WORTH NOTING

Ponte JK. Opened in late 2002, the third bridge crossing Lake Paranoá is consistent with Brasília's commitment to state-of-the-art architecture and engineering. It has become one of the city's most recognizable landmarks. The bridge—a project by Alexandre Chan from Rio de Janeiro—is held aloft by three diagonal arcs that crisscross the deck. Its lakeshore location and pleasant promenade attract many people to stroll or bicycle across and enjoy the sunset. ✉ *Via L4, after SCES, south of Eixo Monumental, Asa Sul* 🎫 *Free.*

WHERE TO EAT

Brasília enjoys what is generally regarded as one of the best restaurant scenes in Brazil, behind only the much larger cities of São Paulo and Rio de Janeiro. The city has by far the highest per capita income in the country, and in recent years this affluence has been reflected in the rapidly expanding range of dining options. Brasília may be relatively small, but nowhere else in the country can you find such a variety of fine regional and international restaurants and cheerful local bars and eateries all in close proximity to oneother.

$$$$ CONTEMPORARY Fodor's Choice ★

🍴 **Aquavit.** In an elegant space on the shores of Lago Paranoá, award-winning Danish chef and owner Simon Lau Cederholm is giving traditional Brazilian ingredients an inspired contemporary twist. The imaginative five-course set menu, which changes every month, transforms seasonal fare from the center and west of Brazil into exotic combinations that never cease to surprise, such as codfish grilled in rare honey from the stingless *jataí* bees of Goiás. All courses come matched with intriguing wines from the old world and the new. [$] *Average main: R$210* ✉ *Setor de Mansões Lago Norte, ML12, Conj. 1, Casa 5, Lago Norte* ☎ *61/3369–2301* 🌐 *restauranteaquavit.com* ✍ *Reservations essential* 🕒 *Closed Sun.–Tues. and Jan. No lunch.*

$$$ PIZZA FAMILY

🍴 **Avenida Paulista.** This attractively located pizzaria, situated right by the futuristic Ponte JK on the shores of Paranoá Lake, has become a favorite since opening in 2011. Diners can choose from a selection of 38 wood-fired pizzas—try the four-flavor *sinfonia di sapori,* or opt for the buffet option of pastas and salads. [$] *Average main: R$58* ✉ *SCES Centro de Lazer, Beira Lago, Trecho, Lote 41, Asa Sul* ☎ *061/3255–6000* 🌐 *www.restauranteavenidapaulista.com.br* 🕒 *No lunch Mon.*

$$$$ PORTUGUESE 🍴 **Bela Sintra.** The city's premier Portuguese restaurant, Bela Sintra has earned a faithful crowd since opening in 2011. The plush furniture and old-world vibe make this a popular option for a rather formal lunch or dinner, and there's an extensive wine list for washing down Portuguese favorites, including a wide range of codfish dishes, such as *bacalhau a largareiro.* [$] *Average main: R$80* ✉ *Asa Sul 105, Asa Sul* ☎ *061/3242–4001* 🌐 *www.abelasintra.com.br* 🕒 *Closed Mon. No dinner Sun.*

$$ ECLECTIC 🍴 **Carpe Diem.** If you're a bibliophile or a fan of the arts, you might enjoy the frequent book parties and art exhibits at this restaurant. On weekdays the lunch buffet is very popular with the business crowd. On weekends people flock here for the *feijoada* (meat stew with black beans). Among the regular entrées, the shrimp risotto is one of the most popular. There are five other locations in Brasília, but the original stands out because of its greenery-filled verandas. [$] *Average main: R$40* ✉ *CLS 104, Bloco D, loja 1, Loja 1, Centro* ☎ *61/3325–5301* 🌐 *www.carpediem.com.br.*

$$ BRAZILIAN 🍴 **Feitiço Mineiro.** Live Brazilian music, from bossa nova to contemporary, is a nightly feature at this restaurant. But the *comida mineira* (food from the state of Minas Gerais) is the best reason to come. One of the most popular dishes is the *costelinha ao Véio Chico* (fried pork ribs with cassava). At lunch, you can help yourself from a large buffet for a set price. The owners run a popular lounge next door, Bar do Feitiço. [$] *Average main: R$30* ✉ *CLN 306 Bloco B, Loja 45 and 51, Asa Norte* ☎ *61/3272–3032* 🕒 *No dinner Sun.*

$$$$ BRAZILIAN Fodor's Choice ★ 🍴 **Fogo de Chão.** One of the most popular fine-dining options in town, this *churrascaria* (steak house) is one of the best of its kind. The sleek ambience of this spacious restaurant adds to the lure. It's famous for its *rodízio* service, in which waiters bring various types of meat on the spit to your table, where they'll carve off as much as you like. The prix-fixe meal includes a large and varied salad bar, but it's the beef that draws the crowds. U.S.-owned since 2012, the restaurant has also introduced some healthier eating options and has stopped serving fried fare altogether. [$] *Average main: R$99* ✉ *SHS Quadra 5, Bloco E, Asa Sul* ☎ *61/3322–4666* 🌐 *www.fogodechao.com.br.*

$$ GERMAN 🍴 **Fritz.** This longtime favorite is the place to go for German cuisine. The laid-back atmosphere and no-frills decor draw those looking for authentic food and a great selection of imported beer and wine. Savor the *rollmops* (rolled thinly cut herring fillets) while you wait for your entrée. Good choices include the *Eisbein* (pig's leg with mashed potatoes) or *Ente mit Blaukraut und Apfelpurée* (duck cooked in wine served with red cabbage and applesauce). [$] *Average main: R$40* ✉ *CLS, Quadra 404, Bloco D, Loja 35, Asa Sul* ☎ *61/3223–4622* 🕒 *No dinner Sun.*

$ FAST FOOD 🍴 **GrandVille.** This spot delivers premium sandwiches to all corners of Brasília. Owner Rodrigo Marcolone is investing in a new, healthier product range and is sprucing up the well-located restaurant for those who prefer to eat on the spot. [$] *Average main: R$15* ✉ *SHSC CL, Q. 105, Bloco B, Lj. 02, Asa Sul* ☎ *061/3242–0008* 🌐 *www.grandvillebsb.com.br.*

$$$$ FRENCH 🍴 **La Chaumière.** For more than 45 years, this small but cozy restaurant has been the mainstay of fine dining *à la française* in the capital. Incredible as it may seem, the friendly owner and chef is a Brazilian who promised the original French owners to keep the original fare and ambience. His resolution still pays off: try the steak *au poivre* (with a green peppercorn and cream sauce). [$] *Average main: R$100* ✉ *SCLS 408, Bloco A Loja 13, Loja 13, Asa Sul* ☎ *61/3242–7599* 🌐 *www.lachaumiere.com.br* 🕒 *Closed Mon. No lunch Sat. No dinner Sun.*

$$$ BRAZILIAN FAMILY 🍴 **Mangai.** One of the largest restaurants you may ever eat in, Mangai specializes in cuisine from Brazil's northeast and has seating for up to 900 people—you still may have to wait for a table. Located near the Ponte JK, Mangai charges R$52.90 for a kilo of food, which you serve up yourself from a vast buffet at the back of the dining hall. Try the *carne de sol com nata* (sun-dried meat in cream) or the tasty shrimp dish *gororoba de camarão.* [$] *Average main: R$60* ✉ *SCE Sul Trecho 2, Cj. 41, Asa Sul* ☎ *061/3224–3079* 🌐 *www.mangai.com.br.*

$$$$ ECLECTIC 🍴 **Universal Diner.** The kitchsy decor is one of the main attractions of this restaurant—bulldog statuettes, miniature porcelain dolls, used vinyl LPs, and other antiques cover the walls and hang from the ceiling. The chef-owner, Mara Alcamim, is always on hand, and regularly checks to make sure patrons have enjoyed the food. Favorite dishes include the intriguingly named "sexy shrimp" (they're with a sauce of Brie, Champagne, and caviar, accompanied by a strawberry-and-sage risotto). [$] *Average main: R$110* ✉ *CLS 210, Bloco B, Lj. 30, Asa Sul* ☎ *61/3443–2089* 🕒 *No lunch Mon. No dinner Sun.*

$$$ ITALIAN 🍴 **Villa Borghese.** The quiet cantina ambience and fantastic cuisine, closely overseen by well-known chef and owner Ana Toscana, make you feel as if you're in Italy. If you're not too concerned about your weight, try the *agnello della nonna* (roasted lamb shank). [$] *Average main: R$60* ✉ *SCLS, Quadra 201, Bloco A, Loja. 33* ☎ *61/3226–5650* 🌐 *www.villaborgheserestaurante.com.br.*

WHERE TO STAY

One thing you don't have to worry about when choosing a hotel in Brasília is location. With the notable exception of a couple of stand-out hotels by the Palacio da Álvoráda, most of the city's hotels are found in the hotel sectors to the south and north of the Eixo Monumental, within walking distance of all the main sights. While some of the original buildings constructed in these sectors in the 1960s are now looking a little tired, new hotels are slated to open before the World Cup. Prices are generally steep, but you'll find rates discounted 50% or more from Friday to Monday, when the politicians are typically away.

$$$ HOTEL 🏨 **Bonaparte Bluepoint.** A sober granite lobby with wood paneling and sophisticated lighting welcomes you to this modern hotel. **Pros:** perfect for longer stays; plush furnishings. **Cons:** neighborhood sketchy at night; small commons area. [$] *Rooms from: R$493* ✉ *SHS, Quadra 02, Bloco J, Asa Sul* ☎ *61/2104–6600, 0800/701–9990* 🌐 *www.bonapartehotel.com.br* 🛏 *97 rooms* 🍽 *Breakfast.*

$$$$ 🏨 **Brasília Palace.** This is your chance to stay in an effortless modernist
HOTEL masterpiece, designed by Oscar Niemeyer, which reopened in 2006 after
Fodor'sChoice a top-to-bottom renovation supervised by Niemeyer himself. **Pros:** inspi-
★ rational, historic building; *Mad Men* cool; great oval-shaped swimming
pool. **Cons:** a little distance from the city center. $ *Rooms from: R$570*
✉*SHTN, Trecho 01, Lote 01, Setor Hoteleiro Norte* 📞*61/3306–9100*
⊕*www.brasiliapalace.com.br* ⏎*156 rooms* ⦿*Breakfast.*

$$$$ 🏨 **Hotel Nacional.** One of Brasília's older hotels, the Nacional is still
HOTEL fondly regarded, although it now needs a makeover. **Pros:** central location; reasonable rates considering what you get. **Cons:** doesn't accept
credit cards; dated and tired decor; some rooms have small bathrooms. $ *Rooms from: R$550* ✉*SHS, Quadra 01, Bloco A, Asa Sul*
📞*61/3321–7575* ⊕*www.hotelnacional.com.br* ⏎*350 rooms* ▭*No*
credit cards ⦿*Breakfast.*

$$$ 🏨 **Kubitschek Plaza.** Originally owned by descendants of Brasília's found-
HOTEL ing father, Juscelino Kubistchek, this hotel is decorated with some of his
own antiques. **Pros:** elegant decor; top-drawer restaurant. **Cons:** small
bathrooms; rooms rather drab. $ *Rooms from: R$490* ✉*SHN, Quadra*
02, Bloco E, Asa Norte 📞*61/3329–3333, 61/3319–3543 reservations*
⊕*www.kubitschek.com.br* ⏎*246 rooms* ⦿*Breakfast.*

$$$$ 🏨 **Meliá Brasil 21.** This property, with an enviable location on the Eixo
HOTEL Monumental, is adjacent to the Brasil XXI convention center and just
steps from the Parque da Cidade, so you often see guests heading out to
enjoy the park. **Pros:** near city's main park; very attentive staff. **Cons:**
neighborhood sketchy at night; can be too busy during conventions.
$ *Rooms from: R$1134* ✉*SHS, Quadra 6, Conjunto A, Bloco D, Asa*
Sul 📞*61/3218–4700, 0800/703–3399 reservations* ⊕*pt.melia.com*
⏎*260 rooms* ⦿*Breakfast.*

$$$$ 🏨 **Naoum Plaza Hotel.** One of Brasília's most sophisticated hotels, this
HOTEL longtime favorite has a faithful clientele that includes heads of state.
Fodor'sChoice **Pros:** luxurious rooms; gorgeous tropical-wood furniture; impeccable
★ and friendly service. **Cons:** neighborhood sketchy at night; lobby a little
cramped; Wi-Fi can be erratic. $ *Rooms from: R$720* ✉*SHS, Quadra*
05, Bloco H/I, Asa Sul 📞*61/3322–4545* ⊕*www.naoumplaza.com.br*
⏎*158 rooms, 16 suites* ⦿*Breakfast.*

$$$$ 🏨 **Royal Tulip Brasília Alvorada.** President Obama's choice when he came
HOTEL to Brasília in 2011, this swank hotel has a prime location next to the offi-
cial residence of the President of Brazil, which has made it a firm favor-
ite for visiting politicians and diplomats. **Pros:** quiet location; lovely
lake views; postmodern architecture by Ruy Ohtake. **Cons:** hectic dur-
ing conventions; far from the city center; impersonal. $ *Rooms from·*
R$1250 ✉*SHTN Trecho 1, Cj. 1B, Bl. C, Asa Norte* 📞*061/3424–7001*
⊕*www.royaltulipbrasiliaalvorada.com* ⏎*395 rooms* ⦿*No meals.*

$$ 🏨 **SIA Park Executive Hotel.** If you're looking for a budget price and a
HOTEL convenient location near the airport, this hotel is a good option. **Pros:**
bargain rates; attentive staff; hearty breakfast. **Cons:** few amenities; far
from city center. $ *Rooms from: R$266* ✉*SIA Sul, Quadra 2C Bloco*
D, Zona Industrial 📞*61/3403–6655* ⊕*www.siapark.com.br* ⏎*50*
rooms ⦿*Breakfast.*

8

NIGHTLIFE AND THE ARTS

Brasília has a young and growing population. The nightlife scene revolves around bars in the Asa Sul and Asa Norte, and festas in the city's various members clubs, especially in the Setor de Clubes Sul.

NIGHTLIFE

BARS

Bar Brasília. If you want to experience a typical Brazilian happy hour, go to the traditional Bar Brasília, known for having the best draft beer in town. Traditional appetizers such as *bolinho de bacalhau* (cod cake) round out the offerings. ⊠ *506 Sul, Bl. A, Lj. 15, Asa Sul* ☎ *61/3443–4323.*

Beirute. An eclectic bar-restaurant with an Arab flair, Beirute has been in business since 1966. During its first decade it drew politicians making deals; today the gay-friendly place attracts a wide range of people. It's known for its ice-cold beer. ⊠ *109 Sul, Bl. A, Lj. 2 e 4, Asa Sul* ☎ *61/3244–1717.*

Libanus. One of Brasília's less pretentious and more relaxed places for a drink, this bustling bar serves cheap and popular Arab snacks as well as the all-important ice cold *chopp* (draught beer). ⊠ *206 Sul, Bl. C, Lj. 36, Asa Sul* ☎ *061/3244–9795.*

Loca Como Tu Madre. This cosmopolitan bar and restaurant has become one of the most popular places in town for Brasília's young and alternative set, drawn here by the stylish interior design, international cuisine, and DJs who know how to read a crowd. ⊠ *SHC 306–0–Bl. C, Lj. 36, Asa Sul* ☎ *061/3244–5828* ⊕ *www.locacomotumadre.com.br.*

Pinella Bistrô. A popular place for winding down after work, Pinella stocks a large selection of beers. Live music or DJs keep things lively. ⊠ *CLN 408, Bl. B, Lj. 20, Asa Norte* ☎ *061/3347–8334* ⊕ *www.pinella.com.br.*

THE ARTS

CULTURAL CENTERS

Caixa Cultural Brasília. One of the city's main cultural spaces, Caixa Cultural Brasília puts on exhibitions, concerts, plays, dance, and multimedia events. ⊠ *SBS, Q. 4, Lt. 3/4 – Edifício anexo à matriz da Caixa, Asa Sul* ☎ *061/3206–9450* ⊕ *www.caixacultural.com.br.*

Centro Cultural Banco do Brasil. This cultural center, aka CCBB, hosts art exhibits, dance shows, and plays. The lunchtime canteen is one of the best dining values in town. ⊠ *SCES, Trecho 02, Lt. 22, Asa Sul* ☎ *061/3108–7600.*

MUSIC CENTERS

Clube do Choro. This is where devotees of *chorinho*, a traditional Brazilian music, perform Wednesday to Saturday. ⊠ *SDC, Bl. G, Eixo Monumental, Zona Cívico-Administrativa* ☎ *61/3224–0599* ⊕ *www.clubedochoro.com.br.*

THEATER

Teatro Nacional Cláudio Santoro. This prominent theater is another Niemeyer construction, with three stages, and is used by—among others—the Orquestra Sinfônica do Teatro Nacional, which performs here from March through November. ⊠ *Setor Cutural Norte S s/n, Asa Norte* ☎ *061/3325–6105.*

SPORTS AND THE OUTDOORS

GOLF

Clube de Golfe de Brasília. At the tip of Eixo Monumental you can golf on this well-respected course at the Clube de Golfe de Brasília. ⊠ *SCES Trecho 2 Lt. 2, Asa Sul* ☎ *61/3224–2718* ⊕ *www.golfebrasilia.com.br* ⅃. *18 holes. 6,788 yards. Par 72. Greens fee: R$120–R$180.* ☞ *Facilities: Driving range, 3 putting greens, pull carts, rental clubs, golf academy, 2 restaurants, bar.*

SOCCER

Estádio Nacional de Brasília Mané Garrincha. This brand-new stadium seats 70,000 people and was inaugurated just in time for the Confederations Cup in 2013. It's due to host seven games during the World Cup. After 2014, the R$1-billion structure will be used mainly for concerts and other cultural events, as Brasília lacks a top-level soccer team. ⊠ *Centro Poliesportivo Ayrton Senna, Centro.*

SHOPPING

There are two major shopping districts along the Eixo Monumental: the Setor Comercial Norte (SCN, Northern Commercial Sector) and the Setor Comercial Sul (SCS, Southern Commercial Sector). In addition, almost every *superquadra* has its own commercial district.

CENTERS AND MALLS

Brasília Shopping. Housed in an odd arch-shape building designed by Ruy Ohtake, Brasília Shopping has several international chain stores as well as movie theaters, restaurants, and snack bars. The mall is close to both hotel sectors and is open till 10 pm daily. ⊠ *SCN, Q. 05 Bl. A, Asa Norte* ☎ *61/2109–2122* ⊕ *www.brasiliashopping.com.br.*

Iguatemi Shopping. Brasília's newest and most upscale shopping mall, Iguatemi opened in the Lago Norte area in 2010. Tony shops—including branches of Burberry, Gucci, and Louis Vuitton—are open daily, with restaurants open until 10 every night. ⊠ *SHIN CA 4, Lt. A, Lago Norte* ☎ *061/3577–5000* ⊕ *www.iguatemibrasilia.com.br.*

Parkshopping. Brasília's largest shopping center has more than 300 shops as well as a Burle Marx–designed central garden, the site of many cultural events. Conveniently located by the main bus station, it's open Monday through Saturday 10–10 and Sunday noon–10. ⊠ *SAI/ Sudoeste, Área 6580 CCCV, Zona Industrial* ☎ *61/3362–1300* ⊕ *www. parkshopping.com.br.*

Pátio Brasil Shopping. This shopping center often has free concerts and is close to most hotels in SHN. It has a full range of shops and movie theaters and is open Monday through Saturday 10–10:30. ⊠ *SCS Q. 07, Bl. A, Asa Sul* ☎ *61/2107–7400* ⊕ *www.patiobrasil.com.br.*

MARKETS

BSB Mix and Feira da Lua (Moon Fair). This retail event is held on alternate weekends 8–4. At more than 100 stalls you can find reasonably priced arts and crafts, furniture, jewelry, clothing, homemade food, and much more. The first weekend of the month the fair is always in the Gilberto Salomão shopping center. ⊠ *Centro Comercial Gilberto Salomão, Bl. D, Sobreloja 12, Sala 5, Lago Sul.*

Feira de Antiguidades (*Antiques Fair*). This market takes place the last weekend of each month from 10 to 7 and offers a great variety of decorative objects. ⊠ *SHIS QI 05 – Centro Comercial Gilberto Salomão, Lago Sul.*

Feira de Artesanato (*Artisans' Fair*). At this lively art market you can find semiprecious-stone jewelry, bronze items, wood carvings, wicker crafts, pottery, and dried flowers. It's held weekends and holidays 8–6. ⊠ *Foot of Torre de TV, Eixo Monumental Oeste, Centro* ⊕ *www.feiradeartesanatodatorredetv.com/sobre_feira.html.*

> ### THE MIGHTY SWAMP
>
> Pantanal literally means "land of swamps." Although the exact size of the Pantanal is a matter of debate among geologists and cartographers, 225,000 square km (96,500 square miles) is a common figure. This is about 3% of all the world's wetlands in one continuous area about 17 times the size of the Florida Everglades. All the water ends up draining through the Paraguay River.

THE PANTANAL

Fodor's Choice ★ Smack in the middle of South America, the **Pantanal Wetlands** cover a gigantic alluvial plain of the Rio Paraguay and its tributaries. Its area is about 225,000 square km (96,500 square miles), two-thirds of which are in Brazil. Much of the land is still owned by ranching families that have been here for generations. The Portuguese had begun colonizing the area by the late 18th century; today it's home to more than 21 million head of cattle and some 4 million people (most of them living in the capital cities). Yet there's still abundant wildlife in this mosaic of swamp, forest, and savanna. From your base at a *fazenda* (ranch) or lodge—with air-conditioning, swimming pools, and well-cooked meals—you can experience the *pantaneiro* lifestyle, yet another manifestation of the cowboy culture. Folklore has it that pantaneiros can communicate with the Pantanal animals.

It's widely held that the Pantanal is the best place in all of South America to view wildlife. (It's slated to become a UNESCO Biosphere Reserve.) More than 600 species of birds live here during different migratory seasons, including *araras* (hyacinth macaws), fabulous blue-and-yellow birds that can be as long as three feet from head to tail; larger-than-life rheas, which look and walk like aging modern ballerinas; the *tuiuiú*, known as the "lords of the Pantanal" and one of the largest birds known (their wingspan is 5–6 feet), which build an intricate assemblage of nests (*ninhais*) on trees; as well as cormorants, ibis, herons, kingfishers, hawks, falcons, and egrets, to name a few. You're also sure to spot *capivaras* (capybaras; the world's largest rodents—adults are about 60 cm/2 feet tall), tapirs, anteaters, marsh and jungle deer, maned wolves, otters, and one of the area's six species of monkeys.

The amphibian family is well represented by *jacarés* (caiman alligators), whose population of 200 per square mile is a large increase from the 1970s, when poaching had left them nearly extinct. (The skin of four animals made just one pair of shoes.) Jacarés are much more tranquil than their North American and African relatives—they don't attack unless threatened. Almost blind and deaf, and lacking a sense of smell, jacarés catch the fish they eat by following vibrations in the water. It's hard to spot jaguars and pumas during the day; a night photographic safari is the best way to try your luck. Native

> ## GO FISH
>
> The Pantanal is a freshwater fishermen's paradise. *Piraputanga* and *dourado* are the most prized catches in the Pantanal, but the abundant *pacú*, *pintado*, and *traíra* are also popular. Piranhas are endemic to the area. Although not the most sought-after catch, locals have some tasty recipes to prepare them. Beginning in November, most fish swim upstream to spawn, a phenomenon called *piracema*. That's why fishing is prohibited November to February.

guides (some are actually converted hunters) take you safely to the animals' roaming areas. Sightings are not uncommon in the fazendas that go the extra mile to protect their fauna. Don't let scary tales about *sucuri* (anacondas), which can grow to 30 feet in length, worry you. Sightings of the snakes are extremely rare and instances of them preying on humans are even rarer.

GETTING AROUND THE PANTANAL

The Pantanal is accessible by car and boat, but flights are the most popular—and easiest—way to reach the the gateway cities. The main airports are in Campo Grande (Pantanal South), and Cuiabá (Pantanal North). Cuiabá is also the starting point for trips to Chapada dos Guimarães.

TOURS

When visiting the Pantanal it's essential to have a guide, as you'll be traversing a remote border region. Before you choose a travel agency, ask questions about the planned route, the kind of vehicle that will be used, and the accommodations. Also ask about the guides, especially about their level of experience and their English-language skills. To avoid being overcharged, compare prices at more than one agency.

You can book longer tours—including river trips in luxurious riverboats (locally known as "hotel-boats") equipped with comfortable air-conditioned cabins. There are several kinds of these boat tours. Some are fishing expeditions on the Paraguay River and its tributaries. Others may combine treks into the wetlands by horseback, 4x4 vehicle, or on foot—whatever it takes to get the best animal sightings. The cost is variable, depending on length, type of accommodation, and equipment. Most tours last four to seven days. If you're pressed for time, there are shorter two-day tours.

TOUR COMPANIES

Agência AR. This agency is a popular tour option among travelers to the Pantanal. ⊠ *Rua Cel. Pilad Rebuá 1890, Bonito* ☎ *67/3255–1008* ⊕ *www.agenciaar.com.br.*

Ecoverde Tours. Affable and multilingual Joel Souza pioneered ecological tours of the Pantanal from Cuiabá in the 1980s, and his Ecoverde agency continues to run good-value, high-quality tours. The agency operates out of the simple but friendly Pousada Ecoverde in the city center. ⊠ *Rua Pedro Celestino 391, Centro, Cuiabá* ☎ *065/9638–1614, 065/3624–1386* ⊕ *www.ecoverdetours.com.br.*

Impacto Turismo. For tours deeper into the north or south Pantanal, this is a good choice. ⊠ *Rua 7 de Setembro, 1090, Centro, Campo Grande* ☎ *67/3325–1333* ✍ *impacto@impactotour.com.br* ⊕ *www. impactotour.com.br.*

Pantanal Discovery. Far and away your best choice in Campo Grande, Pantanal Discovery is one of the most experienced tour operators in the southern Pantanal and works regularly with international television companies. Helpful owner Gil and his friendly crew of multilingual guides can arrange transfers and accommodation in Campo Grande and Bonito as well as in the Pantanal itself. ⊠ *Nacional Hotel, Dom Aquino 610, Campo Grande* ☎ *067/9163–3518, 067/3383–3518* ⊕ *www.gilspantanaldiscovery.com.br.*

Pantanal Nature. Dedicated naturalist and fluent English speaker Ailton Lara is the go-to man for international television companies looking to film in the northern Pantanal as well for travelers from around the world. In the dry season, from June to November, the agency also operates a well-equipped jaguar camp, which provides one of the best chances of spotting these stunning animals. ⊠ *Rua Campo Grande 487, Centro, Cuiabá* ☎ *065/3322–0203, 065/9955–2632* ⊕ *www. pantanalnature.com.br.*

CUIABÁ

1,130 km (700 miles) west of Brasília, 1,615 km (1,000 miles) northwest of São Paulo.

The northern gateway to the Pantanal Wetlands, Cuiabá is also the southernmost gateway to the cerrado and the Amazon beyond. While you're waiting for a tour into the wetlands you can take a jaunt to Chapada dos Guimarães, a mountain range with impressive gorges, waterfalls, and vistas. The capital of Mato Grosso, Cuiabá is well known for being one of the hottest cities in Brazil: mean annual temperature is a sizzling 27°C (81°F). Daily highs surpass 45°C (113°F) several times during the year. The city name comes from the Bororo native people, who lived in the area—it means "place where we fish with spears." It was originally settled in the 18th century, when gold was found in the nearby rivers.

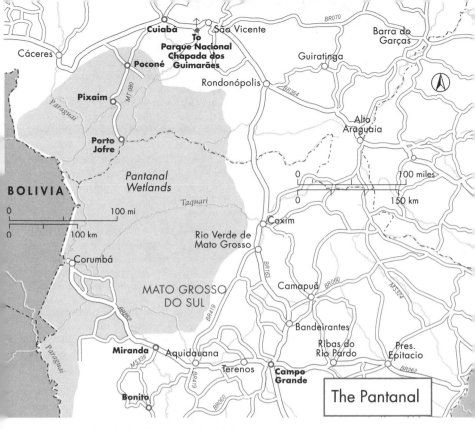

The Pantanal

GETTING HERE AND AROUND

Cuiabá is best reached by air from São Paulo, Rio, or Brasília. Cuiabá's Aeroporto Marechal Rondon is about 10 km (6 miles) from downtown. Taxis from the airport cost R$40. Planned to open by the time of the World Cup, a high-tech tramway will link downtown to the airport.

Andorinha buses travel to Cuiabá from Campo Grande (12 hours; R$83), and Expresso Rubi buses make the trip from Chapada dos Guimarães (1½ hours; R$12).

ESSENTIALS

Airport Aeroporto Marechal Rondon (*CGB*) ✉ *Av. João Ponce de Arruda s/n* ☎ *65/3614–2500.*

Bus Contacts Andorinha ☎ *065/3621–3201* ⊕ *www.andorinha.com.* **Expresso Rubi** ☎ *65/36211764.* **Rodoviária de Cuiabá** ✉ *Rua Jules Rimet 10, Senho dos Passos* ☎ *65/3621–3629.*

Taxi Contacts Rádio Táxi Cuiabana ☎ *65/3322–6664.*

SAFETY AND PRECAUTIONS

Take care in Cuiabá, which has a higher crime rate than other cities. Avoid straying too far from the hotel at night, as mugging can be a problem.

EXPLORING

Museu do Rio Cuiabá. On the west bank of Cuiabá River, this museum has maps and models of the river and photos of its history. Information is in Portuguese only. The building, constructed in 1899, was once the public fish market. The **Aquário Municipal** (Municipal Aquarium), with typical fish of the Pantanal, is part of the complex. ✉ *Av. Beira Rio s/n, Porto* ☎ *65/3617–0928, 65/3617–0929* 🕒 *Tues.–Fri. 9–5, weekends 9–3.*

Sesc Arsenal. Just across the road from the Casa do Artesão, this cultural space in the city's former arsenal stages plays, films, dance, exhibitions, and concerts. ✉ *Rua 13 de Junho, s/n, Centro* ☎ *065/3616–6901* 🕒 *Tues.–Fri. 8 am–11 pm, Sat. 1–11, Sun. 1–5.*

WHERE TO EAT

$$$ STEAKHOUSE 🍴 **Boi Grill.** If you've had your fill of fish, try this *churrascaria* (steak house) for as many beef dishes as you can imagine. The restaurant uses the all-you-can-eat *rodízio* system. Two of the most popular cuts are *picanha* (rump) and *costela* (ribs). Another recommended dish is *paleta de cordeiro* (lamb's rib). [$] *Average main: R$60* ✉ *Av. Miguel Sutil 6741, Despraiado* ☎ *65/3621–4642.*

$ BRAZILIAN 🍴 **Choppão.** A Cuiabá institution since 1974, this open-air eatery is always packed and is the best place in town to go for ice-cold beer and local specialities. This the place to sample *escaldado cuiabano*, a local chicken soup. [$] *Average main: R$20* ✉ *Praça 8 de abril s/n* ☎ *065/3623–9101* 🌐 *www.choppao.com.br* 🕒 *Closed Tues.*

$$ BRAZILIAN 🍴 **O Regionalíssimo.** In the same building as the Museu do Rio, this self-service eatery serves regional cuisine and Brazilian staples such as rice and beans. Try the *mojica de pintado,* a stew made from a local freshwater fish. [$] *Average main: R$37* ✉ *Museu do Rio, Porto* ☎ *65/3623–6881* 🕒 *Closed Mon. No dinner.*

$$$$ SEAFOOD 🍴 **Peixaria Popular.** This is the place to try local fish; don't miss the delicious *piraputanga,* a local fish prepared in a stew or fried. Other options are the *pintado* (a large freshwater fish) and *pacu* (a small piranhalike fish). All orders include a side serving of *pirão* (a thick fish gravy with cassava flour) and *banana frita* (fried bananas). [$] *Average main: R$72* ✉ *Av. São Sebastião 2324, Goiabeiras* ☎ *65/3322–5471* 🕒 *No dinner weekends.*

$$ PIZZA 🍴 **Pizzaria Margherita.** The pizzas here come with thin crusts, generous servings of mozzarella, and fresh ingredients, but it's the candlelit ambience of the restaurant and garden that have made it one of the most popular eateries in town. [$] *Average main: R$30* ✉ *Rua Fernando Correa, next to Bradesco, Chapada dos Guimarães* ☎ *065/9293–9430* 🕒 *Closed Mon. No lunch.*

WHERE TO STAY

$ B&B/INN 🏨 **Catarino's Guest House.** The best budget option in town, this family-run pousada opened in 2012 and has become a favorite with young travelers. **Pros:** attentive, helpful staff; substantial breakfast. **Cons:** basic rooms; can get busy. [$] *Rooms from: R$60* ✉ *Rua 24 de Fevereiro, Centro, Bonito* ☎ *067/3255–2823* 🛏 *8 rooms* 💳 *No credit cards* 🍽 *Breakfast.*

$$$$
HOTEL
Deville. This hotel has a lot to offer, including large rooms attractively decorated with pictures of birds from the Pantanal. **Pros:** great location; big breakfast; a new spa. **Cons:** understaffed at times. *Rooms from: R$678* ⊠ *Av. Isaac Povoas 1000, Centro* ☎ *65/3319–3000* ⊕ *www.deville.com.br* ↩ *174 rooms* ❏❘ *Breakfast.*

$$
HOTEL
Hotel Turismo. This family-run hotel celebrated its 40th anniversary in 2013 and continues to combine a convenient location with a high caliber of service. **Pros:** central location; large breakfasts. **Cons:** swimming pool needs more regular cleaning; uninspiring rooms. *Rooms from: R$283* ⊠ *Rua Fernando Correa 1065, Chapada dos Guimarães* ☎ *065/3301–1176* ⊕ *www.hotelturismo.com.br* ↩ *30 rooms.*

$$$$
HOTEL
InterCity. This is one of Cuiabá's most popular hotels for both business travelers and tourists, mainly because of its location near the city center next to a cluster of restaurants. **Pros:** central location; use of the excellent gym next door. **Cons:** small bathrooms. *Rooms from: R$664* ⊠ *Rua Presidente Arthur Bernardes 64, Centro* ☎ *65/3025–9900* ⊕ *www.intercityhoteis.com.br* ↩ *170 rooms* ❏❘ *Breakfast.*

$$
HOTEL
Paiaguás Palace. The standard rooms at Paiaguás Palace are simple and small, but the large and luxuriously furnished suites suit the rather grandiose name. **Pros:** cozy rooms. **Cons:** neighborhood sketchy at night; very busy during conventions. *Rooms from: R$285* ⊠ *Av. Rubens de Mendonça 1718, Bosque da Saúde, Bosque da Saúde* ☎ *65/3642–5353* ⊕ *www.hotelmt.com.br/hoteis-da-rede/paiaguas-palace-hotel* ↩ *267 rooms* ❏❘ *Breakfast.*

NIGHTLIFE
Confrade. This is one of Cuiabá's liveliest and largest bar/restaurant combinations, with live music every night. Try the *jacaré* (caiman). ⊠ *Av. Mato Grosso 1000* ☎ *065/3027–2000* ⊕ *www.confrade.com.br.*

SHOPPING
Artíndia. For Indian handicrafts try this shop sponsored by the Brazilian Indian agency FUNAI. ⊠ *Rua Pedro Celestino 301* ☎ *65/3623–1675.*

Casa do Artesão. Head here for wicker, cotton, and ceramic crafts from local artists. There's also a small museum in the basement. ⊠ *Rua 13 de Junho 315, Centro Norte* ☎ *65/3611–0500.*

HEALTH CONCERNS IN THE PANTANAL

Malaria is quite rare in tourist areas, but yellow fever has been of greater concern in recent years. If you're traveling to the Pantanal, ask your doctor about getting an inoculation before you leave on your trip. Dengue fever, for which there is no vaccination available, is a worry from November to March. The best way to prevent it is to avoid being bitten by mosquitoes. Lodgings in the Pantanal have screened windows, doors, and verandas. Use strong insect repellent at all times.

8

PARQUE NACIONAL CHAPADA DOS GUIMARÃES

EXPLORING

TOP ATTRACTIONS

Parque Nacional Chapada dos Guimarães. Besides the Pantanal, the areas in and around the Parque Nacional Chapada dos Guimarães are the region's most popular attractions. Traveling northeast of Cuiabá, you see the massive sandstone formations from miles away, rising 3,000 feet above the flat cerrado landscape. Since a fatal rock fall in the park in 2008, some attractions and bathing spots have been closed indefinitely, and all visitors must be accompanied by a guide. The **Cachoeira Véu de Noiva** (Bridal Veil Falls), with a 250-foot freefall, is the most impressive of the falls in the park. You can enjoy lunch at the nearby open-air restaurant. Beyond this point there are hills, caves, more falls, and archaeological sites. The **Circuito das Cachoeiras** (Waterfalls Circuit) is a set of seven waterfalls 3.5 km (2 miles) from the visitor center.

Walk about 30 minutes beyond the Caverna Aroe Jari to **Gruta da Lagoa Azul** (Grotto of Blue Lagoon), a crystal-clear lagoon (bathing is prohibited). You can also walk along the **Vale do Rio Claro** (River Claro Valley) and swim in the river's transparent waters, or climb the **Morro de São Jerônimo** (St. Jerome's Hill), one of the highest points of the Chapada. Entrance to the national park is permitted only with a guide, whom you can hire from an agency in town. ⊠ *MT 251 at Km 51, 74 km (40 miles) north of Cuiabá* ⊕ *www.icmbio.gov.br/parnaguimaraes* ⊗ *Daily 8–5.*

Caverna Aroe Jari. If you have time, arrange a guided visit to Caverna Aroe Jari. The cave's name means "home of souls" in the Bororo language. This mile-long sandstone cave (one of Brazil's largest) can only be reached after a 4.8-km (3-mile) hike through the cerrado. ⊠ *MT 251, 40 km from Guimarães* ⊠ *R$25.*

Eco Turismo Cultural. This is a popular agency for arranging a tour guide in the park. ⊠ *Av. Cipriano Curvo 655a* ☎ *65/3301–1393, 65/9952–1989* ⊕ *www.chapadadosguimaraes.com.br/ecoturis.htm.*

Chapada Explorer. This friendly and efficient travel agency can arrange tours with English-speaking guides to the main sights of the national park and around. ⊠ *Praça Dom Wunibaldo 57* ☎ *065/3301–1290* ⊕ *www.chapadaexplorer.com.br.*

WORTH NOTING

Chapada dos Guimarães. After navigating the steep and winding MT 251 through breathtaking canyons to reach the top of the mesa, you discover the pretty town of Chapada dos Guimarães, which still retains some of its colonial charm. If you're going to Chapada dos Guimarães around the second fortnight of June, don't miss the **Winter Festival,** with art and music workshops and various concerts with local artists. ⊠ *MT 251, 13 km (8 miles) east of national park.*

Igreja de Nossa Senhora de Santana do Sacramento. This handsome colonial church (circa 1779) has some exceptional gold-plated interior flourishes. ⊠ *Praça D. Wunibaldo, Centro* ☎ *65/3301–1213.*

CLOSE UP

The Brazilian Savanna

Brazil's vast *cerrado* (savanna) is the most biologically rich grassland in the world. More than 100,000 species of plants are found in this 500-million-acre (200-million-hectare) territory that covers about 25% of Brazil, and nearly 50% of them are endemic to Brazil. Its small trees, shrubs, and grasses are adapted to the harshness of the dry season, when temperatures in some parts rise well above 38°C (100°F) and humidity drops to a desert low of 13%. Palm species usually stand out among the shrubby vegetation—thick bunches of *buriti* usually grow around springs and creeks. Cacti and bromeliads are also abundant. Look also for the *pequi,* a shrub that produces berries used in local cuisine, which are called souari nuts.

Unfortunately, only about 2% of the cerrado is protected. Since development—mostly in the form of soy and corn farming and cattle ranches—it has become harder to spot such species of cerrado wildlife as deer, jaguars, and giant anteaters. Rheas, however, can be seen wandering through pastures and soybean plantations.

Mirante do Centro Geodésico. In 1972 satellite images proved that the continent's true center was not in Cuiabá, where a monument had been built, but at Mirante do Centro Geodésico on the mesa's edge. If the geodesic center doesn't hold spiritual meaning for you, come for the fantastic view—on a clear day you can see as far as the Pantanal. ✉ *8 km/5 miles southwest of town.*

8

WHERE TO EAT AND STAY

$$$ BRAZILIAN 🍴 **Morro dos Ventos.** Perched on the edge of a cliff, this restaurant has fantastic views. The palm-shaded building and surrounding gardens add to the atmosphere. This is the place for fantastic regional dishes such as *vaca atolada* (literally "cow stuck in the mud"). The strange-sounding dish is actually beef ribs served in cooked cassava chunks. [$] *Average main: R$50* ✉ *Estrada do Mirante Km 1 mile east of town* ☎ *65/3301–1030* 🌐 *restaurantemorrodosventos.com.br* ⏲ *No dinner.*

$$ HOTEL Fodor's Choice ★ 🏨 **Grand Park.** Campo Grande's most modern and sophisticated hotel, the Grand Park opened in 2011 and is helpfully located just across from Shopping Campo Grande. **Pros:** large, bright rooms; sumptuous breakfast; free Wi-Fi. **Cons:** some noise from the main road. [$] *Rooms from: R$365* ✉ *Av. Afonso Pena 5282, Campo Grande* ☎ *067/3044–4444* 🌐 *www.grandparkms.com* 🛏 *129 rooms* 🍽 *Breakfast.*

$$$ RESORT FAMILY 🏨 **Pousada Penhasco.** Clinging to the mesa's edge, this small resort may be far from the Chapada dos Guimarães, but it has tremendous views of the cerrado. **Pros:** many amenities; great sports options. **Cons:** far from downtown; hectic during conventions. [$] *Rooms from: R$479* ✉ *Av. Penhasco s/n, Bom Clima* ☎ *65/3624–1000 in Cuiabá, 65/3301–1555* 🌐 *www.penhasco.com.br* 🛏 *50 rooms* 🍽 *Breakfast.*

POCONÉ

236 km (147 miles) south of Cuiabá.

The hotels here are some of the closest to the Pantanal Wetlands. There are many well-trained guides in town, who have lived here all their lives. (Be sure to specify if you need an English-speaking guide.) The Rodovia Transpantaneira (MT 080) was originally planned to cut a north–south line through the Pantanal. Lack of funds and opposition from environmentalists resulted in a stalemate. Today the road dead-ends at the banks of the Cuiabá River, in a village called Porto Jofre, about 150 km (93 miles) south of the town of Cuiabá. Still, the Transpantaneira makes it possible to observe the abundant fauna and lush vegetation of the northern part of the wetlands. A large number of fazendas and pousadas organize popular activities such as fishing and photo safaris.

GETTING HERE AND AROUND

This "highway" is actually a dirt road with some 125 log bridges, some of which have caved in when cars passed over them. Traversing the Transpantaneira is time-consuming and relatively dangerous. It's best to join an organized tour; leave the driving to experienced guides in four-wheel-drive vehicles.

WHERE TO STAY

$$$ HOTEL 🏨 **Pantanal Mato Grosso Hotel.** Rooms here may be sparsely decorated, but are more than comfortable enough to make your stay pleasant. [$] *Rooms from: R$440* ✉ *Km 65, Rodovia Transpantaneira* ☎ *065/3614–7500* 🌐 *www.hotelmt.com.br* 🛏 *33 rooms* 🍴 *All meals.*

$$$$ B&B/INN 🏨 **Pousada Araras EcoLodge.** Rooms are impeccably clean at this ecolodge, which has comforts unexpected in an area this remote. **Pros:** superb location for wildlife-spotting; great amenities. **Cons:** long distance from nearest airport; few English-speaking guides. [$] *Rooms from: R$656* ✉ *Km 37, Rodovia Transpantaneira* ☎ *065/3682–2800, 065/9983–8633* 🌐 *www.araraslodge.com.br* 🛏 *19 rooms* 🍴 *All meals.*

CAMPO GRANDE

1,025 km (638 miles) west of São Paulo, 694 km (430 miles) south of Cuiabá.

Campo Grande is the gateway to the southern Pantanal and to the water-sports-rich areas around Bonito. Nicknamed the Cidade Morena (Brunette City) because of the reddish-brown earth on which it sits, this relatively young city (founded in 1899) was made the capital of Mato Grosso do Sul in 1978, when the state separated from Mato Grosso. Campo Grande's economy traditionally relied on ranching, but in the 1970s farmers from the south settled in the region, plowed the plateaus, and permanently changed the landscape. Today ecotourism is gaining on agriculture as the main industry. Although not a World Cup city, Campo Grande is all set to open the world's largest freshwater aquarium, an unusually designed structure which is due to open sometime in 2014.

GETTING HERE AND AROUND

Most tourists coming to the southern part of the Pantanal will fly to Campo Grande. Taxi fare from the Campo Grande airport to the town is about R$25. Andorinha has frequent bus service connecting Campo Grande with Cuiabá (12 hours, R$90), and daily service to and from São Paulo (16 hours, R$146).

SEEING CAMPO GRANDE

A double-decker bus whisks travelers past several points of interest, such as historic buildings and museums. A guide gives details of what's to see—only in Portuguese. Tours leave at 9 and 2:30 from the Morada dos Baís daily except Monday. Tickets for the 2½-hour tour cost R$20.

ESSENTIALS

Airport Aeroporto Internacional de Campo Grande ✉ *Av. Duque de Caxias s/n, 7 km (4 miles) west of downtown, Jardim Petrópolis* ☎ *067/3368-6000.*

Bus Contacts Andorinha ☎ *67/3382-3420* 🌐 *www.andorinha.com.* **Terminal Rodoviário de Campo Grande** ✉ *Avenida Guri Marques 1215* ☎ *067/3026-6789* 🌐 *www.socicam.com.br.*

Taxi Contacts Radio Taxi ☎ *67/3361-1111.*

Visitor and Tour Information Morada dos Baís. The municipal tourism office is open Tuesday to Saturday 8 to 7, Sunday 9 to noon. ✉ *Av. Noroeste 5140* ☎ *067/3324-5830* 🌐 *www.turismo.ms.gov.br.*

EXPLORING

Mercado Municipal. The Mercado Municipal is a great place to try *sopa paraguaia* (Paraguayan soup), which, despite its name, is a corn pie with cheese, onions, and spices. There are many shops selling handicrafts from native peoples of Mato Grosso. The market is open daily 6:30 am–8 pm (except for Sunday, when it closes at noon). ✉ *Praça Comendador Oshiro Takemori, Rua 15 de novembro s/n, Centro.*

Museo Dom Bosco. This museum contains more than 5,000 indigenous artifacts of the Bororo, Kadiweu, and Carajás tribes. Noteworthy are the taxidermy exhibits of the Pantanal fauna and the formidable seashell collection (with 12,000 pieces). Don't miss the collection of 9,000 butterflies from all over the world, and the bug room, whose walls are covered from floor to ceiling with insects. ✉ *Av. Afonso Pena 7000* ☎ *67/3326-9788* 🌐 *www.mcdb.org.br* 🎫 *R$5* 🕒 *Tues.–Fri. 8–5, weekends 1–5.*

WHERE TO EAT AND STAY

$$$ BRAZILIAN 🍴 **Casa do Peixe.** Get your fill of the Pantanal's fish varieties at this restaurant run on a fixed-price *rodízio* system. Couples may want to try the *caldo de piranhã* (piranha stew)—it is reputed to have aphrodisiac properties. [$] *Average main: R$60* ✉ *Rua Dr. João Rosa Pires, 1030, Amambaí* ☎ *067/3382-7121* 🌐 *casadopeixe.com.br* 🕒 *No dinner Sun.*

$$$$ BRAZILIAN Fodor's Choice ★ 🍴 **Fogo Caipira.** This is *the* place for regional cuisine, especially grilled and stewed fish dishes. The standout here is the *picanha na chapa* (grilled picanha steak), but the *moqueca de pintado* (a local fish stew) is also recommended. [$] *Average main: R$80* ✉ *Rua José Antônio Pereira 145, Centro, Itanhanga* ☎ *67/3324-1641* 🕒 *Closed Mon. No dinner Sun.*

$$$$ STEAKHOUSE 🍴 **Vermelho Grill.** At Campo Grande's premier steak house, the kitchen takes meat very seriously. All cuts come with certification of origin, and the T-bone steaks are a specialty. The restaurant is right on Campo Grande's swankiest street, but the wooden interior, green spaces, and open barbecue create a relaxing, rustic atmosphere. [$] *Average main: R$180* ✉ *Av. Afonso Pena 6078* ☎ *067/3326–7813* 🌐 *www.vermelhogrill.com.br* 🕒 *No dinner Sun.*

$$ HOTEL 🏨 **Jandaia.** Once the leading hotel in town, the Jandaia has lost its former glory and needs some renovation. **Pros:** central location; attentive staff. **Cons:** in need of investment; hectic when conventions are held. [$] *Rooms from: R$354* ✉ *Rua Barão do Rio Branco 1271, Centro* ☎ *67/3316–7700* 🌐 *www.jandaia.com.br* 🛏 *134 rooms, 6 suites* 🍽 *Breakfast.*

$$ HOTEL 🏨 **Novotel.** A red-tile roof gives this hotel a rustic appeal. **Pros:** good location; sleek rooms. **Cons:** small commons areas. [$] *Rooms from: R$342* ✉ *Av. Mato Grosso 5555, Jardim Copacabana* ☎ *67/2106–5900* 🌐 *www.accorhotels.com.br* 🛏 *88 rooms* 🍽 *Breakfast.*

SHOPPING

Casa do Artesão. For baskets of all shapes, beautiful wood handicrafts, and interesting ceramics made by Pantanal Indians, head to Casa do Artesão. It's open weekdays 8–6 and Saturday 8–noon. ✉ *Avenida Calógeras 2050, Centro* ☎ *67/3383–2633.*

Feira Indígena. The Feira Indígena, adjacent to the Mercado Central and just across Avenida Afonso Pena from the Casa de Artesão, is a good place to shop for locally made crafts. It's open Tuesday through Sunday 8–5.

Shopping Campo Grande. This massive shopping center has everything you'd expect in an American- or European-style mall, but the many boutiques are what make it shine. ✉ *Av. Afonso Pena 4909, Santa Fé* ☎ *67/3389–8000* 🌐 *www.shoppingcampogrande.com.br.*

BONITO

277 km (172 miles) southwest of Campo Grande.

The hills around this small town of 15,000, whose name rightly means "beautiful," are on the southern edge of the Pantanal, not too far from the Bodoquena mountain range. The route to the Pantanal is longer than from Campo Grande, but you are well compensated with top-notch hotels that starkly contrast with the rustic Pantanal lodgings. In Bonito you can swim and snorkel among schools of colorful fish in the headwaters of several crystal clear rivers. Fishing, rafting, rappelling, hiking, and spelunking are popular activities in this area. Tour guides can be hired on Bonito's main avenue.

GETTING HERE AND AROUND

The paved roads to Bonito follow a circuitous route, but they're better than the more direct route on unpaved roads. Take BR 262 west to the town of Anastacio, then head south on BR 419 for about 100 km (66 miles) to Guia Lopes. From there it's about 56 km (35 miles) northwest to Bonito on MS 178. Viação Cruzeiro do Sul buses run here from Campo Grande (5 hours, R$61). There is also regular minivan service to and from Campo Grande airport.

ESSENTIALS

Bus Contacts Estação Rodoviária ⊠ *Rua Pedro Álvares Cabral s/n, Centro*
☎ *67/3255–1606.*

Visitor and Tour Information Centro de Atendimento ao Turista. The "tourist
attention center," is open daily 7 to 5 and has information on hotels, restaurants,
and tour companies. ⊠ *Rodovia Bonito Guia Lopes, Km 0* ☎ *067/3255–1850.*
Vanzella. This company offers twice-daily transfers to and from Campo Grande
airport (3½ hours). They also provide cars and drivers for visiting the sights of
Bonito and getting to the Pantanal. Last transfer from the airport is at 2:30 pm.
⊠ *Rua 31 de Março* ☎ *067/3255–3005* ⊕ *www.vanzellatransportes.com.br.*

EXPLORING

FAMILY **Balneário Municipal.** One of the best-value sights in Bonito is this municipal
baths complex, just 6 km (4 miles) outside town. You can swim with fish
in crystalline waters and get a bite to eat at several simple restaurants, all
at a fraction of the price charged elsewhere in town. ⊠ *Rodovia Bonito
Guia Lopes, Km 6, Centro, Bonito* ☎ *067/3255–1996* ⊠ *R$20.*

Gruta do Lago Azul (*Blue Lagoon Grotto*). The 160-foot-deep Gruta do
Lago Azul has a crystal-clear freshwater lake at the bottom and smaller side
caves in the calcareous rock. The best time to visit is from mid-November to
mid-January at around 8:30 am, when sunlight beams down the entrance,
reflecting off the water to create an eerie turquoise glow. See stalagmites and
stalactites in various stages of development. ⊠ *Fazenda Jaraguá, Rodovia
Três Morros, 12 miles (20 km) west of Bonito* ⊠ *R$36* ☉ *Daily 7–2.*

Parque Ecológico Baía Bonita. At this park just 7 km (4 miles) outside
Bonito, you can go snorkeling along in the 1-km-long (½-mile-long)
Aquario Natural, or "Natural Aquarium." The crystal clear waters
reveal an incredible close-up array of colorful fish. Equipment rental
is included in the admission price. The park is also home to brightly
colored birds and to a handful of captive local mammals. ⊠ *Rodovia
Bonito/Guia Lopes da Laguna, Km 7, Centro, Bonito* ☎ *067/3255–
2160* ⊕ *www.aquarionatural.com.br* ⊠ *R$170* ☉ *Daily 9–5.*

Rio da Prata. One of Bonito's most popular attractions is snorkeling in
the crystalline waters of the Rio da Prata (literally, river of silver). No
sunscreen is permitted, so as not to pollute waters that are home to a
myriad of dazzling tropical fish. Scuba and horseback rides are also
available. ⊠ *BR 267, Km 512, Zona Rural de Jardim, Jardim* ⊕ *www.
riodaprata.com.br/inicio* ⊠ *R$165.*

WORTH NOTING

Rio Formoso. The approximately 1½-hour rafting trip on the Rio Formoso takes you through clear waters and some rapids while you observe
the fish and the birds of the Pantanal. You might also see and hear bands
of *macaco-prego* (capuchin monkeys), the region's largest primates. The
tour ends at Ilha do Padre (Priest's Island), where there's a complex
of rapids emerging through thick riverine vegetation. There's a snack
bar where you can relax after the tour. To best appreciate this attraction, make sure there hasn't been any rain in the previous days—the
river gets quite muddy. ⊠ *Fazenda Cachoeira, Rod do Turismo, Km 08*
☎ *67/3255–1213* ⊠ *R$70* ☉ *Tours by appointment.*

WHERE TO EAT

$$ ✕ **Cantinho do Peixe.** This establishment is one of your best choices for
BRAZILIAN   local fish. The highlight is *pintado*, which is prepared in two-dozen different ways. The cheese sauce is a good accompaniment to any of the fish dishes. $ *Average main: R$40* ⊠ *Cel Pilad Rebua 1437, Centro, Bonito* ☎ *67/3255–3381* ⊘ *Closed Wed.*

$$$$ ✕ **Casa do João.** One of the best places to try local freshwater fish,
BRAZILIAN   this popular wood-furnished eating house is just off the town's main square, behind the Banco do Brasil. The speciality of the house is *traira sem espinha* (fried boneless traira fish). Other favorites include grilled pirarara fish, caiman steaks, and, for dessert, *petit gâteau* (cake) made from guavira, a tasty local fruit. $ *Average main: R$80* ⊠ *Rua Nelson Felicio dos Santos, 664-A, Centro, Bonito* ☎ *067/3255–1212* ⊕ *www.casadojoao.com.br.*

$$ ✕ **Castellabate.** This restaurant at the entrance to Bonito offers an array
BRAZILIAN   of pizza and pasta dishes. The highlights are the caiman and wild boar steaks. These are from farm-raised animals, as hunting is forbidden. $ *Average main: R$40* ⊠ *Rua Pilad Rebuá 2168, Centro, Bonito* ☎ *67/3225–1713.*

$$$ ✕ **Sale e Pepe.** The friendly Japanese owner and chef Masano serves up
JAPANESE   the town's finest Asian food, as well as regional specialties. This may well be your only opportunity to try sashimi of piranha and piraputanga, or spring rolls with pintado and banana. $ *Average main: R$50* ⊠ *29 Maio 971, Centro, Bonito* ☎ *067/3255–1822* ⊘ *Closed Mon. No lunch.*

$$$$ ✕ **Taboá.** Since 1995, this dining and—above all—drinking spot has
BRAZILIAN   evolved from a hole in a wall into a Bonito landmark that can seat nearly 300 for dinner. The regional food is respectable, but it's the artisanal cachaça, the music, and the boisterous atmosphere that keep the crowds coming. Customers are encouraged to write on the walls. $ *Average main: R$65* ⊠ *R. Piad Rebua 1834, Centro, Bonito* ☎ *067/3255–3598.*

WHERE TO STAY

$$ ⊡ **Marruá.** The modern design of this hotel contrasts with others in
HOTEL   town, which lean toward rustic looks. **Pros:** competent staff; soothing atmosphere. **Cons:** few amenities; bland decor. $ *Rooms from: R$268* ⊠ *Rua Joana Sorta 1173, Vila Donária* ☎ *67/3255–1040* ⊕ *www.marruahotel.com.br* ⊅ *56 rooms, 30 suites.*

$ ⊡ **Pousada Rancho Jarinú.** A family-run business, Pousada Rancho Jarinú
B&B/INN   has friendly owners who go to great lengths to make you feel at home. **Pros:** attentive owners; simple but tastful decor. **Cons:** some rooms are dark; small bathrooms. $ *Rooms from: R$210* ⊠ *Rua 24 de Fevereiro, 1895, Centro, Bonito* ☎ *67/3255–2094* ⊕ *www.pousadaranchojarinu.com.br* ⊅ *9 rooms* ⦶ *No meals.*

$ ⊡ **Pousada Remanso.** Run by the town's former secretary of tourism,
B&B/INN   this centrally located pousada has bright rooms and spacious common areas, which make for a comfortable stay. **Pros:** central location; knowledgeable staff. **Cons:** few amenities. $ *Rooms from: R$218* ⊠ *Rua Cel. Pilad Rebuá 1515, Centro, Bonito* ☎ *067/3255–1137* ⊕ *www.pousadaremanso.com.br* ⊅ *21 rooms* ⦶ *Breakfast.*

$$$$ HOTEL Fodor's Choice ★ **Wetiga Hotel.** Large, luxurious, and expertly designed and landscaped, the Wetiga Hotel is the best in downtown Bonito. **Pros:** great amenities; sophisticated decor; excellent service. **Cons:** some bathrooms are small; busy neighborhood. [$] *Rooms from: R$960* ✉ *Rua Pilad Rebuá 679, Centro, Bonito* ☎ *67/3255–5100* 🌐 *www.wetigahotel.com.br* 🛏 *64 rooms, 4 suites* 🍴 *No meals.*

$$$$ RESORT FAMILY **Zagaia Eco-Resort Hotel.** With decorations inspired in the Kadiweu people's traditional crafts, this ecolodge has an authentic feel. **Pros:** great amenities for families; unique decor; spacious common areas; Harrison Ford slept here. **Cons:** hectic during conventions; away from downtown. [$] *Rooms from: R$837* ✉ *Km 0, Rodovia Bonito–Três Morros* ☎ *67/3255–5500* 🌐 *www.zagaia.com.br* 🛏 *100 rooms, 30 suites* 🍴 *Some meals.*

SHOPPING

The town's main avenue has great handicraft shops with native art and other pieces by local artists.

Além da Arte. This shop has beautiful bamboo and feather handicrafts and colorful ceramics made by the Kadiweu and Terena peoples. ✉ *Rua Pilad Rebuá 1966, Centro, Bonito* ☎ *67/3255–1485.*

MIRANDA

205 km (128 miles) west of Campo Grande.

This tiny settlement on the Miranda River grew into a city after the construction of the railway linking São Paulo to Corumbá and on to Bolivia. In its heyday the railway was called Ferrovia da Morte (Death Railway) because of the many cattle thieves, train robbers, and smugglers that rode the rails. Since the 1980s the railway has been closed to passengers.

Ecotourism is Miranda's main source of revenue. Comfortable pousadas and farms allow you to get acquainted with the *pantaneiro* lifestyle. The Rio Miranda area has abundant fauna, including a sizable population of jaguars. Here's a great opportunity to practice *focagem,* a local version of a photographic safari: as night falls, guides take you into the Pantanal in 4x4 pickup trucks with powerful searchlights that mesmerize the animals for some time, so you can get a really close look.

GETTING HERE AND AROUND

You must either drive or take a bus to Miranda from Campo Grande. Direct bus lines from Campo Grande are run by Expresso Mato Grosso (4 hours, R$44) and Andorinha (R$15).

WHERE TO EAT AND STAY

$ BRAZILIAN 🍴 **Zero Hora.** This buffet-style restaurant serves regional fare, including grilled or stewed local fish. There's a large and varied salad bar. [$] *Average main: R$25* ✉ *Rua Barão do Rio Branco 1146* ☎ *67/3242–1330.*

$ B&B/INN **Pousada Águas do Pantanal.** A great budget choice, this inn renovated in 2012 occupies a historic house with lots of antiques. **Pros:** good bargain; attentive staff. **Cons:** few amenities; small bathrooms. [$] *Rooms from: R$170* ✉ *Av. Afonso Pena 367,* ☎ *67/3242–1242* 🌐 *www.aguasdopantanal.com.br* 🛏 *20 rooms* 🍴 *Breakfast.*

$$$$ B&B/INN [🏨] **Refúgio da Ilha.** This pousada is nestled on a 2,000-acre island in the Rio Salobra delta. **Pros:** prime location for wildlife sightings; cozy rooms. **Cons:** extra charge for English-speaking guides; three-night minimum. [$] *Rooms from: R$810* ✉ *31 km (22 miles) west of Miranda, 235 km (146 miles) west of Campo Grande* ☎ *67/3384–3270* 🌐 *www.refugiodailha.com.br* 🛏 *8 rooms* 🍴 *All meals.*

SPORTS AND THE OUTDOORS

RANCHES

The last reluctant ranchers are beginning to see tourism as a viable economic alternative in this region, which means you can visit a working ranch or farm for a day.

Fazenda San Francisco. Fazenda San Francisco is a 37,000-acre working ranch where you can go on a photo safari in the morning and a boat tour on Rio Miranda in the afternoon, when you'll have the chance to fish for piranha. The R$103 fee includes a lunch of rice and beans with beef and vegetables. ✉ *BR 262, 36 km (22 miles) west of Miranda* ☎ *67/3242–1088* 🌐 *www.fazendasanfrancisco.tur.br.*

SALVADOR AND THE BAHIA COAST

Updated by
Lauren Holmes

In "the land of happiness," as the state of Bahia is known, the sun shines almost every day. Its Atlantic Ocean shoreline runs for 900 kilometers (560 miles), creating beautiful white-sand beaches lined with coconut palms. Inland is Parque Nacional da Chapada Diamantina (Chapada Diamantina National Park), with 152,000 hectares (375,000 acres) of mountains, waterfalls, caves, natural swimming pools, and hiking trails. And in Bahia's capital, Salvador, the beat of bongo drums echoing through the narrow cobblestone streets is a rhythmic reminder of Brazil's African heritage.

Bahia's Costa do Coqueiros (Coconut Coast), north of Salvador up to the village of Mangue Seco, on the border of Sergipe State, has 190 kilometers (118 miles) of beautiful beaches. South of Salvador, from Baía de Todos os Santos and its islands (Itaparica and Tinharé) to Itacaré is the Dendê Coast, where you find the African palms that produce the *dendê* oil used in Bahian cooking. The midsection of Bahia's coast is known as the Cocoa Coast, because cocoa plantations dominate the landscape and the economy.

Farther south, the Discovery Coast, from Santa Cruz de Cabrália to Barra do Caí, has many sites linked with the first Portuguese explorers to arrive in Brazil. The last bit of Bahia's coast heading south is the Whale Coast, near the towns of Caravelas and Alcobaça, where humpback whales mate and give birth from June to November.

ORIENTATION AND PLANNING

GETTING ORIENTED

Covering nearly 570,000 square kilometers (220,000 square miles) of eastern Brazil, the state of Bahia is hilly and dry. The vibrant capital of Salvador sits on the Atlantic Ocean about 1,649 km (1,024 miles) north of Rio de Janeiro and 1,962 km (1,219 miles) north of Saõ Paulo. The coastline, with its beautiful beaches, gets most of the attention. The 900 km (560 miles) of coastline is about a third of that in the entire country.

SALVADOR
On the southern tip of a triangular peninsula, Salvador sits at the mouth of the Bahia de Todos os Santos. The peninsula forms a natural harbor and shelters the city from the open waters of the Atlantic Ocean. Salvador is a hilly city, with the Cidade Alta (Upper Town) quite a bit higher than the Cidade Baixa (Lower Town).

TOP REASONS TO GO

■ **Soak Up the Sun:** Warm waters year-round and a continuous lineup of beautiful beaches from south to north make Bahia one of the premier destinations in Brazil for soaking up the sun.

■ **Unique Cuisine:** Bahia's African influence on Portuguese and native Brazilian food has resulted in a distinct regional cuisine.

■ **Carnival:** Salvador is one of the top spots in Brazil to celebrate Carnival—its *trios eléctricos*, street parades, and array of big-name entertainers combine for one long, nonstop party you won't forget.

■ **Afro-Brazilian Culture:** Salvador is the capital of Afro-Brazilian culture and its historic center, Pelourinho, is a World Heritage site with stunning monuments.

■ **Bahian Music:** The top names in Brazilian music, Gilberto Gil, Caetano Veloso, Gal Costa, Maria Bethânia, who were some of the musicians nicknamed *Novo Baianos* (New Bahians), are de facto ambassadors of Bahian music.

THE COCOA COAST

460 km (286 miles) south of Salvador, the Cocoa Coast combines charismatic surf towns and chic beach resorts with cocoa plantations and mineral springs, surrounded by one of Brazil's only remaining sections of primary Mata-Atlantic rain forest. The faded town of Ilhéus, a famous setting for Jorge Amado's romantic novels of Bahian life, was the bustling heart of Brazil's once-booming Cacau region.

THE DISCOVERY COAST

Located 723 km (450 miles) south of Salvador, Porto Seguro provides the gateway to some of Bahia's best beaches, from happening Trancoso to the more remote Caraíva. As idyllic beach villages absorb development, wandering Robinson Crusoes are traveling ever farther south in search of the ultimate deserted white-sand beach.

9

PLANNING

WHEN TO GO

Peak seasons for Brazilians to travel are from December to March (South American summer) and the month of July, when schools have winter breaks. Most international visitors come in the months of August and September. Make reservations far in advance for stays during these months, especially if you plan to visit during Carnival (February or March). As the weather is sunny and warm year-round, consider a trip in the off-season, when prices are lower and the beaches less crowded. Mean temperatures are about 25°C (77°F) in winter (July and August), when there's usually more rainfall, including the occasional tropical downpour. Summer temperatures are a few degrees higher (28°C/82°F), but humidity is somewhat lower.

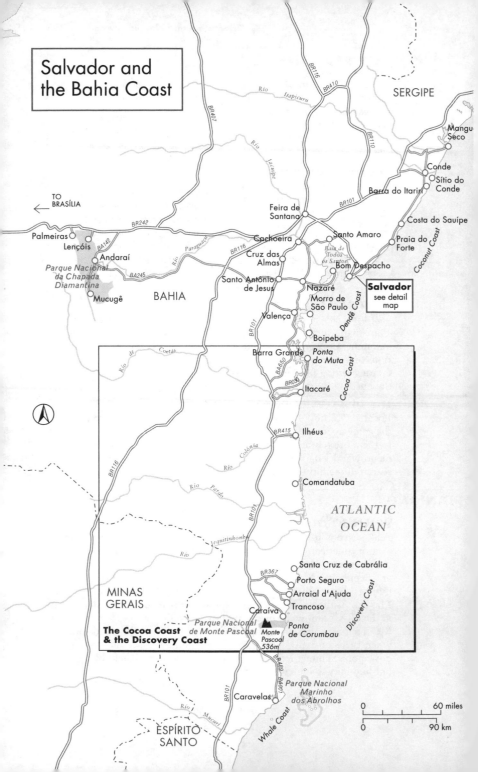

GETTING HERE AND AROUND

Most destinations around Salvador can be easily reached by car. To visit the Discovery Coast, fly to Porto Seguro (723 km [450 miles] south of Salvador), and then rent a car to explore other beaches and attractions. For the Cocoa Coast, you can fly directly to Ilhéus, 460 km (286 miles) south of Salvador.

RESTAURANTS

The laid-back lifestyle of Bahians is reflected in their food. While break-fast in Brazil is traditionally a minor meal, even the simplest of inns will often provide a buffet spread fit for a king—including tropical fruits, eggs, and endless cakes and pancakes made from Tapioca. Lunches are usually casual and not strictly defined by the clock, as the hottest part of the day is not the best for large meals. Dinner is the main meal, and starts late, usually after 9. Bahian cuisine is unique and delicious, and a definite reason to visit. The ever-present *oleo de dendê* (palm oil) is one ingredient that sets it apart from other Brazilian cuisines. *Prices in the reviews are the average cost of a main course at dinner or, if dinner is not served, at lunch.*

HOTELS

Lodging options in Salvador range from modern high-rises with an international clientele and world-class service to cozy, often family-run *pousadas* (inns). While Costa do Sauipe has a concentration of big resorts, the best ones are scattered along the coast. Pousadas are usually the only option in remote beaches or in fishing villages. Apartment hotels, where guest quarters have kitchens and living rooms as well as bedrooms, are available in some places. Low-end pousadas may not have air-conditioning or hot water; be sure to ask before you book. *Prices in the reviews are the lowest cost of a standard double room in high season. For expanded reviews, facilities, and current deals, visit Fodors.com.*

SALVADOR

According to Salvador's adopted son Jorge Amado, "In Salvador, magic becomes part of the every-day." From the shimmering golden light of sunset over the Baía do Todos os Santos, to the rhythmic beats that race along the streets, Salvador, while no longer Brazil's capital, remains one of its most captivating cities.

A large dose of its exoticism comes down to its African heritage—at least 70% of its 2,675,000 population is classified as Afro-Brazilian—and how it has blended into Brazil's different strands, from the native Indians to the Christian colonizers. Salvadorans may tell you that you can visit a different church every day of the year, which is almost true—the city has about 300. Churches whose interiors are covered with gold leaf were financed by the riches of the Portuguese colonial era, when slaves masked their traditional religious beliefs under a thin Catholic veneer. And partly thanks to modern-day acceptance of those beliefs, Salvador has become the fount of Candomblé, a religion based on personal dialogue with the *orixás,* a family of African deities closely linked to nature and the Catholic saints. The influence of Salvador's African heritage on Brazilian music has also turned the city into one of the

A Bit of History

Portuguese navigator and explorer Pedro Alvares Cabral's first sight of Brazil—on Easter Sunday, April 22, 1500—was an isolated mountain of about 530 meters (1,600 feet) immediately named *Monte Pascoal* (Mount Easter), 750 km (466 miles) south of Salvador. The Portuguese flotilla soon dropped anchor most likely at what is now the fishing village of Curumuxatiba. The explorers were met by the native Tupinambá tribe, who were welcoming and eager to accept gifts and provide food and water. Proceeding up the coast about 130 km (81 miles), the ships landed at what is now Santa Cruz de Cabrália. On a knoll on the Coroa Vermelha beach, the first mass on this new-found land was held. In his journal, the journey's log keeper, Pero Vaz de Caminha, extolled the future colony—"where the land is so fertile that all that is sown will give a bountiful harvest." Within a few years more Portuguese expeditions arrived to comb the coastal forests for highly prized *pau-brasil* (brazilwood) trees, the first of many natural resources to be exploited by the colonial landlords.

In 1549 Tomé de Sousa was appointed Brazil's first governor-general, with orders to establish the colony's capital in Bahia. The deep waters at the mouth of Baía de Todos os Santos (All Saint's Bay) and the nearby hills, which provided a commanding view of the region and protection in case of attack by pirates, indicated a favorable site. Within a few decades the city of Salvador had become one of the most important ports in the Southern Hemisphere, and remained so until the 18th century. In 1763 the capital was moved to Rio de Janeiro, and the city lost part of its economic importance and prestige.

Due to its continental dimensions, Brazil has a diverse culture that is sometimes a mosaic but more often a blend of European, African, and indigenous backgrounds. But in Bahia the historical and cultural influence is predominately African. The large African-Brazilian population (comprising more than 70% of the population), the rhythms with mesmerizing percussion, and the scents on the streets of Salvador immediately evoke the other side of the Atlantic.

Until slavery ended officially in 1888, it's estimated that more than 4 million slaves were brought to Brazil from Africa, and the port of Salvador was a major center of the slave trade. By contrast, only around 600,000 slaves were brought to the United States. The large African slave population here and the generally lenient attitude of Portuguese masters and the Catholic Church led to a greater preservation of African customs in Brazil than in other countries. The indigenous tribes, forced to work with the Portuguese to harvest pau-brasil trees, either fled inland to escape slavery or were integrated into the European and African cultures.

Today Bahia faces several challenges. As Brazil's fourth-largest state, it's struggling to juggle population growth and the economic boom that started 50 years ago when oil was found in its territory. The race is on to preserve its way of life and its landscapes, especially the remaining patches of Mata-Atlantica Rain Forest, coral reefs, mangroves, and interior sierras.

musical capitals of Brazil, resulting in a myriad of venues to enjoy live music across the city, along with international acclaim for exponents like Gilberto Gil, Caetano Veloso, and Daniela Mercury.

Salvador's economy today is focused on telecommunications and tourism. The still-prevalent African culture draws many tourists—this is the best place in Brazil to hear African music, learn or watch African dance, and see *capoeira*, a martial art developed by slaves. In the district of Pelourinho, many colorful 18th- and 19th-century houses remain, part of the reason why this is the center of the tourist trade.

GETTING HERE AND AROUND

Salvador's Aeroporto Deputado Luís Eduardo Magalhães (SSA) is one of the busiest in Brazil. In the last few years several international carriers have opened direct service from abroad, especially from Europe. TAM and American Airlines are the only airlines with direct flights from the United States. Most international flights require a change of plane in São Paulo. The airport is quite far from downtown—37 km (23 miles) to the northeast. Taxis to central hotels should cost between R$80 and R$100, with an increase in fare late at night. You can either pay an advanced set fare at the booth inside the terminal or take one of the taxis from the stand outside that run by the meter.

Long-distance buses arrive at Salvador's Terminal Rodoviário. The trips are tortuously long (22 hours from São Paulo, 24 to 28 hours from Rio de Janeiro) and may be more expensive than flying.

Regular buses (R$2.80) serve most of the city, but they're often crowded and rife with pickpocketing. Fancier executivo buses (R$4–R$4.50) are a better option.

Comum taxis (white with a blue stripe) can be hailed on the street or at designated stops near major hotels, or summoned by phone. Taxis are metered, and fares begin at R$3.80. Unscrupulous drivers sometimes "forget" to turn on the meter and jack up the fare. In Salvador tipping isn't expected. A company called Chame Taxi runs taxis that are spacious, air-conditioned, and equipped with modern security devices.

Itaparica and the other harbor islands can be reached by taking a ferry or a *lancha* (a small boat carrying up to five passengers), by hiring a motorized schooner, or by joining a harbor schooner excursion—all departing from two docks. Boats depart from the Terminal Turístico Marítimo or Terminal São Joaquim close to the Feira São Joaquim.

ESSENTIALS

Airport Aeroporto Deputado Luís Eduardo Magalhães (*SSA*)
✉ *Praça Gago Coutinho s/n, São Cristovão* ☎ *071/3204 1010, 071/3204–1444* ⊕ *www.infraero.gov.br.*

Boat Contacts Terminal Marítimo São Joaquim ✉ *Av. Oscar Ponte 1051, São Joaquim.* **Terminal Turístico Marítimo** ✉ *Av da França, Comércio.*

Bus Contact Terminal Rodoviário ✉ *Av. Antônio Carlos Magalhães 4362, Iguatemi* ☎ *071/3450–3871.*

Taxi Cometas ☎ *071/3014–4502.* **Chame Taxi** ✉ *Travessa da Ajuda, 01 Edifício Martins Catarino 3° andar—Sala 302* ☎ *071/3241–8888* ⊕ *www.chametaxisalvador.com.br.*

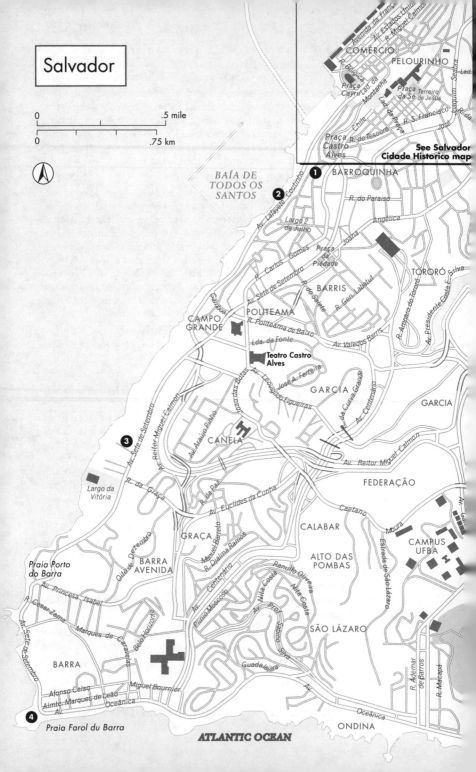

Salvador

0   .5 mile

0   .75 km

BAÍA DE TODOS OS SANTOS

COMÉRCIO

PELOURINHO

Av. Estados Unidos

Av. Miguel Calmon

R. Miguel Calmon

Avenida da Franca

R. Bélgica

Praça Cayru

Lad. da Montanha

Praça da Sé

Terreiro de Jesus

R. S. Francisco

Chile

Lad. da Praça

José

Praça Castro Alves

R. do Tesouro

See Salvador Cidade Historico map

BARROQUINHA

R. do Paraíso

Angélica

Av. Lafayete Coutinho

Largo 2 de Julho

Praça da Piedade

Joana

R. Carlos Gomes

BARRIS

R. do Sodré

R. Gen. Labatut

TORORÓ

Av. Amparo do Tororó

R. Presidente Costa E. Silva

Av. Sete de Setembro

CAMPO GRANDE

POLTEAMA

R. Politeama de Baixo

Gamboa

Lda. da Fonte

Av. Vale dos Barris

Teatro Castro Alves

José A. Ferreira

Leovigildo Figueiras

Largo das Botas

GARCIA

da Curva Grande

Av. Centenário

GARCIA

Av. Sete de Setembro

Av. Reitor Miguel Calmon

CANELA

Av. Araújo Pinho

Av. Reitor Miguel Calmon

FEDERAÇÃO

Largo da Vitória

R. da Graça

R. da Paz

Av. Euclides da Cunha

Caetano

CALABAR

Moura

CAMPUS UFBA

GRAÇA

Manuel Barreto

R. Djalma Ramos

ALTO DAS POMBAS

Estrada de São Lázaro

Praia Porto do Barra

Oito de Dezembro

BARRA AVENIDA

Av. Centenário

Av. Plinio Moscoso

Ranulfo Oliveira

Alta Costa

Av. Nilta Costa

Av. Princesa Isabel

R. César Zama

Marques de Caravelas

Belo Horizonte

SÃO LÁZARO

R. Ademar de Barros

R. Macapá

BARRA

Av. Sete de Setembro

Afonso Celso

Almte. Marques de Leão

Miguel Bournier

Oceânica

Guadalajara

ONDINA

Oceânica

①   **②**   **③**   **④**

Praia Farol du Barra

ATLANTIC OCEAN

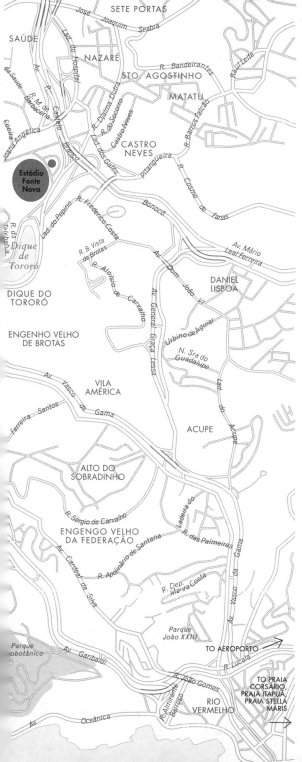

SAFETY AND PRECAUTIONS

In terms of safety, Salvador is no different from most big cities in Brazil—crime is a concern in most neighborhoods. The Centro Histórico area, especially Cidade Alta during daytime, is one of the safest places in Salvador. There are tourist police stationed on almost every corner. At night stick to the main tourist areas and don't walk down deserted streets. It is worth asking at your hotel upon arrival to point out on a map which streets in Pelourinho are the ones to avoid. Elsewhere around the city, take a taxi between neighborhoods. Cidade Baixa and the Comércio neighborhood are notorious for petty crime, and pickpocketing is common on buses and ferries and in crowded places.

TOURS

Do not hire "independent" guides who approach you at churches and other sights, as they are usually not accredited and will likely overcharge you. Also avoid large group tours, which give little information about the sites and are targeted by hordes of street vendors. Private tours with accredited agencies such as Tatur Turismo are your best bet. Prices vary depending on the size of the group; most include hotel pickup and drop-off.

Visitor and Tour Information Bahia Ticket Travel Turismo. An all-around travel company that books buses, cars for hire, internal/international flights, and transfers to Morro de São Paulo/Boipeba. The bilingual office also organizes a selection of city-tours and out-of-town excursions and can rent apartments for longer stays. ⊠ *Largo do Pelourinho 7, Pelourinho* ☎ *071/3322–0809* ⊕ *www.bahiaticket.com.br.* **Disque Bahia Turismo.** A comprehensive and efficient initiative, courtesy of Bahia's Secretary of Tourism, this central portal provides a 24-hour-a-day service for all tourist information—online, through a real-time chat service (launched in 2012) and via a multilingual call center. ⊠ *Secretaria de Turismo, Av Tancredo Neves 776, Camino* ☎ *071/3103–3103* ⊕ *www.bahia.com.br.* **Salvador Bus.** Double-decker tour buses run by Salvador Bus travel around the upper and lower cities and to the beaches. A R$45 wristband lets you hop off and on as many times as you like. ☎ *071/3356–6425* ⊕ *www.salvadorbus.com.br.* **Tatur Tourismo.** Tatur Tourismo offers fantastic tailor-made city tours, including walking tours of the Pelourinho, programs on the city's African heritage, and experiences with local musicians. They are experts in day trips outside the city and can organize travel throughout Bahia. ⊠ *Centro Empresarial Iguatemi, Av. Tancredo Neves 274, Iguatemi* ☎ *071/3114–7900* ⊕ *www.tatur.com.br.*

EXPLORING

Salvador sprawls across a peninsula surrounded by the Baía de Todos os Santos on one side and the Atlantic Ocean on the other. The city has about 50 km (31 miles) of coastline. The original city, referred to as the Centro Histórica (Historical Center), is divided into the Cidade Alta (Upper City), also called Pelourinho, and Cidade Baixa (Lower City).

The Cidade Baixa is a commercial area—known as Comércio—that runs along the port and is the site of Salvador's indoor market, Mercado Modelo. You can move between the upper and lower cities on foot, via the landmark Elevador Lacerda, behind the market, or on the Plano

Inclinado, a funicular lift, which connects Rua Guindaste dos Padres on Comércio with the alley behind Cathedral Basílica.

From the Cidade Histórica you can travel north along the bay to the hilltop Igreja de Nosso Senhor do Bonfim. You can also head south to the point, guarded by the Forte Santo Antônio da Barra, where the bay waters meet those of the Atlantic. This area on Salvador's southern tip is home to the trendy neighborhoods of Barra, Ondina, and Rio Vermelho, with many museums, theaters, shops, and restaurants. Beaches along the Atlantic coast and north of Forte Santo Antônio da Barra are among the city's cleanest. Many are illuminated at night and have bars and restaurants that stay open late.

CIDADE HISTÓRICO

The heart of the original colonial city, the Cidade Alta section, incorporates the Comércio and Pelourinho neighborhoods and is a riveting blend of European and African cultures. More than 500 of the 2,982 buildings have been restored, earning Salvador the reputation of having the finest examples of baroque architecture in South America. Along the winding and sometimes steep streets, whose cobbles were laid by slaves, are restored 17th- and 18th-century buildings. Many of the restored buildings are now occupied by restaurants, museums, bars, and shops that sell everything from clothing, film, musical instruments, and handicrafts to precious stones. They are painted in bright colors, which, along with the sounds of vendors, street musicians, and capoeiristas, add to the festive atmosphere.

The Cidade Baixa (Lower City) is the section of historic Salvador that fronts the Atlantic Ocean. This is where you will find the Mercado Modelo, one of Salvador's landmarks, with dozens of stalls that sell everything from Bahian lace dresses and musical instruments to amulets believed to ward off evil or bring good luck. Around the building gathers a mixed crowd of locals and visitors, impromptu entertainers, fortune tellers, and handicrafts vendors.

In the port of Salvador, ferryboats and catamarans leave from different docks for Ilha de Itaparica (Itaparica Island), Morro de São Paulo, and other destinations within Baía de Todos os Santos. The area is busy during the day but is practically deserted at night, especially near the base of the Lacerda Elevator. Take a taxi at night.

TOP ATTRACTIONS

Catedral Basílica. Recognized as one of the richest examples of baroque architecture in Brazil, this 17th-century masterpiece is a must-visit. The masonry facade is made of Portuguese sandstone, brought as ballast in shipping boats; the 16th-century tiles in the sacristy came from Macau. Inside, the engravings on the altars show the evolution of architectural styles in Bahia. Hints of Asia permeate the decoration, such as the facial features and clothing of the figures in the transept altars and the intricate ivory-and-tortoise shell inlay from Goa on the Japiassu family altar, third on the right as you enter (it is attributed to a Jesuit monk from China). The altars and ceiling are layered with gold—about 10 grams per square meter. ⊠ *Praça 15 de Novembro s/n, Terreiro de Jesus* ☎ *071/3321–4573* 🎟 *R$3* 🕐 *Daily 8–11:30 and 2–5:30.*

WALKING THE PELOURINHO

Showcasing the largest collection of colonial buildings in Latin America, the Pelourinho is perfect for exploring by foot. Begin in the Largo do Pelourinho, which was once the whipping post for runaway slaves, where you can now visit the Fundação de Jorge Amado, the Museu da Cidade, and Senac. Head up Rua Maciel de Baixo, the street that runs past the museum, and stroll the cobblestone streets of the colonial district, flanked by houses in pastel shades, until you reach Largo do Cruzeiro de São Francisco, where you can catch your first glimpse of the exuberant São Francisco Church, the most ornate baroque church in Brazil. Continue through Praça da Sé to the Municipal Square towering above the Lower City, which offers wonderful views of the All Saints bay. Guided tours with a bilingual expert are available through Tatur Turismo.

Fundação Casa de Jorge Amado. This colonial mansion set on the Pelourinho provides a window into the life, work, and inspiration of Bahia's best beloved writer, Jorge Amado. Lovers of his literature will be lost for hours perusing the photos, books, and old belongings, while those yet to delve into Bahia's past through the likes of "Gabriela, Cloves and Cinnamon" will be left hunting for an immediate download. There is also a nice coffee shop that provides great viewing over the square. On Wednesday there's free admission. ⊠ *Largo do Pelourinho, 51, Pelourinho* ☎ *071/3321–0070* ⊕ *www.jorgeamado.org.br* ✉ *R$3* ⊙ *Weekdays 10–6, Sat. 10–4.*

Igreja de Nosso Senhor do Bonfim. Set atop a hill as the Itapagibe Peninsula extends into the bay, Salvador's iconic Igreja de Nosso Senhor do Bomfim is well worth the 8-km (5-mile) detour from the Centro Histórico and marks a crossroads between the Christian and native African religions. Its patron saint, Oxalá, is the father of all the gods and goddesses in the Candomblé mythology. Built in the 1750s, the church has many ex-votos (votive offerings) of wax, wooden, and plaster replicas of body parts, left by those praying for miraculous cures. Outside the church, street vendors sell a bizarre mixture of figurines, from St. George and the Dragon to devils and warriors. The morning mass on the first Friday of the month draws a huge congregation, most wearing white, with practitioners of Candomblé on one side and Catholics on the other. ⊠ *Praça do Senhor do Bonfim, Alto do Bonfim* ☎ *071/3116–2196* ✉ *Free* ⊙ *Services Wed.–Thurs. 9 am; Fri. 6 am, 9:30 am; Sat. 7 am, 8 am, 5 pm; Sun. 6 am, 7 am, 9 am, 10:30 am, 5 pm.*

Igreja de Nossa Senhora do Rosário dos Pretos. Built by and for slaves between 1704 and 1796, the Church of Our Lady of the Rosary has finally won acclaim outside the local Afro-Brazilian community. After extensive renovation, it's worth a look at the side altars to see statues of the church's few black saints. African rhythms pervade the services and the Sunday mass is one not to miss. ⊠ *Largo do Pelourinho s/n, Pelourinho* ☎ *071/3321–6280* ✉ *Free* ⊙ *Weekdays 8–6, Sat. 9–5, Sun. 10–5.*

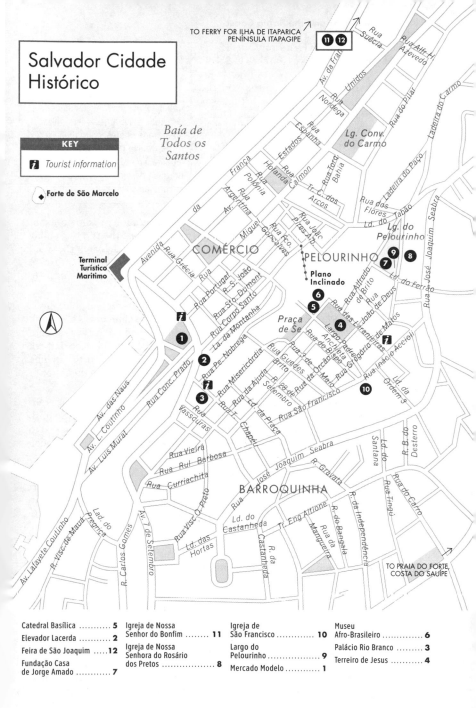

Salvador Cidade Histórico

KEY

i Tourist information

◆ Forte de São Marcelo

Baía de Todos os Santos

TO FERRY FOR ILHA DE ITAPARICA
PENÍNSULA ITAPAGIPE

Lg. Conv. do Carmo

COMÉRCIO

Terminal Turístico Marítimo

PELOURINHO

Plano Inclinado

Praça de Sé

BARROQUINHA

TO PRAIA DO FORTE,
COSTA DO SAUÍPE

FodorsChoice **Igreja de São Francisco.** One of the
★ most impressive churches in Salva-
dor, the Church of St. Francis was
built in the 18th century on the
site of an earlier church that was
burned down during the Dutch
invasion in the early 1600s. The
ceiling was painted in 1774 by José
Joaquim da Rocha, who founded
Brazil's first art school. The ornate
cedar-and-rosewood interior is
covered with images of mermaids
and other fanciful creatures bathed

BAIANAS
Salvadorian street food is prepared and sold by *baianas*, turbaned women in voluminous lace-trim white dresses who take great pride in preserving their Afro-Brazilian culture. Their outfits, an amalgam of African and Afro-Brazilian designs, symbolize peace in Yoruban culture.

in gold leaf. Guides say that there's as much as a ton of gold here, but
restoration experts maintain there's much less. At the end of Sunday
morning mass, the lights are switched off so you can catch the won-
drous subtlety of the gold leaf under natural light. ⊠ *Rua da Ordem
Terceira s/n, Pelourinho* ☎ *071/3322–6430* ⊠ *R$3* ☉ *Mon.–Sat. 7–6.
Sun. 8–noon.*

Convento de São Francisco. With an interior glittering in gold, this is
considered one of the country's most impressive churches. Along with
intricately carved wood-work, the convento has an impressive series of
37 white-and-blue tiled panels lining the walls of the cloister that tell
the tale of the birth and life of St. Francis de Assisi. It is worth catching
Sunday morning mass for the atmosphere alone. ⊠ *Largo do Cruzeiro
de São Francisco s/n, Pelourinho* ☎ *071/3322–6430* ⊠ *R$5*

Ordem Terceira de São Francisco. The Ordem Terceira de São Francisco, on the north side of the complex, has an 18th-century Spanish
plateresque sandstone facade—the only one in Brazil—that is carved to
resemble Spanish silver altars made by beating the metal into wooden
molds. ☎ *071/3321–6968.*

Largo do Pelourinho (*Pelourinho Square*). Once the "whipping post"
for runaway for slaves, this square now serves as the cultural heart
of Salvador's historic center, with regular live music performed in
front of the colorful colonial buildings. The four public stages are
named after characters in Jorge Amado novels; a museum on the
acclaimed author, who lived from 1912 to 2001, borders the upper
end of the square. While summer months see performances nightly,
year-round Tuesdays and Sundays are the days not to miss for music
in the Pelourinho. The small plaza commemorates the day in 1888
when Princesa Isabel, daughter of Dom Pedro II, signed the decree
that officially ended slavery. ⊠ *Intersection of Rua Alfredo de Brito
and Ladeira do Ferrão, Pelourinho.*

Museu Afro-Brasileiro. Next to the Catedral Basílica, this palatial pink
building has a collection of more than 1,100 pieces relating to the
city's religious or spiritual history, including pottery, sculpture, tapestry,
weavings, paintings, crafts, carvings, and photographs. There's an interesting display on the meanings of Candomblé deities, with huge carved-
wood panels portraying each one. The other museum that shares the

CLOSE UP

Spiritual Salvador

Evidence that Brazil is officially a Roman Catholic country can be found everywhere. There are beautiful churches and cathedrals across the nation. Most Brazilians wear a religious medal, bus and taxi drivers place pictures of St. Christopher prominently in their vehicles, and two big winter celebrations (in June) honor St. John and St. Peter. For many Brazilians, however, the real church is that of the spirits.

When Africans were forced aboard slave ships, they may have left their families and possessions behind, but they brought along an impressive array of gods. Foremost among them were Olorum, the creator; Yemanjá, the goddess of the rivers and water; Oxalá, the god of procreation and the harvest; and Exú, a trickster spirit who could cause mischief or bring about death. Of lesser rank but still powerful were Ogun, Obaluayê, Oxôssi, and Yansan, to name a few.

The Catholic Church, whose spiritual seeds were planted in Brazil alongside the rows of sugarcane and cotton, was naturally against such religious beliefs. As a compromise, the slaves took on the rituals of Rome but kept their old gods. Thus, new religions—Candomblé in Bahia, Macumba in Rio, Xangó in Pernambuco, Umbanda in São Paulo—were born.

Yemanjá had her equivalent in the Virgin Mary and was queen of the heavens as well as queen of the seas; the powerful Oxalá became associated with Jesus Christ; and Exú, full of deception to begin with, became Satan. Other gods were likened to saints: Ogun to St. Anthony, Obaluayê to St. Francis, Oxôssi to St. George, Yansan to St. Barbara. On their altars,

crosses and statues of the Virgin, Christ, and saints sit beside offerings of sacred white feathers, magical beads, and bowls of cooked rice and cornmeal.

The famous Afro-Brazilian religion called Candomblé was brought over by slaves from Africa. Based on Yoruban, Fon, and Bantu beliefs from different regions in Africa, the religion has added some aspects of the Catholic faith over the years. One of the parts of the religion is the belief in 13 principle *orixás*, or deities. In addition, each individual is thought to have his or her own orixá to help guide their way.

Salvadorans are eager to share their rituals with visitors, though often for a fee (you can make arrangements through hotels or tour agencies). The Candomblé temple ceremony, in which believers sacrifice animals and become possessed by gods, is performed nightly except during Lent.

Temples, usually in poor neighborhoods at the city's edge, don't allow photographs or video or sound recordings. You shouldn't wear black (white is preferable) or revealing clothing. The ceremony is long and repetitive, and there are often no chairs and there's no air-conditioning; men and women are separated.

A *pãe de santo* or *mãe de santo* (Candomblé priest or priestess) can perform a reading of the *buzios* for you; the small brown shells are thrown like jacks into a circle of beads—the pattern they form tells about your life. Don't select your mãe or pãe de santo through an ad or sign, as many shell readers who advertise are best not at fortune-telling but at saying "100 dollars, please" in every language.

9

building is the Museu Arqueologia e Etnologia (Archaeology and Ethnology Museum). Both have information booklets available in multiple languages. ⊠ *Praça 15 de Novembro s/n, Pelourinho* ☎ *071/3283–5540* ⊕ *www.mafro.ceao.ufba.br* ☜ *R$6* ⊗ *Weekdays 9–5.*

Terreiro de Jesus. This wide plaza lined with 17th-century houses sits in the heart of historic Salvador. Where nobles once strolled under imperial palm trees, there's a crafts fair on weekends. In the afternoons, a group of locals practice *capoeira*—a stylized dancelike fight with African origins—to the sound of the *berimbau,* a bow-shape musical instrument. ⊠ *Intersection of Rua das Laranjeiras and Rua João de Deus, Pelourinho.*

WORTH NOTING

Elevador Lacerda. For a few centavos, ascend 236 feet in about a minute in the world's first urban elevator, which runs between Praça Visconde de Cayrú in the Lower City and the Paço Municipal in the Upper City. Built in 1872, the elevator originally ran on hydraulics. It was electrified when it was restored in the 1930s. Bahians joke that the elevator is the only way to "go up" in life. Watch out for pickpockets when the elevator's crowded. ⊠ *West side of Praça Visconde de Cayrú, Comércio* ☜ *R$0.25* ⊗ *Daily 5 am–midnight.*

Forte de Santo Antonio Além do Carmo. While this fort set at the end of Rua Direita de Santo Antonio may not win prizes for its architecture, its real draw is as a center for capoeira, a type of martial arts practiced in Brazil. Classes led by different capoeria masters take place in the former cells, each with an individiual schedule, while each Saturday night they join together to put on a free demonstration for the public. ⊠ *Praça Barão do Triunfo s/n, Santo Antônio* ☎ *071/3117–1488* ⊕ *fortesantoantonio. blogspot.com.br.*

Fundação Pierre Verger Gallery. At this gallery dedicated to the works of renowned French photographer Pierre Verger you can catch a rotating selection of his captivating black-and-white shots of Afro-Brazilian culture from the 1950s–70s, detailing both daily and religious rituals. A much larger archive is accessible at the foundation, which also hosts workshops and classes and is located on the outskirts of Salvador. ⊠ *Portal da Misericordia 9, Pelourinho* ☎ *071/3321–2341* ⊕ *www. pierreverger.org.*

Palácio Rio Branco. A neoclassic beauty constructed on the site of Brazil's first government building, dating back to 1549, the Palace reopened in 2010 after an extensive, two-year restoration. Today it stands as a cultural center, housing Salvador's Chamber of Commerce, the Cultural Foundation of the State of Bahia, and the state tourist office. On the first floor there's a small memorial museum depicting the last two centuries of local history. Stop by for one of the guided visits around the Palacio's elaborate chambers, led by local graduates. ■ **TIP→ Get a great view of Cidade Baixa and the bay from the east balcony.** ⊠ *Pça. Tomé de Sousa, Pelourinho* ☎ *071/3116–6928* ⊗ *Tues.–Fri. 10–6, weekends 9–1.*

CIDADE BAIXA (THE LOWER CITY)

This historic district was made up of the port of Salvador and adjoining warehouses and businesses. Because of poor planning, most of the original structures were demolished and replaced with private and government office buildings from the early 20th century.

TOP ATTRACTIONS

Fodor's Choice
★

Feira de São Joaquim. A visit to this all-encompassing daily market, the largest in the state, is a headfirst dive into Bahian culture. Dress down and wander labyrinthine alleys of exotic fruits, squawking chickens, dried flamingo pink prawns, and household goods crafted from *palha* (straw), before heading into the undercover section, where you will find an entire lane dedicated to accessories for *Candomblé* practices. Join early-morning vendors for a break at the *barracas* that line the edges and try the local specialty of *passarinha* (fried cow spleen), if you dare, although a cold beer is probably the safer option. ⊠ *Av. Oscar Pontes, Comércio* ☉ *Mon.–Sat. 5 am–6 pm, Sun. 6–1.*

Forte de Santo Antônio da Barra. A symbol of Salvador, St. Anthony's Fort has stood guard over Salvador since 1583. The lighthouse atop the fort wasn't built until 1696, after many a ship wrecked on the coral reefs around the Baía de Todos os Santos entrance. ■ **TIP→ Go in the late afternoon to climb the 22-meter tower before watching the impressive sunset with the crowds who gather on the bank below. Across the road, don't miss stopping by Dinha's barraca for acarajé, her version of the typical Bahian specialty is rumored to be the best in town.** ⊠ *Praça Farol da Barra, Barra* ☎ *071/3264–3296* ⊕ *www.museunauticodabahia.org.br* ⌨ *R$8–10* ☉ *Museum Tues.–Sun. 8:30–7.*

Museu Náutico. Located inside the fort, the Museu Náutico has permanent exhibitions of old maps, navigational equipment, artillery, model vessels, and remnants of shipwrecks found by archaeologists off the Bahian coast. ⊠ *Largo do Farol da Barra, s/n, Barra* ☎ *071/3264–3296.*

Fodor's Choice
★

MAM (Museum of Modern Art). When Italian-Brazilian modernist architect Lina do Bardi set about transforming this 17th-century private *fazenda* overlooking the sea, she created one of the world's most picturesque modern art museums. Original white and blue Portuguese tiles lead up to the former *casarão*, which houses a permanent modernist/contemporary collection, while the former chapel plays host to a rotating schedule of individual shows. Walk through the sculpture garden, with works from artists like Bel Borba and Mario Cravo, before taking a break in the atmospheric basement cafe. JAM no MAM, the Saturday evening alfresco jazz shows, which correspond with the sunset, are something not to miss. ⊠ *Av. Contorno, Comércio* ☎ *071/3117–6132* ⊕ *www.bahiamam.org.*

WORTH NOTING

Mercado Modelo. Set on the bay in Cidade Baixa, this crafts market was once the holding pen for slaves between the 17th and 19th century as they arrived off the boat from Africa. Today it's a convenient place to buy handicrafts, although don't expect a great deal of variety or innovation—this is a market for tourists rather than locals. Bargaining is expected here for goods like *cachaça* (sugarcane liquor), cashews,

9

pepper sauce, cigars, leather goods, hammocks, musical instruments, and semiprecious stones. Head up to the the alfresco terrace on the top-floor restaurant to enjoy a cold beer while watching the boats set off for Morro do Sao Paulo. ⊠ *Praça Visconde de Cayrú 250, Cidade Baixa* ☎ *071/3241–0242* ⊕ *www.mercadomodelobahia.com. br* ⊠ *Mon.–Sat. 9–7, Sun. 9–2.*

Museu de Arte Sacra. Housed in a former Carmelite monastery, the museum and the adjoining **Igreja de Santa Teresa** (St. Theresa Church) are among the best in Salvador. An in-house restoration team has worked miracles that bring alive Salvador's golden age as Brazil's capital and main port, told through thoughtfully cared-for collections of religious objects. See the silver altar in the church, recovered from the fire that razed the original Igreja da Sé in 1933, and the blue-and-yellow-tile sacristy replete with a bay view. Access is recommended via Rua Santa Thereza, and there is a taxi point located nearby. ⊠ *Rua do Sodré 276, Centro* ☎ *071/3283– 5600* ⊕ *www.mas.ufba.br* ⊠ *R$5* ⊘ *Weekdays 11:30–5:30.*

Museu Carlos Costa Pinto. A collection of more than 3,000 objects collected from around the world by the Costa Pinto family, including furniture, crystal, silver pieces, and paintings, is on display at this museum. Included in the collection are examples of gold and silver *balangandãs,* chains with large silver charms in the shapes of tropical fruits and fish, which were worn by slave women around the waist. ⊠ *Av. 7 de Setembro 2490, Corredor da Vitória* ☎ *071/3336–6081* ⊕ *www.museucostapinto. com.br/capa.asp* ⊠ *R$5* ⊘ *Mon. and Wed.–Sat. 2:30–7.*

BEACHES

In general the farther east and north from the mouth of the bay, the better the beaches. To avoid large crowds, don't go on weekends. Regardless of when you go, keep an eye on your belongings and take only what you need to the beach—petty thievery is a problem. There are no public bathrooms. You can rent a beach chair and sun umbrella for about R$10.

Beaches are listed in geographical order, beginning with Piatã, north of the city on the Baía de Todos os Santos, and then to Praia da Barra, near the peninsula's tip, and northeast to other Atlantic beaches.

TOP ATTRACTIONS

Porto da Barra. This popular beach in Barra draws a wide variety of sun-seekers from across the city and is a convenient option if you're staying in the hotel districts of Ondina and Rio Vermelho, where rock outcroppings make swimming dangerous and pollution is often a problem. Chairs and umbrellas are available for rent, and you can purchase food from one of the many restaurants lining the promenade. **Amenities:** food and drink, lifeguards, toilets. **Best for:** partiers, surfing, sunset. ⊠ *Av. Oceânica east of Santo Antônio da Barra, Barra.*

Praia do Flamengo. Clean sand, simple kiosks, and a beautiful view make this long stretch of golden sand a favorite among good-looking locals and surfers drawn to the strong waves. Buses, which run regularly from Barra and the city center, take just over an hour; the journey is well worth it if you are looking for a serious beach day. **Amenities:** food and drink, toilets, lifeguards, parking. **Best for:** surfing, walking, swimming. ⊠ *Thales de Azevedo s/n, Stella Maris.*

FAMILY **Praia Stella Maris.** One of the northermost beaches in the Salvador municipality, Praia Stella Maris's long stretch of sand is ever popular with families in spite of the strong waves. The myriad of food-and-drink kiosks, serving delicious salty snacks and *água de côco* (coconut water), get busy on the weekends. The airport is located just 10 minutes away. **Amenities:** food and drink, lifeguards, toilets, parking. **Best for:** surfing, walking. ⊠ *20 km (12 miles) north of downtown, after Itapuã, Stella Maris.*

WORTH NOTING

Praia Corsário. One of the nicest beaches along Avenida Oceánica is Praia Corsário, a long stretch packed on weekends with a younger crowd. Strong waves make it popular with surfers and bodyboarders, while swimmers should proceed with caution. There are kiosks where you can sit in the shade and enjoy seafood and ice-cold beer. **Amenities:** food and drink, lifeguards, toilets. **Best for:** partiers, surfing. ⊠ *Av. Oceánica, south of Parque Metropolitan de Pituaçu, Pituaçu.*

Praia Itapuã. Frequented by the artists who live in the neighborhood, the Itapuã beach offers an eclectic atmosphere. There are food kiosks—including Acarajé da Cira, one of the best places to get *acarajé* (a spicy fried-bean snack). Although the coconut palms and white sands remain idyllic, it is advisable to be watchful of your belongings. Inland from Itapuã, a mystical freshwater lagoon, the **Lagoa de Abaeté,** and surrounding sand dunes are now a municipal park. Itapuã's dark waters are a startling contrast to the fine white sand of its shores, but it's not suitable for swimming. **Amenities:** food and drink, toilets, parking. **Best for:** walking. ⊠ *16 km (10 miles) northeast of downtown, Itapuã.*

OFF THE BEATEN PATH

Ilha de Itaparica. The largest of 56 islands in the Baía de Todos os Santos, Itaparica was originally settled because its ample supply of fresh mineral water was believed to have rejuvenating qualities. Its beaches are calm and shallow, thanks to the surrounding reefs, which are avidly sought by windsurfers, divers, and snorkelers. The main port of entry on the north of the island is the town of Bom Despacho, where the ferries from Salvador dock. The best beaches are near the villages of Vera Cruz, Mar Grande, and Conceição, the latter almost entirely owned by Club Med Itaparica.

Instead of buses or taxis, small Volkswagen vans (called *kombis*) provide the most convenient local transportation around the island. You can hail vans and hop from beach to beach along the 40 km (25 miles) of BA 001, the coastal highway that connects Itaparica village on the north part of the island to the mainland via Ponte do Funil (Funnel Bridge) on the southwest side. The drive from Salvador to the island takes about four hours. ■ **TIP➔ Bicycle rentals are readily available in the island's towns, so you don't really need a car if you're comfortable with bicycling.**

Terminal Marítimo São Joaquim. Ferries to the island run daily from the Terminal Marítimo São Joaquim. Tickets cost R$3.95 during the week and R$5.20 on the weekend. The ferries run from 5 am to 11 pm and last 40 minutes. ⊠ *Av. Oscar Ponte 1051, São Joaquim.*

WHERE TO EAT

You can easily find restaurants serving Bahian specialties in most neighborhoods. Pelourinho and Barra, full of bars and sidewalk cafés, are good places to start. There are also many good spots in bohemian Rio Vermelho and a slew of places along Orla, the beachfront drive beginning around Jardim de Alah, and surrounding the smarter residential areas of Campo Grande and Vitória. The regional cuisine leans toward seafood, but some meat dishes should be tried. And, like anywhere else in Brazil, there are *churrascarias* for beef lovers. One main course often serves two; ask about portions when you order. Beware that regional food is normally spicy and hot.

JARDIM ARMAÇÃO

$$$$ ✕ **Bargaço.** Delicious Bahian dishes of fresh seafood are served at this
SEAFOOD   longtime favorite, where the ample portions make it great for sharing. *Pata de caranguejo* (vinegary crab claws) is hearty and may do more than take the edge off your appetite for the requisite moqueca *de camarão* (with shrimp) or moqueca *de siri mole* (with soft-shell crab); try the *cocada* for dessert, if you have room. $ *Average main: R$75* ⊠ *Rua Antonio da Silva Coelho s/n, Jardim Armação* ☎ *071/3231–1000* ⊕ *www.restaurantebargaco.com.br.*

$$$$ ✕ **Boi Preto.** For a set price, this top-quality, all-you-can-eat Brazilian
BRAZILIAN   *churrascaria* serves a selection of meat cooked to perfection and a generous choice of sides. A flurry of white-coated waiters appear at your table to carve different options of meat straight on to your plate *rodizio* style, so try not to fill up on the steaming *pao de quiejo* (cheese balls), salads, and seafood from the accompanying buffet—and also know that the best cuts are usually brought toward the end of the meal. $ *Average main: R$90* ⊠ *Av. Otávio Mangabeira s/n, Jardim Armação* ☎ *071/3362–8844.*

CABULA

$$$ ✕ **Paraiso Tropical.** Ask locals and longtime expats alike what not to
BRAZILIAN   miss in Salvador and the response you get will be unanimous: Paraiso
Fodor'sChoice   Tropical. Set in a tropical garden a short taxi ride from the historic
★   center, this relaxed, gourmet spot treats patrons to Bahian classics with a twist. Chef Beto reinvents heavy dishes like *moqueca* and *bobo* using natural dende fruit rather than oil, combined with rare tropical fruits sourced from more than 6,000 square meters of native Mata-Atlantica forest. Go with friends and go hungry, for while the *siri mole* (Bahia soft-shell crab) and prawn moqueca stand out, you'll want to try everything. $ *Average main: R$55* ⊠ *R. Edgar Loureiro, 98-B, Cabula* ☎ *071/3384–7464* ⊕ *www.restauranteparaisotropical.com.br* ⊘ *Closed Sun. dinner.*

CORREDOR DE VITÓRIA

$$$ ✕ **Mar na Boca.** Although this sophisticated Spanish seafood spot is
SPANISH   located right beside the city's top art galleries, the food is reason enough alone to visit the leafy neighborhood of Vitória. Originally from Pamplona, chef Tako darts in and out of the kitchen, consulting with diners on the freshest catch of the day or which wine to select

from the all-Spanish list. Superbly executed dishes such as *gambas al ajillo* (garlic prawns) and *paella negra* make it a top choice for businessmen and the local art crowd alike—even Salvador's answer to Dalí, Bel Borba, regularly drops by for tapas and to say hello to his evocative pieces that line the walls. $ *Average main: R$50* ⊠ *2 Rua Aloísio de Carvalho, Corredor da Vitória* ☎ *071/3022–8580* ⊕ *www. marnaboca.com.br.*

FAST FOOD
Baianas typically make *acarajé*, a delicious street food made of bean dough fried with palm oil and filled with bean paste and shrimp. *Moqueca* is another specialty made with palm oil, coconut milk, and fish or shrimp cooked slowly over a low fire.

PELOURINHO

La Figa. Tucked away on a quiet cobbled street, this lively cantina combines good-value Italian classics with a cozy atmosphere. Owner Salvatore makes the most of fresh local seafood for signature dishes such as *spaghetti ai frutti di mare* and grilled seafood platter to share. Homemade pastas, tasty meat dishes, and endless indulgent desserts have turned this into a local favorite. Come Sunday, regulars spill out onto tables on the street between watching international football on the large TV and sipping Salvatore's special limoncello. The wine list is one of the most varied in town and is well priced. $ *Average main: R$40* ⊠ *17 Rua das Laranjeiras, Pelourinho* ☎ *071/3322–0066* ⊕ *www. ristorantelafiga.com* ⊗ *No dinner Sun.*

Senac. The 30-dish buffet at this lunch-only spot set right on the Pelourinho provides A to Z of Bahian cuisine for the uninitiated at a set price. Start at the small museum on the ground floor, where English-speaking staff will guide you through Bahian food's African roots, before heading up to the breezy dining room to experience it in action. Superbly run by the hospitality school SENAC, the restaurant has students behind the golden moquecas and impossibly sweet desserts—as well as the excellent service. Everything is executed under the watchful eye of professors in suits. ■TIP→ **Vegetarians should make for the Kilo restaurant below.** $ *Average main: R$40* ⊠ *Praça José de Alencar 13/19, Pelourinho* ☎ *071/3324–4550* ⊕ *www.ba.senac.br* ⊗ *Closed for dinner.*

Uauá. Tucked away above a busy street in the Pelourinho, Uauá's tasty, typically Brazilian dishes and reliable service make it one of the most popular restaurants in Salvador—and therefore one of the most crowded. ■TIP→ **Come early to avoid the rush.** Don't skip the Northeastern specialities, like *guisado de carneiro* (minced mutton) or *carne do sol com purê de macaxeira* (salted beef with mandioca puree). $ *Average main: R$45* ⊠ *R. Gregório de Matos 36, Pelourinho* ☎ *071/3321–3089* ⊗ *Closed Sun.*

$$ ITALIAN

$$ BRAZILIAN

$$ BRAZILIAN

9

Afro-Brazilian Heritage

Of all of Brazil's states, Bahia has the strongest links with its African heritage. There are few other countries with such a symphony of skin tones grouped under one nationality. This rich Brazilian identity began when the first Portuguese sailors were left to manage the new land. From the beginning, Portuguese migration to Brazil was predominantly male, a fact that led to unbridled sexual license with Indian and African women.

The first Africans arrived in 1532, along with the Portuguese colonizers, who continued to buy slaves from English, Spanish, and Portuguese traders until 1855. All records pertaining to slave trading were destroyed in 1890, making it impossible to know exactly how many people were brought to Brazil. It's estimated that from 3 million to 4.5 million Africans were captured and transported from Gambia, Guinea, Sierra Leone, Senegal, Liberia, Nigeria, Benin, Angola, and Mozambique. Many were literate Muslims who were better educated than their white overseers and owners.

It was common in the main houses of sugar plantations, which relied on slave labor, for the master to have a white wife and slave mistresses. In fact interracial relationships and even marriage was openly accepted. It was also fairly common for the master to free the mother of his mixed-race offspring and allow a son of color to learn a trade or inherit a share of the plantation.

When the sugar boom came to an end, it became too expensive for slave owners to support their "free" labor force. Abolition occurred gradually, however. It began around 1871, with the passage of the Law of the Free Womb, which liberated all Brazilians born of slave mothers. In 1885 another law was passed, freeing slaves older than 60. Finally, on May 13, 1888, Princess Isabel, while Emperor Dom Pedro II was away on a trip, signed a law freeing all slaves in the Brazilian empire.

The former slaves, often unskilled, became Brazil's unemployed and underprivileged. Although the country has long been praised for its lack of discrimination, this veneer of racial equality is deceptive. Afro-Brazilians still don't receive education on par with that of whites, nor do they always receive equal pay for equal work. There are far fewer black or mixed race professionals, politicians, and ranking military officers than white ones, although this is changing gradually.

Subtle activism to bring about racial equality and educate all races about the rich African legacy continues. For many people the most important holiday is November 20 (National Black Consciousness Day). It honors the anniversary of the death of Zumbi, the leader of the famous *Quilombo* (community of escaped slaves) de Palmares, which lasted more than 100 years and was destroyed by *bandeirantes* (slave traders) in one final great battle for freedom.

WHERE TO STAY

The Cidade Histórico and the nearby neighborhood of Santo Antonio offer a good selection of places to stay, many of which combine a unique atmosphere with immediate access to the colonial charms of the Pelourinho. Heading south into the Vitória neighborhood along Avenida 7 de Setembro there are a number of inexpensive establishments convenient to beaches and sights. In the fashionable Barra neighborhood, many hotels are within walking distance of the beach, while Rio Vermelho is the favored choice of most Brazilians and where the city's best bars, restaurants, and nightclubs can be found, although it is a 20-minute taxi ride from downtown. High seasons are from December to March and the month of July. For Carnival, reservations must be made months in advance, and prices are substantially higher.

BARRA

$ B&B/INN FAMILY

🏨 **Pousada Estrela do Mar.** This pleasant, GLBT-friendly B&B a few steps from Barra beach wins over independent travelers, couples, and families alike with its competitive prices and simple, Mediterranean-style design. **Pros:** near the beach; good value; free Wi-fi. **Cons:** rooms can be noisy. [$] *Rooms from: R$160* ✉ *Rua Afonso Celso 119, Barra* ☎ *071/3022–4882* 🌐 *www.estreladomarsalvador.com* 🛏 *9 rooms* 🕒 *Closed June 15–July 15* 🍴 *Breakfast.*

CAMPO GRANDE

$$$$ HOTEL

🏨 **Sheraton da Bahia.** Opened at the beginning of 2013 with 284 rooms, this business-focused hotel offers sleek, standardized rooms and internationally recognized service, all a short taxi ride from the principal sights and Salvador's business hub. **Pros:** trusted service; sophisticated, modern design. **Cons:** noisy location. [$] *Rooms from: R$550* ✉ *Avenida 7 de Setembro 1537, Campo Grande* ☎ *071/3021–6700* 🌐 *www.starwoodhotels.com* 🛏 *284 rooms* 🍴 *Breakfast.*

SANTO ANTÔNIO

$$$$ HOTEL

🏨 **Aram Yami Hotel.** This intimate boutique hotel on the outskirts of the historic city center—featuring top-level service, spacious rooms, and a unique design—is a favorite among couples celebrating something special. **Pros:** multilingual staff; personalized service. **Cons:** pricey; street-facing rooms are noisy. [$] *Rooms from: R$520* ✉ *132 Rua Direita de Santo Antonio, Santo Antônio* ☎ *071/3242–9412* 🌐 *www.hotelaramyami.com* 🛏 *5 rooms* 🍴 *Breakfast.*

$$$ B&B/INN

🏨 **Casa Amarelindo.** While Aztec-inspired colors may not make this the Peló's most sophisticated choice, it is centrally located and has modern conveniences such as king-size beds and a swimming pool overlooking the Bahia dos Santos. **Pros:** location; attentive service; free high-speed Wi-Fi. **Cons:** bright design not for everyone; bathrooms are outdated; kids must be over 14. [$] *Rooms from: R$420* ✉ *Rua das Portas do Carmo 6, Pelourinho* ☎ *71/3266–8550* 🌐 *www.casadoamarelindo.com* 🛏 *10 rooms* 🍴 *Breakfast.*

$
B&B/INN
FAMILY
Fodor'sChoice
★

⊞ Pousada do Boqueirão. From Brazilian actresses to professors, an assortment of guests have enjoyed this charming, Italian-style pensione, where they linger among tropical plants in the sun-drenched veranda, home to the best breakfast in town. **Pros:** great value; fabulous breakfasts. **Cons:** Wi-Fi only in communal areas; few amenities. $ *Rooms from: R$240* ⊠ *R. Direita de Santo Antonio 48, Santo Antônio* ☎ *071/3241–2262* ⊕ *www.pousadaboqueirao.com.br* ⟳ *11 rooms* ☉ *Closed June and July* ⦿ *Breakfast.*

$
B&B/INN
FAMILY

⊞ Pousada Redfish. A restored mint-green mansion in the heart of San Antonio, this laid-back pousada has spacious rooms and a hip vibe, making it one of the best choices for friends or families on a budget. **Pros:** good value near the Pelourinho; high ceilings; hip design. **Cons:** can be noisy. $ *Rooms from: R$180* ⊠ *Ladeira do Boqueirao N.1, Santo Antônio* ☎ *071/3241–0639* ⊕ *www.hotelredfish.com* ⟳ *9 rooms* ⦿ *Breakfast.*

ONDINA

$$
HOTEL

⊞ Bahia Othon Palace Hotel. Part of a well-respected Brazilian hotel chain, this busy (though tired) hotel sits on a cliff overlooking Ondina Beach and is a short drive from most sights, nightspots, and restaurants. **Pros:** spacious rooms; nice swimming pool; generous buffet breakfast. **Cons:** in need of a refurb; most attractions aren't within walking distance; free Wi-Fi access only in the communal areas. $ *Rooms from: R$270* ⊠ *Av. Oceanica 2294, Ondina* ☎ *071/800–725–0505, 071/2103–7100* ⊕ *www.othon.com.br/en* ⟳ *278 rooms, 13 suites* ⦿ *Breakfast.*

ITAPUÃ

$$$
RESORT
FAMILY

⊞ Catussaba Resort Hotel. A longtime favorite among businessmen and families due to its close proximity to the airport and extensive facilities—including direct access onto the beautiful Itapuã beach—this resort hotel could do with an over-haul. **Pros:** direct access to the beach; ocean views; plenty of amenities. **Cons:** parts of the hotel are tired; the service can be patchy; far from tourist attractions. $ *Rooms from: R$395* ⊠ *Alameda da Praia, Itapuã* ☎ *071/3374–8000* ⊕ *www.catussaba.com.br* ⟳ *253 rooms, 6 suites* ⦿ *Breakfast.*

CORREDOR DA VICTÓRIA

$
B&B/INN

⊞ Hotel Bahia do Sol. There may be little sexy about this B&B aside from the continually competitive pricing, yet it remains one of the city's enduring budget options. **Pros:** a reliable budget option; quiet neighborhood. **Cons:** basic decor; some rooms smell of smoke. $ *Rooms from: R$199* ⊠ *Av. 7 de Setembro 2009, Corredor da Vitória* ☎ *071/3338–8800* ⊕ *www.bahiadosol.com.br* ⟳ *89 rooms, 2 suites* ⦿ *Breakfast.*

RIO VERMELHO

$
B&B/INN

⊞ Hotel Catharina Paraguaçu. A long-standing favorite in the Rio Vermelho district, this 19th-century mansion offers friendly service, delicious breakfasts, and small but comfortable rooms. **Pros:** family-friendly environment; near dining and nightlife. **Cons:** not many amenities. $ *Rooms from: R$212* ⊠ *Rua João Gomes 128, Rio Vermelho* ☎ *071/3334–0089* ⊕ *www.hotelcatharinaparaguacu.com.br* ⟳ *30 rooms, 2 suites* ⦿ *Breakfast.*

$ HOTEL **Hotel Mercure Salvador.** Located in the bohemian district of Rio Vermelho, this high-rise building of serviced apartments with a sleek, modern design offers reliable quality a short distance from some of the city's most happening bars and restaurants. **Pros:** excellent views; great amenities for business travelers. **Cons:** far from the historic district; impersonal feel. [$] *Rooms from: R$235* ✉ *Rua Fonte de Boi 215, Rio Vermelho* ☎ *071/3172–9200* 🌐 *www.accorhotels.com.br* 🛏 *174 rooms* 🍴 *Breakfast.*

THE SAMBA MAN

Dorival Caymmi, one of the greatest Brazilian composers, was born in Salvador in 1914. With his beautiful Bahian sambas, Caymmi brought the sights, smells, and sounds of his native state into the popular imagination. One of his most beautiful compositions is called "Minha Jangada Vai Sair Pro Mar" ("My Boat Will Go Out to Sea").

NIGHTLIFE AND THE ARTS

Pelourinho is the place to catch live music, particularly on Tuesdays and Saturdays, when musicians perform at stages dotted across the various squares, from Largo do Terreiro de Jesus to Largo do Pelourinho and up the Ladeiro do Carmo. Saturday's sunset jazz sessions held at the MAM (Museum of Modern Art) are also a must for music-lovers. For action any night of the week, head to the trendy, bohemian neighborhood of Rio Vermelho, where locals catch up over acarajé in squares like Largo da Santana before heading onto live music spots such as Padaria Bar.

Salvador is considered by many artists as a laboratory for the creation of new rhythms and dance steps. As such, this city has an electric performing arts scene. See the events calendar published on 🌐 *www.bahia.com.br* or check local newspapers for details on live music performances as well as rehearsal schedules.

NIGHTLIFE

BARS

There are many bars in the Pelourinho area, as well as on the beachfront avenues, where the happy hour spots are set overlooking the beach in Pituba and Barra. Rio Vermelho is famous for its botecos, traditional Brazilian pubs where waiters bring around endless trays of ice-cold *chopp* (draught beer).

Cafelier. While this laid-back spot is also recommended for coffee, crepes, and great-value lunches, it is the lime-caipirinhas made from artisanal cachaça that draw the crowds who want to enjoy cocktails while watching the sunset over the Bahia de Todos os Santos. ✉ *Rua do Carmo 50, Santo Antônio* ☎ *071/3241–5095* 🌐 *www.cafelier.com.br.*

O Cravinho. One of the best choices for a cocktail in the Pelourinho, this sophisticated wood-lined bar specializes in clove-infused cachaça, served with tasty snacks and occasional live music. ✉ *Terreiro de Jesus 3, Pelourinho* ☎ *071/3322–6759* 🌐 *www.ocravinho.com.br.*

Carnival in Salvador: Brazil's Wildest Party

Jostling for first place beside Rio and Recife, Salvador is one of Brazil's Carnival kings. While it may have a reputation for being the country's wildest Carnival, it is also the most accessible and authentic large-scale Carnival in Brazil—an explosion of more than 2 million revelers, all dancing in frenzied marching crews, called *blocos*, or hopping parade-side as *pipoca*, or popcorn. At the center of each bloco is the *trio elétrico*, a colossal, creeping stage whose towering speakers blare walls of energetic, ribcage-rattling *axé* music—a danceable and distinctly Bahian mix of African rhythms, rock, and reggae. Top pop stars like Daniela Mercury or Ivete Sangalo perform their party-stoking Carnival favorites, while the Brazilian glitterati enjoy the show from *camarotes* (boxes often sponsored by big name brands), where guests are plied with endless lavish food and champagne.

To be part of the action, and to avoid the hordes of pickpockets that are unfortunately part of the "excitement," join a bloco, which is roped off from the general public. Each bloco has its own all-purpose beer, first-aid, and toilet truck—and you'll have instant camaraderie with your crewmates. (A warning: it's not unusual for women to be kissed by strangers. It might sound feeble, but having a male friend close may deter unwanted groping.)

Favorite bloco themes include Egyptian-garbed percussion band Olodum, and axé acts Are Ketu and Timbalada. Alternatively, there's the peaceful Filhos de Ghandy (Children of Ghandi), a white sea of robes and jeweled turbans. Once you've chosen your bloco, all you have to do is lay down upward of US$100 to buy a crew-specific T-shirt, called an *abadá*, purchased at Central do Carnival kiosks, or at markets from scalpers.

Blocos travel along specific *circuitos* (routes) through the city. Seaside Dodô (about 1 mile, 5 hours) is the route of choice for Carnival's biggest stars and begins at Farol da Barra. Osmar (about 2 miles, 6 hours), beginning near Campo Grande, is large and traditional. The less-populated and calmer Batatinha, which clings to historic Pelourinho, allows an intimate look at smaller percussionist groups and is popular with families. Prepare by checking the official schedule at ⊕ *www. carnaval.salvador.ba.gov.br* (click on "Programação").

Add to all of these fine reasons to patronize Salvador's Carnival the more than 20 pre-Carnival warm-up celebrations and its honor in the *Guinness Book of World Records* as the biggest street carnival on the planet, and it's hard to argue that, come Carnival season, true partiers should be anywhere but Salvador.

—Joe Gould

DANCE SHOWS

Fodor'sChoice ★ **Balé Folclórico da Bahia.** Cited as one of the best dance experiences in Brazil, and at a great value, too, this show lasts just an hour and provides an exhilarating window into the Afro-Brazilian culture. ⊠ *Rua Gregório de Matos 49, Pelourinho* ☎ *071/3322–1962* ⊕ *www. balefolcloricodabahia.com.br.*

NIGHTCLUBS

Padaria Bar. Rock takes to the stage in all forms at this regular hot spot in bomhemian Rio Vermelho. ⊠ *Rua João Gomes 43, Rio Vermelho* ☎ *071/3016–4412* ⊕ *www.padariabar.com.br.*

THE ARTS

CARNIVAL REHEARSALS

Afro-Brazilian percussion groups begin Carnival rehearsals—which are really more like creative jam sessions—around midyear.

Associação Cultural Bloco Carnavalesco Ilê Aiyê. This group, which started out as a Carnival Bloco, has turned itself into much more in its 34-year history. It now has its own school and promotes the study and practice of African heritage, religion, and history. To take part, call ahead to schedule a visit to the school. Contributions are appreciated. ⊠ *Rua do Curuzu 288, Liberdade* ☎ *071/2103–3400* ⊕ *www.ileaiye.org.br.*

Olodum. Salvador's best-known percussion group gained international fame when it participated in Paul Simon's "Rhythm of the Saints" tour and recordings. It is one of Salvador's most popular Carnival schools.

Casa do Olodum. Olodum, Salvador's best-known percussion group, has its own venue, the Casa do Olodum, and performs live shows around town, often on Tuesday or Sunday. ⊠ *Rua Gregorio de Matos, 5, Pelourinho* ☎ *071/3321–5010* ⊕ *www.olodum.com.br.*

Escola Criativa Olodum. Olodum also has a percussion school for kids, Escola Criativa Olodum, where you can arrange a visit to watch the budding students hard at work. ⊠ *Rua das Laranjeiras 30, Pelourinho* ☎ *071/3322–8069.*

MUSIC, THEATER, AND DANCE

Teatro Casa do Comércio. It hosts music performances and some theatrical productions. ⊠ *Av. Tancredo Neves 1109, Pituba* ☎ *071/3273–8543.*

Teatro Castro Alves. Salvador's largest theater holds classical and popular music performances, operas, and plays. ⊠ *Praça 2 de Julho s/n, Campo Grande* ☎ *071/3535–0600* ⊕ *www.tca.ba.gov.br.*

Teatro Vila Velha. Founded in 1969, this is one of the most important cultural venues in Salvador, with workshops, music, dance, and theater. It is also the stage for Bando de Teatro Olodum. ⊠ *Avenida 7 de Setembro s/n, Campo Grande* ☎ *071/3083–4600* ⊕ *www.teatrovilavelha.com.br.*

MEET DONA FLOR

Prepare yourself for Bahia by reading *Dona Flor and Her Two Husbands,* a Jorge Amado novel steeped in the history and culture of Bahia. At the center of the story is a passionate young widow who finds love and propriety with her well-respected second husband, only to face a dilemma when her rogue first husband comes back from the dead and tries to claim her back. Sonia Braga starred in a film that was shot in the streets of Salvador.

9

Capoeira: The Fight Dance

Dance and martial arts in one, *capoeira* is purely Brazilian. The early days of slavery often saw fights between Africans from rival tribes who were thrust together on one plantation. When an owner caught slaves fighting, both sides were punished. To create a smoke screen, the Africans incorporated music and song into the fights. They brought a traditional *berimbau* string-drum instrument (a bow-shape piece of wood with a metal wire running from one end to the other, where there's a hollow gourd containing seeds) to the battles. Tapped with a stick or a coin, the berimbau's taut wire produces a throbbing, twanging sound whose rhythm is enhanced by the rattling seeds. Its mesmerizing reverberations were accompanied by singing and chanting, and when the master appeared, the fighters punched only the air and kicked so as to miss their opponents.

The fights have been refined into a sport that was once practiced primarily in Bahia and Pernambuco but has now spread throughout Brazil. Today's practitioners, called *capoeristas*, swing and kick—keeping their movements tightly controlled, with only hands and feet touching the ground—to the beat of the berimbau without touching their opponents. The goal is to cause one's opponent to lose concentration or balance. Capoeira is traditionally performed in a *roda* (wheel), which refers both to an event of continuous capoeira and to the circle formed by players and instrumentalists. Strength, control, flexibility, artistry, and grace are the tenets of capoeira. In any exhibition the *jogadores,* or players, as they are called—with their backs bending all the way to the floor and their agile foot movements (to avoid an imaginary knife)—as well as the compelling music, make this a fascinating sport to watch.

SPORTS AND THE OUTDOORS

CAPOEIRA

You can see capoeira, a type of martial arts popular in Brazil, in almost any beach or park in Salvador and Bahia. Some places are traditional gathering points for practitioners. One such place is the parking lot of Forte de Santo Antônio on Tuesday, Thursday, and Saturday early evenings. Two schools practice here, of which the Grupo de Capoeira Angola is the best known.

Bimba's Academy. There are several capoeira schools in Salvador for anyone who wants to learn the art that trains both the mind and body for combat. Mestre Bamba (Rubens Costa Silva) teaches at Bimba's Academy. A single hour-long class costs R$20. ⊠ *Rua das Laranjeiras 01, Pelourinho* ☎ *071/3322–0639* ⊕ *www.capoeiramestrebimba.com.br.*

SOCCER

Arena Fonte Nova. This sparklingly new, football-only stadium was created as the replacement for the original Estádio Fonte Nova in order to host the 2014 World Cup and to act as first division team for Bahia's home turf. German architects Brunswick, who redesigned Hanover's stadium for the 2006 World Cup, are behind the new project, while Brazilian beer brand Itaipava is powering its 10-year branding project. ⊠ *R. Lions Club 217–547, Nazar* ⊕ *www.arenafontenova.com.br.*

Estádio Manuel Barradas. Bahia and Vitória are the two local teams that play in the first division of the Brazilian soccer federation. There are games year-round in the Estádio Manuel Barradas, which is also used for other sporting events and concerts. Advance tickets sales are available, but games hardly ever sell out. The best seats are in the higher-priced *arquibancada superior* (upper-level section). ⊠ *Av. Artêmio Valente s/n, Tancredo Neves.*

OUR LADY OF GOOD DEATH

Devotion to Nossa Senhora da Boa Morte (Our Lady of Good Death) began in the slave quarters, where discussions on abolition of slavery took place. The slaves implored Our Lady of Good Death to end slavery and promised to hold an annual celebration in her honor should their prayers be answered. Brazil was the last country in the Western Hemisphere to abolish slavery, in 1888.

SHOPPING

AREAS AND MALLS

Largo do Pelourinho. To pick up contemporary local art, art naïf, and gemstones, visit the many galleries in the Cidade Alta and around the Largo do Pelourinho: Rua do Carmo and Direito do Santo Antonio have some particularly good options. ⊠ *Rua Alfredo de Brito at Ladeira do Taboão.*

Shopping Barra. The best shopping mall in Salvador, Shopping Barra isn't far from the historic center and has cinemas, restaurants, and local boutiques, as well as branches of the major Rio, São Paulo, and Minas Gerais retailers. Many hotels provide transportation to the mall, but you can also take the Rodoviária bus line. ⊠ *Av. Centenário 2992, Chame Chame.*

ART GALLERIES

Atelier Bel Borba. Bahia's answer to Dalí, Bel Borba is one of the region's most famous living artists, and he's picked up a bit of international prestige as well, due to a recent installation of his in New York's Times Square. A visit to his little atelier, where you can also pick up a piece of his work, is a must. ⊠ *Ladeira do Carmo 14, Pelourinho* ☎ *071/3243–9370.*

BOOKS

Livraria Siciliano. The local branch of a major Brazilian chain, Livraria Siciliano has lots of foreign-language books and international magazines. ⊠ *Shopping Iguatemi, Av. Tancredo Neves 148, Camino dos Árvores* ☎ *071/3450–7737* ⊕ *www.livrariasaraiva.com.br.*

HANDICRAFTS

Instituto de Artesanato Visconde de Mauá. Of Salvador's state-run handicrafts stores, the best is the Instituto de Artesanato Visconde de Mauá. Look for exquisite lace, musical instruments of African origin, weavings, and wood carvings. ⊠ *Largo do Porto da Barra 02, Porto da Barra* ☎ *071/3116–6160* ⊕ *www.maua.ba.gov.br* ⊠ *R. Gregorio de Matos 27, Pelourinho* ☎ *071/3116–6700* ⊕ *www.maua.ba.gov.br.*

9

JEWELRY AND GEMSTONES

Bahia is one of Brazil's main sources of gems, with amethysts, aquamarines, emeralds, and tourmalines being the most abundant. Prices for these stones are usually cheaper here than elsewhere in Brazil, but you should have an idea of what stones are worth before you enter a shop.

Bahia Preciosa. The city's most famous jeweler, Bahia Preciosa allows you to peer through a window into the room where goldsmiths work. ⊠ *Rua Terceira Ordem 1, Pelourinho* ☎ *071/3242–5218.*

H.Stern. The well-known, reputable H.Stern has several branches in Salvador, most of them in malls and major hotels. ⊠ *Ave. Centenario 2992, Chame Chame* ☎ *071/3264–3599* ⊕ *www.hstern.net.*

SIDE TRIPS FROM SALVADOR

Although attractions in Salvador can keep you entertained for more than a week, there are a number of easily accessible places for a one- or two-day break in more relaxing environs. Plan a day trip to Praia do Forte or the other northern beaches; they're less crowded and more beautiful than those in and near Salvador, or head out to the charming colonial town of Cachoeira. While two to three days is the minimum you will need to explore the near-pristine beaches and tropical forests of Morro de São Paulo and Boipepa, chances are you will wish you were staying a week.

CACHOEIRA

109 km (67 miles) northwest of Salvador.

This riverside colonial town dates from the 16th and 17th centuries, when sugarcane was the economy's mainstay. It has been designated a national monument and is the site of some of Brazil's most authentic Afro-Brazilian rituals. After Salvador it has the largest collection of baroque architecture in Bahia, with the interior of baroque church Ordem Terceiro do Carmo rivaling São Francisco's in Salvador. A major restoration of public monuments and private buildings was finished in 2003, and included revitalized streets and plazas in town. On an excursion to Cachoeira you can walk through the colorful country market and see architecture preserved from an age when Cachoeira shipped tons of tobacco and sugar downriver to Salvador.

One of the most interesting popular events is the festival held by the Irmandade da Boa Morte (Sisterhood of Good Death). Organized by a religious order created by the black female descendants of 19th-century slaves who were devoted to abolition, it's held on a Friday, Saturday, and Sunday in the middle of August and combines a street parade with a solemn mass, followed by a joyful procession of traditional *samba de roda.*

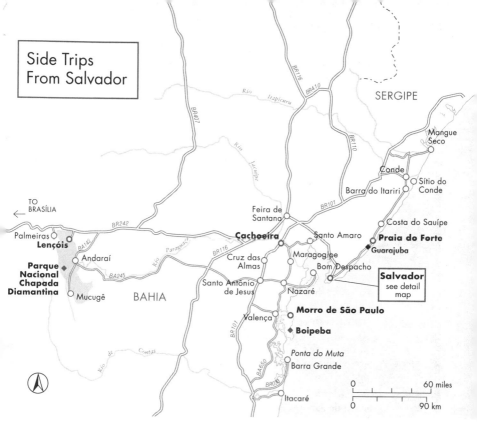

Side Trips
From Salvador

SERGIPE

TO
BRASÍLIA

Mangue
Seco

Conde
Barra do Itariri ○ ○ Sítio do
Conde

Feira de
Santana ○ Costa do Sauípe

Palmeiras ○ ○ Santo Amaro ○ Praia do Forte
Lençóis ◆ Guarajuba

Cachoeira

Andaraí
Cruz das
Almas
Maragogipe

Parque
Nacional
Chapada
Diamantina
Santo Antônio
de Jesus
Bom Despacho

Salvador
see detail
map

○ Mucugê BAHIA Nazaré

Valença ○ **Morro de São Paulo**

◆ **Boipeba**

Ponta do Muta
Barra Grande

Itacaré

0 ─── 60 miles
0 ─── 90 km

GETTING HERE AND AROUND

To drive from Salvador, take BR 324 north for about 55 km (34 miles),
then head west on BR 420 through the town of Santo Amaro. The trip
takes 1½ hours. Santana has daily service from Salvador to Cachoeira
that leaves multiple times per day from the Rodoviaria.

Bus Contacts Santana ☏ *071/3450–4951.*

EXPLORING

Centro Cultural Dannemann. Cross over the rustic wooden bridge to the
small town of São Félix set across the water to pay a visit to Centro Cultural Dannemann. This cultural center is housed in a stunning
colonial building that acts as both a working vintage cigar factory
and a contemporary art space. An art show known as the *Bienale do
Recôncavo* is also held every two years between November and March,
featuring Brazilian and international artists from a variety of disciplines. ⊠ *Av. Salvador Pinto 29, São Félix* ☏ *075/3438–4308* ⊕ *www.
centroculturaldannemann.com.br.*

Igreja da Ordem de Terceiro do Carmo. This gilded baroque splendor from
1702 rivals the interior of Salavdor's São Francisco; watch, too, for the
white and blue Portuguese tiles and sculptures of Christ, dripping in
cow's blood and imported from Macau. ⊠ *Praça de Aclamação s/n.*

Museu da Irmandade da Boa Morte. This small museum located inside the sisterhood's headquarters displays photos and ceremonial dresses worn during their rituals and festivals. You can also meet some of the elderly, energetic women whose ancestors protested slavery. Under renovation at the time of this update, the museum is set to reopen in August 2013. ✉ *Rua 13 de Maio* 🎟 *By donation* 🕒 *Daily 10–6.*

WHERE TO STAY

$ B&B/INN 🏨 **Pousada do Convento.** You can stay overnight in one of the large rooms at this one-time Carmelite monastery that dates back to the 17th century. **Pros:** good food; beautiful colonial furniture. **Cons:** simple accommodations; few amenities. [$] *Rooms from: R$149* ✉ *Praça da Aclamação s/n* ☎ *075/3425–1716* 🌐 *www.pousadadoconvento.com.br* 🛏 *26 rooms* 🍴 *Breakfast.*

NORTH COAST BEACHES

To reach some of Bahia's more pristine and less crowded beaches, head north of Salvador on the Estrada do Coco (Coconut Road), leaving the baroque churches and colonial dwellings behind in favor of miles of quiet road lined with coconut palms.

GETTING HERE AND AROUND

At the fishing village and turtle haven of Praia do Forte, take the Linha Verde (Green Line) up the coast. Buses to this string of beaches are readily available, but the convenience of having your own car is justified here.

BEACHES

Barra do Jacuípe. A river runs down to the ocean at this long, wide, pristine beach lined with coconut palms, where the beachfront snack bars provide the perfect turf for watching the surfers and kite-surfers. The Santa Maria/Catuense bus company operates six buses here daily. **Amenities:** food and drink, parking, toilets. **Best for:** surfing, walking, kite-surfing. ✉ *41 km (25 miles) north of Salvador.*

Guarajuba. With palm trees and calm waters banked by a reef, this is the nicest beach of them all, though it's lined with condos. The bus to Barra do Jacuípe continues on to Guarajuba, which has snack kiosks, fishing boats, surfing, dune buggies, and a playground. **Amenities:** food and drink, toilets, parking. **Best for:** swimming, walking, sunrise. ✉ *60 km (38 miles) north of Salvador* 🌐 *www.guarajuba.com.*

PRAIA DO FORTE

72 km (45 miles) northeast of Salvador.

On a relaxing day trip from Salvador you can visit Praia do Forte's village, get to know the sea-turtle research station, swim, or snorkel. The town also has a beautiful coconut-lined beach. If you decide to stay longer, there are many lodging options, and the nightlife, although toned down a few decibels from that in Salvador, is still lively. Almost everything in town is on the main street, Alameda do Sol. You can book a trip here through any Salvador tour operator or travel agent, or simply take a bus directly on a day trip.

GETTING HERE AND AROUND

To reach Praia do Forte by car from Salvador, take the Estrada do Coco (BA 099) north and follow the signs. From there on, it's called Linha Verde (Green Line), to Costa do Sauípe and the northern beaches all the way to the Sergipe border. Linha Verde has hourly bus service from Salvador to Praia do Forte. The two-hour trip on the un-air-conditioned bus costs R$8.

ESSENTIALS

Visitor and Tour Information Fly and Fun. This outfitter offers charter flights along the coast. ☎ 071/3676–1540 ⊕ www.flyandfun.com.br. **Praia do Forte Turismo.** This bilingual agency specializes in a wide variety of well-organized tours, from whale-watching and canoeing to dune buggy rides to visiting Mangue-Seco. ⊠ Galeria Alga Marinha, Av. ACM ☎ 071/3676–1192 ⊕ www.praiadoforteturismo.com.br.

EXPLORING

FAMILY **Projeto Tamar.** The headquarters of this nationwide turtle preservation project, established in 1980, has turned what was once a small, struggling fishing village into a tourist destination with a mission—to save Brazil's giant sea turtles and their hatchlings. Five of the seven surviving sea-turtle species in the world roam and reproduce on Brazil's Atlantic coast, primarily in Bahia. During the hatching season (September through March), workers patrol the shore at night to locate nests and move eggs or hatchlings at risk of being trampled or run over to safer areas or to the open-air hatchery at the base station. It is here that you can watch adult turtles in the small swimming pools and see the baby turtles that are housed in tanks until they can be released to the sea, something you can take part in between December and February. The headquarters also has educational videos, lectures, and a gift shop. Thirty-three other Tamar stations on beaches across Brazil protect about 15 million hatchlings born each year. If you are looking for a more intimate experience, seek out one of the smaller bases, as this project is certainly the most commercial. ⊠ Av. Farol Garcia D'Ávila s/n ☎ 071/3676–0321 ⊕ www.tamar.org.br ⊠ R$15 ⊗ Daily 9–5:30.

Reserva de Sapiranga. If you have a couple of days to visit Praia do Forte, spend one of them exploring the Reserva de Sapiranga, spread over 600 hectares (1,482 acres) of Atlantic Forest that contains rare orchids and bromeliads. The reserve is a sanctuary for endangered animals. White-water rafting is possible on the Rio Pojuca, which flows through the park, and Lago Timeantube, where more than 187 species of native birds have been sighted. Whether you explore by foot, horseback, or Jeep, going with a guide is recommended. ⊕ www.praiadoforte.org.br/reserva_sapiranga.html.

BEACHES

Papa Gente. Swim or snorkel in the crystal clear (and safe) waters of the Papa Gente, a 3-meter- (10-foot-) deep natural pool formed by reefs at the ocean's edge. Located 1½ km (1 mile) from Projecto Tamar, walk north along the beach when the tide is low and look out for a coconut vendor, who sits in front of the path that leads to the pools and has masks and snorkels for rent. **Amenities:** none. **Best for:** solitude, swimming, snorkeling, walking. ⊠ 1½ km (1 mile) north of the center of Praia do Forte.

WHERE TO EAT AND STAY

$$$ SEAFOOD 🍴 **Sabor da Vila.** It isn't surprising that seafood fresh from the ocean is the specialty at this simple yet ever-popular restaurant on Praia do Forte's main street. Choose between eight different varieties of seafood moqueca, or opt for the lighter option of *ensopado.* [$] *Average main: R$50* ✉ *Alameda do Sol* ☎ *071/3676–1156* 🌐 *www.sabordavila.com* 🕒 *Closed Tues.*

$$ B&B/INN 🏨 **Pousada Sobrado Da Vila.** Located in the center of town, this laid-back pousada offers rooms that are plain but comfortable, a small swimming pool, and a restaurant with Bahian specialties—if you've never tried a *queijo de coalho frito* (roasted cheese ball), this is your chance. **Pros:** relaxing environment; good restaurant. **Cons:** few amenities. [$] *Rooms from: R$369* ✉ *Av. ACM 7* ☎ *071/3676–1088* 🌐 *www.sobradodavila.com.br* 🛏 *23 rooms* 🍽 *Breakfast.*

$$$$ RESORT FAMILY 🏨 **Tivoli Eco Resort Praia do Forte.** Relax in a hammock and contemplate the sea from your private veranda at this chic beachfront resort and wellness center. **Pros:** plenty of amenities; relaxing spa therapies. **Cons:** pricey; some rooms are far from the central facilities. [$] *Rooms from: R$825* ✉ *Av. do Farol s/n, Praia do Forte, Mata de São João* ☎ *071/3676–4000* 🌐 *www.tivolihotels.com* 🛏 *287 rooms* 🍽 *Some meals.*

MORRO DE SÃO PAULO

Eternally popular among travelers seeking fun in the sun, Morro de São Paulo is the largest village on the Ilha de Tinharé, where thick Atlantic Forest protected by a state park helps it remain miraculously car-free. Step off the direct catamarã from Salvador to find wheelbarrows and donkeys waiting to help heavy packers reach the beaches, identified by number. Tourism's footprint can certainly be felt, with beaches lined with accommodation options and restaurants. While Praia Primeria is the most family-friendly, Praia Segunda is party-central, with fresh-fruit *caipi* carts parked directly on the sand and live music every night during high season. Praia Terceira and Praia Quarta provide more peaceful options.

GETTING HERE AND AROUND

To get here from Salvador, take either a *lancha* (small boat carrying up to five passengers) or larger *catamarã* (catamaran) from Salvador's Terminal Maritimo. Lanchas and catamarãs leave daily from 8 am to 2 pm, and return from Morro de São Paulo from noon to 4 pm. Fares range from R$50 to R$75 and are worth booking in advance during high season. Those prone to sea-sickness should come prepared, for the crossing can be rocky.

A handful of small flight operators, including AeroStar, have service to Morro de São Paulo from Salvador. The 20-minute flight costs about R$275 one way. There's only a landing strip at Morro de São Paulo.

ESSENTIALS

Airline Contacts **Aerostar** ✉ *Aeroporto Internacional Dep. Luis Eduardo Magalhães, Praça Gago Coutinho s/n, São Cristovão, Salvador* ☎ *071/3204–1335.*

BEACHES

Popular beaches dot the 40-km (25-mile) Atlantic side of Tinharé. Starting at the village of Morro de São Paulo, beaches begin with Primeira (First) and go on to Segunda, Terceira, and so forth. Local boats offer the best way to explore the island, while horses are also available for hire. Waters are calm thanks to the coral reef just off the surf, whose abundant marine life (mostly in the form of small fish) makes scuba diving or snorkeling worthwhile. The number of tourists nearly triples from December to February, when Brazilians on their summer vacation fill the pousadas for festival and Carnival season. The southernmost beaches near Boca da Barra are usually quieter even during peak season. The government has begun to charge an environmental tourism tax of R$15 per person.

BOIPEBA

5 hours from Salvador.

With few direct transport links, Boipeba's pristine white sand, turquoise waters, and virgin forests have remained something of a Robinson Crusoe's dream. Surrounded by the Atlantic Ocean on one side, and Rio do Infeno (Hell's River) on the other, access to the island from Salvador can be time-consuming and requires a little more effort and planning than most places, but upon arrival, it is well worth it. As yet, no big hotels have found their foothold on the island, and the pousadas here range from the simple to increasingly rustic-chic. Many serve lunch and dinner as well as breakfast. Wi-Fi access is often patchy, so workaholics should come expecting to switch off.

GETTING HERE AND AROUND

From Salvador, there are a number of different options depending on time and budget. Ferries for Bom Despacho (1 hour for R$5) depart regularly from São Joaquim terminal in Salvador. From there you can take a bus (2 hours for R$15) or taxi (1 hour for R$150) to Valença or Gracioso, where small speedboats await to transfer you the final section (1½ hours for R$35). The last speedboat departs at 4 pm, so be sure to leave enough time. The entire journey takes approximately 5 hours. A number of small plane operators also depart 3 times a day and cost R$450 each way.

EXPLORING

The pace on Boipeba is syrupy slow, but if you manage to make it out of your hammock, there is much to explore on and around the 7-km- (4-mile-) wide island. Hire a boat through the local guide's association or via one of the pousadas and spend the day exploring the natural swimming pools that lie before the Ponta dos Castelhanos. After lunch, head to Vila de Moreré, a small beach community of 250 people; some accommodations are available here. Other activities include sunset canoe rides through the mangrove and a visit to Velha Boipeba (the commercial heart of the island). Some pousadas, like Pousada Santa Clara, offer the chance to take part in local environmental and community projects.

WHERE TO STAY

$$$$ ⊞ **Pousada Mangabeiras.** Set amid native forest with views that stretch
B&B/INN over the island and out to sea, the private bungalows at this chic
pousada are Boipeba's most upmarket options. **Pros:** facilities; peaceful atmosphere; lovely views. **Cons:** English not always spoken; a 10-
minute walk to the beach. $ *Rooms from: R$540* ⊠ *Rua Da Praia s/n,
Praia Boca Da Barra* ☎ *075/3653–6214* ⊕ *www.pousadamangabeiras.
com.br* ↴ *9 rooms* ⊙ *Closed June* ⦿| *Breakfast.*

$ ⊞ **Pousada Santa Clara.** This well-run pousada set 50 meters back from
B&B/INN Boca da Barra beach ticks all the boxes for those looking to kick back
FAMILY in paradise: spacious rooms, a tropical garden complete with giant
Fodor's Choice hammocks, and a lavish, homemade breakfast that changes daily.
★ **Pros:** location; bilingual service; a good value. **Cons:** patchy Wi-Fi;
air-conditioning not in all rooms. $ *Rooms from: R$170* ⊠ *Travessa
da Praia no. 5* ☎ *75/3653–6085* ⊕ *www.santaclaraboipeba.com* ↴ *12
rooms* ⊙ *Closed mid May–early June* ⦿| *No meals.*

LENÇÓIS

*427 km (265 miles) west of Salvador; 1,133 km (704 miles) northeast
of Brasília.*

In 1822 a precious-stone frenzy began with the discovery of diamonds
in riverbeds around the town of Mucugê. Hordes of people hoping to
make their fortune flooded into the region. This golden age lasted until
late in the 1800s, when gems ran out. What remained were towns such
as Lençóis, Igatu, and Mucugê, where cobblestone streets are lined with
19th-century colonial houses. Because of the historic and architectural
importance of the region, buildings are being restored to give travelers
a taste of what life was like in those heady days.

The largest community in the Chapada Diamantina area, as well as
the gateway to Chapada Diamantina National Park, Lençóis arose
from the hundreds of makeshift tents of white cotton fabric built by
garimpeiros (gold- and precious stone-seekers). (*Lençóis* means "bed-
sheet"). The settlement quickly became an important trade hub for
precious stones, attracting merchants from as far away as England,
France, and Germany. Many fortunes were made, but the golden age
ended in 1889, when most of the stones had been hauled away, and
the city was forgotten.

The small town enjoyed a renaissance after it was designated a national
monument in 1973. Several *sobrados* (houses) have been restored to
their original grandeur. The *mercado municipal* (municipal market),
where most of the diamonds were sold, has been completely renovated.

GETTING HERE AND AROUND

When driving, the route to Chapada Diamantina from Salvador is fairly
straighforward: take BR 342 west to Feira de Santana, then BR 242 to
Lençóis. Both roads are in good condition, but expect irregular pavement in some spots. Real Expresso buses make the six-hour trip from
Salvador to Lençóis for about R$60, with departures at 7 am, 1 pm,
4:30 pm, and 11:30 pm daily. Return is at 7:30 am, 1:15 pm, 3:30 pm,
and 11:30 pm daily.

ESSENTIALS

Bus Contacts Estação Rodoviária ⊠ *Av. Senhor dos Passos s/n* ☎ *075/3334–1112.* **Real Expresso** ☎ *075/3334–1112 in Lençóis, 071/3450–9310 in Salvador* ⊕ *www.realexpresso.com.br.*

Visitor and Tour Information Fora da Trilha. This adventure specialist offers a range of "off the beaten track" experiences across Chapada Diamantina, from guided walks to rappeling and climbing, as well as longer hikes of two to eight days. Groups are arranged on level of expertise and fitness. The company can also organize lodging and transfers for you. ⊠ *Rua das Pedras 202* ☎ *75/3334–1326* ⊕ *www.foradatrilha.com.br.* **LenTur Turismo Ecológico.** Pioneer of trekking expeditions in the remote backcountry areas of the Chapada, LenTur Turismo Ecológico, aimed at adventurous travelers, also now provides bilingual guided tours and motorbike trails. ⊠ *Av. 7 de Setembro 10* ☎ *075/3334–1271* ⊕ *www.lentur.com.br.*

EXPLORING

Igatú. A steep 6-km (4-mile) cobblestone road connects the BA 142 highway with the village of Igatú, a former boomtown of the 19th century where the faded ruins of hundreds of abandoned mansions surround contemporary pastel cottages. A pretty museum, Galeria Arte e Memoria, combines contemporary art with relics, while at the Mina Brejo-Veruga, you can venture into what was once the area's largest diamond mine. ⊠ *113 km (70 miles) south of Lençóis.*

FAMILY **Lapa Doce.** A 30-minute hike takes you down to the mouth of the Lapa Doce cave. Along the easy walk through the cave you'll see a stunning collection of large stalagmites and stalactites. Because it's so accessible, Lapa Doce is especially recommended for children. The entrance fee includes a local guide. ✛ *From Lençóis, take BR 242 west 25 km (16 miles), then take BA 432, the road to Irecê, for about 18 km (11 miles)* ☎ *075/3625–1084* 🖃 *R$15* ☉ *Daily 9–6.*

Rio Serrano. One of the region's most popular hiking trails runs along a section of Rio Lençóis called Rio Serrano. It's surrounded by exuberant forest, now protected as a municipal park. The reddish-color water is due to organic matter from the forest floor. You can bathe and relax in several natural pools—they look a bit like hot tubs—formed on the rock-strewn riverbed. There are also three waterfalls along the way to a scenic overlook of the town and surrounding hills. The trailhead is about 1 km (½ mile) north of Lençóis, after the gate to Portal de Lençóis hotel. ⊠ *End of Rua Altina Alves.*

Torrinha. The cave's name, which means "Little Tower," refers to a rock formation outside the entrance. Here you can find a diverse collection of cave formations; besides the usual stalactites and stalagmites, aragonite flowers, clusters of helectites, and chandeliers abound. There are three different guided tours ranging from 1 to 2½ hours that explore different sections of the cave. ✛ *From Lençóis, take BR 242 west 25 km (16 miles), then take BA 432, the road to Irecê, for about 13 km (8 miles)* ☎ *075/9996–7782* 🖃 *R$20* ☉ *Daily 9–6.*

9

WHERE TO EAT AND STAY

There are a growing number of hotels and pousadas in the area. Ranch-style accommodations, complete with hearty meals, appeal to many visitors.

$$$ MODERN ITALIAN 🍴**Maria Bonita Casa de Massas.** Three sisters from Lençóis teamed up under the supervision of their Italian father to open this restaurant offering lasagna and other pasta dishes. Try the ravioli stuffed with ricotta and tomato sauce. [$] *Average main: R$55* ✉ *Rua das Pedras s/n* ☎ *075/3334–1850* 🌐 *www.mariabonitalencois.blogspot.com* 💳 *No credit cards.*

$ B&B/INN 🏨**Estalagem de Alcino.** Guests rave about the endless gourmet breakfasts at this beautiful house, where owner artist Alcino is on hand to provide insider information and personalized service. **Pros:** charming host; fantastic homemade breakfast; romantic atmosphere. **Cons:** some rooms have a shared bathroom; few amenities. [$] *Rooms from: R$190* ✉ *139 Rua Tomba Surrao* ☎ *075/3334–1171* 🌐 *www.alcinoestalagem.com* 🛏 *12 in total: 5 suites, 3 with shared bathroom, 4 bedrooms in a private house* 🍽 *Breakfast.*

$$ B&B/INN 🏨**Hotel Canto das Águas.** One of the first hotels to open after the creation of the national park, Canto das Águas is inspired by the colonial architecture of the nearby historic district, with stone archways opening to a garden that surrounds the main building. **Pros:** superb location near the main plaza. **Cons:** noisy during festivals. [$] *Rooms from: R$345* ✉ *Av. Sr. dos Passos 1* ☎ *075/3334–1154* 🌐 *www.lencois.com.br* 🛏 *36 rooms, 8 suites* 🍽 *Breakfast.*

$$ HOTEL FAMILY 🏨**Portal de Lençóis.** Overlooking Lençóis—west-facing accommodations have magnificent views of the forest-covered river valley—this distinctive hotel has a Portuguese tile roof and stone facade. **Pros:** interesting architecture; plush accommodations; good for groups. **Cons:** rather pricey; property is starting to age. [$] *Rooms from: R$270* ✉ *Av. Sr. dos Passos 1* ☎ *075/3334–1233* 🌐 *www.portalhoteis.tur.br* 🛏 *84 rooms* 🍽 *Breakfast.*

$ B&B/INN 🏨**Pousada Casa da Geléia.** If you're seeking a home away from home, look no further than this simple pousada's clean, spacious, white-walled rooms, where the English-speaking owners will entertain you with tales of the history of the Chapada. **Pros:** fantastic breakfast; friendly owners; spacious grounds. **Cons:** no in-room TVs; a 10-minute walk into town. [$] *Rooms from: R$165* ✉ *Rua General Viveiros 187* ☎ *075/3334–1151* 🌐 *www.casadageleia.com.br* 🛏 *6 rooms* 💳 *No credit cards* 🍽 *Breakfast.*

PARQUE NACIONAL CHAPADA DIAMANTINA

60 km (37 miles) west of Lençóis

The Chapada Diamantina (Diamond Highlands) in Central Bahia was once famous for its precious gems, but it's now recognized as one of the country's best spots for ecotourism. In this chain of mountain ranges with an average altitude of 3,000 feet you'll find historic mining towns, rivers, and creeks with natural pools and waterfalls, and the largest number of caves in any part of Brazil.

GETTING HERE AND AROUND

The town of Lençóis is by far the best gateway to the park.

ESSENTIALS

Visitor and Tour Information Associação dos Condutores de Visitantes. Based in Lençóis, Associação dos Condutores de Visitantes has certified guides to take you to the national park. Itineraries can be arranged to suit your interests and level of fitness. ☎ *075/3334–1425.*

SAFETY AND PRECAUTIONS

Traversing the roads and especially the trails within the park definitely requires experienced guides, as trails are not well marked.

EXPLORING

Parque Nacional Chapada Diamantina. Established in 1985, the 1,520-square-km (593-square-mile) national park is one of the most scenic places in Brazil. Here you can find crystal clear creeks, rivers with abundant rapids and waterfalls, and more than 70 grottos and caverns. There are also the tall peaks of the Sincorá Range, the highest point being Barbados Peak (2,080 meters/7,000 feet). The flora and fauna of the area, which include many varieties of cacti, orchids, and bromeliads, and more than 200 bird species, have been the subject of two extensive studies by the Royal Botanical Gardens at Kew in England. The best time to visit the park is in the dry season from March to October, but expect high temperatures during the day (rarely above 36°C/100°F). From May to July, temperatures might drop to near 10°C (45°F). The park does not have a visitor center, but there's a small ranger headquarters in the town of Palmeiras. ⊕ *www.guiachapadadiamantina.com.br.*

Cachoeira da Fumaça. One of the most popular hikes in the national park leads to the country's tallest waterfall, 1,312-foot Cachoeira da Fumaça (Smoke Waterfall). Most of the falling water evaporates before reaching the ground, hence the odd name. A 4-kilometer (2-mile) path from the village of Caeté-Açú takes you to the canyon's rim. The most scenic route is a longer trail that leaves Lençóis and reaches the gorge below the falls. The path goes past the impressive Capivara Falls. ⊠ *25 kilometers (14 miles) west of Lençóis.*

Vale do Pati. One of the country's most scenic treks, this onetime pilgrim trail of the Tupi Indians takes you between towering sierras, through caves, and past waterfalls. The 70-km (43-mile) trail starts in Bomba, climbs to Candombá hills, follows a plateau at Gerais de Vieira, then goes alongside the steep Rio Paty toward Andaraí. A six-day trek in total, this is best suited for more serious walkers. ⊠ *20 km (12 miles) west of Lençóis.*

THE COCOA COAST

180 kilometers (112 miles) of golden beaches, flanked by coconut groves, dense Mata-Atlantica rain forest, and exotic cocoa plantations stretch between the hip surf town of Itacaré and sleepy Canavieras, making the Cocoa Coast one of Bahia's best driving routes. Along the way are fishing villages, fresh seafood, and luxurious beach resorts, where you could happily get lost for weeks. Regional bus service to towns on the Cocoa Coast departs from Salvador's Terminal Rodoviário.

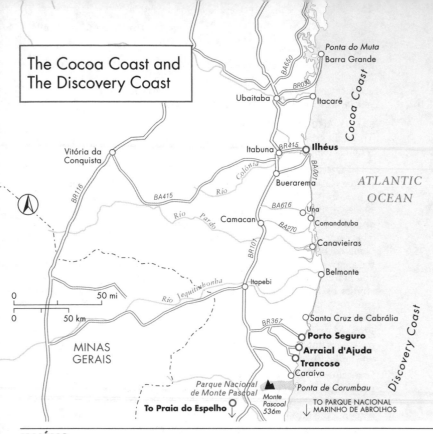

The Cocoa Coast and
The Discovery Coast

Ponta do Muta
Barra Grande
Ubaitaba
Itacaré
Vitória da
Conquista
Itabuna
Ilhéus
Buerarema
ATLANTIC
OCEAN
Camacan
Una
Comandatuba
Canavieiras
Belmonte
Itapebi
Santa Cruz de Cabrália
Porto Seguro
Arraial d'Ajuda
Trancoso
Caraíva
MINAS
GERAIS
Parque Nacional
de Monte Pascoal
Monte
Pascoal
536m
Ponta de Corumbau
To Praia do Espelho
TO PARQUE NACIONAL
MARINHO DE ABROLHOS

Cocoa Coast
Discovery Coast

0   50 mi
0   50 km

ILHÉUS

460 km (286 miles) south of Salvador.

In Brazil, Ilhéus (literally meaning "islanders") is synonymous with cocoa and Jorge Amado, one of Brazil's best-known 20th-century writers. Amado spent his childhood here, and the house he lived in is now a cultural center. Many of his world-famous novels are set in places in and around Ilhéus, and bring to life the "golden age" of the region, when cocoa production was so prosperous that it was nicknamed "black gold." Catedral de São Sebastião (San Sebastian Cathedral) is the heart of the central area—a plaza surrounded by colonial-period buildings akin to those in Pelourinho. While Ilhéus has many beaches, it is worth escaping to the white sands that lie along the north and south coast rather than settling in Ilhéus.

GETTING HERE AND AROUND

There are flights to Ilhéus from Rio de Janeiro, Saõ Paulo, and Salvador. Águia Branca buses travel from Salvador to Ilhéus in about six hours. The cost is R$90 for a regular bus and R$125 for an executive bus. By car take Rodovia BR 101 south.

ESSENTIALS

Airport Aeroporto de Ilhéus Jorge Amado ✉ *Rua Brigadeir o Eduardo Gomes s/n, Pontal* ☎ *73/3234–4000* 🌐 *www.infraero.gov.br.*

Bus Contact Águia Branca ☎ *073/3288–1039, 073/4004–1010* 🌐 *www.aguiabranca.com.br.*

Taxi Contacts Rádio Taxi ☎ *73/3634–4213.*

Visitor Information Associação de Turismo de Ilhéus. Known as ATIL, the Associação de Turismo de Ilhéus has information on local attractions and lodging options. ✉ *Av. Soares Lopes s/n Sala 3, Centro de Convenções Luis Eduardo Magalhaes, Centro,Ilhéus* ☎ *073/3234–6515* 🌐 *www.atil.tur.br.*

WHERE TO STAY

The Cocoa Coast has a few upscale resorts and hotels and many budget pousadas with good-quality, ranch-style accommodations, complete with hearty meals and a wide array of activities such as horseback riding, tennis, and swimming.

$$$$ RESORT Fodor'sChoice ★ 🏨 **Makenna.** Located on a nature reserve between Ilhéus and Itacaré (30 minutes from Ilhéus), this design-focused lodge offers spacious, minimalist wooden cabins that open directly onto the beach. **Pros:** stunning design; good service; beach location. **Cons:** Internet can be slow. [$] *Rooms from: R$650* ✉ *Rodovia Ilheus Itacare Km 16* ☎ *073/2101–6400* 🌐 *www.makenna.com.br* 🛏 *16 rooms* 🍴 *Breakfast.*

$$$$ RESORT 🏨 **Txai Resorts.** This sprawling, high-luxury eco-resort sits among 100 hectares of coconut groves on one of the region's most beautiful beaches and it has delightful facilities, including a hilltop spa with views over the ocean and virgin Mata-Atlantica rain forest. **Pros:** beautiful beach location; great for families; good service. **Cons:** can feel isloated; rustic bathrooms. [$] *Rooms from: R$990* ✉ *Rodovia Ilheus Itacare, Km 48, Ilheus* ☎ *73/2101–5000* 🌐 *www.txai.com.br* 🛏 *40 rooms* 🍴 *Breakfast.*

$$$$ RESORT FAMILY 🏨 **Transamérica Ilha de Comandatuba.** On an island with a giant coconut grove, this grande-dame of Brazilian beach resorts remains a favorite choice for families with kids and golf lovers. **Pros:** beautiful building; nicely furnished rooms; lovely beach. **Cons:** far from nightlife options. [$] *Rooms from: R$999* ✉ *Ilha de Comandatuba s/n, Una* ☎ *073/3686–1122, 0800/012–6060* 🌐 *www.transamerica.com.br* 🛏 *231 rooms, 115 bungalows, 16 suites* 🍴 *All meals.*

THE DISCOVERY COAST

Protected areas where you can experience nature in its pristine state form the backdrop of the birthplace of Brazil.

PORTO SEGURO

730 km (453 miles) south of Salvador.

Not too long ago, Porto Seguro (Safe Harbor) was a serene fishing village. Now it's one of the prime tourist destinations in the country for Brazilians, and the access point for travelers eager to visit deserted beaches and small villages that encapsulate what Porto Seguro once

Beach Savvy

- As a rule, the farther away from the downtown area, the better the beach in terms of water cleanliness and number of people, especially on weekends.

- Beaches in Bahia, as in most of Brazil, tend not to have facilities like bathrooms or showers.

- Pickpocketing and minor theft can be a problem. Bring as few items to the beach as possible, and just enough money for the day. Be cautious about leaving anything unattended.

- Vendors, especially in Salvador, had a reputation for being overly persistent, but this is something that has changed considerably and you should now find that you can shop in peace.

- Larger cities such as Salvador, Ilhéus, and Porto Seguro have quick and comfortable public transportation to beaches, like the *ônibus executivo* (executive bus; a minibus or van, usually labeled "roteiro das praias").

- Be careful when entering the water for the first time—a few steps in can put you in deep waters.

- Be aware of rock outcroppings and coral reefs that can cut your feet.

- If you plan to snorkel, bring your own gear. Rentals are not always available.

- Food and drink are available at almost every beach, except those you have to hike to. However, if you're squeamish about eating food from a beach vendor, bring your own.

---

was. Hotels, inns, and restaurants have risen to please nearly every need or taste, although many former fans argue it has become too busy and commercial.

Porto Seguro has an intense atmosphere comparable only to Salvador in Bahia. Picture a city whose main drag is called "Passarela do Alcool" (Booze Walkway). Carnival is a major event here, drawing hundreds of thousands of tourists. The beaches north of the city are recommended for those looking for calmer grounds.

GETTING HERE AND AROUND
From Salvador, Águia Branca offers daily overnight bus service to Porto Seguro (11 hours, R$120). There are daily flights from Salvador, Rio de Janeiro, and Saõ Paulo on Tam, GOL, Azul and Trip.

ESSENTIALS
Airport Aeroporto Porto Seguro ⊠ *Estr. Aeroporto 1500* ☎ *73/3288–1880.*

Bus Contacts Águia Branca ☎ *73/3288–1039, 4004–1010* ⊕ *www.aguiabranca.com.br.* **Rodoviária** ⊠ *Rua José Borges Souza 35* ☎ *071/3288–1914.*

Taxi Contacts Porto Táxi ☎ *73/3288–1010.*

Visitor and Tour Information Pataxó Turismo. This local agency specializes in private and group tours of the region, including visits to the neighboring Pataxó Indian reserve and tours for whale-watching. ⊠ *Shopping Rio Mar, loja 3 – Passarela do Alcool, Centro* ☎ *073/3288–1256* ⊕ *www.pataxoturismo.com.br.*

CLOSE UP

Eating Bahian

When African slaves arrived in Bahia, they added coconut milk, palm oil, and hot spices into Portuguese and Indian dishes, transforming them into something quite new. Additional basic raw materials are lemon, coriander, tomato, onions, dried shrimp, salt, and hot chili peppers. Seafood is the thing in Bahia, and most regional seafood dishes are well seasoned, if not fiery hot. Bahia's most famous dish is *moqueca*, a seafood stew made with fish and/or shellfish, dendê oil, coconut milk, onions, and tomatoes, cooked quickly in a clay pot over a high flame. *Bobó* is an equally tasty but creamier version of moqueca due to the addition of cassava flour. Other classics include *vatapá*, a thick puree-like stew made with fish, shrimp, cashews, peanuts, and a variety of seasonings; *caruru*, okra mashed with ginger, dried shrimp, and palm oil; *ximxim de galinha*, chicken marinated in lemon or lime juice, garlic, and salt and pepper, then cooked with dendê and peanut oil, coconut milk, tomatoes, and seasonings; and *efo*, a bitter chicory-like vegetable cooked with dried shrimp. *Sarapatel* is a Portuguese dish, a stew of pig meat and inner organs that has been incorporated seamlessly into Bahian cuisine.

A popular snack is *acarajé*, a pastry of *feijão fradinho* (black-eyed beans) flour deep-fried in dendê oil and filled with *camarão* (sun-dried shrimp) and *pimenta* (hot-pepper sauce). A variation is *abará*, peas or beans boiled in a banana leaf instead of fried. Note that palm oil is high in saturated fat and hard to digest; you can order these dishes without it. Restaurants in Bahia usually serve hot pepper sauce on the side of all dishes, which is unusual elsewhere in Brazil.

WHERE TO EAT AND STAY

$$$ ITALIAN
🍴 **Recanto do Sossego.** Run by three Italians, this beach restaurant combines fresh seafood with homegrown classics, such as fish carpaccio and gnocchi with pesto sauce. On Friday evenings, reservations are a must. [$] *Average main: R$50* ✉ *Av. Beira Mar, 10130, Praia do Mutá* ☎ *073/3677–1266* 🌐 *www.recantodosossego.com.*

$$$$ RESORT ALL-INCLUSIVE
🏨 **La Torre Resort.** This all-inclusive hotel is popular with international visitors because of its location on quiet Mutá Beach and its wide range of activities. **Pros:** all-inclusive property; on the beach. **Cons:** basic rooms; impersonal. [$] *Rooms from: R$660* ✉ *Praia do Mutá, Av. Beira Mar 9999* ☎ *073/2105–1700* 🌐 *www.resortlatorre.com* 🛏 *230 rooms* 🍽 *All-inclusive.*

$$$$ RESORT
🏨 **Villagio Arcobaleno.** Porto Seguro's five-star choice is right on hip Taperapuã Beach. **Pros:** nicely furnished rooms; free Internet. **Cons:** a bit removed from the center; a minimum two-night stay. [$] *Rooms from: R$530* ✉ *Av. Beira Mar, at Km 6.5* ☎ *073/2105–5050, 0800/284–5222* 🌐 *www.hotelarcobaleno.com.br* 🛏 *159 rooms, 4 suites* 🍽 *Breakfast.*

ARRAIAL D'AJUDA

10-minute ferry ride from Porto Seguro.

The municipality of Arraial starts just across Rio Buranhém from Porto Seguro. The town is about 4 km (2½ miles) south of the river. It was founded by Jesuits that arrived in 1549 with the Portuguese official Tomé de Souza, the first governor-general of Brazil. Its name is a tribute to Our Lady of Help, a much-revered saint in Portugal. The church and parish were the center of the Catholic church in Brazil for more than a century.

In the 1970s, laid-back Arraial d'Ajuda attracted Brazilian hippies, and then a slew of foreign adventurers moved here, giving the place an eclectic atmosphere and the nickname "Corner of the World."

Coroa Vermelha beach, to the south, is where the first mass in Brazil was celebrated. Other great beaches are Mucugê, Parracho, and Pitinga.

GETTING HERE AND AROUND

Take one of the ferries that depart from Porto Seguro every half hour. The five- to 10-minute trip costs R$2.50.

WHERE TO EAT AND STAY

$$
ECLECTIC
✕ A Portinha. This popular buffet-style restaurant attracts both locals and foreign visitors drawn to the generous salad bar and the variety of "slow-cooked" options. The restaurant daily serves a different type of cuisine, so the fare for any given day might include Brazilian, Italian, or Asian specialties. $ *Average main: R$30* ⊠ *Rua do Mucugê 333 – Shopping d´Ajuda* ☎ *073/3575–1289* ⊕ *www.portinha.com.br.*

$$$
RESORT
FAMILY
▦ Arraial d'Ajuda Eco Resort. This resort should be your choice if you're looking for a beachfront hotel offering ample activities plus a gorgeous beach complete with natural pools. **Pros:** water park admission included in rates; comfortable rooms; great for kids. **Cons:** can be crowded with day-trippers. $ *Rooms from: R$500* ⊠ *Ponta do Apaga Fogo* ☎ *073/3575–8500* ⊕ *www.arraialresort.com.br* ⇄ *160 rooms* ❑ *Some meals.*

$
B&B/INN
▦ Manacá Pousada Parque. The main draw at this charming pousada is the rooms, which are large, comfortable, well-decorated, and appointed with king-size beds, balconies, and hammocks. **Pros:** pleasant rooms; reasonable prices. **Cons:** not on the beach. $ *Rooms from: R$167* ⊠ *Estrada Arraial 500* ☎ *073/3575–1442* ⊕ *www.pousadamanaca.com.br* ⇄ *29 rooms* ❑ *Breakfast.*

TRANCOSO

725 km (450 miles) from Salvador.

Smaller than its northern neighbors Arraial and Porto Seguro, Trancoso moves at a much slower pace. Founded by Jesuit missionaries in 1586, its first name was St. John Baptist of the Indians. Life here circles around the downtown plaza called "Quadrado" (the Square), where pedestrians have the right of way—no cars allowed. This is where everybody goes for shopping, dining, and people-watching. In recent years Trancoso has become something of a jet-set destination—a haven for high-society Brazilians from São Paulo, especially between Christmas and early January when the laid-back Quadrado is overrun by glamorous dresses, high-heels, and endless events. As a result, it now has several high-end hotels, such as the Casa Uxua, as well as an increasing number of private villas to rent, to cater to the clientele. Outside these peak periods, the village remains as charming as ever.

GETTING HERE AND AROUND

Take a ferry to from Porto Seguro Arraial D'Ajuda. From here take a bus or van to Trancoso. If you're driving, take BA 101 from Arraial d'Ajuda to Trancoso.

ESSENTIALS

Visitor and Tour Information **Brazilian Beach House.** This bilingual travel specialist rents some of Brazil's most beautiful private houses, from intimate fisherman's cottages to fully staffed beachfront mansions for groups of 20. Many options are available in and around Trancoso. ✉ *Visconde de Piraja 95, Ipanema, Rio de Janeiro* ☎ *021/2225–9476* 🌐 *www.brazilianbeachhouse.com.* **Porto Mondo.** This professional agency can organize everything from airport transfers to eco-sports and day trips to the area's most beautiful and secluded beaches. It's located in Porto Seguro, but it's your best option for finding activities around Trancoso. ☎ *073/3575–3686* 🌐 *www.portomondo.com.*

WHERE TO EAT

$$$ SEAFOOD 🍴 **Capim Santo.** Located in the heart of the quadrado, *Capim Santo*—which means lemongrass in Portuguese—is one of the best restaurants in town. Open since 1985, the family-run business, which includes lodging, retains an essence of informality and coziness, even though service is super sharp and the seafood-based menu sophisticated enough to warrant a second branch in São Paulo. Reservations in high season are a must, where the flickering candlelight and jabuticaba caiprinhas make this one of the hottest, and most romantic, spots in Trancoso. If you decide to stay the night, you will find the good-value rooms are spread over a tropical garden with fruit trees and an outdoor pool. [$] *Average main: R$60* ✉ *Rua do Beco 55* ☎ *073/3668–1122* 🌐 *www.capimsanto.com.br* 🕒 *Closed Sun.*

$$$ ITALIAN 🍴 **Pizzeria Maritaca.** Fabulous thin-crust pizza, homemade pasta, and a happening scene keep this lively local spot ever popular. It's only open for dinner. [$] *Average main: R$50* ✉ *Rua Carlos Alberto Parracho s/n* ☎ *073/3668–1258* 🕒 *Closed Mon.*

$$$$ ECLECTIC Fodor's Choice ★ 🍴 **Restaurante da Sylvinha.** This colorful cottage with some of the most innovative food in Bahia, set right on Praia do Espelho beach, draws Trancoso's jet set, who get here via a bumpy 40-minute drive on dirt roads. Sylvinha serves a generous set menu that blends Brazilian and Asian flavors (think ginger-infused fish and tropical fruit chutneys) to diners who gather around a few big tables on the terrace of her house. Daybeds are set under the coconut palms for post-lunch snoozing. ■ **TIP→ Reservations are essential at this lunch-only spot.** [$] *Average main: R$75* ✉ *Praia do Espelho s/n* ☎ *075/9985–4157* ✍ *Reservations essential* 🕒 *Closed Sun.*

WHERE TO STAY

Trancoso offers some of the most sophisticated accommodation options in Bahia, from beach-shack chic pousadas to high-end resorts. Between December and March, make sure you book well in advance.

$$ B&B/INN **Mata N'ativa Pousada.** Location is prime here, right on the banks of Trancoso's river, three minutes' walk from the beach and the downtown square. **Pros:** pleasant rooms; ecofriendly environment. **Cons:** rather rustic; very secluded. [$] *Rooms from: R$270* ✉ *Estrada do Arraial s/n* ☎ *073/3668–1830* 🌐 *www.matanativapousada.com.br* 🛏 *8 rooms* 🍴 *Breakfast.*

$$$ HOTEL Fodor's Choice ★ **Pousada Etnia.** While just a few minutes' stroll from Trancoso's happening square, this intimate pousada feels like a world of its own. **Pros:** intimate feel; romantic spot; lovely furnishings. **Cons:** not for families (children must be over 14); a short walk to the beach. [$] *Rooms from: R$400* ✉ *Av. Principal, 25* ☎ *073/3668–1137* 🌐 *www.etniabrasil.com.br* 🛏 *8 bungalows* 🕓 *Closed May and June* 🍴 *Breakfast.*

$$$$ HOTEL Fodor's Choice ★ **Uxua Casa Hotel & Spa.** The imaginative genius of Wilbert Das, Diesel's creative director, found his calling with this exceptional hotel: the 10 private bungalows encapsulate the original, colorful character of Trancoso's former fishermen's cottages while remaining impeccably furnished, with king-size beds, plasma TVs, and iPod docks. **Pros:** inspirational design; sophisticated facilities; friendly local staff. **Cons:** expensive restaurant. [$] *Rooms from: R$990* ✉ *Quadrado* ☎ *073/3668–2277* 🌐 *uxua.com* 🛏 *10 rooms* 🍴 *Breakfast.*

PRAIA DO ESPELHO

40 minutes south of Trancoso.

One of the regions' most idolized spots and a regular winner of Brazil's best beach, Praia do Espelho is reached from Trancoso through fields of buffalo and communities of Pataxó Indians. During sunny days, the giraffe-like coconut palms provide shade for bathers, while a smattering of simple-chic restaurants serve cold agua de coco and fresh seafood. Come during the week and you will have the perfect horseshoe bay all to yourself. Beach strollers will want to head right, where more deserted coves of golden sand await. *Espelho* means "mirror" in Portuguese and alludes to the shimmering layer of water that reflects the sky during low-tide. The more adventurous can continue on to the small town of Caraiva, accessible only by wooden boat.

WHERE TO STAY

$$$$ B&B/INN **Cala e Divino.** One of the only options to sleeping overnight on Praia do Espelho, this former artist's residence offers 10 Santorini-esque private chalets scattered up the bluff overlooking the beach. **Pros:** access to one of Brazil's most beautiful beaches; great food; tranquillity. **Cons:** can feel isloated; poor Wi-Fi. [$] *Rooms from: R$600* ✉ *Estrada Trancoso/Caraíva, Km 22* ☎ *073/3668–1380* 🌐 *www.divinoespelho.com.br* 🛏 *10 rooms* 🍴 *Breakfast.*

THE NORTHEAST

Updated by
Lauren Holmes

Like the whole of Brazil, the Northeast is a place of contrasts. Churches, villas, and fortresses in Recife, Natal, and
Fortaleza tell the tale of Portuguese settlers who fought Dutch
invaders and amassed fortunes from sugar. The beaches in
and around these cities evoke Brazil's playful side and its
love affair with sun, sand, and sea. West of the cities, the
rugged, often drought-stricken *sertão* (bush) shows Brazil's
darker side—one where many people struggle for survival.
This warp and weave of history and topography is laced
with threads of culture: indigenous, European, African, and
a unique blend of all three that is essentially Brazilian.

Brazil's northeastern cities are experiencing a renaissance whose
changes strike a balance between preservation and progress. Recife
remains a place of beautiful waters, and nearby Olinda is still a charming enclave of colonial architecture—though bohemians have long
since replaced sugar barons. On Ceará State's 570-km-long (354-mile-
long) coast, Fortaleza continues to thrive against a backdrop of fantastic beaches with both new amenities and timeless white dunes.
Although smaller and with less-storied pasts, Natal and surrounding
beach towns like Praia da Pipa have cemented their status as some of
the country's most beautiful and popular tourist destinations. Meanwhile little-known Alagoas, Brazil's smallest state, is gaining recognition as the place where white-sand beaches and fisherman villages still
remain gloriously underexplored.

ORIENTATION AND PLANNING

GETTING ORIENTED

The Northeast of Brazil includes the coastal states of Bahia, Sergipe,
Alagoas, Pernambuco, Rio Grande do Norte, Paraiba, Ceará, Maranhão and the landlocked state of Piauí. In the middle of this region are
two large and vibrant cities, Recife and Fortaleza. The region, which
covers an area of 1,554,257 square km (600,102 square miles), is home
to a little less than a third of the population of the entire country.

RECIFE

In the state of Pernambuco, the sprawling city of Recife is bounded by
the Beberibe and the Capibaribe rivers, which flow into the Atlantic.
The city is known for the dozens of bridges linking its many boroughs.
It is 2,392 km (1,486 miles) from Rio de Janeiro and 2716 km (1,688
miles) from São Paulo.

TOP REASONS TO GO

■ **Idyllic Beaches:** Relax on some of Brazil's most beautiful beaches, with warm water all year and sand dunes high enough to ski down.

■ **Gorgeous Olinda:** Wander along the winding streets of Olinda as you gaze up at the beautiful colonial-era architecture.

■ **Star-gaze:** Star-gaze and watch the full moon rise in some of the world's clearest skies.

■ **Carnival:** The energetic Carnival in Olinda is considered to be among the best in Brazil, rivaling those in Rio and Salvador.

■ **Northeastern Eats:** Try the amazing *carne de sol*, or sun-dried beef, as well as the other unique Northeastern dishes using lobster, shrimp, and crabs.

NATAL
The capital of Rio Grande do Norte, Natal has a population of 1,234,819. The city is surrounded by dunes on both sides, which gives it a unique appearance. It's 2,680 km (1,665 miles) from Rio de Janeiro and 3,011 km (1,871 miles) from São Paulo.

FORTALEZA
A thriving economic center, Fortaleza is the entry point for the state of Ceará. The population is 2,416,920, and is growing at a rapid pace. On the Atlantic Ocean, it's 2,808 km (1,744 miles) from Rio de Janeiro and 3,109 km (1,932 miles) from São Paulo.

FERNANDO DE NORONHA
An archipelago in the state of Pernambuco, the national marine park of Fernando de Noranha consists of 21 sparsely populated islands. About 354 km (219 miles) from the coast of Brazil, these islands have a population of roughly 2,000.

PLANNING

WHEN TO GO
High season corresponds to school vacations (July) and the period between Christmas and Carnival (late December–mid-March). Prices are better off-season, but if you've come to partake in festivities, Olinda has one of the best Carnival celebrations in the country. Also, the region has two of the most popular out-of-season Carnival celebrations: Carnatal in Natal, on the first weekend in December; and Fortal in Fortaleza, on the last weekend in July. Temperatures hover between about 20°C and 35°C (70°F and 95°F) year-round—temperatures get hotter the farther north you go. Rain is heaviest from May to August in Recife. In Fortaleza, March and April are the rainiest months. Natal sits at about 25°C (75°F) year-round; it sees much less rain than Fortaleza or Recife, but April through July are the wettest months.

10

GETTING HERE AND AROUND

The distances between the cities in Northeast Brazil make flying the best way to get around. Even then, the times involved are not small. Flying to Fortaleza from Salvador, for example, takes 2½ hours. That's nothing compared to the 24 hours you'd spend on a bus. Once you've reached your destination, there's often no reason to rent a car. In Natal or Fortaleza you can easily get around by taxi or bus.

RESTAURANTS

The Northeast has little of the hustle and bustle you'll find in the southern cities of Rio de Janeiro and São Paulo. Residents enjoy a relaxed lifestyle, so in restaurants you'll find that casual attire is the norm. The many *batidas* (tropical fruit cocktails) are the highlights of the local cuisine, but many restaurants serve foods from other parts of Brazil. You'll also have many other options, including Italian, Dutch, and French restaurants set up by expats who never left. Dinner begins around 8 pm. Most hotels include breakfast in the cost of your room. Restaurants not in hotels are usually not open for breakfast. *Prices in the reviews are the average cost of a main course at dinner or, if dinner is not served, at lunch.*

HOTELS

Hotels are plentiful throughout the Northeast. Prices range from moderate to pricey, depending on season. Many hotels are sleek and modern, comparable to those you'd find in tourist destinations around the world. Pousadas tend to have a bit more charm and personalized service. Making reservations is advisable during high seasons. Keep in mind that prices listed at the hotel reception are often considerably higher than those that can be find online. Many business hotels in Boa Viagem will also drop their rates on the weekends. *Prices in the reviews are the lowest cost of a standard double room in high season. For expanded reviews, facilities, and current deals, visit Fodors.com.*

RECIFE

Just over 3.6 million people make their home in the capital of Pernambuco State. This vibrant metropolis 829 km (515 miles) north of Salvador has a spirit that's halfway between that of the modern cities of Brazil's south and of the traditional northeastern centers. It offers both insight on the past and a window to the future.

It was in Pernambuco State, formerly a captaincy, that the most violent battles between the Dutch and the Portuguese took place. Under the Portuguese, the capital city was the nearby community of Olinda. But beginning in 1637 and during the Dutch turn at the reins (under the powerful count Maurício de Nassau), both Olinda and Recife were greatly developed.

The city has beautiful buildings alongside the rivers that remind many visitors of Europe. Unfortunately, huge swathes of 19th-century buildings were razed to make way for modern structures. As a result, the center of the city has pockets of neocolonial splendor surrounded by gap-toothed modern giants. Today Recife is a leader in health care and

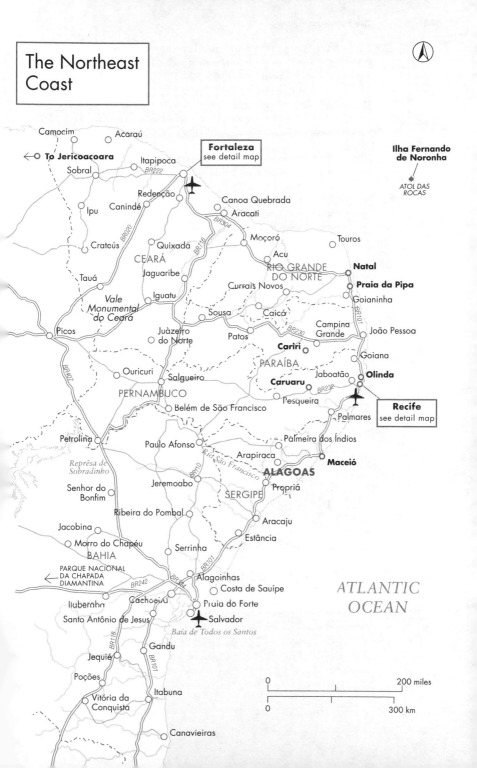

The Northeast Coast

Camocim
Acaraú
←○ To Jericoacoara
Itapipoca
BR222
Sobral
Fortaleza
see detail map

Ilha Fernando de Noronha

ATOL DAS ROCAS

Redenção
Ipu   Canindé
BR020
Canoa Quebrada
Aracati
BR304

Cratéus
Quixadá
BR116
Moçoró
Touros

CEARÁ
Acu
RIO GRANDE DO NORTE
Natal

Tauá
Jaguaribe
Iguatu
Currais Novos
Caicá
Praia da Pipa
Goianinha
BR101

Vale Monumental do Ceará
Sousa
Campina Grande
João Pessoa

Picos
Juàzeiro do Norte
Patos
BR230
Cariri ○
Goiana

BR407
Ouricuri
Salgueiro
PARAÍBA
Jaboatão
Olinda

PERNAMBUCO
Caruaru
BR232
Belém de São Francisco
Pesqueira
Recife
see detail map

Petrolina
Paulo Afonso
Palmares
Pálmeira dos Índios

Represa de Sobradinho
Rio São Francisco
Arapiraca
Maceió

Senhor do Bonfim
BR110
Jeremoabo
ALAGOAS
Propriá

Ribeira do Pombal
SERGIPE

Jacobina
Estância
Aracaju

Morro do Chapéu
Serrinha
BAHIA
PARQUE NACIONAL DA CHAPADA DIAMANTINA
BR242
BR116
BR101
Alagoinhas

ATLANTIC OCEAN

Ituberaba
Cachoeira
Costa de Sauípe
Praia do Forte

Santo Antônio de Jesus
Salvador
Baía de Todos os Santos

Jequié
BR116
BR101
Gandu

Poções
Itabuna
0   200 miles

Vitória da Conquista
0   300 km

Canavieiras

has benefitted from significant government investment in recent years, resulting in a boom in infrastructure and construction industries. It's also Brazil's third-largest gastronomic center—it's almost impossible to get a bad meal here.

Recife is built around three rivers and connected by 49 bridges. Its name comes from the *recifes* (reefs) that line the coast. Because of this unique location, water and light often lend the city interesting textures. In the morning, when the tide recedes from Boa Viagem Beach, the rocks of the reefs slowly reappear. Pools of water are formed, fish flap around beachgoers, and the rock formations dry into odd colors. And if the light is just right on the Rio Capibaribe, the ancient buildings of Recife Antigo (Old Recife) are reflected off the river's surface in a watercolor display.

GETTING HERE AND AROUND

The Aeroporto Internacional Guararapes is 10 km (6 miles) south of Recife, just five minutes from Boa Viagem, and 15 minutes from the city center. There are numerous daily flights from São Paulo and Rio de Janeiro to Recife on GOL, TAM, Avianca, and Azul. Recife has also developed into the northeastern hub for international flights, with direct daily flights to Miami with American Airlines, and to Lisbon with Tap. In the airport lobby, on the right just before the exit door, is a tourist-information booth, and next to that is a taxi stand. You can pay at the counter; the cost is about R$30 to Boa Viagem and R$40 to downtown. There are also regular buses and microbuses (more expensive). The bus labeled "aeroporto" runs to Avenida Dantas Barreto in the center of the city, stopping in Boa Viagem on the way.

The Terminal Integrado de Passageiros (TIP), a metro terminal and bus station 14 km (9 miles) from the Recife city center, handles all interstate bus departures and some connections to local destinations. To reach it via metro, a 30-minute ride, enter through the Museu do Trem, opposite the Casa da Cultura, and take the train marked "rodoviária". Expresso Guanabara has several buses a day to Fortaleza (12 hours, R$130) and Natal (four hours, R$61) and frequent service to Caruaru (two hours, R$12). Itapemerim has buses to Rio de Janeiro (36 hours, R$358) and Salvador (14 hours, R$140).

Recife is the only northeastern city with a subway system. A single ride on the metro is R$1.50. You can find a map at the Metrorec website (click on "Mapa da Rede"). Transfer tickets and city bus tickets cost about R$1.75. Buses are clearly labeled and run frequently and past midnight. Many stops have signs indicating the routes. To reach Boa Viagem via the metro, get off at the Joana Bezerra stop (a 20-minute ride) and take a bus or taxi (R$20) from here. Buses are free when using the metro and vice-versa.

Taxis are cheap (fares are higher on Sunday and at night), but drivers seldom speak English. All use meters. You can either hail a cab on the street or call for one.

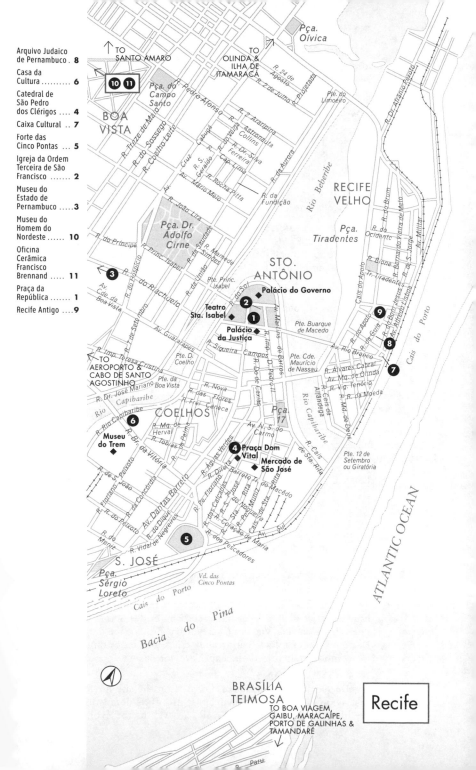

Recife

ESSENTIALS

Airport Aeroporto Internacional Guararapes (REC) ⊠ Praça Ministro Salgado Filho s/n, Imbiribeira ☎ 081/3322–4188.

Boat Contacts Catamaran Tours. Catamaran cruises along the Rio Capibaribe take you past Recife's grand houses, bridges, and mangrove forests. Catamaran Tours offers two such excursions: an hour-long afternoon trip goes through the old rotating bridge and passes Recife Antigo and São José, the customs quay, the Santa Isabel Bridge, and the Rua da Aurora quays to the area near the Casa da Cultura. A two-hour-long night tour is aboard a slower—but more lively—vessel. It passes the quays of São José Estelita. Prices range between R$38 and R$50. ⊠ Praça Marco Zero, Recife Antigo ☎ 081/3424–2845, 081/9973–4077 ⊕ www.catamarantours.com.br.

Bus Contacts Expresso Guanabara ⊠ R. Min Mário Andreazza 30 ☎ 081/2101–1992 ⊕ www.expressoguanabara.com.br. **Itapemerim** ⊠ Estr. do Bongi 388 ☎ 081/3445–7555 ⊕ www.itapemirim.com.br. **Terminal Integrado de Passageiros** ⊠ Km 15, Rodovia BR 232 ☎ 081/3452–1211.

Subway Contacts Metrorec ☎ 081/2101–8502 ⊕ www2.cbtumetrorec.gov.br.

Taxi Contacts Coopetáxi ☎ 081/3424–8944 ⊕ www.coopetaxi.com.br. **Ouro Táxi Recife** ☎ 081/3423–7777. **Teletáxi** ☎ 81/2121–4242 ⊕ www.teletaxirecife.com.br.

Visitor and Tour Information Agência Luck. This agency specializes in tours of the region. ⊠ Avenida Conselheiro Aguiar 2205, Boa Vista ☎ 081/3366–6222 ⊕ www.luckviagens.com.br.

SAFETY AND PRECAUTIONS

With the exception of Recife Antigo, Recife's downtown area is dead at night and should be avoided as a safety precaution.

EXPLORING

Recife is spread out and somewhat hard to navigate. The Centro—with its mixture of high-rises, colonial churches, and markets—is always busy during the day. The crowds and the narrow streets can make finding your way around even more confusing. The Centro consists of three areas: Recife Antigo (the old city); Recife proper, with the districts of Santo Antônio and São José; and the districts of Boa Vista and Santo Amaro. The first two areas are on islands formed by the rivers Capibaribe, Beberibe, and Pina; the third is on an island created by the Canal Tacaruna.

Six kilometers (4 miles) south of Centro is the upscale residential and beach district of Boa Viagem, reached by bridge across the Bacia do Pina. Praia da Boa Viagem (Boa Viagem Beach), the Copacabana of Recife, is chockablock with trendy clubs and restaurants as well as many moderately priced and expensive hotels.

TOP ATTRACTIONS

Arquivo Judaico de Pernambuco. Located on the site of the America's first synagogue, this excellent museum offers detailed insight into the history and culture of the city, as well as the evolution of the

Jewish experience in Brazil. All that remains of the original sanctuary, built in 1641, is the walls and the ground, which can be viewed through glass floor panels. Some guides speak English, and the informative signs are bilingual. ⊠ *Rua do Bom Jesus 197, Recife Antigo* ☎ *081/3224–8351* ⊕ *www.arquivojudaicope.org.br* ⊠ *R$4* ⊙ *Tues.– Fri. 9–5, Sun. 2–6.*

Catedral de São Pedro dos Clérigos. The facade of this cathedral, which was built in 1728, showcases fine wooden sculptures and a splendid trompe-l'oeil ceiling. The square surrounding the cathedral is lined with many restaurants, shops, and bars, and is a hangout for local artists, who often read their poetry or perform music, particularly on Tuesday evening. ⊠ *Rua Patio de São Pedro, São José* ☎ *081/3224–2954* ⊠ *Free* ⊙ *Tues.–Fri. 8–11 and 2–4, Sat. 8–10:30.*

Igreja da Ordem Terceira de São Francisco. Built in 1606, this church has beautiful Portuguese tile work, while the adjoining Capela Dourada (Golden Chapel), constructed in 1697, is an outstanding example of Brazilian baroque architecture. The complex also contains a convent—the Convento Franciscano de Santo Antônio—and a museum displaying sacred art. ⊠ *Rua Imperador Dom Pedro II s/n, Santo Antônio* ☎ *081/3224–0530* ⊠ *R$2* ⊙ *Weekdays 8–11:30 and 2–5, Sat. 8–11:30.*

Museu do Estado de Pernambuco. The state historical museum, in a mansion once owned by a baron, seems more like a home filled with beautiful antiques than a museum. Among the 14,000 objects on display, there is a grand piano, a dining-room table set with 18th-century china, an ornate 19th-century crib, and many beautiful paintings. ⊠ *Av. Rui Barbosa 960, Graça* ☎ *081/3184–3174* ⊠ *R$2* ⊙ *Tues.–Fri. 9–5, weekends 2–5.*

Fodor'sChoice ★ **Museu do Homem do Nordeste.** Offering rich insight into the history and cultural influences of Brazil's Northeast, this museum's collection ranges from utensils crafted by indigenous tribes and artifacts from European colonizers, to religious items from African slaves and ceramics by artists such as Mestre Vitalino and Mestre Zê. For those interested in learning more about this region of Brazil, the Museu do Homem do Nordeste is essential. ⊠ *Av. 17 de Agosto 2187, Casa Forte* ☎ *081/3073–6340* ⊕ *www.fundaj.gov.br* ⊠ *R$5* ⊙ *Tues.–Fri. 8:30–5, weekends 1–5* ⊙ *Closed Mon.*

10

FAMILY **Oficina Cerâmica Francisco Brennand.** In the old São José sugar refinery, this museum houses more than 2,000 ceramic pieces by the great (and prolific) Brazilian artist Francisco Brennand. Having studied in France, he was influenced by Pablo Picasso and Joan Miró, among others, and his works also include paintings, drawings, and engravings. About 15 km (9 miles) from Recife Antigo, the museum's location amid forests and fountains is almost as appealing as its displays. ⊠ *Km 16, Propriedade Santo Cosme e Damião s/n, Várzea* ☎ *081/3271–2466* ⊕ *www. brennand.com.br* ⊠ *R$4* ⊙ *Mon.–Thurs. 8–5, Fri. 8–4.*

Praça da República. The city's original cultural and political meeting point of the 17th century, this historic square was given a new lease of life by landscape architect Burle Marx in the 1930s, and now features rows of Imperial palms and a hundred-year-old baobab tree among the elaborate 19th- and 20th-century architecture. Highlights include the Teatro Santa Isabel (St. Isabel Theater, 1850); the Palácio do Campo das Princesas, also known as the Palácio do Governo (Government House, 1841); and the Palácio da Justiça (Court House, 1930). ⊠ *Recife Antigo.*

Fodor's Choice
★

Recife Antigo. Most of Old Recife's colonial-era public buildings and houses have been restored. The area between Rua do Bom Jesus and Rua do Apolo is full of shops, cafés, and bars, making it the hub of downtown life both day and night; on weekends there's live *maracatu* music and dancing, and a handicrafts fair is held every Sunday from 2 to 8 on Rua do Bom Jesus.

WORTH NOTING

Casa da Cultura. The old cells of this former 19th-century prison have been transformed into shops that sell works from Pernambuco's artisans, including clay figurines, wood sculptures, carpets, leather goods, and items made from woven straw. One of the cells has been kept in its original form to give visitors an idea of how the prisoners there lived. ⊠ *Rua Floriano Peixoto, Santo Antônio* ☎ *081/3224–0557* ⊠ *Free* ⊘ *Mon.–Sat. 9–7, Sun. 9–2.*

Forte das Cinco Pontas. Originally constructed from mud in 1630, the "Fort of Five Points" was rebuilt in 1677 with stone and mortar; even though it now has only four sides, the fort has retained its original name. One of the last buildings built duing the era of Dutch dominance, this military fort now houses the **Museu da Cidade,** where an array of maps and photos illustrates Recife's history. ⊠ *Praça das Cinco Pontas, São José* ☎ *081/3224–8492* ⊘ *Tues.–Fri. 9–6, weekends 1–5.*

BEACHES

Boa Viagem. Coconut palms line Recife's most popular beach, the 9-km-long (4-mile-long) Praia da Boa Viagem. A steady Atlantic breeze tames the hot sun, and reef formations create pools of warm water that are perfect for swimming. Sailors and fishermen beach their *jangadas* (handcrafted log rafts with beautiful sails), and vendors sell coconut drinks from kiosks. Avenida Boa Viagem separates a row of hotels and apartments from the beach, which is lined by a wide blue *calçadão* (sidewalk) that's perfect for running, bike rides, or evening promenades. On weekend afternoons there's a handicrafts fair in Praça da Boa Viagem. Surfing and swimming beyond the reef are not recommended because of the presence of sharks. **Amenities:** food and drink, lifeguards, parking (fee). **Best for:** partiers, walking, sunrises. ⊠ *Boa Viagem.*

Cabo de Santo Agostinho. Some of Pernambuco's finest beaches are clustered around the small town of Cabo de Santo Agostinho, 35 km south of the city. The town's namesake beach, Cabo de Santo Agostinho, is better for soaking up the view of the cliffs and surrounding colonial houses rather than sun-bathing, as there is very little sand to sit on. Buses to and from Recife depart regularly and cost R$2. **Amenities:** food and drink; toilets. **Best for:** sunsets. ⊠ *35 km (22 miles) southeast of Recife.*

Gaibu. Surrounded by palm trees and favored by local surfers, beautiful Gaibu has become one of the area's most happening hangout spots. Volleyball competitions, fishing, and surfing are all practiced along the shore, while at the end of the beach, you can visit the ruins of the Fort of San Francisco Xavier. Some parts of the beach are not recommended for swimming. **Amenities:** food and drink; lifeguards. **Best for:** partiers; surfing. ⊠ *30 km (19 miles) south of Recife.*

FAMILY **Ilha de Itamaracá.** This island is set off the coast of the historic city of Igarassu and has a number of beautiful beaches with calm waters for swimming, as well as a protected area for manatees. The best beach is Forte Orange, next to Coroa do Avião; it has a historic fort that kids love to explore. Buses to Igarassu and Ilha de Itamaracá leave from the center of Recife, at the Cais de Santa Rita in front of the Fórum Thomas de Aquino. **Amenities:** food and drink; toilets. **Best for:** walking; swimming. ⊠ *39 km (24 miles) north of Recife.*

Maracaípe. South of Recife on the road past Porto das Galinha lies serene Maracaípe beach. The excellent waves and happening *Quiosques* (beach bars) have made this a popular weekend spot with younger crowds. **Amenities:** food and drink; lifeguards; parking; toilets; water sports. **Best for:** partiers; surfers; windsurfing. ⊠ *73 km (46 miles) southwest of Recife.*

Porto de Galinhas. Once considered one of the most beautiful beaches in Brazil, this historic port has lost a considerable dose of its original charm because of the increasingly heavy influx of tourists drawn to the beach's transparent natural swimming pools. If you don't mind sharing the beauty, there is a good variety of accommodation options and restaurants, as well as *jangadas* (small boats) for hire. The beach, which follows the curve of a bay lined with coconut palms and cashew trees, gets crowded on weekends year-round. You shouldn't expect to spot any chickens—Porto das Galinhas (Port of Chickens) earned its name as a hub of illegal slave trading after abolition, when slaves from Africa would arrive hidden under guinea-fowl crates, and traders would be alerted that the "chickens had arrived." **Amenities:** food and drink; lifeguards; parking (fee); showers; toilets; water sports. **Best for:** partiers; snorkeling; sunrise; surfing. ⊠ *70 km (43 miles) south of Recife.*

10

Tamandaré. Situated 109 km (68 miles) south of Recife, this beach region shares the same calm, warm waters and natural pools as Porto das Galinhas, yet lacks the crowds. The postcard-perfect **Praia dos Carneiros** is regularly elected as one of Brazil's best. Its brilliantly clear emerald waters are home to shoals of tropical fish, and the beach huts there serve fresh coconut water and seafood snacks. **Amenities:** food and drink; lifeguards; parking (fee); toilets. **Best for:** solitude; snorkeling; swimming; sunrises. ⊠ *109 km (68 miles) south of Recife.*

WHERE TO EAT

An integral part of the city's culture, Recife's culinary scene has a well-earned reputation as one of the best in Brazil. Among the specialties not to miss are *carne do sol* (salted beef, dried in the sun for 1–2 days), tapioca pancakes (white flour made from cassava root) with fried cheese and caramelized banana, and *caldeirada* (seafood stew with octopus and parsley).

$$$
SEAFOOD
✕**Bargaço.** For those looking for an authentic taste of Bahia, this pleasant restaurant serves up golden *moquecas baianas* (fish cooked with onion, tomatoes, peppers, parsley, and coconut milk) and flavorful *caju caipirinhas* (cocktails made with cashew fruit). Service can be slow, so make sure you aren't in a hurry here. $ *Average main: R$60* ⊠ *Av. Antonio de Góes 62, Pina* ☎ *081/3466–5026* ⊕ *www.restaurantebargaco.com.br.*

$
BRAZILIAN
FAMILY
✕**Parraxaxá.** Waiters at this popular restaurant wear the bent orange hats of Lampião, a Jesse James–like folk hero who made his way through the interior of northeastern Brazil during the early 20th century. The buffet has a wide selection of the regional specialties that Lampião might have encountered back then. The food is priced per kilogram, so the cost will depend on how hungry you are. Try the amazing *escondinho* (a wonderful meat and cheese dish), *charque* (dried beef), and *carne sol* (brisket). $ *Average main: R$28* ⊠ *Av. Fernando Simoes Barbosa 1200, Boa Viagem* ☎ *081/3463–7874* ⊕ *www.parraxaxa.com.br* ⊙ *Daily 11:30 am–11 pm.*

$$$
PORTUGUESE
✕**Tasca.** As popular now as when it opened more than 30 years ago, this elegant, old-school restaurant serves up Portuguese classics such as *bacalhau a calí*—codfish cooked with olive oil, onion, garlic, tomatoes, potatoes, and white wine. Save room for sugary Portuguese desserts like *pastel de belém* (a creamy custard tart). $ *Average main: R$55* ⊠ *165 Rua Dom José Lopes, Boa Viagem* ☎ *081/3326–6309* ⊙ *Tues.–Thurs. 6:30 pm–midnight, Fri.–Sat. 6:30 pm–1 am, Sun. 12–5* ⊙ *Closed Mon. No lunch Tues.–Sat. No dinner Sun.*

$$$
BRAZILIAN
Fodor's Choice
★
✕**Tio Pepe.** Specializing in innovative yet traditional dishes, this lively restaurant has loyal locals queuing out the door for juicy portions of *carne de sol* (sun-dried beef) and *porco vulcanico* (pork fillet served with a special house sauce, beans, and manioc). The menu revolves around the grill, with a wide variety of fish as well as meat dishes generous enough to be shared. Opt for a table among the tropical plants on the breezy terrace, where colorful tablecloths and eclectic design add to the character. $ *Average main: R$60* ⊠ *Rua Almirante Tamandare 170, Boa Viagem* ☎ *081/3341–7153* ⊕ *www.tiopepe.com.br* ⊙ *Closed Mon. No dinner Sun.*

WHERE TO STAY

Most of Recife's top hotels are between 10 and 20 minutes from the airport, across from the Boa Viagem and Pina beaches or along Piedade Beach, in the municipality of Jaboatão dos Guararapes.

$$$$
HOTEL
Fodor's Choice
★
🏨 **Atlante Plaza Hotel.** The city's smartest business hotel, this glimmering high-rise looks directly over Recife's most popular beach. **Pros:** superlative service; rooftop pool; superior facilities. **Cons:** can be overrun by business folk and flight crews. $ *Rooms from: R$525* ⊠ *Av. Boa Via-*

gem 5426, Boa Viagem ☎ 081/3302–3333 🌐 www.atlanteplaza.com.br 🛏 214 rooms, 27 suites 🍴 Breakfast.

$$$ HOTEL 🏨 **Beach Class Suites.** Located in one of the trendiest parts of Boa Viagem and right across from the beach, this modern hotel has elegantly designed rooms and the sort of smiling, efficient service you would expect from one of Brazil's largest hotel groups. **Pros:** hip design; trendy location; free Wi-Fi and free parking. **Cons:** small swimming pool faces directly on to busy traffic; pricey. [$] *Rooms from: R$450* ✉ *Avenida Boa Viagem 1906, Boa Viagem* ☎ *081/2121–2626* 🌐 *www.atlanticahotels.com.br* 🛏 *152 rooms, 12 suites* 🍴 *Breakfast.*

$$$ HOTEL FAMILY 🏨 **Mar Hotel Recife.** A five-minute walk from Boa Viagem beach, this slightly dated hotel offers spacious rooms that all come with a small, private veranda. **Pros:** near the beach; fun pool area. **Cons:** dated design; much higher room rates when booking directly at the counter. [$] *Rooms from: R$395* ✉ *Rua Barão de Souza Leão 451, Boa Viagem* ☎ *081/3302–4444* 🌐 *www.marhotel.com.br* 🛏 *188 rooms, 19 suites* 🍴 *Breakfast.*

$ HOTEL 🏨 **Recife Monte Hotel.** A block from Boa Viagem Beach, this hotel's outdated lobby and basic decor is balanced by great rates, a good location, and a lovely outdoor pool. **Pros:** pleasant rooms; affordable rates. **Cons:** dated decor; some rooms smell of smoke. [$] *Rooms from: R$199* ✉ *Rua dos Navegantes 363, Boa Viagem* ☎ *081/2121–0909* 🌐 *www.recifemontehotel.com.br* 🛏 *155 rooms, 16 suites* 🍴 *Breakfast.*

$ B&B/INN 🏨 **Recife Plaza.** Overlooking the Rio Capibaribe, this simple downtown hotel emphasizes function over form and is one of the few lodging options within walking distance of Recife Antigo. **Pros:** inexpensive rates; river views. **Cons:** parts of the hotel in serious need of renovation; infrequent hot water and Wi-Fi. [$] *Rooms from: R$240* ✉ *Rua da Aurora 225, Boa Vista* ☎ *081/3059–1200* 🌐 *www.recifeplazahotel.com.br* 🛏 *73 rooms* 🍴 *Breakfast.*

$$ HOTEL 🏨 **Transamérica Prestige.** Since opening in 2011, this spacious, modern hotel has been a favorite among both businesspeople and families for its comfortable facilities and professional service. **Pros:** large rooms; clean and modern decor; 24-hour room service **Cons:** restaurant lacks atmosphere; no pool bar. [$] *Rooms from: R$325* ✉ *Avenida Boa Viagem 420, Boa Viagem* ☎ *081/3039–9000* 🌐 *www.transamericagroup.com.br* 🛏 *191 rooms, 4 suites* 🍴 *Breakfast.*

NIGHTLIFE AND THE ARTS

NIGHTLIFE

Pólo Pina, the calçadão in the Pina district, is a popular area near the beach for nighttime activities. Along the streets off Rua Herculano Bandeira you can find close to two-dozen bars and restaurants. Between Rua do Apolo and Rua do Bom Jesus (or Rua dos Judeus) in Recife Antigo, people gather in a seemingly endless variety of bars, cafés, and nightclubs.

BARS

Boteco. Chilled draft beer, tasty snacks, and excellent service make Boteco one of the most popular bars in town. ✉ *Av. Boa Viagem 1660, Boa Viagem* ☎ *081/3325–1428.*

Depois. In the heart of a bohemian neighborhood, Depois takes up three floors of an old building. Hits from the 1960s to the '90s keep the crowd glued to the dance floor. ⊠ *Av. Rio Branco 66, Recife Antigo* ☎ *081/3424–7451* ⊙ *Mon.–Thurs. 11 pm–3 am, Fri.–Sat. 9 pm–5 am.*

UNDER THE SEA
More than a dozen shipwrecks make good destinations for underwater explorers of all experience levels. The *Vapor de Baixo* is one such dive site. Bombed by the Germans during World War II, it's 20 meters (65 feet) down and is crawling with lobsters and turtles.

Galeria Joana D'Arc. A favorite hangout for local gay men and lesbians, Galeria Joana D'Arc is a cluster of small cafés and bars, among them Café Poire, Anjo Solto, Barnabé, and Oriente Médio. ⊠ *Rua Herculano Bandeira 513, Pina* ☎ *81/3325-0862.*

O Biruta. Repeatedly selected as Recife's best beach bar, O Biruta is a great spot to watch the moon rise over the beach while enjoying a refreshing cocktail. There's live samba music every Saturday. ⊠ *Rua Bem-te-vi 15, Brasília Teimosa* ☎ *081/3326–5151* ⊕ *www.birutabar.com.br* ⊙ *Mon. from 5 pm, Tues.–Sun. from 11 am.*

DANCE CLUBS

Downtown. A club with a London pub look, Downtown is a good place to be on Saturday night when local bands play. The club is especially popular with teenagers and twentysomethings. ⊠ *Rua Vigário Tenório 105, Recife Antigo* ☎ *081/3424–6317* ⊕ *www.downtownpub.com.br* ⊙ *Wed.–Sun. 10 pm–5 am.*

THE ARTS

Caixa Cultural. Opened in 2012 in a beautifully restored belle-epoque mansion in Recife Antigo, this huge arts space includes three exhibitions rooms, a theater, a coffee shop, dance studios, and a roof-terrace with wonderful views over the city. ⊠ *Avenida Alfredo Lisboa no. 505, Recife Antigo* ☎ *081/3425–1906* ⊕ *www.caixacultural.com.br* ⊙ *Closed Mon.*

Teatro Santa Isabel. Built in 1850, lovely Teatro Santa Isabel looks splendid after a major restoration. The neoclassical theater is the setting for operas, plays, and classical concerts, as well as the home of the Recife Symphony Orchestra. ⊠ *Praça da República s/n, Santo Antônio* ☎ *081/3355–3323, 081/3355–3324* ⊕ *www.teatrosantaisabel.com.br.*

SPORTS AND THE OUTDOORS

SCUBA DIVING

For centuries the treacherous offshore reefs that gave Recife its name have struck fear into the hearts of sailors. Many a vessel has failed to navigate the natural harbor successfully. Though diving is practiced year-round, visibility is best between October and May, when the wind and water are at their calmest.

Seagate. This tour operator offers diving courses, rents equipment, and runs trips for certified divers. ⊠ *Av. Herculano Bandeira 287, Pólo Pina* ☎ *081/3463–0523* ⊕ *www.seagaterecife.com.br.*

SOCCER

Arena Pernambuco. In anticipation of the 2014 World Cup, Recife has built a new, multipurpose stadium in the city's western suburbs. Arena Pernambuco will have a capacity of 46,160 people and act as the home for Pernambuco's top football team, Clube Náutico Capibaribe. The country's first "green" arena, the stadium will be run by the electricity from a nearby solar power plant. ⊠ *Recife Antigo* ⊕ *www. cidadedacopa.com.br.*

SHOPPING

Centro de Artesenato de Pernambuco. Opened in 2012, this shop occupies an entire warehouse and contains the work of more than 15,000 regional artisans. It is a wonderful place to pick up local souvenirs, from ceramics to original prints. Prices are reasonable and there is a nice buffet restaurant and auditorium in the adjoining warehouses. ⊠ *Avenida Alfredo Lisboa 11, Recife Antigo* ☎ *081/3181–3450* ⊕ *www. portaldoartesanato.pe.gov.br* ☉ *Mon. 2–8, Tues.–Sat. 10–8.*

Mercado de São José. In the city's most traditional market, vendors sell handicrafts, clothing, produce, and herbs. It's housed in a beautiful cast-iron structure that was imported from France in the 19th century. ⊠ *Praça Dom Vital s/n, São José* ☎ *081/3355–3398* ☉ *Mon.–Sat. 6–5, Sun. 6–noon.*

Shopping Center Recife. The enormous Shopping Center Recife is the place to go if you are looking for a shopping fix. There are more than 450 stores, along with a 10-screen cinema and a food court. The center is not far from Boa Viagem Beach. ⊠ *Rua Padre Carapuceiro 777, Boa Viagem* ☎ *081/3464–6000* ⊕ *www.shoppingrecife.com.br* ☉ *Mon.–Sat. 10–10, Sun. 1–9.*

SIDE TRIP TO OLINDA

7 km (4 miles) north of Recife.

The name of Pernambuco State's original capital means "beautiful," and this must have been what came to mind when the first Europeans stood atop the forested hills and gazed at ocean and beach spread out before them. Today the town's natural beauty is complemented by colonial buildings painted in a rainbow of colors, making it a stunning slice of the old Northeast.

Founded by the Portuguese in 1535, Olinda was developed further by the Dutch during their brief turn at running Pernambuco in the 1600s. The narrow cobblestone streets of this UNESCO World Cultural Site curve up and down hills that, at every turn, offer spectacular views of both Recife and the Atlantic. The scenery is just as nice up close: many houses have latticed balconies, heavy doors, and stucco walls. The zoning laws are strict, resulting in a beautiful, compact city that artists, musicians, and intellectuals have made their own.

The city center is hilly but fairly easy to explore by foot. You may want to hire a guide to help provide some historical background on the city and its principal sites. Look for the official guides (they have ID cards

10

OLINDA'S CARNIVAL

Many rate Carnival in Olinda as one of the best in Brazil, rivaling those in Rio de Janeiro and Salvador. It's considered Brazil's most traditional Carnival—meaning there's noticeably less skin exposed. Music is generally the slower-paced *forró or the frenetic frevo*, in contrast to Rio's *samba* and Salvador's *axé*.

Carnival here lasts a full 11 days. Highlights include the opening events—led by a bloco of more than 400 "virgins" (men in drag)—and a parade of *bonecos de pano* (huge dolls) and *mamulengos* (marionettes) in the likenesses of famous Northeasterners. The dolls and puppets are made of Styrofoam, fabric, and papier-mâché, and are often so elaborate that they take neighborhood artists most of the year to make.

and bright orange or blue T-shirts) who congregate in the Praça do Carmo. They are former street children, and half the R$45 fee for a full city tour goes to a home for kids from the streets.

GETTING HERE AND AROUND
A cab from the airport in Recife costs between R$50 and R$65. Alternatively, you can take the "aeroporto" bus to Avenida Nossa Senhora do Carmo in Recife and transfer to the "casa caiada" bus bound for Olinda.

Visitor Information Casa Da Turista. This bilingual center provides information and advice, as well as acting as a lost-and-found pickup point in Olinda. ⊠ *R. Prudente de Morais 472, Carmo Olinda, Olinda* ☎ *081/3305–1060.*

SAFETY AND PRECAUTIONS
To be on the safe side, don't hire sightseeing guides who approach you on the street. Hire one through the museum or sight you're visiting, a tour operator, the tourist board, your hotel, or a reputable travel agency.

EXPLORING
TOP ATTRACTIONS
Alto da Sé. This is the most scenic spot for soaking up Olinda's views of Recife and the ocean, particularly during sunset. It's also a good place to see some historic churches as well as to sample Bahia-style *acaraje* (black-eyed pea fritters) and Pernambuco's famous tapioca cakes. Make sure you try the *cartola*, a heavenly combination of fried cheese, banana, cinnamon, and condensed milk. Have a seat at one of the outdoor tables here, or browse in the shops that sell handicrafts—including lace—and paintings. To get here, just walk up on Ladeira da Sé. ⊠ *Ladeira da Sé, Carmo Olinda.*

Igreja da Sé. Built in 1537, the Igreja da Sé has been restored as much as possible to its original appearance. From its side terrace you can capture a postcard-perfect view of the Old City and the ocean. ⊠ *Alto da Sé, Carmo* ▣ *Free* ☉ *Daily 8–12 and 2–4:30.*

Fodor's Choice **Mosteiro de São Bento.** The main chapel of the Mosteiro de São Bento, a
★ Benedictine monastery, is Olinda's richest church and considered to be one of Brazil's most beautiful. Brilliant gold covers the elaborately carved

wooden altar and frames the sumptously furnished private balconies that overlook it, providing a dramatic contrast with the white walls and frescoed ceilings. It once housed the nation's first law school. Sunday's 10 am mass features Gregorian chants. ✉ *Rua de São Bento s/n, Varadouro* ☎ *081/3316–3290* 🎟 *Free* 🕒 *Daily 8:30–11:45 and 2–6:30.*

TAPIOCA STANDS

While in Olinda, try the food at stands selling *tapioca,* or patties made from shaved coconut. Many claim that the tapioca made here is the best in the country. Try the savory chicken and catupiry tapioca, then follow it up with a cartola (grilled cheese, banana, and cinnamon) tapioca for dessert.

WORTH NOTING

Convento de São Francisco. Built in 1577, the Convento de São Francisco was the first Franciscan convent in Brazil. The floors are Portuguese tile work, ceilings are frescoed, and walls are made of ground-up local coral. ✉ *Rua São Francisco 280, Carmo Olinda* ☎ *081/3429–0517* 🎟 *R$3* 🕒 *Weekdays 8–noon and 2–5, Sat. 8–12.*

Igreja da Misericórdia (*Mercy Church*). Built in 1540 and restored in 1654, the Igreja da Misericórdia has rich sculptures of wood, gold, and silver. It sits atop the Alto da Sé and offers magnificent views of Recife. The church is open for visits of 20 minutes only, at 11:45 am and 5:30 pm, and during mass, held daily at 6:20 am and on Sunday at 7:30 am. ✉ *Rua Bispo Coutinho, Carmo* ☎ *081/3494–9100* 🎟 *Free* 🕒 *Mon.–Sat. 6:20 am, 11:45–12:05, 5:30–5:50; Sun. 7:30 am.*

Museu do Mamulengo-Espaço Tiridá. At this whimsical museum, you can soak up the essence of Northeastern folk tales through shows featuring puppets crafted from wood and felt that were used in street theater in the 19th century. ✉ *Rua do São Bento 344* ☎ *081/3493–2753* 🎟 *R$2* 🕒 *Tues.–Sun. 10–5.*

WHERE TO EAT AND STAY

$$$ BRAZILIAN 🍴 **Oficina do Sabor.** Settle down in the leafy dining room of this regional restaurant, and take in the views of the coconut palms of Olinda while sampling the house speciality of stuffed pumpkin for two. While there are 15 different fillings, it is the *abóbora com camarão* (pumpkin stuffed with shrimp and served with a *pitanga* cherry sauce) that really stands out. [$] *Average main: R$55* ✉ *Rua do Amparo 335* ☎ *081/3429–3331* 🌐 *www.oficinadosabor.com* 🕒 *Closed Mon. No dinner Sun.*

$$ HOTEL FAMILY 🏨 **Hotel 7 Colinas.** Named after the seven hills that surround the hotel, 7 Colinas is a sprawling oasis that sits amid the trees and flowers of a tropical estate that once belonged to the São Francisco religious order. **Pros:** cozy rooms; nice atmosphere; fantastic swimming pool. **Cons:** no Internet connection in the rooms. [$] *Rooms from: R$290* ✉ *Ladeira de São Francisco 307* ☎ *081/3493–7766* 🌐 *www.hotel7colinasolinda.com.br* 🛏 *44 rooms* 🍽 *Breakfast.*

10

$ B&B/INN 🏨 **Hotel Pousada Quatro Cantos.** In a converted mansion, this pousada has rooms that vary considerably in size, quality, and price; the suites, with hardwood floors, rival those at the best hotels, but the standard rooms are just average. **Pros:** wonderful suites; good rates. **Cons:** not all rooms are equal. [$] *Rooms from: R$230* ✉ *Rua Prudente de Morais*

441 ☎ *081/3429–0220* 🌐 *www.pousada4cantos.com.br* 🛏 *16 rooms, 2 suites* 🍴 *Breakfast.*

$$$ HOTEL 🏨 **Pousada do Amparo.** This lovely pousada is made up of two colonial houses with soaring ceilings; wood and brick details, original artwork, and an indoor garden lend considerable warmth to the cavernous spaces. **Pros:** atmospheric buildings; lovely rooms; helpful staff. **Cons:** poor Wi-Fi connection; breakfast could be improved. [$] *Rooms from: R$460* ✉ *Rua do Amparo 199, Varadouro* ☎ *081/3439–1749* 🌐 *www.pousadadoamparo.com.br* 🛏 *18 rooms.*

SHOPPING

Casa do Artesão. For regional crafts, head to the Casa do Artesão. It's open weekdays 9–6 and Saturday 9–2. ✉ *Rua Prudente de Morais 458, Carmo* ☎ *081/3053–1927* 🌐 *casadoartesaoolinda.blogspot.com.br.*

Rua do Amparo. Along Rua do Amparo, one of the cultural hubs of Olinda, you will find an eclectic collection of artists' workshops. The artists themselves will happily welcome you inside and let you browse through their work. ✉ *Rua do Amparo, Varadouro, Olinda.*

SIDE TRIP TO CARUARU

134 km (83 miles) west of Recife.

Caruaru and its crafts center, Alto do Moura (6 km/4 miles south of Caruaru), became famous in the 1960s and '70s for clay figurines made by local artisan Mestre Vitalino. There are now more than 500 craftspeople working in Alto do Moura. All are inspired by Vitalino, whose former home is now a museum, open Monday through Saturday 8–noon and 2–6 and Sunday 8–noon. At the crafts center you can buy not only figurines, which depict Northeasterners doing everyday things, but also watch the artisans work.

GETTING HERE AND AROUND

A shuttle bus runs between Recife and Caruaru every half hour. Caruaruense buses cost R$12. To reach Caruaru from Recife by car, take BR 232 west; the trip takes two hours.

ESSENTIALS

Bus Contacts Caruaruense ☎ *81/3722–1611.*

EXPLORING

Feira de Caruaru. This fantastic open-air market, the largest in Northeast Brazil, takes place daily. Here, as the songwriter Luis Gonzaga put it, "it is possible to find a little of everything that exists in the world." Look for pottery, leather goods, ceramics, hammocks, and baskets. On Saturday, roving musicians provide a soundtrack to shopping with violins and folk music. ✉ *Parque 18 de Maio.*

WHERE TO STAY

$ B&B/INN 🏨 **Caruaru Park Hotel.** On the outskirts of town, the Caruaru Park's colorful rooms and chalets are sparsely decorated but neat and clean. **Pros:** pleasant rooms; good breakfast. **Cons:** basic decor. [$] *Rooms from: R$134* ✉ *Rod br 232, 201 – Agamenon Magalhãe* ☎ *081/3727–9494* 🌐 *www.caruaruparkhotel.com.br* 🛏 *76 rooms* 🍴 *Breakfast.*

SIDE TRIP TO ALAGOAS

For a long time, Brazil's smallest state was known for little else than sugar production and as the breeding ground (and favored retreat) of some of the country's most corrupt politicians. However, in the last five years, the state has begun to gain ground as one of the country's emerging tourist destinations, particularly for Brazilians who have tired of the increasing commercialization of Bahia's beach towns.

From Barra de São Miguel south of the capital Maceio up through the *rota ecológica* toward Recife, the coast is lined with coconut palms and remarkably free, thus far, of large resorts. Instead, you will find small communities of fisherman's villages, boutique pousadas, and deserted beaches. The *rota ecológica,* also known as the Costa dos Corais after the coral reef that runs along its shore, is one of the area's highlights: 20 km of road that veer off from the main highway and pass through villages such as São Miguel de los Milagres, which have thus far remained a far better kept secret than the natural pools of nearby Maragogi. The predominantly calm warm waters here make it a great choice for kids.

GETTING HERE AND AROUND

Buses run regularly between the two capitals of Recife and Maceio, with the "conventional" class stopping off at beach towns along the way. To get the best out of hopping between the different beaches, hiring a car is recommended. A taxi from São Miguel dos Milagres to Recife will cost around R$250 reais and take between 2 and 3 hours.

ESSENTIALS

Bus Contacts Real Alagoas ☎ *081/3452–9400* ⊕ *www.realalagoas.com.br.*

Visitor and Tour Information Gato do Mato. This professional agency specializes in a wide range of eco-tours and adventure activities throughout the region. They can also arrange transfers. ⊠ *Praia dos Frances, Alagoas, Recife* ☎ *082/3033–1040* ⊕ *www.gatodomato.com.*

EXPLORING

Saõ Miguel dos Milagres. This fisherman's village is surrounded by some of the region's most charming independent pousadas, most of which face directly onto the sand and are focused on preserving the natural surroundings. The beaches along this part of the coast form one long trail of coconut palms perfect for long walks and soaking up the natural beauty, while the sea itself is protected by a fringe of coral that keeps conditions continuously calm. One thing not to miss is the Sea-Cow Sanctuary, which rehabilitates wounded manatees and is one of the best places in Brazil to get close to these endangered animals. Look for signs on the main road that point toward the workshops of local artisans, where you can find furniture and handicrafts carved from local materials. ⊕ *Access via BR101 South of Recife, 233 KM.*

BEACHES

Praia do Patacho. Almost always deserted, this long stretch of white sand is the Coral Coast's most beautiful beach, with warm waters calm enough for even small kids to feel like they are taking a bath. The landscape changes significantly between high and low tide, when the water retreats from the coconut-lined shore up to 500 meters, leaving

10

an iridescent layer of water that reflects the sunlight. **Amenities:** none. **Best for:** solitude; snorkeling; sunrises; swimming; walking. ⊠ *Porto das Pedra (140 km/87 miles from Recife via BR-101 South).*

WHERE TO STAY

$$$$
RESORT
Fodor's Choice
★

🏨 **Kenoa.** Brazil's first eco-design resort, this remarkable property provides high-end luxury while maintaining its dedication to the preservation of nature and the local culture. **Pros:** stunning design; five-star service; spa; well-priced restaurant **Cons:** far from the nearest town. $ *Rooms from: R$1490* ⊠ *Rua Escritor Jorge de Lima nº 58, Barra de São Miguel* 🕾 *082/3272–1285* ⊕ *www.kenoaresort.com* 🛏 *23 rooms* 🍴 *Breakfast.*

$$$
B&B/INN
FAMILY

🏨 **Pousada Amendoeira.** Perched on a deserted white-sand beach, this pousada is a contender for Brazil's most tranquil place to unwind. **Pros:** romantic atmosphere; excellent location; stellar service. **Cons:** rooms can be a little small; no pool. $ *Rooms from: R$490* ⊠ *Praia do Toque, São Miguel dos Milagres* 🕾 *082/3295–1213* ⊕ *www.pdamendoeira.com.br* 🛏 *8 rooms* 🍴 *Some meals.*

$$$
B&B/INN
FAMILY
Fodor's Choice
★

🏨 **Pousada Xuê.** This beach-chic pousada stands out for its exceptional food and bungalows that open directly onto beautiful beaches. **Pros:** excellent service; fantastic food; great for families. **Cons:** far from the nearest town; Internet only in communal areas. $ *Rooms from: R$450* ⊠ *Praia do Patacho, Porta das Pedra* 🕾 *082/3298–1197* ⊕ *www.pousadaxue.com.br* 🛏 *5 bungalows* 🍴 *Some meals.*

NATAL

Natal has been growing by leaps and bounds over the past decade. The capital of Rio Grande do Norte has become an important industrial center, yet no industry has had more effect on the economy than tourism. The past few administrations have invested heavily in the infrastructure and promotion, effectively placing it on the map as one of the prime tourism destinations in Brazil.

Although it has little in the way of historical or cultural attractions, the city's main asset is its location along one of the most beautiful stretches of coast in Brazil. In fact, Natal's foundation and much of its history have been all about location. In 1598 the Portuguese began construction of the Fortaleza dos Reis Magos in present-day Natal. Its location was strategic for two reasons. First, it was at the mouth of the Rio Potengi. Second, it was near the easternmost point of the continent and therefore was closest to Europe and Africa. On December 25, 1599, the city was founded and named Natal, Portuguese for "Christmas."

While bustling Ponta Negra and the sprawling nearby holiday resorts may conjure up summer destinations in Southern Europe, the towns and beaches that lie to the north and south of the city are distinctly Brazilian.

GETTING HERE AND AROUND

Aeroporto Internacional Augusto Severo is 15 km (9 miles) south of the town center. Taxis to Ponta Negra or downtown Natal cost around R$40 to R$50. Vans from the airport to downtown costs R$2.20

Natal has two bus stations. For almost all destinations you use the Rodoviário de Natal, 5 km (3 miles) from Ponta Negra. It's often referred to as the *terminal nova* (new terminal). Several buses daily go to Praia da Pipa (1½ hours; R$11.50), Recife (four hours; R$61), Fortaleza (eight hours; R$88–R$110), and Rio de Janeiro (44 hours; R$400). Buses to Genipabu and Ponta Negra beaches leave from Natal's other bus station, the Rodoviário Velho (old bus station), downtown.

Natal lies at the northern end of BR 101, making it an easy trip by car from Recife, which is due south on BR 101. To reach Praia da Pipa, head south on BR 101 and then take RN 003 to the east. To Fortaleza, take BR 304 northwest and then head north on BR 116.

Natal's few museums and historic buildings are mostly clustered in the Cidade Alta (Upper City), within easy walking distance of each other. Ponta Negra is still small enough that it can easily be explored on foot—most hotels and restaurants are very close to the beach. All taxis have meters and are easy to locate in Ponta Negra and downtown.

ESSENTIALS

Airport Aeroporto Internacional Augusto Severo (*NAT*) ⊠ *R. Rio Xingu, Parnamirim* ☎ *84/3087–1200.*

Bus Contacts Terminal Rodoviário de Natal ⊠ *Av. Capitão Mor. Gouveia 1237, Cidade de Esperança* ☎ *084/3205–2931.*

Taxi Contacts Rádio Táxi ☎ *084/3221–5666* ⊕ *www.radiotaxinatal.com.br.* **Rádio Táxi Relámpago** ☎ *084/3223–5444.*

Visitor and Tour Information Cariri Ecotours. This ecotourism operator arranges trips throughout the Northeast, including to Praia da Pipa and Fernando do Noronha. ⊠ *Av. Prudente de Morais 4262, Loja 3B, sala 1, Lagoa Nova* ☎ *084/9660–1818* ⊕ *www.caririecotours.com.br.* **Natal Tur.** This tour operator has dune-buggy trips to Genipabu and other local beaches, as well as trips to Fernando de Noronha. ⊠ *Av. Deodoro da Fonseca 424, Cidade Alta* ☎ *084/3211–0177* ⊕ *www.nataltur.com.br.* **SETUR** ⊠ *Rua Mossoró 359, Tirol* ☎ *084/3232–2785* ⊕ *www.rn.gov.br.* ⊠ *Praia Shopping, Av. Engenheiro Roberto Freire 8790, Ponta Negra* ☎ *084/3232–7248*

10

EXPLORING

Few tourists stay in the city itself, and many do not even visit, and instead head straight to Ponta Negra, a considerably developed beach area 10 km (6 miles) south of the city center.

TOP ATTRACTIONS

Museu Câmara Cascudo. This well-conceived museum, named after one of Brazil's greatest folklorists, showcases exhibits from a variety of disciplines: archaeology, paleontology, mineralogy, ethnography, and popular culture. A highlight is the collection of dinosaur fossils. ⊠ *Av. Hermes da Fonseca 1398, Tirol* ☎ *084/3215–4195* ⊕ *www.mcc.ufrn. br/wordpress* ☒ *R$3* ⊙ *Weekdays 9–6.*

WORTH NOTING

Forte dos Reis Magos. Natal owes its existence to this impressive five-sided fort. It was built by the Portuguese in 1598, one year before the founding of Natal, and controlled by the Dutch between 1633 and 1654. Visitors can see the old quarters, the chapel, and rusted cannons. ⊠ *Northern end of Av. Praia do Forte, continuation of Via Costeira that extends to Ponta Negra, Praia do Meio* ☎ *084/3202–9006* ⊠ *Free* ⊗ *Daily 8–4:30.*

Maracajaú. The principal draw at Maracajaú is the large coral reef 6 km (4 miles) off the coast. Teeming with marine life, the sizable reef offers the best snorkeling in the Natal area, and the natural pools are some of Brazil's most beautiful. Visitors can catch a van from Natal, followed by a small boat or catamaran across to the reefs. A round-trip with Natal Vans costs R$110 per person. ⊠ *Take BR 101 north to Maracajaú access road; 55 km (34 miles) north of Natal, (Ma-noa Aquatic Park) Enseada Pontas dos Anéis, Maracajaú.*

Ma-noa Parque Aquático. This water park has all that day-trippers require: a restaurant, water rides, a huge pool, boat trips to the reef with snorkeling equipment provided, and even transport to and from Natal hotels. ☎ *084/3211–2140* ⊕ *www.ma-noa.com.br.*

BEACHES

Búzios. This beach has been endowed with great natural beauty, yet does not usually have many visitors. On the left side of the beach, the barrier reef creates an area of clear, calm waters ideal for bathing, snorkeling, and scuba diving. The right side of the beach is best for surfing, and the middle best avoided due to occasional currents. In the background are some impressive dunes, covered with palm trees and other vegetation. The modest infrastructure consists of just a few small pousadas and restaurants. **Amenities:** food and drink; toilets; lifeguards; parking. **Best for:** swimming; snorkeling; solitude. ⊠ *RN 063 (Rota do Sol); 35 km (21 miles) south of Natal.*

Fodor'sChoice **Genipabu.** Massive dunes have made this one of the best-known beaches
★ in the country. The area is most commonly explored on thrilling day-trips across the dune by buggy, stopping off at three lakes and two further parks along the way. You have two choices: *com emoção* (literally, "with emotion"), which rivals any roller-coaster, or *sem emoção* (without emotion), a little calmer but still fairly hair-raising. Buggy operators, who usually find you before you find them, charge around R$75 per person. You can also explore the dunes on camels imported from southern Spain. Other activities include half-hour boat rides and sky-boarding (also called sky-surfing)—which is basically snowboarding down the dunes. The beach is attractive, although it gets very crowded

during high season. Because Genipabu is close to Natal, it's primarily a day-trip destination. There are a few small pousadas and restaurants near the beach, but the town shuts down at night. Buses leave from the Rodoviário Velho every half hour or so for the 45-minute trip. **Amenities:** food and drink; toilets. **Best for:** walking. ✉ *Take BR 101 north to Pitanguí access road; 10 km (6 miles) north of Natal.*

Pirangi do Norte. This long white-sand beach is an extremely popular summer vacation destination for residents of Natal. Boat rides to nearby coral reefs and beaches run frequently. Near the beach is the world's largest cashew tree, according to the *Guinness Book of World Records.* Its circumference measures 500 meters (1,650 feet), and it's as big as roughly 70 normal cashew trees. The entrance fee is R$4, and includes free cashew nuts and a cashew juice. There is a small market nearby for souvenirs. **Amenities:** food and drink; parking; toilets. **Best for:** walking; water sports. ✉ *RN 063, 28 km (17 miles) north of Natal.*

Ponta Negra. Nearly all tourism development has focused on or around this beach in the past decade, with both negative and positive repercussions. It has a multitude of pousadas, restaurants, and shops, and even a few large resorts at the northern end. The beach itself, around 2½ km (1½ miles) long, can no longer be called pristine, but is still attractive and reasonably clean. If you seek a connection with nature, you would be best advised to head to one of the city's outer beaches during the day and venture to Ponta Negra for the nightlife, which ranges from buzzy to seedy. Ponta Negra's distinguishing feature is the Morro da Careca (Bald Man's Hill), a 120-meter (390-foot) dune at the southern end. You can catch a taxi or a bus (look for buses marked "ponta negra") at various stops along the Via Costeira south of Natal. Buses run fairly frequently. From Ponta Negra to downtown Natal, look for buses marked "centro" or "cidade alta." **Amenities:** food and drink; lifeguards; parking (fee); toilets. **Best for:** partiers. ✉ *Via Costeira; 10 km (6 miles) south of Natal.*

WHERE TO EAT

$$ BRAZILIAN Fodor's Choice ★ 🍴 **Mangai.** Choose from more than 40 delicious regional specialties at this immensely popular buffet restaurant. Tourists and town residents eat together at communal wood tables, which fit the typical rustic decor of the sertão. To top off your meal, consider ordering the *cartola,* a popular dessert made of caramelized banana, cheese, and cinnamon. [$] *Average main: R$30* ✉ *Av. Amintas Barros 3300, Lagoa Nova* ☎ *084/3206–3344* 🌐 *www.mangai.com.br.*

$$ SEAFOOD 🍴 **Peixada da Comadre.** If you were wondering where locals go for the town's best fish, this is it. Recipes here have been passed down from the owners' mother, and dishes like the tasty fried fish fillets are easily large enough for two. [$] *Average main: R$35* ✉ *Av. Praia de Ponta Negra 9048, Ponta Negra* ☎ *084/3219–3016* 💳 *No credit cards* 🕒 *Closed Mon. No dinner Sun.*

$$$ ITALIAN FAMILY 🍴 **Piazzale Itália.** During the high season (July and December to mid-March), make a reservation, or you'll be among the many waiting outside, salivating from smells of fresh tomato sauce and garlic. The

restaurant's popularity is a result of reasonable prices, proximity to the Ponta Negra Beach, and skillful preparation of pasta and seafood dishes. Particularly recommended is the *tagliolini allo scoglio* (pasta with lobster, shrimp, and mussels). [$] *Average main: R$50* ✉ *Av. Deputado Antônio Florêncio de Queiroz 12, Ponta Negra* ☎ *084/3236–2697* 🌐 *www.piazzaleitalia.com.br* ⏲ *Closed Mon. No lunch Tues.–Thurs.*

WHERE TO STAY

$ B&B/INN FAMILY 🏨 **Divi-Divi.** One block from the beach, this small hotel is a great value if you're willing to forgo a beachside location. **Pros:** affordable rates; friendly atmophere. **Cons:** not on the beach. [$] *Rooms from: R$170* ✉ *Rua Elias Barros 248, Ponta Negra* ☎ *084/4006–3900* 🌐 *www.dividivi.com.br* 🛏 *32 rooms, 2 suites* 🍴 *Breakfast.*

$$$ HOTEL Fodor's Choice ★ 🏨 **Manary Praia Hotel.** It's hardly surprising that this small hotel was chosen as a member of Brazil's prestigious Roteiros de Charme group; both the service and decor reflect tremendous attention to detail. **Pros:** good location; beautiful building. **Cons:** not all rooms have great views. [$] *Rooms from: R$385* ✉ *Rua Francisco Gurgel 9067, Ponta Negra* ☎ *084/3204–2900* 🌐 *www.manary.com.br* 🛏 *23 rooms* 🍴 *Breakfast.*

$ B&B/INN 🏨 **O Tempo e o Vento.** The four-star rooms at this hotel are highly incongruous with the two-star-quality lobby; luckily, prices are more representative of the latter. **Pros:** pleasant rooms; great views. **Cons:** shabby lobby; not on the beach. [$] *Rooms from: R$200* ✉ *Rua Elias Barros 66, Ponta Negra* ☎ *084/3219–2526* 🌐 *www.otempoeovento.com.br* 🛏 *22 rooms.*

$$$$ RESORT FAMILY 🏨 **Pestana Natal Beach Resort.** This attractive accomodation manages to avoid some of the problems associated with massive resort complexes: its beige color allows it to blend into its sandy surroundings, rooms have original artwork and other strokes of personality, and personalized service makes you feel like more than just a number. **Pros:** pleasant atmosphere; doting service. **Cons:** a bit noisy; minimum stay of 3–5 nights. [$] *Rooms from: R$501* ✉ *Rua Senador Dinarte Mariz 5525, Via Costeira, 6 km (4 miles) north of Ponta Negra* ☎ *084/3220–8900* 🌐 *www.pestana.com* 🛏 *188 rooms, 5 suites* 🍴 *No meals.*

$ B&B/INN FAMILY 🏨 **Residence Praia Hotel.** A block away from Praia dos Artistas, this modern hotel is a good option for those who want all major amenities but don't want to pay Ponta Negra prices. **Pros:** comfortable accommodations; affordable rates; swimming pool. **Cons:** area is a bit sketchy at night. [$] *Rooms from: R$170* ✉ *Av. 25 de Dezembro 868, Praia dos Artisas* ☎ *084/3202–4466* 🌐 *www.residencepraia.com.br* 🛏 *117 rooms* 🍴 *Breakfast.*

$$ RESORT FAMILY 🏨 **Rifóles.** At the end of Ponta Negra beach, this resort offers extensive facilities, family-oriented entertainment, and the chance to unwind in the blazing Northeastern sun in one of the six swimming pools. **Pros:** on the beach; friendly atmosphere. **Cons:** lacks personal service; can be noisy. [$] *Rooms from: R$333* ✉ *Rua Coronel Inácio Vale 8847, Ponta Negra* ☎ *084/3646–5000* 🌐 *www.rifoles.com.br* 🛏 *204 rooms* 🍴 *Breakfast.*

NIGHTLIFE AND THE ARTS

NIGHTLIFE

Natal has a fairly active night-life, supported by nearly year-round tourists. Some of the most frequented bars and clubs are in Praia dos Artistas. Other popular spots are scattered downtown and in Ponta Negra. Every Thursday the Centro de Turismo hosts a live forró band as part of the long-running "Forró com Turista" program, which is aimed at acquainting tourists with this important piece of local culture. Natal has a reputation for being one of the country's most prominent places for sex-tourism. Recently police have made an active effort to crack down heavily on underage prostitution, but it is a side to the city that tourists should be aware of, particularly at night.

COUNTRY MUSIC

Forró is the name of what was considered Northeast country music. It became a national favorite in the 1950s, and is still played and danced to up and down the coast. It features *zarumba* (African drum), accordion, and triangle accompaniments. As the story goes, U.S soldiers or British engineers stationed in the Northeast during World War II always invited the townsfolk to their dances, saying they were "for all." This term, when pronounced with a Brazilian accent, became "forró." But music historians trace the origin of the term to an abbreviation of an Indian word *forróbodo*, or craziness.

BARS

Taverna Pub. A bar with character, Taverna Pub is in the basement of a stylized medieval castle. It's popular with locals in their twenties and tourists who stay in the partnering hostel upstairs (Lua Cheia). ⊠ *Rua Dr. Manuel Augusto Bezerra de Araújo 500, Ponta Negra* ☎ *084/3236–3696* ⊕ *www.tavernapub.com.br.*

DANCE CLUBS

Downtown. Inspired by London's rock and roll scene, Downtown has live rock music Thursday through Saturday. ⊠ *Rua Chile 11, Bairro da Ribeira* ☎ *84/3424–6317* ⊕ *www.downtownpub.com.br.*

Guinza Blue. A great choice for romantic drinks, this tucked-away spot opens only on Friday night, when DJs spin tracks from the '80s and the caipirinhas flow. Below the bar is a good sushi restuarant that serves satisfied customers from Tuesday to Sunday. ⊠ *Rua Ana Porto, 4, Ponta Negra* ☎ *084/3219–2002* ⊕ *www.guinza.com.br.*

Seven Pub. This two-story mansion is the place to be on weekends, when live local bands and DJs take to the floor. There is also a spacious area for chilling during breaks from the dance floor. ⊠ *Rua Seridó 722, Petrópolis* ☎ *084/3202–3838.*

10

SHOPPING

Centro de Turismo. The best place to go for local crafts and artwork is the Centro de Turismo, where little shops are housed within the cells of a former prison. ⊠ *Rua Aderbal de Figueiredo 980, Petrópolis* ☎ *084/3211–6149* ⏱ *Daily 8–7.*

Praia Shopping. The most convenient shopping mall for those staying in Ponta Negra, Praia Shopping offers a 3-D cinema and a food hall, alongside all the classic brands. ⊠ *Av. Engenheiro Roberto Freire 8790, Ponta Negra* ☎ *084/4009–0842* ⊕ *www.praiashopping.com.br.*

SIDE TRIP TO PRAIA DA PIPA

85 km (51 miles) south of Natal

Praia da Pipa was a small fishing village until it was "discovered" by surfers in the '70s. Word of its beauty spread, and it's now one of the most famous and fashionable beach towns in the Northeast. It's also rapidly gaining a reputation for having an extremely active nightlife. Praia da Pipa receives a truly eclectic mix of people: hippies, surfers, foreign backpackers, Brazilian youth, and, most recently, high-end visitors attracted by the increasingly upscale restaurants and pousadas.

On either side of the town is a string of beaches with amazingly varied landscapes created by stunning combinations of pink cliffs, black volcanic rocks, palm trees, and natural pools. You can spend hours exploring the various beaches, most of which are deserted because they fall within environmentally protected areas. Another recommended activity is the boat ride to see dolphins, which often frequent the surrounding waters, although if you wait till low-tide, you can walk along the shore to the breathtaking Baía dos Golfinhos and swim with them for free.

Experienced surfers will find continually challenging conditions and boards for hire at the hip Praia do Amor, while beginners will benefit from the calm waters and surf schools at nearby Praia do Madeiro, a 10-minute ride by van on the road to Tibau do Sul (R$2). Tibau do Sul is also a hot spot for kite-surfers and the only place in the area where you can watch the sunset.

GETTING HERE AND AROUND
Take BR 101 South from Natal. Buses leave from the Rodoviário de Natal several times daily (1½ hours; R$11.50).

ESSENTIALS
Bus Contacts Oceano. Buses between Natal and Praia da Pipa depart every hour or two from Rodoviaria Velho and cost R$9.75. The journey takes just under two hours. ⊠ *Av. Capitão Mor Gouveia 125, Natal* ☎ *084/3311–3333* ⊕ *www.expresso-oceano.com.br.*

EXPLORING
FAMILY
Fodor's Choice
★

Santuário Ecológico de Pipa (*Pipa Ecological Sanctuary*). Nature lovers will enjoy the Santuário Ecológico de Pipa, a 120-hectare (300-acre) protected area. Sixteen short, well-maintained trails pass through Atlantic Forest vegetation and allow for some great views of the ocean. Between January and June, visitors can take part in baby turtle conservation effort organized by Projecto Tamar. Call ahead for details and availability. ✉ *Estrada para Tibau do Sul, 2 km (1 mile) northwest of town* ☎ *084/3201–2007* 🌐 *www.ecopipa.com.br* 🎫 *R$5* ⏲ *Daily 8–4.*

Praia das Minas. Walk 30 minutes north of Pipa's main street via terracotta dirt road or along the beach (depending on the tide) and you will arrive at the deserted, rugged beauty of Praia das Minas. During high season, a beach bar and restaurant serving delicious fresh fish and caipirinhas is open between 10 am and 5 pm to reward your efforts. Big waves and strong currents make the water best for paddling. **Amenities:** food and drink; toilet; shower. **Best for:** solitude; walking; sunrise.

Praia do Amor. The reliably strong waves at Praia do Amor are what makes Pipa such a surfer's town. Surf schools offer boards and lessons, as well as lounge chairs, umbrellas, and waiter service for avid spectators. At the right-hand side of the beach, the water is calmer and offers great swimming, particularly in the natural pools that are formed during low tide. Stand atop the dusky red cliffs and look down over Praia do Amor and you will see that the shoreline curves in the shape of a heart. **Amenities:** food and drink; toilets; showers; parking; lifeguards. **Best for:** surfers; sunrise; swimming; walking; partiers.

Praia do Madeiro. The soft, white sand and calm, warm waters of Praia do Madeiro make it an eternal favorite for long days swimming and soaking up the sun. The steep path that winds through the trees down from the road offers glimpses of the glistening sea through the forest and keeps the masses at bay. Beginner surf schools and beach barracas serving ice-cold coconut water and crispy shrimp are clustered at the right-hand side of the beach; but if you head left along the long curve of sand, you'll have the coconut plams all to yourself. To get there, catch one of the minivans that run between Praia da Pipa and Tibau do Sul and request to stop at Madeiro. **Amenities:** food and drink. **Best for:** surfing; walking; swimming; solitude. ✉ *Avenida Antonio Florencio 2695, Estrada para Pipa.*

Praia dos Golfinhos. One of Northeast Brazil's most magical spots, this locals' favorite is only accessible during low tide and the most likely place to swim with wild dolphins outside Fernando do Noronha. There is no access point down from the salmon-pink cliffs that frame the long slip of sand, which means that aside from a lone water seller who makes the trek daily, the beach's pristine beauty is preserved. To get there, consult the tide-chart and head northwest from Pipa's central beach. **Amenities:** food and drink. **Best for:** swimming; walking; solitude.

10

WHERE TO EAT AND STAY

$$ ITALIAN FAMILY

🍴 **Pizzeria dall'Italiano.** The thin-crust pizza at this lively spot is a serious contender for the best in Brazil. Originally from Italy, owners Paulo and Michela designed and built their own wood-fire oven to ensure that their secret recipe for pizza dough turned out just like at home. Regulars are happy to wait over caiprinhas in a queue that often snakes out the door, making it a great spot to chat with the locals. [$] *Average main: R$30* ✉ *Rua de Ceu 17* ☎ *084/9152–8651* ⏲ *Closed Tues.*

$$ × **Tapas.** There are several good reasons why this hole-in-the-wall res-
ECLECTIC   taurant has an almost religious following: their tapas dishes fuse Span-
Fodor'sChoice   ish and Asian flavors and make the most of local seafood, and the wine
★   list is one of Pipa's most varied and reasonably priced. Choose from
favorites like sesame-crusted seared tuna alongside daily specials writ-
ten on a blackboard menu hanging from the crimson walls. The relaxed
yet sophisticated design creates the perfect spot for sharing food with
friends—two to three plates per person should do it. $ *Average main:
R$45* ⊠ *Rua dos Bem te Vis s/n* ☎ *084/9414–4675* ⊙ *Closed Mon.
Dinner only.*

$ ⌨ **Pousada Xamã.** A calm oasis tucked away near Praia do Amor,
B&B/INN   this well-run pousada offers friendly service, charming rooms, and
Fodor'sChoice   a beautiful swimming pool surrounded by tropical trees. **Pros:** beau-
★   tiful garden and swimming pool; excellent value; great breakfast.
Cons: 10-minute walk into town. $ *Rooms from: R$150* ⊠ *Rua dos
Cajueiros* ☎ *084/3246–2267* ⊕ *www.pousadaxama.com.br* ⇵ *19
rooms* ⦿*Breakfast.*

$$$$ ⌨ **Toca da Coruja.** One of the first properties to open in Praia da Pipa
HOTEL   and a pioneer of the eco-hotel movement in Brazil, this luxury retreat
Fodor'sChoice   remains the best in the area. **Pros:** beautiful, colonial-style bungalows;
★   eco-friendly; superb service. **Cons:** slow Internet in the rooms; not the
best place for families with small children. $ *Rooms from: R$580* ⊠ *Av.
Baía dos Golfinhos 464* ☎ *084/3246–2226* ⊕ *www.tocadacoruja.com.
br* ⇵ *28 bungalows* ⦿*Breakfast.*

FORTALEZA

Called the "City of Light," Fortaleza claims that the sun shines on
it 2,800 hours a year. And it's a good thing, too, as the coastline
stretches far beyond the city. To the east, along the Litoral Leste or the
Costa Sol Nascente (Sunrise Coast) are many fishing villages. To the
west, along the Litoral Oeste or the Costa Sol Poente (Sunset Coast),
there are pristine stretches of sand. The shores here are cooled by
constant breezes and lapped by waters with an average temperature
of 24°C (72°F).

Today Fortaleza, a large, modern state capital with more than 2 million
inhabitants, is Brazil's fifth-largest city. It's also on the move, with one
of the country's newest airports, a modern convention center, a huge
cultural center with a planetarium, large shopping malls, several muse-
ums and theaters, and an abundance of sophisticated restaurants. At
Praia de Iracema there's a revitalized beachfront area of sidewalk cafés,
bars, and dance clubs. But if you wander along the shore, you're still
bound to encounter fishermen unloading their catch from traditional
jangadas—just as they've done for hundreds of years.

GETTING HERE AND AROUND

Tap is the only international airline that flies directly to Fortaleza from
Europe (Lisbon); all flights to the U.S. connect in São Paulo or Rio
de Janeiro. Aeroporto Internacional Pinto Martins is 6 km (4 miles)
south of downtown. After clearing customs, those headed downtown
should take an *especial* (special) taxi that costs between R$45 and

$60. For reliable taxis to Iracema, Aldeota, or Beira Mar, cross the street in front of the terminal. These taxis should cost about $36. City buses run frequently from the airport to the main bus station, Terminal Rodoviário João Tomé, 6 km (4 miles) south of the Centro, and Praça José de Alencar in the Centro. In low season you can buy tickets at the station right before leaving. São Benedito runs three daily to Aracati and Canoa Quebrada (3½ hours; R$17). Expresso Guanabara has five daily buses to Recife (12 hours; R$91–R$177). Itapemerim has one daily to Salvador (20 hours; R$206) and daily buses to Rio de Janeiro (43 hours; R$397).

The easiest way to get around the city is by bus and taxi. All taxis have meters, so make sure they have been restarted and are turned on before you set off. Fares from Beira Mar to Fortaleza Centre and Praia do Futuro will be between R$12 and R$20. Rides to Das Dunas will be between R$60 and R$80. The fare on city buses is R$2.

ESSENTIALS

Airport Aeroporto Internacional Pinto Martins (*FOR*) ⊠ *Av. Senador Carlos Jereissati, Serrinha* ☎ *085/3392-1200.*

Bus Contacts Expresso Guanabara ☎ *085/4005-1992* ⊕ *www.expressoguanabara.com.br.* **Itapemirim** ☎ *085/3235-2678* ⊕ *www.itapemirim.com.br.* **São Benedito** ☎ *085/3444-9999* ⊕ *www.gruposaobenedito.com.br.* **Terminal Rodoviário Engenheiro João Tomé** ⊠ *Av. Borges de Melo 1630, Fátima* ☎ *085/3230-1111.*

Taxi Contacts Disquetáxi ☎ *085/3287-7222* ⊕ *www.disquetaxifortaleza.com. br.* **Radio Táxi Fortaleza** ☎ *085/3254-5744* ⊕ *www.radiotaxifortaleza.com.br.*

Visitor and Tour Information Ernanitur. This company offers city tours and arranges transportation to Jericocoara, Canoa Quebrada, and a number of other beaches. ☎ *085/3533-7700* ⊕ *www.ernanitur.com.br.* **Lisatur Viagens e Turismo Ltda** ⊠ *Av. Monsenhor Tabosa 1067, Praia Iracema* ☎ *085/3219-5000* ⊕ *www.lisatur.com.br* ◷ *Daily 8–7.* **OceanView Tours and Travel.** This tour company offers trips to Flexeiras, Jericoacoara, and other beach areas outside Fortaleza. It also organizes city tours and transfers. ⊠ *Av. Monsenhor Tabosa 1165, Meireles* ☎ *085/3219-1300* ⊕ *www.oceanviewturismo.com.br.* **SETUR.** SETUR has a branch in the airport open daily 6 am–11 pm, one in the bus station open daily 6 am–9 pm, one in the Centro open Monday to Saturday 8 to 6 and Sunday 8 to noon, and one in Cambeba open weekdays 8 to 5. These offices can help with maps and local info. The airport contact number is the main number to call for any tourist queries as there are multilingual staff available. ⊠ *Centro Administrativo Virgílio Távora, Cambeba* ☎ *085/3101-4688* ⊕ *www.ceara.gov.br* ⊠ *Aeroporto Internacional Pinto Martins, Av. Senador Carlos Jereissati, Serrinha* ☎ *085/3392-1667* ⊠ *Centro de Turismo, Rua Senador Pompeu 350, Centro* ☎ *085/3101-5508* ⊠ *Terminal Rodoviário João Tomé, Av. Borges de Melo 1630, Fátima* ☎ *085/3230-1111.*

10

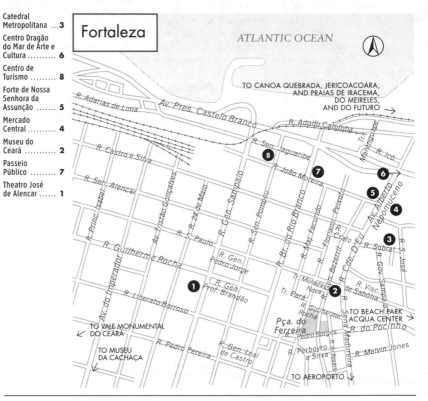

EXPLORING

Fortaleza is fairly easy to navigate on foot because its streets are laid out in a grid. Its business center lies above the Centro Histórico (Historic Center) and includes the main market, several shopping streets, and many government buildings. East of the center, urban beaches are lined with high-rise hotels and restaurants. Beyond are the port and old lighthouse, from which Praia do Futuro runs 5 km (3 miles) along Avenida Dioguinho. Be on guard against pickpockets—particularly in the Historic District.

TOP ATTRACTIONS

Catedral Metropolitana. Inspired by the famous cathedral in Cologne, the Catedral Metropolitana was built between 1937 and 1963 and has a dominant Gothic look. Its two spires are 75 meters (250 feet) high, and it can accommodate 5,000 worshipers, who no doubt draw inspiration from its beautiful stained-glass windows. Don't be put off by the grimy exterior—the interiors gleam brilliant white. ⊠ *Rua Sobral, 1, Centro* ☎ *085/3388–8702* ⊕ *www.arquidiocesedefortaleza.org.br* 🖃 *Free* ☉ *Weekdays 8–5, weekends 8–11.*

Centro de Turismo. Originally a prison, this building was structurally changed in 1850 along simple, classical lines. It's now the home of the state tourism center, with handicraft stores as well as the Museu de

Minerais (Mineral Museum) and the Museu de Arte e Cultura Populares (Popular Art and Culture Museum), whose displays of local crafts and sculptures are interesting. ⊠ *Rua Senador Pompeu 350, Centro* ☎ *085/3101–5508* 📨 *R$2* ☉ *Weekdays 8–6, Sat. 8–4, Sun. 8–noon.*

Fodor's Choice
★
Centro Dragão do Mar de Arte e Cultura. Not far from the Mercado Central, this majestic cultural complex is an eccentric mix of curves, straight lines, and angular and flat roofs. What's inside is as diverse as the exterior. There's a planetarium as well as art museums with permanent exhibitions of Ceará's two most famous artists, Raimundo Cela and Antônio Bandeira. Another museum presents Ceará's cultural history, with exhibits of embroidery, paintings, prints, pottery, puppets, and musical instruments. When you need a break, head for the center's romantic Santa Clara Café Orgânico, which serves a variety of cocktails made with coffee as well as little meat or vegetarian pies. There are also some great bars installed in the converted colonial houses that surround the complex. The center's bookstore has English-language titles as well as souvenirs and cards. ⊠ *Rua Dragão do Mar 81, Praia de Iracema* ☎ *085/3488–8600* ⊕ *www.dragaodomar.org.br* 📨 *Museums R$2, planetarium R$8* ☉ *Tues.–Fri. 9–6:30, Sat.–Sun. 2–8:30.*

Mercado Central. With four floors and more than 600 stores, this is *the* place to find handicrafts and just about anything else. It has elevators to take you from one floor to the next, but since it's built with an open style and has ramps that curve from one floor to the next, it's just as easy to walk up. ⊠ *Av. Alberto Nepomuceno 199, Centro* ☎ *085/3454–8586* ⊕ *www.mercadocentraldefortaleza.com.br* ☉ *Weekdays 8–6, Sat. 8–4, Sun. 8–noon.*

Fodor's Choice
★
Passeio Público. Also called the Praça dos Mártires, this landmark square dates from the 19th century. In 1824 many soldiers were executed here in the war for independence from the Portuguese crown. It has a central fountain and is full of century-old trees and statues of Greek deities. Look for the ancient baobab tree.

Fodor's Choice
★
Theatro José de Alencar. This theater is a rather shocking example (especially if you come upon it suddenly) of the eclectic phase of Brazilian architecture, showcasing a mixture of neoclassical and art nouveau styles. The top of the theater, which looks as if it was designed by the makers of Tiffany lamps, really stands out against Ceará's perpetually blue sky. It was built in 1910 of steel and iron (many of its cast-iron sections were imported from Scotland) and was restored in 1989. It's still used for cultural events—including concerts, plays, and dance performances—and houses a library and an art gallery. Some of the tour guides speak English; call ahead for reservations. ⊠ *Praça do José Alencar s/n, Centro* ☎ *085/3101–2583* ⊕ *www.secult.ce.gov.br* 📨 *R$4* ☉ *Weekdays 8–5, Sat. 8–3.*

10

WORTH NOTING

Beach Park Acqua Center. Just 30 minutes from downtown on the idyllic Porto das Dunas Beach is this enormous water park. A 14-story-high waterslide dumps you into a pool at a speed of 105 kph (65 mph), or if you prefer slow-paced attractions, visit its museum, which has the country's largest collection of *jangadas*, the wooden sailing rafts used by fishermen. An open-air restaurant at the beach serves excellent seafood dishes. There is no bus from downtown, and a taxi costs around R$50. ⊠ *Rua Porto das Dunas 2734, Aquiraz* ☎ *085/4012–3000* ⊕ *www. beachpark.com.br* ⧉ *R$130* ⊘ *Daily 11–5.*

Forte de Nossa Senhora da Assunção. Built by the Dutch in 1649, this fort was originally baptized Forte Schoonemborch. In 1655 it was seized by the Portuguese and renamed after the city's patron saint, Nossa Senhora da Assunção. It was rebuilt in 1817 and is now a military headquarters. The city took its name from this fortress (*fortaleza*), which still has the cell where the mother of one of Ceará's most famous writers, José de Alencar, was jailed. Guided tours are led by the soldiers themselves. ⊠ *Av. Alberto Nepomuceno s/n, Centro* ☎ *085/3255–1600* ⧉ *Free* ⊘ *Daily 8–4.*

Museu da Cachaça. It's a toss-up for whether coffee or cachaça is Brazil's national drink. This museum just west of Fortaleza offers tastings of the latter after you tour the plant and learn about the history of this liquor made from sugarcane juice that has been fermented and distilled; most notably, cachaça is the primary ingredient for the *caipirinha,* widely considered as Brazil's national cocktail. In the tavern you can see a 98,736-gallon wooden barrel, the largest in the world. The museum is located inside the I-Park, which has a variety of fun activities, from paddleboats to a climbing wall. ⊠ *Turn left off CE 65 just before small town of Maranguape* ☎ *085/3341–0407* ⧉ *R$28* ⊘ *Tues.–Sun. 8–5.*

Museu do Ceará. Housed in the former Assembléia Provincial (Provincial Assembly Building), this museum's exhibits are devoted to the history and anthropology of Ceará State. ⊠ *Rua São Paulo 51, Centro* ☎ *085/3101–2609* ⧉ *Free* ⊘ *Tues.–Sat. 9–5.*

BEACHES

Fortaleza's enchanting coast runs 22 km (14 miles) along the Atlantic between the Rio Ceará, to the west, and the Rio Pacoti, to the east. The feel of this great urban stretch of sand along with its scenery varies as often as its names: Barra do Ceará, Pirambu, Formosa, Iracema, Beira-Mar, Meireles, Mucuripe, Mansa, Titanzinho, Praia do Futuro, and Sabiazuaba.

In the city center and its immediate environs, feel free to soak up the sun and the ambience of the beaches, but stay out of the water—it's too polluted for swimming. However, you can find clean waters and amazing sands just a little way from Centro and beyond. Surfing is fine at several beaches, including those near the towns of Paracuru and Pecém, to the west of Fortaleza, and Porto das Dunas, to the east.

Fodor's Choice ★ **Canoa Quebrada.** Hidden behind dunes, the stunning Canoa Quebrada Beach was "discovered" in the 1970s by French doctors working in the area. The spectacular scenery includes not only dunes but also jangadas, red cliffs, and groves of palm trees. Carved into a cliff is the symbol of Canoa: a crescent moon with a star in the middle. Although it was originally settled by Italian hippies, the village itself has moved on with the times and now has good roads, several comfortable pousadas, and bars and restaurants. The best way to get here is on a trip offered by one of Fortaleza's many tour operators, but bus companies also have daily departures from Fortaleza and Natal. Try to avoid coming here on Brazilian holidays, when the small town is overrun with tourists. **Amenities:** food and drink; parking; toilets; water sports. **Best for:** swimming; walking; surfing; windsurfing. ⊠ *Take BR 116 to BR 304; 164 km (101 miles) east of Fortaleza.*

Iguape. The white-sand dunes at this beach are so high that people actually ski down them. The water is calm and clean. In the nearby village of Aquiraz, you'll find both fishermen and lace makers (lace is sold at the Centro de Rendeiras). There's also a lookout at Morro do Enxerga Tudo. Buses depart from Fortaleza for this beach several times daily on the route to Aquiraz. **Amenities:** food and drink; parking; toilets. **Best for:** solitude; swimming. ⊠ *CE 040, 50 km (31 miles) east of Fortaleza, Aquiraz* ⊕ *www.iguapece.com.br.*

Flecheiras. The ocean is always calm at this beach, which is surrounded by coconut trees, lagoons, and sand dunes. During low tide the reefs surface, and you can see small fish and shells in the rocks. When the tide comes in and the natural pools form, you can grab your mask and go snorkeling. In a 5-km (3-mile) stretch between Flexeiras and Mundaú—another almost-deserted beach—there are several fishing villages and a working lighthouse. A river joins the ocean at Mundaú, forming a large *S* on the sand; on one side is a line of coconut trees and on the other, fishermen with their jangadas—the scene conveys the very essence of Ceará. Flexeiras is about a 90-minute drive from Fortaleza. You can take the Rendenção bus or arrange a trip here with a tour operator. As yet there are no luxury resorts here, but there are several simple, clean pousadas. **Amenities:** food and drink; parking; toilets. **Best for:** solitude; snorkeling; swimming. ⊠ *CE 085, 177 km (110 miles) northwest of Fortaleza.*

Porto das Dunas. Tourists and locals alike flock to this beach to enjoy the many water sports (including surfing) and gawk at the lovely sand dunes. South of Fortaleza in the municipality of Aquiraz, Porto das Dunas also has a golf course overlooking the beach. You can get here on the *jardineira* bus from the Centro or along Avenida Beira-Mar. **Amenities:** food and drink; lifeguards; parking; toilets. **Best for:** water sports; surfing; windsurfing. ⊠ *Take Av. Washington Soares, then follow signs to Estrada da Cofeco and Beach Park; 22 km (14 miles) southeast of Fortaleza.*

Praia do Futuro. Hands-down the city's best beach for swimming, this long curve of golden sand lines the only part of Fortaleza's sea regularly clean enough to take a dip. Framing the beach are *mega-barracas*, sophisticated beach huts that have restaurants, bathrooms, bars, and even swimming pools with slides for kids. The regular waves attract local surfers. If returning after dark, it is best to take a taxi. **Amenities:** food and drink; lifeguards; parking (fee); showers; toilets. **Best for:** partiers; walking; swimming; surfing.

Taíba. Kite-surfers and surfers who want optimum conditions but lack the time to travel to Jericoacora should head to this little beach town up the coast from Fortaleza. The recent construction of the Porto de

> **LOCAL SPECIALTIES**
>
> When in Fortaleza, be sure to try *lagosta ao natural* (lobster served with homemade butter), sun-dried meat with *paçoca* (manioc flour seasoned with herbs and red onions), and *caldeirada* (shrimp and vegetable soup with strong spices).

Pecém has upgraded the infrastructure of this little fisherman's village, although local fisherman still grill their daily catches directly on the seashore. The vibe here is very much geared toward relaxing. In August, the village hosts the Festival of Escargot, where local restaurants set up stands on the main street and serve snails and wine. You can stay overnight in one of the few simple yet comfortable pousadas, or rent your own beach house. **Amenities:** food and drink; lifeguards; parking; toilets; water sports. **Best for:** surfing; windsurfing; kite-surfing. ✉ *CE 085, 74 km (45 miles) northwest of Fortaleza.*

WHERE TO EAT

In the last decade, Fortaleza's gourmet scene has caught up with neighboring Recife. Stylish seafood restaurants set on the shore now compete with upmarket *churrascarias* (all-you-can-eat meat barbecues). At laid-back local spots, Brazilian dishes such as *feijoada* (pork and black bean stew) reign supreme alongside Fortaleza's specialty, *baião-de-dois* (seasoned rice and black beans served with soft cheese).

$$ SEAFOOD 🍴 **Cemoara.** A sophisticated decor with clean lines adds to the appeal of this traditional seafood restaurant. Although the *bacalão* (salt cod) selections are fabulous, you can't go wrong with the grilled lobster in a caper sauce or any of the flambéed dishes. The piano in the corner is there for a purpose: a musician accompanies your dinner with nice, soft music. [$] *Average main: R$40* ✉ *Rua Joquim Nabuco 166, Meireles* ☎ *085/3242–8500* 🌐 *www.cemoara.com.br* 🕒 *No dinner Sun.*

$$ SEAFOOD FAMILY 🍴 **Coco Bambu Frutos do Mar.** Lovers of seafood should look no further than this speciality spot overlooking the beach, which serves prawns in all imaginable forms. Start with the giant king prawns encrusted in coconut and served with mango chutney, and then follow that up with grilled lobster with Sicilian lemon risotto. The spacious restaurant has a number of different areas for dining, from the ample open-air terrace to an air-conditioned salon. [$] *Average main: R$40* ✉ *Avenida Beira-Mar 3698, Meireles* ☎ *085/3198–6000* 🌐 *www.restaurantecocobambu.com.br.*

$ BRAZILIAN 🍴 **Colher de Pau.** Ana Maria Vilmar and her mother opened Colher de Pau over a decade ago in a small rented house in the Varjota district. The regional cuisine here has become so popular that there is now a sister spot in São Paulo. The sun-dried meat is served not only with *paçoca* but also with banana and *baião-de-dois*. The shellfish dishes, many prepared with regional recipes, are also standouts. Generous portions serve two or three people, and live music is performed nightly in the atmospheric country house. [$] *Average main: R$27* ✉ *Rua Ana Bilhar 1178, Varjota* ☎ *085/3267–6680* 🌐 *www.restaurantecolherdepau.com.br.*

$$$$ ✗**Santa Grelha.** In a restored colonial house about a mile from the
STEAKHOUSE beach, Santa Grelha is off the tourist path and specializes in exceptional grilled meat and fish. Black-suited waiters and a climatized wine cellar of more than 600 options add to the air of elegance. ⓢ *Average main: R$76* ✉ *R. Tibúrcio Cavalcante 790, Meireles* ☎ *085/3224–0249* ⊗ *Closed Mon.*

WHERE TO STAY

Most hotels are along Avenida Beira-Mar (previously known as Avenida Presidente John Kennedy). Those in the Praia de Iracema are generally less expensive than those along Praia do Mucuripe. Iracema, however, is also a more interesting area to explore, and it's full of trendy restaurants and bars.

$$ 🏨**Casa na Praia.** True to its name, which translates as "house on the
B&B/INN beach," this intimate pousada opens right onto the sand and has one of
Fodor's Choice the best views in town over the dune. **Pros:** personalized service; delicious breakfast. **Cons:** rooms lack TVs. ⓢ *Rooms from: R$360* ✉ *Av.*
★ *Beira Mar s/n, Jericoacoara* ☎ *088/9921–5089* ⊕ *www.casanapraiajeri. com* ⇆ *7 rooms* ⦿*Breakfast.*

$$$ 🏨**Gran Marquise.** Overlooking trendy Praia do Mucuripe, just a 15-
HOTEL minute drive from the Centro, this luxury resort hotel can certainly trumpet its "convenient location." **Pros:** great location; good dining choices; excellent amenities. **Cons:** not all rooms have views. ⓢ *Rooms from: R$380* ✉ *Av. Beira-Mar 3980, Mucuripe* ☎ *085/4006–5000* ⊕ *www.granmarquise.com.br* ⇆ *230 rooms, 26 suites* ⦿*Breakfast.*

$$ 🏨**Hotel Luzeiros.** With modern rooms, a rooftop pool, two restaurants,
HOTEL and a bar, this stylish hotel is one of the best options in town. **Pros:** views; design; location. **Cons:** slow Wi-Fi connection; lower rooms can be noisy. ⓢ *Rooms from: R$306* ✉ *Av. Beira Mar 2600, Meireles* ☎ *085/4006–8585* ⊕ *www.hotelluzeiros.com.br* ⇆ *202* ⦿*No meals.*

$$ 🏨**Mercure Fortaleza Meireles.** These comfortable apartments are perfect
HOTEL for families and visitors in the city for a long stay. **Pros:** family-friendly environment; good breakfast. **Cons:** plain decor. ⓢ *Rooms from: R$257* ✉ *Rua Joaquim Nabuco 166, Meireles* ☎ *085/3486–3000* ⊕*www. accorhotels.com* ⇆ *166 apartments* ⦿*Breakfast.*

$$$ 🏨**Othon Palace Fortaleza.** The Othon Palace Fortaleza sits on a small
HOTEL hill right where the beach makes a big curve, affording guests a spectacular view of the beach and Mucuripe Bay. **Pros:** spacious accommodations; excellent beach. **Cons:** fewer amenities than at other hotels; extra charge for Wi-Fi. ⓢ *Rooms from: R$384* ✉ *Av. Beira-Mar 3470, Meireles* ☎ *085/3466–5500* ⊕ *www.othon.com.br* ⇆ *121 rooms, 13 suites* ⦿*Breakfast.*

$$$ 🏨**Pousada Vila Kalango.** Out of the many upmarket pousadas that have
HOTEL opened in Jericoacoara in the last five years, Vila Kalango stands above
FAMILY the crowd with its private bungalows propped on stilts. **Pros:** unique design; connection with nature; excellent service. **Cons:** can be noisy due to passing beach buggies. ⓢ *Rooms from: R$460* ✉ *Rua das Dunas 30, Jericoacoara* ☎ *088/3669–2289* ⊕ *www.vilakalango.com.br* ⇆ *24 bungalows* ⦿*Breakfast.*

10

$$ ▦ **Vila Galé Fortaleza.** This family-friendly resort is the most upscale
HOTEL   hotel in the Praia do Futuro area. **Pros:** direct access to a good beach;
great amenities. **Cons:** far from the action; could benefit from more
maintenance. $ *Rooms from: R$250* ⊠ *Av. Dioguinho 4189, Praia do
Futuro* ☎ *085/3486–4400* ⊕ *www.vilagale.com.br* ⊷ *285 rooms, 15
suites* ❍| *No meals.*

NIGHTLIFE AND THE ARTS

NIGHTLIFE
Fortaleza is renowned for its lively nightlife, particularly along Avenida
Beira-Mar and Rua dos Tabajaras in the vicinity of Praia de Iracema.
The action often includes live forró, the traditional and very popular
music and dance of the Northeast.

BARS AND CLUBS
Domínio Público. A young crowd grooves to the latest music at this
trendy bar, one of many good options that surround the Cultural Cen-
tre. ⊠ *Rua Dragão do Mar 212, Praia de Iracema* ☎ *085/3253–3881.*

Mucuripe Club. With a sophisticated infrastructure and packed schedule
of events and DJs, this dance club remains one of the most happening
places in town. Music tends to vary between axé, electro music, and
pop-rock, but check the website to confirm. ⊠ *Travessa Maranguape
108, Centro* ☎ *085/3254–3020* ⊕ *www.mucuripe.com.br.*

THE ARTS
Centro Cultural Banco do Nordeste. The Centro Cultural Banco do Nor-
deste hosts plays, concerts, and art exhibitions. ⊠ *Rua Floriano Peixoto
941, Centro* ☎ *085/3464–3108.*

Centro Dragão do Mar de Arte e Cultura. The large Centro Dragão do
Mar de Arte e Cultura, near the Mercado Central, has several the-
aters and an open-air amphitheater that host live performances. There
are also classrooms for courses in cinema, theater, design, and dance.
⊠ *Rua Dragão do Mar 81, Praia de Iracema* ☎ *085/3488–8600* ⊕ *www.
dragaodomar.org.br.*

SPORTS AND THE OUTDOORS

The sidewalk along Avenida Beira-Mar is a pleasant place for a walk,
run, or bike, and there's usually a pickup volleyball or soccer game in
progress on the beach—although beware of asking to join in unless
your skills are up to scratch. There are also running tracks and sports
courts in the 25-km-long (16-mile-long) Parque do Cocó, on Avenida
Pontes Vieira.

SOCCER
Castelão Stadium. The first of Brazil's 12 stadiums to open after renova-
tions for the 2014 World Cup, the Castelão Stadium now seats 66,700
people and hosts music concerts for international stars such as Paul
McCartney, as well as football games. ⊠ *Avenida Alberto Craveiro s/n*
⊕ *www.arenacastelao.com.*

SHOPPING

Fortaleza is one of the most important centers for crafts—especially bobbin lace—in the Northeast. Shops sell a good variety of handicrafts, and others have clothing, shoes, and jewelry along Avenida Monsenhor Tabosa in Praia de Iracema. Shopping centers both large and small house branches of the best Brazilian stores.

> ### SAY BONGIORNO!
>
> If you make it to Jericoacoara, you might feel you're in the heart of Italy. It's a great place to practice your Italian, as it's spoken far more widely than Portuguese as a result of the multitude of expats who have made it their home.

Markets and fairs are the best places to look for lacework, embroidery, leather goods, hammocks, and carvings.

Aquiraz. For lace aficionados, a trip to the town of Aquiraz is a must. Ceará's first capital (1713–99) is today a hub for artisans who create the famous *bilro* (bobbin) lace. On the beach called Prainha (6½ km (4 miles) east of Aquiraz) is the Centro de Rendeiras Luiza Távora. Here, seated on little stools, dedicated and patient lace makers explain how they create such items as bedspreads and tablecloths using the bilro technique. ✉ *30 km/19 miles east of Fortaleza.*

Ceart. First-class artisan work from across the region is featured at this upmarket workshop, where you can often catch the craftspeople at work. Even though the prices for wood, straw, and ceramic work may be steeper than at the Mercardo Central, the high quality more than makes up for this. ✉ *Av. Santos Dumont, Aldeota.*

Feirinha Noturna. More than 600 artisans sell their work at this nightly fair. ✉ *Av. Beira-Mar, Meireles* ⊕ *www.ceara.com.br.*

SIDE TRIP TO JERICOACOARA

Fodor's Choice
★

300 km (186 miles) northwest of Fortaleza.

It could be the sand dunes, some more than 30 meters (100 feet) tall; it could be the expanse of ocean that puts no limits on how far your eyes can see; or it could be that in the presence of this awesome display of nature, everyday problems seem insignificant. Jericoacoara, a rustic paradise on Ceará State's northwest coast, affects everyone differently but leaves no one unchanged—just like the sand dunes that change their shape and even their colors as they bend to the will of the winds.

In Jericoacoara, or Jerí, time seems endless. It's the ultimate relaxing vacation, and not because there isn't anything to do. You can surf down sand dunes or ride up and down them in a dune buggy. You can take an easy hike to the nearby Pedra Furada, or Arched Rock, a gorgeous formation sculpted by the waves. Jerí is also Brazil's premier destination for kite-surfing and windsurfing.

10

GETTING HERE AND AROUND

From Fortaleza, Fretcar buses depart at 8 am or 6:30 pm and arrive in Jijoca around 6½ hours later. From there an open-air bus drives you the rest of the way to Jericocoara. The journey costs between R$42 and R$58. Buy your return ticket as soon as you arrive in Jericocoara, as they sell out quickly.

ESSENTIALS

Bus Contacts **Fretcar** ☎ *085/3402–2222* 🌐 *www.fretcar.com.br.*

Visitor and Tour Information **Brazilian Beach House.** This bilingual villa specialist rents private beach houses along the Northeast coast—a good option for a group of friends or those looking for a longer stay. ✉ *Visconde de Piarajá 95, Ipanema, Rio de Janeiro* ☎ *021/2225–9476* 🌐 *www.brazilianbeachhouse.com.* **Hard Tour Ecotourismo.** This tour operator offers three-day, off-road trips to Jericoacoara that stop at all the beaches and hamlets along the way. ✉ *Rua Francisco Holanda 843, Fortaleza* ☎ *085/9925–6262* 🌐 *www.hardtour.com.br.* **OceanView Tours and Travel.** This company can arrange tours to Ceara's beaches, as well as transfers to Jericoacoara. ✉ *Av. Monsenhor Tabosa 1165, Fortaleza* ☎ *085/3219–1300* 🌐 *www.oceanviewturismo.com.br.*

WHERE TO EAT AND STAY

$$ SEAFOOD 🍴 **Carcará.** This highly regarded restaurant has a wide variety of seafood dishes, from local specialties to international favorites such as sashimi and ceviche. You can choose between pleasant indoor and outdoor seating areas. [$] *Average main: R$30* ✉ *Rua do Forró 530* ☎ *088/3669–2013* 🌐 *restaurantecarcara.com.br* 🕓 *Closed May. No lunch Sun.*

$ ITALIAN 🍴 **Na Casa Dela.** Slip off your flip-flops and settle down to excellently priced pizza, pasta, and regional specialties in the charming garden of this friendly restaurant. The wood-fire oven and homemade dishes keep locals and tourists alike coming back for more. [$] *Average main: R$25* ✉ *Rua Principal 20* ☎ *088/9717–8649* 🕓 *Closed Sun.*

$ B&B/INN 🏨 **Pousada Ibirapuera.** Wind chimes, candles, and mobiles help create a sense of peace and tranquility at this splendid pousada. **Pros:** pleasant rooms; lots of privacy. **Cons:** few amenities. [$] *Rooms from: R$200* ✉ *Rua S da Duna 06* ☎ *088/3669–2012, 088/9602–2020* 🌐 *www.pousadaibirapuera.com.br* 🛏 *8 apartments* 🍽 *Breakfast.*

SPORTS AND THE OUTDOORS

BUGGY RIDES

Buggy Tours. One of the highlights of Jericoacoara's is exploring the dunes by beach buggy. There are various possible routes depending on the amount of time you have. First-timers should journey to the village of Tatajuba, passing through mangroves and stopping off at the Rio Camboa to spot sea horses. On arrival at Tatajuba, lunch is served while you relax in hammocks suspended on the edges of the Lagoa da Torta. The average price is R$250 for four people. Other itineraries include a trip to the Lagoa Azul (Blue Lake) to bathe in the crystalline waters, or across the dunes at Praia do Préa. Ask for a recommendation from your pousada for the best *bugueiro*.

KITE-SURFING

Rancho do Kite. Windy all year-round, Jericoacoara is considered one of the world's premier destinations for kite-surfing, especially between July and January, when conditions are the most consistent. Regular wind and a glut of good teachers also make Jericoacoara a great place for beginners to get started. Rancho do Kite, the best kite school, offers equipment and various levels of training (from beginning to advanced) in over five languages. Courses take place on Praia do Préa and last between one and three days. ⊠ *Rua da Praia s/n, Preá Beach* ☎ *088/3669–2080* ⊕ *www.ranchodokite.com.br.*

FERNANDO DE NORONHA

322 km (200 miles) off the coast of Recife.

This group of 21 islands is part of the Mid-Atlantic Ridge, an underwater volcanic mountain chain more than 15,000 km (9,315 miles) long. It was discovered in 1503 by the Italian explorer Amérigo Vespucci, but was taken over by Fernando de Noronha of Portugal. Its attackers have included the French, Dutch, and English, but the Portuguese built several fortresses and, with cannons in place, fought them off.

Brazil used these islands for a prison and as a military training ground. As word of its beauty and spectacular underwater wonders spread, it was designated a protected marine park. Today stringent regulations protect the archipelago's ecology.

The mountainous, volcanic main—and only inhabited—island of Fernando de Noronha is ringed by beaches with crystal clear warm waters that are perfect for swimming, snorkeling, and diving. In summer surfers show up to tame the waves. There are shipwrecks to explore and huge turtles, stingrays, and sharks (14 species of them) with which to swim. Diving is good all year, but prime time is from December to March on the windward side (facing Africa) and from July to October on the leeward side (facing Brazil).

If you're an experienced diver, be sure to visit the *Ipiranga,* a small Brazilian destroyer that sank in 1987. It sits upright in 60 meters (200 feet) of water and is swarming with fish, and you can see the sailors' personal effects, including uniforms still hanging in closets. Another good site is the Sapata Cave, which has an antechamber so large that it has been used for marriage ceremonies (attended by giant rays, no doubt).

Well-maintained trails and well-trained guides make for enjoyable hikes. You can also enjoy the landscape on a horseback trek to the fortress ruins and isolated beaches where hundreds of seabirds alight. In addition, Projeto Tamar has an island base for its work involving sea turtles. One of the most fascinating exploring experiences, however, is an afternoon boat trip to the outer fringes of the Baía dos Golfinhos (Bay of the Dolphins), where dozens of spinner dolphins swim south each day to hunt in deep water.

There are two daily departures to Fernando de Noronha from Natal and three from Recife; flight time from either is around an hour. Only

10

90 visitors are allowed here each day, and there's a daily tourist tax of R$43.20, including the day you arrive and the day you leave. Divers pay an additional R$20 a day. In 2012, a new tourist tax (R$130 for foreigners and R$65 for Brazilians) was introduced by Econoronha, the company that administers the national park, for those who want to visit the island's most popular beaches. The money is to improve infrastructure and increase preservation. Bring enough reais to last the trip, as credit cards are not widely accepted and changing money is difficult. There is only one bank in Fernando de Noronha, so withdraw cash before your trip here.

AN ISLAND PRISON

Brazil took advantage of Fernando de Noronha's isolated location and built a prison on one of the islands. The vegetation on the island was cut down so that prisoners wouldn't be able to build rafts on which to escape. In the 1930s and 1940s the prison was used to house political prisoners, specifically communists and anarchists.

GETTING HERE AND AROUND
Flights on Gol and Trip from Recife and Natal usually cost around R$1,000.

Taxis from the airport cost about R$30.

ESSENTIALS
Airport Aeroporto de Fernando de Noronha ☎ 081/3619–1311.

Visitor and Tour Information Ilha de Noronha. This tour operator can organize complete package visits (often the cheapest option), as well as various other excursions around the island. ✉ *Alameda das Acácias 566, Floresta Nova* ☎ *081/3076–9777* ⊕ *www.ilhadenoronha.com.br.*

BEACHES

Fodor'sChoice
★
Baía dos Porcos (*Bay of Pigs*). The best showcase for the island's stunning natural beauty, the "Bay of Pigs" is a literal paradise tucked away on the north ridge of the island. Strict conservation laws ensure that its crystalline waters are rarely crowded. Grab a mask and dive into the natural swimming pools here to glimpse starfish, sea urchins, and even the occasional turtle or stingray as they wait for the tide to rise and take them back out to sea. The view over the rugged rocks in the bay is awe-inspiring. Further down the rocky path, there is a small trail that leads to the Baía dos Sanchos and allows you to avoid the R$130 entrance fee to that beach. Buggy drivers (*bugueiros*) are the local means of transportation for accessing the different beaches here. **Amenities:** none. **Best for:** solitude; snorkeling; swimming.

Baía do Sancho. Surrounded by cliffs draped in lush green vegetation, Baía do Sancho is one of the country's most breathtakingly beautiful beaches. Its crystal clear waters shift in tonality from sparkling blue to emerald green, while the coral reefs make it a prime spot for snorkeling. Be prepared for a lengthy descent down a natural stairway to reach the shore, although those with mobility problems can access the beach by boat trip. In 2012, the local government introduced a R$130 tourist tax to cover the costs of maintenance and preservation of the park; however, you can avoid the fee by accessing the beach via Baía dos Porcos. **Amenities:** none. **Best for:** solitude; snorkeling; swimming.

Praia da Conceição. This beach is one of the island's best spots for watching the sunset. From April to November, calm, transparent waters make this a good beach for walking; during the summer months, the tall waves draw surfers from across the country. **Amenities:** food and drink; lifeguards; toilets. **Best for:** sunsets; surfing; walking.

WHERE TO EAT AND STAY

$$$ SEAFOOD 🍴 **Ecologiku's.** This very small restaurant is known for its seafood, especially lobster. If you can't decide what to order, the *sinfonia ecologiku* is a sampling of every type of seafood on the menu. Call ahead and they will send a transfer to collect you, since finding this tucked-away establishment can be a challenge. [$] *Average main: R$60* ✉ *Estrada Velha do Sueste, near airport* ☎ *081/3619–0031, 081/3619–1200* ⏲ *No lunch. Closed every 2nd Sun.*

$$$$ SEAFOOD 🍴 **Mergulhão.** This contemporary restaurant serves fresh seafood with attentive service. With deck chairs, a breezy terrace, and beautiful views over the port during sunset, this is a great spot for a romantic date. [$] *Average main: R$70* ✉ *Porto Santo Antonio s/n* ☎ *081/3619–0215* 🌐 *www.mergulhaonoronha.com.br.*

$$$$ B&B/INN 🏨 **Pousada Dolphin.** A five-minute walk from the beach, this well-run pousada has large, attractively decorated rooms, a small swimming pool, and hearty, home-cooked breakfasts. **Pros:** lots of space. **Cons:** not on the beach. [$] *Rooms from: R$550* ✉ *Alameda Boldró s/n, BR 363* ☎ *081/3366–6601* 🌐 *www.dolphinhotel.tur.br* 🛏 *11 rooms* 🍽 *Breakfast.*

$$$$ HOTEL Fodor's Choice ★ 🏨 **Pousada Teju-Acu.** Resembling tropical tree houses constructed from reclaimed wood, this eco-pousada's comfortable bungalows were designed with couples in mind. **Pros:** ambience; excellent servic. **Cons:** small pool. [$] *Rooms from: R$1141* ✉ *Estrada da Alamoa s/n* ☎ *81/3619–1277* 🌐 *www.pousadateju.com.br* 🛏 *12 bungalows* 🍽 *Breakfast.*

SPORTS AND THE OUTDOORS

SCUBA DIVING

Atlantis Divers. For dive trips, Atlantis Divers has excellent English-speaking staffers and good boats. ✉ *Fernando de Noronha, Caixa Postal 20* ☎ *084/3206–8840, 084/3206–8841* 🌐 *www.atlantisdivers.com.br.*

THE AMAZON

Updated
by Rasheed
Abou-Alsamh

The world's largest tropical forest seems an endless carpet of green that's sliced only by the curving contours of rivers. Its statistics are as impressive: the region covers more than 10 million square km (4 million square miles) and extends into eight other countries (French Guiana, Suriname, Guyana, Venezuela, Ecuador, Peru, Bolivia, and Colombia). It takes up roughly 40% of Brazil in the states of Acre, Rondônia, Amazonas, Roraima, Pará, Amapá, and Tocantins. The Amazon forest is home to 500,000 cataloged species of plants and a river that annually transports 15% of the world's available freshwater to the sea.

Although there are regular flights and some bus routes through the Amazon, many visitors opt for the area's primary mode of transportation—boat (⇨ *Amazon by Boat, below)*. Though much slower, boats offer a closer look at Amazon culture, nature, and the river system, and they go just about everywhere you'd want to go.

ORIENTATION AND PLANNING

GETTING ORIENTED

A trip along the Amazon itself is a singular experience. From its source in southern Peru it runs 6,300 km (3,900 miles) to its Atlantic outflow and averages more than 3 km (2 miles) in width, but reaching up to 48 km (30 miles) across in the rainy season. Of its hundreds of tributaries, 17 are more than 1,600 km (1,000 miles) long. The Amazon is so large it could hold the Congo, Nile, Orinoco, Mississippi, and Yangtze rivers with room to spare. In places it is so wide you can't see the opposite shore, earning it the appellation Rio Mar (River Sea). Although there has been increasing urbanization in the Amazon region, between one-third and one-half of the Amazon's residents live in rural settlements, many of which are along the riverbanks, where transportation, water, fish, and good soil for planting are readily available.

MANAUS

Manaus is the Amazon's largest city as well as its main entrance. It was built largely on the good fortune of a couple of economic booms. The first was rubber. The second was the creation of a tax-free zone. Getting around the city or heading north to Venezuela is done by car or bus. To go anywhere else, you must use a boat or plane. Don't plan to drive south to Porto Velho or Bolivia. The road will be gone in a number of places.

11

TOP REASONS TO GO

■ **The Rain Forest:** Experience the largest tropical forest in the world and one of the wildest places on the planet.

■ **The River:** Explore the largest river in the world (by volume) and the second-longest, spanning more distance than the continental U.S.; the Amazon is also the earth's biggest freshwater ecosystem, and home to more fish than the Atlantic Ocean.

■ **Exotic Foods:** Dig into water-buffalo steak, duck in manioc sauce (*pato no tucupi*), fried piranha, and other river fish with exotic Indian names such as *tucunaré* and *pirarucú*.

■ **Handicrafts:** Shop for traditional indigenous crafts, such as wood-crafted and woven items, bows, arrows, blowguns, and jewelry and headdresses of seeds and feathers.

BETWEEN MANAUS AND BELÉM

As one would expect, distances between the major cities are huge. Traveling from one to another is done mostly by boat and plane, since there are no roads connecting them. Boats commonly run from Belém to Manaus and back, though the 1,150-mile journey takes four or five days. Large planes connect cities and larger towns. Small planes reach some smaller towns, though they are costly. While the Trans Amazônica highway is intended to connect the eastern and western regions, nature is still in control. Much of it is still dirt, mud, or dust. Consider it impassable and even dangerous in places.

BELÉM

Belém lies 60 miles upstream from the ocean at the confluence of several rivers. It was one of the first areas to be settled by the Portuguese. Its blend of river, ocean, and tropical forest makes for interesting geography and traveling. Buses run to landlocked villages northeast and southwest of the city, while boats run elsewhere. Boats are slow, so add extra time to your travel plans.

PLANNING

Visiting outlying areas in the Amazon usually results in unforgettable adventures, but tropical environments can be hostile, so prepare well and go with a companion if possible. It's a good idea to hire a guide or go with a tour company specializing in backcountry adventures. To join a tour or to choose a destination, contact one of the tour companies we suggest, or consult with a state-run tour agency. Before departure make sure someone knows exactly where you are going and when you are returning. Tell them you will contact them as soon as you have phone access. Research important health and safety precautions before your trip. A small cut, for example, can turn into a bad infection, and a painful encounter with a stingray's barb can result in a ruined vacation. The more remote your destination, the more seriously you should heed the travel advice and health precautions in this book. Your adventure can be wonderful, but you have to prepare well.

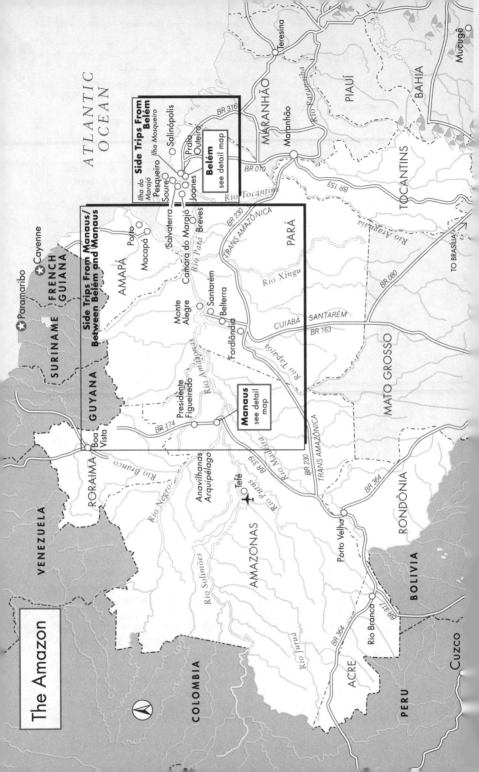

A Bit of History

Spaniard Vicente Pinzón is credited with being the first to sail the Amazon, in 1500. But the most famous voyage was undertaken by Spanish conquistador Francisco de Orellano, who set out from Ecuador on a short mission to search for food in 1541. Instead of gold or a lost kingdom, however, Orellano ran into natives, heat, and disease. When he emerged from the jungle a year later, his crew told a tale of women warriors they called the Amazons (a nod to classical mythology), and the story lent the region its name. In the late 19th century, rubber production transformed Belém and Manaus into cities. Rubber barons constructed mansions and monuments and brought life's modern trappings into the jungle. Since the rubber era, huge reserves of gold and iron have been discovered in the Amazon. Land-settlement schemes and development projects, such as hydroelectric plants and major roadworks, have followed. In the process, vast portions of tropical forest have been indiscriminately cut; tribal lands have been encroached upon; and industrial by-products, such as mercury used in gold mining, have poisoned wildlife and people. The Brazilian government has established reserves and made some efforts to preserve the territory, but there is much more to be done.

WHEN TO GO

The dry season (low water) between Belém and Manaus runs roughly from mid-June into December, and it's often brutally hot. Shortly before the new year, rains come more often and the climate cools a bit. The average annual temperature is 80°F (27°C) with high humidity. The early morning and the evening are always cooler and are the best times for walking around. The rainy season (high water) runs from December to June. "High water" means flooded forests and better boat access to lakes and wetlands for wildlife spotting. It also means flooded river beaches. Fishing is prime during low water, when fish move from the forest back into rivers and lakes, making them more accessible. Keep in mind that even the driest month has an average rainfall of 2 inches (compared with up to 13 inches during the wet season), so some kind of raingear is always recommended. Depending on where you are in the Amazon, during the rainy season it may rain every day, or three out of every four days, whereas during the dry season it may rain only one out of four days or less.

PACKING

For remote travel in the Amazon, a small backpack is the most efficient way to carry your gear. Plan for drenching downpours by bringing sufficient plastic bags, especially for important items. Specific things to consider packing for an off-the-grid Amazon vacation are: water bottle, filter, and purification tablets, sunscreen, insect repellent, hat, a good medical kit, knife, lightweight gold-miner's hammock (*rede de garimpeiro*), mosquito netting, sheet, 3 yards of ¼-inch rope, tent (if you're planning to camp), rain poncho, light shorts, pants (important for warding off pests while hiking), jacket, flashlight, batteries, matches, earplugs, sunglasses, and a waterproof camera case (good old plastic bags work, too!)

GETTING HERE AND AROUND

Given the enormous size of the region and the difficulty of traveling large distances, most visitors travel through only one region. For example, you can visit Manaus and its surrounding area or choose the Belém region. If you fly into Manaus, see the Meeting of the Waters, walk through the Adolfo Lisboa market, and take a tour in Teatro Amazonas. Then take a boat to a jungle lodge for a few days for trekking, swimming, and wildlife viewing. Conversely, fly into Belém and explore historic sites for a couple of days and then take a boat and van to a ranch on Marajó Island for a cultural experience and some wildlife spotting.

AMAZON BY BOAT

Sleep in a hammock on the middle deck of a thatch-roof riverboat or in the air-conditioned suite of an upscale tour operator's private ship. Keep in mind that wildlife-viewing is not good on boats far from shore. Near shore, however, the birding can be excellent. Binoculars and a bird guide can help, and shorebirds, raptors, and parrots can be abundant. Common in many parts of the river system are *boto* (pink dolphins) and *tucuxi* (gray dolphins).

ADVENTURE CRUISES

Adventure cruises combine the luxury of cruising with exploration. Their goal is to get you close to wildlife and local inhabitants without sacrificing comforts and amenities. Near daily excursions include wildlife-viewing in smaller boats with naturalists, village visits with naturalists, and city tours.

OCEANGOING SHIPS

Some cruise ships call at Manaus, Belém, and Santarém as part of their itineraries. Most trips take place October through May. They range in length from 10 to 29 days, and costs vary. Two major lines making such journeys are Princess Cruises and Royal Olympic Cruises.

TOURIST BOATS

Private groups can hire tourist boats that are more comfortable than standard riverboats. They generally travel close to the riverbank and have open upper decks from which you can observe the river and forest. The better tour operators have an English-speaking regional expert on board—usually an ecologist or botanist. You can either sleep out on the deck in a hammock or in a cabin, which usually has air-conditioning or a fan. Meals are generally provided.

SPEEDBOATS

You can take a speedboat to just about anywhere the rivers flow. Faster than most options, speedboats can be ideal for traveling between smaller towns, a morning of wildlife-viewing, or visiting a place that doesn't have regular transportation, such as a secluded beach or waterfall. You design the itinerary, including departure and return times. Prices and availability vary with distance and locale. Contact tour agencies, talk with locals, or head down to the docks to find a boat willing to take you where you want to go. Work out the price, destination, and travel time before leaving. You may have to pay for the gas up front, but don't pay the rest until you arrive. For trips longer than an hour, bring water, snacks, and sunscreen.

Health in the Amazon

Several months before you go to the Amazon, visit a tropical medicine specialist to find out what vaccinations you need. Describe your planned adventure, and get tips on how to prepare.

BITES AND STINGS

Tropical forests are home to millions of biting and stinging insects and other creatures. Most are harmless and many, such as snakes, are rarely seen. Mosquitoes can carry malaria and dengue, so it's important to protect yourself. To avoid snake bites, wear boots and pants in the forest and watch closely where you step. Escaping the Amazon without a few bites is nearly impossible—some anti-itch ointment will help you sleep at night.

FOOD AND WATER

In rural areas, avoid drinking tap water and using ice made from it. In the cities most restaurants buy ice made from purified water. Beware of where you eat. Many street stands are not very clean. Over-the-counter remedies can ease discomfort. For loose bowels, Floratil can be purchased without a doctor's prescription. Estomazil and Sorrisal (which may contain aspirin) are remedies for upset stomach.

INFECTIONS AND DISEASES

Dehydration and infections from insect bites and cuts are common. Get plenty of (bottled or purified) water and treat infections quickly. Rabies, Chagas' disease, malaria, yellow fever, meningitis, hepatitis, and dengue fever are present in the Amazon. Research tropical diseases in the Amazon so you know the symptoms and how to treat them should you fall ill. You shouldn't have problems if you take precautions.

HEALTH TIPS

■ If you're allergic to stings, carry an adrenaline kit.

■ Use screens on windows and doors, and sleep in rooms with air-conditioning, if possible.

■ Apply strong repellents containing picaridin or DEET (diethyl toluamide) when hiking in rural or forested areas.

■ A *mosquiteiro* (netting for hammock or bed) helps tremendously at night—to be effective it must reach the floor and not touch your skin.

■ Cover up with long pants and a shirt at night indoors, and wear pants, a long-sleeve shirt, and boots in the forest.

■ Check inside your shoes every morning for small guests.

■ Do not leave water in sinks, tubs, or discarded bottles. Dengue mosquitoes thrive in urban areas and lay their eggs in clean water.

■ If you have dengue symptoms, *do not* take aspirin, which can impair blood clotting.

■ If you find a tick on your skin, carefully remove it, treat the site with disinfectant, and see a doctor as soon as possible.

■ To avoid hard-to-see chiggers, which inhabit grassy areas, spray repellent or sprinkle powdered sulfur on shoes, socks, and pants.

■ Don't bathe in lakes or rivers without knowing the quality of water and the risks involved.

MACAMAZON BOATS

Longer boat routes on the lower Amazon are covered by MACAMA-ZON. Regular departures run between Belém, Santarém, Macapá, Manaus, and several other destinations. The boats are not luxurious but are a step above regional boats. You can get a suite for two from Belém to Manaus with air-conditioning and bath. Camarote (cabin) class gets you a tiny room for two with air-conditioning and a shared bath. Rede (hammock) class is the cheapest and most intimate way to travel, since you'll be hanging tight with the locals on the main decks. Hammocks are hung in two layers very close together, promoting neighborly chats. Arrive early for the best spots, away from the bar, engine, and bathrooms. Keep your valuables with you at all times and sleep with them. Conceal new sneakers in a plastic bag. In addition to a hammock (easy and cheap to buy in Belém or Manaus), bring two 4-foot lengths of 3/8-inch rope to tie it up. Also bring a sheet, since nights get chilly.

REGIONAL BOATS

To travel to towns and villages or to meander slowly between cities, go by *barco regional* (regional boat). A trip from Belém to Manaus takes about five days; Belém to Santarém is two days. The double- or triple-deck boats carry freight and passengers. They make frequent stops at small towns, allowing for interaction and observation. You might be able to get a cabin with two bunks (around R$400 for a two-day trip), but expect it to be claustrophobic. Most passengers sleep in hammocks with little or no space between them. Bring your own hammock, sheet, and two 4-foot sections of rope. Travel lightly and inconspicuously.

Booths sell tickets at the docks, and even if you don't speak Portuguese, there are often signs alongside the booths that list prices, destinations, and departure times. Sanitary conditions in bathrooms vary from boat to boat. Bring your own toilet paper, sunscreen, and insect repellent. Food is sometimes served, but the quality ranges from so-so to deplorable. Consider bringing your own water and a *marmita* (carry-out meal) if you'll be on the boat overnight. Many boats have a small store at the stern where you can buy drinks, snacks, and grilled *mixto quente* (ham-and-cheese) sandwiches. Fresh fruit and snacks are available at stops along the way. Be sure to peel or wash fruit thoroughly with bottled water before eating it.

RESTAURANTS

Reservations and dressy attire are rarely needed in the Amazon (indeed, reservations are rarely taken). Tipping isn't customary except in finer restaurants. Call ahead on Monday night, when many establishments are closed. *Prices in the review are the average cost of a main course at dinner or, if dinner is not served, at lunch.*

HOTELS

Amazon hotel prices tend to be reasonable and include breakfast. Services and amenities such as laundry, however, may cost quite a bit extra. Don't expect to be pampered. When checking in, ask about discounts (*descontos*). During the slow season and midweek, you may get a break.

Cry a little, as the Brazilians say, and you may get a larger discount. Paying with cash may lower the price. Rooms have air-conditioning, TVs, phones, and bathrooms unless we indicate otherwise, but showers don't always have hot water. Jungle lodges and smaller hotels in outlying areas often lack basic amenities. *Prices in the reviews are the lowest cost of a standard double room in high season. For expanded reviews, facilities, and current deals, visit Fodors.com.*

MANAUS

Manaus, the capital of Amazonas State, is a hilly city of around 1.8 million people that lies 766 km (475 miles) west of Santarém and 1,602 km (993 miles) west of Belém on the banks of the Río Negro 10 km (6 miles) upstream from its confluence with the Amazon. Manaus is the Amazon's most popular tourist destination, largely because of the many jungle lodges in the surrounding area. The city's principal attractions are its lavish, brightly colored houses and civic buildings—vestiges of an opulent time when the wealthy sent their laundry to be done in Europe and sent for Old World artisans and engineers to build their New World monuments.

Founded in 1669, Manaus took its name, which means "mother of the Gods," from the Manaó tribe. The city has long flirted with prosperity. Of all the Amazon cities and towns, Manaus is most identified with the rubber boom. In the late 19th and early 20th centuries it supplied 90% of the world's rubber. The industry was monopolized by rubber barons, whose number never exceeded 100 and who lived in the city and spent enormous sums on ostentatious lifestyles. They dominated the region like feudal lords. Thousands of *seringueiros* (rubber tappers) were recruited to work on the rubber plantations, where they lived virtually as slaves. A few of the seringueiros were from indigenous tribes, but most were transplants from Brazil's crowded and depressed northeast. Eventually conflicts erupted between barons and indigenous workers over encroachment on tribal lands. Stories of cruelty abound. One baron is said to have killed more than 40,000 native people during his 20-year "reign." Another boasted of having slaughtered 300 Indians in a day.

The 25-year rubber era was brought to a close thanks to Englishman Henry A. Wickham, who took 70,000 rubber-tree seeds out of Brazil in 1876. (Transporting seeds across borders has since been outlawed.) The seeds were planted in Kew Gardens in England. The few that germinated were transplanted in Malaysia, where they flourished. Within 30 years Malaysian rubber ended the Brazilian monopoly. Although several schemes were launched to revitalize the Amazon rubber industry, and many seringueiros continued to work independently in the jungles, the high times were over. Manaus entered a depression that lasted until 1967, when the downtown area was made a free-trade zone. The economy was revitalized, and its population jumped from 200,000 to 900,000 in less than 20 years.

In the 1970s the industrial district was given exclusive federal free-trade-zone status to produce certain light-industry items. Companies moved in and began making motorcycles and electronics. In the mid-1990s the commercial district lost its free-trade-zone status. Thousands of workers lost their jobs and businesses crumbled, but the light-industrial sector held strong and even grew. Today it employs over 100,000, has the largest motorcycle factory in South America, and makes 90% of Brazilian-made TVs.

GETTING HERE AND AROUND

Brigadeiro Eduardo Gomes Airport is 17 km (10 miles) north of downtown. Most flights connect in São Paulo. TAM and GOL have regular flights to and from Brasília, Rio, and São Paulo. TAM also has flights from Santarém and Belém. Azul flies to Manaus from its base in Campinas. The trip to Manaus Centro from the airport takes 25 minutes and costs about R\$58 by taxi. A trip on one of the city buses, which depart regularly during the day and early evening, costs R\$2.75 for a normal bus and R\$4.20 for an air-conditioned one.

If you're looking for a boat from Manaus to another town, a lodge, or a beach, go to the Hidroviária Regional Terminal. At the ticket or tourist information booths you can get information about prices and departure times and days to all the locations. You can also walk down to Porto Flutuante via the bridge behind the terminal to take a look at the regional boats. Their destinations and departure times are listed on plaques.

MACAMAZON boats run from Manaus to Santarém on Wednesday and Friday from the Porto São Raimundo (west of downtown) or the Porto Flutuante. The journey takes two days and cost R\$120 for a hammock and R\$600 for a two-person cabin. Boats from Manaus to Belém run three times a week; the trip takes five days and costs R\$320 for a hammock, and R\$1,100 for a two-person cabin.

The bus station in Manaus, Terminal Rodoviário Huascar Angelim, is 7 km (4 miles) north of the city center. From Manaus, BR 174 runs north (471 miles) to Boa Vista in Roraima State. BR 319 travels south to Porto Velho in Rondônia State but involves a ferry crossing and is only paved for about 100 km (63 miles); the road is eventually invaded by rivers and lakes. Even if you're after adventure, don't think about driving to Porto Velho.

The city bus system is extensive, easy to use, and inexpensive (R\$3). Most of the useful buses run along Avenida Floriano Peixoto, including Bus 120, which goes to Ponta Negra and stops near the Hotel Tropical. From the airport a taxi to Hotel Tropical costs R\$58; a trip from the Tropical to the center of town also costs R\$58. Manaus has its share of traffic and parking problems, but the driving is calmer than in Belém.

ESSENTIALS

Airport Information Aeroporto Brigadeiro Eduardo Gomes ⊠ *Av. Santos Dumont 1350, Tarumã* ☎ *092/3652–1210.*

Boat Contacts MACAMAZON ☎ *091/3222–5604, 091/3228–0774* ⊕ *www.macamazon.com.br.*

Bus Contacts Terminal Rodoviário Huascar Angelim ⊠ *Rua Recife 2784, Flores* ☎ *092/3642–5805.*

Emergencies and Medical Assistance Hospital e Pronto Socorro ⊠ *Alameda Cosme Ferreira 3775, São Jose* ☎ *092/3249–9000.*

Taxi Contacts Recife Rádio Táxi ☎ *092/3238–7301.* **Tucuxi** ☎ *092/2123–9090, 092/3622–4040* ⊕ *www.tucuxitaxi.com.br.*

Visitor and Tour Information Centro de Atendimento ao Turista (CAT) ⊠ *Av. Eduardo Ribeiro 666, Centro* ☎ *092/3182–6250* ⊗ *Weekdays 8–5, weekends 8–noon.* **Fontur.** This trusted operator has boat and city tours, as well airplane flights to various locations. Fontur can also arrange trips to jungle lodges. ⊠ *Hotel Tropical, Av. Coronel Teixeira 1320, Ponta Negra* ☎ *092/3658–3052, 092/8114–8136* ⊕ *www.fontur.com.br* ⊗ *Daily 7–5.* **Selvatur** ⊠ *Av. Constantino Nery 761, Sala 05, Presidente Vargas* ☎ *092/3231–1471.*

EXPLORING

Manaus is a sprawling city with a couple of high-rise buildings. There are a lot of hotels and sights are in the small city center (Centro), but the area is congested and not very attractive.

CENTRO

Manaus's downtown area has a lot going on. The floating docks are here, with tourist shops nearby. Open markets sell fish, meats, and all sorts of produce, while general stores ply machetes, hoes, hardtack, cassava flour, and boat motor parts to those pursuing a livelihood outside the city. The Centro is also the most important historic section of the city. The Teatro Amazonas and the Adolfo Lisboa Market are here, along with old churches, government buildings, and mansions. The result is a mix of neoclassical, Renaissance, colonial, and modern architecture.

TOP ATTRACTIONS

FAMILY **Museu do Índio.** The Indian Museum is maintained by Salesian Sisters, an order of nuns with eight missions in the upper Amazon. It displays handicrafts, weapons, ceramics, ritual masks, and clothing from the region's tribes. The gift shop sells traditional crafts such as necklaces made from seeds and feathers and baskets. ⊠ *Rua Duque de Caxias 356, Centro* ☎ *092/3635–1922* ☜ *R$5* ⊗ *Weekdays 8:30–11:30 and 2–4:30, Sat. 8:30–11:30* ⊗ *Closed Sun.*

Palácio Rio Negro. The extravagant Rio Negro Palace was built at the end of the 19th century as the home of a German rubber baron and was later used as the official governor's residence. Today it houses some of the city's finest art exhibits and a cultural center. The Museu da Imagem e do Som, on the same property, has three daily screenings of art films and documentaries Tuesday through Friday and four screenings daily on weekends. Don't miss the cultural exhibits out back, which include a caboclo home, an indigenous home, and a cassava-processing house. ⊠ *Av. 7 de Setembro 1546, Centro* ☎ *092/3232–4450* ☜ *Free* ⊗ *Tues.– Fri. 10–4, Sun. 5–8* ⊗ *Closed Mon. and Sat.*

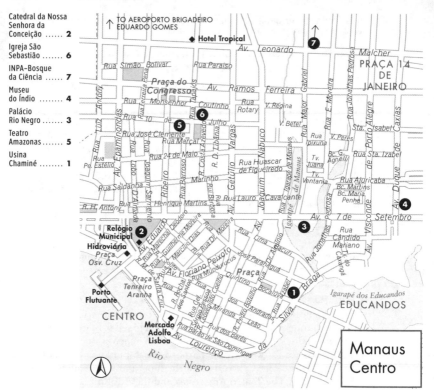

Manaus
Centro

Fodor's Choice **Teatro Amazonas.** Built during the rubber boom of the late 1800s, the
★ grandiose Teatro Amazonas was financed by wealthy Brazilian rub-
ber barons who wanted a cultural gem rivaling those in Europe. All
the bricks for the building were brought over in ships as ballast from
England, and the crystal chandeliers and mirrors were imported from
France and Italy. Don't miss the awe-inspiring ceiling murals in the main
hall. Operas and other events are presented regularly. Monday-evening
performances are free and usually feature local artists of various musical
genres. The Amazonas Philharmonic Orchestra plays Thursday night
and can be seen and heard practicing in the theater weekdays 9 to 2.
A variety of foreign entertainers also have performed here. Half-hour
tours are conducted daily 9 to 4. ⊠ *Praça do Congresso s/n, Centro*
☎ *092/3622–1880* 🎫 *R$10* ☉ *Mon.–Sat. 9–6.*

Usina Chaminé. Transformed from a sewage-treatment plant that never
functioned, this art gallery displays exhibits and holds dance and theater
performances. Its elegant neo-Renaissance–style interior, with hard-
wood floors and massive wood beams, is reason enough to visit. ⊠ *Av.
Lourenço da Silva Braga, Centro* ☎ *092/3633–3026* 🎫 *Free* ☉ *Tues.–
Fri. 10–5, weekends 4–8.*

WORTH NOTING

Catedral da Nossa Senhora da Conceição. Built originally in 1695 by Carmelite missionaries, the Cathedral of Our Lady of Immaculate Conception (also called Igreja Matriz) burned down in 1850 and was reconstructed in 1878. It's a simple, predominantly neoclassical structure with a bright, colorful interior. ⊠ *Praça Osvaldo Cruz 1, Centro* ☎ *092/3234–7821* ☜ *Free* ☉ *Usually Mon.–Sat. 9–5, but hrs vary.*

Igreja São Sebastião. With its charcoal-gray exterior and medieval style, this neoclassical church (circa 1888) seems foreboding. Its interior, however, is luminous and uplifting, with white Italian marble, stained-glass windows, and beautiful ceiling paintings. The church has a tower on only one side. No one is sure why this is so, but if you ask, you may get one of several explanations: the second tower wasn't built because of lack of funds; it was omitted as a symbolic gesture to the poor; or the ship with materials for its construction sank. As you stroll through the church plaza, note the black-and-white Portuguese granite patterns at your feet. They are said to represent Manaus's meeting of the waters. ⊠ *Rua Tapajós, 54, Centro* ☎ *092/3232–4572* ☜ *Free* ☉ *Usually Mon.– Sat. 9–5, but hrs vary.*

ELSEWHERE IN MANAUS

Most of the area surrounding downtown Manaus is not very attractive to visit. The few places of interest include the Natural History Museum and INPA's Bosque da Ciência in Aleixo. The Bosque and nearby Parque Municipal do Mindu in Parque 10 are both forested and good for walks. A taxi will cost around R$30 one-way from downtown to these sites. Ponta Negra along the Río Negro has several restaurants and is super for evening strolls. Also, Hotel Tropical is on its upstream end. Taxis charge R$58 from downtown.

TOP ATTRACTIONS

FAMILY **INPA–Bosque da Ciência.** Used as a research station for the INPA (Instituto Nacional de Pesquisa da Amazônia), this slice of tropical forest is home to a great diversity of flora and fauna. Some highlights include manatee tanks, caiman ponds, a museum, a botanical garden with an orchidarium, and nature trails. It's a great place for a walk in the shade. ⊠ *Rua Otávio Cabral s/n, Petropolis* ☎ *092/3643–3192* ⊕ *www.inpa. gov.br* ☜ *R$5* ☉ *Weekdays 9–12 and 2–5, weekends 9–4.*

FAMILY
Fodor's Choice
★
Meeting of the Waters. Outside of Manaus, the slow-moving, muddy Amazon and the darker, quicker Río Negro flow side by side for 6 km (4 miles) without mixing. If you run your foot in the water at the meeting place, you can feel the difference in temperature—the Amazon is warm and the Negro is cold, the consistencies of the rivers are different, and the experience is magical. At the CEASA port you can rent a boat, or go with a tour company. It takes about an hour to go from CEASA to the Meeting of the Waters, spend some time there, and return. A taxi to CEASA from downtown is about R$30.

CLOSE UP

A Vanishing People

In 1500, when the Portuguese arrived in Brazil, the indigenous population was 4.5 million, with an estimated 1,400 tribes. From the beginning the Portuguese divided into two camps regarding the native people: the missionaries, who wanted to "tame" them and convert them to Catholicism, and the colonizers, who wished to enslave and exploit them. The missionaries lost, and when it became apparent that the indigenous people couldn't be enslaved, the infamous *bandeirantes* (assault forces) relentlessly persecuted them so as to "liberate" tribal lands. Many lost their lives defending their land and their way of life, but the greatest killers were smallpox and influenza—European diseases against which they had no immunity. Slow but steady integration into Portuguese society caused the native population to dwindle.

Today, of Brazil's 328,000 remaining indigenous people, about 197,000 live in the Amazon. Each of the 220 societies has its own religious beliefs, social customs, and economic activities. The larger groups include the Manaó, Yanomami, Marajó, Juma, Caixana, Korubo, and Miranha. Each speaks one of the 170 distinct languages spoken by the indigenous peoples of Brazil; Tupi (with seven in-use derivations, including Tupi-Guaraní) is the most widely spoken, followed by Macro Jê, Aruák, Karíb, and Arawá.

Throughout Brazil's history sporadic efforts were made to protect indigenous people, but it was only in 1910 that the government established an official advocacy agency, the Service for the Protection of the Indians (SPI), to support Indian autonomy, ensure respect for traditional practices, and help indigenous peoples to acquire Brazilian citizenship. In 1930 the SPI was abolished due to corruption and lack of funds. It was replaced in 1967 by the current governmental advocacy group, FUNAI (Fundação Nacional do Indio, or the National Indian Foundation). Although it has been highly criticized, FUNAI helped to get the first (and, thus far, only) indigenous person elected into office: Mario Juruna, an Indian chief, served as federal deputy from 1983 to 1987. The foundation has also defended the rights of indigenous people to protect their lands (it allows only legitimate researchers to visit reservations), which are increasingly targeted for logging, rubber extraction, mining, ranching, or the building of industrial pipelines and hydroelectric plants.

The indigenous people of the Amazon have always respected and understood their environment; their plight and that of the rain forest are closely linked. Conservation efforts to preserve the rain forest have called attention to some of FUNAI's issues, but for the Brazilian government the issue is complicated: rain-forest conservation is often overshadowed by economic development. Further, the indigenous people still lack many basic human rights, and violence (such as the 1998 murder of prominent activist Francisco de Assis Araujó) still sporadically occurs as the indigenous people continue to defend their way of life against outsiders.

—Melisse Gelula and Althia Gamble

WHERE TO EAT

If you expect to find much regional cuisine using local, exotic ingredients in Manaus, you may be disappointed. Belém has a much more vibrant and creative eating scene. Here expect to find rather bland, brightly lit restaurants serving much fish caught in Amazonian rivers and served with the ubiquitous *farofa,* the ground manioc flour that is fried in oil and served crispy and dry as a side dish.

$$$$ BRAZILIAN Fodor's Choice ★

🍴 **Banzeiro.** Run by the brothers Felipe and Thiago Schaedler, this restaurant has twice won the *Veja* magazine award for best regional Amazon cuisine. Fresh fish from the Amazon rivers reigns supreme here—you can't go wrong with the tambaqui fried chops served with *farofa* (manioc). For dessert, try the banana cake drizzled with molasses. Very popular with locals, the place fills up on weekends. **■ TIP→ Check the restaurant's website before going for English descriptions of their main dishes, as no menus in English are available in the restaurant, and most staff speak only Portuguese.** [$] *Average main: R$64* ✉ *Rua Libertador 102, Vieralves* ☎ *092/3234–1621* 🌐 *www.restaurantebanzeiro.com.br* 🕒 *Daily 11:30–3 and 6:30–11:30.*

$$ LATIN AMERICAN

🍴 **Canto da Peixada.** When Pope John Paul II came to Manaus in 1981, this restaurant was chosen to host him. The dining areas aren't elegant, but the fish dishes are outstanding. Be sure to come hungry, as one platter comes with enough food for two people. [$] *Average main: R$37* ✉ *Rua Emilio Moreira 1677, Praça 14* ☎ *092/3234–1066* 🌐 *www.cantodapeixada.com* 🕒 *Mon.–Sat. 10:30–3:30 and 6:00–10:30, Sun. 10:30–3:30.*

$$ STEAKHOUSE Fodor's Choice ★

🍴 **Churrascaria Búfalo.** Twelve waiters, each with a different cut of chicken, beef, or goat, scurry around this large, sparkling clean restaurant. As if the delectable meats weren't enough, tables are also stocked with side dishes, including manioc root, pickled vegetables, and caramelized bananas. [$] *Average main: R$45* ✉ *Rua Pará, 490, Vieralves* ☎ *092/3131–9000* 🌐 *www.churrascariabufalo.com.br* 🕒 *Mon.–Thurs. 11:30–3 and 7–11, Fri.–Sat. 11:30–4 and 7–11, Sun. 11:30–4.*

$$$ BRAZILIAN

🍴 **Fiorentina.** The green awning and red-and-white-check tablecloths are hints that this restaurant serves authentic Italian cuisine. Pasta dishes are delicious, especially the lasagna *fiorentina* (with a marinara and ground-beef sauce). A buffet is also available everyday for lunch. [$] *Average main: R$50* ✉ *Praça da Polícia 44, Centro* ☎ *092/3215–2233* 🕒 *Daily 10 am–11 pm.*

$ BRAZILIAN

🍴 **Restaurante Aves Grill.** For a quick, cheap bite, you can't beat this pay-per-kilo restaurant. Most main courses contain some kind of bird, whether quail, turkey, duck, or chicken. Side dishes include lovely salads, fries, beans, and rice. [$] *Average main: R$20* ✉ *Rua Henrique Martins 366, Centro* ☎ *092/3233–3809* 🕒 *No dinner.*

WHERE TO STAY

Manaus has several decent in-town hotels, but the jungle lodges outside town are where you should base yourself if you're interested in Amazon adventures. Most jungle lodges have naturalist guides, swimming, caiman searches, piranha fishing, and canoe trips. Many jungle lodges are near the Río Negro, where mosquitoes are less of a problem because they can't breed in its acidic black water.

$ HOTEL **Central Hotel Manaus.** A good option if you're on a budget, this hotel has simple, clean rooms with standard amenities. **Pros:** inexpensive; pleasant. **Cons:** rooms are plainly decorated. [$] *Rooms from: R$130* ✉ *Rua Dr. Moreira 202, Centro* ☎ *092/3622–2600* 🌐 *www.hotelcentralmanaus.com.br* 🛏 *50 rooms* 🍴 *Breakfast.*

$ B&B/INN **Chez les Rois.** You'll truly feel like you're staying in a friend's house at this popular and cozy bed-and-breakfast. **Pros:** friendly, laid-back staff. **Cons:** you may get lost trying to find this place as it's located on a small side street. [$] *Rooms from: R$165* ✉ *Travessa Dos Cristais 01, Conjunto Manauense off of Rua Acre, Vieralves* ☎ *092/3584–3549* 🌐 *www.chezlesrois.com.br* 🛏 *11 rooms* 🍴 *Breakfast.*

$ HOTEL **Hotel Manaós.** Across from Teatro Amazonas and just up the street from the busy part of downtown, Hotel Manaós is an excellent base for exploring Manaus. **Pros:** one of best locations in town. **Cons:** rooms are small. [$] *Rooms from: R$189* ✉ *Av. Eduardo Ribeiro 881, Centro* ☎ *092/3633–5744* 🛏 *39 rooms* 🍴 *No meals.*

$ HOTEL Fodor's Choice ★ **Hotel Tropical.** Nothing in the Amazon can match the majesty of this resort hotel, which is located 20 km (12 miles) northwest of downtown and overlooks the Río Negro, with a short path to the beach. **Pros:** beautifully appointed rooms; luxurious furniture; all the amenities of a high-class resort. **Cons:** far from all points of interest; expensive commute by taxi. [$] *Rooms from: R$159* ✉ *Av. Coronel Teixeira 1320, Ponta Negra* ☎ *092/2123–5000* 🌐 *www.tropicalhotel.com.br* 🛏 *525 rooms* 🍴 *No meals.*

$$ HOTEL **Park Suites Manaus.** This 20-story hotel has a spectacular infinity pool that overlooks the Rio Negro. **Pros:** great views. **Cons:** far from the center of town; few shopping or eating options nearby. [$] *Rooms from: R$363* ✉ *Avenida Coronel Teixeira 1320A, Ponta Negra* ☎ *092/3306–4500* 🌐 *www.atlanticahotels.com.br* 🛏 *250 rooms* 🍴 *Breakfast.*

$ HOTEL **St. Paul Apart Service.** Although the exterior and lobby of this hotel aren't much to write home about, its central location and helpful staff more than make up for it. **Pros:** modern facilities. **Cons:** bland food at breakfast. [$] *Rooms from: R$196* ✉ *Av. Ramos Ferreira 1115, Centro* ☎ *092/2101–3800* 🌐 *www.manaushoteis.com.br* 🛏 *70 apartments* 🍴 *Breakfast.*

$$ HOTEL **Taj Mahal.** With a rooftop pool, a revolving restaurant with a view, and a convenient location, the Taj Mahal is one of the most comfortable choices in central Manaus. **Pros:** good location; pleasant rooms. **Cons:** hotel is a bit unkempt. [$] *Rooms from: R$250* ✉ *Av. Getúlio Vargas 741, Centro* ☎ *092/3627–3737* 🌐 *www.grupotajmahal.com.br* 🛏 *144 rooms, 26 suites* 🍴 *Breakfast.*

NIGHTLIFE AND THE ARTS

NIGHTLIFE

Manaus em Tempo (🌐 *www.emtempo.com.br*) is a newspaper that lists nightlife events in Manaus. *Boi bumbá* (ox legend) music and dance—native to the central Amazon region—tells stories with tightly choreographed steps and strong rhythms. The amphitheater at Praia da Ponta Negra holds regular boi-bumbá performances.

CLOSE UP

Chico Mendes: Environmental Pioneer

11

Born in 1944 in the northwestern state of Acre, Chico Mendes was the son of a *seringueiro* (rubber-tree tapper) who had moved across the country in the early 20th century to follow the rubber boom. Chico followed in his father's footsteps as a seringuero in Xapuri, close to the Bolivian border. In the 1960s rubber prices dropped dramatically, and tappers began to sell forests to cattle ranchers who cut them for pastures. In the '70s, to protect forests and the tappers' way of life, Mendes joined a group of nonviolent activists who managed to prevent many ranch workers and loggers from clearing the rubber trees. On the local council of Xapuri, he promoted the creation of forest reserves for rubber and Brazil-nut production. He founded the Xapuri Rural Workers Union and the National Council of Rubber Tappers to educate tappers on forest issues.

In 1987 Mendes was invited to Washington, D.C., to help convince the Inter-American Development Bank to rescind its financial support of a planned 1,200-km (750-mile) road to be constructed through the forest. That same year, Mendes was awarded the Global 500 environmental achievement award from the United Nations, making him an international celebrity.

In 1988 Mendes stopped rancher Darly Alves da Silva from extending his ranch into a reserve. On December 22, 1988, da Silva and son Darcy murdered Mendes outside his home. Upon his death, Chico Mendes made the front page of the *New York Times* and numerous other publications worldwide. Subsequently, Brazil created the Chico Mendes Extractive Reserve near Xapuri, along with 20 other reserves covering more than 8 million acres.

BARS
Cervejaria Fellice. Food, live music every night, and a variety of homemade beer is made at microbrewery Cervejaria Fellice. ✉ *Studio 5 Festival Mall, loja 5, Av. Rodrigo Otavio 3555, Distrito Industrial* ☎ *92/3216–3400* ⊕ *www.cervejariafellice.com.br.*

DANCE CLUBS
Botequim. Near the Teatro Amazonas, Botequim features live bands that play a mix of MPB (*música popular brasileira,* or Brazilian pop music), samba, bossa nova, and other Brazilian styles on Thursday, Friday, and Saturday. ✉ *Rua Barroso 279, Centro* ☎ *092/3232–1030* ⊗ *Thurs.–Sat. 8 pm–3 am.*

THE ARTS
Secretaria da Estado de Cultura (SEC). Secretaria da Estado da Cultura (SEC) provides information on cultural activities and festivals in Manaus. ✉ *Av. 7 de Setembro 1546, Centro* ☎ *092/3633–2850* ⊕ *www. culturadoam.blogspot.com.br* ⊗ *Weekdays 8–1, 2–5.*

Teatro Amazonas. Teatro Amazonas draws some of the biggest names in theater, opera, and classical music. Monday-evening performances are free, and the Amazonas Philharmonic Orchestra plays every Thursday night. The Teatro holds an opera festival every year in April and May. ✉ *Rua Tapajos 5, Centro* ☎ *092/3232–1768* ▣ *R$10.*

Elusive El Dorado

The search for El Dorado (which means, in Spanish, "The Gilded Man") and his supposedly wealthy kingdom began with the arrival of the conquistadors to South America in the 1500s and continued into the 1900s. The suspected location of El Dorado (as the kingdom came to be called) changed depending on who was searching. The most captivating story placed it in Colombia, in a village where each year Chibcha natives rolled a chieftain in gold dust. The chieftain then paddled to the middle of sacred lake Gustavita and bathed. So powerful was the lure of finding riches there, that when conquistadors Gonzalo Pinzarro and Francisco de Orellana heard the story, they mounted an expedition of hundreds of men, horses, and dogs. They went east over the Andes, descended its steep slopes, and dropped into Amazon rain forest. Along the way they lost most of their men and animals. They never found El Dorado or any gold. Nor did Sir Walter Raleigh, Colonel Fawcett, or numerous others who searched. Many, like Fawcett, succumbed to illness or arrows and never returned.

SHOPPING

Here, as in other parts of the Amazon, you can find lovely indigenous artisanal items made from animal parts. Macaws, for example, are killed in the wild for feathers to make souvenir items for tourists. As a result, there are no longer many macaws in the forests close to Manaus. Traveling home with items made from animal parts, certain types of wood, or plant fibers can result in big fines and even jail time, so beware.

SHOPPING AREAS AND MALLS

Amazonas Shopping. With more than 300 stores and restaurants, Amazonas Shopping is the largest, most upscale mall in the region. ⊠ *Av. Djalma Batista 482, Chapada* ☎ *092/3303–9000* ⊕ *www. amazonasshopping.com.br* ⊙ *Mon.–Sat. 10–10, Sun. 2–9.*

Studio 5 Festival Mall. Part of a larger commercial complex, Studio 5 Festival Mall contains many clothing stores, restaurants, cinemas, a hotel, and even a convention center. ⊠ *Av. Rodrigo Octavio 2555, Distrito Industrial* ☎ *092/3216–3527.*

SPECIALTY SHOPS

Ecoshop. Ecoshop sells regional art and a variety of indigenous crafts made from wood, seeds, and straw. ⊠ *Amazonas Shopping, Chapada* ☎ *092/3642–2026* ⊕ *www.ecoshop.com.br.*

Mercado Adolfo Lisboa. One of the best places to buy all kinds of things, from fresh fish to hammocks and souvenirs, is Mercado Adolfo Lisboa, down along the river. Built between 1880 and 1883, the building was based on Les Halles in Paris and has intricate ironwork that was made in France and shipped over by boat. It was made an historical landmark in 1987. ⊠ *Rua Dos Barés 46, Centro* ☎ *092/3663–8342.*

SIDE TRIPS FROM MANAUS

Not far from Manaus you can explore black-water rivers, lakes, and beaches on the Río Negro; muddy-water rivers and lakes on the Amazon River; and waterfalls and streams north of Manaus. You can also visit caboclo villages along the rivers. Perhaps your guide or boat driver will walk through the village with you to introduce you and show you around. Wildlife watching can be done anywhere, though it gets better the farther you get from the city.

Whichever tour you choose, be sure your experience includes wildlife viewing with a guide, contact with locals, and regional foods and drinks. The most popular tours run from Manaus, since it's the best organized for tourism and has the best jungle lodges. It can feel clogged with tourists at times though, which can make the less-popular starting points of Santarém and Belém more appealing.

MANAUS-AREA BEACHES

Praia da Lua is 23 km (14 miles) southwest of Manaus; Praia do Tupé is 34 km (20 miles) northwest of Manaus.

To reach most Manaus-area beaches, catch a boat from Porto Flutuante in downtown or from Ponta Negra. Boats are available throughout the week—just make sure to inquire about return trips, especially on weekdays when there are fewer departures. Look for people wearing the green vests of the Associação dos Canoeiros Motorizados de Manaus near the Porto Flutuante or at the Marina de David. They can set you up with local boat trips at reasonable prices.

Praia da Lua. Named after its crescent-shaped beach, Praia da Lua is on the Río Negro, and is located 10 minutes away from Ponta Negra in Manaus. Avoid this beach on the weekends when it is overcrowded and noisy. During the week you should expect warm waters, and is one of the few beaches open year-round. Don't expect any frills here, just wooden tables and benches to eat your food at, and small restaurants selling pricey food and drinks from tents. Catch boats from the Marina do David at the end of Coronel Teixeira Avenue in Ponta Negra near the Tropical Hotel and expect to pay R$10 round-trip, per person. **Amenities:** food and drink. **Best for:** sunsets; swimming; people-watching.

Praia do Tupé. This beach on the Río Negro is popular with locals and tends to fill up on Sunday and holidays. Visitors will usually be greeted by members of a local tribe dancing, but beware that you will be charged to take part in the festivities (around R$10 per person). You must bring your own food and drink. Expect to pay around R$25–30 per person round-trip to get here from Manaus. You can hire boats either from the main port in Manaus or from Ponta Negra. **Amenities:** none. **Best for:** views of the Rio Negro; swimming. ⊠ *34 km (20 miles) northwest of Manaus.*

PRESIDENTE FIGUEIREDO

107 km (64 miles) north of Manaus.

One of the Amazon's best-kept secrets is a two-hour drive north of Manaus. The town of Presidente Figueiredo (founded 1981) has dozens of waterfalls—up to 32 meters (140 feet) in height—and caves with prehistoric paintings and pottery fragments. The area was stumbled on during the construction of BR 174, the only highway that takes you out of the state (to Roraima and on to Venezuela), and was ultimately discovered by explorers looking for minerals, who had based themselves in Presidente Figueiredo. The area is excellent for swimming in blackwater streams and hiking through upland forest. The town has several hotels and restaurants, and there's a hydropower plant and reservoir and an archaeology museum in the area. The Centro de Proteção de Quelonias e Mamiferos Aquaticos (Center for the Protection of Turtles and Aquatic Mammals) is in Balbina, 82 km (51 miles) north of town. Get cash in Manaus because there are only two banks here, and they do not always accept international cards.

GETTING HERE AND AROUND

To get to Presidente Figueiredo from Manaus, take the bus labeled "Aruanã", which runs twice a day (105 km, 1 hour and 30 minutes) from the Terminal Rodoviário Huascar Angelim and costs around R$22.

AMAZON EXCURSIONS FROM MANAUS

The Amazon, home to more than 200 species of mammals and 1,800 species of birds, and providing 30% of the earth's oxygen, is the world's largest and densest rain forest. Stretching 6,300 km (3,900 miles), the Amazon is the world's longest river. From its source in the Peruvian Andes, the river and its tributaries snake through parts of Bolivia, Ecuador, Colombia, and Brazil before emptying into the Atlantic.

Though Belém, Santarém, and other communities are great for jungle and river excursions, they don't have nearly the selection or number of visitors that Manaus has. The most common excursion is a half- or full-day tourist-boat trip that travels 15 km (9 miles) east of Manaus to where the coffee-colored water of the Río Negro flows beside and gradually joins the coffee-with-cream-color water of the Rio Solimões. According to Brazilians, this is where the Amazon River begins. The waters flow alongside one another for 6 km (4 miles) before merging. Many of these Meeting-of-the-Waters treks include motorboat side trips along narrow streams or through bayous. Some also stop at the Parque Ecológico do Janauary, where you can see birds and a lake filled with the world's largest water lily, the *vitória régia*.

Nighttime boat trips into the forest explore flooded woodlands and narrow waterways. Some stop for trail hikes. Some companies take you by canoe on a caiman "hunt," where caimans are caught and released. Trips to the Rio Negro's upper reaches, where wildlife is a little wilder, are also offered. Such trips usually stop at river settlements to visit with local families. They may include jungle treks, fishing (they supply the gear and boat), and a trip to Anavilhanas, the world's largest freshwater archipelago. It contains some 400 islands with amazing Amazon flora, birds, and monkeys.

Whatever your style of travel, there's a boat plying the river to suit your needs. Sleep in a hammock on the deck of a thatch-roof riverboat or in the air-conditioned suite of an upscale vessel. A typical river program includes exploring tributaries in small boats; village visits, perhaps with a blowgun demonstration; piranha fishing; nocturnal wildlife searches; and rain-forest walks with a naturalist or indigenous guide to help you learn about plants, wildlife, and traditional medicines. River

> **THE RAREST BEER**
>
> Amazonian tribes have been making manioc and corn beers for about 2,000 years. The most popular of these is a hearty dark beer used during social and religious festivals. All types of celebrations are accompanied with beer drinking in the Amazon. The Tapajó tribe used to add the unique ingredient of cremated human bones to ensure that their ancestors would carry on in them. Try the Xingu beer that is sold all over.

journeys along the Brazilian Amazon typically begin in Manaus and feature 3 to 10 days on the water, plus time in Manaus and, sometimes, Rio de Janeiro.

TOUR OPERATORS

Though most tour companies will pick you up at the airport and drop you off following your adventure, airport pickup should not be assumed in all situations. It's often included in tour packages, but ask while making arrangements. Local naturalist guides are often available at lodges. Though knowledgeable, they're neither biologists nor teachers and may not always impart accurate information.

Amazon Jungle Tours. This Manaus-based tour operator offers a variety of jungle excursions: four- to six-night riverboat cruises, four-night stays at jungle lodges, and seven-day jungle survival trips. Trips start from US$100 a night per person and include airport pickup, English-speaking guides, three meals a day and mineral water, activities, and accommodation at basic, no-frills lodges. ⊠ *10 de Julho Street 708, Centro, Manaus* ☎ *092/3087–0689, 092/9184–8452* ⊕ *www.amazonjungletours.com.br.*

Amazon Tours Brazil. Specializing in boat cruises, this tour operator is run out of Manaus by Carlos Damasceno, who was born in the Amazon jungle and personally leads many of the tours. Amazon Tours Brazil has cruises ranging from three to five days, with prices starting at US$1,000 per person for a three-day cruise on a regular river boat, to US$3,500 per person for a four-day cruise on a luxury boat with special air-conditioned cabins. ⊠ *Manaus* ☎ *092/915–67185* ⊕ *www. amazontoursbrazil.com.*

JUNGLE LODGES NEAR MANAUS

Because the Amazon and its tributaries provide easy access to remote parts of the jungle, river transport often serves as the starting point for camping and lodge excursions. Many lodges and camps are within or near national parks or reserves. Accommodations range from hammocks to comfortable rooms with private, hot-water baths. Nature walks, canoe trips, piranha fishing, and visits to indigenous villages are typically part of rainforest programs led by naturalists or indigenous guides.

> ### THE AMAZON CANOPY
>
> Trees in the Amazon are not only connected at the roots, but they're linked at the branches as well. This creates an enormous ecosystem far above the ground. The canopy holds more species of insects than any other part of the rain forest.

$$$$
RESORT

Amazon Eco Lodge. Rustic floating cabins with air-conditioning and baths make up this remote lodge. **Pros:** beautiful cabins; close to nature. **Cons:** steeply priced. $ *Rooms from: R$2996* ⊠ *74 km (50 miles) south of Manaus, Lago Juma* ☎ *092/3308–8393, 092/3236–1181* ⊕ *www.amazonlodgeamazonas.com.br* ↯ *16 rooms, 2 wedding suites* ⊟ *No credit cards* ❘○❘ *All meals.*

$$$$
RESORT

Amazon Ecopark Lodge. With air-conditioned rooms, hot showers, and mosquito nets this lodge offers a comfortable jungle experience, and includes visits to monkeys in rehabilitation, hikes with a naturalist guide on 10 km (6 miles) of trails through several habitat types with enormous trees, and dips in streams and natural pools. **Pros:** elegant, well-appointed rooms; lots of activities. **Cons:** no TVs, refrigerators, or Internet. $ *Rooms from: R$675* ⊠ *Rio Tarumã* ☎ *021/2547–7742 Reservations, 092/9146–0594 Lodge* ⊕ *www.amazonecopark.com.br* ↯ *64 rooms* ❘○❘ *Some meals.*

$$$$
RESORT

Amazon Jungle Palace. It's quite a sight to cruise down the Rio Negro and see the façade of this luxurious "flotel," built on a steel barge, looming on the horizon. **Pros:** right on the river; excellent amenities. **Cons:** large number of rooms makes it crowded at times. $ *Rooms from: R$1570* ⊠ *35 km (20 miles)/1 hr west of Manaus, Río Negro* ☎ *092/3212–5610, 092/3212–5650* ⊕ *www.amazonjunglepalace.com.br* ↯ *68 rooms* ❘○❘ *All meals.*

$$$$
RESORT
Fodor's Choice
★

Anavilhanas Lodge. Right off the shore of the mighty Rio Negro, this luxurious resort is near many prime spots for spotting wildlife and the numerous islands of the Anavilhanas archipelago. **Pros:** excellent service. **Cons:** more expensive than most. $ *Rooms from: R$1645* ⊠ *Around 180 km (112 miles) northwest of Manaus, Rodovia Am 352, Km 1, Igarapé do Monteiro, Novo Airão* ☎ *092/3365–1180* ⊕ *www.anavilhanaslodge.com* ↯ *16 rooms, 4 bungalows* ❘○❘ *All meals.*

$$$$
RESORT

Ariaú Amazon Towers. The most famous of the Amazon jungle lodges, Ariaú consists of four-story wooden towers on stilts and linked by catwalks—an effect that is even more dramatic when the river floods the ground below from December to June. **Pros:** excellent food; nicely furnished rooms. **Cons:** large complex; small rooms. $ *Rooms from: R$782* ⊠ *60 km (40 miles)/2 hrs northwest of Manaus, Rio Ariaú* ☎ *092/2121–5000* ⊕ *www.ariautowers.com.br* ↯ *300 rooms, 8 suites* ❘○❘ *All meals.*

CLOSE UP

What to Expect at a Jungle Lodge

11

Most of the jungle lodges near Manaus are around 200 kilometers northwest of the city, in the district known as Novo Airão. Whether luxurious or rustic, they offer similar activities that revolve around boat rides along the Rio Negro. Here's what you can expect from a stay in a jungle lodge:

Night sighting of animals and caimans: Although the Amazon jungle is full of wildlife, some visitors may be disappointed at how few animals they actually encounter. Your best bet at spotting wildlife comes from night tours of riverbank areas, where you might find large snakes in the treetops, sloths, and small owls. Caimans, a smaller type of alligator, are also usually sighted at night.

Spotting pink dolphins: Tours to see Amazon river dolphins, also called pink dolphins or boto in Portuguese, are popular. Some lodges include such excursions in their packages, others charge extra. Some lodges will allow you to stand in the water and interact with the dolphins, but be careful not to move your hands or legs suddenly, as they might bite. Their long beaks have sharp rows of teeth on each side of the jaws.

Hiking through the jungle: Led by knowledgeable local guides, usually of indigenous origin, these hikes offer visitors the chance to learn about various Amazonian plants and insects. The massive ant hills and ground-level homes of tarantulas are especially impressive. Be sure to wear long pants and long-sleeved shirts, and bring along insect repellent and bottled drinking water.

Fishing for piranha: Although there are more than 30 varieties of piranhas, you will probably be fishing for the smaller variety of these carnivorous fish. Some lodges will gladly cook any fish you catch, most likely in a fish stew since their bodies have little flesh and are full of spiky bones.

Watching the sunrise: Expect a wake-up knock at your cabin at 5 am in order to glimpse the spectacular colors of the sunrise over the Rio Negro.

Visiting riverside communities: At these communities, visitors often learn how to make manioc flour, a staple of the Amazonian diet, and sample fruit from Amazonian trees such as the tucuman, which has round fruit with a fleshy, orange-colored inside. Riverside communities carve the pits of these fruit to make black-colored bracelets and rings.

OFF THE BEATEN PATH

Mamirauá Sustainable Development Reserve. The largest wildlife reserve in Brazil, Mamirauá is about 1,050 km (650 miles) west of Manaus on the Rio Solimões. The reserve is known for its abundant wildlife, including the endemic, and endangered, red-faced uakari monkey. Guided tours (from Pousada Flutuante Uakari) take you through the *várzea* (flooded forest) in canoes during the rainy season (January–April) and on foot the rest of the year. Plan to get muddy if you're hiking. Frequent animal sightings include three species of monkeys, colorful birds, and pink river dolphins. Dry season is the best time to see caimans and fish. Since Mamirauá encompasses several communities, the cooperation and assistance of local inhabitants in the areas of research, ecotourism, maintenance, and fiscalization help make it successful as a sustainable development reserve.

To get to the reserve, you'll need to fly to Tefé (a one-hour flight from Manaus) and take Mamirauá's boat from there. It's a bit of an effort but well worth it. ☎ *097/3343-4160* 🌐 *www.mamiraua.org.br*.

$$$$ RESORT 🏨 **Pousada Flutuante Uakari.** This lodge takes great pride in its efforts to exist in harmony with the local population and the environment—for instance, local guides are hired and most of the lodge uses solar power. **Pros:** rustic rooms with lots of light. **Cons:** few amenities. [$] *Rooms from: R$1600* ✉ *One hour by boat from Tefé* ☎ *097/3343–4160, 097/8123–1800* 🌐 *www.mamiraua.org.br and www.uakarilodge.com.br* 🛏 *10 rooms* 🍴 *All meals* ☞ *R$1,600 per person double occupancy, 4 days and 3 nights.*

$$$$ RESORT 🏨 **Tariri Amazon Lodge.** On the shores of Lake Acajatuba, this family-owned resort consists of charming wooden rooms built on stilts above the jungle floor. **Pros:** personal attention from the owners; delicious food. **Cons:** no air-conditioning, hot water, Internet, or television. [$] *Rooms from: R$950* ✉ *Around 180 km (112 miles) northwest of Manaus, Lago de Acajatuba, Municipio de Iranduba* ☎ *092/9137–1925* 🌐 *www.taririamazonlodge.com.br* 🛏 *6 cabins for couples, 4 cabins for families* 🕒 *Closed Oct. 15–Nov. 15 due to dry season* 🍴 *All meals.*

BETWEEN MANAUS AND BELÉM

The smaller communities between the Amazon's two major cities give the best picture of pure Amazonian culture. Life tends to be even more intertwined with the river, and the center of activity is the dock area in village after village. Even a brief stop in one of these towns provides an interesting window into the region's day-to-day life.

ILHA DO MARAJÓ

Soure (the islands largest town) is 82 km (49 miles) northwest of Belém.

With an area of roughly 49,600 square km (18,900 square miles), Ilha do Marajó is reputedly the world's largest river island. Its relatively unspoiled environment and abundant wildlife make it one of the few accessible places in the Amazon that feel isolated.

Ilha do Marajó's western half is dominated by dense forest and its eastern half by expansive plains, wetlands, and savannas. The island is ideal for raising cattle and water buffalo and has a half-million water buffalo and more than a million head of cattle; the human head count is about 250,000. According to local lore, the arrival of the water buffalo was an accident, the result of the wreck of a ship traveling from India to the Guianas. A day trip to a local ranch or a stay at Fazenda Carmo gives you a close-up look at the unique lifestyle of the island's people as well as the chance to view some of its animals, both domesticated and wild. You may see caiman, toco toucans, monkeys, and capybara, the world's largest rodent. Hiking is better in the dry season and boating in the rainy season.

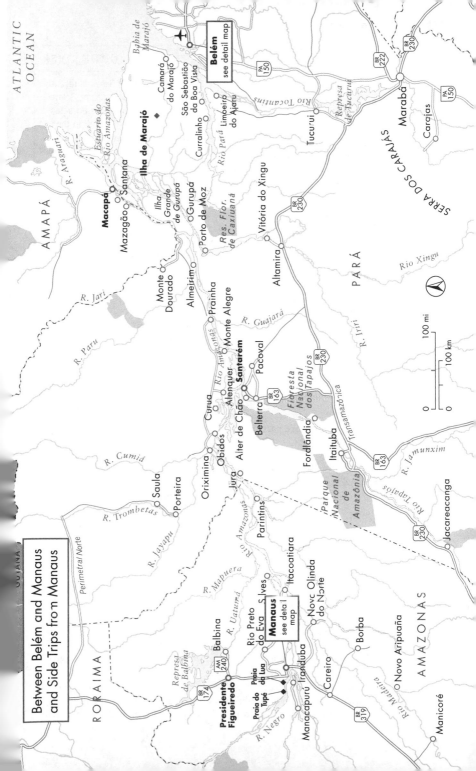

Between Belém and Manaus
and Side Trips from Manaus

ATLANTIC OCEAN

Estuário do Rio Amazonas

Bahia de Marajó

Belém see detail map

Camará do Marajó

São Sebastião da Boa Vista

Curralinho

Limoeiro do Ajaru

Ilha de Marajó

Rio Pará

AMAPÁ

Macapá

Mazagão Santana

Ilha Grande de Gurupá

Gurupá

Porto de Moz

Monte Dourado

Almeirim

R. Jari

R. Paru

R. Cumiá

Res. Flor. de Caxiuanã

Tucuruí

Represa de Tucuruí

Marabá

Carajás

SERRA DOS CARAJÁS

PARÁ

Rio Xingu

Vitória do Xingu

Altamira

R. Iriri

Prainha

Monte Alegre

R. Guajará

Santarém

Pacoval

Alenquer

Curuá

Rio Amazonas

Alter de Chão

Belterra

Floresta Nacional dos Tapajos

Fordlândia

Itaituba

Transamazônica

R. Jamunxim

Óbidos

Oriximiná

Juruá

Parintins

Rio Amazonas

Parque Nacional de Amazônia

Rio Tapajos

Jacareacanga

Saúba

Porteira

R. Trombetas

R. Jauapu

R. Mapuera

Itacoatiara

GUIANA

Perimetral Norte

RORAIMA

Balbina

Represa de Balbina

R. Uatumã

Rio Preto do Eva

Silves

Nova Olinda do Norte

Manaus see detail map

AMAZONAS

Presidente Figueiredo

Praia do Tupé

Praia da Lua

Manacapuru

Iranduba

Careiro

Borba

Novo Aripuanã

R. Negro

Rio Madeira

Manicoré

0 — 100 mi
0 — 100 km

PA 150

BR 222

BR 230

PA 150

BR 230

BR 230

BR 163

BR 230

BR 163

BR 174

AM 240

BR 319

Local cuisine invariably involves the water buffalo, whether in the form of a succulent steak or in cheeses and desserts made with buffalo milk. There's also an array of local fish to try. Bring cash in small bills, as breaking large ones can be a challenge and credit cards are rarely accepted. In a pinch, beer vendors can usually make change.

> **VAMPIRES IN THE RIVER**
>
> A new species of fish was recently discovered in the Amazon. Related to the candiru (which is attracted to urine and lodges itself in the urinal tract of a swimmer) this little catfish clamps onto the host and sucks its blood. Always wear snug swimming trunks and bikinis to keep the little critter from going any farther.

GETTING HERE AND AROUND
Arapari operates boats between Belém and Camará, on Ilha do Marajó, twice daily Monday through Saturday (R$43.44 round-trip in economy, and R$69.48 in the VIP section). A one-way trip from Belém to Ilha de Marajó takes two hours and costs about R$21 in economy class, and R$34 in the VIP section. A ferry takes cars to Ilha do Marajó.

On Ilha do Marajó one of the best ways to reach the beaches or to explore towns is to use a bike. Rates are R$2 an hour. You can find motorcycles to rent for R$60–R$70, though you'll have to ask around, since they're not advertised. The locals usually know who has equipment for rent.

ESSENTIALS
Boat Contacts Arapari ⊠ *Rua Siqueira Mendes 120, Cidade Velha, Belém* ☏ *091/3242–1870, 091/3241–4977.*

Visitor and Tour Information Iara Turismo. This company provides packages to Ilha de Marajó, and passages from Belém to the island; it also makes reservations for the Hotel Ilha de Marajó. ⊠ *Av. Gov. José Malcher 815, Ed. Palládium Center, Loja 8, Nazaré, Belém* ☏ *091/4006–3852* ⊕ *www.iaraturismo.com.br* ⊗ *Weekdays 8–6.* **Muiraquitã Turismo** ⊠ *Trav. São Pedro 566, Batista Campos, Belém* ☏ *091/4006–1999* ⊗ *Weekdays 9–5* ⌨ *Muiraquitã has a 3-day package to Ilha de Marajó with hotel and transportation included.*

SAFETY AND PRECAUTIONS
Wear sandals on the beach, as the sand is known to hide worms, known locally as *bichos-do-pé,* which can burrow into the soles of your feet and breed.

EXPLORING
Marajó is a huge island, but most human activity is clustered on its eastern coast, due to proximity to Belém. The western side of the island is beachless and floods during the rainy season.

Caju Una. The beach at Caju Una, a secluded fishing village, is breathtaking: a long strip of white sand with no vendors and few people. The village and its neighbor, Vila do Céu, are about a 45-minute drive (19 km/11 miles) north of Soure.

Joanes. Roughly 23 km (14 miles) southwest of Soure, Joanes was the island's first settlement. Poke around the ruins of a 16th-century Jesuit mission blown-up by the Portuguese when they expelled the order from the area, bask on a beach, and have a meal in one of the town's seafood restaurants. A taxi from Soure costs about R$60 round-trip.

Salvaterra. A quarter-mile boat ride across the narrow Rio Paracauari, Salvaterra is smaller than Soure but equally charming, and boats called *rabetas* cost R$1. Make sure you taste their sweet pineapples, which are grown locally.

Soure. With almost 20,000 people, Soure (20 miles north of Camará) is Ilha do Marajó's largest town. Its many palm and mango trees, simple but brightly painted houses, and shore full of fishing boats make it seem more Caribbean than Amazonian. Make sure to try the local white cheese, called *queijo de Marajó*, made from buffalo's milk.

BEACHES

Praia do Araruna. Coconut trees line the 8-km (5-mile) length of this beach, about 20 minutes (a 4-km/2-mile taxi ride) northeast of Soure. Here you may see flocks of scarlet ibis that appear out of nowhere. This beach tends to be much emptier than the nearby Praia da Barra, and you can swim in the small tributaries away from the main river. **Amenities:** none. **Best for:** solitude; walking; swimming; sunset.

Praia do Pesqueiro. Eight miles north of Soure, Praia do Pesqueiro is the island's most popular beach. When you stand on the white-sand expanse looking out at the watery horizon, the waves lapping at your feet, it's hard to believe you're not on the ocean. The beach has several thatch-roof restaurant-bars, making this an ideal place to spend an afternoon. You can travel here from Soure by taxi, by mototaxi (for one passenger), or by bike. Ask locals or hotel staff about bike rentals when you arrive in Soure. **Amenities:** food and drink. **Best for:** swimming; walking.

WHERE TO STAY

$$$ B&B/INN 🏨 **Fazenda Carmo.** As a guest in this small, antiques-filled farmhouse, you're privy to wonderful hospitality in a simple and rustic setting, and homestyle meals prepared with farm-fresh ingredients. **Pros:** a bed-and-breakfast experience; fresh food; uniquely decorated rooms. **Cons:** lacks basic creature comforts, like hot water, private bathrooms, and sometimes electricity. [$] *Rooms from: R$460* ✉ *Salvaterra* ☎ *091/3241–1019* 🌐 *www.carmocamara.com.br* 🛏 *8 rooms* 🍴 *All meals.*

$ HOTEL 🏨 **Hotel Ilha do Marajó.** Great verandas, solid creature comforts, and excellent facilities, including a lovely pool, make this hotel popular. **Pros:** airy hotel; immaculate rooms; excellent amenities. **Cons:** during the rainy season (December–June) mosquitoes infiltrate rooms. [$] *Rooms from: R$150* ✉ *Trv. 2 No. 10, Soure* ☎ *091/3741–1315* 🌐 *www.ilaraturismo.com.br* 🛏 *36 rooms.*

$ B&B/INN 🏨 **Pousada & Camping Boto.** This pousada offers lovely gardens, clean, modern rooms, friendly staff, and good food for a reasonable price. **Pros:** pleasant surroundings; well-kept rooms. **Cons:** the restaurant is open only on the weekend; the rooms are small. [$] *Rooms from: R$94* ✉ *Av. Alcindo Cacela, Salvaterra* ☎ *091/3765–1539* 🌐 *www.pousadaboto.com.br* 🛏 *9 rooms* 🍴 *Breakfast.*

SHOPPING

There are a few stores that sell sundries along Travessa 17 and Rua 3 in Soure.

Curtume Marajó. For sandals, belts, and other leather goods, head to Curtume Marajó, a five-minute walk from downtown Soure and next to the slaughterhouse. The workers here can give you a tour of the tannery. ⊠ *Rua Primeira 450, Bairro Novo, Soure* ☎ *091/8156–6818, 091/8870–3804* ⊕ *www.curtumeartcouromarajo.com.br.*

Núcleo Operário Social Marilda Nunes. Núcleo Operário Social Marilda Nunes has stalls with everything from marajoara pottery and woven items to T-shirts and liquor. In theory, the hours are daily 7–noon and 2:30–6; the reality may be something else entirely. ⊠ *Rua 3 between Trv. 18 and Trv. 19, Soure.*

MACAPÁ

330 km (198 miles) northwest of Belém.

Macapá is on the north channel of the Amazon Delta and, like Belém, was built by the Portuguese as an outpost. Today it's the capital of and the largest city in the Amapá State, with 150,000 people. It's also one of only five metropolises in the world that sit on the equator. Macapá's main lure is as a base for trips to see an extraordinary phenomenon—the *pororoca* (riptide).

GETTING HERE AND AROUND

Domestic carriers TAM, GOL and Azul-Trip have flights to Macapá. Aeroporto de Macapá is 4 km (2 miles) northwest of town. Take a taxi for the short, inexpensive ride.

Although Macapá is close to Ilha do Marajó's western side, most boats traveling to Macapá, including MACAMAZON and Bom Jesus, originate in Belém. Trips are 24 hours and you can get hammock space for around R$130, and a two-person cabin for R$400. Boats dock in the nearby port town of Santana, where taxis await. The fare to Macapá is R$67.50. Buses in Macapá cost R$2.30 and taxi rides around major tourist points cost around R$50 maximum.

ESSENTIALS

Airport Aeroporto de Macapá ⊠ *Rua Hildemar Maia s/n* ☎ *096/3223–2323.*

Boat Contacts Bom Jesus ⊠ *Saida da Avenida Bernardo Saião, Belém* ☎ *091/3272–1423.* **MACAMAZON** ☎ *091/3222–5604, 091/3031–5899* ⊕ *www.macamazon.com.br.*

Bus Contacts Terminal Rodoviário ⊠ *R. Barão de Mauá 156* ☎ *096/3251–2009.*

Tour Information Casa Francesa Viagens e Turismo. This tour operator offers trips to the capital city of Macapá, ecological tours, and two-day excursions to see the *pororoca* tidal bore (the most continuous wave in the world). ⊠ *Rua Independência 232* ☎ *096/3223–0889* ☾ *Weekdays 8–6, Sat. 8–noon.*

EXPLORING

Fortaleza de São José de Macapá. The top man-made attraction in Macapá also happens to be Brazil's largest fort. Completed in 1782 after 18 grueling years, Fortaleza de São José de Macapá is constructed of stones brought from Portugal as ship ballast. The well-preserved buildings house a visitor center, an art gallery, a meeting room, and a dance-music recital room. ⊠ *Rua Cândido Mendes s/n* ☎ *096/3212–5118* 💲 *Free* ⊗ *Tues.–Sun. 9–6.*

Marco Zero do Equador. The Marco Zero do Equador is a modest monument to the equatorial line that passes through town. Although it consists of only a tall, concrete sundial and a stripe of red paint along the equator, there's a distinct thrill to straddling the line or hopping between hemispheres. The soccer stadium across the street uses the equator as its centerline. From Macapá's outdoor bus terminal on Rua Antônio Coelho de Carvalho, a block from the fort, catch the bus labeled "b. novo/universidade" to the Marco Zero, a 20-minute ride. ⊠ *Av. Equatorial 0288* 💲 *Free* ⊗ *Daily 9–noon and 2–8.*

WHERE TO EAT AND STAY

$$$
BRAZILIAN

✕**Cantinho Baiano.** To shake up the conservative cuisine scene on Macapá, the Salvador-born owner of Cantinho Baiano began cooking specialties from Bahia State. These dishes, especially the seafood *moqueca* (fried fish in vegetable, coconut milk, and dendê oil), are not to be missed. The excellent river view, soft music, and colorfully clad waiters add to the ambience. 💲 *Average main: R$49* ⊠ *Rua Beira Rio 328, Santa Ines* ☎ *096/3223–4153* ⊗ *No dinner Sun.*

$
HOTEL

🏨**Hotel Atalanta.** Garishly pink and supported by towering Roman columns, there's nothing else in town that looks like the Hotel Atalanta. **Pros:** comfortable guest rooms; near shopping center. **Cons:** inconvenient location (10 blocks from the river in a residential neighborhood). 💲 *Rooms from: R$205* ⊠ *Av. Coaracy Nunes 1148, Centro* ☎ *096/3223–1612* ⊕ *www.atalantahotel.com.br* ⇗ *33 rooms, 3 suites* ⊙❘ *No meals.*

$
HOTEL

🏨**Macapá Hotel.** Partially obscured by palm trees, this three-story, white, colonial-style hotel is on well-manicured grounds, and comes with many amenities, including hard-to-find wireless Internet in the rooms. **Pros:** suites have balconies with exceptional river views. **Cons:** the interior is slightly worn; guest rooms aren't very impressive, despite modern amenities. 💲 *Rooms from: R$120* ⊠ *Av. Azarias Neto 17, Centro* ☎ *096/2101–1350* ⇗ *74 rooms, 2 suites* ⊙❘ *No meals.*

NIGHTLIFE AND THE ARTS

Macapá has a surprisingly active nightlife. If you like to bar-hop, head for the riverfront, where about 10 bars, some with music, are busy nearly every night.

Teatro das Bacabeiras. Most weekends and even sometimes during the week there's a play, a philharmonic concert, or a dance recital in the Teatro das Bacabeiras. ⊠ *Rua Cândido Mendes 368.*

SHOPPING

Although Macapá has a free-trade zone, neither the prices nor the selection is anything special. The largest concentration of shops is on Rua Cândido Mendes and Rua São José.

Associação dos Povos Indígenas do Tumucumaque (APITU). The Associação dos Povos Indígenas do Tumucumaque (APITU) has textiles, baskets, and other objects made by Amapá natives. ⊠ *Rua Francisco Azarias Silva C Neto 1* ☎ *96/3222–4329.*

Casa do Artesão. The Casa do Artesão sells works by local craftspeople and artists—from tacky souvenirs to exquisite paintings and pottery. ⊠ *Rua Francisco Azarias Neto* ☎ *096/3223–7545* ⊕ *www.ap.gov.br/amapa/site/index.jsp.*

SANTARÉM

836 km (518 miles) west of Belém; 766 km (475 miles) east of Manaus.

Since its founding in 1661, Santarém has ridden the crest of many an economic wave. First wood, then rubber, and more recently minerals have lured thousands of would-be magnates hoping to carve their fortunes from the jungle. The most noteworthy of these may have been Henry Ford. Although he never actually came to Brazil, Ford left his mark on this country in the form of two rubber plantations southwest of Santarém—Fordlândia and Belterra.

Today this laid-back city of 300,000 has a new boom on the horizon: soybeans. As highway BR 163 from Mato Grosso State improves (a federal government priority is to pave the rest of this road closer to Santarém), it's becoming the fastest, cheapest route for hauling soybeans from Santarém to Atlantic seaports for international export. To meet the global demand for soybeans and to make enormous profits, Brazilian farmers are clearing vast tracts of forest south of town and all along the way to Mato Grosso. With this new boom, Santarém may change drastically in coming years.

Santarém-based trips can take you into a little-known part of the Amazon, with few foreign visitors, to places where the ecosystem is greatly different from those around Belém and Manaus. The area receives much less rain than upstream or downstream, and has rocky hills, enormous wetlands, and the Amazon's largest clear-water tributary, the Rio Tapajós.

GETTING HERE AND AROUND

Domestic carriers TAM, GOL and Azul-Trip have flights to Santarém, and Santarém is easily accessible by air via Belém or Manaus. Aeroporto Maestro Wilson Fonseca is 14 km (23 miles) west of town, and buses and taxis from the airport are plentiful; a taxi ride costs around R$43.

MACAMAZON makes the two-day trip from Macapá to Santarém and onward to Manaus, R$70 for a hammock, and R$400 for a two-person cabin. The Belém to Santarém boat costs R$160 for a hammock, R$500 for a two-person cabin, and the ride takes three days. Sleeping arrangements are the same as on the Belém–Macapá route. Taxis are always at the docks in Santarém. The cost to any of the nearby hotels in town is less than R$10.

ESSENTIALS

Airport Aeroporto Maestro Wilson Fonseca ✉ *Rodovia Fernando Guilhon, Praça Eduardo Gomes s/n* ☎ *093/3522–4328.*

Boat Contacts MACAMAZON ☎ *091/3222–5604, 091/3031–5899.*

Visitor and Tour Information Santarém Tur. This tour company offers boat trips on the Amazon and Arapiuns rivers, day trips to Alter do Chão, and city tours. ✉ *Rua Adriano Pimentel 44, Central* ☎ *093/3522–4847, 093/3523–1836* 🌐 *www.santaremtur.com.br.* SANTUR ✉ *Rua Inácio Corrêa 22* ☎ *093/3523–2434* 🕓 *Weekdays 8–noon.*

EXPLORING

Centro Cultural João Fona (*João Fona Cultural Center*). To learn more about Santarém's culture and history, head for the Centro Cultural João Fona. This small museum has a hodgepodge of ancient ceramics, indigenous art, and colonial-period paintings and a library for more in-depth studies. It also houses the Secretary of Tourism. ✉ *Praça Barão de Santarém* ☎ *093/3523–2934* 🎟 *Free* 🕓 *Weekdays 8–5.*

Meeting of the Waters. In Santarém, for about 5½ miles, the beautiful, aquamarine Rio Tapajós floats next to the murkier waters of the Amazon, until the larger river finally absorbs it. Seeing the meeting of the waters here is breathtaking. It's best viewed from the **Praça Mirante do Tapajós**, on the hill in the center of town and just a few blocks from the waterfront.

WHERE TO EAT AND STAY

$ BRAZILIAN 🍴 **Mistura Brasileira.** Excellent sandwiches and a self-service buffet keep the Mistura Brasileira hopping. Try the beef fillet sandwich or the lasagna. The restaurant is housed in a hotel of the same name. [$] *Average main: R$18* ✉ *Travessa Quinze de Novembro, Centro* ☎ *093/3522–4819* 💳 *No credit cards* 🕓 *Daily 11–4.*

$ HOTEL 🏨 **Rio Dourado.** The reasonable rates at Rio Dourado get you simple but attractive accommodations, a convenient location, and friendly service. **Pros:** good prices; pleasant rooms. **Cons:** not many modern facilities. [$] *Rooms from: R$100* ✉ *Rua Floriano Peixoto 799* ☎ *093/3522–4021* 🛏 *30 rooms* 🍽 *Breakfast.*

NIGHTLIFE

Mascotinho. One of the best places in Santarém to get a drink is Mascotinho. It has passable food and is usually breezy since it's on the river. There's Brazilian pop music all nights except when it rains, since the seats are outside. ✉ *Rua Adriano Pimentel, Centro* ☎ *093/3523–2399* 🕓 *Daily 5 pm–midnight.*

SHOPPING

Loja Regional Muiraquitã. One of three artisan shops grouped together, Loja Regional Muiraquitã sells an incredible variety of regional items, including native musical instruments, locally mined minerals, and wood carvings. ✉ *Rua Senador Lameira Bittencourt 131* ☎ *093/3522–7164* 🕓 *Weekdays 9–7, Sat. 9–6* 🕓 *Closed Sun.*

Ford's Impossible Dream

Henry Ford spent millions of dollars to create two utopian company towns and plantations to supply his Model T cars with rubber tires. In 1927 he chose an area 15 hours southwest of Santarém. A year later all the materials necessary to build a small town and its infrastructure were transported by boat from Michigan to the Amazon. Small Midwestern-style houses were built row after row. *Seringueiros* (rubber tappers) were recruited with promises of good wages, health care, and schools for their children. Fordlândia was born. Despite all the planning, the scheme failed. The region's climate, horticulture, and customs weren't taken into account. Malaria and parasites troubled the workers; erosion and disease plagued the trees.

Convinced that he had learned valuable lessons from his mistakes, Ford refused to give up. In 1934 he established another community in Belterra, 48 km (30 miles) outside Santarém. Although some rubber was extracted from the plantation, production fell far short of original estimates. World War II caused further disruptions as German boats cruised the Brazilian coast and prevented food and supplies from arriving. Advances in synthetic rubber struck the final blow. Today some rusted trucks and electric generators, a few industrial structures, and many empty bungalows are all that remain of Ford's impossible dream.

BELÉM

The capital of Pará State, Belém is a river port of around 1.4 million people on the south bank of the Rio Guamá, 120 km (74 miles) from the Atlantic, and 2,933 km (1,760 miles) north of Rio de Janeiro. The Portuguese settled here in 1616, using it as a gateway to the interior and an outpost to protect the area from invasion by sea. Because of its ocean access, Belém became a major trade center. Like the upriver city of Manaus, it rode the ups and downs of the Amazon booms and busts. The first taste of prosperity was during the rubber era. Architects from Europe were brought in to build churches, civic palaces, theaters, and mansions, often using fine, imported materials. When Malaysia's rubber supplanted that of Brazil in the 1920s, wood and, later, minerals provided the impetus for growth.

Belém has expanded rapidly since the 1980s, pushed by the Tucuruvi hydroelectric dam (Brazil's second largest), the development of the Carajás mining region, and the construction of the ALBRAS/Alunorte bauxite and aluminum production facilities. Wood exports have risen, making Pará the largest wood-producing state in Brazil. As the forests are cut, pastures and cattle replace them, resulting in an increase in beef production. In 2000 the state government began construction of a bridge network connecting Belém to outlying cities. The resulting increase in commerce has spurred economic growth in the region, though there's still considerable poverty and high unemployment.

In the city, high-rise apartments are replacing colonial structures. Fortunately, local governments have launched massive campaigns to preserve the city's rich heritage while promoting tourist-friendly policies. This effort has earned state and federal government funds to restore historical sites in the Belém area. Tourism is on the rise in the city and is becoming increasingly important for the city's economic well-being.

GETTING HERE AND AROUND

There are several daily flights to Belém from Rio and São Paulo. TAM offers discounted flights most weekends, and GOL has frequent

> ### A BEAR IN THE AMAZON
>
> Having lost a presidential election to Woodrow Wilson in November 1912, Teddy Roosevelt decided to drown his sorrows in the Amazon River. He traveled with an expedition of renowned scientists and Amazon explorers to take a closer look at the River of Doubt (Rio de Duvida), an unexplored tributary. Though Roosevelt had always been an intrepid adventurer, the Amazon almost brought him to his end. The expedition lacked meat, lost boats in the whirling river, and was ravaged by disease.

promotions. Azul-Trip flies to Belem from Campinas. All airlines arrive at the Aeroporto Internacional Val-de-Cans, 11 km (7 miles) northwest of the city. Varig and TAM sometimes offer direct flights from Miami. TAM and GOL fly regularly from Rio, São Paulo, Brasília, and Manaus.

During the Brazilian summer flights to Belém can be cheap since this is the rainy season and most flock to the beaches instead. If time is not an issue, there are daily buses from Rio and São Paulo on Transbrasilia (45 hours).

Most long-distance ships arrive and depart from the Terminal Hidroviário (Ave. Marechal Hermes). MACAMAZON and Bom Jesus (based in Macapá) have ships and standard riverboats to Macapá, Santarém, Manaus, and other places. The Belém to Santarem boat on MACAMAZON takes three days and costs R$160 for a hammock, and R$500 for a two-person cabin. The Belém to Manaus boat on MACAMAZON takes five days and costs R$250 for a hammock and R$1,000 for a two-person cabin. A trip to Ilha de Marajo from Belém takes two hours and costs R$21.72. From Belém to Macapá the boat takes 24 hours and the hammock costs R$130, and R$400 for a two-person cabin.

Belém's local bus service is safe (though you should keep an eye on your belongings) and comprehensive, but a little confusing. Ask a resident for guidance. The bus costs R$2.20.

ESSENTIALS

Airport Information Aeroporto Internacional Val-de-Cans ⊠ *Av. Julio Cesár s/n* ☎ *091/3210–6000, 091/3257–3780.*

Boat Contacts Bom Jesus ☎ *091/3272–1423, 091/3223–2342.* **MACAMAZON** ⊠ *Boul Castilhos França 744, Campina* ☎ *091/3222–5604, 091/3228–0774.*

Bus Contacts Rodoviário São Brás ⊠ *Praça do Operário, São Brás* ☎ *091/3266–2625.*

Taxi Contacts Coopertáxi ☎ 091/3257–1041, 091/3257–1720.

Visitor and Tour Information Sightseeing boats leave from Estação das Docas Ave. Marechal Hermes, and from behind Hotel Beira Rio on Rua Bernardo Saião, 20 minutes southeast of town near the Federal University.

Amazon Star Tours ✉ *Rua Henrique Gurjão 210, Reduto* ☎ *091/3241–8624* ⊕ *www.amazonstar.com.br* ☞ *Wide range of tours and transport options, trips on boats, and to different islands. They also have excursions to Ilha de Marajo (2 days, R$400; 3 days, R$550).* ◐ *Weekdays 8–6, Sat. 8–noon.* **BELEMTUR** ✉ *Av. Governador José Malcher 38, Palacete Bolonha, Nazaré* ☎ *091/3283– 4865* ⊕ *www.belem.pa.gov.br/belemtur* ◐ *Weekdays 8–noon and 2–6.* **Lusotur** ✉ *Av. Brás de Aguiar 471, Nazaré* ☎ *091/3323–1100* ⊕ *www.lusotur.com.br* ☞ *City tours and ecotours.* **PARATUR** ✉ *Praça Maestro Waldemar Henrique s/n, Reduto* ☎ *091/3212–0575, 091/3212–0669* ⊕ *www.paraturismo.pa.gov. br* ◐ *Weekdays 8–6.* **Valeverde Turismo** ✉ *Av. Alcindo Cacela 104, Cremação* ☎ *091/3218–7333* ⊕ *www.valeverdeturismo.com.br* ☞ *They offer city tours in Belém (3 hrs), tours to the Island of Marajó, tours to Salinas (12 hrs), tours to Mosquiero, and to ecological sites in the city.*

SAFETY AND PRECAUTIONS
In Belém watch out for pickpockets everywhere, but especially at Ver-o-Peso, on Avenida President Vargas, and in Comércio. Avoid walking alone at night or on poorly lighted streets, and don't wear jewelry, especially gold.

EXPLORING

Belém is more than just a jumping-off point for the Amazon. It has several good museums and restaurants and lots of extraordinary architecture. Restored historic sites along the waterfront provide areas to walk, eat, and explore. Several distinctive buildings—some with Portuguese *azulejos* (tiles) and ornate iron gates—survive along the downtown streets and around the Praça Frei Caetano Brandão, in the Cidade Velha (Old City). East of here, in the Nazaré neighborhood, colorful colonial structures mingle with new ones housing trendy shops.

CIDADE VELHA
Cidade Velha (Old City) is the oldest residential part of Belém. Here you'll find colonial houses made of clay walls and tiled roofs, the tallest being only three stories high. However, there are more and more 15-floor apartment buildings invading from the north. Much of Cidade Velha is middle-income with a variety of hardware, auto-parts, and fishing-supply stores. On its northwestern edge, the Forte Presépio lies along the bank of the Rio Guamá.

TOP ATTRACTIONS
Casa das Onze Janelas. At the end of the 18th century, sugar baron Domingos da Costa Barcelar built the neoclassical House of Eleven Windows as his private mansion. Today Barcelar's mansion is a gallery for contemporary arts, including photography and visiting expositions. The view from the balcony is impressive. Take a walk through the courtyard and imagine scenes of the past. This is where the aristocracy took tea and watched

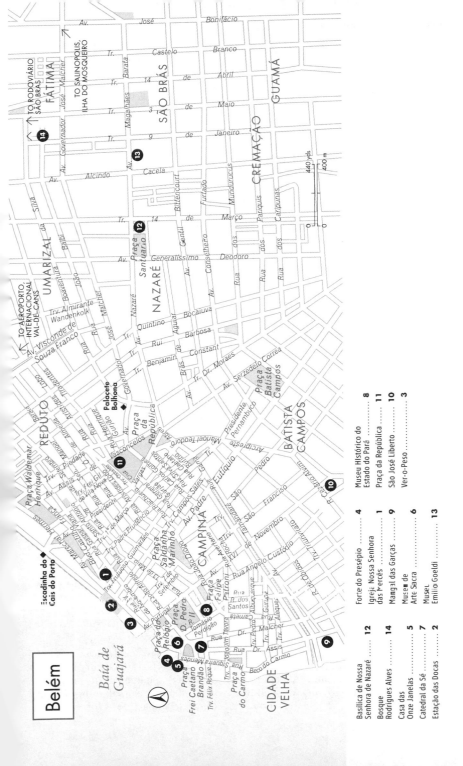

Belém

Baía de Guajará

CIDADE VELHA

REDUTO

UMARIZAL

FÁTIMA

SÃO BRÁS

NAZARÉ

CREMAÇÃO

GUAMÁ

CAMPINA

BATISTA CAMPOS

↑ TO RODOVIÁRIO SÃO BRÁS

← TO SALINÓPOLIS, ILHA DO MOSQUEIRO

↖ TO AEROPORTO, INTERNACIONAL, VAL-DE-CANS

440 yds

400 m

over the docks as slaves unloaded ships from Europe and filled them with sugar and rum. ✉ *Praça Frei Caetana Brandão, Cidade Velha* 🕾 *91/4009–8821* ▣ *R$2, free Tues.* ⊙ *Tues.–Sun. 10–4.*

Estação das Docas. Next to Ver-o-Peso market on the river, three former warehouses have been artfully converted into a commercial–tourist area. All have one wall of floor-to-ceiling glass that provides a full river view when dining or shopping. The first is a convention center with a cinema and art exhibits. The second has shops and kiosks selling crafts and snacks, and the third has a variety of restaurants

---

DANCE THE LAMBADA

This musical form, popular among Brazilians in the '80s and early '90s, originated in the state of Pará in the 1970s. The first lambada was composed by the Pinduca, who had written a number of carimbós. The music swept the North and Northeast, and even became popular outside of the country. Two American movies popularized the genre but were made only after the craze began to wane—*Lambada* (1990) and *The Forbidden Dance* (1990).

---

and bars. The buildings are air-conditioned and connected by glass-covered walkways and contain photos and artifacts from the port's heyday. A stroll outside along the docks provides a grand view of the bay. Tourist boats arrive and depart at the dock, making it a good place to relax both day and night. ✉ *Ave. Boulevard Castilho França s/n, Campina* 🕾 *091/3212–5525* ▣ *Free* ⊙ *Noon–midnight or later, Sat. open at 10 am.*

FAMILY
Fodor'sChoice
★
Forte do Presépio (*Fort of the Crèche*). Founded January 12, 1616, this fort is considered Belém's birthplace. From here the Portuguese launched conquests of the Amazon and watched over the bay. The fort's role in the region's defense is evidenced by massive English- and Portuguese-made cannons pointing out over the water. They are poised atop fort walls that are 3 yards thick in places. Recent renovations unearthed more than two-dozen cannons, extensive military middens from the moat, and native Tupi artifacts. A small museum of prefort indigenous cultures is at the entrance. Just outside the fort, cobblestone walkways hug the breezy waterfront. ✉ *Praça Frei Caetano Brandão, Cidade Velha* 🕾 *091/4009–8828* ▣ *R$2, Tues. free* ⊙ *Tues.–Fri. 10–6, weekends 10–8.*

FAMILY
Mangal das Garças. City beautification efforts to increase tourism and encourage environmental conservation led to the creation of the Mangrove of the Egrets. A great place for a short stroll, it has an aviary, a tower with a view, a navigation museum, a boardwalk leading to a lookout over the Rio Guamá, a live butterfly exhibit, ponds with aquatic plants, food vendors, a gift shop, and a restaurant. ✉ *Praça Carneiro da Rocha, Cidade Velha* 🕾 *091/3242–5052* ⊕ *www.mangalpa.com.br* ▣ *R$9 admission to interior facilities, Tues. free* ⊙ *Weekdays 9–5.*

Museu de Arte Sacra. A guided tour (call 48 hours in advance to reserve an English-speaking docent) begins in the early-18th-century baroque Igreja de Santo Alexandre (St. Alexander's Church), which is distinguished by intricate woodwork on its altar and pews that they taught the Native Indians to do. The church was abandoned for 40 years, resulting in much of the wood ceiling being lost to termites and water damage, but the areas that were restored are spectacular. On the second half of the tour you see the museum's collection of religious sculptures and paintings. ⊠ *Praça Frei Caetano Brandão, Cidade Velha* ☎ *091/4009–8805* ⌨ *R$4, Tues. free* ⊙ *Tues.–Sun. 10–6, holidays 9–1.*

Museu Histórico do Estado do Pará. The Pará State Muscum is in the sumptuous Palácio Lauro Sodré (circa 1771), an Antônio Landi creation with Venetian and Portuguese elements. Consistently outstanding visiting exhibits are on the first floor; the second floor contains the permanent collection of furniture and paintings. ⊠ *Praça Dom Pedro II, Cidade Velha* ☎ *091/4009–8805* ⌨ *R$2, Tues. free* ⊙ *Tues.–Fri. 10–6, weekends 10–2* ⊙ *Closed Mon.*

Fodor's Choice ★ **Ver-o-Peso.** Its name literally meaning "see the weight" (a throwback to the time when the Portuguese weighed everything entering or leaving the region), this market is a hypnotic confusion of colors and voices. Vendors hawk tropical fruits, regional wares, and an assortment of tourist kitsch. Most interesting are the *mandingueiras,* women who claim they can solve any problem with "miracle" jungle roots and charms for the body and soul. They sell jars filled with animal eyes, tails, and even heads, as well as herbs, each with its own legendary power. The sex organs of the pink river dolphin are a supposedly unrivaled cure for romantic problems. In the fish market you get an up-close look at pirarucu, the Amazon's most colorful fish and the world's second-largest freshwater species. Look for bizarre armored catfish species, such as the *tamuatá* and the huge *piraiba.* Across the street is a small arched entrance to the municipal meat market. Duck in and glance at the French-style pink-and-green-painted ironwork, imported from Britain. Be sure to visit Ver-o-Peso before noon, when most vendors leave. It opens around 6 am. Leave your jewelry at home and beware of pickpockets. ⊠ *Av. Castilhos França s/n, Comércio.*

WORTH NOTING

NEED A BREAK?

Cairu. The many regional flavors at ice-cream shop Cairu include some unique to the Amazon, such as *taperebá, graviola,* and *cajá* (cashew fruit), as well as the more familiar *cocó* (coconut), mango, and chocolate. Juices, sandwiches, and soft drinks are also served. ⊠ *Estação das Docas, Blvd. Castilhos França s/n, Campina.*

Catedral da Sé. In 1755 Bolognese architect Antônio José Landi, whose work can be seen throughout the city, completed this cathedral's construction on the foundations of an older church. Carrara marble adorns the rich interior, which is an interesting mix of baroque, colonial, and neoclassical styles. The high altar was a gift from Pope Pius IX. ⊠ *Praça Dom Frei Caetano Brandão s/n, Cidade Velha* ☎ *091/3241–6282, 091/3223–2362* ⌨ *Free.*

Igreja Nossa Senhora das Mercês (*Our Lady of Mercy Church*). Another of Belém's baroque creations, this church is notable for its pink color and convex facade. The shell dates from the 17th century, and the rest attributed to Antônio Landi's restoration. It's part of a complex that includes the Convento dos Mercedários, which has served both as a convent and a prison, though not simultaneously. ✉ *Gaspar Viana e Frutuosa Guimarães, Comércio* ☎ *091/3212–3102* ➰ *Free.*

São José Liberto. Belém's old prison began as a monastery, became a brewery, then an armory, a nunnery, and eventually the final stop for many criminals. Today's museums and garden are an attempt to redeem long years of tortuous conditions and bloody rebellions. Behind the enormously thick walls are a gem museum, a prison museum, and several shops. ✉ *Praça Amazonas, Jurunas* ☎ *091/3344–3500* ⊕ *www.espacosaojoseliberto. blogspot.com* ➰ *R$4* ⊙ *Tues.–Sat. 10–10, Sun. 3–10.*

NAZARÉ

Just east of the Cidade Velha, Nazaré's mango tree–lined streets create the sensation of walking through tunnels. Among the historic buildings there's a tremendous variety of pastel colors and European styles. Many of the newer buildings house elegant shops.

TOP ATTRACTIONS

Fodor's Choice
★

Basílica de Nossa Senhora de Nazaré. It's hard to miss this opulent Roman-style basilica—not only does it stand out visually, but there's an enormous *samauma* tree (kapok variety) filled with screeching white-winged parakeets in the plaza out front. The basilica was built in 1908 as an addition to a 1774 chapel, on the site where a *caboclo* (rural, riverside dweller) named Placido is said to have seen a vision of the Virgin in the early 1700s. The basilica's ornate interior is constructed entirely of European marble and contains elaborate mosaics, detailed stained-glass windows, and intricate bronze doors. ✉ *Praça Justo Chermont, Nazaré* ☎ *091/4009–8436, 091/4009–8407 museum* ➰ *Free.*

FAMILY
Museu Emílio Goeldi. Founded by a naturalist and a group of intellectuals in 1866, this complex contains one of the Amazon's most important research facilities. Its museum has an extensive collection of Indian artifacts, including the distinctive and beautiful pottery of the Marajó Indians, known as *marajoara*. A small forest has reflecting pools with giant *vitória régia* water lilies. But the true highlight is the collection of Amazon wildlife, including manatees, anacondas, macaws, sloths, and monkeys. ✉ *Av. Magalhães Barata 376, São Braz* ☎ *091/3219–3300* ⊕ *www.museu-goeldi.br* ➰ *Park R$1.50 or R$4.50 for the park, aquarium, and museum together* ⊙ *Park Tues.–Sun. 9–5, museum and acquarium Tues.–Sun. 9–12 and 2–5.*

WORTH NOTING

FAMILY
Bosque Rodrigues Alves. In 1883 this 40-acre plot of rain forest was designated an ecological reserve. Nowadays it has an aquarium and two amusement parks as well as natural caverns, a variety of animals (some in the wild), and mammoth trees. ✉ *Av. Almirante Barroso 2453, Marco* ☎ *091/3277–1112* ➰ *R$2 for adults, R$1 for students and children* ⊙ *Tues.–Sun. 8–5.*

Praça da República. At this square you'll find a large statue that commemorates the proclamation of the Republic of Brazil, an amphitheater, and several French-style iron kiosks. On Sunday vendors, food booths, and musical groups create a festival-like atmosphere that attracts crowds of locals. ✉ *Bounded by Av. Presidente Vargas, Trv. Osvaldo Cruz, and Av. Assis de Vasconcelos.*

CLOSE UP

Tales from the Mist

The immense Amazon region is fertile ground not only for flora and fauna but also for legends, which are an integral part of local culture and are remarkably consistent throughout the region.

One particularly creepy legend is that of Curupira, who appears as a nude and savage indigenous child whose feet are turned backward. He is said to lure people into the jungle, causing them to become irreversibly lost. As the story goes, white men cut off his feet before killing him; a god sewed Curupira's feet on backward and returned him to the forest to exact revenge. Some people claim you can solicit Curupira's help for hunting and crop failures. As payment, you must bring him tobacco, matches, and a bottle of liquor—the latter of which he will down in one swig to seal the pact. If you ever tell anyone about the agreement, Curupira will hunt you down and stab you to death with his long, sharp fingernails.

Several tales explain the origins of important fruits and vegetables. Guaraná, for example, was the name of a young child beloved by all. As the story goes, he was killed by the jealous god Jurupari, who disguised himself as a snake. Lightning struck as the village gathered around Guaraná's body and wept. At that moment the lightning god, Tupã, ordered the villagers to bury the child's eyes. The *guaraná* fruit (which actually resembles eyes) sprouted from the burial spot.

In a legend explaining the origins of the *açaí* fruit (a rich, dark-purple fruit endemic to the Amazon), the chief of a starving tribe ordered all babies to be sacrificed to end the famine. The chief's daughter, Iaça, had a beautiful baby. Before its sacrifice, she found the child holding a palm tree, and then he suddenly vanished. The tree then became full of açaí (which is Iaça spelled backward), from which a wine was made that saved the tribe and ended the sacrifices. To this day, Amazonians call the cold soup made from the fruit *vinho* (wine).

The legend of the native water flower *vitória régia* begins with a beautiful girl who wished to become a star in the heavens. She trekked to the highest point in the land and tried in vain to touch the moon. Iaci—the god of the moon—was awed by the girl's beauty. He knew that a mortal could never join the astral kingdom, so he decided to use his powers to immortalize the girl on earth instead. He transformed her into a stunning flower with an alluring scent. Realizing that he needed something fitting to help display this "star," he stretched a palm leaf and created a lily pad, and thus the vitória régia came to be.

WHERE TO EAT

$ BRAZILIAN

🍴 **Boteco das Onze.** In the Casa das Onze Janelas, the Boteca das Onze has thick stone and mortar walls stylishly adorned with antique instruments. The full bar has a complete drink menu with one of the largest selections of wines in the city. The patio has a view of the garden and river. A house favorite is the seafood platter for two. The all-you-can-eat lunch buffet is a good deal, and includes dessert but not drinks. [$] *Average main: R$28* ✉ *Praça Frei Caetano Brandão, Cidade Velha* ☎ *091/3224–8599, 091/3241–8255* 🌐 *botecodasonze.com.br* ⏲ *No lunch Mon.*

$ BRAZILIAN 🍴**Casa do Caldo.** Eight soups (out of 36) are featured every night for family dining in the "House of Soup." One price (R$20) covers the rodizio of unlimited soup, toast, and dessert porridge. Try the crab soup with cilantro and the cow's-foot soup. It's air-conditioned and casual, with superb service. [$] *Average main: R$11* ✉ *Rua Diogo Moia 266, Umarizal* ☎ *091/3224–5744* 🌐 *www.casadocaldo.com.br.*

BIBLICAL NAMES

Belém is the Portuguese name for Bethlehem. One of its main neighborhoods, Nazaré, is Portuguese for Nazareth. The city was renamed three times before it assumed its current name: Feliz Lusitânia, Santa Maria do Grão Pará, Santa Maria de Belé do Grão Para.

$ ITALIAN 🍴**Famiglia Sicilia.** From gnocchi to ravioli, flawless preparation of the basics distinguishes this Italian eatery from others. Everyone in town knows this, so reservations are a good idea—particularly on weekends. Be sure to try one of their 600 varieties of wine on offer. Don't leave without ordering a scrumptious *dolce Paula* (ice cream–and–brownie dessert). [$] *Average main: R$29* ✉ *Av. Conselheiro Furtado 1420, Batista Campos* ☎ *091/4008–0001* 🌐 *www.domgiuseppe.com.br* ✍ *Reservations essential* 🕓 *Mon.–Sat. 6:30–midnight and Sun. 11:30–4.*

$$ BRAZILIAN 🍴**Garrote.** A traditional *churrascaria* (Brazilian barbecue restaurant), Garrote serves up as much grilled and roasted beef, pork, and other meat as you can eat for a reasonable fixed price. A salad buffet and dessert are also included. The service is excellent. [$] *Average main: R$42* ✉ *Av. Governador José Malcher 258, Centro* ☎ *091/3225–2776* 🌐 *www.churrascariagarrote.com.br* 🕓 *Daily 11–4 and 7–10:30* 🕓 *No dinner Sun.*

$ BRAZILIAN Fodor's Choice ★ 🍴**Lá em Casa.** Regional cuisine, prepared to exacting specifications, has earned Lá em Casa its stellar reputation and made it a favorite of the locals. Consider trying Belém's premier dish, *pato no tucupi* (duck in a yellow manioc–herb sauce served with the mildly intoxicating *jambu* leaf). Crabs on the half-shell covered with *farofa* (finely ground manioc fried in margarine) is another good choice, as is açaí sorbet for dessert. Sitting on the patio overlooking the river and fringed by tropical vines and bromeliads, you feel like you're dining in the middle of the forest. [$] *Average main: R$25* ✉ *Estação das Docas, Boul Castilhos França 707* ☎ *091/3212–5588* 🌐 *www.laemcasa.com* 🕓 *Sun.–Wed. noon–midnight, Thurs.–Sat. noon–2 am.*

$$ BRAZILIAN 🍴**Remanso do Bosque.** The hippest restaurant in Belém, Remanso do Bosque specializes in local Paranese cuisine with a contemporary twist. They use fish caught in the nearby Amazonian rivers and varieties of *farofa,* a fried ground manioc topping. Try the excellent tasting menu for such dishes as baby fish cooked over coals with a fantastically crunchy açaí farofa, and smoked pirarucu fish served with bananas. Finish with the tangy Amazonian fruit *bacuri* in a puree served with local honey and pollen. If you'd rather order from the menu, you can't go wrong with the pork pancetta cooked in a wood stove and served with a molasses sauce and farofa. [$] *Average main: R$45* ✉ *Av. Rômulo Maiorana com Perebebui 2350, Marco* ☎ *091/3347–2829* 🌐 *www.restauranteremanso.com.br* 🕓 *Tues.–Sat. 12–3 and 7–11, Sun. 12–3* 🕓 *Closed Mon.*

WHERE TO STAY

$$ **Golden Tulip Belém.** This four-star hotel has sleek but understated
HOTEL rooms, with all the amenities one would want. **Pros:** great furnish-
ings; friendly staff; free parking and Wi-Fi. **Cons:** tiny lobby; small
bathrooms. $ *Rooms from: R$292* ⊠ *Travessa Dom Romualdo de*
Seixas 1560, Umarizal ☎ *091/3366-7575* ⊕ *www.goldentulipbelem.*
com ↩ *127 rooms* ⫯⃝ *Breakfast.*

$$$ **Hilton International Belém.** Centrally located on the Praça da República,
HOTEL this Hilton is very similar to the others—comfortable rooms, good
facilities, and lots of amenities. **Pros:** great location; excellent facilities. **Cons:** rooms don't have free Internet and the Wi-Fi signal is weak;
noisy central air-conditioning. $ *Rooms from: R$380* ⊠ *Av. Presidente*
Vargas 882 ☎ *091/4006-7000 in U.S.* ⊕ *www.belem.hilton.com* ↩ *361*
rooms ⫯⃝ *No meals.*

$ **Hotel Grão Pará.** The oldest hotel in town may have few amenities,
HOTEL but it makes up for this with low prices and modern, clean rooms with
marble sinks in the bathrooms. **Pros:** inexpensive hotel in a central location; free Internet. **Cons:** no-frill rooms; simply furnished. $ *Rooms*
from: R$120 ⊠ *Av. Presidente Vargas 718* ☎ *091/3321-2121* ⊕ *www.*
hotelgraopara.com.br ↩ *150 rooms* ⫯⃝ *Breakfast.*

$ **Hotel Regente.** This hotel has excellent service and a prime central
HOTEL location for a reasonable price. **Pros:** lovely views; great location.
Cons: there is a charge for Internet access in the rooms. $ *Rooms from:*
R$238 ⊠ *Av. Governador José Malcher 485, Nazaré* ☎ *091/3181-5000*
⊕ *www.hotelregente.com.br* ↩ *219 rooms* ⫯⃝ *Breakfast.*

$ **Itaoca Hotel.** It comes as no surprise that this small, reasonably priced
HOTEL hotel has the highest occupancy rate in town: It's in the center of town,
on the city's main street and right next to the Estação das Docas and
Ver-o-Peso. **Pros:** inexpensive; great views; well-equipped rooms; free
Wi-Fi. **Cons:** outdated furnishings. $ *Rooms from: R$138* ⊠ *Av. Presi-*
dente Vargas 132, Centro ☎ *091/4009-2400, 091/4009-2402* ⊕ *www.*
hotelitaoca.com.br ↩ *32 rooms, 4 suites* ⫯⃝ *Breakfast.*

NIGHTLIFE AND THE ARTS

NIGHTLIFE

Umarizal is Belém's liveliest neighborhood at night, with a good selection of bars, clubs, and restaurants. Other nightlife hot spots are scattered around the city.

BARS

Água Doce. This busy bar specializes in *cachaça* (Brazilian sugarcane
liquor). Listed on its menu are 182 kinds of cachaça and 605 different drinks, along with appetizers and entrées. Softly lighted with lots
of tables, this place gets busy on weekends. ⊠ *Rua Diogo Móia 283*
☎ *091/3222-3383* ⊘ *Tues.-Sat. 5 pm-3 am.*

Bar Casa do Gilson. This bar has excellent live choro and samba on Friday
from 8 pm to midnight and also on weekends from midday to midnight.
Lunch is served weekends as well. ⊠ *Travessa Padre Eutíquio 3172,*
Condor ☎ *091/3272-7306.*

Cosanostra Caffé. If you prefer music in a relaxed environment, head to Cosanostra Caffé, which has live MPB (*música popular brasileira*) and jazz. Catering to locals and expatriate foreigners alike, it serves food from an extensive menu until late in the night. ✉ *Travessa Benjamin Constant 1499, Nazaré* ☎ *091/3241–1068* ⏱ *Daily 12 pm–3 am.*

SATERÊ MAUÉ

An indigenous language from the Amazon, *saterê Maué* has contributed many words to Brazil's language. For example, the root word for fish is "pira." The fish species that use this indigenous root are: piramutaba, piranambu, piranha, pirapitinha, and pirarara.

Roxy Bar. This bar tops nearly everyone's list of hip places to sip a drink and people-watch. ✉ *Av. Senador Lemos 231, Umarizal* ☎ *091/3224–4514* ⊕ *www.roxybar.com.br.*

THE ARTS
Estação das Docas. Live music is played nightly at the Estação das Docas. Weekday shows usually consist of acoustic singers and/or guitarists. On weekends rock, jazz, and MPB bands play on a suspended stage that moves back and forth on tracks about 8 meters (25 feet) above patrons of the microbrewery and surrounding restaurants. ✉ *Ave. Boulevard Castilho França s/n, Campina* ☎ *091/3212–5525* ⊕ *www. estacaodasdocas.com.br.*

SHOPPING

Indigenous-style arts and crafts are popular souvenir items in Belém. Some of them, however, can create problems with customs when returning home. Import regulations of Australia, Canada, New Zealand, the United Kingdom, and the United States strictly prohibit bringing endangered species (dead or alive) into those countries, and the fines can be hefty. Nonendangered wildlife and plant parts are also illegal to import, though there are some exceptions. Wooden and woven items, for example, are usually not a problem. Avoid headdresses and necklaces of macaw feathers and caiman teeth, and go for the marajoara pottery and the tropical fruit preserves (pack them carefully). The main shopping street in Belém is Avenida Presidente Vargas, especially along the Praca da Republica. In addition, there are many boutiques and specialty shops in Nazaré.

SHOPPING AREAS AND MALLS
Icoaraci. A riverside town 18 km (11 miles) northeast of Belém, Icoaraci is a good place to buy marajoara pottery. ⊕ *www.anisioartesanato.com.br.*

Shopping Patio Belem. To shop in air-conditioning, head for the upscale Shopping Patio Belem, a mall in the truest sense of the word. There are 198 stores, including four department stores—Y. Yamada, Visão, Lojas Americanas and C&A—with a bit of everything. The mall also includes a multiscreen cinema, banks, a food court, and currency exchange shops. ✉ *Trv. Padre Eutíquio 1078, Batista Campos* ☎ *091/4008–5800* ⊕ *www.patiobelem.com.br* ⏱ *Mon.–Sat. 10–10, Sun. 2–10.*

11

MARKETS

Praça da República. This town square is busy only on Sunday, when *barracas* (small shops) pop up to sell paintings, snacks, artisanal items, and regional foods. You can watch the action from a park bench while sipping a cold coconut or eating a slice of *cupuaçú* cake. It's a local favorite for morning family strolls. ✉ *Bounded by Av. Presidente Vargas, Trv. Osvaldo Cruz, and Av. Assis de Vasconcelos, Nazaré.*

SPECIALTY SHOPS

Casa Amazônia Artesanatos. Though small, Casa Amazônia Artesanatos is packed with natural soaps, regional fruit preserves, pottery, and wood carvings. ✉ *Av. President Vargas 512, Nazaré* 🕾 *091/3225–0150.*

> ### CARIMBÓ
>
> The carimbó is an indigenous dance and music form, originating in Belém and the island of Marajó that later gave way to the rhythms of the lambada. This music is steeped in the sounds of the Amazon and its folklore, but has also been influenced by African culture. It's accompanied by wooden tambourines. During the dance the woman passes her skirt over the man.

São José Liberto. São José Liberto is a combination museum (⇨ *Cidade Velha in Exploring Belém, above*) and high-price jewelry and craft shops with Amazonian wares of gold, amethyst, and wood; pottery; and seeds and plant fibers. ✉ *Praça Amazonas, Jurunas* ⊕ *espacosaojoseliberto. blogspot.com* 🕙 *Tues.–Sat. 10–10, Sun. 3–10.*

SIDE TRIPS FROM BELÉM

If you're interested in beaches, fishing, forests, wildlife, or rural communities, there are some great spots to visit beyond the sidewalks of Belém. Buses and boats can take you to all of these spots and there's always a taxi driver willing to take you where you want to go.

ILHA DO MOSQUEIRO

60 km (36 miles) from Belém; about 2 hours by bus or car.

Most Belém residents head for one of 18 beaches on Mosqueiro Island, along the Rio Pará. Mosqueiro is easily accessible by car or intermunicipal bus Beira-Dão.

GETTING HERE AND AROUND

Beira-Dão buses leave every half hour from Belém and cost R$4. To reach the beaches at Ilha Mosqueiro from Belém, take BR 316 and then head north on PA 191.

ESSENTIALS

Bus Contacts Beira-Dão ✉ *Travessa Vileta 2110, Belém* 🕾 *091/3771– 1207.* **Estação Rodoviária Arthur Pires Teixeira** ✉ *Rua Juvênia Silva* 🕾 *91/3771–3624.*

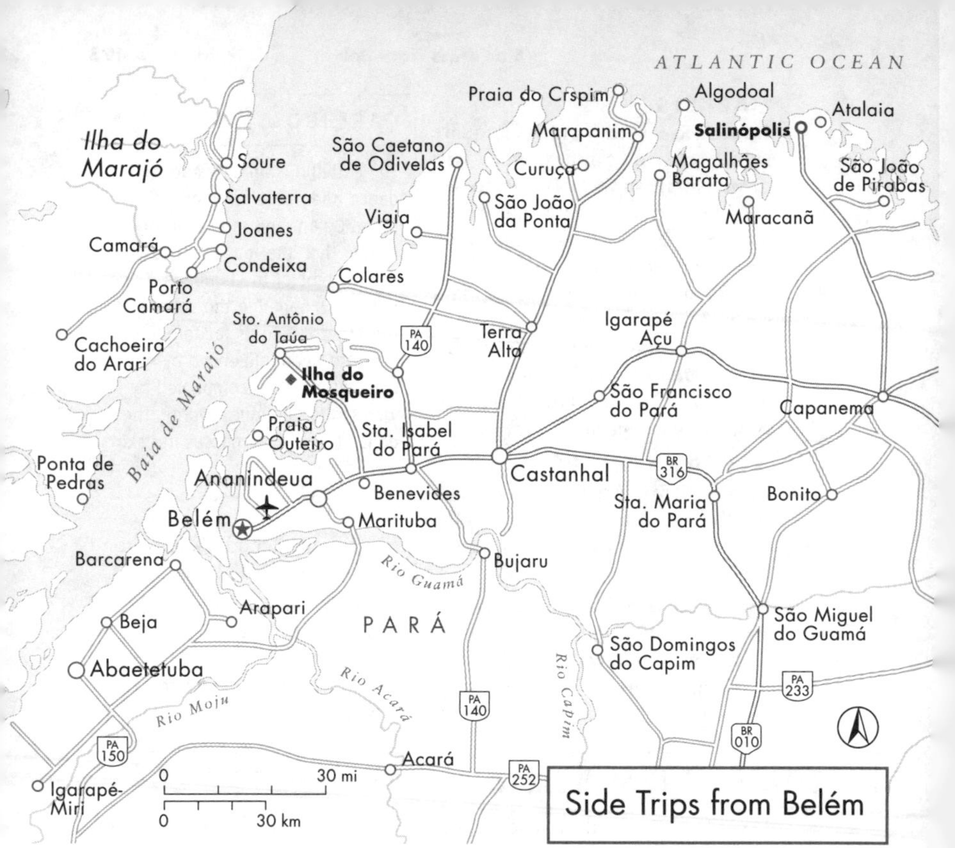

BEACHES

One of Ilha do Mosqueiro's most popular beaches, **Praia Farol,** is often crowded because it's close to **Vila,** the island's hub. At low tide you can walk to tiny, rocky Ilha do Amor (Love Island). In October and March the waves are high enough for river-surfing competitions. **Praia Morubira,** also close to Vila, has beautiful colonial houses and many restaurants and bars. The water is clear and the shore clean at **Praia Marahú,** but no bus from Belém travels here directly. You have to disembark in Vila and hop another bus.

Praia Paraíso. This beach is lined with trees and has soft white sands and clear emerald waters that stretch for miles. If you can't bear to leave at day's end, consider a stay at the Hotel Fazenda Paraíso. **Amenities:** food and drink. **Best for:** solitude; sunset; walking; swimming. ✉ *Buses depart from Rodoviário São Brás, Av. Almirante Barroso s/n, São Brás, Mosqueiro, Belém.*

WHERE TO STAY

$ RESORT 🏨 **Hotel Fazenda Paraíso.** At this popular beachside hotel, wood-and-brick chalets with red-tile roofs accommodate as many as five people. **Pros:** beachside location. **Cons:** simple rooms with little space. [$] *Rooms from: R$198* ✉ *Beira-Mar, Praia do Paraíso, Ilha Mosqueiro* ☎ *091/3204–4666, 091/3618–2022* 🌐 *www.hotelfazendaparaiso.com.br* 🛏 *28 rooms, 22 chalets* 🍴 *No meals.*

SALINÓPOLIS

200 km (120 miles) east of Belém.
Commonly known as **Salinas,** this old salt port on the Atlantic coast is loaded with beaches. It lies south of the mouth of the Amazon River, three to four hours from Belém on good roads, making it accessible to weekend beachgoers.

GETTING HERE AND AROUND

Buses run every couple of hours from the Belém *rodoviário* (bus terminal) and drop you off at the Salinas terminal. Boa Esperança makes the 220-km (125-mile) journey from Belém to Salinópolis every couple of hours daily and costs R$20. There are also many alternative vans that leave from the same terminal for R$20.

PINK DOLPHINS

Legend has it that the *botos cor de rosa* (pink river dolphins) can take human form. As humans, they are always handsome men, dressed immaculately in white, and very seductive. After dancing with the youngest and most beautiful girls, they lure them outside, have their way with them, and then return to the water just before dawn. You can always tell a boto from its slightly fishy smell and the hole in the top of its head, which is covered by a hat. Or at least this is what the pregnant girls tell their parents.

Once there, take a taxi about a mile to Centro and Maçarico Beach, or travel 20 minutes to Atalaia. A rickety old bus travels between the beaches every hour, from around 6:30 am to 10 pm. It takes some work to get to Salinas's more secluded beaches. Praia Maria Baixinha and Praia Marieta require a boat, as do island beaches. Ask your hotel to make arrangements for you. To reach Salinas Beach from Belém by car, take BR 316 to PA 324 and head north on PA 124.

ESSENTIALS

Bus Contacts Boa Esperança ⊠ *Avenida João Paulo II 1047, Marco, Belém* ☎ *091/3266–0033* ⊕ *www.boaesp.com.br.* **Terminal Rodoviário** ⊠ *Ave. Dr. Miguel Santa Brigada s/n* ☎ *091/3423–1148.*

EXPLORING

Praia Atalaia is Salinas's largest and most popular beach. The 14-km (9-mile) white-sand beach is expansive; the highest dunes have nice views. Behind them is the black-water pond Lago Coca Cola, which sometimes dries up between September and January. Also visible are dunes encroaching on hotels and businesses, signs of poor coastal management. Atalaia has several restaurant-bars with simple, low-price rooms for rent; expect no amenities, and bring your own towel and soap. The best places to eat and stay are in the middle of the beach, and some accept credit cards. Shop around and choose a room with a secure window. A 10-minute walk from Atalaia is a quieter beach, **Praia Farol Velho,** which has few services. To get here, turn left at the entrance and walk around the point.

In the old section of downtown Salinas, known as **Centro,** life revolves around the Farol Velho (the old light tower). The scene changes dramatically at the beginning of the **Praia Maçarico.** The Maçarico strip, which sits back from the beach, is broad, clean, and dotted with benches and coco palms. On the strip are a couple of playgrounds, exercise stations, and some restaurants and hotels. The beach can get crowded. Maçarico is about a 10-minute walk downhill on João Pessoa toward the water. As you walk toward the beach, beware of the sidewalk on the left that occasionally drops off and has deep exposed gutters. **Praia Corvina,** near Maçarico, is a calmer spot. Upon entering Maçarico Beach, turn left and round the point to Corvina.

Ecotours can be arranged to mangrove forests to see scarlet ibis and other species. Talk to your hotel manager.

WHERE TO STAY

$ RESORT 🏨 **Hotel Clube Privé do Atalaia.** Just off the beach, this place has more amenities than any other in town; breezy, spacious public areas, a wet bar, and water slides help you keep cool. **Pros:** beachside location; lots of water activities. **Cons:** few amenities; no in-room Internet or phones. [$] *Rooms from: R$180* ✉ *Estrada do Atalaia 10* ☎ *91/3464–1244* 🌐 *www.privedoatalaia.tur.br* 🛏 *141 rooms* 🍴 *No meals.*

$ HOTEL 🏨 **Hotel Salinópolis.** Right above Maçarico Beach, this hotel has the best location in town: You can look down the length of the beach from the pool. **Pros:** rooms are pleasant; brightly colored; doors open onto water. **Cons:** windows are small. [$] *Rooms from: R$150* ✉ *Av. Beira Mar 26* ☎ *091/3423–3000, 091/9114–5248* 🌐 *www.hotelsalinopolis.com.br* 🛏 *26 rooms* 🍴 *No meals.*

$ HOTEL 🏨 **Rango do Goiano.** Well situated on the Maçarico strip, this family-run place has compact but comfortable rooms. **Pros:** beachside location; good seafood menu at hotel restaurant. **Cons:** small rooms; few amenities. [$] *Rooms from: R$100* ✉ *Rua João Pessoa 2165* ☎ *091/3423–3572, 091/3788–2054, 091/3241–1099* 🌐 *www.pousadarangodogoiano.com* 🛏 *19 rooms* 🍴 *No meals.*

SHOPPING

Hotel Clube Privé do Atalaia. The high-end boutique at Hotel Clube Privé do Atalaia has sunscreen, hats, crafts, T-shirts, and Salinas memorabilia. ✉ *Estrada do Atalaia 10* ☎ *091/3464–1244* 🌐 *www.privedoatalaia.tur.br.*

UNDERSTANDING BRAZIL

BRAZILIAN PORTUGUESE VOCABULARY

BRAZILIAN PORTUGUESE VOCABULARY

	ENGLISH	PORTUGUESE	PRONUNCIATION
BASICS			
	Yes/no	Sim/Não	**see**ing/nown
	Please	Por favor	pohr fah-**vohr**
	May I?	Posso?	**poh**-sso
	Thank you (very much)	(Muito) obrigado	(**moo**yn-too) o-bree-**gah**-doh
	You're welcome	De nada	day **nah**-dah
	Excuse me	Com licença	con lee-**ssehn**-ssah
	Pardon me/what did you say?	Desculpe/ O que disse?	des-**kool**-peh/ o.k. **dih**-say
	Could you tell me?	Poderia me dizer?	po-day-**ree**-ah mee dee-**zehrr**
	I'm sorry	Sinto muito	**seen**-too **moo**yn-too
	Good morning!	Bom dia!	bohn **dee**-ah
	Good afternoon!	Boa tarde!	**boh**-ah tahr-dee
	Good evening!	Boa noite!	**boh**-ah nohee-tee
	Goodbye!	Adeus!/Até logo!	ah-**deh**oos/ah-**teh loh**-go
	Mr./Mrs.	Senhor/Senhora	sen-**yor**/sen-**yohr**-ah
	Miss	Senhorita	sen-yo-**ri**-tah
	Pleased to meet you	Muito prazer	**moo**yn-too prah-**zehr**
	How are you?	Como vai?	**koh**-mo **vah**-ee
	Very well, thank you	Muito bem, obrigado	**moo**yn-too **beh**-in, o-bree-**gah**-doh
	And you?	E o(a) Senhor(a)?	eh oh sen-**yor** (**yohr**-ah)
	Hello (on the telephone)	Alô	ah-**low**
NUMBERS			
	1	um/uma	oom/**oom**-ah
	2	dois	**doh**ees
	3	três	**treh**ys
	4	quatro	**kwa**-troh
	5	cinco	**seen**-koh

ENGLISH	PORTUGUESE	PRONUNCIATION
6	seis	**seh**ys
7	sete	**seh**-tee
8	oito	**oh**ee-too
9	nove	**noh**-vee
10	dez	**deh**-ees
11	onze	**ohn**-zee
12	doze	**doh**-zee
13	treze	**treh**-zee
14	quatorze	kwa-**tohr**-zee
15	quinze	**keen**-zee
16	dezesseis	deh-zeh-**seh**ys
17	dezessete	deh-zeh-**seh**-tee
18	dezoito	deh-**zoh**ee-toh
19	dezenove	deh-zeh-**noh**-vee
20	vinte	**veen**-tee
21	vinte e um	**veen**-tee eh **oom**
30	trinta	**treen**-tah
32	trinta e dois	**treen**-ta eh **doh**ees
40	quarenta	kwa-**rehn**-ta
43	quarenta e três	kwa-**rehn**-ta e **treh**ys
50	cinquenta	seen-**kwehn**-tah
54	cinquenta e quatro	seen-**kwehn**-tah e **kwa**-troh
60	sessenta	seh-**sehn**-tah
65	sessenta e cinco	seh-**sehn**-tah e **socn**-ku
70	setenta	seh-**tehn**-tah
76	setenta e seis	seh-**tehn**-ta e **seh**ys
80	oitenta	ohee-**tehn**-ta
87	oitenta e sete	ohee-**tehn**-ta e **seh**-tee
90	noventa	noh-**vehn**-ta
98	noventa e oito	noh-**vehn**-ta e **oh**ee-too

ENGLISH	PORTUGUESE	PRONUNCIATION
100	cem	**seh**-ing
101	cento e um	**sehn**-too e **oom**
200	duzentos	doo-**zehn**-tohss
500	quinhentos	key-**nyehn**-tohss
700	setecentos	seh-teh-**sehn**-tohss
900	novecentos	noh-veh-**sehn**-tohss
1,000	mil	meel
2,000	dois mil	**doh**ees meel
1,000,000	um milhão	oom mee-lee-**ahon**

COLORS

black	preto	**preh**-toh
blue	azul	a-**zool**
brown	marrom	mah-**hohm**
green	verde	**vehr**-deh
pink	rosa	**roh**-zah
purple	roxo	**roh**-choh
orange	laranja	lah-**rahn**-jah
red	vermelho	vehr-**meh**-lyoh
white	branco	**brahn**-coh
yellow	amarelo	ah-mah-**reh**-loh

DAYS OF THE WEEK

Sunday	Domingo	doh-**meehn**-goh
Monday	Segunda-feira	seh-**goon**-dah **fey**-rah
Tuesday	Terça-feira	**tehr**-sah **fey**-rah
Wednesday	Quarta-feira	**kwahr**-tah **fey**-rah
Thursday	Quinta-feira	**keen**-tah fey-rah
Friday	Sexta-feira	**sehss**-tah fey-rah
Saturday	Sábado	**sah**-bah-doh

	ENGLISH	PORTUGUESE	PRONUNCIATION
MONTHS			
	January	Janeiro	jah-**ney**-roh
	February	Fevereiro	feh-veh-**rey**-roh
	March	Março	**mahr**-soh
	April	Abril	ah-**breel**
	May	Maio	**my**-oh
	June	Junho	jy**oo**-nyoh
	July	Julho	jy**oo**-lyoh
	August	Agosto	ah-**ghost**-toh
	September	Setembro	seh-**tehm**-broh
	October	Outubro	owe-**too**-broh
	November	Novembro	noh-**vehm**-broh
	December	Dezembro	deh-**zehm**-broh
USEFUL PHRASES			
	Do you speak English?	O Senhor fala inglês?	oh sen-**yor fah**-lah een-**glehs**
	I don't speak Portuguese.	Não falo português.	nown **fah**-loh pohr-too-**ghehs**
	I don't understand (you)	Não lhe entendo	nown ly**eh** ehn-**tehn**-doh
	I understand	Eu entendo	**eh**-oo ehn-**tehn**-doh
	I don't know	Não sei	nown say
	I am American/ British	Sou americano (americana)/inglês (inglêsa)	sow a-meh-ree-**cah**-noh (a-meh-ree-**cah**-nah)/ een-**glehs** (een-**gleh**-sa)
	What's your name?	Como se chama?	**koh**-moh seh **shah**-mah
	My name is . . .	Meu nome é . . .	mehw **noh** meh eh
	What time is it?	Que horas são?	keh **oh**-rahss **sa**-ohn
	It is one, two, three . . . o'clock	É uma/São duas, três . . . hora/horas	eh **oom**-ah/**sa**- ohn **doo**-ahss, **treh**ys **oh**-rah/ **oh**-rahs
	Yes, please/ No, thank you	Sim por favor/ Não obrigado	seing pohr fah-**vohr**/ nown o-bree-**gah**-doh
	How?	Como?	**koh**-moh

ENGLISH	PORTUGUESE	PRONUNCIATION
When?	Quando?	**kwahn**-doh
This/Next week	Esta/Próxima semana	**ehss**-tah/**proh**-see-mah seh-**mah**-nah
This/Next month	Este/Próximo mêz	**ehss**-teh/**proh**-see-moh mehz
This/Next year	Este/Próximo ano	**ehss**-teh/**proh**-see-moh **ah**-noh
Yesterday/today/ tomorrow	Ontem/hoje/amanhã	**ohn**-tehn/**oh**-jeh/ ah-mah-**nyan**
This morning/ afternoon	Esta manhã/tarde	**ehss**-tah mah-**nyan**/ **tahr**-deh
Tonight	Hoje a noite	**oh**-jeh ah **noh**ee-tee
What?	O que?	oh **keh**
What is it?	O que é isso?	oh **keh** eh **ee**-soh
Why?	Por quê?	pohr-**keh**
Who?	Quem?	**keh**-in
Where is . . . ?	Onde é . . . ?	**ohn**-deh **eh**
the train station?	a estação de trem?	ah es-tah-**sah**-on deh train
the subway station?	a estação de metrô?	ah es-tah-**sah**-on deh meh-**tro**
the bus stop?	a parada do ônibus?	ah pah-**rah**-dah doh **oh**-nee-boos
the post office?	o correio?	oh coh-**hay**-yoh
the bank?	o banco?	oh **bahn**-koh
the hotel?	o hotel . . . ?	oh oh-**tell**
the cashier?	o caixa?	oh **kahy**-shah
the museum?	o museo . . . ?	oh moo-**zeh**-oh
the hospital?	o hospital?	oh ohss-pee-**tal**
the elevator?	o elevador?	oh eh-leh-vah-**dohr**
the bathroom?	o banheiro?	oh bahn-yey-roh
the beach?	a praia de . . . ?	ah prahy-yah deh
Here/there	Aqui/ali	ah-**kee**/ah-**lee**

ENGLISH	PORTUGUESE	PRONUNCIATION
Open/closed	Aberto/fechado	ah-**behr**-toh/ feh-**shah**-doh
Left/right	Esquerda/direita	ehs-**kehr**-dah/ dee-**ray**-tah
Straight ahead	Em frente	ehyn **frehn**-teh
Is it near/far?	É perto/longe?	eh **pehr**-toh/**lohn**-jeh
I'd like to buy . . .	Gostaria de comprar . . .	gohs-tah-**ree**-ah deh cohm-**prahr**
a bathing suit	um maiô	oom mahy-**owe**
a dictionary	um dicionário	oom dee-seeoh-**nah**-reeoh
a hat	um chapéu	oom shah-**peh**oo
a magazine	uma revista	oomah heh-**vees**-tah
a map	um mapa	oom **mah**-pah
a postcard	cartão postal	kahr-**town** pohs-**tahl**
sunglasses	óculos escuros	ah-koo-loss ehs-**koo**-rohs
suntan lotion	um óleo de bronzear	oom **oh**-lyoh deh brohn-zeh-**ahr**
a ticket	um bilhete	oom bee-lyeh-teh
cigarettes	cigarros	see-**gah**-hose
envelopes	envelopes	eyn-veh-**loh**-pehs
matches	fósforos	**fohs**-foh-rohss
paper	papel	pah-**pehl**
sandals	sandália	sahn-**dah**-leeah
soap	sabonete	sah-bow-**neh**-teh
How much is it?	Quanto custa?	**kwahn**-too **koos**-tah
It's expensive/cheap	Está caro/barato	ehss-tah **kah**-roh/ bah-**rah**-toh
A little/a lot	Um pouco/muito	oom **pohw**-koh/ **mooy**n-too
More/less	Mais/menos	**mah**-ees /**meh**-nohss
Enough/too much/ too little	Suficiente/demais/ muito pouco	soo-fee-see-**ehn**-teh/ deh-**mah**-ees/**mooy**n-toh **pohw**-koh

ENGLISH	PORTUGUESE	PRONUNCIATION
Telephone	Telefone	teh-leh-**foh**-neh
Telegram	Telegrama	teh-leh-**grah**-mah
I am ill.	Estou doente.	**ehss**-tow doh-**ehn**-teh
Please call a doctor.	Por favor chame um médico.	pohr fah-**vohr** shah-meh oom **meh**-dee-koh
Help!	Socorro!	soh-**koh**-ho
Help me!	Me ajude!	mee ah-**jyew**-deh
Fire!	Incêndio!	een-**sehn**-deeoh
Caution!/Look out!/ Be careful!	Cuidado!	kooy-**dah**-doh

ON THE ROAD

Avenue	Avenida	ah-veh-**nee**-dah
Highway	Estrada	ehss-**trah**-dah
Port	Porto	**pohr**-toh
Service station	Posto de gasolina	**pohs**-toh deh gah-zoh-**lee**-nah
Street	Rua	**who**-ah
Toll	Pedagio	peh-**dah**-jyoh
Waterfront promenade	Beiramar/orla	behy-rah-**mahrr/ohr**-lah
Wharf	Cais	**kah**-ees

IN TOWN

Block	Quarteirão	kwahr-tehy-**rah**-on
Cathedral	Catedral	kah-teh-**drahl**
Church/temple	Igreja	ee-**greh**-jyah
City hall	Prefeitura	preh-fehy-**too**-rah
Door/gate	Porta/portão	**pohr**-tah/porh-**tah**-on
Entrance/exit	Entrada/saída	ehn-**trah**-dah/sah-**ee**-dah
Market	Mercado/feira	mehr-**kah**-doh/**fey**-rah
Neighborhood	Bairro	**buy**-ho
Rustic bar	Lanchonete	lahn-shoh-**neh**-teh
Shop	Loja	**loh**-jyah
Square	Praça	**prah**-ssah

ENGLISH	PORTUGUESE	PRONUNCIATION

DINING OUT

ENGLISH	PORTUGUESE	PRONUNCIATION
A bottle of . . .	Uma garrafa de . . .	oomah gah-**hah**-fah deh
A cup of . . .	Uma xícara de . . .	oomah **shee**-kah-rah deh
A glass of . . .	Um copo de . . .	oom **koh**-poh deh
Ashtray	Um cinzeiro	oom seen-**zehy**-roh
Bill/check	A conta	ah **kohn**-tah
Bread	Pão	**pah**-on
Breakfast	Café da manhã	kah-**feh** dah mah-**nyan**
Butter	A manteiga	ah mahn-tehy-gah
Cheers!	Saúde!	sah-**oo**-deh
Cocktail	Um aperitivo	oom ah-peh-ree-**tee**-voh
Dinner	O jantar	oh **jyahn**-tahr
Dish	Um prato	oom **prah**-toh
Enjoy!	Bom apetite!	bohm ah-peh-**tee**-teh
Fork	Um garfo	**gahr**-foh
Fruit	Fruta	**froo**-tah
Is the tip included?	A gorjeta esta incluída?	ah gohr-**jyeh**-tah ehss-**tah** een-clue-**ee**-dah
Juice	Um suco	oom **soo**-koh
Knife	Uma faca	**oo**mah **fah**-kah
Lunch	O almoço	oh ahl-**moh**-ssoh
Menu	Menu/cardápio	me-**noo**/kahr-dah-peeoh
Mineral water	Água mineral	**ah**-gooah mee-neh-**rahl**
Napkin	Guardanapo	gooahr-dah-**nah**-poh
No smoking	Não fumante	nown foo-**mahn**-tch
Pepper	Pimenta	pee-**mehn**-tah
Please give me	Por favor me dê	pohr fah-**vohr** mee **deh**
Salt	Sal	sahl
Smoking	Fumante	foo-**mahn**-teh
Spoon	Uma colher	**oo**mah koh-**lyehr**

ENGLISH	PORTUGUESE	PRONUNCIATION
Sugar	Açúcar	ah-**soo**-kahr
Waiter!	Garçon!	gahr-**sohn**
Water	Água	**ah**-gooah
Wine	Vinho	**vee**-nyoh

PRONOUNCING PLACE NAMES

NAME	PRONUNCIATION
Amazônia	ah-mah-**zoh**-knee-ah
Bahia	bah-**ee**-ah
Belém	beh-**lein**
Belo Horizonte	**beh**-loh ho-rih-**zon**-teh
Brasília	brah-**zee**-lee-ah
Fortaleza	for-tah-**leh**-zah
Manaus	mah-**nah**-oos
Minas Gerais	**mee**-nahs jyeh-**rah**-ees
Paraná	pah-rah-nah
Porto Alegre	**pohr**-toh ah-**leh**-greh
Recife	heh-**see**-fee
Rio de Janeiro	**hee**-oh day jah-**ne**-roh
Rio Grande do Sul	**hee**-oh **gran**-deh doh sool
Salvador	sahl-vah-**dohr**
Santa Catarina	sahn-**tah** kah-tah-reeh-nah
São Paulo	saohn **pow**-low

TRAVEL SMART
BRAZIL

GETTING HERE AND AROUND

Brazil is one of the biggest countries in the world, and larger than the continental U.S. In fact, the Amazon jungle alone is slightly larger than India. This means that you'll be hard-pressed to see the Amazon, Bahia, Rio, and São Paulo during a weeklong vacation. You can, however, cover a lot of territory if your trip is well planned. If you want to start from the North/Northeast and then later on go southward, go ahead. We just recommend spending a little time gaining a clear idea of the often vast distances between destinations.

Road conditions in Brazil vary widely throughout the country, and passenger train travel is almost nonexistent. Private cars and public buses are the main modes of inter-city road travel. Buses can range (depending on the route and the price) from luxurious and well maintained to basic and mechanically unsound. Traveling by plane is a good option, especially considering the large distances between cities. It's fast, safe, and you can get good prices on tickets.

TRAVEL TIMES FROM SÃO PAULO TO	BY AIR	BY BUS
Rio de Janeiro	1 hour	6 hours
Salvador	1 hour, 30 minutes	24 hours
Manaus	2 hours	60 hours
Florianópolis	1 hour, 15 minutes	9 hours
Brasília	1 hour, 45 minutes	13 hours

■ AIR TRAVEL

Within a country as big as Brazil, it's especially important to plan your itinerary with care. Book as far in advance as possible, particularly for weekend travel. Planes tend to fill up on Friday, especially to or from Brasília or Manaus. For more booking tips and to check prices and make online flight reservations, log on to ⊕ *www.infraero.gov.br.*

■**TIP→** Ask the local tourist board or hotel staff about hotel and local transportation packages that include tickets to major museum exhibits or other special events.

The flying time from New York is 10 hours to Rio and 10½ hours to São Paulo. From Miami it's 8½ hours to Brasília (the nation's capital), 9½ hours to Rio de Janeiro, 9 hours to São Paulo, and 8 hours to Salvador. Bear in mind that most flights to Rio or other Brazilian cities stop in Miami. From Miami, if flying with a Brazilian airline, you'll be able to fly nonstop to Brasília, Manaus, São Paulo, and Rio de Janeiro. Most flights from Los Angeles go through Miami, and flight times are about 13 hours, not including layover in Miami. Usually the connection time in São Paulo is an hour to 90 minutes.

Reconfirm flights within Brazil, even if you have a ticket and a reservation, as flights tend to operate at full capacity.

When you leave Brazil, be prepared to pay a hefty departure tax, which runs about R$86 ($43) for international flights. A departure tax also applies to flights within Brazil; amounts run as high as about R$22 ($11). Although some airports accept credit cards to pay departure taxes, it's wise to have the appropriate amount in reais.

Airlines and Airports Airline and Airport Links.com has links to many of the world's airlines and airports. ⊕ *www.airlineandairportlinks.com.*

Airline Security Issues Transportation Security Administration ⊕ *www.tsa.gov.*

Air Travel Resources in Brazil National Civil Aviation Agency (ANAC) ☎ *55/61–3905–2645, 080/0725–4445 toll-free within Brazil* ⊕ *www.anac.gov.br.*

TRANSFERS BETWEEN AIRPORTS

Some airports offer transfers to another airport, such as Guarulhos-Congonhas, in São Paulo, and Galeão-Santos Dumond, in Rio de Janeiro. Because the country is so big, this type of service is not common outside of Rio and São Paulo, although most other Brazilian cities have only one commercial airport.

FLIGHTS
TO BRAZIL

Miami, New York, and Toronto are the major gateways for flights to Brazil—typically to São Paulo and Rio, and sometimes Brasília as well—from North America. United Airlines flies nonstop from Houston, Newark, and Chicago; American Airlines has direct service from Dallas, Miami, and New York; and Delta offers nonstop service from Atlanta and New York. Air Canada has nonstop service between Toronto and São Paulo.

LATAM Airlines (still known as TAM within Brazil), created in 2012 by the merger of Chile's LAN Airlines and Brazil's TAM Airlines, flies nonstop from New York and Miami to São Paulo, with continuing service to Rio and connections to many other cities. TAM also offers nonstop service between Miami and Manaus. The Colombian airline Avianca flies from Washington, DC to São Paulo, with a brief stopover in Bogotá.

Airline Contacts Air Canada ☎ *11/3254–6630 in Brazil, 888/247–2262 in North America* ⊕ *www.aircanada.com.* **American Airlines** ☎ *800/433–7300, 0300/789–7778 in Brazil* ⊕ *www.aa.com.* **Avianca Airlines** ☎ *0800/891–8668 in Brazil, 800/284–2622 in North America* ⊕ *www.avianca.com.* **Delta Airlines** ☎ *800/241–4141 in North America, 0800/881–2121 in Brazil* ⊕ *www.delta.com.* **TAM** ☎ *888/235–9826 in the U.S., 55/21 3212–9400 in Rio, 55/11 3274–1313 in São Paulo* ⊕ *www.tam.com.br.* **United Airlines** ☎ *800/864–8331 in North America, 11/3145–4200 in São Paulo, 0800/16–2323 in Rio de Janeiro and other cities within Brazil* ⊕ *www.united.com.*

WITHIN BRAZIL

There's regular jet service within the country between all major and most medium-size cities. Remote areas are also accessible—as long as you don't mind small planes. Flights can be long, lasting several hours for trips to the Amazon, with stops en route. Reliable domestic airlines include TAM and GOL, a reliable low-cost airline with routes that cover most major and medium-size Brazilian cities (GOL also has service to some Latin American countries). Another option is TRIP Azul Linhas Aéreas, Brazil's newest airline, with service to about 100 domestic destinations.

The flight from Rio to São Paulo or Belo Horizonte is 1 hour; Rio to Brasília is 1½ hours; Rio to Salvador is 2 hours; Rio to Belém or Curitiba is 2½ hours. From São Paulo it's 4 hours to Manaus and 1½ hours to Iguaçu Falls.

Domestic Airlines GOL ☎ *0800/704–0465 in Brazil* ⊕ *www.voegol.com.br.* **TAM** ☎ *888/235–9826 in North America, 0800/570–5700 in Brazil* ⊕ *www.tam.com.br.* **TRIP Azul Linhas Aéreas** ☎ *4003–1118 from major Brazil cities, 0800–884–4040 toll-free from other cities within Brazil* ⊕ *www.voeazul.com.br.*

AIR PASSES

If you reside outside Brazil, you're eligible to purchase air passes from TAM or GOL. If you're planning four or more flights within the country within 30 days, these passes—available online through Miami-based travel agency and tour operator Brol—can save you hundreds of dollars. Prices start around $540 (plus tax), and you must purchase these passes before you enter Brazil. Passes that include flights between Brazil and some other South American countries (Argentina, Paraguay, and Uruguay) are also available.

Air Pass Information Brol ☎ *888/527–2745* ⊕ *www.brol.com.*

▌ BUS TRAVEL

The nation's *ônibus* (bus) network is affordable, comprehensive, and efficient—compensating for the lack of trains and the high cost of air travel. Every major city can be reached by bus, as can most small to medium-size communities. The quality of buses in Brazil is good; in many cases better than in the U.S. The number of stops at roadside cafés depends on the length of the journey. A trip from São Paulo to Curitiba, for example, which takes about six hours, has only one 20-minute stop. Usually buses stop at large, nice outlets with food, souvenirs, and magazines.

Lengthy bus trips can involve travel over some bad highways, a fact of life in Brazil. Trips to northern, northeastern, and central Brazil tend to be especially trying; the best paved highways are in the southeast and the south. When traveling by bus, bring water, toilet paper or tissues, and an additional top layer of clothing (handy if it gets cold or as a pillow). Travel light, dress comfortably, and keep a close watch on your belongings—especially in bus stations. If your bus stops at a roadside café, take your belongings with you.

When buying a ticket, you'll be asked whether you want the *ônibus convencional*, the simplest option; the *ônibus executivo*, which gets you a/c, coffee, water, a sandwich, more space between seats, and a pillow and blanket; or the *ônibus-leito*, where you have all facilities of an executive bus plus a seat that reclines completely. If you're over 5'10", it's prudent to buy the most expensive ticket and try for front-row seats, which usually provide more space.

Most buses used for long trips are modern and comfortable, usually with bathrooms and a/c. Note that regular buses used for shorter hauls may be labeled "ar condicionado" ("air-conditioned") but often are not.

Bus fares are substantially cheaper than in North America or Europe. Between Rio and São Paulo (6½–7 hours), for example, a bus departs every half hour and costs about $34; a night sleeper will run about $60. Sometimes competing companies serve the same routes, so it can pay to shop around.

Tickets are sold at bus-company offices, at city bus terminals, and in some travel agencies. Larger cities may have different terminals for buses to different destinations, and some small towns may not have a terminal at all (you're usually picked up and dropped off at the line's office, invariably in a central location). Expect to pay with cash, as credit cards aren't accepted everywhere. Reservations or advance-ticket purchases generally aren't necessary except for trips to resort areas during high season—particularly on weekends—or during major holidays (Christmas, Carnival, etc.) and school-break periods (July and December/January). In general, arrive at bus stations early, particularly for peak-season travel.

Traveling between Argentina and Brazil by bus is also a good idea if time is not an issue. The same can be said for Uruguay, Chile, Peru, and other neighboring countries. It's inexpensive and you can enjoy the landscapes. Expect to pay $200 USD for the 14-hour trip between São Paulo and Buenos Aires.

▌TIP→ **To ensure that your destination is understood, write it down on a piece of paper and present it to bus or taxi drivers, most of whom don't speak English.**

Bus Information Expresso Brasileiro
☎ *0300/700–9000* ⊕ *www.expressobrasileiro. com.* **Itapemirim** ☎ *800/723–2121* ⊕ *www. itapemirim.com.br.* **Pluma International** ☎ *41/3212–2689 from the U.S., 0800/646– 0300 within Brazil* ⊕ *www.pluma.com.br.*

▌ CAR TRAVEL

Traveling by car is recommended if you meet the following criteria: you're not pressed for time, you enjoy driving even in places you do not know well, and you do not want to be limited by airline or bus schedules. Traveling by car is, especially if you avoid driving at night, reasonably safe in most areas, and it's a wonderful way to see the country and access lesser-known areas.

GASOLINE

Gasoline in Brazil costs around R$2.80 ($1.40) per liter, or about $5.30 per gallon. Unleaded gas, called *especial,* costs about the same. Brazil also has an extensive fleet of ethanol-powered cars, *carro a álcool,* and you might end up with one from a rental agency. Ethanol fuel is sold at all gas stations and is a little cheaper than gasoline. However, these cars get lower mileage, so they offer little advantage over gas-powered cars. Stations are plentiful within cities and on major highways, and many are open 24/7. In smaller towns few stations take credit cards, and their hours are more limited. If you want a receipt, ask for a *recibo.*

PARKING

Finding a space in most cities—particularly Rio, São Paulo, Brasília, Belo Horizonte, and Salvador—is a major task. It's best to head for a garage or a lot and leave your car with the attendant. The cost of parking depends on the city and the neighborhood: downtown garages, close to stores, will certainly be more expensive than those in residential areas. There are no meters; instead, there's a system involving coupons that you must post in your car's window, which allows you to park for a certain time period (one or two hours). You can buy them from uniformed street-parking attendants or at newsstands. Should you find a space on the street, you'll probably have to pay a fee for parking services.

> ### WARNING
>
> It can be risky to drive at night, especially in Rio and São Paulo, where drivers commonly run stop signs and traffic lights to avoid robbery. Take special note of motorcycles at night—they're often used in robberies for a quick getaway. We strongly recommend that women do not drive alone at night. Note that Brazil has a zero-tolerance policy when it comes to drinking and driving. The legal limit is a miniscule 0.01%, so it's best not to drive if you've recently consumed even a tiny amount of alcohol; these laws are strictly enforced.

No-parking zones are marked by a crossed-out capital letter E (which means *estacionamento,* Portuguese for "parking").

ROAD CONDITIONS

Road conditions in Brazil vary widely throughout the country. Roads in the South are often excellent, while federal, interstate roads (also known as BR) in other parts of the country are often poor, with occasional potholes and uneven surfaces. Passenger car travel is reasonably safe in most areas, while passenger-bus robberies, usually nonviolent, do randomly occur in some areas. In major cities, traffic jams are common in rush hours (8 am, 6 pm); the problem is especially bad in São Paulo and Rio de Janeiro. In Brasília there are special roads for those driving faster (the so-called Eixão, where the limit is 80 kph/49 mph). At rush hour you may find the local driving style more aggressive, but still, driving in major cities is easier than in small ones.

The Brazilian Federal Government maintains a (Portuguese-language) website with up-to-date information on road conditions throughout the country (⊕ *www.dnit.gov.br*); the site also has downloadable state roadmaps. A private Brazilian company, Quatro Rodas (⊕ *www.guia4rodas.com.br*), publishes road maps that list local phone numbers for obtaining current road conditions; these cost about R$30 ($15). Apart from toll roads, which generally have their own services, roadside assistance is available only sporadically and informally through local private mechanics. There's a group called the "Angels of the Pavement" that provides roadside assistance on the main highway between São Paulo and Rio de Janeiro.

FROM	TO	DISTANCE
São Paulo	Rio de Janeiro	430 km
Rio de Janeiro	Búzios	180 km
Rio de Janeiro	Salvador	1,650 km
São Paulo	Belo Horizonte	590 km
São Paulo	Florianópolis	705 km
São Paulo	Foz do Iguaçu	1,050 km

ROADSIDE EMERGENCIES

The Automóvel Clube do Brasil (Automobile Club of Brazil) provides emergency assistance to foreign motorists, but only if they're members of an automobile club in their own nation. If you're not a member of an automobile club, you can call 193 from anywhere in the country. This is a universal number staffed by local fire departments. The service is in Portuguese only. Many motorists in major urban areas and more developed parts of the country carry cell phones, and can be asked to assist in calling for help. In case of emergency, the fastest way to summon assistance is to call one of the following services: Fire Brigade (193); Police (190); Federal Highway Patrol (191); Ambulance (192); Civil Defense (199).

RULES OF THE ROAD

Brazilians drive on the right, and in general traffic laws are the same as those in the United States. The use of seat belts is mandatory. The national speed limit ranges from 60 to 80 kph (36 to 48 mph). There are cameras on the streets of most cities to enforce the speed limit. Make sure you wear seat belts at all times and do not speak on your cell phone. The minimum driving age is 18 and children should always sit in the backseat.

SAFETY

If you get a ticket for some sort of violation, be polite with the police officer and try to solve the issue either by accepting the ticket (if you committed the violation) or by explaining your position (if you did not commit a violation). Even though it's common to see scams in cases like this, the best option is to solve the problem as honestly as possible, especially if you're a foreigner.

CAR RENTAL

When you reserve a car, ask about cancellation penalties, taxes, drop-off charges (if you're planning to pick up the car in one city and leave it in another), and surcharges (for being under or over a certain age, for additional drivers, or for driving across state or country borders or beyond a specific distance from your point of rental). All these things can add substantially to your costs. Request car seats and extras such as a GPS when you book.

Rates are sometimes—but not always—better if you book in advance or reserve through a rental agency's website. There are other reasons to book ahead, though: for popular destinations, during busy times of the year, or to ensure that you get certain types of cars (vans, SUVs, exotic sports cars). At many airports, agencies are open 24 hours.

■ TIP→ Make sure that a confirmed reservation guarantees you a car. Agencies sometimes overbook, particularly for busy weekends and holiday periods.

Driving can be chaotic in cities like São Paulo, but much easier in cities like Curitiba and Brasília. In the countryside the usually rough roads, lack of clearly marked signs, and language difference can make driving a challenge. Further, the cost of renting can be steep. All that said, certain areas are most enjoyable when explored on your own in a car: the beach areas of Búzios and the Costa Verde (near Rio) and the Belo Horizonte region; the North Shore beaches outside

São Paulo; and many of the inland and coastal towns of the south, a region with many good roads.

Brazil has more than 1.7 million km (1.05 million miles) of highway, about 10% of it paved. The country's highway department estimates that 40% of the federal highways (those with either the designation *BR* or a state abbreviation such as *RJ* or *SP*), which constitute 70% of Brazil's total road system, are in a dangerous state of disrepair. Evidence of this is everywhere: potholes, lack of signage, inadequate shoulders. Landslides and flooding after heavy rains are frequent and at times shut down entire stretches of key highways. Recent construction has improved the situation, but independent land travel in Brazil definitely has its liabilities.

Increasing traffic adds to the system's woes, but fortunately in large cities like Curitiba and Brasília there are now cameras to detect and fine abusive drivers. This has decreased traffic accidents significantly, but you should be careful anyway. Some drivers slow down only when close to these cameras. The worst offenders are bus and truck drivers. For these reasons, we recommend that you rely on taxis and buses for short distances and on planes for longer journeys. In cities be very careful around motorcycles, as their drivers are notorious for flouting traffic rules.

Some common-sense tips: before you set out, establish an itinerary and ask about gas stations. Be sure to plan your daily driving distance conservatively and don't drive after dark. Always obey speed limits and traffic regulations.

Always give the rental car a once-over to make sure the headlights, jack, and tires (including the spare) are in working condition.

Although international car-rental agencies have better service and maintenance track records than local firms (they also provide better breakdown assistance), your best bet at getting a good rate is to rent on arrival, particularly from local companies. But reserve ahead if you plan to rent during a holiday period, and check that a confirmed reservation guarantees you a car. You can contact local agencies through their websites in advance.

Consider hiring a car and driver through your hotel concierge, or make a deal with a taxi driver for extended sightseeing at a long-term rate. Often drivers charge a set hourly rate, regardless of the distance traveled. You'll have to pay cash, but you may actually spend less than you would for a rental car.

You need an international driver's license if you plan to drive in Brazil. International driving permits (IDPs) are available from the American and Canadian automobile associations. These international permits, valid only in conjunction with your regular driver's license, are universally recognized.

Tollbooths, better known as *pedagio* in Portuguese, are common in Brazil. These are located along many highways, especially in the southeast and around São Paulo. Fees depend on the type of vehicle you're driving. Make sure you carry cash, including some small change.

CAR-RENTAL INSURANCE

Car insurance is not compulsory when renting a car, but if you have plans to drive in more than one city we strongly recommend buying car insurance, given the bad conditions of Brazilian roads in some states and the risk of accidents. Most car-rental companies offer an optional insurance against robbery and accidents. Minimum age for renting a car is 21, but some companies require foreign clients to be at least 25 or charge extra for those under 26.

If you own a car, your personal auto insurance may cover a rental to some degree, though not all policies protect you abroad; always read your policy's fine print. If you don't have auto insurance, then seriously consider buying the collision- or loss-damage waiver (CDW or LDW) from the car-rental company, which eliminates your liability for damage to the car.

Some credit cards offer CDW coverage, but it's usually supplemental to your own insurance and rarely covers SUVs, minivans, luxury models, and the like. If your coverage is secondary, you may still be liable for loss-of-use costs from the car-rental company. But no credit-card insurance is valid unless you use that card for *all* transactions, from reserving to paying the final bill. All companies exclude car rental in some countries, so be sure to find out about the destination to which you are traveling.

■TIP➔ Diners Club offers primary CDW coverage on all rentals reserved and paid for with the card. This means that Diners Club's company—not your own car insurance—pays in case of an accident. It doesn't mean your car-insurance company won't raise your rates once it discovers you had an accident.

Some rental agencies require you to purchase CDW coverage; many will even include it in quoted rates. All will strongly encourage you to buy CDW—possibly implying that it's required—so be sure to ask about such things before renting. In most cases it's cheaper to add a supplemental CDW plan to your comprehensive travel-insurance policy than to purchase it from a rental company. That said, you don't want to pay for a supplement if you're required to buy insurance from the rental company.

■TIP➔ You can decline the insurance from the rental company and purchase it through a third-party provider such as Travel Guard (⊕ *www.travelguard.com*), which can cost significantly less than coverage offered by car-rental companies.

ESSENTIALS

■ ACCOMMODATIONS

All hotels in Brazil have bathrooms in their rooms. The simplest type of accommodation usually consists of a bed, TV, table, bathroom, a little fridge, a telephone, and a bathroom with a shower. (Budget hotels in the Amazon or Northeast don't always have hot water.) In luxury hotels you'll also generally have Internet, cable TV, and a bathroom with a bathtub and shower. Hotels listed with EMBRATUR, Brazil's national tourism board, are rated using stars. Staff training is a big part of the rating, but it's not a perfect system, since stars are awarded based on the number of amenities rather than their quality.

If you ask for a double room, you'll get a room for two people, but you're not guaranteed a double mattress. If you'd like to avoid twin beds, ask for a *cama de casal* ("couple's bed").

Carnival, the year's principal festival, takes place during the four days preceding Ash Wednesday. ■TIP→ For top hotels in Rio, Salvador, and Recife during Carnival you must make reservations a year in advance. Hotel rates rise by at least 30% for Carnival. Not as well known outside Brazil but equally impressive is Rio's New Year's Eve celebration. More than a million people gather along Copacabana Beach for a massive fireworks display and to honor the sea goddess Iemanjá. To ensure a room, book at least six months in advance.

In the hinterlands it's good to look at any room before accepting it; expense is no guarantee of charm or cleanliness, and accommodations can vary dramatically within a single hotel. Also, be sure to check the shower: some hotels have electric-powered showerheads rather than central water heaters. In theory, you can adjust both the water's heat and its pressure. In practice, if you want hot water you have to turn the water pressure down; if you want pressure, expect a cool rinse. ⚠ Don't adjust the power when you're under the water—you can get a little shock. Note that in the Amazon and other remote areas what's billed as "hot" water may be lukewarm at best—even in higher-end hotels.

Most hotels and other lodgings require you to give your credit-card details before they will confirm your reservation. However you book, get confirmation in writing and have a copy of it handy when you check in.

Be sure you understand the hotel's cancellation policy. Some places allow you to cancel without any kind of penalty—even if you prepaid to secure a discounted rate—if you cancel at least 24 hours in advance. Others require you to cancel a week in advance or penalize you the cost of one night. Small inns and B&Bs are most likely to require you to cancel far in advance. Most hotels allow children under a certain age to stay in their parents' room at no extra charge, but others charge for them as extra adults; find out the cutoff age for discounts.

Prices in the reviews are the lowest cost of a standard double room in high season, including tax, service, and breakfast only. For expanded reviews, facilities, and current deals, visit Fodors.com.

BED AND BREAKFASTS

B&Bs in Brazil are comfortable, friendly, and offer a modicum of privacy. They're a nice option if you're looking for something a little more intimate than a hotel.

Contacts Bed & Breakfast.com ☎ 800/462–2632, 512/322–2710 ⊕ www.bedandbreakfast. com. **BnB Finder.com** ☎ 888/469-6663 ⊕ www.bnbfinder.com.

FAZENDAS

Another accommodation option is to stay on a *fazenda* (farm), or *hotel fazenda*, where you can experience a rural environment. They are ideal for families with kids, as most have adventure sports and programs for children. Some farms in the state of São Paulo date back to colonial times, when they were famous Brazilian coffee farms. Prices range from around $70 to $150 per day for adults, but the actual cost depends a lot on which facilities and activities you choose. The prices we give usually include all meals (but be sure to check this beforehand) and are valid for the months of January, February, July, and December (high season). You can get discounts of up to 30% during the low season.

POUSADAS

If you want the facilities of a hotel plus the family environment of an apartment, but at a lower cost, a *pousada* is a good option. Cheaper than hotels and farms, pousadas are simple inns, often in historic houses. They usually offer breakfast and have swimming pools, parking lots, air-conditioning and/or fans, TVs, refrigerators, and common areas such as bars, laundry, and living rooms. Some have a common kitchen for guests who prefer to cook their own meals. Hidden Pousadas Brazil is a helpful website for locating pousadas.

Contacts Hidden Pousadas Brazil 🖃 *21/ 8122–2000* ⊕ *www.hiddenpousadasbrazil.com.*

▮ ADDRESSES

Finding addresses in Brazil can be frustrating, as streets often have more than one name and numbers are sometimes assigned haphazardly. In some places street numbering doesn't enjoy the wide popularity it has achieved elsewhere; hence, you may find the notation "s/n," meaning *sem número* (without number). In rural areas and small towns there may only be directions to a place rather than a formal address (i.e., street and number). Often such areas do not have official addresses.

In Portuguese *avenida* (avenue), *rua* (street) and *travessa* (lane) are abbreviated (as *Av., R.,* and *Trv.* or *Tr.*), while *estrada* (highway) often isn't abbreviated, and *alameda* (alley) is abbreviated (Al.). Street numbers follow street names. Eight-digit postal codes (CEP) are widely used.

In some written addresses you might see other abbreviations. For example, an address might read, "R. Presidente Faria 221-4°, s. 413, 90160-091 Porto Alegre, RS," which translates to 221 Rua Presidente Faria, 4th floor, Room 413 ("s." is short for *sala*), postal code 90160-091, in the city of Porto Alegre, in the state of Rio Grande do Sul. You might also see *andar* (floor) or *edifício* (building).

The abbreviations for Brazilian states are: Acre (AC); Alagoas (AL); Amapá (AP); Amazonas (AM); Bahia (BA); Ceará (CE); Distrito Federal (Federal District, aka Brasília; DF); Espírito Santo (ES); Goiás (GO); Maranhão (MA); Minas Gerais (MG); Mato Grosso do Sul (MS); Mato Grosso (MT); Pará (PA); Paraíba (PB); Paraná (PR); Pernambuco (PE); Piauí (PI); Rio de Janeiro (RJ); Rio Grande do Norte (RN); Rio Grande do Sul (RS); Rondonia (RO); Roraima (RR); Santa Catarina (SC); São Paulo (SP); Sergipe (SE), Tocantins (TO).

▮ COMMUNICATIONS

INTERNET

In most of Brazil (particularly at hotels popular with international travelers), North American–style plugs work fine, as long as your plug doesn't have a third-prong grounder, but Brazil recently adopted its own three-prong outlet, so it's a good idea to travel with a universal adapter. Be discreet about carrying laptops, smart phones, and other obvious displays of wealth, which can make you a target of thieves; conceal your laptop in a generic bag and keep it close to you at all times.

Internet access, both high-speed and wireless, is widespread. Cybercafés and hotels with business centers or in-room Internet are common; sometimes hotels charge a daily fee of $5 to $10, but free access is increasingly common. 3G iPad, tablet, and smart-phone access in big cities like São Paulo and Rio is common, but check with your local provider to find a plan that mitigates the often-steep roaming charges.

PHONES

The good news is that you can now make a direct-dial telephone call from virtually any point on earth. The bad news? You can't always do so cheaply. Calling from a hotel is almost always the most expensive option; hotels usually add huge surcharges to all calls, particularly international ones. In remote areas you can phone from call centers or sometimes even the post office, but in big cities these call centers don't exist anymore. Calling cards usually keep costs to a minimum, but only if you purchase them locally. And then there are mobile phones, which are sometimes more prevalent—particularly in the developing world—than landlines; as expensive as mobile phone calls can be, they are still usually a much cheaper option than calling from your hotel.

The number of digits in Brazilian telephone numbers varies widely. The country code for Brazil is 55. When dialing a Brazilian number from abroad, drop the initial zero from the local area code.

Public phones are everywhere and are called *orelhões* (big ears) because of their shape. The phones take phone cards only.

CALLING WITHIN BRAZIL

Local calls can be made most easily from pay phones, which take phone cards only. A bar or restaurant may allow you to use its private phone for a local call if you're a customer.

If you want to call from your hotel, remember long-distance calls within Brazil are expensive, and hotels add a surcharge.

With the privatization of the Brazilian telecommunications network, there's a wide choice of long-distance companies. Hence, to make direct-dial long-distance calls, you must find out which companies serve the area from which you're calling and then get their access codes—the staff at your hotel can help. (Some hotels have already made the choice for you, so you may not need an access code when calling from the hotel itself.) For long-distance calls within Brazil, dial 0 + the access code + the area code and number. To call Rio, for example, dial 0, then 21 (for Embratel, a major long-distance and international provider), then 21 (Rio's area code), and then the number.

CALLING OUTSIDE BRAZIL

International calls from Brazil are extremely expensive. Hotels also add a surcharge, increasing this cost even more. Calls can be made from public phone booths with a prepaid phone card. You can also go to phone offices. Ask your hotel staff about the closest office, as they are less common in Brazil than pay phones.

For international calls, dial 00 + 23 (for Intelig, a long-distance company) or 21 (for Embratel, another long-distance company) + the country code + the area code and number. For operator-assisted international calls, dial 00–0111. For international information, dial 00–0333. To make a collect long-distance call (which will cost 40% more than a normal call), dial 9 + the area code and the number.

The country code for the United States is 1.

AT&T and Sprint operators are also accessible from Brazil; get the local access codes before you leave home for your destinations.

Access Codes AT&T Direct ☎ *0800/703–6335 for individuals* ⊕ *www.att.com/esupport/traveler.jsp.* **Sprint International Access** ☎ *866/866–7509, 866/805–9890 From Canada* ⊕ *mysprint.sprint.com.*

CALLING CARDS

All pay phones in Brazil take phone cards only. Buy a phone card, a *cartão telefônico*, at a *posto telefônico* (phone office), newsstand, drugstore, or post office. Cards come with a varying number of units (each unit is usually worth a couple of minutes), which will determine the price. Buy a couple of cards if you don't think you'll have the chance again soon. These phone cards can be used for international, local, and long-distance calls within Brazil. Be aware that calling internationally using these cards is extremely expensive and your units will expire pretty quickly. It's advisable to buy several cards with the maximum number of units (75 minutes). A 20-minute card costs about $1.25, a 50-minute card about $3.25, and a 75-minute about $5.

In big cities like São Paulo and Rio de Janeiro you can buy an international phone card, which is around the same price as the 75-minute local card.

MOBILE PHONES

If you have a multiband phone and your service provider uses the world-standard GSM network, you can likely use your phone in Brazil, although the costs of international roaming can be high, both for placing calls and using data. Check with your provider back home for details on international plans—some companies, like Verizon and AT&T, have reasonably affordable international data plans, but it's still always a good idea, if you have a Wi-Fi-enabled phone, to use local Wi-Fi when you're able to find it. Also keep in mind that you can use a Wi-Fi-enabled phone to make international calls using Skype or Viber.

If you plan only to make local calls, consider buying a new SIM card (note that your provider may have to unlock your phone for you)—this especially makes sense if you'll be in the country for more than a few days. You'll then have a local number and can make calls at local rates. Be aware that as a non-Brazilian you must show proof of citizenship (such as a passport) to buy a SIM card, which costs around $10. Note that you'll use up the credit on your SIM card more quickly when calling numbers in a Brazilian state other than the one in which you purchased the card. Many travelers buy a new SIM card in each state they visit.

▌ EATING OUT

Food in Brazil is delicious, inexpensive (especially compared with North America and Europe), and bountiful. Portions are huge and presentation is tasteful. A lot of restaurants prepare plates for two people; when you order, be sure to ask if one plate will suffice—or even better, glance around to see the size of portions at other tables.

In major cities the variety of eateries is staggering: restaurants of all sizes and categories, snack bars, and fast-food outlets line downtown streets and fight for space in shopping malls. Pricing systems vary from open menus to buffets where you weigh your plate. In São Paulo, for example, Italian eateries—whose risottos rival those of Bologna—sit beside pan-Asian restaurants, which, like the chicest spots in North America and Europe, serve everything from Thai *satay* to sushi. In addition, there are excellent Portuguese, Chinese, Japanese, Arab, and Spanish restaurants.

Outside the cities you find primarily typical, low-cost Brazilian meals that consist simply of *feijão preto* (black beans) and *arroz* (rice) served with beef, chicken, or fish. Manioc, a root vegetable that's used in a variety of ways, and beef are adored everywhere.

Many Brazilian dishes are adaptations of Portuguese specialties. Fish stews called *caldeiradas* and beef stews called *cozidos* (a wide variety of vegetables boiled with different cuts of beef and pork) are popular, as is *bacalhau*, salt cod cooked in sauce or grilled. *Salgados* (literally, "salteds") are appetizers or snacks served in sit-down restaurants as well as at stand-up *lanchonetes* (luncheonettes). Dried salted meats form the basis of many dishes from the interior and northeast of Brazil, and pork is used heavily in dishes from Minas Gerais. Brazil's national dish is *feijoada* (a stew of black beans, sausage, pork, and beef), which is often served with rice, shredded kale, orange slices, and manioc flour or meal—called *farofa* if it's coarsely ground, *farinha* if finely ground—that has been fried with onions, oil, and egg.

One of the most avid national passions is the *churrascaria,* where meats are roasted on spits over an open fire, usually *rodízio* style. Rodízio means "going around," and waiters circulate nonstop carrying skewers laden with charbroiled hunks of beef, pork, and chicken, which are sliced onto your plate with ritualistic ardor. For a set price you get all the meat and side dishes you can eat. Starve yourself a little before going to a rodízio place. Then you can sample everything on offer.

At the other end of the spectrum, vegetarians can sometimes find Brazil's meat-centric culture challenging, especially outside of larger cities. Increasingly, though, salads and vegetarian options are offered at nicer restaurants in areas catering to foodies, tourists, and those with more international tastes. You'll also find salads at buffet restaurants, called *quilos,* found throughout Brazil.

Brazilian *doces* (desserts), particularly those of Bahia, are very sweet, and many are descendants of the egg-based custards and puddings of Portugal and France. *Cocada* is shredded coconut caked with sugar; *quindim* is a small tart made from egg yolks and coconut; *doce de banana* (or any other fruit) is banana cooked in sugar; *ambrosia* is a lumpy milk-and-sugar pudding.

Coffee is served black and strong with sugar in demitasse cups and is called *cafezinho.* (Requests for *descafeinado* [decaf] are met with a firm shake of the head "no," a blank stare, or outright amusement.) Coffee is taken with milk—called *café com leite*—only at breakfast. Bottled water (*agua mineral*) is sold carbonated or plain (*com gás* and *sem gás,* respectively).

Prices in the reviews are the average cost of a main course at dinner or, if dinner is not served, at lunch.

MEALS AND MEALTIMES

Between the extremes of sophistication and austere simplicity, each region has its own cuisine. You find exotic fish dishes in the Amazon, African-spiced dishes in Bahia, and well-seasoned bean mashes in Minas Gerais.

It's hard to find breakfast (*café da manhã*) outside a hotel restaurant, but in bakeries (*padarias*) you can always find something breakfast-like. At lunch (*almoço*) and dinner (*jantar*) portions are large. Often a single dish will easily feed two people; no one will be the least bit surprised if you order one entrée and ask for two plates. In addition some restaurants automatically bring a *couvert* (an appetizer course of such items as bread, cheese, or pâté, olives, quail eggs, and the like). You'll be charged extra for this, and you're perfectly within your rights to send it back if you don't want it.

Mealtimes vary according to locale. In Rio and São Paulo, lunch and dinner are served later than in the United States. In restaurants lunch usually starts around noon and can last until 3. Dinner is always eaten after 7 and in many cases not until 10. In Minas Gerais, the Northeast, and smaller towns in general, dinner and lunch are taken at roughly the same time as in the States.

Unless otherwise noted, the restaurants listed in this guide are open daily for lunch and dinner.

PAYING

Credit cards are widely accepted at restaurants in the major cities. In the countryside all but the smallest establishments generally accept credit cards as well, but check before you order. Smaller, family-run restaurants are sometimes cash-only. Gratuity is 10% of the total sum, and it's sometimes included in the bill; when it's not, it's optional to give the waiter a tip. Restaurants in Brazil generally don't accommodate requests for separate checks.

For guidelines on tipping see Tipping below.

RESERVATIONS AND DRESS

Appropriate dress for dinner in Brazil can vary dramatically. As a general rule, dress more formally for expensive restaurants. In most restaurants dress is casual, but even moderately priced places might frown on shorts.

Regardless of where you are, it's a good idea to make a reservation if you can. We only mention them specifically when reservations are essential (there's no other way you'll ever get a table) or when they're not accepted. For popular restaurants, book as far ahead as you can (often 30 days), and reconfirm as soon as you arrive. (Large parties should always call ahead to check the reservations policy.) We mention dress only when men are required to wear a jacket or a jacket and tie.

WINES, BEER, AND SPIRITS

The national drink is the *caipirinha,* made of crushed lime, sugar, and *pinga* or *cachaça* (sugarcane liquor). When whipped with crushed ice, fruit juices, and condensed milk, the pinga/cachaça becomes a *batida.* A *caipivodka,* or *caipiroska,* is the same cocktail with vodka instead of cachaça. Some bars make both drinks using a fruit other than lime, such as kiwi and *maracujá* (passion fruit). Brazil has many brands of bottled beer. In general, though, Brazilians prefer tap beer, called *chopp,* which is sold in bars and restaurants. Be sure to try the carbonated

soft drink *guaraná,* made using the Amazonian fruit of the same name. It's extremely popular in Brazil.

▌ELECTRICITY

The current in Brazil isn't regulated: in São Paulo and Rio it's 110 or 120 volts (the same as in the United States and Canada); in Recife and Brasília it's 220 volts (the same as in Europe); and in Manaus and Salvador it's 127 volts. Electricity is AC (alternating current) at 60 Hz, similar to that in Europe. To use electric-powered equipment purchased in the U.S. or Canada, it's wise to bring a converter and adapter, although these days, increasingly, most electronics are designed to convert themselves—if your device specifies a range of 100 to 240 volts, you won't have any problem using it in Brazil. Wall outlets take Continental-type plugs, with two round prongs. Consider buying a universal adapter, which has several types of plugs in one handy unit. Some hotels are equipped to handle various types of plugs and electrical devices. Check with your hotel before packing converters and adapters.

▌EMERGENCIES

In case of emergency, call one of the services below. Calling the fire brigade is a good option, since they're considered one of the most efficient and trustworthy institutions in Brazil. If you need urgent and immediate support, talk to the people around you. Brazilians are friendly and willing to help. They'll go out of their way to speak your language and find help.

If you've been robbed or assaulted, report it to the police. Unfortunately, you shouldn't expect huge results for your trouble. Call your embassy if your passport has been stolen or if you need help dealing with the police.

General Emergency Contacts Federal Highway Patrol ☎ *191.* Fire Brigade (Bombeiros) ☎ *193* ⊕ *www.bombeirosemergencia.com. br.* Police ☎ *190.* Ambulance ☎ *192.* Civil Defence ☎ *199.*

■ HEALTH

The most common types of illnesses are caused by contaminated food and water. Especially in developing countries, drink only bottled, boiled, or purified water and drinks; don't drink from public fountains or use ice. It's even prudent to use bottled water to brush your teeth. Make sure food has been thoroughly cooked and is served to you fresh and hot; avoid vegetables and fruits that you haven't washed (in bottled or purified water) or peeled yourself. If you have problems, mild cases of traveler's diarrhea may respond to Imodium (known generically as loperamide) or Pepto-Bismol. Be sure to drink plenty of fluids; if you can't keep fluids down, seek medical help immediately.

Infectious diseases can be airborne or passed via mosquitoes and ticks and through direct or indirect physical contact with animals or people. Some, including Norwalk-like viruses that affect your digestive tract, can be passed along through contaminated food. If you're traveling in an area where malaria is prevalent, use a repellent containing DEET and take malaria-prevention medication before, during, and after your trip as directed by your physician. Condoms can help prevent most sexually transmitted diseases, but they aren't absolutely reliable and their quality varies from country to country. Speak with your physician and/or check the CDC or World Health Organization websites for health alerts,

particularly if you're pregnant, traveling with children, or have a chronic illness.

English-speaking medical assistance in Brazil is rare. It's best to contact your consulate or embassy if you need medical help. Seek private clinics or hospitals, since getting an appointment in the government's health-care system is a slow process.

■ **TIP→** If you're traveling to the Amazon, extra precautions are necessary.

DIVERS' ALERT

Do not fly within 24 hours of scuba diving. Neophyte divers should have a complete physical exam before undertaking a dive. If you have travel insurance that covers evacuations, make sure your policy applies to scuba-related injuries, as not all companies provide this coverage.

FOOD AND DRINK

The major health risk in Brazil is traveler's diarrhea, caused by eating contaminated fruit or vegetables or drinking contaminated water. So watch what you eat—on and off the beaten path. Avoid ice, uncooked food, and unpasteurized milk and milk products, and drink only bottled water or water that has been boiled for at least 20 minutes, even when brushing your teeth. The use of bottled water for brushing your teeth is not necessary in large cities, where water is treated. Don't use ice unless you know it's made from purified water. (Ice in city restaurants is usually safe.) Peel or thoroughly wash fresh fruits and vegetables. Avoid eating food from street vendors.

Choose industrially packaged beverages when you can. Order tropical juices only from places that appear clean and reliable.

INFECTIOUS DISEASES AND VIRUSES

The Amazon and a few other remote areas are the only places in Brazil where you really need worry about infectious diseases. Most travelers to Brazil return home unscathed, apart from a bit of traveler's diarrhea. However, you should visit a doctor at least six weeks prior to traveling to discuss recommended vaccinations, some of which require multiple shots over a period of weeks. If you get sick weeks, months, or in rare cases, years after your trip, make sure your doctor administers blood tests for tropical diseases.

Meningococcal meningitis and typhoid fever are common in certain areas of Brazil—and not only in remote areas like the Amazon. Meningitis has been a problem around São Paulo in recent years. Dengue fever and malaria—both caused by mosquito bites—are common in Brazil or in certain areas of Brazil, like Rio de Janeiro. Both are usually only a problem in the Amazon, but dengue can affect urban areas and malaria is sometimes found in urban peripheries. Talk with your doctor about what precautions to take.

PESTS AND OTHER HAZARDS

You'll likely encounter more insects than you're used to in Brazil, but they generally only present health problems in the Amazon.

Heatstroke and heat prostration are common though easily preventable maladies throughout Brazil. The symptoms for either can vary but always start with headaches, nausea, and dizziness. If ignored, these symptoms can worsen until you require medical attention. In hot weather be sure to rehydrate regularly, wear loose lightweight clothing, and avoid overexerting yourself.

OVER-THE-COUNTER REMEDIES

Mild cases of diarrhea may respond to Imodium (known generically as loperamide) or Pepto-Bismol (not as strong), both of which can be purchased over the counter at a *farmácia* (pharmacy). Drink plenty of purified water or *chá* (tea)—*camomila* (chamomile) is a good folk remedy, as is dissolving a tablespoon of cornstarch in a mix of lime juice and water. In severe cases rehydrate yourself with a salt–sugar solution: ½ teaspoon *sal* (salt) and 4 tablespoons *açúcar* (sugar) per quart of *agua* (water).

An effective home remedy for diarrhea is the same as the rehydrating concoction: a teaspoon of sugar plus a quarter teaspoon of salt in a liter of water.

Aspirin is *aspirina*; Tylenol is pronounced *tee*-luh-nawl.

SHOTS AND MEDICATIONS

■ TIP→ If you travel a lot internationally—particularly to developing nations—refer to the CDC's Health Information for International Travel (aka Traveler's Health Yellow Book). Info from it is posted on the CDC website (*wwwnc.cdc.gov/travel*).

The best recommendation to avoid health problems is to see a doctor before and after traveling, just to be on the safe side. Some vaccines must be applied long before traveling so that their protective effect is guaranteed, and some prophylactic medicines must be taken also in advance so that the doctor and the patient are aware of possible side effects.

Vaccinations against hepatitis A and B, meningitis, typhoid, and yellow fever are highly recommended. Consult your doctor about whether to get a rabies vaccination. Check with the CDC's International Travelers' Hotline if you plan to visit remote regions or stay for more than six weeks.

Discuss the option of taking antimalarial drugs with your doctor. Note that in parts of northern Brazil a particularly aggressive strain of malaria has become resistant to one antimalarial drug—chloroquine. Some antimalarial drugs have rather unpleasant side effects—from headaches, nausea, and dizziness to psychosis, convulsions, and hallucinations.

For travel anywhere in Brazil, it's recommended that you have updated vaccines for diphtheria, tetanus, and polio. Children must additionally have current inoculations against measles, mumps, and rubella.

Yellow fever immunization is compulsory to enter Brazil if you're traveling directly from one of the following countries in South America (or from one of several

African countries): Bolivia; Colombia; Ecuador; French Guiana; Peru; or Venezuela. You must have an International Certificate of Immunization proving that you've been vaccinated.

Health Warnings National Centers for Disease Control & Prevention (*CDC*) ☎ *800/232–4636* ⊕ *www.cdc.gov.* **World Health Organization** (*WHO*) ⊕ *www.who.int.*

▮ MONEY

Brazil's unit of currency is the *real* (R$; plural: *reais*). One real is 100 *centavos* (cents). There are notes worth 2, 5, 10, 20, 50, and 100 reais, together with coins worth 1, 5, 10, 25, and 50 centavos and 1 real.

ATMS AND BANKS

Your own bank will probably charge a fee for using ATMs abroad; the foreign bank you use may also charge a fee. Nevertheless, you'll usually get a better rate of exchange at an ATM than you will at a currency-exchange office or even when changing money in a bank. And extracting funds as you need them is a safer option than carrying around a large amount of cash.

▮TIP➜ **PIN numbers with more than four digits are not recognized at ATMs in many countries. If yours has five or more, remember to change it before you leave.**

Nearly all the nation's major banks have ATMs, known in Brazil as *caixas eletrônicos*, for which you must use a card with a credit-card logo. MasterCard/Cirrus holders can withdraw at Banco Itaú, Banco do Brasil, HSBC, and Banco24horas ATMs; Visa holders can use Bradesco ATMs and those at Banco do Brasil. American Express cardholders can make withdrawals at most Bradesco ATMs marked "24 horas". To be on the safe side, carry a variety of cards. For your card to function in some ATMs, you may need to hit a screen command (perhaps, *estrangeiro*) if you are a foreign client.

Banks are, with a few exceptions, open weekdays 10 to 4. Avoid using ATM machines alone and at night, and use ATMs in busy, highly visible locations whenever possible.

CREDIT CARDS

It's a good idea to inform your credit-card company before you travel, especially if you're going abroad and don't travel internationally very often. Otherwise, the credit-card company might put a hold on your card owing to unusual activity—not a good thing halfway through your trip. Record all your credit-card numbers—as well as the phone numbers to call if your cards are lost or stolen—in a safe place, so you're prepared should something go wrong. Both MasterCard and Visa have general numbers you can call (collect if you're abroad) if your card is lost, but you're better off calling the number of your issuing bank, since MasterCard and Visa usually just transfer you to your bank; your bank's number is usually printed on your card.

If you plan to use your credit card for cash advances, you'll need to apply for a PIN at least two weeks before your trip. Although it's usually cheaper (and safer) to use a credit card abroad for large purchases (so you can cancel payments or be reimbursed if there's a problem), note that some credit-card companies *and* the banks that issue them add substantial percentages to all foreign transactions, whether they're in a foreign currency or not. Check on these fees before leaving home, so there won't be any surprises when you get the bill. Credit card fraud does happen in Brazil, so always conceal PIN numbers and keep your receipts.

▮TIP➜ **Before you charge something, ask the merchant whether he or she plans to do a dynamic currency conversion (DCC). In such a transaction the credit-card processor (shop, restaurant, or hotel, not Visa or MasterCard) converts the currency and charges you in dollars. In most cases you'll pay the merchant a 3% fee for this service in addition to any credit-card company and issuing-bank foreign-transaction surcharges.**

Dynamic currency conversion programs are becoming increasingly widespread. Merchants who participate in them are supposed to ask whether you want to be charged in dollars or the local currency, but they don't always do so. And even if they do offer you a choice, they may well avoid mentioning the additional surcharges. The good news is that you *do* have a choice. And if this practice really gets your goat, you can avoid it entirely thanks to American Express; with its cards, DCC simply isn't an option.

In Brazil's largest cities and leading tourist centers, restaurants, hotels, and shops accept major international credit cards. Off the beaten track, you may have more difficulty using them. Many gas stations in rural Brazil don't take credit cards.

For costly items use your credit card whenever possible—you'll come out ahead, whether the exchange rate at which your purchase is calculated is the one in effect the day the vendor's bank abroad processes the charge or the one prevailing on the day the charge company's service center processes it at home.

Reporting Lost Cards American Express ☎ 800/528-4800 in U.S., 336/393-1111 collect from abroad ⊕ www.americanexpress.com. **Diners Club** ☎ 800/234-6377, 514/881-3735 collect from abroad ⊕ www.dinersclub. com. **MasterCard** ☎ 800/627-8372 in U.S., 636/722-7111 collect from abroad, 0800/891-3294 in Brazil ⊕ www.mastercard.com. **Visa** ☎ 800/847-2911 in U.S., 410/581-9994 collect from abroad, 0800/99-0001 in Brazil ⊕ www.visa.com.

CURRENCY AND EXCHANGE

At this writing, the real is at about 2 to the U.S. dollar and 1.9 to the Canadian dollar.

For the most favorable rates, change money through banks. Although ATM transaction fees may be higher abroad than at home, ATM rates are excellent because they're based on wholesale rates offered only by major banks. You won't do as well at *casas de câmbio* (exchange houses), in airports or bus stations, in hotels, in restaurants, or in stores. ATMs also allow you to avoid the often long lines at airport exchange booths.

Outside larger cities, changing money in Brazil becomes more of a challenge. When leaving a large city for a smaller town, bring enough cash for your trip.

■TIP➔ Even if a currency-exchange booth has a sign promising no commission, rest assured that there's some kind of huge, hidden fee. (Oh, that's right. The sign didn't say no fee.) And as for rates, you're almost always better off getting foreign currency at an ATM or exchanging money at a bank.

■ PACKING

For sightseeing, casual clothing and good walking shoes are appropriate; most restaurants don't require formal attire. For beach vacations, bring lightweight sportswear, a bathing suit, a beach cover-up, a sun hat, and waterproof sunscreen that is at least SPF 20. A sarong or a light cotton blanket makes a handy beach towel, picnic blanket, and cushion for hard seats, among other things.

If you're going to coastal cities like Rio, Florianópolis, and Salvador in summer (December, January, and February), dress more informally and feel free to wear flip-flops (thongs) all day—and don't forget your sunglasses. Southeastern cities like São Paulo, Curitiba, and Porto Alegre, which have lower temperatures, tend to be more formal and more conservative when it comes to clothing (sometimes even Brazilians are shocked by the way people in Rio dress). In urban areas it's always a good idea to have some nice outfits for going out at night.

Travel in rain-forest areas requires long-sleeve shirts, long pants, socks, waterproof hiking boots (sneakers are less desirable, but work in a pinch), a hat, a light waterproof jacket, a bathing suit, and plenty of strong insect repellent. (Amazonian bugs tend to be oblivious to non-DEET or non-picaridin repellents.) Other useful items include a screw-top water container that you can fill with bottled water, a money pouch, a travel flashlight and extra batteries, a Swiss Army knife with a bottle opener, a medical kit, binoculars, a pocket calculator, spare camera batteries, and a high-capacity memory card.

PASSPORTS AND VISAS

At this writing, passports and visas are required for citizens—even infants—of the U.S. and Canada for entry to Brazil. Business travelers may need a special business visa. It has all the same requirements as a tourist visa, but you'll also need a letter on company letterhead addressed to the embassy or consulate and signed by an authorized representative (other than you), stating the nature of your business in Brazil, itinerary, business contacts, dates of arrival and departure, and that the company assumes all financial and moral responsibility while you're in Brazil.

PASSPORTS

When in Brazil, carry your passport or a copy with you at all times. Make two photocopies of the data page (one for someone at home and another for you, carried separately from your passport). If you lose your passport, promptly call the nearest embassy or consulate and the local police.

If your passport is lost or stolen, first call the police—having the police report can make replacement easier—and then call your embassy. You'll get a temporary Emergency Travel Document that will need to be replaced once you return home. Fees vary according to how fast you need the passport; in some cases the fee covers your permanent replacement as well. The new document will not have your entry stamps; ask if your embassy takes care of this, or whether it's your responsibility to get the necessary immigration authorization.

Contacts Brazilian Embassy ✉ *3006 Massachusetts Ave. NW, Washington, District of Columbia, USA* ☎ *202/238–2700* ⊕ *washington. itamaraty.gov.br/en-us* ✉ *450 Wilbrod St., Ottawa, Ontario, Canada* ☎ *613/237–1090* ⊕ *ottawa.itamaraty.gov.br/en-us.*

VISAS

A visa is essentially formal permission to enter a country. Visas allow countries to keep track of you and other visitors—and generate revenue (from application fees).

Go to the website for the Brazilian embassy or consulate nearest you for the most up-to-date visa information. At this writing, tourist visa fees are US$160 for Americans and C$81.25 for Canadians. Additional fees may be levied if you apply by mail. Obtaining a visa can be a slow process, and you must have every bit of paperwork in order when you visit the consulate, so read instructions carefully. (For example, in the U.S., the fee can only be paid by a U.S. Postal Service money order.)

To get the location of the Brazilian consulate to which you must apply, contact the Brazilian embassy. Note that some consulates don't allow you to apply for a visa by mail. If you don't live near a city with a consulate, consider hiring a concierge-type service to do your legwork. Many cities have these companies, which not only help with the paperwork, but also send someone to wait in line for you.

When you apply by mail, you send your passport to a designated consulate, where your passport will be examined and the visa issued. Expediters—usually the same ones who handle expedited passport applications—can do all the work of obtaining your visa for you; however, there's always an additional cost (often at least $50 per visa).

Most visas limit you to a single trip—basically during the actual dates of your planned vacation. Other visas allow you to visit as many times as you wish for a specific period of time. Remember that requirements change, sometimes at the drop of a hat, and the burden is on you to make sure that you have the appropriate visas. Otherwise, you'll be turned away at the airport or, worse, deported after you arrive in the country. No company or travel insurer gives refunds if your travel plans are disrupted because you didn't have the correct visa.

U.S. Passport Information U.S. Department of State ☎ 877/487–2778 ⊕ *travel.state.gov/ passport.*

U.S. Passport and Visa Expediters A. Briggs Passport & Visa Expediters ☎ 800/806–0581, 202/338–0111 ⊕ *www. abriggs.com.* **American Passport Express** ☎ 800/455–5166 ⊕ *www.americanpassport. com.* **Passport Express** ☎ 800/362–8196 ⊕ *www.passportexpress.com.* **Travel Document Systems** ☎ 800/874–5100, 202/638–3800 ⊕ *www.traveldocs.com.* **Travel the World Visas** ☎ 866/886–8472, 202/223–8822 ⊕ *www.world-visa.com.*

GENERAL REQUIREMENTS FOR BRAZIL	
Passport	Must be valid for 6 months after date of arrival.
Visa	Required for Americans (US$160) and Canadians (C$81.25)
Vaccinations	Yellow fever and diptheria
Driving	International driver's license required; CDW is compulsory on car rentals and will be included in the quoted price
Departure Tax	Approximately US$43, payable in cash only

▌RESTROOMS

The word for "bathroom" is *banheiro,* though the term *sanitários* (toilets) is also used. *Homens* means "men" and *mulheres* means "women." Around major tourist attractions and along the main beaches in big cities, you can find public restrooms that aren't necessarily clean. In some smaller beach cities, there are no facilities at the beach, so be prepared to walk a bit to find a bathroom. In other areas you may have to rely on the kindness of local restaurant and shop owners. If a smile and polite request (*"Por favor, posso usar o banheiro?"*) doesn't work, become a customer—the purchase of a drink or a knickknack might just buy you a trip to the bathroom. Rest areas with relatively clean, well-equipped

bathrooms are plentiful along major highways. Still, carry a pocket-size package of tissues in case there's no toilet paper. Tip bathroom attendants with a few spare centavos.

▌TAXES

Sales tax is included in the prices shown on goods in stores but listed separately on the bottom of your receipt. Hotel, meal, and car rental taxes are usually tacked on in addition to the costs shown on menus and brochures. At this writing, hotel taxes are roughly 5%, meal taxes 10%, and car-rental taxes 12%.

Departure taxes on international flights from Brazil aren't always included in your ticket and can run as high as R$86 ($43); domestic flights may incur a R$22 ($11) tax. Although U.S. dollars are accepted in some airports, be prepared to pay departure taxes in reais.

▌TIME

Brazil covers four time zones. Most of the country—including Rio, São Paulo, Porto Alegre, Salvador, Brasília, and Belo Horizonte—is three hours behind GMT (Greenwich mean time). Manaus and Pantanal are an hour behind those cities, and the far western Amazon is an hour behind Manaus. Fernando de Noronha, an archipelago off Brazil's northeast coast, is two hours behind GMT. From October to March (exact days vary), Brazil observes daylight saving time in most of the country, so in many areas it stays light until 8:30 pm.

▌TIPPING

Wages can be paltry in Brazil, so a little generosity in tipping can go a long way. Tipping in dollars is not recommended—at best it's insulting; at worst, you might be targeted for a robbery. Large hotels that receive lots of international guests are the exception. Some restaurants add a 10% service charge onto the check. If there's no service charge, you can leave as much as you want, but 15% is a good amount. In deluxe hotels tip porters R$2 per bag, chambermaids R$2 per day, and bellhops R$4–R$6 for room and valet service. Tips for doormen and concierges vary, depending on the services provided. A good tip is around R$30, with the average at about R$15. For moderate and inexpensive hotels, tips tend to be minimal (salaries are so low that virtually anything is well received). If a taxi driver helps you with your luggage, a per-bag charge of about R$1 is levied in addition to the fare. In general, you don't tip taxi drivers. If a service station attendant does anything beyond filling up the gas tank, leave him a small tip of some spare change. Tipping in bars and cafés follows the rules of restaurants, although at outdoor bars Brazilians rarely leave a gratuity if they have had only a soft drink or a beer. At airports and at train and bus stations, tip the last porter who puts your bags into the cab (R$1 a bag at airports, 50 centavos a bag at bus and train stations).

▌ VISITOR INFORMATION

EMBRATUR, Brazil's national tourism organization, doesn't have offices overseas, though its website is helpful. For information in your home country, contact the Brazilian embassy or the closest consulate, some of which have websites and staff dedicated to promoting tourism. The official consular website in New York, ⊕ *novayork.itamaraty.gov.br/en-us*, has details about other consulates and the embassy as well as travel information and links to other sites. Cities and towns throughout Brazil have local tourist boards, and some state capitals also have state tourism offices.

Contacts Brazilian Consulate–New York ☎ *917/777–7777* ⊕ *novayork.itamaraty.gov.br/en-us.* **EMBRATUR** ☎ *61/2023–7146 in Brazil* ⊕ *www.visitbrazil.com.*

ONLINE RESOURCES

The like-minded travelers on Fodors.com are eager to answer questions and swap travel tales. For further information you may have to search by region, state, or city—and hope that at least one of them has a comprehensive official site of its own.

The online magazine *Brazzil* and Internet newspaper the Rio Times Online have interesting English-language articles on culture and politics. Gringoes.com is an online forum for foreigners living in or traveling to Brazil, where you'll find info about everything from security to getting a driver's license. And VivaBrazil.com provides background and travel info on Brazil's different regions as well as links that will help you arrange your trip.

All About Brazil
Gringoes.com ⊕ *www.gringoes.com.br.*
Brazzil Magazine ⊕ *www.brazzil.com.*
Rio Times Online ⊕ *www.riotimesonline.com.*
VivaBrazil.com ⊕ *www.vivabrazil.com.*

Currency Conversion Google. Google does currency conversion. Just type in the amount you want to convert and an explanation of how you want it converted (e.g., "14 Swiss francs in dollars"), and then voilà. ⊕ *www.google.com.* **Oanda.com.** The site allows you to print out a handy table with the current day's conversion rates. ⊕ *www.oanda.com.* **XE.com.** Currency conversion website. ⊕ *www.xe.com.*

Weather Accuweather.com. A reliable weather-forecasting website. ⊕ *www.accuweather.com.* **Weather.com** is the website for the Weather Channel. ⊕ *www.weather.com.*

INDEX

A

Academia de Cachaça (dance club), 96
Acaso 85 Scotch Bar e Restaurante, 312
Addresses, 516
Afro-Brazilian heritage, 384
Águas de São Pedro, 219–221
Air travel, 18, 508–509
  Rio de Janeiro, 43
  São Paulo, 149, 152
Al Dente Ristorante ✕, 271
Alagoas, 427–428
Alambique Cachaçaria e Armazém (bar), 298
Alto da Sé, 424
Amantikir Garden, 222
Amazon, 17, 452–496
  beaches, 469, 477, 494, 495–496
  dining, 458, 465, 479, 481, 487, 489–490
  guided tours, 471
  health precautions, 457
  history, 455
  language, 492, 495
  legends, 489
  lodging, 458–459, 465–466, 472–473, 474, 477, 479, 481, 491, 494, 496
  nightlife and the arts, 466–467, 479, 481, 491–492
  packing, 455
  safety and precautions, 476, 484
  shopping, 468, 478, 480, 481, 492–493, 496
  timing the visit, 455
  transportation, 456, 458
Anavilhanas Lodge 🖃, 472
Angra dos Reis, 136–137
Antiquarius ✕, 78
Arcos de Lapa, 54
Argentina, 245–246, 249, 253
Arquivo Judaico de Pernambuco, 416–417
Arraial d'Ajuda, 406
Arraial do Cabo, 124
Art galleries. ⇨ See Museums and art galleries
Artisan Market (Belo Horizonte), 294
Arts. ⇨ See Nightlife and the arts
Atlante Plaza Hotel 🖃, 420–421

ATMs, 523

Auditório do Ibirapuera, 168
Auto racing, 198
Avenida Paulista (São Paulo), 147, 163–164

B

Baden-Baden ✕, 223
Bahia Coast. ⇨ See Salvador and the Bahia Coast
Baía do Sancho, 448–449
Baía dos Porcos, 448
Balé Folclórico da Bahia, 388
Balneário Municipal, 359
Balneário Municipal Dr. Octávio Moura Andrade, 221
Bandeirantes, 224
Banks, 523
Banzeiro ✕, 465
Bar do Arnaudo ✕, 85
Bardot, Brigitte, statue, 129
Barra da Tijuca, 40, 59–60, 85, 93, 115
Barra do Jacuípe, 394
Barra do Sahy, 213
Barra Funda, 147
Bars and lounges
  Amazon, 467, 491–492
  Minas Gerais, 298
  Northeast Brazil, 421–422, 433, 444
  Rio de Janeiro, 94–95, 96–97, 98–99
  Rio de Janeiro side trips, 130
  Salvador and the Bahia Coast, 387
  São Paulo, 190–192, 193, 194, 195
Basílica Bom Jesus do Matosinho, 315
Basílica de Lourdes, 293
Basílica de Nossa Senhora de Nazaré, 488
Beach Park Acqua Center, 439–440
Beaches, 22–23, 30, 404
  Amazon, 469, 477, 494, 495–496
  Northeast Brazil, 418–419, 427–428, 430–431, 440–442, 448–449
  Rio de Janeiro, 41, 65–71
  Rio de Janeiro side trips, 124–125, 127–128, 139

Salvador and the Bahia Coast, 380–381, 394, 395, 397
São Paulo side trips, 213–214, 215–216, 219
Southern Brazil, 262–263
Beco do Comércio (Rio de Janeiro), 52
Bed and breakfasts, 515
Beer, 471
Bela Vista (São Paulo), 183, 190
Belém, 453, 482–493
Belo Horizonte, 285, 288–302
Biblioteca Nacional, 48, 50
Bicycling, 105, 200
Bishop, Elizabeth, 310
Bixiga (São Paulo), 148, 169, 170
Blue Coast, 118, 121–132
Blue Lagoon, 139
Boa Viagem, 418
Boat and ferry travel, 456, 458
  Rio de Janeiro, 104
  Rio de Janeiro side trips, 131, 137
  São Paulo side trips, 217
  Southern Brazil, 263, 265
Boipeba, 397–398
Bom Retiro, 201
Bonito, 358–361
Bosque Alemão, 237
Bosque Municipal Dr. Octávio Moura Andrade, 221
Bosque Rodrigues Alves, 488
Botafogo (Rio de Janeiro), 39, 55–57, 77–78, 95, 109
Brasília and the west, 17, 326–362
  dining, 327, 342–344, 352, 355, 357–358, 360, 361
  festivals and seasonal events, 354
  guided tours, 349–350, 354, 357
  health concerns, 353
  history, 331, 341
  lodging, 330, 344–345, 352–353, 355, 356, 360–362
  nightlife and the arts, 346, 353
  outdoor activities and sports, 347, 349, 362
  safety and precautions, 334, 351
  shopping, 347–348, 353, 358, 361

534 <   Index

PHOTO CREDITS

NOTES

NOTES

NOTES

NOTES

NOTES

NOTES

NOTES

NOTES

NOTES

NOTES

NOTES

NOTES

Fodor's BRAZIL 2014

Publisher: Amanda D'Acierno, *Senior Vice President*

Editorial: Arabella Bowen, *Executive Editorial Director*; Linda Cabasin, *Editorial Director*

Design: Fabrizio La Rocca, *Vice President, Creative Director*; Tina Malaney, *Associate Art Director*; Chie Ushio, *Senior Designer*; Ann McBride, *Production Designer*

Photography: Melanie Marin, *Associate Director of Photography*; Jessica Parkhill and Jennifer Romains, *Researchers*

Maps: Rebecca Baer, *Senior Map Editor*; Mark Stroud, Moonstreet Cartography, *Cartographers*

Production: Linda Schmidt, *Managing Editor*; Evangelos Vasilakis, *Associate Managing Editor*; Angela L. McLean, *Senior Production Manager*

Sales: Jacqueline Lebow, *Sales Director*

Marketing & Publicity: Heather Dalton, *Marketing Director*; Katherine Fleming, *Senior Publicist*

Business & Operations: Susan Livingston, *Vice President, Strategic Business Planning*; Sue Daulton, *Vice President, Operations*

Fodors.com: Megan Bell, *Executive Director, Revenue & Business Development*; Yasmin Marinaro, *Senior Director, Marketing & Partnerships*

Writers: Rasheed Abou-Alsamh, Juliana Barbassa, Taylor Barnes, Mark Beresford, Lucy Bryson, Angelica Mari Hillary, Lauren Holmes, Joshua Eric Miller, Sheena Rossiter, Blake Schmidt

Editors: Luke Epplin, Andrew Collins, Debbie Harmsen, Daniel Mangin

Production Editor: Carrie Parker

ISBN 978-1-4000-0439-3

ISSN 0163-0628

SPECIAL SALES

This book is available at special discounts for bulk purchases for sales promotions or premiums. For more information, e-mail specialmarkets@randomhouse.com

PRINTED IN THE UNITED STATES OF AMERICA

10 9 8 7 6 5 4 3 2

ABOUT OUR WRITERS

Rasheed Abou-Alsamh is a Brasília resident who was a newspaper editor in Saudi Arabia and the United Arab Emirates for 20 years. He is now a columnist for *O Globo*. He has written for the *New York Times, Washington Times,* and *Christian Science Monitor.* Rasheed grew up in Brasília, and after spending years traveling throughout Asia, he returned to Brazil in 2008. For this edition, he updated The Amazon chapter.

Juliana Barbassa is Brazilian and returned to her home country after years abroad to cover it as correspondent for the Associated Press. She's currently working on a book about the changes in Rio de Janeiro as it prepares for the Olympics. She loves exploring Brazil's wild side, from the pristine mountains of Itatiaia National Park to the lesser-known beaches along the coastline. She wrote the Experience Brazil and soccer insert for this edition.

Taylor Barnes is a foreign correspondent based in Rio de Janeiro who covers Brazil for several English-language outlets. She challenges cariocas da gema (Rio's born and raised) to name a corner of the city she has not visited, written about, or had a meal in. She writes and reviews Rio's gastronomical scene at www.CulinaryBackstreets.com. She can be found most days jogging along the Flamengo beach. For this edition, she wrote the Experience Brazil chapter.

Born in Scotland, **Mark Beresford** has been a resident of the warmer climes of Rio de Janeiro since 2007. He regularly writes about Brazil and Latin America for supplements of the *Wall Street Journal, Barron's,* and other publications. When not cycling along the beaches of the Zona Sul, Mark likes to escape to the hills and old towns of Goiás, his home-away-from-home in Brazil. For this edition, Mark updated the Brasília and the West chapter.

Lucy Bryson is a freelance British travel writer who has been living in Rio de Janeiro since 2007. She works as a Rio expert for a range of online guides including 10Best @ *USA Today,* and has also written for several print guides to Brazil and South America. She lives in the beautiful historic neighborhood of Santa Teresa with her Brazilian partner, their British-Brazilian daughter, and their lively carioca dog. For this edition, Lucy updated the Rio de Janeiro and Side Trips from Rio chapters.

Angelica Mari Hillary is a São Paulo native who now lives in Serra Negra. As well as regularly writing for major business and technology publications, she also contributes to various travel and lifestyle magazines worldwide. But her main pleasure and focus is her own business, Gift Brazil, a start-up focused on promoting Brazilian crafts to a global audience. For this edition, Angelica updated the Minas Gerais and Side Trips to São Paulo chapters.

Growing up in London, long-time Rio resident **Lauren Holmes** couldn't resist the lure of Brazilian beach life. Working as a freelance journalist for publications like *Monocle, Condé Nast Traveler,* and the *South China Morning Post,* Lauren loves traveling through Brazil, tracking down the best botecos and emerging beach hotspots. For this edition, Lauren updated the Salvador and the Bahia Coast and The Northeast chapters.

Joshua Eric Miller is a resident of São Paulo who is, at heart, a runaway with a bindle stick. Miller has lived in Delhi, Caracas, Havana, Mexico City, Miami, Chicago, Washington, DC, and his hometown Philadelphia. Miller has a BSJ from the Medill School of Journalism at Northwestern University, and has contributed to PBS.org, the Associated Press, and Forbes. He currently works in IT management while moonlighting as a freelancer. For this edition, Miller updated the São Paulo chapter.

Sheena Rossiter is a São Paulo resident who enjoys the city's urban arts and culture scene. She is the Brazil correspondent for Monocle 24 radio. Sheena is also the co-owner and creative director of Dona Ana Films & Multimedia, a São Paulo-based production company, which has acted as the local producer for international television stations such as CBC and Bloomberg TV, among others. For this edition, Sheena updated the Travel Smart section.

Blake Schmidt is a São Paulo resident who loves surfing off the sun-drenched beaches in southern Brazil. After covering Latin America for nearly a decade, from a coup in Honduras to the emergence of Colombia's economy from a half-decade conflict, he is now based in Brazil, where he often surprises local soccer players with his penchant for scoring goals. For this edition, he updated The South chapter.

DISCARD